INVITATION TO

WORLD
MISSIONS

Invitation to Theological Studies

Published

1. *Invitation to Biblical Hebrew: A Beginning Grammar*
   Invitation to Biblical Hebrew DVDs
   Invitation to Biblical Hebrew Workbook
   Russell T. Fuller and Kyoungwon Choi

2. *Invitation to Biblical Preaching: Proclaiming Truth with Clarity and Relevance*
   Donald R. Sunukjian

3. *Invitation to World Missions*
   Timothy C. Tennent

Forthcoming

1. *Invitation to Biblical Interpretation*
   Andreas Köstenberger and Richard D. Patterson

2. *Invitation to Christian Apologetics*
   Douglas Geivett

3. *Invitation to Christian Ethics*
   Kenneth Magnuson

4. *Invitation to Christian Theology*
   Craig A. Blaising

5. *Invitation to Church History*
   John Hannah

6. *Invitation to Evangelism*
   Timothy K. Beougher

7. *Invitation to Historical Theology: A Survey of Christian Thought*
   Steven A. McKinion

8. *Invitation to New Testament Greek*
   Buist Fanning, Jay Smith, and Jon Laansma

9. *Invitation to the New Testament*
   Michael J. Wilkins and Alan Hultberg

10 *Invitation to the Old Testament*
   David M. Howard Jr.

11. *Invitation to the Theology of Paul*
   C. Marvin Pate

Stimulating the mind and nourishing the soul, each volume in the Invitation to Theological Studies series is written to provide a primary textbook for core graduate-level courses.

INVITATION TO THEOLOGICAL STUDIES SERIES

INVITATION TO
WORLD
MISSIONS

*A Trinitarian Missiology
for the Twenty-first Century*

TIMOTHY C. TENNENT

Kregel
Academic & Professional

Invitation to World Missions: A Trinitarian Missiology for the Twenty-first Century

© 2010 by Timothy C. Tennent

Published by Kregel Publications, a division of Kregel, Inc., P.O. Box 2607, Grand Rapids, MI 49501

Figure 1.1 was originally published in Todd M. Johnson and Sun Young Chung, "Tracking Global Christianity's Statistical Centre of Gravity, A.D. 33–A.D. 2100" in *International Review of Mission*, Vol. 93, No. 369, April 2004, pp. 166–181. Used by permission.

The Hebrew font used in this book is New JerusalemU and is available from www .linguistsoftware.com/lgku.htm, +1-425-775-1130.

ISBN 978-0-8254-3883-7

Printed in the United States of America

12 13 14 / 5 4 3 2

To
J. Christy Wilson Jr.,
who first lit the fire
of missions in me;

Norman Allison,
who first introduced me
to the discipline of missiology;

and Peter Kuzmic,
my beloved colleague,
who simultaneously embodies the "fire of missions"
and the "discipline of missiology" better than anyone I know.

Contents

Preface

CENTRAL TO MY CONCERN in writing this book is that the way missions mostly has been conceptualized over the last generation is no longer adequate for the peculiar challenges and exciting opportunities that await us in the unfolding of twenty-first-century missions. This book seeks to bridge the gap between a practical-oriented missions textbook and a more reflective missiology that explores the undergirding foundations of missions practice. It contains much of what is normally found in traditional introductory texts on missions but seeks to place it all within a Trinitarian framework. Key theological foundations such as the *missio dei*, the Trinity, the New Creation, and a vision for a truly global church form the basis and structure of the entire work. It will assist those who teach missions to think more carefully about how missions is biblically and theologically undergirded. In the past, it was not uncommon for mission textbooks to contain a "biblical foundations for missions" section, which typically preceded the remaining content of the book. However, it was not always clear how the biblical and theological foundations were related to all that followed. This book seeks to integrate biblical and theological reflection throughout the entire work.

Having been a missions practitioner for over twenty years, as well as having taught missions in a seminary for over a decade, I have become concerned that missions practice has drifted quite a long way from intentional, disciplined missiological reflection. Thus, this book seeks to encourage the reuniting of missions practice with missiological reflection rooted in sound theology. The very word *missiology* can be daunting, even to some missionaries. The discipline of missions as a field of study seems somewhat removed from the practice of missions in the field of the world. Nevertheless, the world of practice and the world of disciplined reflection must be brought together if the increasingly global missionary movement is to be faithful to the high calling of being Christ's ambassadors in the world.

The word *missiology* has been called a "verbal monstrosity" because it is the joining of a Latin root—*missio*—with a Greek ending—*logos*.[1] However, perhaps the very word *missiology* reminds us that missions is, at its heart, about bridging cultures, crossing frontiers, and celebrating the marvelous translatability of the gospel of Jesus Christ in an increasingly global context. This book is written in celebration of the one hundredth anniversary of the 1910 World Missionary Conference held in Edinburgh, Scotland. It is a call to faithful remembrance as we look back on those who have gone before us, and it is also a call to look ahead and reenvision what it means to be called into the world. This book is part of the Invitation to Theological Studies series being published by Kregel. Therefore, it stands as an invitation to rejoice in God's abiding faithfulness and to engage afresh in the world mission of the church as global participants in the *missio dei*.

---

1. Johannes Verkuyl, *Contemporary Missiology: An Introduction* (Grand Rapids: Eerdmans, 1978), 2, quoting Raoul Allier, "Missions and the Soul of a People," *International Review of Missions* 18 (1929): 282–84.

Acknowledgments

I WOULD LIKE TO EXPRESS MY GRATITUDE to the trustees of Gordon-Conwell Theological Seminary for granting me a sabbatical to write this book. Their commitment to theological education built on the highest standards of excellence and fidelity to the Scriptures is one of the most enduring legacies of Gordon-Conwell, and one of which I am a grateful beneficiary. I will also cherish the months spent as a visiting fellow at the University of Edinburgh throughout much of 2008. My wife and I counted it as a great privilege to return to Edinburgh, where I did my doctoral work. The collegial hospitality I enjoyed at the Centre for the Study of Christianity in the Non-Western World will not soon be forgotten.

I also want to acknowledge my gratitude to George Chavanikamannil, with whom I have had the privilege of laboring in India since 1988. George models the best of missions practice and thoughtful reflection and does it right in the heart of North India, which is a remarkable testimony to his wisdom and vision. He is truly one of the most inspiring and visionary leaders I have ever known. I am privileged also to count him as one of my dearest friends.

During my sabbatical in Edinburgh, my wife, Julie, spent the time writing beautiful and theologically informed hymns for the church. One of the greatest joys of my sabbatical was coming home each day to discover fresh insights from the Scriptures that Julie had so ably turned into an act of worship for the church. Julie's whole life is a faithful reminder to all who know her that worship will always be at the center of the life of the church. We were also delighted to have both of our children, now adults, visit us while we were in Scotland. Jonathan and Bethany are two of God's wonderful gifts to us, for which we are so grateful.

I also want to express my gratitude to Brian Indrelie and Daniel Wang, both students at Gordon-Conwell, who ably assisted me in various phases of my research and writing of this book. Thanks also to Kelly McCuaig from Asbury Theological Seminary who helped me with the indexing.

I am also appreciative of the many hours discussing theology with my good friend Kevin Scott. Despite our very busy lives and most of the time living on two different continents, we have somehow managed to meet weekly by phone or Skype for the last ten years to study the Scriptures together. My life has been deeply enriched by his friendship and insights.

Since the writing of this book, I have accepted the call to serve as the President of Asbury Theological Seminary. I am deeply grateful to God for this wonderful new opportunity to serve Him alongside so many deeply committed Christians in my new Asbury family.

Finally, I want to give praise and honor to our Lord Jesus Christ, who graciously summons us forth to participate in His mission.

Timothy C. Tennent
Soli Deo Gloria

PART ONE
INTRODUCTION

Section A

Megatrends That Are Shaping Twenty-first Century Missions

From Moratorium and Malaise to *Selah* and Rebirth

MISSIONARIES ARE OFTEN KNOWN to be excellent storytellers. As a child, I remember sitting in rapt attention as missionaries would visit my home church and tell stories of exotic peoples in some faraway place. The mission fields that were described were always in some distant land where people spoke strange languages and had even stranger customs. I remember visiting one missionary who wore a colorful African headdress and riveted us with a string of electrifying stories about some remote part of tribal Africa. Suddenly—to the delight of most and to the horror of some—he unrolled the skin of a large snake out across the floor. It must have been at least twenty feet long, because it stretched across most of the floor of the fellowship hall where we were gathered. We were all dazzled. I knew right then and there that no other occupation in the world could possibly compare with being a missionary—learning strange languages, traveling to distant lands, telling exotic stories back home, and maybe even getting to dramatically roll a snakeskin across the floor! That, to me, was missions.

Even today, I can still recall those unforgettable images (usually projected by endless slide carousels) of remote jungles, smiling, white-faced missionaries holding Bibles, and strange-looking people rowing up a river as they stood upright in a hollowed-out canoe. It all seemed so strange and so foreign. Indeed, in those days, people rarely used the word *missions* without the adjective *foreign* attached to it—*foreign missions*. Clearly, the mission field was somewhere *"over there,"* something "*foreign.*" We in the West sat quite confidently and securely at the center of Christian gravity. *We* were the ones who sent the missionaries to all the *other* places. Growing up in the "Bible Belt" of the southern United States, I never recall hearing about Korean or Indian missionaries. I never even imagined the possibility that anyone might come to North America as a missionary.

Years later, as a seminary student I began to formally study missions for the first time. I had the privilege of studying missions at Gordon-Conwell Theological Seminary under J. Christy Wilson Jr., a living saint, and one of the most remarkable missionaries of his generation. To this day, he remains one of my missionary heroes. It was from Christy Wilson that I learned about unreached people groups in the "10/40 Window,"[1] dedicated missionaries doing Bible translation in Papua New Guinea, and people doing "tentmaking" in "restricted access countries." His lectures still nourish and inform my thinking today. However, I don't recall hearing anything about what the church in Brazil or China might have been doing in response to the Great Commission. Instead, missions was conceptualized in my mind as moving outward from its sending center in the Western world to the unreached world. *We* were the bearers of the missionary mandate and message, and those outside the West were the object of missions, the mission field. I had no idea that, even then, the Christian church was quietly undergoing some of the most dramatic changes in its history. Indeed, many of the paradigms that had largely defined and conceptualized Protestant missions since the eighteenth century were fading away. In short, the world of missions as I had known it was turning upside down. Perhaps a few quick illustrative "snapshots" will serve to underscore the point.

- *Christianity Today* reported a few years ago that 85 percent of the members of Yale University's Campus Crusade for Christ chapter are Asian, whereas "the university's Buddhist meditation meetings are almost exclusively attended by whites."[2]

---

1. The actual terminology of the "10/40 window" was not coined until 1989 when Luis Bush introduced the concept at the 1989 Lausanne II conference in Manila. When I was being trained, it was still called the "resistance belt."
2. "Go Figure," *Christianity Today* 47, no. 7 (2003): 13.

- The *World Christian Encyclopedia* recorded that more Anglican Christians worship in Nigeria in any given week than all the Episcopal and Anglican churches of Europe and North America combined![3]
- An examination of *World Christian Trends* reveals that there are now more evangelical Christians in Nepal than in Spain.[4] The historic William Carey Memorial Church in Lester, England, is now a Hindu temple, while the church in India, the traditional home of Hinduism, now sends out over 41,000 cross-cultural missionaries. In fact, today there are nearly half a billion Christians who are crossing cultural boundaries with the gospel from the Majority World.[5]
- All ten of the most gospel-resistant people groups in the world are located in Western Europe, whereas all ten of the most gospel-receptive people groups in the world today are located in either China or India. In fact, China can now boast of the fastest growing church in the world, with an estimated 16,500 new Christians every day.[6]

Philip Jenkins, in *The Next Christendom*, sums up this new "upside-down" world we live in when he states that "in another generation the phrase 'a white Christian' may sound like a curious oxymoron, as mildly surprising as a 'Swedish Buddhist.' Such people can exist, but a slight eccentricity is implied."[7]

None of these developments were predicted fifty years ago. Today, as I survey the landscape of contemporary missions and missiological reflection, it is clear that those who live in the West are facing a serious

---

3. Christopher Wright, "An Upside-Down World," *Christianity Today* 51, no. 1 (2007): 42.
4. David B. Barrett and Todd M. Johnson, eds., *World Christian Trends, AD 30–AD 2200: Interpreting the Annual Christian Megacensus* (Pasadena, CA: William Carey Library, 2001), 415, table 12-1.
5. This book uses the phrase "the Majority World" to refer collectively to all the Christians who inhabit Asia, Africa, and Latin America. For a full discussion concerning the pros and cons of various terms, including *Third World, Two-Thirds World, non-Western World,* and *Global South,* see my *Theology in the Context of World Christianity* (Grand Rapids: Zondervan, 2007), xviii–xx.
6. David B. Barrett, Todd M. Johnson, and Peter F. Crossing, "Missiometrics 2008: Reality Checks for Christian World Communions," *International Bulletin of Missionary Research* 32, no. 1 (January 2008): 29, table B.
7. Philip Jenkins, *The Next Christendom: The Coming of Global Christianity* (Oxford: Oxford University Press, 2002), 2.

crisis concerning missions and Christian identity within the larger global Christian movement. This is not to be overly negative or alarmist, for I am reminded of the great Dutch missiologist Hendrick Kraemer (1888–1965), who famously commented that "the church is always in a state of crisis; its greatest shortcoming is that it is only occasionally aware of it."[8] My purpose is simply to point out some of the contours of the crisis of *our* time and help make us aware of it.

In order to better grasp the sheer magnitude of the changes that confront the church and the need for a completely different approach to the discourse, conceptualization, and execution of missions by Christians around the world, I will examine the "crisis" under seven megatrends. Many of these trends will be developed or applied in some way later in the book, but they are presented in summary form here so that, from the beginning, we will be learning some of the new vocabulary and trajectories that are influencing missions in the twenty-first century.

These seven megatrends should not be viewed as seven distinct developments but as seven major shifts that are all related to, intertwined with, and built upon the others.

SEVEN MEGATRENDS THAT ARE SHAPING TWENTY-FIRST CENTURY MISSIONS

Megatrend #1: *The Collapse of Christendom*
The Western world can no longer be characterized as a Christian society/ culture in either its dominant ethos or in its worldview. Christendom has collapsed, and twenty-first-century missions must be reconceptualized on new assumptions.

Christendom refers to a political and ecclesiastical arrangement that reinforces a special relationship between the church and the state. The state strengthens the church by promoting Christian hegemony over the religious and cultural life. The church, in turn, gives legitimacy to the state by supporting the political establishment and tacitly granting divine sanction to the actions of the state.

---

8. As quoted in David Bosch, *Transforming Mission* (Maryknoll, NY: Orbis, 1991), 2. Kraemer insisted that this is true because of the "abiding tension between [the church's] essential nature and its empirical condition." See Kraemer, *The Christian Message in a Non-Christian World* (London: Edinburgh House, 1938), 24–25.

In the context of *official* Christendom, the church receives protection from the civil authorities (the king/queen of the United Kingdom has the title *"Defender of the Faith"*) and receives many privileges because it is the "established" religion of the realm. The classic phrase was *cuius regio, eius religio,* broadly meaning, the faith of the ruler is the religion of the realm.[9] The ruler is responsible for the spiritual welfare of his/her people, and in his or her dominion, uniformity of faith and practice is considered normative.[10]

To embrace a different faith is to be a "dissenter," with all of the explicit and implicit sanctions that term implies. Because of the connection with the state, Christendom often (even unconsciously) conceptualizes the Christian church—the *corpus Christianum*—in *territorial* ways. To belong to the "realm" means, by definition, that you share the faith of the "realm." Particular embodiments of the gospel, therefore, are linked to specific geographic regions and particular peoples.

Christendom has existed in both official, legally binding ways and in unofficial, more implicit, expressions. In certain regions, most notably Europe and Latin America, Christianity was legally and/or constitutionally granted special status and, therefore, we find Christendom there in its most explicit forms.[11] In other regions, such as the United States, church and state are officially kept separate, but a form of civil religion exists that finds innumerable ways to extend special status to Christianity over other non-Christian religions. In its ideal form, civil religion serves to unify the society and give the state legitimizing authority by providing a kind of moral cement for the culture. In the United States, for example, state funerals take place in the National Cathedral, God's name is invoked in public speeches, the president takes the oath of office with his hand on the Bible, and so forth.

Even now the flickering shadow of Christendom looms over America in the heated debates about crèches in public squares during Christmas, or whether it is legal for Alabama, Kentucky, and Ohio to display the Ten Commandments on courthouse walls.[12] I was in India in July 2007,

---

9. Literally, "whose the region is, his religion."

10. In the United Kingdom, for example, the Church of England is Anglican and the Church of Scotland is Presbyterian.

11. A contemporary European example would be Greece, whose constitution recognizes the Orthodox Church and the government pays clerical salaries.

12. Very public cases concerning the public display of the Ten Commandments in Kentucky, Ohio, and Alabama have elevated this issue in the wider national discourse.

when I read on the front page of the *Hindu Times* that for the first time in American history a Hindu priest named Rajan Ned from Nevada had been asked to open the U. S. Senate in prayer.[13] During the 2008 presidential election campaign, early presidential hopeful and Mormon, Mitt Romney from Massachusetts, was asked whether America was "ready" to elect a Mormon as president of the United States. In a few years, these types of debates will seem incredulous.

Official and unofficial Christendom arrangements have powerfully shaped our understanding of evangelism and missions, over many centuries. The worldview of Christendom also assumes that every important question has already been canvassed and answered. Christendom eventually lost the capacity to listen to new questions.[14] With the collapse of Christendom, the structures built on its paradigms are no longer viable. To illustrate this point, I will highlight three examples of major paradigm shifts, followed by a few examples of how these shifts might influence contemporary missionary preparation in the Western world.

MOVING FROM THE CENTER TO THE PERIPHERY

Christendom sees Christianity at the center of the culture and the mission field along the periphery, beyond the edges of the culture. Because Christianity is part of the prevailing plausibility structure and lies at the center of all public discourse, evangelism occurs passively. It is assumed that citizens grow up as Christians. Christianity is the normative expression of religious faith and ethical action, and there are no major dissenting voices or alternative religious worldviews. Therefore, the "gospel" does not need to robustly defend itself against either secular humanism or some alternative religious worldview such as Islam or Hinduism. Islamic or Hindu counterclaims are virtually nonexistent within the boundaries of Christendom. The most common encounters Christendom-type Christianity has with non-Christian faiths are either when it has engaged them as a cultural "other" in military campaigns (such as the Crusades or the Gulf Wars) or sponsored a missionary who is sent forth as an agent to transmit the gospel from the host culture to the new, "foreign" culture.

---

13. This took place in Congress on July 12, 2007.

14. I have developed the theological (not just missiological) implications for this in my book *Theology in the Context of World Christianity*.

However, with the collapse of the Christian center in the West, we find ourselves standing in the middle of a newly emerging mission field. We now stand more on the periphery of the world Christian movement. This demands a complete restructuring of how we understand and conceptualize missions.

MOVING FROM "JERUSALEM" TO "ATHENS"

Tertullian once famously asked, "What has Athens to do with Jerusalem . . . what has the academy to do with the church?"[15] Tertullian envisioned a culture with the revelation of God's Word at its center. In such a culture, divine self-disclosure received in and through the Bible trumps all other knowledge and discourse. For Tertullian, "Jerusalem" symbolically represents a society framed by revelation and, therefore, theological and cultural stability. "Jerusalem" signifies a redeemed congregation of the faithful gathered to hear God's Word, the centrality of the pulpit, and a shared consensus of the truthfulness and transformative nature of the gospel.

In contrast, "Athens" represents skepticism, dialogue, and speculative enquiry. "Athens" is the place of religious pluralism, doubt, and dialogic speculation. Tertullian did not want to live in "Athens" because it was messy, spiritually lost, and a far more unpredictable place than Jerusalem. However, as much as we may look back wistfully on simpler times, we must recognize that we are no longer proclaiming the gospel from the "Temple Mount" of our "Jerusalem." Instead, we are seeking to persuade the gospel into people's lives in the midst of the raucous, pluralistic, experimental, skeptical environment of the "Mars Hill" of their "Athens." There are competing deities and purported "revelations" that clamor for attention in this new post-Christendom marketplace.

MOVING FROM A GEOGRAPHIC,
PARTICULARISTIC IDENTITY TO A GLOBAL IDENTITY

Christendom, as we observed, conceptualizes Christian and non-Christian identity in geographic terms. Christendom represents the "Christian world," and everything outside those boundaries represents the "pagan world." A century ago, the famous 1910 Edinburgh World Missionary Conference divided the entire globe into two spheres: the Christian sphere and the

---

15. Tertullian, *De Praescriptione Haereticorum* 7.9.

non-Christian sphere. The implication was that "here" is a culture shaped by the gospel, and we are all Christians; and out "there" are cultures not yet under the sway of Christian hegemony, and that is where all the non-Christians reside. This perspective still hangs over Western missions like a shroud. *Here* we do "ministry," and *out there* we do "missions." We are simply not able to grasp the full force of the collapse of Christian faith in the West and the simultaneous emergence, as we shall explore later, of Christian vitality among new people groups throughout much of the Majority World.

We must recognize that the Western world can no longer be characterized as a Christian society. The important and operative phrase in the statement is "no longer." Many societies have never had anything remotely reflecting a dominant Christian ethos. Yet, some of those societies, like India and China, are still able to produce generations of vibrant expressions of Christian identity and faithfulness. Indeed, having taught in India for many years, I have observed how Indian Christians develop an understanding quite early about what it means to be part of a small, often misunderstood, Christian community who live out their faith within the larger context of a religious, cultural, and social life dominated by Hinduism. In short, they understand profoundly how to live *counter* to the culture and have become accustomed to living as a minority community and daily negotiating its nuances. Indian Christians, especially in North India, do not *expect* encouragement from the wider governmental and social structures. Their identity and self-understanding occupies the margins rather than the mainstream of the culture.[16] Christians in India don't have to pass through the fiery furnace of adapting to life in a post-Christendom world because they never had a Christendom arrangement to begin with.

In contrast, the collapse of Christendom has left Western Christians in an uncomfortable position because most have no real preparation or precedent for how to live on the margins, *counter* to the culture. For the most part, we don't know how to think about missions without ourselves being at the center (including sending structures, personnel, money, and strategic planning). Our long sojourn under the spell of Christendom has also meant that

---

16. Undoubtedly, this has spawned a wide array of Christian subcultural ghettos in India, who seek to live in isolation from the larger social and political context. This is particularly evident in South India. However, there are other Indian Christians who seem to reflect quite profoundly on what it means to live authentically as a Christian in the midst of a pluralistic, multireligious, Hindu-dominated India.

we find ourselves adhering to a rather domesticated version of the gospel. One of the legacies of Christendom is that it is willing to provide a safe haven for Christianity, but only at the cost of the steady domestication of Christianity, gradually smoothing down most of its rough prophetic edges, so that Christian identity and cultural identity became virtually seamless.[17]

Today missions, and indeed the gospel itself, have to be rediscovered in the West apart from Christendom. We must understand what it means to live in a world where Christian identity no longer has any particular geographic center. We can learn much from many of our Majority World brothers and sisters who have learned over many centuries how to live out their faith as a minority faith or, oftentimes, even in a context where there is a state-sponsored religion other than Christianity.[18]

How might the collapse of Christendom and these accompanying paradigm shifts practically influence the conceptualization and preparation of a new generation of missionaries? First, we must better train our students to critique culture. In the past, mission strategy has been very strong in the area of "contextualization." We emphasized the need to blend in and to cause as little cultural disruption as possible. While this is laudable and was an important corrective to a legacy of past cultural imperialism, it nevertheless conceptualizes the gospel as moving from one cultural *center* to another cultural *center*. It does not prepare students to move from one cultural *periphery* to another cultural *periphery*. We have to learn how to occupy the cultural periphery with prophetic authenticity.

Second, the gospel must become more robust in responding to very specific challenges that hitherto went unnoticed. In a Christendom context, the challenges of non-Christian religions or apathetic unbelief are distant and remote. Christians in this kind of setting lose their edge and the gospel becomes domesticated. Today the West is witnessing the rise of

---

17. Religious plurality in the United States became more pronounced after the passage of the Immigration Reform Act in 1965 under President Lyndon Johnson.

18. Many countries with a predominately Islamic population have their own version of "Christendom." However, rather than calling it something like "Islamdom," it is often best observed by the presence of Islamic *Sharia* as the governing arrangement and the effective merging of "mosque and state." Even in a place like India, which is governed by a secular constitution, Hinduism consistently receives special recognition and protection. Similar examples could be given with countries like Bhutan, Nepal, or Thailand. For example, Nepal has traditionally been a "Hindu kingdom," Bhutan a "Buddhist kingdom," and Saudi Arabia an "Islamic kingdom."

many new challenges: postmodern relativistic secularism, Islamic fundamentalism, aggressive atheism, and the seeping pluralism of Hinduism, to name a few. These challenges will inevitably force faithful Christians to articulate more clearly what constitutes genuine Christian identity. Christians in general, and future missionaries in particular, must be far more culturally articulate, globally aware, and theologically perceptive than they have been in the past.

Third, since the mission field is now everywhere, the classic (and important) distinction between monocultural *evangelism* and cross-cultural *missions* has become more nuanced. As we shall see, the distinction must be retained, but we have to separate it from its long association with geography. Indeed, even after Ralph Winter "dropped a bombshell on the playground" of the missionaries at Lausanne I in 1974 when he declared that missions is about *peoples*, not *places*, we still labor quite heavily under geographic paradigms and assumptions regarding the world, the church, and the mission field.[19] Christians in the West have not been prepared well to inhabit the mission field. Yet in post-Christendom society we can no longer assume that our own next-door neighbor understands even basic theological categories such as "God" or "sin" or "faith." Their knowledge of Jesus Christ is far more likely to come from a popular book like Dan Brown's *The Da Vinci Code* than from the Bible. Basic Christian discourse once sat comfortably behind the secure walls of Christendom. That day is now past. Christendom has collapsed. With the removal of these high walls, we will face many new challenges, but we will, increasingly, also have a better view of the world.[20]

Megatrend #2: The Rise of Postmodernism: Theological, Cultural, and Ecclesiastical Crisis

The Western church has responded in very different ways to the collapse of Christendom and the emergence of postmodernity, but none has managed the transition without experiencing some form of crisis.

---

19. In speaking at missions conferences across the country, I regularly hear people ask missionaries, "*Where* are you a missionary?" implying a geographic reply. Only rarely does anyone ask "*To whom* are you a missionary?" which would imply a people-group reply.
20. For further reading on this theme, I would highly recommend Bryan Stone's *Evangelism After Christendom: The Theology and Practice of Christian Witness* (Grand Rapids: Brazos, 2007) and David Smith's *Mission After Christendom* (London: Darton, Longman and Todd, 2003).

The West is experiencing a growing skepticism about the certainty of knowledge, an increasing distrust in history, and a general cultural malaise caused by the loss of meaning. In 1979, the French philosopher Jean-Francois Lyotard coined the term *postmodernism* to describe these changes.[21] According to Lyotard, the twin forces of Christendom and the Enlightenment provided the foundations for the modern world and gave Western societies a cohesive sense of an overarching truth informed either by a theistic, Judeo-Christian worldview or a secular belief in the inevitability of progress, the reliability of human reason, and the perfectibility of humanity. Western Christianity and the Enlightenment were never completely separate forces; each often supported and drew strength and energy from the other. The key shift from modernism to postmodernism, argues Lyotard, is marked by the collapse of what he calls these "grand narratives," which had guided and produced stability in the formation of modernity.

Today, the rise of relativistic pluralism, the loss of faith in the inevitable progress of the human race, and an increasing uncertainty about normative truth claims have resulted in a cultural, theological, and ecclesiastical crisis.[22] When the old plausibility structures began to collapse, the church was uncertain how to respond. There had been little preparation in the West for either occupying the margins of society or proclaiming the gospel in an increasingly postmodern milieu. Suddenly, a whole host of unresolved questions arose in the church. How much resistance should be applied, and in what areas? Is the loss of Christendom and the rise of postmodernity a tragedy or a gift? Would the collapse of Christendom produce a smaller but more robust church? Does postmodernism mark the end of religious faith in the West? These are a few of the questions that demanded the attention of the church.

The mainline Protestant churches[23] were desperate to make certain that the church retained its position at the cultural center. The mainline churches, and particularly the university divinity schools, which trained most of the pastors for mainline churches, wanted to make certain that Christianity remained intellectually respectable. The older denominations had long en-

---

21. Jean-Francois Lyotard, *The Postmodern Condition: A Report on Knowledge* (Minneapolis: University of Minnesota Press, 1985).
22. This "crisis" is often referred to as "postmodernity" but is sometimes characterized as a crisis within modernity.
23. The so-called "mainline" churches refers to the older established denominations such as Lutheran, Methodist (UMC), Episcopal, Presbyterian (PCUSA), and Congregational.

joyed a privileged position at the heart of Western culture and, understandably, they did not want to lose that influence. However, as the postmodern worldview continued to challenge the reliability of any overarching canopy of meaning or objective truth claims beyond one's personal narrative, the mainline churches felt that it was necessary to compromise the distinctive truth claims of historic Christian faith in order to retain credibility within the culture. What, under Christendom, had been a gradual, mild domestication became, under post-Christendom and postmodernity, a virulent attack upon the very heart of Christian identity. The scandalous particularity of the Christian message was increasingly unacceptable to those at the center of the culture. Tragically, the mainline churches were all too willing to accommodate those concerns in order to remain at the center. Through a long series of shifts that continues to the present, the mainline churches quietly abandoned their confidence in the trustworthiness and authority of Scripture, which led to an erosion of confidence in the supremacy of Jesus Christ and in the universal relevance of the gospel message.

Soon, relativistic pluralism was almost as rampant in the mainline churches as it was in the wider culture. This naturally led to the discrediting of any plausible rationale for missions and evangelism. Many Christians, along with the wider culture, began to associate the terms *missions* and *missionaries* with intolerance, inquisitions, colonial abuses, the Crusades, forced conversions, and so forth. Missionaries were more likely portrayed as purveyors of Western imperialism than as bearers of the good news of Christ's redemption. Put bluntly, missionaries were an embarrassment to this newly enlightened, tolerant church, and the church grew increasingly timid about commending the faith to those of other faiths. Not unsurprisingly, at a meeting in Bangkok in 1972, the World Council of Churches called for a moratorium on missions, and the mainline churches responded. Many missionaries were brought home and missionary activity, particularly evangelism and church planting, was largely discredited. The result was a precipitous decline of missionaries sent out from mainline, Western churches, especially missionaries who were committed to the traditional work of evangelism and church planting. There are, of course, a number of exceptions to this general trend, but this has been the broad story.[24]

---

24. These trends also have affected church membership. The decrease in membership in the mainline churches has been nothing less than staggering. For a few examples, note that between the

The Roman Catholic Church is centered in the heart of Western Europe and is the most obvious symbol of the Christendom project. Vatican II,[25] which was initiated by Pope John XXIII (1958–1963) and continued through the first two years of the papacy of Paul VI (1963–1978), sought to accommodate the church to many of the new postmodernist trends. The writings of liberal Roman Catholic theologians such as Karl Rahner (1904–1984), Edward Schillebeeckx (b. 1914), and Hans Kung (b. 1928) reflected many of the theological trends that were emerging in mainline Protestant thought. However, John Paul II (1978–2005) became increasingly concerned that the church was being overly influenced by secularism and the postmodern collapse of normative truth claims. John Paul II and Benedict XVI (2005–present)[26] regularly challenged the moral relativism, materialistic consumerism, unrestrained capitalism, and sexual promiscuity of the West. However, rather than taking up this challenge and offering a powerful Christian critique on the margins of an increasingly secular society, Roman Catholics in the West left the church in staggering numbers.[27] Many of those who did not formally leave the church simply became (or remained) only nominally Roman Catholic and in time generally shared the relativistic values of the larger culture.[28] The shocking sex scandals that exposed pedophile priests in Roman Catholicism in both Europe and North America served to further discredit the church. Craig Carter comments that the current Pope Benedict XVI "appears to favor a smaller church with a more distinctive witness rather than a culturally accommodated one."[29] However, it appears that despite the efforts of John

---

years 1970 and 2005, the following mainline denominations experienced significant loss: American Baptist, from 2,100,000 to 1,762,000; United Methodist, from 14,353,000 to 8,075,010; Presbyterian Church (USA), from 4,766,941 to 3,098,842. See http://www.worldchristiandatabase.org/wcd/esweb.asp?WCI=Results&Query=339 (accessed January 5, 2008).

25. Vatican II refers to the twenty-first ecumenical council of the Roman Catholic Church. It began under Pope John XXIII in 1962 and concluded with Pope Paul VI in 1965.

26. It was Cardinal Ratzinger (later, Benedict XVI) who coined the phrase "dictatorship of relativism." See, Philip Jenkins, *God's Continent* (Oxford: Oxford University Press, 2007), 71.

27. Ireland has always boasted the highest Roman Catholic affiliation and devoted church attendance in the world. However, Philip Jenkins quotes one Dublin professional who reflected the imploding state of Roman Catholicism in Ireland when he said, "I don't go to church, and I don't know one person who does. Fifteen years ago, I didn't know one person who didn't." See ibid., 32.

28. In Europe, for example, the average percentage of Roman Catholics who claim to regularly attend mass is less than 15 percent.

29. Craig A. Carter, *Rethinking Christ and Culture: A Post-Christendom Perspective* (Grand Rapids: Brazos, 2006), 24.

Paul II and Benedict XVI, the Roman Catholic Church of the early twenty-first century is in a difficult battle to forestall being both smaller in numbers *and* culturally accommodated.

Many who left the mainline Protestant churches and the Roman Catholic Church found themselves in one of the more conservative, growing evangelical churches. These churches purported to maintain their commitment to Scripture and the historic teachings of the church. In many of these churches, missions continued to be idealized, even if it was mostly understood within the now disappearing paradigms of Christendom. However, the evangelical churches were just as unprepared to respond to the collapse of the cultural center as the mainline Protestants. They have not known how to respond to the loss of confidence in the gospel in many of their youth, who are growing up in a relativistic, pluralistic, entertainment-oriented culture. Many members of evangelical churches, who had been joyfully ushered into the church on a kind of minimalistic basis, remained poorly equipped theologically and were no longer convinced that those without Christ are lost. Evangelicals have not been immune to the general cultural malaise. They were ill equipped for the robust catechesis (theologically and experientially) that was required to counteract the wider cultural attitudes.[30]

Some evangelical churches became more aware of the emerging vibrancy of the Majority World churches. This knowledge, coupled with a growing embarrassment about the ethnocentrism of nineteenth-century Western missionaries, led many to think that Western missionaries were either not needed or not wanted, or both. Therefore, it seemed best to stay home and support the indigenous missionaries through prayer and finances. Some mission agencies in the West tapped into this malaise by encouraging Western Christians just to stay home and "support the nationals" by sending in their monthly checks. One such agency boldly greeted visitors to their Web site with the words, "Thank you for staying home."[31] Many evangelicals felt that they had done their part by sending their "e-mails and dollars" rather than the traditional response of sending their "sons and daughters." The result

---

30. For more on the decline of orthodoxy among evangelicals, see David F. Wells, *Above All Earthly Pow'rs: Christ in a Postmodern World* (Grand Rapids: Eerdmans, 2005).

31. As reported in Stan Guthrie, *Missions in the Third Millennium: 21 Key Trends for the 21st Century* (Waynesboro, GA: Paternoster, 2000), 11.

was that a sort of missionary vision survived, but it was weak and passive at best.

The evangelical churches that identified themselves with the so-called "megachurch" movement faced their own challenges. To their credit, these churches understood that the traditional Christendom framework had collapsed. They realized that Western people were living in an increasingly postmodern milieu and inhabited a world that was highly skeptical of normative truth claims and had very little idea of what Christianity is. However, the megachurch movement was not prepared to occupy the margins of the culture. Instead, they were committed to impacting the culture by portraying Christianity as useful, relevant, and user-friendly.

The megachurch movement found that by abolishing the "strangeness" of the church and not challenging the overt materialistic commercialization of life in the West, they could bring in large numbers of people. Church services and programs became increasingly entertaining and pragmatic. Who wouldn't want to belong to a church that offered good music, family life centers, weight rooms, free counseling, exciting children's programs, and a Starbucks just inside the main entrance? Søren Kierkegaard once famously declared that "Christianity is the profoundest wound that can be inflicted upon a man, calculated on the most dreadful scale to collide with everything."[32] In contrast, the megachurch movement had learned to make the gospel's entrance into one's life almost seamless and unnoticeable. Their instinct has been to uncritically embrace the entertainment culture and the abandonment of Christian vocabulary and historical roots. Furthermore, with the exception of short-term missions, which were conceptualized as a "vacation with a purpose," very little attention has been paid to cross-cultural missions, either in creating sending and support structures for full-time career missionaries or seeing themselves as part of the wider global church. The megachurch movement unwittingly became just another illustration *of* popular culture, rather than a prophetic call to a radical gospel and the Jesus of the prophetic imagination. As megachurch pastor, Walt Kallestad declared in his popular megachurch

---

32. Søren Kierkeegaard, *Kierkegaard's Attack upon "Christendom" 1854–1855*, trans. Walter Lowrie (Princeton, NJ: Princeton University Press, 1944), 258.

guide, *Entertainment Evangelism*, "The Christian church needs to be friendlier than Disneyland."[33]

The "emergent" churches, like the megachurch, understand that we are living in a post-Christendom society. However, they have rejected the "spiritual Darwinism" of the megachurches, which assumes that bigger is better, and the one-size-fits-all veneer of spirituality that is characteristic of that movement. Instead, they emphasize more intimate relationships, authentic experiences, and images. The sermon is not as central in the emergent churches, because postmoderns mistrust authoritative statements and regard metanarratives as nothing more than propaganda. If megachurches are targeting the "seekers," the "emergent" churches are targeting the "*post*-seekers." However, the emergent churches, like the megachurches, have generally held an uncritical attitude toward postmodern epistemology. Like the megachurch, they are focused almost exclusively on those disillusioned with Christianity and the church in the West, that is, the *post*-Christian. Whether either of these movements (or "conversations" as the emergent people like to say) will be able to stimulate reproducible, orthodox Christianity remains to be seen. Furthermore, it is too early to tell whether or not the emergent church will engage with the larger, world Christian movement and be willing to support long-term cross-cultural missionaries.

This overview, of course, does not tell the whole story. Although this survey may appear overly pessimistic about Western Christianity, I will later explore the basis for my optimism about the future of the church in the West, once the transition to the margins has been negotiated. Furthermore, several thrilling models are emerging, which effectively proclaim the gospel to postmoderns. It also must be said that throughout all quarters of the church and throughout history, one finds heroic examples of self-sacrificing Christians whose lives faithfully bear witness to the gospel. My present point, however, is that we must candidly admit that the overall transition for Western Christians from occupying the center of the modern world to occupying the margins of a postmodern world has not gone particularly well,

---

33. Walt Kallestad, *Entertainment Evangelism: Taking the Church Public* (Nashville: Abingdon, 1996), 81. Karl Barth rightly commented, as follows: "Throughout the world, the Church is concerned today with the problem of the secularization of modern man. It would perhaps be more profitable if the Church were at least to begin to become concerned with the problem of its own secularization" (Karl Barth, *God in Action*, trans. E. G. Homrighausen and Karl J. Ernst [Manhasset, NY: Round Table, 1936], 15).

the inspiring and prophetic examples notwithstanding. One of the goals of this book is to rearticulate the missionary mandate to a church that no longer occupies the cultural center and has largely lost the biblical and theological moorings that have traditionally supported missionary endeavors.[34]

Megatrend #3: *The Collapse of the "West-Reaches-the-Rest" Paradigm*

Western Christians have been slow to grasp the full missiological implications of the simultaneous emergence of a post-Christian West and a post-Western Christianity.

The loss of Christian vitality in the West inevitably led to a dramatic loss in formal Christian identity. During the fifteen-year period between 1970 and 1985, at least people left the church every day in North America and Western Europe.[35] This pace shows no signs of abating. The old mission-sending center is collapsing.[36] One has to go back many centuries in church history to discover a dominant mission-sending paradigm that did not have the Western world at its center. Protestants have never known a dominant non-Western mission-sending paradigm, and we are at a loss as to how to make the transition to something different. Indeed, the "West-reaches-the-rest" paradigm was the unchallenged assumption behind the famous "white man's burden" of the nineteenth century.

The notion that areas that were once the traditional "mission field" could become, over time, the new heartland of Christian vitality was hardly contemplated by most Western Christians. Yet, Jerusalem, Antioch, North Africa, and Constantinople were at one time all at the center of Christian vibrancy, but today these places have only a very tiny remnant of Christianity remaining and, with the exception of Jerusalem, are almost completely Islamic.[37] In contrast, places like Lagos, Nigeria, and Seoul,

---

34. For an insightful examination of the destructive effects of secularization, see the Roman Catholic author George Weigel, *The Cube and the Cathedral: Europe, America, and Politics without God* (New York: Basic Books, 2006).

35. Lamin Sanneh, *Whose Religion Is Christianity? The Gospel Beyond the West* (Grand Rapids: Eerdmans, 2003), 15. Elizabeth Isichei says that the number leaving the church in the West was 7,500 per day. See Elizabeth Isichei, *A History of Christianity in Africa* (Grand Rapids: Eerdmans, 1995), 1.

36. This will be nuanced significantly later on in the text. There are many ways in which the West continues to remain a Christian center, even while the numbers decline.

37. For an excellent study of the decline of Christianity in the East, see Bat Ye'or, *The Decline of Eastern Christianity Under Islam: From Jihad to Dhimmitude* (London: Associated University Press, 1996).

South Korea, where the presence of Christianity at one time seemed almost unimaginable, are today vibrant centers of Christian faith. Furthermore, the idea that North America and Western Europe, which for centuries represented the center of Christian gravity and the most prolific mission-sending church in history, could lose the very faith they once espoused seemed remote.

There were those who predicted that the whole modern world would become one big "secular city" and modernization would inevitably lead to the collapse of religious faith everywhere. However, even in the West, "post-Christian" should not be assumed to be secular. Indeed, the eminent sociologist Peter Berger has noted that the "secularization theory is essentially mistaken" because "the assumption that we live in a secularized world is false." Berger goes on to say that the key assumption of the secularization theory, which insists that "modernization necessarily leads to a decline of religion, both in society and in the minds of individuals ... turned out to be wrong."[38] In recent years the West has produced a new, virulent stream of atheism, evidenced by the popularity of such books as Richard Dawkins's *The God Delusion* and Sam Harris's *The End of Faith* and *Letter to a Christian Nation.*[39] However, the larger trend has been a movement toward a dizzying array of new and old spiritualities. The greatest surprise has been the emergence of a vibrant, Majority World Christianity. Indeed, this is the great new fact of our time. This seismic change, which will be explored from a historical perspective in more detail in chapter 10, has enormous implications for what it means to study missions today, especially if you are living in North America or Western Europe. We have to learn about missions from the new perspective of living where the center has collapsed while new mission-sending centers are emerging. The new reality of mission is both multidirectional and multicontinental.

Missiologists as early as Johannes Verkuyl (1908–2000) saw the need for a multidirectional mission, even if he underestimated the full nature of the collapse of the Western center. In the preface to his well-known

---

38. Peter L. Berger, "The Desecularization of the World: A Global Overview," in *The Desecularization of the World: Resurgent Religion and World Politics,* ed. Peter L. Berger (Grand Rapids: Eerdmans, 1999; Washington, DC: Ethics and Public Policy Center, 1999), 2–3.

39. These new atheists are not, for the most part, atheist in the classical sense of the word, but they are more *etsi Deus non daretu* (living as if God does not exist), baptized in anti-Christian rhetoric, which mostly caricatures actual Christian positions.

Contemporary Missiology, he explains why he felt the need to write a new missiology to replace that of his mentor, John Bavinck's *Introduction to the Science of Missions* published in 1954.[40] Verkuyl said, "My predecessor's book reflects the age when missions were still seen as one direction only—from the West to the other continents. That time is past; the traffic now proceeds in many directions. We now live in an age of growing mutual assistance as together we fulfill our worldwide task."[41] However, despite his foresight, the basic textbooks used to train missionaries remained largely unchanged. Sometimes chapters were tacked onto the end to provide some perspective on the global church, but the overall framework for studying missions was still only a minor tweaking of the "West-reaches-the-rest" paradigm, and on the whole they still assumed a Christendom framework and were overly beholden to social science categories. This textbook seeks to be conceptualized entirely within the context of a post-Christendom, multidirectional missionary movement.

Megatrend #4: *The Changing Face of Global Christianity*
The simultaneous emergence of multiple new centers of Christian vitality has created a multidirectional mission with six sending and receiving continents.

In 1974 Walbert Buhlmann in *The Coming of the Third Church*[42] predicted a major demographic shift of the church to the global South. Later, missiologists such as Andrew Walls and Lamin Sanneh frequently spoke of the surprising emergence of a vital postcolonial church in the Majority World. David Barrett, the well-known demographer and editor of the *World Christian Encyclopedia,* provided the statistical support for this shift in 1982. However, as late as the year 1990, when *Christian History* magazine listed the one hundred most significant events in the history of Christianity, there was not a single reference to any event taking place in the Majority World or initiated by Majority World Christians.[43] There seemed to be little awareness that one of the most dramatic developments in the history of Christianity was unfolding in the Majority World.

---

40. John Bavinck, *Introduction to the Science of Missions*, trans. David H. Freeman (Philadelphia: Presbyterian and Reformed, 1960).
41. Johannes Verkuyl, *Contemporary Missiology: An Introduction* (Grand Rapids: Eerdmans, 1978), xiii.
42. Walbert Buhlmann, *The Coming of the Third Church* (Maryknoll, NY: Orbis, 1978).
43. Jenkins, *The Next Christendom*, 4. See *Christian History* 28 (1990): 51.

Philip Jenkins did more than anyone else to increase the general awareness among Western Christians about the rise of the Majority World church. With Jenkins's popularly written, best-selling books, *The Next Christendom, The New Faces of Christianity,* and *God's Continent,* it seemed that almost overnight the discourse about global Christianity changed and the general awareness increased significantly. Increasingly, I am more likely to receive nods of understanding than looks of disbelief when I speak about the shift in the "center of gravity" of the world Christian movement.

The statistical center of gravity refers to that point on the globe with an equal number of Christians living north, south, east, and west of that point. After its birth in Asia, Christianity had its most vigorous growth as it moved steadily westward and northward. As more and more people in the West embraced Christianity, the statistical center of gravity moved north and west. However, beginning in 1900, the statistical center began to shift dramatically southward, and in 1970 it began to move eastward for the first time in 1,370 years (see Figure 1.1)! Today, the statistical center of Christianity is located in Timbuktu! This means that for the first time since the mid-fourteenth century, the majority of Christians (approximately 67 percent) are now located outside the Western world. Some specific examples of how the church is changing will help to illustrate this shift better. At the turn of the twentieth century, the Christian church was predominately white and Western. In 1900, there were over 380 million Christians in Europe and less then 10 million on the entire continent of Africa.[44] Today there are over 367 million Christians in Africa, comprising one-fifth of the entire Christian church. Throughout the twentieth century a net average gain of 16,500 people were coming to Christ every day in Africa. From 1970 to 1985, for example, the church in Africa grew by over six million people. During that same time, as noted earlier, 4,300 people per day were leaving the church in Europe and North America.[45]

The church is not just moving southward, it is also moving eastward. In Korea, for example, despite the fact that Christianity was not formally

---

44. The World Christian Database notes that there were 380,641,890 Christians in Europe and 9,938,588 Christians in Africa. See www.worldchristiandatabase.org.

45. Sanneh, *Whose Religion Is Christianity?* 15. Elizabeth Isichei give the highter number of 7,500 per day leaving the church in the West. See Isichei, *History of Christianity in Africa,* 1.

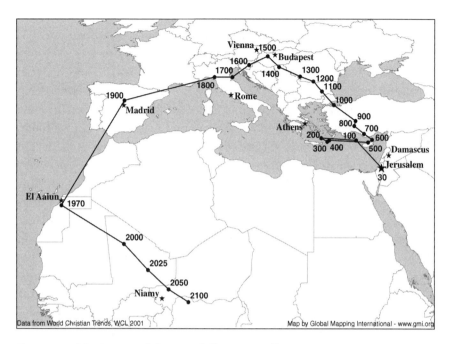

Figure 1.1. The Statistical Center of Christianity[46]

introduced within the country until the eighteenth century, today there are over 20 million Christians in South Korea alone with a total population of 49 million. In fact, South Korea is widely regarded as the home of the modern church growth movement, which is exemplified by the remarkable story of the Yoido Full Gospel Church founded by Dr. "David" Paul Yonggi Cho (b. 1936). Founded in 1958 with only five people in a small living room, the church now claims over 700,000 members, by far making it the largest church in the world.

India has been called the cradle of the world's religions, having given birth to Hinduism, Buddhism, Jainism, and Sikhism. Yet today this land of exotic Eastern religions is also the home of over 60 million Christians.[47]

46. Chart originally published in Todd M. Johnson and Sun Young Chung, "Tracking Global Christianity's Statistical Centre of Gravity, AD 33–AD 2100," *International Review of Mission* 93, no. 369 (April 2004): 167.

47. Todd M. Johnson, Sarah Tieszen, and Thomas Higgens, "Counting Christians in India, AD 52–2200," *Dharma Deepika* (forthcoming). This research was conducted at the Center for the Study of Global Christianity at Gordon-Conwell Theological Seminary, which produces the data for the *World Christian Encyclopedia*. This represents 6.15 percent of the population of India, far above the official 3 percent figure given by the government. However, the official

Church planting in India, particularly in the traditionally Hindu north, is taking place at such a blistering pace that many missiologists predict that by the year 2050 India will have over 100 million Christians.[48] However, even Korea and India cannot match the dramatic rise of the Chinese church. Even as recently as Mao Zedong's (Tse-tung) famous Cultural Revolution in China (1966–1976), there were only about one million Christians in China. Today, the Chinese church comprises over 90 million believers and is the fastest growing church on the planet with an average growth rate of 16,500 per day.[49]

You will have missed the main significance of these statistics if you only recognize that the church is *growing* in the Majority World. Throughout its history the church has experienced unexpected advances among new people groups and civilizations. Andrew Walls, among others, has pointed out the peculiar nature of Christian expansion through history.[50] The spread of Christianity has been one of serial, not progressive, growth. In other words, Christianity has not had an even, steady growth beginning with a central, cultural and geographic center from which it subsequently spread to its present position as the largest, most ethnically diverse religion in the world. Instead, Christian history has been one of advance and recession. Christian history has witnessed powerful penetrations of the gospel into certain geographic and cultural regions, only to later experience a major recession in that region and sometimes even wither away almost to extinction.[51]

---

figures disenfranchise millions of Christians who are counted as "tribals" or are remaining within Hindu communities.

48. This is the current projection of the Center for the Study of Global Christianity. This will represent 8.94 percent of the population of India.

49. David B. Barrett, George T. Kurian, and Todd M. Johnson, *World Christian Encyclopedia: A Comparative Survey of Churches and Religions in the Modern World,* 2nd ed. (New York: Oxford University Press, 2001), 191.

50. Andrew Walls, *The Missionary Movement in Christian History: Studies in the Transmission of Faith* (Maryknoll, NY: Orbis, 1996), 22–25.

51. This advance-and-recession motif is such a major theme in Christian history that the imminent church historian Kenneth Scott Latourette uses it as a major organizing motif for his famous multivolume work, *A History of Christianity.* See Kenneth Scott Latourette, *A History of Christianity,* vols. 1 and 2 (Peabody, MA: Prince Press, 2000). Latourette uses as his heading for A.D. 500–A.D. 950 the following: "The Darkest Hours: The Great Recession." The next section for A.D. 950–1350, he titles, "Four Centuries of Resurgence and Advance." The next section for 1350–1500 is titled, "Geographic Loss and Internal Lassitude, Confusion, and Corruption, Partly Offset by Vigorous Life." Many of the subheadings also reflect this theme as, for example, chapter 28, "Western Europe: Decline and Vitality," and chapter 40, "Stagnation and Advance: The Eastern Churches."

The major point to recognize, however, is that never before has the church had so many dramatic and *simultaneous* advances into *multiple* new cultural centers. It is not as if the story of our time were the withering away of Christianity in the West and the dramatic growth of Christianity in Africa, which will become the new standard-bearer of Christian vitality. Instead, we are now experiencing what John Mbiti calls multiple new "centers of universality."[52] Koreans, Chinese, Indians, Latinos, and Africans, among others, can all legitimately claim that *they* are at the center of the world Christian movement. We now have the collapse of the old center and the simultaneous emergence of multiple new centers. This is having a dramatic influence on the whole missionary movement. In fact, no longer can Christian history be understood from only one vantage point, whether cultural, geographic, or confessional. The new reality of the church is that it can only be fully appreciated from a global perspective.

Most Western missionary training and support structures assume a Western initiative in the development of strategy and assume a movement from the West out to the peripheries of missional engagement. From the perspective of the turn of the twentieth century, that made sense since in 1900 the vast majority of the world's 16,000 missionaries were from the West. However, the dawn of the twenty-first century witnessed a world with over 420,000 missionaries, of which only 12 to 15 percent were from the West.[53] This fact alone requires—and, thankfully, has already begun to stimulate—important changes in the existing structures of mission societies based in the West.[54]

Megatrend #5: The Emergence of a Fourth Branch of Christianity

We can no longer conceptualize the world Christian movement as belonging to Roman Catholic, Protestant, or Eastern Orthodox communions exclusively. The twenty-first century is characterized by enormous changes in Christian self-identity, which influence how the Christian message is understood and shared.

---

52. As quoted in Kwame Bediako, *Christianity in Africa: The Renewal of a Non-Western Religion* (Maryknoll, NY: Orbis, 1995), 157.
53. Guthrie, *Missions in the Third Millennium*, xii.
54. The dramatic shift in the center of gravity of the world Christian movement and the shift to multiple centers of universality have already begun to influence the books being used to train Western missionaries. One of the more helpful publications is Michael Pocock, Gailyn Van Rheenen, and Douglas McConnell, *The Changing Face of World Missions: Engaging Contemporary Issues and Trends* (Grand Rapids: Baker Academic, 2005).

The early followers of Jesus were simply known as followers of "The Way." The term "The Way" referred to a small movement *within Judaism* that regarded Jesus as the fulfillment of Jewish hopes and expectations. In this early period there was no concept of Christianity as a separate religion. The earliest followers of Jesus were Jews, and they understood Jesus and His message within that context. However, with the dramatic influx of Gentile believers, it became necessary to reconceptualize what it meant to be a follower of Jesus Christ. Thus, it was in Antioch, the home of the first major Gentile ingathering of believers, that the followers of Jesus were first called Christians (Acts 11:26).

In A.D. 330 the emperor Constantine relocated the capital of the Roman Empire to Byzantium in the East, renaming it Constantinople (modern-day Istanbul). Gradually, the church developed two distinct traditions, one Eastern and Greek and the other Western and Latin. Conflicts between these two traditions over (among other things) the authority of the pope and the Western insertion of the *filioque* clause[55] into the Nicene Creed eventually created a disruption in the church's unity. The "Great Schism," which formally separated Roman Catholic from Eastern Orthodox, occurred in 1054. From this point onward, it was necessary for Christians to reconceptualize the church, taking into account these very different expressions of Christianity, each with their own traditions, doctrinal emphases, understanding of ecclesiology, liturgy, and so forth.

The sixteenth century witnessed the culmination of a long-standing dissent movement within the church that finally broke out into what became known as the Reformation. Once the Reformers officially severed their ties with Rome and the movement grew in size and scale, it became necessary for Christians to, once again, reconceptualize the church in new ways. The current threefold configuration has served the church for nearly five hundred years.

The point of this is not to provide an overview of church history, as much as it is to recognize that the identity of the church has gone through major upheaval and transformation over time. If you grew up in the late twentieth century, even a cursory glance at most church history texts will confirm that since the time of the Reformation the Christian church has

---

55. A reference to the phrase "and the Son," which was added to the Nicene Creed affirmation about the Holy Spirit: "who proceeds from the Father *and the Son*."

been broadly conceptualized into three major divisions: Roman Catholic, Eastern Orthodox, and Protestant. This is a basic conceptual grid that dramatically influences how we understand the world Christian movement, and every student of church history learns it quite early on. Indeed, one's self-identity as a "Roman Catholic" or as a "Protestant" or as an "Orthodox" carries with it the enormous weight and force of history, the legacy of past decisive struggles, and the peculiarities of our own doctrinal and liturgical distinctiveness.

Because of the territorial legacy of Christendom discussed earlier, these three divisions also are used to identify ethnic, cultural, and political orientations that have very little to do with the Christian gospel but remain crucial to one's self-identity. The struggle between the Republic of Ireland and the six Protestant counties of Northern Ireland that belong to the United Kingdom is a classic example. The breakup of former Yugoslavia into Catholic Croatia, Islamic Bosnia, and Eastern Orthodox Serbia was determined largely by the association of ethnic particularity with religious identity.

However, the dramatic shift in the center of Christian gravity makes this tripartite framework increasingly untenable. It is time for another major reconceptualization of the church. Millions of new Christians are pouring into the church throughout the Majority World. Many of these new Christians cannot be easily categorized under any of the traditional headings. The basic practice for many years has been to regard any group that was not explicitly Roman Catholic or Eastern Orthodox to be, by default, Protestant. However, as the numbers grow, it becomes increasingly problematic to lump every non-Roman Catholic, non-Eastern Orthodox Christian movement into the "Protestant" camp when they clearly have no link whatsoever to any European "protest" movement. Yet, equally, they are neither related to the pope or to the magisterium in Rome nor do they submit to or receive any oversight from any Eastern Orthodox patriarch.

Many of these new Christians belong to various independent, Pentecostal-oriented movements. Others belong to independent, prophetic movements that are difficult to classify. Some of these movements are currently only quasi-Christian but are moving toward orthodoxy. Other quasi-Christian movements are emerging as independent movements outside the boundaries of historic orthodoxy. Still others claim to be following

Christ from within the boundaries of Hinduism or Islam, a phenomenon known as "insider movements," which has received considerable attention in missiological literature over the last decade.

In response to these trends, the 1982 edition of the *World Christian Encyclopedia* added several new categories, including "nonwhite indigenous" and "crypto-Christian." The 2001 edition of the same work changed the name of the "nonwhite indigenous" category to "independent" and added an additional category of "hidden" believers. The encyclopedia also reclassified millions of believers from the "Protestant" category to this new "independent" category.[56]

If the numbers of those in this "independent" category remained small, then perhaps the traditional tripartite division might find a way to survive the twenty-first century. However, the "independents" are easily the fastest growing segment of global Christianity and must become a central part of our larger conceptual framework. At the turn of the twentieth century, the largest blocks of Christian affiliation were the Roman Catholics at 266 million, followed by Eastern Orthodox at 115 million and Protestants at 103 million. It is estimated that at the turn of the twentieth century, there were less than 8 million "independent" Christians in the entire world. However, in the opening decade of the twenty-first century, there are currently 1.1 billion Roman Catholics, 423 million independents, followed by 386 million Protestants and 252 million Orthodox. Thus, independent Christians now form the second largest segment of Christian identity.[57]

This new Christian megablock is not easy to categorize. The other major branches were largely defined because of a historical separation with Roman Catholicism, which emerged due to particular, identifiable historical developments. This brought a certain kind of cohesion, historically and doctrinally, to these movements, which, in turn, forms the main backbone of the narrative that is rehearsed and, in time, shapes and forms

---

56. The 1981 edition (p. 6) projected 154 million Christians in the "nonwhite indigenous" category. The name of this category was changed to "independent" in the 2001 edition, and the number of Christians in this category was revised to 385 million "independent" believers. The *World Christian Encyclopedia* also found "hidden" believers within Hinduism in seven countries and "hidden" believers within Islam in fifteen countries.

57. David B. Barrett, Todd M. Johnson, and Peter F. Crossing, "Missiometrics 2008: Reality Checks for Christian World Communions," *International Bulletin of Missionary Research* 32, no. 1 (January 2008): 29. The estimated 423 million Christians classified as "Independent" does not include an additional 36 million Christians who are classified as "marginal" Christians.

the identity of the movement. However, in the case of the independent churches, there is no single, pervasive point of identity. It is true that there are certain broad trends that sometimes are cited. For example, sometimes it is noted that the independent churches are normally led by laypeople without formal training and have very informal leadership structures. Others point out that they are frequently Pentecostal/charismatic in their experience, rely heavily on powerful, prophetic figures for guidance, and have little sense of the larger sweep of church history. Still others point out the emphasis that is sometimes placed on certain legalistic taboos, strange new liturgies, peculiar doctrines, worship practices, or missionary zeal. The point is that there is no single galvanizing "mark" of these new Christians.

Nevertheless, the term *independent* seems an insufficient and somewhat inaccurate descriptor, even though it is a vast improvement from "crypto" or "marginal" Christian.[58] It probably will take several more decades before it becomes evident whether there might be enough shared perspectives or some grand narrative that will carry enough ballast to galvanize these various independent strands to recognize larger points of coherence, connectedness, and identity. For example, what distinctive features might be found in movements as diverse as the Asian house church network, the African Initiated Churches of the apostolic variety, the Fourth Watch in the Philippines, the City Harvest Church in Singapore, the Fill the Gap Healing Centers in South Africa, the Meiti in India, the Cooneyites of Australia, the Igreja ev Pente of Brazil, and the Han house churches in China? Eventually, leaders from these various independent movements will find ways of describing themselves as they interact with other segments of the global church. As dialogue increases they may discover deeper points of convergence. Until then, phrases like the independent churches, the Majority World Church, the house churches, the indigenous churches, the emerging Global South churches, or the Younger Churches will continue to be used. The important point is that, whatever nomenclature we use, this "fourth branch" of Christianity must become central in our understanding of the twenty-first-century church and what it means to be a participant or global player in God's mission in the world.

---

58. The word *independent* implies sovereignty and self-sufficiency, both of which cannot properly be applied to a church, which by definition is submitted to the authority of Christ.

Megatrend #6: Globalization: Immigration, Urbanization,
and New Technologies
Globalization has fostered dramatic changes in immigration, urbanization,
and technological connectivity. The result is that the traditional sending
structures and geographic orientation that have dominated missions since
the nineteenth century are no longer tenable.

In every generation, Christian ministry has never occurred in a vacuum but has fundamentally been a contextual event. However, the forces of globalization have created a new situation in which there is no such thing as a mere local ministry context. Every local context today is informed by the larger global context. The long-held distinction of "home" missions and "foreign" missions is passing away, not just because of the collapsing center noted above, but also because of forces set into motion by globalization, which have had such a profound effect on all of us.

Globalization has been summarized as a "complex connectivity,"[59] whereby local events and social relationships are influenced and shaped by distant events. This "complex connectivity" has influenced every sphere of life, including politics, social relationships, economics, technology, science, culture, and religion. I will highlight three areas that are having a profound effect on how we understand and conceptualize missions in the twenty-first century: immigration, urbanization, and technological connectivity.

IMMIGRATION

The European people groups of the Western world are experiencing a demographic crisis that has been aptly described as autogenocide, a slow form of cultural suicide. In order for any society to maintain its existing population, it is necessary to maintain a minimum fertility rate of 2.1 children per woman. Currently, the average fertility rate in Western Europe falls well below that, averaging 1.4.[60] To provide some perspective, these statistics translate to a one-fifth drop in the population in just one generation. In fact, Europe's "old stock" population is, according to Philip Jenkins, declining faster than it did during the worst years of World War II, when it

---

59. John Tomlinson, *Globalization and Culture* (Chicago: University of Chicago Press, 1999), 2.
60. Jenkins, *God's Continent*, 6. Some representative samples in Europe are, on the low end, Spain 1.28, Italy 1.28, and Germany 1.39; and on the higher end, Ireland 1.86, and France 1.9.

suffered the brunt of Hitler's atrocities. When the European Union was founded, it collectively represented approximately 14 percent of the world's population. Currently, those same European countries represent about 6 percent of the world population, and by 2050 it will be down to 4 percent.[61]

These statistics also mean that the median age of Europeans is steadily rising. With the rise of an elderly, graying Europe, the only way to maintain a viable society where young people are working and paying taxes is through massive immigration. For Europe the shortage of workers has been supplied by immigrants from Africa, Asia, and the Middle East. This is slowly leading to significant changes in religious affiliation and practice in Europe. The challenge has been summarized well by Mark Steyn, who wrote that "the design flaw of the secular social-democratic state is that it requires a religious-society birthrate to sustain it."[62] Since the vast majority of predominantly Islamic countries have population rates ranging well above 2.1, they have an excess population in reasonable proximity to Europe and are eager to migrate.[63] Thus, one of the major trends in Western Europe over the last sixty years has been the collapse of Christendom and the rise of Islam.[64] According to the Pew Forum on Religion in Public Life, there are now some countries in Western Europe where the number of Muslims attending a mosque in a given week outnumbers those who attend church.[65] The anxiety this is producing in Europe is one explanation for the popularity of recent publications such as *Eurabia* by Bat Ye'or and Walter Laqueur's *The Last Days of Europe*.[66]

The United States also is facing a declining birthrate among people groups of European descent, but not nearly at the alarming rate of Europe. In fact, because of immigration, the overall population of the United

---

61. Robert Spencer, "Eurabia?" Dhimmi Watch, posted April 4, 2004, http://www.jihadwatch.org/dhimmiwatch/archives/001432.php.

62. As quoted in Jenkins, *God's Continent*, 7.

63. A few examples include Somalia at 6.76, Afghanistan 6.69, Yemen, 6.5, Iraq 4.18, and 3.4 in Egypt. In contrast to Europe, the Arab world has grown from 80 million to 320 million over the last fifty years.

64. Interestingly, even after Muslims immigrate to Europe, they do not mirror the European birthrate. The birthrate among Muslims living in Europe is currently 3.5 children per woman.

65. "An Uncertain Road: Muslims and the Future of Europe," Pew Forum on Religion and Public Life, 6. See http://pewforum.org/docs/index.php?DocID=60. See, also, Timothy M. Savage, "Europe and Islam," *Washington Quarterly* 27, no. 3 (summer 2004): 25–50.

66. Bat Ye'or, *Eurabia: The Euro-Arab Axis* (Madison: Fairleigh Dickinson University Press, 2005); Walter Laqueur, *The Last Days of Europe: Epitaph for an Old Continent* (New York: Thomas Dunne Books/St. Martin's, 2007).

States is on the rise, and remarkably, the median age of 35 in the United States is not expected to drop over the next fifty years. Contrast that with the average median age in Europe, which, over the same time period, will rise from 37 to 52.3.[67] The population of the United States is currently around 300 million but is projected to rise to 400 million by 2050 and 570 million by 2100.[68] The United States continues to be a destination of choice for immigrants and, like Europe, is becoming less European and less white. Indeed, since the 1965 Immigration Reform Act, the ethnic diversity of American society has increased dramatically. However, the most significant difference between immigration in the United States and European immigration is that the United States draws far more heavily on Latino, African, Filipino, Korean, and Chinese groups, who are far more likely to be Christians or to become Christians after immigration than their counterparts in Europe. Indeed, the fastest growing religious demographic in the United States are the non-Anglo Christian churches.[69]

How will these dramatic changes in immigration influence missions in the twenty-first century? First, as the old Christendom center collapses, the immigration population represents the most important new wave of future missionaries to the West. Later, this textbook will explore some of the strategic differences between "Old Northern" and "New Southern" missionaries, but the new missionaries, for example, are far more likely to target the West as a mission field than the 10/40 window, which has received so much attention and focus by evangelical missions from the West. Despite the recent anti-immigration sentiment in the United States, Christians should understand that immigration represents the most important hope not only for the ongoing viability of our society but also for the reevangelization of the West. In *The Next Christendom*, Jenkins suggests somewhat tongue-in-cheek that Diana Eck's book, *How a "Christian Country" Has Become the World's Most Religiously Diverse Nation* should really be titled *How Mass Immigration Ensured that a Christian Country Has Become an Even More Christian Country.*[70] Second, the old geographic distinctions that associate certain regions of the world with particular ethnic populations are no

---

67. Jenkins, *God's Continent*, 7.
68. Jenkins, *The Next Christendom*, 100.
69. In Boston where I lived, there are more people who worship Jesus Christ in languages other than English than those who worship in English.
70. Jenkins, *The Next Christendom*, 105.

longer viable. Latinos now make up the majority of California's population. Texas has become a majority-minority state. By 2050 the minority groups will statistically outnumber the whites in the whole country. John Wesley once said, "The world is my parish." In today's new global context, we must amend that and say, "The world is *in* my parish."[71]

URBANIZATION

The corollary to the dramatic rise in immigration has been the equally dramatic rise in global urbanization. Urbanization undoubtedly has been one of the megatrends of the twentieth century. The forces of globalization have collapsed the traditional space and time barriers, allowing for increased travel and relocation. Globalization has shifted increasingly higher percentages of the world away from agrarian farming and toward urban centers. At the turn of the twentieth century, the top twenty-five most populated cities in the world were in Europe and North America. Today, none are in Europe and only two in North America (Los Angeles and New York). The megacities of the world are now places like Tianjin, Tokyo, Osaka, Karachi, Lagos, Seoul, and Mumbai, to name a few.[72] Today more people live in urban areas than rural areas (55 percent), a remarkable statistic given that at the turn of the twentieth century only 16 percent lived in urban areas. [73]

Urbanization has far-reaching implications for twenty-first-century missiological strategy. First, most evangelistic and church-planting strategies were formulated for and implemented in rural settings because that was the dominant context of nineteenth-century missions. Twentieth-century strategies often simply made minor adjustments to the nineteenth-century models. Today, entirely new paradigms of

---

71. By 2050, according to Jenkins, one-third of America will be Asian and Latinos who are inclined toward, not away from, Christianity. See *God's Continent*, 284. For more on the ways immigration is transforming our lives, see Weigel, *The Cube and the Cathedral*.

72. The World Christian Database projects that the top fifteen most populated cities in the world in the year 2025 will be as follows: Mumbai, 30 million; Lagos, 30 million; Tokyo, 28 million; Karachi, 24 million; Dhakka, 23 million; Calcutta, 21 million; Mexico City, 21 million; Sao Paulo, 20 million; Shanghai, 20 million; Delhi, 19 million; New York, 18 million; Beijing, 17 million; Cairo, 16 million; Tianjin, 15 million; Manila, 15 million. Please note that no European cities are even on this list and New York is the only Western city to make the list. See www.worldchristiandatabase.org.

73. Barrett and Johnson, eds., *World Christian Trends, AD 30–AD 2200*, 393, table 10-10. Barrett and Johnson project that the trend towards urbanization will continue well into the twenty-first century. By 2025 they project that the percentage of urban dwellers will be close to 60 percent.

mission strategy must emerge that conceptualize a mission field that is primarily urban. Even today, despite the dramatic rise in urbanization, I find that many people continue to assume that an "unreached" people group must live in a remote or tribal region of the world.

Second, the peoples of the Majority World often live in urban areas characterized by widespread corruption, poverty, disease, and oppression. Today's missionaries must have a more nuanced understanding of how to communicate and proclaim the gospel in a holistic way in order to address the complex challenges of urban life and experience. Finally, urbanization often means that people live in the midst of religious pluralism and cultural diversity. Today's missionaries must be culturally savvy, conversant with non-Christian religions, and aware of the complexities of urban social interactions and the ways in which information is passed on and assimilated, which are profoundly different than in traditional agrarian, rural societies.

TECHNOLOGY

The "complex connectivity" that is integral to globalization is made possible by technology. Twentieth-century missions was profoundly changed by technological advances in travel and communication, most notably the advent of affordable jet travel and the laying of the transatlantic telephone lines. Twenty-first-century technology has exponentially transformed our lives even more, especially in the information and communication technologies. We live in a world of iPods, instant messages, YouTube, chat rooms, Twitter, MySpace, and Facebook. Cellular or satellite phones and e-mail have placed almost every missionary in the world in a position of potential, instantaneous access.[74] The Web and easily transported CD-ROMs have put an unprecedented amount of information at our fingertips with the click of a mouse. Technology has been the source of many opportunities that would have seemed unthinkable to previous generations. For example, I was a member of the faculty of Gordon-Conwell Theological Seminary in the United States as well as the faculty of the New Theological College in Dehra Dun, North India. For the last twenty years, I have trained missionaries in both

---

74. This also has been aided by the availability of radio-based e-mail for areas of the world without telephone lines.

places, teaching annually on both continents, a practice unthinkable in any previous generation.

However, despite all the benefits, technology also has created fresh challenges. Technology has produced a new kind of grassroots global connectivity that has helped to uproot the "top-down" metanarratives of modernism, which had produced a single "grand canopy" of meaning and *telos* for an entire civilization. In the twenty-first century, the church and the message of the gospel often are reduced to just another message among thousands that might give meaning to a person's personal narrative but can no longer pretend to be a normative claim for the world. We live in a world saturated with information and overwhelmed by choices. In an information-saturated world, framed by personal preferences and immersed in the commoditization of all of life, it becomes extremely difficult for the gospel to be properly heard.

Effective twenty-first-century missions requires a new determination to proclaim and herald the "grand narrative" framed by creation, fall, incarnation, redemption, and a final eschatological climax of the divine/human drama to an increasingly postmodern world. All people, in all times and places, need to discover the life-transforming narrative that is rooted in the person and work of Christ. Jesus Christ and the biblical message do not change, but how we communicate the gospel effectively in such a new context requires some significant changes. We must resist the pressure to treat people as "religious consumers" to whom we "market" the gospel and create some kind of "market share." This inevitably compromises the church, tempting her to proclaim a kind of minimalistic gospel that focuses on the *least* one has to do to be a Christian. This approach must be decisively abandoned and replaced with intensive discipleship objectives that produce a leaner, far more robust, culturally savvy, and theologically literate church.

Megatrend #7: A Deeper Ecumenism
The simultaneous emergence of postdenominational identity among many, as well as the emergence of thousands of new denominations, requires the forging of new kinds of unity that transcend traditional denominational and confessional identities.

Old Christendom was built upon alliances that were determined by pivotal political and historical developments, confessional/theological agreements, and/or shared missional objectives. This eventually produced not only the major tripartite structure noted earlier but also a myriad of deeper alliances such as Roman Catholic religious orders and Protestant denominations. As noted earlier, this has had a profound influence on how we traditionally have conceptualized the global church and our particular place in it.

Andrew Walls has insightfully pointed out that there is an enormous difference between writing church history and writing *Christian* history. Walls says, "Church history writing requires ecclesiological choice; it assumes, consciously or unconsciously, a specific identification of the church, or at least a particular manifestation of it."[75] When students sign up for a course in church history, what is actually being studied is a well-defined selection of themes within the history of Christianity that are relevant to a particular group of Christians who share a particular geographic and confessional heritage.[76] This has been even more obvious in books on, or courses about, missions history.

However, as global Christianity becomes increasingly made up of peoples from Asia, Africa, and Latin America, and as these newly emerging indigenous expressions become normative, the whole structure of our understanding and discourse about Christian history and mission history must also undergo a dramatic change. In the West our cultural and ecclesiastical history flows primarily from the Roman Empire, so what happened in Western Europe dominates our understanding of history. However, after having spent considerable time with Christians from various parts of Asia, I can testify that the Roman Empire does not loom nearly as large in the perspective of peoples shaped by the Persian, Ashokan, or Han Empires. This background influences how Christian history is understood and told. Thus, the narratives that rehearse mission history need to be reconceptualized so that they reflect a more global perspective on the church, particularly as African and Asian Christianity become increasingly normative and Western Christianity becomes more ancillary to the larger global movement.

One of the most important transformations that this shift offers is a new basis for ecumenism within the global church that transcends the

---

75. Andrew F. Walls, *The Cross-Cultural Process in Christian History* (Maryknoll, NY: Orbis, 2002), 5.
76. Ibid.

traditional barriers. We must find new ways—which may actually be a recovery of more ancient ways—of engaging in a more globally informed discourse with committed Christians from around the world. We need to discover a *deeper* ecumenism for the twenty-first century.

Let me clarify what I mean by "deeper ecumenism" because the term *ecumenical* has been used in a wide variety of ways.[77] I am not using the term *ecumenical* in reference to any attempt to find some grand, eternal, structural unity for the church. There are over thirty-eight thousand distinct denominations in the world, and the deeper ecumenism I am referring to does not necessarily mean that this number will dramatically decrease. I am not using the term to refer to any vision of the church that models an uncritical accommodation to modernity by sacrificing *kerygmatic* essentials of the historic Christian proclamation. The kind of ecumenism I am referring to is the deeper, older ecumenism that finds its roots in historic Christian confessions. A case for this has been effectively set forth in Thomas Oden's excellent work, *The Rebirth of Orthodoxy*.[78][78]

We can no longer afford the kind of entrenched sectarianism that has often characterized fundamentalism and evangelicalism. This does not mean that we must relinquish our distinctive theological convictions. On the contrary, being in conversation with the global church will not only serve to enrich our own theological perspectives, but, more importantly, it will also lead us to a deeper understanding of the *depositum fidei*, that ancient apostolic faith that forms our common confession.

However, it will mean that we must distinguish more explicitly and publicly between the *kerygmatic* truths that unite all true Christians and the *adiaphora,* where there are legitimate differences. Sadly, the old world of Christendom permitted the kind of divisions that have marred the church's witness and her obedient response to Jesus' high priestly prayer that we "may be one" (John 17:11). The advent of global Christianity with multiple centers of vitality means that we have an opportunity to see ourselves first and foremost as *Christians* proclaiming the apostolic faith and only secondarily as Reformed Christians, Pentecostal

---

77. For a full exposition of my understanding of ecumenism and how it compares and contrasts with various usages of the word, see my *Theology in the Context of World Christianity,* 184–88.
78. Thomas Oden, *The Rebirth of Orthodoxy* (New York: Harper SanFrancisco, 2003). See also, J. I. Packer and Thomas Oden, *One Faith: The Evangelical Consensus* (Downers Grove, IL: InterVaristy Press, 2004).

Christians, Dispensational Christians, Arminian Christians, or independent Christians. We also need to invest more time in constructive engagement with our Roman Catholic and Eastern Orthodox brothers and sisters. We cannot, and should not, simply deny the defining struggles that produced the Protestant movement. Nevertheless, we must learn to listen better to the perspectives and struggles of other Christians and to endeavor to see ourselves as members of a global Christian movement.

The global church is a tapestry of diversity. Despite our many differences, however, there are certain great truths that unite us. Christ Himself, who is the Truth, unites all Christians in every age around those affirmations that have been held *semper ubique ab omnibus.*[79] This is more than the unity expressed by a creed, although it should not be less than that. Rather, it refers to a deeper, spiritual unity that acknowledges our catholicity because we are all members of the body of Christ and share a common union with Jesus Christ and a burden to bear witness to Him in authentic ways throughout the whole world. This has important implications for twenty-first-century missions, including the meaning of collaboration and partnership, our understanding of ecclesiology in a global context, and our conceptualization of Christian identity.

THE NEED FOR A *SELAH* AND REBIRTH

The collective force of these seven megatrends means that we have to do much more than just tweak our existing missiological paradigms, training programs, and methodological assumptions. Rather, these themes call for the need to completely rethink, not only how we train and prepare missionaries, but also how we conceptualize both the global church and the mission field. What we must resist is a kind of "business-as-usual" approach to missions, which offers only a few minor adjustments or missiological window dressing while our main assumptions go unchallenged.

Earlier I noted that in 1972 the World Council of Churches called for a moratorium on missions. To this day, the very word *moratorium* still makes me shudder because I associate the word primarily with the loss of the central biblical mandate to evangelize and plant new churches. Nevertheless, at the risk of being misunderstood by those who may not know of my lifetime commitment to missions, I think there is wisdom in calling for

---

79. "always, everywhere, by everyone."

a *temporary* period of readjustment and reassessment. I am not calling for a moratorium but rather what I prefer to call a "missions *selah*." The word *selah* occurs throughout the Psalms. The precise meaning of *selah* is unknown. However, most believe that it signifies some kind of musical pause or interlude. This is precisely what I have in mind. We in the West have been accustomed to playing the melody. We directed the orchestra and decided what pieces would be played and where, and the players were mostly from the West. Now, the orchestra is far more diverse, and we are being asked to play harmony, not melody. This requires a temporary interlude—a time to pause and reassess, a time to think about what we are doing in fresh ways.

Like any healthy heart, we must have a proper balance between the active pumping of blood (systolic) and the brief period of rest (diastolic), when the blood is being reoxygenated and prepared to be pumped out in ways that give life and nourishment. The heart of missions needs this time of rest if we are to maintain long-term vitality. This textbook is designed to help during this transitional interlude. This transition, like the word *selah*, is somewhat ambiguous and no one knows precisely what this will mean for missions. Nevertheless, I am convinced that if we are attentive to the refreshing winds of the Holy Spirit during this tumultuous and yet thrilling time, we will have a missiological rebirth where, side by side with the global church, we will see a remarkable renewal of the church's life and faith like we have not known. This textbook seeks to envision what this new and exciting chapter of missionary training, preparation, and collaboration might look like.

Section B

The Triune God and
the Missio Dei

— 2 —
A Trinitarian, Missional Theology

TWO STUDENTS, LARRY PAGE and Sergey Brin, sat in their dorm room at Stanford University and pledged themselves to the following mission statement: "To organize the world's information and make it universally accessible and useful." The result was *Google*, the most powerful and widely used search engine in the world.[1] Today, it seems that both large and small businesses are all adopting mission statements. Even businesses with an unambiguous and widely known purpose such as Federal Express, Barnes & Noble, and Nike all have mission statements. Nike's mission statement, for example, is "to bring inspiration and innovation to every athlete in the world." The mission craze has even begun to influence the government. For example, the state department now has a mission statement.[2] Some marriage counselors are now encouraging couples to write up their own personal mission statement. It seems that it is no longer only the church that has a mission. We live in a world awash with mission statements—everybody is on a mission. Clearly the word *mission* has lost its identity as an exclusively Christian term.

In formulating a missiology for the twenty-first century, the word *mission* needs very careful definition if it is to continue as a useful word for the church. Despite the challenges, the word can continue to serve the church well into the twenty-first century, although it needs renovation. This becomes clear when we begin to realize the changing history of the word even within the church. The word *mission* (or *missions*) as a reference

---

1. *Google* is a term coined by Milton Sirotta for the number 1 followed by 100 zeros. It symbolizes the vast amount of information in the world.
2. The mission statement of the U.S. Department of State is "to create a more secure, democratic and prosperous world for the benefit of the American people and the international community."

to people sharing their faith around the world, extending the church, and fulfilling the Great Commission is a relatively recent application of that word. It was in the sixteenth century that the Jesuits first began to use the term *mission* in reference to spreading the gospel to people who were not Christians. Until that time *mission* was "used exclusively with reference to the doctrine of the Trinity, that is, of the sending of the Son by the Father and of the Holy Spirit by the Father and the Son."[3] In short, the word *mission* was originally about God and *His* redemptive initiative, not about us and what we are doing. However, in its popular usage within the church, it seems that *mission* has now come to refer almost exclusively to various tasks the *church* is doing.

In recent years, especially with the advent of the church mission statement, the word has been broadened even further to mean "everything the church should be doing," thus robbing the word of any distinctive emphasis or character. Carlos Cardoza-Orlandi, in *Mission: An Essential Guide,* even cites this as one of the five models of mission in the church today. He calls it the "mission-is-everything model" and points out what many of us have observed, namely, that *mission* has come to mean everything from basketball in the church gym, to a day-care center, to church planting in Papua New Guinea, and everything in between.[4] The word has slowly migrated from a theocentric connotation to a more anthropocentric one. In other words, there is a vital difference between a word that is applied primarily to the Trinity and the inner life of *God's* action and a word that is primarily understood to refer to human endeavors and the actions of the church. Clearly, the word *mission* needs a twenty-first century renovation. However, I suggest that what we need is not a renovation to a new meaning but rather a reclaiming of something closer to the original meaning of the word.

MISSION AND MISSIONS

In this book the word *mission* refers to *God's redemptive, historical initiative on behalf of His creation. Mission* is first and foremost about God and His redemptive purposes and initiatives in the world, quite apart from any actions or tasks or strategies or initiatives the church may

---

3. David Bosch, *Transforming Mission* (Maryknoll, NY: Orbis, 1991), 1.
4. Carlos F. Cardoz-Orlandi, *Mission: An Essential Guide* (Nashville: Abingdon, 2002), 24–25.

undertake. To put it plainly, *mission* is far more about *God* and *who He is* than about *us* and *what we do.*

In some ways, the call for this renovation of the word *mission* is new, and in other ways it is not. Let me begin by explaining how it is not new. In 1910, the first major world missionary conference in modern times took place in Edinburgh, Scotland. This was the beginning of a series of major worldwide conferences sponsored by the International Missionary Council, which were held in various parts of the world, including Jerusalem (1928), Tambaram (near Chennai, India) (1938), Whitby, Ontario (1947), Willengen, Germany (1952), and Accra, Ghana (1957/58).[5] It was at the Willengen conference in July 1952 that a new model of mission was proposed that clearly articulated that God's redemptive action in the world *precedes* the church, meaning that the church should not perceive itself as the starting point for mission activity in the world. The defining phrase that was later used to conceptualize this view of mission was *missio dei*, a phrase originally coined by German missiologist Karl Hartenstein in 1934. The phrase *missio dei,* or the "mission of God," was later popularized by Georg Vicedom as a key concept in missions with the publication of his 1963 landmark book, *The Mission of God: An Introduction to the Theology of Mission.* Vicedom insightfully conceptualized mission as our participation in the Father's mission of "sending the Son." Vicedom declared that "the missionary movement of which we are a part has its source in the Triune God Himself."[6]

The idea of understanding mission through the lens of the *missio dei* is fundamentally sound, and it will be the foundation of the Trinitarian missiology that this book proposes. The problem with the twentieth-century ecumenical notion of *missio dei* was not so much in the concept itself as in the application of the concept and how it was actually understood and practiced. Certainly in his classic articulation of the *missio dei,* Vicedom

---

5. In the 1961 meeting of the World Council of Churches in New Delhi, the IMC became a department of the WCC. The year 2010 marks the one hundredth anniversary of the original conference. To celebrate the event, there will be two major global missionary conferences dedicated to reflecting on how missions has changed over the last century and what the next century might look like. One, with broad ecumenical sponsorship, will take place in Edinburgh in June of 2010; and another, sponsored jointly by Lausanne and the World Evangelical Association, will take place in Cape Town, South Africa, in October of 2010.

6. Georg Vicedom, *The Mission of God: An Introduction to the Theology of Mission,* trans. Gilbert A. Thiele and Dennis Hilgendorf (Saint Louis: Concordia, 1965), 5. Vicedom is quoting Hans Hartenstein.

in no way intended for God's mission to be separated from the church's proclamation and activity. When Vicedom declared that we can no longer speak of the "mission of the church,"[7] he meant that the church should not see its work in the world apart from its source in the *missio dei*. Nevertheless, a flaw occurred in the application of the *missio dei* in the last century because of the undue separation of God's mission from the church. It is here that my proposal is fundamentally different from what took place in the wake of Willengen in 1952.

It is one thing to propose that mission should not be a subset of the doctrine of the church; it is entirely another to disconnect the *missio dei* altogether from a robust ecclesiology. It is one thing to see the Trinitarian basis for mission; it is entirely another to fail to see that the church has been ordained by God to reflect the Trinity through redemptive actions in the world. Yet this is essentially what happened in the post-Willengen period. The world was the stage of God's redemptive action, and the church was effectively sidelined. God's redemptive activity was more likely to be seen in a political revolution, economic trend, or social movement, than through the faithful witness of the church in the world. Indeed, in the post-Willengen view of missions, the world set the agenda for the church.[8] The church's role, at best, was merely to point out where society was "struggling for humanization" or where "God's *shalom*" was emerging in the world. Thus, the *missio dei* had the effect of untethering the church from God's presence and work in the world.

This "world-focused" rather than "church-focused" emphasis in the church's understanding of mission was officially adopted at the Uppsala Assembly of the WCC in 1968. We must recall that these developments within the World Council of Churches were taking place at the same time as similar trends in the Roman Catholic Church with Vatican II (1962–1965) and the writings of Karl Rahner, Edward Schillebeeckx, and Hans Kung,

---

7. Ibid., 8.

8. Vicedom's statement (ibid.) that "the entire Heilsgeschichte exhibits itself as a history of the *missio Dei*" did seem to effectively sideline the church. However, Vicedom also seems to envision the church being "sent out" as a reflection of Christ being "sent" into the world by the Father. Vicedom also says that "His activity is always a messenger that conveys the call" (p. 11). He also speaks candidly of the need to "carry out the assignment of God" (p. 18) and that "the death and resurrection of Jesus are the presupposition for the mission to the heathen" (p. 41). All of this implies a proclaiming church, although, admittedly, Vicedom only rarely uses the word *church* in his seminal work. At one point Vicedom does state quite plainly that "the church must regard herself as the carrier of the message to the world" (p. 47). Nonetheless, the trend was to equate salvation history with world history—*geschichte was heilsgeschichte*.

as noted in chapter 1.[9] The line that separates the world from the church was slowly being erased in both mainline Protestantism and Roman Catholicism. But there were voices of dissent. The main groups opposing this trend were the Eastern Orthodox and the evangelical Protestants.

The Eastern Orthodox Church has long resisted any trend that seeks to downplay the line that separates the world from the church. Eastern Orthodox missiology has remained committed to a strong connection between mission and the nature of the church. It may come as a surprise to evangelical readers that Eastern Orthodox history reveals a remarkably robust practice of mobilizing and sending out missionaries as an extension of the church's witness. For example, Orthodox missionary Makary Glucharev spent his ministry doing things normally associated with nineteenth-century Protestant missions: Bible translation, church planting, establishing hospitals and schools, and so forth. His publication, *Thoughts on the Methods to be followed for a successful dissemination of the Faith among Muhammadans, Jews and Pagans in the Russian Empire*, is similar in many ways to writings published by nineteenth-century Protestants.[10]

However, in the twentieth century, under pressure to survive under the yoke of oppressive political regimes, Orthodox missiology became more passive, gradually equating mission and the church. This is seen in the writings of the Romanian Orthodox missiologist Ion Bria (1929–2002). Commenting on the relationship of mission to the church, Bria said, "When one says that mission is the function of the Church, Orthodox are very suspicious, because they are against such instrumentalistic interpretations of the Church. Mission is not an act of profession, but an ecclesial one."[11] It became difficult to distinguish between missions and liturgy. Thus, if the mainline

---

9. Even though the Roman Catholic Church is not a member of the World Council of Churches, the Vatican's Pontifical Council for Promoting Christian Unity is permitted to place twelve full members onto the *Faith and Order Commission*.

10. Orthodox Bishop Anastasios Yannoulatos of Androussa, in "Discovering the Orthodox Missionary Ethos," comments as follows: "The Russian Church adopted Byzantine missionary tradition. With originality and daring, they continued and developed missionary methods inherited from the Byzantines: i.e. catholicity in their view of missionary obligations within and outside the borders of the empire; participation of both clergy and laity, and even a general mobilization of the faithful; education for native clergy; translation of liturgical and religious books into native languages ... [and] the celebration of the Divine Liturgy in the local language." Citation found in Ion Bria, ed., *Martyria/Mission: The Witness of the Orthodox Churches Today* (Geneva: World Council of Churches, 1980), 23.

11. Ibid., 9.

Protestant and Roman Catholics tended to *separate* God's mission from the church, the Eastern Orthodox Church went to the opposite extreme, to the point of *equating* mission and the church. The Orthodox eventually reduced the evangelistic and missionary mandate to the "internal witness" signified through the recitation of the liturgy, the first part of which is "consecrated to the preaching of the Gospel to unbelievers."[12] Thus, by completely subsuming their missiology into their ecclesiology, the Orthodox have largely adopted a "come-and-see" rather than a "go-and-tell" approach to missions.

The evangelical opposition was spearheaded by leading missiologists such as Donald McGavran and Arthur Glasser.[13] McGavran and Glasser stressed traditional themes of evangelism, conversion, and church growth. They raised legitimate concerns about the secularization of the gospel and the tendency to reduce the mission of the church "to social and political activism."[14] However, they were not able to appreciate the insights of the *missio dei* emphasis; nor were they able to fully envision the biblical witness of the church in the social and political sphere.[15] Furthermore, the missiology they offered in its place was overly driven by pragmatic, sociological principles, rather than a positive theological vision of God's work in the church.

Of course, this is not to imply that we should affirm that God works *only* in and through His church. Indeed, God often works both beyond and despite of the church to accomplish His redemptive plans. Nevertheless, central to a biblical vision of God's mission is that God *does, in fact, work in*

---

12. Ibid.

13. The evangelical response to the post-Willengen trends was also partly responsible for the formation of the first Lausanne International Congress on World Evangelization held July 16–25 in 1974. It was sponsored by two well-known evangelical leaders, John Stott and Billy Graham. The congress drew more than 2,300 leaders from 150 countries under the theme, "Let the Earth Hear His Voice." The Lausanne Covenant, which emerged out of the congress, is widely regarded as the most significant legacy of Lausanne I. Section five of the Lausanne Covenant does an excellent job articulating how soteriology relates to the social order.

14. Arthur Glasser, "Salvation Today and the Kingdom," as found in Donald McGavran, ed., *Crucial Issues in Mission Tomorrow* (Chicago: Moody, 1972), 33 [full chapter, pp. 33–53]. It should be noted that this growing trend to secularize the church's mission was developing in tandem with the general theological shift of the time, which was to rearticulate the Christian faith in the light of secular presuppositions. See, for example, John Robinson's *Honest to God* (Philadephia: Westminster, 1963) and Harvey Cox's *The Secular City: Secularization and Urbanization in Theological Perspective* (New York: Macmillan, 1966).

15. Nineteenth-century evangelicalism had a far more integrated view of "evangelism" and "social action." However, the shift in the mainline churches tended to harden each side against the insights of the other. Interestingly, both liberal and evangelical theologies became increasingly narrow, reductionistic, and imbalanced, but in very different ways.

and through His church and that it is central, not ancillary, to His mission. Indeed, the church is the only community Jesus Christ has specifically instituted to reflect the Trinity and to participate in His mission in the world.[16]

So, a biblical missiology must be built firmly on the foundation of Trinitarian theology. Furthermore, it must be simultaneously God centered and church focused. In order to capture both of these realities, we need to make an important distinction between the words *mission* and *missions*. In this book, as noted earlier, *mission* refers to *God's redemptive, historical initiative on behalf of His creation.* In contrast, *missions* refers to *all the specific and varied ways in which the church crosses cultural boundaries to reflect the life of the triune God in the world and, through that identity, participates in His mission, celebrating through word and deed the inbreaking of the New Creation.*[17] Missions is made possible only at God's invitation. The title of this book, *Invitation to World Missions,* refers to God's gracious invitation to the church to participate in His mission in the world.

God-Centered *and* Church-Focused Missions

Missions should never be conceptualized apart from the *missio dei.* As an evangelical, I am painfully aware of how we are among the first to verbalize that missions flows out of God's heart and God's initiative but still remain quite busy with our own initiatives, high-powered strategies, and endless missional[18] tasks with little reflection on how what we are doing may or may not relate to God's redemptive action in the world.

---

16. This affirmation will be defended in my later expositions of the Great Commission texts in chapter 5. It also should be noted that Lesslie Newbigin was the primary author of the adopted document at Willengen, "The Missionary Calling of the Church," which sought to ground the new emphasis in a strong ecclesiology. However, in the post-Willengen period, the antiecclesiological emphasis of major leaders such as Johannes Hoekendijk carried the day. In response, Newbigin delivered his ecclesiology lectures, later published as Household of God in 1953 to express his concern that the modern ecumenical movement was losing its ecclesiological grounding. David Bosch argues, convincingly, that the antichurch mood continued from 1952 until the Nairobi Assembly of the World Council of Churches in 1975. See Bosch, *Transforming Mission*, 388, and Lesslie Newbigin, *Household of God: Lectures on the Nature of the Church* (London: SCM, 1953).

17. I am including the phrase "crosses cultural boundaries" because, as will be developed later in the book, I am not willing to completely abandon the distinction between evangelism and missions as long as it is removed from its long-standing association with geography. The phrase is included here in anticipation of my emphasis on the importance of maintaining a distinction between those with and those without access to the gospel.

18. *Missional* is an adjective form of *mission* indicating something that is characterized by mission.

There are many different reasons why the church has struggled with conceptualizing and understanding a view of mission(s) that is simultaneously God centered *and* church focused. However, three key reasons will be explored.

Missiology and the Social Sciences

First, almost from its inception, missiology as a modern discipline has been dominated by the social sciences. There are, undoubtedly, many wonderful insights that the social sciences bring to missiology. I would not want to deny the church the insights of cultural anthropology any more than I would want to deny Christian counselors the insights of the latest family systems theory or urban pastors the insights from sociology as they seek to understand what it means to minister in complex urban settings. The point is simply that we cannot build our missiology on a social science foundation any more than we could make Christian counseling a mere subset of counseling in general. The reason is that Christianity, as a whole, is built on an entirely different foundation and worldview. Therefore, anything that flows out from the church must be clearly situated in relation to deeper Christian wellsprings, or it will ultimately prove to be anthropocentric and shallow. First and foremost, the controlling categories of missions must be theological, not sociological. As noted above, this was the key failure in the missiology of figures such as Donald McGavran, who tried to articulate an evangelical reply to the growing secular emphasis within the church.

Theology of Mission Versus Missional Nature of All Theology

Second, we have tended to construct elaborate biblical theologies to support missions, rather than seeing the fundamental missional nature of all theology. In other words, we have tended to develop a cadre of biblical texts that are then used to support the various activities we call "missions" rather than seeing the entire Bible as revealing the missionary nature of God in relation to the world and the larger missional context of the *whole* of Scripture. From this perspective, all theology is fundamentally missional because biblical theology reveals God as a missionary God.

We owe a great debt to Christopher Wright and his excellent book, *The Mission of God*, which points out the inherent problems with all of the "biblical foundation for missions" projects.[19] Drawing on earlier work done by

---

19. Christopher J. H. Wright, *The Mission of God* (Downers Grove, IL: IVP Academic, 2006), 34ff.

David Bosch, Wright argues that through this kind of proof-texting, "we have already decided what we want to prove (i.e. that our missionary practice is biblical), and our collection of texts simply ratifies our preconception."[20] In its place, Wright proposes what he calls a "missional hermeneutic" that sees the whole of Scripture as a "missional phenomenon in the sense that it witnesses to the self-giving movement of this God toward his creation and us."[21] Wright contrasts the two approaches as follows. He describes a "biblical basis of mission" as the attempt to "seek out those biblical texts which express or describe the missionary imperative, on the assumption that the Bible is authoritative." In contrast, a missional hermeneutic of the Bible "proceeds from the assumption that the whole Bible renders to us the story of God's mission through God's people in their engagement with God's work for the sake of the whole of God's creation."[22] Missions, therefore, arises not simply as a response of obedience to a command given to the church (although it is never less than that) but as a joyful invitation to *participate with God* in His redemptive work in the world. God the Father is unfolding a grand narrative, of which His Son, Jesus Christ, is the central figure and we, as the church, are being called and empowered through God the Holy Spirit to participate in the unfolding of this grand narrative. Kevin Vanhoozer calls this unfolding grand narrative a "theodrama," which he argues is "essentially missional, consisting in a series of historical entrances and exoduses (e.g. incarnation, crucifixion, resurrection, ascension, Pentecost)."[23] Therefore, missions is about simultaneously entering into the inner life of God as a missionary God, as well as entering into the world where the triune God is actively at work.

Individualistic Conceptions of Soteriology
Third, the theology of missionaries, especially Protestant missionaries, has tended to be influenced by an overly individualistic and pietistic understanding of salvation. It is important to remember that Protestant missions

---

20. Ibid. See also David Bosch's "Reflections on the New Testament as a Missionary Document" as found in *Transforming Mission*. Bosch is also critical of introductions to missiology that contain a "Biblical Foundation for Missions" section that inadvertently obscures the missionary character of the New Testament. See pp. 15–16.
21. Wright, *The Mission of God*, 48.
22. Ibid., 51.
23. Kevin J. Vanhoozer, "'One Rule to Rule Them All?' Theological Method in an Era of World Christianity," in *Global Theologizing*, ed. Harold Netland and Craig Ott (Grand Rapids: Baker Academic, 2006), 110.

was born out of the larger context of seventeenth-century pietism. The founding fathers of the modern Protestant missionary movement were leaders such as August Francke, Nicholas von Zinzendorf, and William Carey. They were all deeply influenced by pietistic theology. At the core of their theology was the belief in the necessity of individual conversion. Let me clearly say at the outset of this point that I believe in the necessity of personal conversion and its centrality to the New Testament *kerygma*. However, let me also clearly state that biblical salvation encompasses much *more* than individual conversion. Salvation also inherently implies incorporation into a community. We are not just baptized *by* faith; we are baptized *into* a faith that is shared by a *community* that exists in space around the world and back through time. Indeed, there are aspects of salvation that can be experienced and known only within the church as the redeemed community and cannot be realized in isolation from that community. The New Testament celebrates a salvific transformation that has both vertical and horizontal dimensions. Personal salvation in the New Testament is inextricably linked to becoming part of the new humanity of Ephesians 2:15.

The emphasis on personal conversion in pietism was often tied to an underlying mistrust of the church and the ordained clergy. This is why pietism saw itself as a lay movement that served as a "church within the church." On the whole, the emphases of pietism were an important and needed correction to the dry theological abstractions that its leaders inherited. However, one of the long-term legacies of pietism that has deeply influenced Protestantism, especially contemporary evangelicalism, has been a weak ecclesiology. In their view, the central work of God in the world was between God and individuals who were being called to repent and believe. At best, the church had only an *instrumental* role in God's plan. What was often missed is the *ontological* identity of the church. As Simon Chan says in *Liturgical Theology*, the church is not merely an instrument to accomplish God's purposes; the church is the "expression of God's ultimate purpose itself."[24] This perspective has been missed by many Protestants.

Once reconciliation is conceptualized within the relatively narrow locus of the individual person, it becomes increasingly difficult to see how God's work is related in an ongoing way to the church as the redeemed community, the living reflection of the triune God in the world.

---

24. Simon Chan, *Liturgical Theology* (Downers Grove, IL: IVP Academic, 2006), 21.

Once salvation is privatized and the church is understood as having merely an instrumental role, then the gospel story is seen to have been completed at the Cross and the Resurrection. From a theological perspective, an overly privatized view of salvation unduly separates soteriology from both ecclesiology and pneumatology. In this fragmented vision, the church's role—and therefore the task of missions—is merely to look back and tell the world what happened at the Cross and the Resurrection. Of course, the Cross and the Resurrection always must remain central to the church's proclamation. However, it is important to recognize that the gospel does not stop at the Cross and the Resurrection but continues to unfold in God's ongoing initiatives at Pentecost and in the life of the church.

The undue separation of soteriology from pneumatology and ecclesiology dramatically diminishes the significance of Pentecost and the inbreaking of God the Holy Spirit. The role of the church as the body of Christ, the redeemed community in the world, and the ongoing reflection of the Trinity in the world is largely lost. We see ourselves as commissioned to *tell* the story, but we don't see ourselves as intrinsically *part* of the story. However, the church must do more than tell the gospel; we must embody it. As Chan says, "We need to see ecclesiology as an intrinsic part of the doctrine of the gospel of Jesus Christ, not an administrative arrangement for the sake of securing practical results."[25]

The separation of soteriology from ecclesiology also tends to isolate the missions mandate, making it ancillary to the life of the church. From this perspective, missions applies only to an elite group of individual, professional missionaries rather than the whole church as participants in God's redeeming mission. This is why the 1952 Willengen conference declared that, "there is no participation in Christ without participation in His mission to the world."[26] In fact, in an overly privatized soteriology, even the Holy Spirit is granted only an instrumental role in empowering the church for effective witness. However, in the biblical view, the Holy Spirit is the one who actualizes the New Creation in the life of the church, bringing the eschatological "not yet" into the "already." The Spirit

---

25. Ibid., 36.
26. Norman Goodall, ed., *Missions Under the Cross: Addresses Delivered at the Enlarged Meeting of the Committee of the International Missionary Council at Willlingen, in Germany,* 1952 (London: Edinburgh House, 1953), 190.

doesn't just empower us for some extrinsic task we call the "mission of the church." Rather, the mission of the church *is* the mission of the Spirit acting in and through the church, enabling us to manifest the "body of Christ." This means that missions must first understand what the church *is* before it can articulate what the church *does*; the church is by nature a missionary church. A proper understanding of the Holy Spirit's role in bringing into the "already" the firstfruits of the New Creation that still awaits us in the "not yet" also transforms and properly links the church to a more robust eschatology that transcends the popular, reductionistic eschatology that sees eschatology only in terms of one's personal escape from condemnation in the afterlife. Robert Speer, the great missionary statesman and prolific author, once said that "the Holy Spirit alone can reveal to the Church her missionary character; He alone can prepare the world for the Church's mission. It is the Spirit who must lift the Church out of her self-centeredness into a vision of life and service in imitation of Christ."[27]

This distinction between *mission* and *missions* helps the church to avoid triumphalism by keeping missions God centered. We must have the humility to remember that we can never claim that missions is always identical with the *missio dei*. As David Bosch comments in his magisterial work, *Transforming Mission*, "Our missionary activities are only authentic insofar as they reflect participation in the mission of God."[28] Yet, even though we acknowledge the mystery of God's mission, we are reminded through the use of the word *missions* that God has invited the church to be a central player in His work in the world. Maintaining the distinction between mission and missions enables the church to be both God-centered *and* church-focused. The importance of this should now be clear since history has revealed that whenever the church fails to keep missions *both* God centered and church focused, both a truncated view of God and a diminished view of the church inevitably follow. This is why it is essential that missions be reconceptualized within a Trinitarian framework.

---

27. Quoted in Harry Boer, *Pentecost and Missions* (Grand Rapids: Eerdmans, 1961), 60. Robert Speer (1867–1947) was a Presbyterian leader in the International Missionary Council. He was a popular speaker and prolific author, probably best known for his work, *The Unfinished Task in Foreign Missions.*
28. Bosch, *Transforming Mission*, 391.

TRINITY AND *MISSIO DEI* IN LESSLIE NEWBIGIN
AND KWAME BEDIAKO

A cursory look at the standard books introducing world missions (or missiology as a discipline) to a new generation of students reveals that a Trinitarian framework has not figured predominately in how missions has been conceptualized. Typically, missions is examined under the rubrics of theology, history, anthropology, and practice. The normal progression is as follows. First, the biblical basis for missions is examined, which is then used to establish a theology of missionary practice. Second, a brief overview of the history of missions is explored so that students can understand their place in the overall sweep of the church's obedience to the Great Commission. Third, an anthropological section is included, which deals with many of the classic challenges to our understanding and communicating the gospel within the context of a culture other than our own. Finally, some missionary textbooks include a practical section dedicated to such important issues as how a Christian discerns a call from God to be a missionary, how a missionary should relate to his or her sending church, what to do about educating one's children abroad, or even tips about fund-raising. Clearly, all this information is vital to the proper training of missionaries, and we certainly need it. However, the lack of a Trinitarian structure tends to make it very difficult to keep the necessary link between mission and missions.

As one who has taught missions and trained future missionaries for over twenty years in the United States and in India,[29] I have sometimes felt like the earlier part of a missions course in which I introduced the concept of mission and the *missio dei* was largely forgotten once we got into all of the seemingly more practical and applicable aspects of missionary training. I eventually came to recognize that the only way to maintain the link between God's mission and missions in the church is to immerse the *entire training* in a thoroughly Trinitarian and ecclesial framework, so that everything is ultimately related to God (*missio dei*) and His church (*missio ecclesiae*).

---

29. Toccoa Falls College in Georgia (1993–1998), Gordon-Conwell Theological Seminary in Massachusetts (1998–2009), Asbury Theological Seminary (2009–present), and the Luther W. New Jr. Theological College in Dehra Dun, India (1988–present).

Lesslie Newbigin's Trinitarian Framework for Missiology

One of the most important pioneers in formulating a Trinitarian missiology was Bishop Lesslie Newbigin (1909–1998). He is known for his leadership in the church (especially his conciliar work[30]), as well as in the academy. He was educated at Cambridge University and went to India as a missionary (1936–1946), eventually serving as a bishop in the Church of South India (1947–1958, 1965–1974). Newbigin served as the general secretary of the International Missions Council (1959–1965) and as a lecturer in the Selly Oak Colleges in Birmingham, England (1974–1979), and he even pastored an inner-city United Reformed Church (1980–1988). He remained active in writing and speaking in the "gospel and culture" movement until his death in 1998.

Newbigin continues to impact missiology today because of his prolific publications, which continue to nourish his readers.[31] For example, his *Foolishness to the Greeks* established Newbigin as one of the first missiologists to recognize that the Western world was emerging as a post-Christian civilization and, therefore, should be regarded as a newly emerging mission field. Newbigin's *The Gospel in a Pluralist Society* remains an excellent resource in understanding how Christians who are committed to historic Christian faith can best live out their faith in the midst of a pluralistic society. During his years at Selly Oak, Newbigin also wrote a theology of missions that was published under the title *The Open Secret*.

As general secretary of the International Missions Council (1959–1965), Newbigin was a central figure during the post-Willengen period, when it was becoming increasingly clear that the *missio dei* theme was being used to separate God's mission from the church.[32] Gradually, Newbigin began to emphasize the importance of developing missiology within the framework of Trinitarianism. He said, "The mission of the Church is to be understood, can only be rightly understood, in terms of the Trinitarian model."[33]

---

30. Conciliar work broadly refers to attempts to help the larger church discover areas of common agreement rather than focus only on our differences.
31. For a full bibliography of Lesslie Newbigin's voluminous writings, see www.newbigin.net.
32. Michael Goheen has made the helpful point that even though the Willengen conference endorsed a Trinitarian basis for mission, it became a generic "Cosmo-centric Trinitarianism" rather than understanding the Trinity through God the Father's specific revelation through His Son, Jesus Christ, and the sending of the Holy Spirit. See Michael W. Goheen, *As the Father Has Sent Me, I Am Sending You: J. E. Lesslie Newbigin's Missionary Ecclesiology* (Zoetermer: Uitgeverij Boekencentrum, 2000), 117.
33. Lesslie Newbigin, *The Gospel in a Pluralist Society* (Grand Rapids: Eerdmans, 1989), 118.

For Newbigin, one of the key texts in the New Testament that exemplifies the basis for a Trinitarian missiology is found in John's gospel. In John 20:21–22 Jesus says, "'Peace be with you! As the Father has sent me, I am sending you.' And with that he breathed on them and said, 'Receive the Holy Spirit.'" This passage demonstrates the continuity between the Father's mission and Jesus' mission and the ongoing mission of the Holy Spirit in the life and witness of the church.

For Newbigin, the Trinity is the starting point for the church's understanding of missions and how it relates to the mission of God. He argued that "a fresh articulation of the missionary task in terms of a pluralistic, polytheistic, pagan society of our time may require us likewise to acknowledge the necessity of a Trinitarian starting point."[34] Earlier in this chapter we established that missions must flow out of mission, which means that we have no missional authority apart from the mission of the triune God. The Trinity remains the only authority by which we proclaim the gospel to the world. The difficulty comes in that the Trinity, for many Christians, represents nothing more than a vague, confusing theological conundrum.[35] If Christians do not even understand the Trinity, it is reasoned, then how can it possibly become the basis for our proclamation to a postmodern, relativistic world? The idea of the Trinity being the starting point and basis for missions seems counterintuitive. Yet it is precisely at this point that we need to remember that the old Christendom structures have collapsed. As long as the church lived within the context of Christendom, then the question "By what authority do you preach the Christian gospel?" was hardly asked; the authority was assumed. Slowly, under the domesticating influence of Christendom, the biblical, Trinitarian authority for the missionary mandate was replaced by a cultural, institutional, or pragmatic one. However, with the collapse of Christendom, this is no longer tenable because these sources of authority have been utterly discredited.

It is precisely at this point that we must recognize that we cannot meet

---

34. Lesslie Newbigin, *The Relevance of Trinitarian Doctrine for Today's Mission*—CWME Study pamphlet #2 (London: Edinburgh House, 1963), 32–34.
35. This is not to underestimate the difficulty in understanding the Trinity. Augustine insightfully commented that anyone who denies the Trinity is in danger of losing their salvation, but anyone who tries to understand the Trinity is in danger of losing their mind. Quoted in Roger E. Olson and Christopher A. Hall, *The Trinity* (Grand Rapids: Eerdmans, 2002), 1.

a relativistic, postmodern world on *their* terms. Following Jesus cannot be built on a pragmatic, cultural, or institutional footing. The key features of a distinctively Christian message cannot be conformed and reshaped into the image of a relativistic, postmodern worldview. Therefore, as noted in the last chapter, we must learn how to be *counter*cultural. We cannot hide from the "scandal of particularity." Being countercultural is not merely a new technique. Rather, it is fundamental to our own understanding of the Christian message in the midst of a non-Christian world. When the world, in derision, asks us, "By what authority do you preach the gospel?" our answer must be unequivocal: "We have been commissioned by God in Jesus Christ and we preach in the name of and by the authority of the Father, Son, and Holy Spirit!" The twenty-first century, no less than the first century, may regard it as "a stumbling block" or as "foolishness" (1 Cor. 1:23), but it remains "the power of God unto salvation" (Rom. 1:16 KJV).

As noted above, the best overall sketch of Newbigin's Trinitarian missiology can be found in his work *The Open Secret*, which he wrote while at Selly Oak. After a chapter on the "Mission of the Triune God," he organized his theology of mission under three chapters. The first was, "Proclaiming the Kingdom of the Father: Mission as Faith in Action." This was followed by a chapter entitled, "Sharing the Life of the Son: Mission as Love in Action." Finally, he concluded with a chapter entitled, "Bearing the Witness of the Spirit: Mission as Hope in Action." These three chapters were followed by a series of chapters outlining contemporary issues that Newbigin analyzed, to use his words, "from the point of view of this Trinitarian faith."[36]

However, Newbigin's project was never fully worked out. *The Open Secret* was based on lecture notes from Selly Oak and never attempted anything more than the broad outlines of a Trinitarian theology of mission. Furthermore, Newbigin never really worked out the particulars of the Father's role in mission, and there were many current missiological problems that were not related in any way to the Trinity. Nevertheless, Newbigin's prophetic realization about the need for a Trinitarian missiology remains one of his important legacies.

---

36. Lesslie Newbigin, *The Open Secret: An Introduction to the Theology of Mission*, rev. ed. (Grand Rapids: Eerdmans, 1995), 29.

Kwame Bediako and the Context of the Trinity

The Yale historian Lamin Sanneh[37] has long argued that the story of the Western missionary movement is far more complex and multifaceted than the widely accepted assertion that it was merely a minor subplot in the history of Western imperialism.[38] As an African, Sanneh brought a fresh perspective in understanding the missionary movement from one who was on the receiving end. In keeping with this theme, Sanneh wrote an important article in 1983 entitled, "The Horizontal and Vertical in Mission: An African Perspective."[39] In the article, Sanneh observes that historians of the nineteenth-century missionary movement had failed to recognize that the missionary movement involved two distinct forces. The first force is what he calls the "historic transmission" of the gospel. This refers to the missionaries who brought the gospel to specific contexts. Sanneh says that this historical narrative, spearheaded by the missionaries, has dominated the literature.

The second force is what Sanneh calls the "indigenous assimilation." This is the force that, after receiving the gospel, adapts it and applies it to the local context, sometimes in surprising ways. In other words, we should not equate gospel transmission with gospel reception and assimilation because the latter often has transformed and empowered people in ways the missionary could never have anticipated. Sanneh particularly sees this evidenced in the Bible translation movement, which "imbued the local culture with eternal significance" in ways the missionary never imagined. As the gospel was assimilated and internalized by those who received it, the Africans unquestionably became the dominant players. When one sees the whole process of the missionary movement from the arrival of the missionary to the point when the Africans themselves become preachers and missionaries, Sanneh says that "the process of the historical transmission of Christianity under western missionary agency should be subordinated to that of local assimilation."[40] In other words, the missionaries set into motion a process of religious change in which the Africans themselves became the key players.

---

37. Lamin Sanneh is from The Gambia and currently serves as the D. Willis James Professor of Missions and World Christianity and professor of history at Yale Divinity School. He is the author of over a dozen books and over one hundred articles in the area of world Christianity.
38. Sanneh's groundbreaking book on this topic was *Translating the Message: The Missionary Impact on Culture* (Maryknoll, NY: Orbis, 1989).
39. Lamin Sanneh, "The Horizontal and Vertical in Mission: An African Perspective," *International Bulletin of Missionary Research* 7, no. 4 (October 1983): 165–71.
40. Ibid., 166.

Sanneh argues that this is evidence that the *missio dei* must transcend *mere* human agency.[41] He observes that "the God whom the missionary came to serve had actually preceded him or her on the field and that to discover His true identity the missionary would have to delve deep into the local culture" to discover "the hidden reality of this divine presence."[42]

Kwame Bediako, the Ghanian historian, later followed up on Sanneh's article and more explicitly framed it within the *missio dei*. In his landmark book, *Christianity in Africa: The Renewal of a Non-Western Religion*, Bediako argues that Sanneh's insights should all be seen as aspects of the *missio dei*. Bediako says that the entire missionary enterprise should be understood as a divine process that encompasses three distinct phases. First is the divine initiation "through the pre-Christian tradition" of a people group. Second is the "historical missionary transmission" through the church's witness in the world. Last is the "indigenous assimilation" of the gospel in the communities of those who receive it.[43] By more explicitly bringing Sanneh's ideas within the framework of the *missio dei*, Bediako furthers the discussion by moving us from "two forces" to three distinct actions of God in the world. It could be visualized as an unfolding divine drama that encompasses three acts. The three distinct acts each have their own integrity but are also seen as part of the overall drama of God's initiative.

While Bediako effectively conceptualizes missions within the larger framework of the *missio dei,* he does not go on to specifically develop this in a Trinitarian way. In my view, this is where we can cross a new threshold and perhaps gain a fresh vista on the missionary enterprise. Each of these three phases or acts of God does have a natural orientation in each of the three persons of the triune God.

Act I: Divine Initiation in Creation and Preparatio Evangelica

Divine initiation, or Act I, is the work of God the Father. The Father designs the plan of redemption. He is the one who takes the initiative to unfold His

---

41. Sanneh goes as far as to say that "historical missions were the side effects of the *missio dei*" (ibid.). In my view this is a poor choice of phrases for Sanneh, because the overall impact of his writings has been to take very seriously the historical process. This phrase does emphasize the priority of divine agency but could be interpreted to diminish the importance of the church's work in the world, as occurred in the post-Willengen period.

42. Ibid.

43. Kwame Bediako, *Christianity in Africa: The Renewal of a Non-Western Religion* (Maryknoll, NY: Orbis, 1995), 121.

plan. As the Creator, the Father sows seeds into the fabric and design of creation that anticipate the plan of redemption that will eventually unfold. Furthermore, in the particular historical development of people groups, God the Father is working to prepare and anticipate the later full revelation of Jesus Christ. These divine initiatives have been collectively referred to as the *preparatio evangelica*—all of the ways in which God prepares people to receive the gospel before any missionary agent arrives. The most obvious example of *preparatio evangelica* is in God the Father's work in and through the Jewish people, as evidenced in the Hebrew Scriptures. The earliest Christians were Jews, and they readily testified how God, through the prophets, had prepared them to receive the full revelation of Christ. Even the Law was a "tutor" to lead them to Christ. Later, followers of Jesus who came from Gentile backgrounds recognized that God was at work in *their* pre-Christian past, preparing them to receive the gospel. For example, Justin Martyr calls this the "seed of the Word," or *logos spermatikos*, which God has implanted "in every race of men." In his *Second Apology*, Justin Martyr demonstrates that just as God used the Law to help the Jews see their need for Christ, He likewise used the insights of Greek philosophers as stepping-stones to lead him to Christ.[44] Philosophy raised ultimate questions for which they had no ready solution. Justin saw how Christ fulfilled and answered many of the aspirations and unanswered questions that the philosophers had posed.

This acknowledgement of God's work prior to any action by human agents is an important but often neglected aspect of the *missio dei*. Yet, there is a persistent testimony to its truth throughout the Christian tradition. For example, in his *Confessions*, Augustine speaks of the "loving memory" of God that lies latent even in unbelievers.[45] The Scholastic tradition distinguished between the *cognitio actualis* (actual knowledge) and the *cognitio habitualis* (latent knowledge) of God.[46] In his *Institutes*, the Reformer John

---

44. Justin Martyr, *Second Apology*, 8, in *Ante-Nicene Fathers*, ed. Alexander Roberts and James Donaldson (Peabody, MA: Hendrickson, 1999), 1:191.

45. Augustine, *Confessions* 7.17.23, in *The Nicene and Post-Nicene Fathers*, ed. Philip Schaff and Henry Wace (Peabody, MA: Hendrickson, 1999), 1:111.

46. This is not to be confused with the Scholastic *cognitio Dei intuitive*, which is available only through the beatific vision, nor should this be confused with the Platonizing language of *cognitio innata* since, for the Scholastics, this knowledge is ultimately rooted in God's free activity. The Scholastics further distinguished between *cognitio infusa* (infused knowledge) and *cognitio insita* (implanted knowledge). The former refers to knowledge gained by the ordinary process of the mind and senses. The latter, however, refers to knowledge implanted by God.

Calvin points out that God Himself "has endued all men with some idea of his Godhead, the memory of which he constantly renews and occasionally enlarges." In this context, Calvin refers to the "sense of the Divine" (*sensus divinitaitis*) and the universal "germ of religion" (*semen religionis*).[47] This is an important testimony to the Father's prior work, long before any human agent is involved in the historical transmission of the gospel.

ACT II: HISTORIC TRANSMISSION OF THE GOSPEL THROUGH THE CHURCH

The second act, the historical transmission of the gospel through the witness of the church, finds its focus in God the Son. The drama of the Father's unfolding redemptive plan gives the pivotal historical role to the Son. The Father sends the Son into the world to secure the redemption of fallen humanity. In the Incarnation, the Son of God's history intersects in specific ways with human history. The story of the Incarnation is not merely that God became a man but that God became a *particular* man. There is no generic incarnation. Jesus entered the history and culture of a particular group at a particular time. Jesus learned and spoke the languages of His time, and He fully entered into the "shared consciousness" and "shared traditions" and "mental processes and patterns of relationships" that make up the particularities of the Jewish culture in which He grew up.[48] It is important to see that Jesus' life, death, resurrection, and ascension occur within the context of real history. He fulfills the Father's plan *in history*.

One of the most important but often neglected phrases in the Apostles' Creed is the statement, "He suffered under Pontius Pilate." Some have wondered why the early church would include in this very ancient confession of faith the name of the very Roman governor who presided over Jesus' trial and ordered His crucifixion. Upon reflection, however, it is clear that this phrase is a strategic, ongoing reminder that the gospel intersects real human history. In a similar way, the church is sent out by Jesus Christ to proclaim and embody the redemption that has been wrought through Christ, but it must intersect with the actual histories and narratives of those to whom we are sent. So in this second act, the historical transmission, we find many of

---

47. John Calvin, *Institutes of the Christian Religion*, vol. 20, book 1, chapter 3.1. For an English translation of the *Institutes*, see John T. McNeill, ed., *Calvin: Institutes of the Christian Religion* (Philadelphia: Westminster Press, 1960).

48. Andrew F. Walls, *The Missionary Movement in Christian History: Studies in the Transmission of Faith* (Maryknoll, NY: Orbis, 1996), 27.

the acts that are normally associated with missions. However, when placed within the *missio dei*, the church becomes an agent of God's redemptive initiative in the world whereby He acts in and through His church.

ACT III: INDIGENOUS ASSIMILATION OF THE GOSPEL IN A PARTICULAR CONTEXT

The third act, the "indigenous assimilation" of the gospel, demonstrates the central role of the Holy Spirit in convicting the world regarding sin, empowering the preaching of the gospel, and bringing people to faith in Christ. Furthermore, just as God's work precedes the historical transmission of the gospel via the *preparatio evangelica*, so God's work continues long after the missionary departs. It is God the Holy Spirit who is charged with assimilating the gospel into the life and experience of the communities who receive the gospel. It is the Holy Spirit who is central in the work of discipling and maturing communities of believers. Seeing the work of missions within the larger framework of the *missio dei* keeps the church from an unwarranted reductionistic view of soteriology that equates salvation with justification and fails to see the more comprehensive, holistic work of the triune God in regeneration, justification, sanctification, and final glorification, culminating in the New Creation.

CONCLUSION

It is clear from this overview that the *missio dei*, when set within a more explicitly Trinitarian understanding, has profound implications for the transmission, reception, and assimilation of the Christian gospel into the lives of people, societies, and nations. Thus, the Trinitarian framework this book proposes seeks to build on the ideas initiated by Newbigin, Bediako, and others[49] and to provide a structure whereby the overall work of missions can be understood within that Trinitarian framework. The specifics of how a Trinitarian conception of the *missio dei* applies to missions will be explored more fully in chapter 3.

---

49. Some of the other thinkers I am indebted to are Alan Roxburgh and Ajith Fernando. Alan Roxburgh's "Rethinking Trinitarian Missiology" and the missiological reflections on the Trinity that Ajith Fernando gave at the Iguassu Missiological Consultation in Brazil in October of 1999 both set forth the need to reorient missiological studies toward a Trinitarian basis. See William Taylor, ed., *Global Missiology for the 21st Century: The Iguassu Dialogue* (Grand Rapids: Baker Academic, 2000), 179–88 (Roxburgh) and 189–256 (Fernando).

— 3 —

A Trinitarian Framework
for Missions

THE DOCTRINE OF THE TRINITY is the church's attempt to tell the truth about God and about ourselves. If God really is triune, this powerfully resolves many of the classic tensions in intellectual thought between unity and diversity, rationality and relationality, the material and the spiritual, autonomy and dependence, the one and the many, and so forth. God's self-disclosure also demands that the Trinity be at the center of all our theology, lest we slip into the monadic conception of God—the "man upstairs," which resides in the popular imagination, or the impersonal "God of the Philosophers."

In chapter 2, we demonstrated how the Trinity enlivens all theological discussions, demanding that they be seen from a missional perspective. The triune God is on a "mission." The mission of the triune God, which we are summarizing with the shorthand phrase *missio dei,* must be understood as the generative center of our understanding of missions. The purpose of this chapter is to outline the specifics of how the missiology that this textbook proposes flows out of a Trinitarian framework.

The purpose here is not to provide a theological reflection on the Trinity in a broad way. There are many excellent works that already provide this.[1] This chapter seeks to examine the Trinity with a particular focus on the implications that it holds for the theory and practice of

---

1. For example, see David S. Cunningham, *These Three Are One: The Practice of Trinitarian Theology* (Malden, MA: Blackwell, 1998).

missions. It can be summarized as follows: The Father is the Sender, the "Lord of the harvest"; the incarnate Son is the model embodiment of mission in the world; and the Holy Spirit is the divine, empowering presence for all of mission. To demonstrate this, each person of the Trinity will be explored, along with four themes that are distinctive for that member of the Trinity.

GOD THE FATHER: THE SOURCE, INITIATOR, AND GOAL OF THE *MISSIO DEI*

Broadly speaking, there are four major themes in missions that can be identified as having their locus in God the Father.

God the Father as the Initiator of Missions

God the Father is the source and initiator of missions. This is a very liberating perspective, especially when seen through the eyes of those who have traditionally been the "object" of Western missionary activity. For those who have been the recipients of missionary activity, it is easy to fall into the trap of seeing only through the narrowest of historical lenses that the gospel came through the missionary agents. A statement such as "the missionaries brought the gospel to us in 1823" makes perfect sense historically but is far less coherent theologically. A theological perspective helps to liberate the gospel from the sometimes painful associations with the historical transmission process, which, like all human endeavors, is tainted with sin. Some of those who were the "objects" of the missionary impulse may associate the gospel with their culture being devalued or intertwined with colonialism, and so forth. This is why it is so comforting to hear the African theologian John Mbiti poignantly remind us all that the missionaries did not bring God to Africa, it was God who brought the missionaries to Africa! This is, of course, a vital distinction, since it unhinges the gospel from *mere* human agency, with its undue emphasis on human initiatives, and returns the focus to God's initiative. Indeed, as Kwame Bediako observes, only the *missio dei* can rescue Christianity from "the western possessiveness of it."[2] Thus, rooting missions in God the Father as the source and originator of mission delivers all past, present,

---

2. Kwame Bediako, *Christianity in Africa: The Renewal of a Non-Western Religion* (Maryknoll, NY: Orbis, 1995), 122.

and future agents of the gospel from a sense of triumphalism. Missions is ultimately the work of the triune God, initiated by God the Father for His eternal glory.

God the Father as the Sender of Missions

God the Father is the Sender and, therefore, the ultimate source of all missionary sending. The Father sent His word through the prophets. He sent miraculous signs and wonders to reveal His glory. Ultimately, He sent His Son into the world as the greatest revelation of Himself. It is quite common for the church, and even missions textbooks, to associate Jesus Christ with "sending" since He is the one who commissions and sends the church out in those dramatic, postresurrection appearances to His disciples. After all, it is Jesus who declared to His disciples those famous texts such as, "Go into all the world," "preach the gospel to all creation," and "send I you." However, from the perspective of the triune God, Jesus is the one who Himself was sent into the world by the Father. It is only as a "sent one" that Jesus is granted the authority to send.[3]

Here we are reminded of the important distinction that is made in Trinitarian theology between the *economic* and the *immanent* Trinity. The *immanent* Trinity refers to the inner life of the Trinity within God's own self—the ontology or aseity of God, apart from His actions in relation to human history. In contrast, the *economic* Trinity refers to the various ways the triune God acts in history and interacts with humanity. So, in human history it is Jesus who sends the church, but from the deeper perspective of the inner nature of the triune God, it is God the Father who is the source of all sending. It is sufficient to recall a few of the famous sending formulas of the New Testament.

> For what the law was powerless to do because it was weakened by the sinful nature, God did by *sending his own Son* in the likeness of sinful humanity to be a sin offering. (Rom. 8:3 TNIV)

> But when the set time had fully come, *God sent his Son*, born of a woman, born under the law. (Gal. 4:4 TNIV)

---

3. This point will be more fully developed and defended in chapter 5 when John 20:21–22 is examined within the larger setting of John's Gospel.

This is how God showed his love among us: *He sent his one and only Son into the world* that we might live through him. (1 John 4:9)[4]

When the church sends out missionaries into the world, we are not only obeying the command of Jesus Christ but are also reflecting the glory of the Father, who is the ultimate source, initiator, and sender.

History as the Stage for God the Father's Actions

Rooting missions in the *missio dei* and in God the Father as the source and initiator of mission enables us to see missions within the framework of the grand narrative of God's work and not just from the perspective of the sent church. In other words, contrary to popular notions, missions does *not* begin after the Resurrection or with the witnessing church streaming out into the world in obedience to the Great Commission. Even the "Great Commission" texts must be seen within the larger context of the *missio dei* and as one part (albeit a very crucial part) of the unfolding drama of God's redemptive plan, which started even before creation in the design of God and will not find its culmination until the eschaton and the consummation of the New Creation. From this larger perspective, the Father's redemptive intentions for the world are made known to humanity in the covenant He made with Abraham, found in Genesis 12. The particulars of this covenant and its significance for missions will be explored later. It will be demonstrated that the entire missional impulse of the church is *already present* in the Abrahamic covenant in seed form. However, at this juncture it is important to keep the larger vista in view. It is theologically significant to note that God the Father took the initiative, not only to reveal His purposes to Abraham, but also to enter into a covenant that firmly links those purposes with the unfolding history of a specific and named nation, through whom all nations will be blessed.

This demonstrates that human history is the stage upon which the divine drama unfolds. Human history has a *telos*, a destination under the *missio dei*. Human history will culminate in the full realization of the New Creation. This not only validates the significance of human history in God's plan, but it also provides the basis for a robust theology of human culture. The divine

---

4. This doctrine of the Father "sending" the Son is a central theme in John's Gospel that will be explored in more detail in chapter 5.

affirmation of human history and culture is a necessary prelude, not only to such sublime realities as the divine inbreaking into human history that we call the Incarnation, but also to a whole host of daily activities that are crucial to the church's understanding of missions. Indeed, such familiar themes as church planting across cultural boundaries, Bible translation into new vernacular languages, and the formulation of contextual strategies could not be accredited without the high view of history and culture that is first revealed in God's creation and subsequent covenant with Abraham. To put it plainly, God's plan does not remain some ephemeral, hidden concept known only within the mysterious, inner counsel of the triune God. Rather, God's grand narrative intertwines with all the particularities of human narratives. It is made public and concrete on the plain of human history.

Missions as an Expression of God's Relational, Holy Love

The foundational assumption of this textbook is that a Trinitarian missiology is fundamental to a post-Christendom engagement with a relativistic, postmodern world. Increasingly, people are no longer willing to affirm a doctrinal or creedal statement, however orthodox, simply because the church declares it to be true. We live in a world that has a latent mistrust of authority skepticism toward all institutions. The notion of an overarching canopy of objective truth has collapsed, leaving only tiny islands of subjective experience. There is a growing dissatisfaction with the inability of postmodernity to make any moral discrimination. However, this generation also longs for authentic relationships. Therefore, there is a renewed longing for ethical and relational moorings.

This is precisely where Trinitarian theology is so abundantly rich and remains, in my view, the greatest hope for the twenty-first century. The Trinity is not merely some abstract concept. The Trinity is the seminal *relationship* that lies behind all human relationships. One of the greatest triumphs of the renewal of Trinitarian theology in recent years has been the emphasis on the *relational* aspect of the Trinity. God is not the solitary monad of popular imagination, or Aristotle's Unmoved Mover, or three individual "somethings." Rather, He is "a complex network of relations."[5] As the Puritans said,

---

5. Cunningham, *These Three Are One*, 20. Cunningham comments that the historic affirmation that "God was a 'single divine substance' tended to evoke an image of an isolated, passionless monad—thus obscuring both God's internal relationality and God's loving relationship with the

"God is, within Himself, a sweet society."[6] Although the Trinity is only revealed in seed form in the Old Testament, we do see its reflection. From the
dawn of creation itself, we see God the Father calling people into relationship
with Himself. One of the most basic revelations of the Old Testament is that
God is *personal* and that He calls us into relationship with Himself.

This is in stark contrast to other major world religions.[7] The highest
reality in Buddhism is *sunyata*, which is either defined as "emptiness"
(Madhyamika view) or "mind/consciousness" (Yogacara view). In either
case, Buddhism is nontheistic, affirming no God; therefore, any affirmation of a personal God who undergirds the universe is denied. The "destiny" of a Buddhist is the "nothingness" or "emptiness" of nirvana, not the
fullness (*plērōma*) of the New Creation.

In Hinduism, the most prominent school of philosophy is known as
advaita (nondualism), which draws from the great Hindu philosopher-theo-
logian Śankara (788–820). According to Śankara, the highest conception of
God or Ultimate Reality is *nirguna Brāhman*, meaning God *without* qualities. Śankara teaches that we cannot know if God is personal, nor can we
confidently attribute qualities such as holiness or justice or love to *Brāhman*
because, to use Śankara's words, *Brāhman* is "non-connected with the world
and is devoid of all qualities."[8] Whenever Hindus speak of God with personality, or with various qualities or attributes, this is a lower level of *Brāhman*
known as *saguna Brāhman*, meaning God *with* qualities and attributes.
However, for Śankara, this lower level of *Brāhman* is ultimately illusory.
This so-called "personal God," known as Iśvara, has no actual reality and
is merely a projection of imperfect and limited human descriptions of God.[9]

---

world" (p. 25). This is why Trinitarianism is essential to a robust response to the passionless
monad of Islamic theism.

6. Timothy George, "Letters," *Christianity Today* 46, no.4 (2002): 12.

7. For a full discussion that compares the Christian conception of God with the conceptions of ulti-
mate reality in Hinduism, Buddhism, and Islam, see my *Christianity at the Religious Roundtable:
Evangelicalism in Conversation with Hinduism, Buddhism and Islam* (Grand Rapids: Baker Aca-
demic, 2002). See especially chapters 2, 4, and 6. For a full treatment of the viability of identifying
Allah with the God of biblical revelation, see chapter 2 of my *Theology in the Context of World
Christianity* (Grand Rapids: Zondervan, 2007).

8. E. Deutsch and J. A. B. van Buitenen, eds., *A Source Book of Advaita Vedanta* (Honolulu: University of Hawaii Press, 1971), 160.

9. For more on the personhood of God in advaitism, see R. G. Panikkar, "The Brāhman of the Upanishads and the God of the Philosophers," *Religion and Society* 7, no. 2 (September 1960): 12–19;
and see B. Malkovsky, "The Personhood of Śankara's Para Brāhman," *Journal of Religion* 77, no.
4 (October 1997): 541–62.

Islam affirms the doctrine of *tawhid*, meaning the absolute oneness of God. This doctrine is incompatible with the Christian affirmation of the Trinity, which the Muslims regard as *shirk* (unwarranted associations with God)[10] or crass tritheism (Surah 5:73). However, the Islamic doctrine of monotheism (*tawhid*) protects God's otherness at the high cost of sacrificing the relational aspect of God's nature. Allah does not enter into relationship with Muslims. The very word *Islam* means "to submit" to the will of Allah. A Muslim is called to *obey* Allah, not to *know* Him. The well-known Iranian theologian of Islam, Al-Ghazali (1058–1111), summed it up well when he said, "Allah does not reveal Himself, He only reveals His will."

All of this is in stark contrast to the biblical revelation of Yahweh who is determined not only to reveal His will but also to reveal *Himself* and to enter into a relationship with His people. This is because God, by His triune nature, is inherently relational. The fall of man was not merely the entrance of rebellion into the world; it was, at a deeper level, the tragic fracturing of a relationship.[11] This has important implications for missions. Missionaries are "ambassadors of reconciliation," heralding how Christ has reconciled us with the Father. But this message must not become overly privatized. Missions must flow out of the very lifeblood of the church, which is the corporate expression of the community of God's inner life in the world. Missions, at its best, calls people into the new community.

Not only does God reveal Himself from creation as relational, but He also reveals Himself as holy. "Be holy, for I am holy" is one of the foundational revelations of Yahweh to His covenant people. There is no relationship with God apart from holiness. The redeemed community is to be a holy community. There is very little emphasis on holiness in the church today, and even less in missions literature. Because the focus of missions has been on proclaiming the message in a way that

---

10. *Shirk* in Islam is considered an unforgivable sin.
11. Eastern Orthodox theologian John Zizioulas has observed that the Trinity is best understood from the perspective of "personhood and communion." What defines a "person" (as with the Trinity) is being in relationship. For Zizioulas, a person does not become a person and then enter into relationships. Rather, to exist is to be in relationship. From this perspective, the triune God is related to history, not just in matters of salvation history such as the Red Sea, Sinai, Incarnation, Resurrection, and Ascension, but also in the very matrix of creation itself, since the Trinity is the archetype for all personhood and is reflected in the *imago dei*. For a full discussion on this, see Veli-Mati Karkkainen, *Trinity and Religious Pluralism* (Burlington, VT: Ashgate, 2004), 5–6; and J. Zizioulas, *Being and Communion: Studies in the Personhood and Church* (New York: St. Vladimir's Seminary Press, 1985).

has not been properly connected to the Trinity, we easily forget that we must reflect the message that we are proclaiming. Once the church is conceptualized as the earthly reflection of the Trinity, then holiness becomes central to missions. As Lamin Sanneh has noted, "The idea of the kingdom was at bottom the idea of a fellowship, chastened, redeemed and elected to exhibit the marks of love and forgiveness. The reality of God was thus intertwined with the ethical life of the fellowship of believers who were narrowly fenced off from the world."[12]

This has enormous ramifications for missionary practice. Much of our practice has been overly privatized and focused almost exclusively on conversion as the "end" of the missionary engagement. This has produced an individualistic and minimalistic view of what it means to follow Christ. Today's emphasis on "soul winning" must become an emphasis on church planting (community building),[13] and "conversion" must be broadened to include the end of spiritual exile and the inbreaking of the reign of God (kingdom of God) and the firstfruits of the New Creation.

In my experience of working in India, I have found that discipleship often *precedes* conversion by many years. This seems counterintuitive in the West, because Christendom always assumed a larger Christian context, making it easy to live as a Christian, since Christian ethics and values were presumably infused throughout the whole of society. However, in India, it often takes many years for someone to comprehend the gospel message and what it means to follow Jesus Christ. Lengthy periods of instruction and modeling often take place long before someone receives Christian baptism. This is closer to Jesus' model exemplified in the Gospels, whereby intensive instruction took place with His disciples for several years before they fully understood and accepted His lordship.

The renewed emphasis on holiness, intensive discipleship, and learning to live *counter* to the culture is all rooted in the Old Testament revelation of God's holiness, which forms the basis for entering into a covenantal relationship with God. In fact, by going back to the initial revelation of God in the Old Testament, we are able to fully capture the "end"

---

12. Lamin Sanneh, *Translating the Message: The Missionary Impact on Culture* (Maryknoll, NY: Orbis, 1989), 12.
13. Christ dwells in community (e.g., 1 Cor. 5:4) as the church has declared, *ubi Christus, ibi ecclesia*—where the church is, there is Christ (Ignatius, *Epistle to the Smyrnaeans* 8.2).

goal of missions: a holy people, a community that reflects the colloquy of the triune God. This is why one of the great images of the eschaton is that of a great feast, a holy banquet, where together as the redeemed community, we celebrate the arrival of the New Creation in the presence of the triune God.

God the Son: The Embodiment of the *Missio Dei*

Lesslie Newbigin observes that "the mission of Jesus was not only to proclaim the Kingdom of God, but also to *embody* the presence of the Kingdom of God in his own person."[14] One of the fundamental lessons of the Incarnation is that Jesus is not merely a messenger of good news but the embodiment of it. In Islam, Muhammad, at best, can only be the "messenger of Allah." In fact, even Allah's message to Muhammad must be mediated through the angel Gabriel because Allah cannot come down from his throne. The non-Trinitarian monotheism of Islam renders the kind of divine invasion represented by the Incarnation an impossibility. However, it is precisely this radical inbreaking of the New Creation that is embodied in Jesus Christ. This has important theological implications for those of us who proclaim, "Jesus is Lord!" The church as a missionary community must not only bear the message but also embody it. The church must reflect the Incarnation as an ongoing expression of the unfolding drama of God's mission in the world.

The Son of God's central role in the *missio dei* must be reflected in missions. In this overview, I will identify four major themes in missions that have their locus in God the Son.

Christian Missions in History as a Reflection of the Incarnation

We have already demonstrated in our reflection on God the Father that history is the stage for the unfolding of the *missio dei*. Nowhere is this revealed more profoundly than in the Incarnation. In the presence of Jesus of Nazareth, we find the final, definitive evidence that the Trinity is not merely some interiorized, abstract speculation about a remote being but the very means through which God Himself intersects with human history to accomplish His redemptive plan.[15]

---

14. Lesslie Newbigin, *The Open Secret: An Introduction to the Theology of Mission*, rev. ed. (Grand Rapids: Eerdmans, 1995), 40.

15. God in Himself certainly contains mysteries not yet known in the "economy" of salvation history and His intersection with His creation. Nevertheless, nothing about Himself that is revealed "in

Likewise, Christian missions happens in particular, real-time, historical and cultural settings. Missionaries are both bearers of a message and embodiments of that message. Whenever a missionary crosses cultural boundaries, learns a new language and culture, and seeks to communicate the gospel, this is a reflection of the Incarnation itself. From the perspective of the Trinity, Jesus is the archetypal missionary. The first Western missionaries to arrive in Papua New Guinea may have believed that no one had ever traversed such a vast cultural divide as they. However, their experience pales in comparison to the great gulf that the Son of God crossed in the Incarnation. The apostle Paul captures this well in his rendering of the ancient Christ hymn, found in Philippians 2.

> Who, being in very nature God, did not consider equality with God something to be used to his own advantage; rather, he made himself nothing by taking the very nature of a servant, being made in human likeness. And being found in appearance as a human being, he humbled himself by becoming obedient to death—even death on a cross! (Phil. 2:6–8 TNIV)

This early hymn is probably based on that well-known Servant Song of Isaiah found in Isaiah 52:13 to 53:12.[16] This Christian reflection on Isaiah's fourth Suffering Servant Song, demonstrates not only Jesus' solidarity with those among the faithful Jewish remnant who were suffering, but also His fulfillment of the eschatological hope that Jews held for their future deliverance from bondage and exile. Christians realized that this eschatological hope had already broken into the present age through Jesus Christ who, through His suffering, had rescued the human race from its bondage and exile.

The conclusion of the Christ hymn makes even more explicit the connection between the exaltation of the Suffering Servant and the unfolding Gentile mission.

---

history" will ever contradict that which is not yet known or revealed. Thus, while affirming the great continuity between the "immanent" and the "economic" Trinity, I would not affirm Karl Rahner's famous "rule" that the "economic Trinity" *is* the "immanent Trinity" and the "immanent Trinity" is the "economic Trinity." See Karl Rahner, *Trinity* (New York: Seabury, 1997), 22.

16. James Ware, *The Mission of the Church in Paul's Letter to the Philippians in the Context of Ancient Judaism* (Leiden, Netherlands; Boston: E. J. Brill, 2005), 225. See Richard Bauckham, *God Crucified: Monotheism and Christology in the New Testament* (Grand Rapids: Eerdmans, 1998), 58–60.

Therefore God exalted him to the highest place and gave him the name that is above every name, that at the name of Jesus every knee should bow, in heaven and on earth and under the earth, and every tongue confess that Jesus Christ is Lord, to the glory of God the Father. (Phil. 2:9–11)

The allusions to the Suffering Servant of Isaiah extend only through verse 9. Beginning with verse 10 the focus shifts from a description of Christ's sufferings to a Christological reflection upon the ultimate purposes of God. In short, it is a glimpse into the *missio dei*. The hymn anticipates the cosmic victory of Christ, His reign over all nations, and the eschatological universal worship of the triune God, which is anticipated in Isaiah 45:22–23 and ultimately finds its fulfillment in the New Creation.[17]

Authentic, biblical missions must envision itself as a reflection, as well as an ongoing extension, of this hymn in the world. From this perspective, missions represents countless reenactments of the Incarnation on a small scale. The church, of course, has not always been faithful to this vision. Nevertheless, it is essential that as a new generation of missionaries crosses cultural boundaries and enters the histories and narratives of new people groups, that they be trained to go forth as servants. Missionaries should be a reflection of the Suffering Servant, who entered our history and embedded Himself in our narratives, for the sake of our salvation. Missions also must constantly bear in mind the goal, the final vision, of all missions, which is the cosmic exaltation of Christ and the worship of the triune, living God by all nations. Thus, the historical presence of the church in the world, which both bears and embodies the gospel, finds its locus in the Son.

Incarnation as Translation

The Incarnation is the ultimate act of translation. Andrew Walls, who has made translatability a centerpiece of his missiology, comments that "when God in Christ became man, Divinity was translated into humanity, as though humanity were a receptor language."[18] As noted

---

17. Ware, *The Mission of the Church*, 229.
18. Andrew F. Walls, *The Missionary Movement in Christian History: Studies in the Transmission of Faith* (Maryknoll, NY: Orbis, 1996), 27.

in chapter 2, the story of the Incarnation is not merely that God became a man but that God became a *particular* man. This act of divine
translation in the Incarnation provides the theological foundation for
our commitment to the infinite translatability of the gospel in all of
the real and specific historical contexts and narratives that make up
our world.

The primary way Christians think about the "translatability" of the
gospel is in terms of linguistics. This remains a good place to start, because
there are several important features of translatability that are illustrated
quite well by the process of linguistic translation. Even a cursory knowledge of church history will reveal that the church has sometimes struggled
over the notion that the Scriptures could be (or should be) translated into
vernacular languages. Because the *Koine* Greek of the New Testament did
not conform to classical Greek, there was a long period of time when it was
regarded as a kind of specialized, sacred language of the Holy Spirit. This
view was used by some as a theological argument either against translating the New Testament at all or limiting translation only to Latin, which
was also considered a sacred language in the West. However, in the late
nineteenth century, scholars such as Adolph Deissmann and A. T. Rob-
ertson demonstrated persuasively that the Greek of the New Testament
was not specialized at all but was actually the common language of the
first-century marketplace. This underlined the powerful theological point
that God was prepared not just to speak to humanity but to do so in the
common language of the streets. This has helped the church to recognize
that the gospel of Jesus Christ potentially can be translated into any language in the world.

Another important lesson from the linguistic translatability of the
gospel is the reminder that Christianity is the only world religion whose
primary source documents are in a language other than the language of
the founder of the religion. This is one of the many stunning differences
between Christianity and all other world religions. Muhammad spoke
Arabic, and the Qur'ān is in Arabic; the Brahmin priests in India spoke
Sanskrit, and the Upanishads are in Sanskrit. Jesus taught in Aramaic, and
yet the primary documents that record Christ's teachings are not in Aramaic but in Koine Greek. This vitally important theological point about the
translatability of the Christian gospel dramatically contrasts, for example,
with the Muslims, who maintain that the Qur'ān is untranslatable and the

Word of Allah can be conveyed only in Arabic.[19] In contrast, at the very outset of the Christian message, the linguistic translatability of the message was testified to and even enshrined in our primary source documents.

The translatability of the gospel, however, extends far beyond linguistics.[20] Not only is the gospel *linguistically* translatable, but the gospel also is *culturally* translatable. In other words, Christ's entry into the world and taking on "the very nature of a servant," as the hymn reminds us, serves to destigmatize *all* cultures, making the whole world a potential extension of the inbreaking kingdom. If the Son of God could enter into the backwaters of an oppressed, despised people living on the margins of a first-century empire, then, by extension, the gospel can enter with confidence into any and every culture. This is the theological basis for the whole field of contextualization. Indeed, Lesslie Newbigin links the Incarnation with contextualization when he says that "true contextualization happens when there is a community which lives faithfully by the gospel and in that same costly identification with people in their real situations as we see in the earthly ministry of Jesus."[21] Thus, the Incarnation effectively throws open the door for all the strategic, missiological reflections on contextualization and how the gospel maintains its universal qualities even when it is embodied within a potentially infinite array of cultural particularities.

Incarnation and the Global "Ephesians Moment"

India received her independence on August 15, 1947, at midnight. Reports of the event noted that at the stroke of midnight crowds numbering up to a million, including Nehru and Mountbatten, gathered at the Viceroy's House to celebrate. However, there was one man who was not there and did not celebrate. That was Mahatma Gandhi. He said that despite all his labors, marches, protests, and imprisonments, he saw August 15 as a day of mourning, because India was partitioned and divided. India could not dwell together in unity. This, it seems, is one of the marks of our time. Our

---

19. This is why the persistence by pre-Vatican II Roman Catholics to keep the Mass in Latin was closer to the Islamic conception of the nontranslatablility of the Qur'an than the Christian position that has prevailed.

20. Missiologists are indebted to Lamin Sanneh for his work in moving the concept of translatability outside the technical world of linguistics and textual work.

21. Lesslie Newbigin, *The Gospel in a Pluralist Society* (Grand Rapids: Eerdmans, 1989), 154.

world is full of discord and disunity, whether it is in Sudan, the Balkans, Iraq, or in the towns and cities in our own backyard.

Jesus Christ initiated a new community that began within the rather narrow confines of first-century Jewish culture but quickly spread beyond it. As the church crossed more and more cultural frontiers, the community of those who followed Christ became increasingly more diverse, and the potential for division rose.[22] Early on, there was considerable pressure placed on the new Gentile believers to completely conform to all the Jewish social and cultural practices. In fact, there were those who insisted that they take on the full requirements of the Torah. However, once the Jerusalem Council (Acts 15:1–35) allowed the Gentiles to enter the church without leaving their own culture, the church had to find creative ways to simultaneously celebrate its unity and its diversity. The church was to be as diverse as the human race but still be one in Jesus Christ. The barrier between Jew and Gentile in the New Testament prefigures all such ethnic, cultural, and caste barriers that separate people of all times and places. However, in the gospel, those who were enemies and "far away" have now been brought near in Jesus Christ. For, as Paul declares in Ephesians 2:14, "He himself is our peace, who has made the two one and has destroyed the barrier, the dividing wall of hostility." This is what Andrew Walls called the "Ephesians Moment"—the coming together of diverse cultures into a new identity in Jesus Christ.[23] The dominant metaphor of the Christian community, which simultaneously celebrates diversity and unity, is the *body*—diverse parts and varied functions but one body. The church is the body of Christ (1 Cor. 12:27). This radical extension of the Incarnation should transform our conception of Christian missions.

Once the church really experiences the "Ephesians Moment," missions is liberated from being merely the aggrandizement of a religious institution or organization. Missions becomes an extension of a dynamic, living *community*, the body of Christ. Andrew Walls points out the two dangers that afflict missionaries when they fail to conceptualize missions within the biblical vision of the church as the body of Christ. First, there

---

22. The Acts 6 dispute between the Aramaic-speaking Jews and the Greek-speaking Jews or the Acts 15 dispute between the Judaizers and Paul's party are early examples of how the early church effectively responded to division.

23. Andrew Walls, "The Ephesians Moment," in *The Cross-Cultural Process in Christian History* (Maryknoll, NY: Orbis, 2002), 72–81.

is the attempt to make our particular version of Christianity the norm for everyone, thereby linking the gospel with some form of cultural imperialism. Second, there is the postmodern attempt to make every version of Christianity equally "valid and authentic," and "we are therefore each at liberty to enjoy our own in isolation from the others."[24] Christian unity is not a celebration of uniformity, but neither is diversity a celebration of fragmentation. Despite our many failures to realize this vision, the Christian church remains the most ethnically, racially, and culturally diverse movement on earth. Missions should be the greatest force for racial and ethnic reconciliation, as more and more peoples of the world experience the "Ephesians Moment."

In fact, the more ethnically and culturally diverse the church becomes, the greater the realization of the glory of the triune God. Walls says that "if the incarnation of the Son represents a divine act of translation, it is a prelude to repeated acts of re-translation *as Christ fills the Pleroma again.*"[25] In other words, as missionaries transmit the gospel, it is not merely a one-way street, because as we witness the reception of Christ among new peoples, it becomes part of our own discovery and rediscovery of even greater insights into the fullness of Christ. We would be underestimating the full significance of Acts 10 if we read it only as Peter's communication of the gospel to Cornelius followed by the conversion and baptism of Cornelius's household. Acts 10 is certainly a testimony to the cultural translatability of the gospel as it crosses the barrier between Jew (Peter) and Gentile (Cornelius), but it also demonstrates that gospel communication is never a one-way street. Cornelius was converted and became a follower of Christ. However, Peter also was transformed by the encounter. His preconceived theological categories were shaken. Peter was surprised and caught off guard by the magnitude of the *missio dei*. God's plan was bigger than Peter had realized. In that sense, Acts 10 is the story of a double conversion—Cornelius became a follower of Christ, and Peter gained a deeper insight into the fullness of the *missio dei*.[26]

---

24. Ibid.

25. Walls, *The Missionary Movement in Christian History*, xvii, emphasis mine.

26. This pericope in the New Testament has an interesting parallel with the encounter of Jonah with the Ninevites. Jonah, like Peter, would not have gone to the Gentiles except through divine prompting and initiative. Jonah, the reluctant and resistant missionary, finds unexpected faith and responsiveness among the "pagan Gentiles." The text is unclear how Jonah's faith was

All authentic missionary exchanges should reflect this "double conversion" as we think more and more globally about God's work. As the Christian community expanded beyond Jewish and Hellenistic culture and began to enter into Chinese, Indian, African, Korean, and others, we gained more insights into the beauty and fullness of Jesus Christ. In this vein, Jonathan Edwards saw the church as an "emanation" of God's glory in the same way that a tree puts forth buds, branches, leaves, and fruit to display its glory. The more the church grows, writes Edwards, the more it testifies to the "abundant diffusion" of His own "fullness" and "glory."[27] Although God is complete in Himself, His inner life continues to "flow forth," making more and more people "partakers of him."[28] Consequently, our understanding and insight into the full nature of God in Jesus Christ continually expands as more and more people groups come to the feet of Jesus. This is why missions cannot be relegated to merely a task of the church. Missions is the very means by which the church becomes the body of Christ, realizing and manifesting the fullness of Christ.

Hebrews 11 famously celebrates the men and women of the old covenant who lived by faith. However, the chapter concludes by saying that they did not receive the promise because God had an "even better plan for us. His purpose was that only in company with us would they be made perfect" (Heb. 11:40 GNT). Apparently, it is also true that only in the company of the full global church will any of us be made complete in Christ.

Incarnation and Holistic Missions
As noted in chapter 1, one of the tragedies of the transition to a post-Christendom context was an increasing emphasis on the privatization of faith. Postmodernism embraces only the subjectivism of one's personal narrative and not any claim for an objective metanarrative that is binding on all. Thus, Christianity was banished from the public square, "except when it was trotted out as part of a civil religion designed to rally the

---

expanded by the experience, but the opportunity was there for Jonah to experience a deeper conversion as he saw the surprising expansiveness of God's work in the world.

27. Jonathan Edwards, "Some Objections Considered Which May Be Made Against the Reasonableness of What Has Been Said of God's Making Himself His Last End," in *The Works of Jonathan Edwards*, ed. John E. Smith et al., vol. 8, *Ethical Writings* (New Haven: Yale University Press, 1972), 433, 439.

28. Ibid., 461–62.

citizens in time of war."[29] As broadly surveyed in chapter 1, the collapse of Christendom and the rise of postmodernism took its toll on all the major expressions of Christianity. However, the movement toward the privatization of faith among evangelical Christians is a particularly complex story. The common assertion that liberal Protestants embrace a "social gospel" while evangelicals embrace "personal evangelism" is not only historically inaccurate but also grossly unfair to the diversity within both traditions. Historically, evangelicals have been at the forefront of many major social changes, including child labor laws, the abolition of slavery, and prison reform. Evangelical missionaries built schools, orphanages, and hospitals all over the world. Likewise, mainline Protestant churches have produced some of the most inspiring examples of evangelistic fervor and dedicated church planting.

The fundamentalist-modernist controversies of the 1920s and 1930s did tend to reinforce the evangelical emphasis on personal conversion. Furthermore, the popular, pietistic stream within evangelicalism had always tended to emphasize that change happens "from within" and social change occurs "one person at a time." Thus, evangelicals were more likely to privatize social responsibility than to reject the notion of social action. For example, they were far more likely to engage in practical social assistance, such as a homeless shelter or a soup kitchen, than to address the larger, institutional and systemic root causes of evil.

The evangelical renewal that occurred after World War II was quite vocal in rejecting an overly privatized gospel and emphatically opposed popular fundamentalist notions of cultural separationism.[30] In 1954, Harold Ockenga, widely regarded as the leader of evangelicalism, spoke at the inauguration of E. J. Carnell as president of Fuller Theological Seminary, the early flagship school of evangelicalism. In the speech, Ockenga coined the phrase "new evangelical" when he said,

> The new evangelical embraces the full orthodoxy of fundamentalism in doctrine, but manifests a social consciousness and responsibility which was strangely absent from fundamentalism.

---

29. Craig A. Carter, *Rethinking Christ and Culture: A Post-Christendom Perspective* (Grand Rapids: Brazos, 2006), 19.

30. I am referring to the evangelical movement centered on Carl F. Henry, Harold J. Ockenga, Billy Graham, the National Association of Evangelicals (1943), and *Christianity Today* (1956).

The new evangelicalism concerns itself not only with personal salvation, doctrinal truth, and an external point of reference, but also . . . believes that orthodox Christians cannot abdicate their responsibility in the social scene.[31]

A "new evangelical," by definition, was someone who was doctrinally orthodox *and* socially engaged. In the last decade, the increased awareness of globalization has made everyone, including evangelicals, aware that companies like Nike and the GAP used "sweatshops" in the developing world to produce their goods. Younger evangelicals were deeply concerned when they learned, for example, that a woman in Haiti makes only six cents for sewing a "101 Dalmatians" outfit that Disney sells for twenty dollars. The result was a dramatic interest and participation in social involvement that addressed structural and systemic sources of evil, not just the outward symptoms. Robert Webber in the *Younger Evangelicals* has documented the growing interest in social engagement at every level by the newest generation of evangelicals.[32]

The best thing about these changes is that they have stimulated a renewed interest in the holistic ministry of Jesus as a model for Christian engagement in the world. It is hard to make a convincing case that missionaries have not been actively engaged in social concerns. Where missionaries have had difficulty is in articulating the *relationship* between evangelism and social action. Some missionaries have tended to see social action as a foothold or platform to evangelize, thus creating a hierarchy that validates social action only if it leads to explicit evangelism. Others have seen social action as a natural expression of Christ's love and, therefore, as a valid expression of the good news, even if it is not accompanied by, or does not lead to, a specifically articulated evangelistic call.

The holistic ministry of Jesus fully embodies both evangelism *and* social action, integrating them and putting an end to any lingering mistrust between the two. In a summary of Jesus' ministry, Matthew records that

---

31. Harold John Ockenga, "Theological Education," *Bulletin of Fuller Theological Seminary* 4 (October–December 1954): 4. Similar statements can be found in Carl Henry, *The Uneasy Conscience of American Fundamentalism* (Grand Rapids: Eerdmans, 1947).
32. Robert Webber, *The Younger Evangelicals: Facing the Challenge of a New World* (Grand Rapids: Baker, 2002).

Jesus went about "preaching the good news of the kingdom and healing every disease and sickness" (Matt. 9:35). Later, Jesus sent His disciples out to "preach the kingdom of God and to heal the sick" (Luke 9:2). Once missiology is reconceptualized within a Trinitarian framework, then Jesus is seen as the archetypal missionary who embodies the *missio dei*. Thus, a fresh examination of Jesus' ministry has a way of resolving many of the traditional tensions that have caused unnecessary discord. Jesus represents the inbreaking of the reign of God, the firstfruits of the New Creation. There are no disembodied souls in the New Creation. The lordship of Jesus Christ lays hold of the whole of creation, body *and* soul, humanity *and* the environment. We need to be constantly rescued from our natural tendency toward an overly parochial view of the *missio dei*.

In chapters 15 to 17 of this text, we will encounter a wide range of missionary models of witness, some of which seem to focus more on evangelism and church planting, while others seem to focus more on our social and cultural witness in the world. However, it is important to recognize that effective Christian ministry in any particular setting must be viewed through the broadest lens. No one ministry can fully reflect the expansiveness of the *missio dei* in the world. Only *together* can we manifest the fullness of Christ to a lost world.

GOD THE HOLY SPIRIT:
THE EMPOWERING PRESENCE OF THE *MISSIO DEI*

In his survey of the development of Christian doctrine, Jaroslav Pelikan observes that the doctrine of the Trinity represents the apex of doctrinal development in the early church. However, the recognition of the full deity of Jesus Christ came far more quickly than the recognition of the Holy Spirit's full deity within the triune Godhead. The Nicene Creed of 325 reflects the late emergence of pneumatology by simply stating, "We believe in the Holy Spirit," without further commentary. This rather sparse affirmation is often attributed to two reasons. First, the first ecumenical council that met at Nicea was preoccupied with responding to a wide range of challenges to the deity of Jesus Christ and was not in a position to consider the deity of the Holy Spirit. Second, New Testament evidence supporting the deity of the Holy Spirit is considerably less than the testimony to the Father and the Son, so it took longer to fully consider the case. As Gregory of Nazianzus commented, the Scripture did not "very often call him God in so many words, as it does first the Father and later on the Son."[33] As late as 380, Gregory admitted that "to be only slightly in error [about the Holy Spirit] was to be orthodox."[34] It was not until 381, in the Niceno-Constantinopolitan Creed, that the church articulated the version of the Nicene Creed that is so widely affirmed today: "We believe in the Holy Spirit, the Lord and Giver of Life, who proceedeth from the Father, who with the Father and the Son together is worshipped and glorified, who spoke by the prophets."[35]

Even though the deity of the Holy Spirit was resolved by 381, discussions about the exact nature and relations of the Trinity continued for almost a century.[36] All of this had a profound, cumulative, effect on theological discourse concerning the Holy Spirit. Because the ecumenical discussions about the Holy Spirit were focused primarily on the *person* of the Holy Spirit (i.e., His deity and relationship within the Trinity), there was a serious neglect throughout the patristic period of a full development of His *work*. In short, the "immanent" discourse about the Holy Spirit consistently trumped the needed "economic" discussions. Because these discussions emphasized the person of the Holy Spirit more than His work, the deliberations and writings of the patristic period were more weighted toward technical, abstract formulations. The result was that the Holy Spirit often was not thought of in personal terms. The dominant images of wind, fire, water, and oil are all impersonal images, which suggest an impersonal force rather than the empowering presence of the living God. Yet, in the New Testament, the Holy Spirit is the acting, personal subject of more than a dozen verbs.[37]

---

33. Jaroslav Pelikan, *The Christian Tradition: A History of the Development of Doctrine*, vol. 1, *The Emergence of the Catholic Tradition (100–600)* (Chicago: University of Chicago Press, 1971), 212. For a fresh analysis of Paul's understanding of the deity of the Holy Spirit and his Trinitarian theology, see Gordon D. Fee, *God's Empowering Presence* (Peabody, MA: Hendrickson, 1994), 827–45.

34. Pelikan, *Emergence of the Catholic Tradition*, 213.

35. Philip Schaff and Henry Wace, eds., *Nicene and Post-Nicene Fathers*, vol. 14, *The Seven Ecumenical Councils* (Peabody, MA: Hendrickson, 1999), 163. It should be noted that the phrase "and the Son" (*filioque*) was not inserted after the phrase "who proceedeth from the Father" until the year 589 at the third council of Toledo in Spain, although it was not included in the liturgical Latin version of the creed until 1014. The Eastern Church does not accept the addition of this phrase.

36. We should also remember that an acknowledgment of the deity of the Holy Spirit must not be confused with a full affirmation of the Trinity. The Trinity was not officially declared until the fifth ecumenical council in Constantinople in 553.

37. For example, the Spirit searches (1 Cor. 2:10), knows (1 Cor. 2:11), teaches (1 Cor. 2:13), dwells (1 Cor. 3:16; Rom. 8:11; 2 Tim. 1:14), accomplishes (1 Cor. 12:11), gives life (2 Cor. 3:6), cries out (Gal. 4:6), leads (Gal. 5:18; Rom. 8:14), bears witness (Rom. 8:16), has desires (Gal. 5:17), helps us

The Reformation's emphasis on the authority of Scripture, ecclesiology, and Christology, as crucial as it was, meant that there was a further delay in a full theological development of the doctrine of the Holy Spirit, and several vital aspects of His work were neglected in post-Reformation Protestant theology, which focused on solidifying and organizing the theological developments of the Reformers. Over time, Western theological traditions that developed greatly limited the active role of the Holy Spirit in the life of the church. The result was a pneumatological deficit that is only now becoming painfully apparent. A typical example can be found in Louis Berkhof's *Systematic Theology*, a classic text in Reformed theology that is still in use today. Berkhof discusses the work of the Holy Spirit but limits it to applying the work of Christ into our lives (e.g., regeneration) and in personal holiness (e.g., sanctification). In his development of ecclesiology, Berkhof is silent about the role of the Holy Spirit in empowering the church for witness and mission or in enabling the church as a whole to live out in the present the eschatological realities of the New Creation. It is not unusual to find Western systematic theologies that do not even develop the person and work of the Holy Spirit as a separate category of study but develop their theology of the Holy Spirit as subsets under the doctrine of God and the doctrine of soteriology.[38]

The twentieth century has simultaneously ushered in a renewed emphasis on the work of the Holy Spirit as well as a major renaissance in Trinitarian theology.[39] The emergence of global Pentecostalism has stimulated an unprecedented emphasis on the *work* of the Holy Spirit. Likewise, such influential theologians such as Karl Barth, Karl Rahner, and Jürgen Moltmann have all made the doctrine of the Trinity the centerpiece of their theological work. The result of both of these developments has served to mature our understanding of the Holy Spirit and thereby to understand better the role of the Holy Spirit in the *missio dei*. As with the other persons of the Trinity, four themes will now be examined.

(Rom. 8:26), intercedes (Rom. 8:26–27), works (Rom. 8:28), strengthens (Eph. 3:16), and grieves (Eph. 4:30).

38. See, for example, Henry C. Thiessen, *Lectures in Systematic Theology*, rev. ed. (Grand Rapids: Eerdmans, 1979).

39. Space does not permit a discussion of significant preparatory movements that laid the groundwork in the eighteenth and nineteenth centuries, such as the Wesleyan Holiness Movement and the Keswick revivals.

God the Spirit Empowers the Church for Witness

The church is, fundamentally, a community of proclamation. In this respect, Pentecost is the crucial dividing line between the Old Testament *kahal* (congregation) and the New Testament *ekklēsia* (church). The Old Testament was centered on the temple, the priest, the altar, the sacrifice, and the gathered congregation. After the Resurrection, the church was sent out into the world, as each of the postresurrection appearances of Jesus to His church made clear. However, just prior to His ascension, Jesus instructed His disciples to wait for the presence and empowerment of the Holy Spirit before they went forth as His community of proclamation. Jesus said, "I am going to send you what my Father has promised; but stay in the city until you have been clothed with power from on high" (Luke 24:49). At Pentecost the church was equipped to be the community of proclamation that embodies in word and deed the inbreaking of God's reign. The Cross, the Resurrection, and Pentecost collectively serve to mark the fulfillment of the old covenant. The new order is breaking into the present, and it must be proclaimed to all nations. As Harry Boer in *Pentecost and Missions* says, "Pentecost was the death-knell of temple, priest, altar, sacrifice, law and ceremony."[40] The term "death-knell" should not be taken to mean the end of these realities but the culminating fulfillment of them all into the greater reality that is found in Jesus Christ. In comparison to the new reality of Jesus Christ, those former realities are only a shadow (Heb. 8:5; 10:1). The result was a transformation in the people of God from a geographically defined, ethnically narrow movement to a global movement that was being extended to every nation on earth.

This new proclamation was explicitly understood as an extension of the ministry of the Holy Spirit in and through the church. While this global dimension was foreshadowed from the beginning, it was the death and resurrection of Christ, followed by Pentecost and the coming of the Holy Spirit, that marked the end of shadows, types, and anticipations and

---

40. Harry Boer, *Pentecost and Missions* (Grand Rapids: Eerdmans, 1961), 113. With one exception, the Greek term for a Jewish gathering or community, *sunagōgē*, is never used of a Christian gathering in the New Testament. Paul uses the word *ekklēsia* to describe Christians who are gathered in a particular place for worship. Later, he extends the meaning of *ekklēsia* to include all Christians everywhere, even those who are in heaven. For a full discussion on the use and development of *ekklēsia* in Pauline writings, see Robert J. Banks, *Paul's Idea of Community*, rev. ed. (Peabody, MA: Hendrickson Publishers, 2007), especially chapters 2 and 3, pp. 26–46.

began the actual inbreaking of the New Creation.[41] The central way the Holy Spirit brings the New Creation into the present is through empowering the church to proclaim the gospel in word and deed in the midst of all contextual challenges that the present evil order presents.

Catechesis into the Life and Ethos of the Kingdom/New Creation

In the Farewell Discourse recorded in John 14–17, Jesus places a great emphasis on the coming of the Holy Spirit. Jesus promises that when the Holy Spirit comes, He will "guide you into all truth" (16:13). The Holy Spirit is the divinely appointed catechist for the church. The word *catechesis* comes from a Greek word meaning "to instruct." It also can mean "to resound" or "to echo." Traditionally, the church has prepared small guidebooks, known as catechisms, which summarize the basic teachings of Christianity in order to help priests (later, pastors) to instruct new believers and to help parents in raising their children. Probably the most famous Protestant catechism is Martin Luther's *Shorter Catechism*, which was written to provide very basic instruction on the Ten Commandments, the Sermon on the Mount, and the Lord's Prayer. Through careful and patient instruction, the disciple was able to "echo" the apostolic faith, thus providing continuity in the life and teaching of the church over the centuries.

Seeing the Holy Spirit as the great catechist for the church reminds us of the ongoing need to teach and instruct the church. The Holy Spirit teaches the church the meaning and significance of the person and work of Jesus Christ. Jesus said that the Holy Spirit would help us "remember all that I have told you" (John 14:26 GNT). Jesus Christ did not usher in merely a "way of salvation" but a "New Creation." Gordon Fee, in his magisterial work on the Holy Spirit, *God's Empowering Presence*, correctly observes that "the one feature that distances the New Testament church the most from its contemporary counterpart is the thoroughly eschatological perspective of all of life."[42] For us, eschatology is about some vague, distant events that scholars and laypeople argue about. In contrast, the early church realized that the future had already been set into motion and was breaking into the

---

41. It will be explored in detail in chapter 4 how the promise to bless all nations/people groups was part of God's original plan, as promised in the Abrahamic covenant.
42. Fee, *God's Empowering Presence*, 803.

present. This is why we are defining missions as the global announcement and embodiment, through word and deed, of the inbreaking of God's reign and the New Creation. This is why Paul declares that we are those "upon whom the end of the ages has come" (1 Cor. 10:11 RSV). The most basic prayer of the church is the Lord's Prayer, a portion of which says, "May your Kingdom come; may your will be done on earth as it is in heaven" (Matt. 6:10 GNT). This is not a prayer that merely anticipates a future, eschatological event, when God's kingdom comes and God's will is done. It is a prayer for the church to embody the present realization of the future kingdom in the midst of the present, evil order.

The Holy Spirit, as the great catechist, teaches us and empowers us to live the life of the future in the present. Of course, the Holy Spirit's work of teaching is evident all over the world and in the whole church. However, it seems that since the missionary movement represents the extension of God's reign among new people groups, many of whom have no knowledge of Christianity, it is particularly important that we reflect the Spirit's catechesis in all that we do.

Suffering and Persecution and the Missio Dei

The expectation that Christians will be persecuted was among the first casualties of the domesticating influence of Christendom. In Christendom, the line between the church and the world was virtually erased, thereby blunting important aspects of the Holy Sprit's work. Paul makes regular references to his suffering and the suffering of others for the sake of the gospel.[43] In fact, suffering and persecution form an integral part of Paul's understanding of the public witness of the gospel. In mission studies, persecution often has been understood only within the context of particular resistant people groups and/or political situations that prohibit the public profession of Christ. However, for Paul, suffering is an ongoing reflection of and participation in the sufferings of Christ (Rom. 8:17; 2 Cor. 1:5–7; Phil. 3:10; Col. 1:24) wherever the true church is. Persecution produces perseverance (Rom. 5:3), enables us to rely upon God (2 Cor. 1:9), and prepares us to share in the eschatological glory that is to be revealed (Rom. 8:18–25). For Paul, suffering is a normal expectation

---

43. Rom. 5:3; 8:17–18; 2 Cor. 1:5–7; 11:21–29; Eph. 3:13; Phil. 3:10; Col. 1:24; 1 Thess. 1:6; 2 Thess. 1:4–5; 2 Tim. 1:8, 12; 2:3, 9, 11.

for Christian witness (Rom. 8:35; 2 Cor. 12:10; 2 Tim. 1:8, 11–12; 2:3, 9). In fact, Paul states this explicitly when he instructs Timothy, saying, "Everyone who wants to live a godly life in Christ Jesus *will be perse-cuted*" (2 Tim. 3:12).[44] This language must seem like an alien world to those who have only known the cheap grace of Christendom.

In contrast, we discover in the New Testament that suffering is one of the ways in which we embody the gospel and reflect Christ's work in the world. Jesus anticipates that the church would be "brought to trial be-fore rulers and kings." When that occurs, He admonishes us to not worry "about what you are going to say or how you will say it . . . for the words you will speak will not be yours; they will come from the Spirit of your Father speaking through you" (Matt. 10:18–20 GNT). Jesus envisions perse-cution as one of the ways in which the Spirit of God proclaims the gospel, through His church, to the rulers of this present age. As we move into a post-Christendom, increasingly post-Christian context, we need to better prepare students to understand the dynamics of persecution and to de-velop a theological understanding of persecution as a normative part of the church's life and witness. This transition can be greatly aided as we learn valuable lessons from the emerging new generation of missionaries coming from the Majority World. Many of these missionaries come from contexts where Christianity is a persecuted and misunderstood minority. These new missionaries are proving to be far more adept at helping new Christians understand how to inhabit a post-Christendom world or a culture where some other world religion dominates the religious and political landscape.

Missionary Witness as a Dynamic Overflow of the Spirit

Since the advent of Protestant missions, the dominant motivation for mis-sions has been an appeal to the "missionary mandate." Thus, missions became a response of obedience to a particular set of commands, most no-tably those texts commonly referred to as embodying the Great Commis-sion. In contrast, Lesslie Newbigin pointed out that in the New Testament, we do not witness the burden of obeying a command but rather a vast "explosion of joy."[45] Jürgen Moltmann describes missions as the joyous

---

44. Emphasis mine.
45. Lesslie Newbigin, "The Logic of Missions," in *New Directions in Mission and Evangelization*, vol. 2, ed. James Scherer and Stephen Bevans (Maryknoll, NY: Orbis, 1994), 16. Original context found in *The Gospel in a Pluralist Society*, 116–27.

invitation to all peoples to come to a "feast without end."[46] Missions, of course, is never *less* than a command of Christ, but it is certainly far *more* than that. The perspective of the New Testament is never, "How can we motivate someone to go?" but rather, "Who could possibly be silent in light of the resurrection of Jesus Christ?"

Harry Boer (in his *Pentecost and Missions*) rightly points out that none of the key figures in the book of Acts ever makes a direct appeal to any of the Great Commission passages to justify his preaching, even when questions are raised about the emerging Gentile mission. He further points out that the earliest believers who took the initiative to preach the gospel to Gentiles (Acts 11:20) were very likely not even present at any of those postresurrection commissioning events.[47] However, this is less a statement about the importance of Jesus' final commission in their minds than a statement about the effect of the transformative events of the Resurrection and Pentecost in the lives of those earliest witnesses. The nineteenth-century missiologist Gustav Warneck (1834–1910) was probably correct when he stated that "the Great Commission was the silent presupposition underlying the witness of the earliest Christian community."[48] However, the point is that the Great Commission cannot, and should not, be viewed in isolation from either of the two determinative, supernatural events that precede and follow the commission; namely, the resurrection of Jesus Christ and the coming of the Holy Spirit on the Day of Pentecost. It was the transforming reality of these two supernatural events that thrust the early church outward into that "explosion of joy."

Understanding missions as an extension of the Holy Spirit's life and work through the church and into the world carries with it a wide range of implications for missions, many of which will be developed in more detail in chapters 14 through 16. However, in a more general way, three representative examples will be noted here. First, this new perspective should help to liberate missionaries from an undue emphasis on human strategies that have been articulated in isolation from the Spirit's work. Contemporary missiology places great emphasis on the skill of human efforts, sociological models, and elaborate strategies, but comparatively

---

46. Jürgen Moltmann, *The Church in the Power of the Spirit* (London: SCM, 1975), 75.
47. Boer, *Pentecost and Missions*, 43.
48. As quoted in Boer, *Pentecost and Missions*, 36.

less emphasis on conceptualizing missions as *primarily* an extension of the ministry of the Holy Spirit. We need to prepare missionaries not only in what to say and do, but more importantly, in how to *live* as a disciple of Jesus Christ in the world.

Moonjang Lee, one of my colleagues who teaches missions at Gordon-Conwell, once surprised some of our students in a chapel service where he was preaching. He commented that no missionaries should go out onto the field until they are certain that their own spirituality is deeper than those to whom they are being sent. We have emphasized so much the inherent power of the Christian message that we sometimes forget the importance of the messenger whose life fully reflects what it means to live in the power of the Holy Spirit under the lordship of Jesus Christ.

Second, the underdeveloped doctrine of the Holy Spirit has limited the church's ability to integrate missionary training with important biblical themes such as the role of persecution or the role of signs and wonders in the proclamation of the gospel. Yet even a casual reading of the book of Acts reveals that signs and wonders and persecution often accompany and attest to the faithful preaching of the gospel.

Third, placing missions within the larger context of the Holy Spirit's work in bringing in the New Creation has important implications for how we understand and define the "task" or "goal" of missions. In missions writings dating back to the nineteenth century, there is a great deal of emphasis on "completing the task" and "fulfilling the Great Commission." Probably the most famous missionary slogan emerged out of the Student Volunteer Missionary Movement: "*The Evangelization of the World in This Generation.*" Since that time, the language of "completion" and "fulfillment" has typified evangelical missions literature. In the twentieth century, the most important movement that focused the church's energy on "completing" the Great Commission was the A.D. 2000 movement. The motto of the A.D. 2000 movement was "A Church for Every People and the Gospel for Every Person by 2000."

All these movements have wonderfully served the church. Indeed, the global church is stronger today because of the zeal, commitment, and the genuine Christian fruit these movements produced. However, we must increasingly recognize that the language of "completion" can be comprehended only when missions is built on the foundation of Christendom, not on the foundation of the Trinity. Through the lens of the *missio dei,* we no longer isolate soteriology from pneumatology and es-chatology. Therefore, even when every person has had an opportunity to hear the gospel, or even if a church is planted in every people group of the world, missions will not be over. Once missions is linked inseparably to the triune God, then the church recognizes that the ultimate goal of mis-sions can be found only in the New Creation. This does not negate impor-tant goals such as planting a church in every people group in the world. However, it does mean that the church must always live in the tension of "unfinished business." The mission of the church (missions) is to partici-pate in the *missio dei* by continuing the mission of Jesus throughout the world until the end of history.

CONCLUSION

This chapter has sought to provide a broad framework for the reconcep-tualization of missions within a Trinitarian framework. Once the *missio dei* becomes the generative center of all missiological reflection, it changes the way we think and conduct ourselves as ambassadors of God's mission in the world. We find ourselves transcending the competitive aggrandize-ment of a particular denominational work. Instead, we become heralds who embody the inbreaking of the New Creation. The triumphalism of human agency and ingenuity are replaced by a deepened humility and awe that God would use us, alongside Christians from all over the world, in the accomplishment of His unfolding plan of redemption in the world. As David Bosch said in the conclusion of his *Transforming Mission,* "It is not the church which 'undertakes' mission; it is the *missio dei* which constitutes the church. The mission of the church needs constantly to be renewed and re-conceived."[49] The chapters that follow are an attempt to renew missions for the twenty-first century by reconceiving each element within the larger context of the Trinity and the *missio dei.*

---

49. David Bosch, *Transforming Mission* (Maryknoll, NY: Orbis, 1991), 519.

PART TWO

GOD THE FATHER:
THE PROVIDENTIAL SOURCE
AND GOAL OF THE
MISSIO DEI

A Missional Perspective
on the Bible

— 4 —
The God of Mission Reveals His Plan

NEILL MCGREGOR, THE FORMER DIRECTOR of the National Gallery of Art in London, noted a few years ago that roughly one-third of the greatest European paintings in the collection depict an explicitly biblical theme.[1] This reflects the historical impact Christianity has had on Western civilization. The irony is that the majority of Europeans who daily file past these magnificent displays of art today have no idea what biblical scenes are being depicted. The once-familiar biblical narrative that winds its way along the grand canal of creation, fall, redemption, and New Creation has receded into the background, leaving in its place only the vaguest notions of a distant, monadic God who has neither a name nor a biography. In a post-Christendom world, we can no longer take for granted that the English word *God* has any necessary association with the God who has revealed Himself in the Bible.

Thus, it must be an amazing experience for new readers of the Bible to encounter the living God who has revealed Himself in those sacred pages. From the opening chapters of Genesis, all of the vacuity of the generic *God* that inhabits the consciousness of the contemporary world is powerfully swept aside. Instead, we are confronted with a personal God who is *not silent*, a God who *acts*, and a God who *sends*. The entire structure of this book is based on the assumption that God has engaged human history with a mission. This is why missions is ultimately not about what we do but about who God is. Our actions emerge only as we are enabled to

---

1. Neill MacGregor, *The Image of Christ* (London: National Gallery, 2000), 6, as quoted in David Smith, *Mission After Christendom* (London: Darton, Longman and Todd, 2003), 1.

enter into and are called to participate in His grand, unfolding narrative. The God who reveals Himself in the Bible is the God of mission. This is why mission is defined in this text as *God's redemptive, historical initiative on behalf of His creation.* This chapter explores how, beginning with Abraham, God has taken the initiative and revealed His plan.

THE ABRAHAMIC COVENANT

The Covenant with Abraham and the Tower of Babel
God's covenant with Abraham,[2] found in Genesis 12, is such a remarkable event in the history of redemption that Paul describes it as God preaching the gospel "in advance" to Abraham (Gal. 3:8). Genesis 12 becomes the cornerstone of God's covenant with the Jewish people, as well as the initial self-disclosure concerning His mission. Later, chapter 5 will explore how the Abrahamic covenant serves as the foundation upon which missions in the New Testament is built and engaged.

Yahweh's covenant with Abraham must be seen within the larger context of the preceding chapters. Genesis 3 depicts what is known as the Fall, the entrance of sin, and the brokenness of the human race apart from God. The subsequent chapters develop cycles of human wickedness and rebellion that culminate in the narratives about Noah (Gen. 6–9) and the Tower of Babel (Gen. 11). The effects of human rebellion are shown to be both personal and systemic, not only separating individuals from God (e.g., Adam and Eve), but also fracturing all relationships (e.g., Cain and Abel) and society as a whole (e.g., Noah's world).[3] Indeed, even the soil is cursed, demonstrating that the whole of creation is affected by the willful assertion of human autonomy.

The Tower of Babel narrative in Genesis 11 represents the wider effects of the Fall and serves as an important theological backdrop to the covenant God makes with Abraham in Genesis 12. Three facets of the Babel narrative should be noted. First, the peoples who had settled on the plains of Mesopotamia wanted—through their own efforts and ingenuity—to build

---

2. I.e., Abram, but I am using the later amended name Abraham, since this is how he is commonly known.
3. One of the deficits in contemporary theology has been to see the Fall only through the lens of Adam's personal guilt. In other writings, I develop in some detail how the Fall produces fear, guilt, and shame, all of which have their own personal and societal implications. See my *Theology in the Context of World Christianity* (Grand Rapids: Zondervan, 2007), 77–104.

"a city with a tower that reaches the sky" (11:4 GNT).[4] Second, the purpose of the city and the tower was to "make a name" for themselves (11:4). Finally, this event has global ramifications. The worldwide significance of this event is underscored by the fact that five times the narrative mentions "the whole earth" (כל־הארץ, 11:1, 4, 8, 9 [2x]). This is an important backdrop to the Abrahamic covenant, which represents God's initiative to "make a name for Abraham," and to bless "the whole earth." In fact, Abraham lives by faith, anticipating the reverse of Babel in that eschatological city "whose architect and builder is God" (Heb. 11:10).

Genesis 12, therefore, should be seen as both God's initiative with Abraham and His response to the culminating effects of worldwide, human rebellion. The covenant is simultaneously personal *and* global, local, *and* universal. The covenant of Genesis 12:1–3 begins with an imperative. God commands Abraham to "get up and go." It is an imperative that suggests decisive action in sending Abraham out to that which is unknown. It is in direct contrast to those at Babel, who were determined to "settle down" (11:2) and "not be scattered" (11:4). In contrast, God commands Abraham, saying, "leave your country, your relatives, and your father's house, and go to a land that I am going to show you" (12:1 GNT). As Abraham obeys, God declares a series of blessings that He will bring about.

> I will make you into a great nation and I will bless you; I will make your name great. (12:2)

At the Tower of Babel, the people were determined to make a name *for themselves*. Here, God declares that *He* will make Abraham's name great. The city and tower of Genesis 11 were built to prevent being "scattered all over the earth" (GNT) but resulted in precisely that, as God scattered them in 11:9. In contrast, Abraham allowed himself to be scattered out into the world (12:4–9), in order to become the father of a great and gathered nation.

---

4. Commentators are divided about whether there was anything inherently wrong in building a city. Some argue that their stopping to build any kind of city was rebellion against the command to "multiply and fill the earth." This would put greater emphasis on the second part of their reason for building the tower, namely, so as not to be "scattered over all the earth." Others insist that there was nothing inherently wrong in building a city, but this particular city and tower were seen as an act of human rebellion, revealed by the first part of the phrase, their wanting to "make a name for themselves." Both reasons are important and are reflected by how they contrast with the Abrahamic covenant in Genesis 12.

As Abraham goes out, God's divine blessing will likewise go forth and increase. Abraham will be blessed, the nation that comes from him will be blessed, and indeed the whole world will be blessed. The overall structure of the passage is chiastic.[5] A close examination of Genesis 12 reveals that the order of what Abraham is called to forsake begins in the largest frame and gets increasingly narrow. He is to leave his *land*, his *relatives*, and his *father's house*. However, the corresponding blessing is in direct reverse, encompassing an ever-widening circle of blessing. As Abraham obeys, God will personally bless *Abraham*, He will bless the *nation* that will come from him, and, finally, *all the families and peoples of the earth will be blessed through him*.[6] It is the latter phrase that is of particular importance in our understanding of the *missio dei*, as well as all the missions that ultimately emerge as a reflection of it. God is promising to bless not only Abraham and the nation of Israel but also, through Abraham's obedience, all the nations of the world.

The phrase in Genesis 12:3 that is used to describe this largest sphere of blessing is *kol mishpehot*. The phrase is sometimes translated "all the nations," but it is actually a more specific phrase, which means, "all the extended families" or "all the kinship groups." In either case, it does not refer to the larger geopolitical units we often refer to as nations today. The word *mishpehot* is a *people* word, not a political or geographic word. It refers to ethnic and kinship groupings, just as the Greek word *ethnē* does in the New Testament.

The threefold structure of the blessing is even more vividly portrayed in subsequent repetitions of the covenant at strategic points in the lives of each of the patriarchs, Abraham, Isaac, and Jacob. After Abraham's unwavering faith in God's promise, shown in his willingness to sacrifice his own son, followed by the equally dramatic intervention of God, who provides the substitute, the covenant is renewed as follows:

---

5. A chiasm refers to a particular grammatical structure where the order of words in one clause is inverted in a parallel clause. The term comes from the Greek letter *chi* (X), indicating a "crisscross" arrangement of words or phrases.

6. The verb "to bless" in Genesis 12:3 is sometimes incorrectly translated as a reflexive, "all peoples on earth will bless themselves," rather than as a passive, "all peoples on earth will be blessed." Walter Kaiser, among others, has persuasively argued that it should be translated as passive, not reflexive. Kaiser points out that "it is not without significance that all five of the Genesis passages recording the Abrahamic promise are rendered as passives in the Samaritan Version, the Babylonian (Onkelos) Targum, the Jerusalem (Pseudo-Jonathan) Targum, and all citations of these references in the inter-testamental literature, as well as in the New Testament." See Walter C. Kaiser Jr., *Mission in the Old Testament: Israel as a Light to the Nations* (Grand Rapids: Baker, 2000), 19–20.

> I swear by myself, declares the LORD, that because you have done this and have not withheld your son, your only son, I will surely bless you and make your descendants as numerous as the stars in the sky and as the sand on the seashore. Your descendants will take possession of the cities of their enemies, and through your offspring all nations on earth will be blessed, because you have obeyed me." (Gen. 22:16–18)

The threefold blessing is once again made explicit: First, Abraham will be personally blessed through the dramatic increase of his descendents. His descendents will be as numerous as the stars in the sky. Second, his descendents will be a blessed nation, even taking "possession of the cities of their enemies." Finally, through Abraham's seed "all nations on earth will be blessed" because of his obedience. The phrase used as the object of this third part of the ever-increasing blessing is *kol goye*, meaning "all the nations." Although the word *goye* (nations) is used instead of *mishpehot* (extended families), it is nevertheless a reference to people groups, not geographic or political units.[7]

When Yahweh repeats the covenant with Isaac, it follows the same threefold pattern, blessing him personally through the multiplication of his descendents, giving the future nation of Israel "all these lands," and through his seed blessing "all nations on earth":

> I will make your descendants as numerous as the stars in the sky and will give them all these lands, and through your offspring all nations on earth will be blessed, because Abraham obeyed me and kept my requirements, my commands, my decrees and my laws. (Gen. 26:4–5)

The same threefold blessing occurs when the covenant is repeated to Jacob in Genesis 28:11–17 during his dramatic vision of angels ascending and descending on a staircase between earth and heaven. The key difference between the way the covenant is articulated to Isaac in Genesis 26 and to Jacob in Genesis 28 is that the word used in Genesis 28:14 to describe this global blessing reverts to the original language of Genesis 12:3:

---

7. In the Old Testament, the Hebrew terms "people" (*'am*) and "nation" (*goye*) are used interchangeably in reference to Israel.

"all the familes (*mishpehot*) on earth will be blessed."[8] While this does not alter the meaning, it is an example of a stylistic chiastic structure that is found in the repetition of the covenant to each of the patriarchs:

families (12:3) → nations (22:18) ← nations (26:4) ← families (28:14)

Three Key Themes in the Abrahamic Covenant

There are three important themes that should be identified in this overview of the Abrahamic covenant.

First, God is the source and initiator of mission. The Abrahamic covenant is initiated by God and stands in utter contrast to human initiatives and plans for greatness, and to "make a name" for ourselves. The Tower of Babel represents human pride, leading to confusion and scattering (Gen. 11:9). The Abrahamic covenant represents God's sovereign, providential initiative, leading to the ultimate gathering and blessing of all nations (Rev. 7:9–10). It is here, at the initial unfolding of the covenant, that we derive the general heading for this section of the book: God the Father is the providential source, as well as the goal, of the *missio dei*. *Providence* is an important word that has been neglected in post-Enlightenment Christian discourse. The word *providence* means "to see beforehand." It captures the idea that God not only designed and initiated a plan—a mission—but also foresaw in advance that this plan would ultimately unfold to be a blessing to all nations or people groups. To speak of God's providence means that He knows the final goal of the *missio dei* and that He is able to guide history toward that final goal. Because God already has ordained the final goal, He actually confirms it with an oath, swearing by His own self that all nations will be blessed through the seed of Abraham (Gen. 22:16–18). Thus, the Abrahamic covenant represents an initiative by God with a view to a final goal or particular end. The initiation by God and the final goal are linked together by God's sovereign providence.

---

8. There are several other minor variations between all three articulations of the covenant in Gen. 22, 26, and 28. For example, in Genesis 22 the numerical blessing is pictured with the dual metaphors of "stars in the sky and as the sand on the seashore." In Genesis 26 a single metaphor is used, "the stars in the sky." In Genesis 28 the metaphor is "the dust of the earth." These are all stylistic variations with the same meaning. The other difference is that the order of the three blessings is switched in Genesis 28, emphasizing the giving of the land first, followed by the numerical blessing. However, this is driven by the context of the passage since this particular rearticulation of the covenant is in response to Jacob's sojourn through the land.

Second, the Abrahamic covenant reveals Yahweh as a sending God. When God speaks to Abraham, He begins with the imperative "Go!" The Old Testament scholar Christopher Wright translates the opening phrase of the covenant, "Get yourself up and go!"[9] God the Father is the source of all sending. The Hebrew verb meaning "to send" is *salah.* Over two hundred occurrences of the verb have God as the subject of the sending.

Ferris McDaniel, in "Mission in the Old Testament," provides an overview of the usages of *salah* and points out four facets of how the word is understood.[10] (1) Sending is connected with *purpose*; it is an extension of the will of the sender. God sends Abraham because He has a divine purpose that is going to be accomplished through this act of sending. In the New Testament, when Jesus sends the church to all nations, it must be seen as an extension of the original purpose, which finds its source in the Abrahamic covenant. (2) Sending is often associated with *authority.* In over three hundred of its usages, it is "a judge or other person of rank, especially a king, who sends."[11] For a king, to send is the same as to give a command. Whether God sends Adam and Eve out of Eden (Gen. 3:23), or sends Moses to confront Pharaoh (Exod. 3:10; 4:21; 7:13, 15) or sends His fiery arrows against David's enemies (2 Sam. 22:15; Ps. 18:15), the act of sending implies a command.

(3) Because sending is connected with authority, there is a *reluctance to disobey.* McDaniel points out how few times people refuse once they have been sent. Perhaps the most famous example of reluctance is when Moses is sent to lead the Israelites out of Egypt and he asks that someone else be sent (Exod. 4:13). Nevertheless, obedience is a normative expectation of those being sent out by a greater authority, and even Moses' reluctance cannot withstand God's authoritative call. (4) Sending often involves the *use of messengers.* God frequently sends His word through emissaries. Normally, this is done through human agency. For example, God's word to Pharaoh is sent through Moses, and God's word to His people is sent through the prophets. Sometimes God sends an entire nation, such as the Assyrians or Babylonians, to judge His people and extend His purposes. However, God extends His "sending" through a wide variety of agents,

---

9. Christopher J. H. Wright, *The Mission of God* (Downers Grove, IL: IVP Academic, 2006), 200.

10. Ferrris L. McDaniel, "Mission in the Old Testament," in *Mission in the New Testament: An Evangelical Approach,* William J. Larkin Jr., ed. and Joel F. Williams (Maryknoll, NY: Orbis, 1998), 12–15.

11. Ibid., 13.

including angels (Gen. 19:13), plagues (Exod. 9:14; Jer. 24:10), wild beasts (Ezek. 14:21), abundant harvests (Joel 2:19), and even Gentile rulers such as Rezin (2 Kings 15:37) and Nebuchadnezzar (Jer. 43:10). The picture is of a divine sovereign who has the whole of creation at His disposal to accomplish His divine purpose. This "whole creation" perspective helps to situate world missions and the church's obedience to the Great Commission within the larger context of God's sovereignty as the Sender.

Third, the Abrahamic covenant reveals God's heart for all nations. There is a persistent misunderstanding by many that the Old Testament is somehow narrowly particularistic, revealing a God who gives preferential treatment to Israel while totally ignoring or disdaining all other nations and that it is not until the New Testament that we discover God's love and compassion for all the nations of the world. This perspective reveals a deficient understanding of the Old Testament. As we have demonstrated, God's revelation to Abraham, which is the cornerstone of the entire covenant relationship Israel has with God, declares that God chose and sent Abraham so that all the peoples of the earth would be blessed! Abraham and all of Israel were blessed in order to be a blessing. In other words, God's election of Israel should not be understood as a rejection of other nations; it should be seen as the means by which God would fulfill His ultimate (and stated) purpose of blessing all nations.

It is important to see here (as well as later on in the Great Commission passages in the New Testament) that the movement of history that is revealed in this glimpse into the *missio dei* is not the individual but the *nations* (people groups) of the world.[12] One of the dangerous tendencies in post-Enlightenment thought has been to view God's actions and initiatives as ultimately finding their locus in the individual rather than in the larger social network of ethnic identity within *communities*. This does not downplay the work of God in our own personal lives, or diminish how Christ as the "seed" of Abraham blesses us in profoundly personal ways with eschatological significance. The point is that while the *missio dei* is never *less* than personal, it envisions something that is *more* than merely personal. To reduce the *missio dei* to God's work among individuals neglects the larger frame of community that joins us

---

12. Whenever the word *nation* is used, unless otherwise noted, the usage will be the biblical understanding of nation as a people group, not a geopolitical concept as found in popular discourse.

as individuals to the church, the body of Christ, the corporate expression of the Trinity in the world, and the bride of Christ in the eschaton.

Evangelical soteriology, in particular, has often understood salvation in terms of God's action of grace within a human heart and the individual response to God's work. Without minimizing the necessity of a personal response, I do want to address an imbalance that has focused almost exclusively on the vertical aspects of salvation and neglected the horizontal. As noted in chapter 2, only by reuniting the Cross and the Resurrection with the inbreaking of the Holy Spirit at Pentecost are we able to see *both* the individual and the corporate dimensions of a biblical soteriology. Only by reuniting the two can we gain a biblical perspective on human history and the glorious diversity in human cultures. Thus, in chapters 5 and 6, we will examine in more detail how the missionary activity of the church needs to be focused on *nations*, not just individuals within nations.

GOD'S BLESSING OF THE NATIONS IN THE OLD TESTAMENT

Once we rediscover the centrality of God's heart for the nations within the *missio dei*, we can have the proper perspective on the dozens of passages in the Old Testament that make reference to the nations. It is beyond the scope of this study to fully explore the rich and multifaceted theme of the nations in the Old Testament. Our focus will be specifically on those texts that are particularly relevant to the mission of God, as revealed in the Old Testament. In a broad sense, these texts fall into four general categories. First, there are texts that reveal Israel's understanding that God is sovereign over all nations, not just Israel. Second, some texts set forth Israel's call to proclaim and embody the glory of God to all nations. Third, there are specific messianic passages in the Hebrew Scriptures that reveal and anticipate how God will manifest His glory to the nations. Finally, there are eschatological promises embedded within the whole tapestry of the Old Testament that remind us of the goal that was originally articulated in the initial covenant to Abraham but will not be finally realized until the eschaton. There is, of course, considerable overlap within these categories, especially since the messianic prophecies represent the inbreaking of the future eschaton into human history. Nevertheless, this will provide a general framework for understanding how the *missio dei* continues to be unfolded within the context of God's covenant with Israel. As explored in chapter 2, the purpose of this overview is not to provide a theology of

missions in the Old Testament but to demonstrate how a missional theology is found throughout every strand of the Hebrew Scriptures.

God's Sovereignty over the Nations

There are dozens of texts that demonstrate that although God has entered
into a particularistic covenant with one nation, Israel, He enjoys sovereign
dominion over all the nations of the world. This means God retains the
right to judge, as well as to bless, the nations. Psalm 47:8 declares, "God
reigns over the nations, God is seated on his holy throne." He is "exalted
over all the nations," declares the psalmist in Psalm 113:4, and He has determined to reveal "his righteousness to the nations" (Ps. 98:2). The Lord
sits in judgment over all nations within the context of human history. The
prophet Joel declares, "Let the nations be roused; let them advance into
the Valley of Jehosphaphat, for there I will sit to judge all the nations" (Joel
3:12). Israel prays with confidence in God's sovereignty over the nations,
which is why they declare, "Arise, O LORD, let not man triumph, let the
nations be judged in your presence" (Ps. 9:19). Undoubtedly, the Old Testament reveals God's sovereignty over all nations on earth.

Declaring God's Glory Among the Nations

Those unfamiliar with the Old Testament often mistakenly assume that the
mandate to declare God's glory among the nations emerges only in the New
Testament. However, Israel is commanded to "make known among the nations what he has done" (1 Chron. 16:8) and to "declare his glory among the
nations" (1 Chron. 16:24; Ps. 96:3). The Old Testament exhorts the "families
of nations" to "ascribe to the Lord glory and strength" (1 Chron. 16:28).
Far from a mere particularistic vision, God regularly asserts the original
Abrahamic promise that His glory will be revealed among all nations (Ps.
96:7; 105:1). The Lord says to Malachi, "My name will be great among the
nations, from the rising of the sun to the setting of the sun. In every place
incense and pure offerings will be brought to my name, because my name
will be great among the nations" (Mal. 1:11). Even the Jewish temple, probably the most visible sign of God's particular presence among Israel, will be
called "a house of prayer for all nations" (Isa. 56:7).[13]

---

13. New Testament scholar Greg Beale, in *The Temple and the Church's Mission*, has convincingly demonstrated that the symbolism of the temple in the Old Testament has eschatological

Messianic Prophecies of the Old Testament

Prophecies about a coming Messiah are a rich category of Old Testament texts that have been explored in several important studies.[14] For our purposes here, we will focus on a few representative texts that are significant in our understanding of the unfolding of the *missio dei*. What makes these texts important for Christians who are a part of an ethnically diverse, multicentered, global church is that the Jewish messianic hope is *simultaneously* particularistic and universal. In other words, Jesus fulfills very specific Jewish expectations for one who will come and redeem Israel. Jesus is the fulfillment of very particular Jewish hopes and expectations that had been predicted by the prophets and anticipated and prayed for by the faithful within Israel. This particularistic strand is summed up by the title "Messiah" (Christ) and, therefore, is sometimes known as the messianic strand. However, Jesus also comes as a universal Savior for the world. The Jewish Messiah will be the "hope of the nations" (cf. Isa. 42:4; Matt. 12:21). He is the "seed" of Abraham through whom God blesses *all nations* on earth. One can easily hear the universal promise of the Abrahamic covenant in Israel's praise: "May his name endure forever; may it continue as long as the sun. All nations will be blessed through him, and they will call him blessed" (Ps. 72:17). This universal strand would later be summed up by the early Christians with the title "Lord," and the early confession, "Jesus is Lord." Jesus is Savior and Lord of all nations.

These two strands, one particularistic, one universal, were never completely separate. The Jews always believed that God would bless the nations of the world through Israel's Messiah. What was unanticipated was the sheer magnitude of the Gentile role in God's plan.[15] This is why

---

connotations that find various strands of fulfillment in Jesus Christ, the church, the coming of the Holy Spirit, and in the world. See Greg Beale, *The Temple and the Church's Mission* (Downers Grove, IL: InterVarsity Press, 2004).

14. Philip E. Satterthwaite, Richard S. Hess, and Gordon J. Wenham, eds., *The Lord's Anointed: Interpretation of Old Testament Messianic Texts* (Grand Rapids: Baker, 1995); R. S. Hess and M. Daniel Carroll R., eds., *Israel's Messiah in the Bible and the Dead Sea Scrolls* (Grand Rapids: Baker, 2003).

15. There is a natural universalistic perspective that is inherent in any thoroughgoing monotheism. The Jews believed that Yahweh was the Creator and, therefore, Lord of heaven and earth. In that sense, Jewish particularity always had a universalistic perspective. However, E. P. Sanders goes beyond this to argue convincingly that the majority of Jews were united in their thinking that, in the end, *some* Gentiles would be admitted to the people of God, although it was always envisioned as sufficiently small in numbers to never threaten the ethnic solidarity of Judaism. The debate was only over the terms and conditions. Apparently the magnitude of their admission

Paul would later declare his insight into the "mystery of Christ," which was only then being revealed "by the Spirit to God's holy apostles and prophets." The mystery is that "through the gospel the Gentiles are heirs together with Israel, members together of one body, and sharers together in the promise in Christ Jesus" (Eph. 3:5, 6).

The scope and the terms under which the Gentiles became full participants in the blessings of the Jewish Messiah caused the early Jewish Christians to go back and reread their Scriptures with fresh eyes. They discovered the profound connection between the missional and the messianic strands of the old covenant. This explains why the apostle Paul, in his testimony before Festus, sums up the Old Testament promises as follows:

> I am saying nothing beyond what the prophets and Moses said would happen—that the Christ [Messiah] would suffer and, as the first to rise from the dead, would proclaim light to his own people and to the Gentiles [nations]. (Acts 26:22–23)

Understanding the missional (universal) and messianic (particularistic) strands is essential to a proper understanding of the unfolding theme of God's mission in the world. These strands are present in each of the three major structures of the Old Testament: the Law, the Prophets, and the Writings. We have already developed how the original Abrahamic covenant functioned on both of these levels. The covenant was simultaneously a choosing of Abraham and his descendents (Jews) and a promise to bless all nations. As representative samples of the other two major sections of the Old Testament, we will examine the Suffering Servant passages from the prophecy of Isaiah, and two psalms as a representative selection from the Writings.

THE SUFFERING SERVANT SONGS OF ISAIAH

There are four passages in Isaiah that have been widely identified as a distinct collection of texts because they highlight a "suffering servant."[16] These

---

was not fully anticipated. See E. P. Sanders, *Jesus and Judaism* (Philadelphia: Fortress, 1985), 220–21.

16. The first commentator to isolate these texts and refer to them as the "servant of Yahweh songs" was Bernard Duhm (1847–1928). See Bernard Duhm, *Das Buch Jesaia* (Tubingen: Tubingen University Press, 1892) and Leroy Andrew Huizenga, "The Incarnation of the Servant: The 'Suffering Servant' and Matthean Christology," *Horizons in Biblical Theology* 27, no. 1 (2005): 25–28.

texts are found in Isaiah 42:1–9; 49:1–6; 50:2–9; and 52:13–53:12. They are important for our understanding of the *missio dei* because of the prominence of four central themes. First, the Servant is sent on a mission from Yahweh. Second, the mission involves vicarious suffering. Third, although the Servant will suffer and be rejected, He will be exalted and vindicated. Finally, His suffering will bring justice, salvation, and blessing to all nations.

In the first passage, Yahweh's messenger is called His "servant" and His "chosen one" (42:1). He will be endowed with the "Spirit" (42:1) so that He will "bring justice to the nations" (42:1). The word translated "justice" is *mishpat,* which, in the context of Isaiah, represents a legal judgment between Yahweh and the Gentiles. The passage just prior to the song is a court scene that pictures a lawsuit between Yahweh and all the other "gods" of the nations (41:21–29). The rival claims of the Gentile deities are declared to be as nothing. In response to the verdict, Yahweh announces in the Suffering Servant Song His plan to send His Servant to the nations: "Behold my servant . . . my chosen . . . he will bring forth justice (*mishpat*) to the nations" (42:1 rsv). "Bring forth" (in the *Hiphil*) is the most frequently used phrase to describe Israel being brought out of Eygpt.[17] However, here it is the nations of the world who are being brought forth out of bondage. All the nations of the world are being invited to participate in the salvation and justice that comes through Yahweh's Servant. The text not only envisions a greater exodus but also an enlarged covenant and a global mission. Through His Servant, Yahweh will embody and bring "a covenant for the peoples" and through Him He will be a "light for the Gentiles [nations]" (42:6). The whole song reverberates with liberation and light as the Servant "opens eyes that are blind," "frees captives from prison," and "releases from the dungeon those who sit in darkness" (42:7).

The second Suffering Servant Song is found in Isaiah 49:1–6. This song is explicitly addressed to the nations of the world, reinforcing the point made earlier that Yahweh is sovereign over the nations. He declares, "Listen to me, you islands; hear this, you distant nations" (49:1). The Servant's mouth has been made "like a sharpened sword" (49:2). Through Him, Yahweh will display His glory (49:3). Throughout the song, the Servant is the speaker, but He only tells the reader what Yahweh has declared. The declaration falls into two separate sections, which vividly highlight the particularistic and

---

17. Klaus Baltzer, *Deutero-Isaiah* (Minneapolis: Augsburg Fortress, 2001), 127.

universalistic strands that are embodied in God's mission through His Servant. Verse 5 focuses on the particularistic mission of the Servant to Israel. He is being sent by Yahweh to "bring Jacob back to him and gather Israel to himself" (49:5). We have already demonstrated how the theme of gathering is central to the Abrahamic covenant, in contrast to the scattering of the nations who stand in opposition to God's sovereignty. However in verse 6, as with the first song, there is a widening of the mission to include the salvation and gathering of the nations of the world:

> He says, "It is too small a thing for you to be my servant to restore the tribes of Jacob and bring back those of Israel I have kept. I will also make you a light for the Gentiles (to the nations), that you may bring my salvation to the ends of the earth."

This passage gives a remarkable glimpse into the *missio dei*. Without diminishing God's mission to Israel, there is an even greater mission that encompasses all the nations. Thus, despite the setbacks regarding Israel (rebellion, exile, and judgment), the original promise given to Abraham to bless the nations is still in full view. However, the unique contribution of Isaiah is the insight that this blessing will be revealed in and through the Servant of Yahweh.

The third Suffering Servant Song is found in Isaiah 50:2–9. This song continues the unfolding biography of the Servant but shifts from an articulation of the final goal to the suffering the Servant will bear. The song begins by picturing an empty stage upon which no player is present and no voice is heard: "When I came, why was there no one? When I called, why was there no one to answer?" (50:2). Then, in verse 4, the Suffering Servant enters. He has been given "an instructed tongue" and, unlike Israel, He is eager to listen and to obey (50:4–5). However, the Servant, like Yahweh, will be rejected. He will be beaten, insulted, and shamed. He will offer His back to those who beat Him, His cheeks to those who pull out His beard. He does not turn His head, although they mock Him and spit upon His face (50:6). Quite surprisingly, the Servant willingly accepts this hostility and suffering as part of Yahweh's plan. Because He trusts in Yahweh, the Servant knows that ultimately He will be vindicated, His shame lifted, and His disgrace removed (50:7). The song ends, as it began, with silence. However, this time there is silence because Yahweh has vindicated His Servant and silenced all His accusers (50:8). They will all come to nothing, like a garment eaten up by moths (50:9).

The fourth Suffering Servant Song is found in Isaiah 52:13–53:12. The preceding context is a picture of a new exodus; Israel is solemnly and triumphantly processing up out of exile. The song opens with a scene in heaven, where Yahweh's Servant is presented: "See, my servant!" (52:13). The Servant is granted a threefold (or three-stage) honoring by being "raised and lifted up and highly exalted" (52:13). The language reflects the coronation and exaltation of a king, but the Servant is exalted into the very presence of God. However, this extraordinary exaltation is set against the backdrop of suffering. He is "marred" and "disfigured" (52:14). He is "despised and rejected by men, a man of sorrows, and familiar with suffering" (53:3). The theme resonates with the third song, but it is now explicitly declared that the suffering of the Servant is vicarious: "Surely he took up our infirmities and carried our sorrows" (53:4). "He was pierced for our transgressions, he was crushed for our iniquities; the punishment that brought us peace was upon him, and by his wounds we are healed" (53:5). The song also makes clear that it was the will of Yahweh that His Servant suffer (53:10). For, it was only through vicarious suffering that the Servant would "justify many" (53:11) and bear the sin of many, making intercession for the transgressors (53:12).[18] From the outset of this fourth song, the setting is before the eyes of both heaven and the entire world. The unfolding picture of the Servant will cause astonishment among the nations and silence the kings of the earth (52:15).

Reflecting on the songs as a whole, several key themes emerge that are important in our understanding of the *missio dei*. First, God the Father is the initiating source of this redemptive mission. He sends the Suffering Servant on a mission that involves vicarious suffering. Second, the scope of this mission is clearly global, encompassing all the nations of the world, over whom God is sovereign. Third, despite the opposition to God's plan, He will use even the suffering of His Servant to bring justice, salvation, and blessing to all nations, thereby fulfilling His original promise to Abraham: "through your offspring all nations on earth will be blessed, because you have obeyed me" (Gen. 22:18).

The quotation of the Suffering Servant Songs in the New Testament and other early Christian writings demonstrates decisively that the early

---

18. In the Old Testament, the concept of vicarious suffering is found in both the sacrificial system and the intercession of the prophets on behalf of the people. The Suffering Servant embodies both forms of vicarious suffering.

church understood that Jesus Christ was the Suffering Servant through whom the nations would be redeemed and the mission of God accomplished. Various strands of the Suffering Servant Songs are quoted by Matthew, Luke, Paul, Peter, Clement, and Justin Martyr, among others.[19] The more surprising development comes in Paul's quotation of Isaiah 49:6 in connection with the expansion of the gospel to the Gentiles. In Acts 13:46–47 Paul and Barnabus declare to the Jews,

> We had to speak the word of God to you first. Since you reject it and do not consider yourselves worthy of eternal life, we now turn to the Gentiles. For this is what the Lord has commanded us: *"I have made you a light for the Gentiles, that you may bring salvation to the ends of the earth."*

The apostle Paul, along with other early Christians, believed that Jesus was the fulfillment of Isaiah's promise that the Suffering Servant would be a "light for the Gentiles" and bring salvation "to the ends of the earth." What is surprising is that Paul understood his own ministry as an extension of that fulfillment. Note carefully that Paul introduces the quotation from Isaiah not by saying that this is what the Lord commanded concerning *him* but "this is what the Lord has commanded *us*." Paul understood his turning to the Gentiles (the context of Acts 13) and, indeed, the entire unfolding global witness of the church as an extension of Christ's light to the Gentiles. In other words, the global witness of the church is the *very means* through which Jesus Christ will bring His light and salvation to the ends of the earth.

In Romans, Paul declares, "It has always been my ambition to preach the gospel where Christ was not known, so that I would not be building on someone else's foundation" (15:20). Paul then establishes the basis for his not preaching the gospel where Christ was already known with a quotation from the fourth song.

> Rather, as it is written: "Those who were not told about him will see, and those who have not heard will understand." (Rom. 15:21)

---

19. See, for example, 1 Clement 16 (quotes Isa. 53 almost in its entirety); 1 Peter 2:22–24 (Isa. 53:7); Luke 22:37 (quoting Isa. 53:12); Acts 8:32–33 (Isa. 53:7–8); Didache 8.9, 11; 9:1; 14:1–3; Rom. 10:16 (Isa. 53:1); 15:21 (Isa. 52:15); Matt. 8:17 (Isa. 53:4); and 12:18–21 (Isa. 42:1–4).

These citations demonstrate that Paul understood the global witness of the church to all nations to be an extension of Christ's mission in the world. This is possible only because the risen Christ continues to work in and through His church. The church is the extension of the *missio dei*—missions flows out of God's mission.

PSALM 67 AND PSALM 2

The representative texts from the Writings will be taken from the Psalms. In the context of Israel's worship, there are over seventy references to the nations in the Psalms, making it a rich resource for understanding the place of the nations in the *missio dei*. Certainly a key theme is that nations are fallen and are full participants in the global rebellion against God (e.g., Ps. 9). We often think only of individuals standing under the judgment of God. However, the Psalms makes it clear that all nations, including Israel, stand under God's judgment. Likewise, the nations are objects of God's mercy (Ps. 72:17). God's dealing with Israel was like a small-scale model that represented His larger intentions for the nations of the world. In fact, the Psalms make clear that the very reason God has chosen and blessed Israel is so that they will be a blessing to the nations. This is evident, for example, in the priestly extension of the famous Aaronic blessing found in Psalm 67. In Numbers, Aaron was commanded to bless Israel, using these familiar words:

> The LORD bless you and keep you; the LORD make his face shine upon you and be gracious to you; the LORD turn his face toward you and give you peace. (Num. 6:24–25)

However, in Psalm 67:1–2 the blessing is extended to include the *purpose* of God's blessing of Israel; namely, that they be a blessing to the nations:

> May God be gracious to us and bless us and make his face shine upon us, that your ways may be known on earth, your salvation among all nations.[20]

As Christopher Wright has observed, the redemption and blessing of

---

20. To make the Aaronic blessing usable in public worship, the psalmist changed the covenantal name for God, YHWH, to *elohim*, the broad word for God in Hebrew.

Israel was to be "the first-fruits of God's wider harvest among all nations on earth."[21] God regularly sought to move Israel to embrace a wider, more global understanding of His ultimate plan.[22]

The second representative text is Psalm 2. The reason for this selection is twofold. First, Psalm 2 is one of the most frequently quoted psalms in the New Testament.[23] The early Christians understood the significance of this psalm for God's unfolding mission in and through the church. Second, Psalm 2 is a coronation psalm and therefore is not related to the suffering motif we explored with Isaiah. Psalm 2 represents an important and distinctive strand of the Old Testament.

Psalm 2 opens with a picture of the nations in rebellion against God: "Why do the nations conspire and the peoples plot in vain?" The rulers of the world have taken their stand "against the LORD and against his Anointed One." However, since the Lord is sovereign over the nations, we are told that "the One enthroned in heaven laughs." Then, in contrast to the schemes and plans of the rebellious nations, the LORD declares His decree, "I have installed my King on Zion, my holy hill." The King sits enthroned as God's regent, His "son," on earth.

In its original setting as a coronation psalm, it must have seemed audacious for a tiny backwater nation like Israel to declare that God would "make the nations your inheritance, the ends of the earth your possession. You will rule them with an iron scepter; you will dash them to pieces like pottery." However, this psalm envisions the ultimate inbreaking of God's rule, His kingdom, in the incarnation of His Son, Jesus Christ. The New Testament identifies the "You are my Son" of Psalm 2 with Jesus at His incarnation (Heb. 1:5), His baptism (Matt. 3:17), the Transfiguration (Matt. 17:5; 2 Peter 1:17), and the Resurrection (Acts 13:33). The early Christians saw the official opposition to Christ (i.e., the Anointed One) as a fulfillment of Psalm 2 (Acts 4:25–28). God has decreed to give His "anointed one," meaning the Messiah or the Christ, the "nations" as an inheritance and the "ends of the earth" as His possession (see Rev. 19:15).

---

21. Wright, *The Mission of God*, 477.
22. This parallels what we observed in the Servant Songs of Isaiah. Pivotal themes such as the Exodus, covenant, temple, and redemption are all broadened from a particularistic view that was overly parochial to a view that understood that Israel was the small-scale model, or the first-fruits, of what God intended to do among all the nations of the world.
23. Psalm 2 is quoted in Matthew 3:17; 17:5; Acts 4:25–26; 13:33; Hebrews 1:5; 2 Peter 1:17; and Rev. 19:15.

Psalm 2 envisions the end goal of the *missio dei*: all nations acknowledging the lordship of God's Anointed One. This messianic fulfillment is anticipated in several other places in the Psalter, including Psalm 72:11, which declares, "All kings will bow down to him and all nations will serve him." However, while we experience the inauguration of the kingdom in the incarnation of Jesus Christ, it will not be fully realized until the eschaton. This end goal of the *missio dei* ultimately is found in the eschaton, which securely positions missions within an eschatological context.

Eschatological Expectations

A "whole Bible" perspective on the *missio dei* reveals that while the final end or *telos* of the mission of God is fully present in seed form in the Abrahamic covenant, it will not be fully realized until the eschaton. Therefore, missiology rests in the tension between the "already" and the "not yet." Missions does not start with the church, nor does it end when all of our missional tasks are completed. Missions always must unfold within the context of, and the anticipation of, God's work, which He alone initiated and which He alone can bring to final completion. This perspective, if properly understood, should not render us passive or our work inconsequential. Rather, it puts all of our work within the larger and more ennobling context of God's action and the certainty of the final outcome.

There are a number of texts in the Old Testament that envision this kind of eschatological fulfillment that all the missional vitality of the church eventually joins with and moves toward. For example, Daniel sees the Son of Man given "authority, glory and sovereign power" (Dan. 7:14). He sees the nations submitting to the lordship of the Son of Man, when he declares, "All peoples, nations and men of every language worshiped him. His dominion is an everlasting dominion that will not pass away, and his kingdom is one that will never be destroyed" (Dan. 7:14). Isaiah envisions the day when "nations will come to your light, and kings to the brightness of your dawn" (Isa. 60:3). The "firstfruits" of the streaming of the nations to the Messiah is, of course, seen on a small scale with the visit of the Magi to Christ as recorded in Matthew 2:1–12. As more nations have been gathered to the feet of Christ through the missional life of the church, the full harvest comes closer to being realized (Matt. 24:14). However, the goal of missions will be experienced eschatologically only when, as recorded in Psalm 22:27–28: "All the ends of the earth will remember and turn to the LORD, and all the families of the nations will bow down before him." Yahweh repeatedly reminded His people of the final vision: "Before me every knee will bow; by me every tongue will swear" (Isa. 45:23). It is this vision that is carried forward in that beautiful hymn of the early church, which anticipates the day when "every knee [shall] bow . . . and every tongue confess that Jesus Christ is Lord" (Phil. 2:10–11). It finds its final culmination in the eschaton, which John prophetically sees when he says that "there before me was a great multitude that no one could count, from every nation, tribe, people and language, standing before the throne and in front of the Lamb" (Rev. 7:9). Missions finds its fulfillment as the nations of the world gather in the power of the Holy Spirit to worship Jesus Christ and give glory to the Father in the New Creation.

CONCLUSION

The purpose of this chapter has been to demonstrate how God the Father is the initiator and final goal of the *missio dei*. This chapter has focused on the Old Testament and God's covenant with Abraham, in which Yahweh promises to choose and to bless Abraham (and Israel) as a means by which He will bring blessing to all nations. The promise to Abraham, which includes the expectation that all nations on earth will be blessed, eventually becomes embedded into every strand of the Old Testament revelation. It is gradually understood that this blessing to the nations is made possible through God's Suffering Servant, His Anointed One, whom the Father will send into the world. Furthermore, it becomes clear that even the Old Testament understands the fulfillment of the *missio dei* within a larger eschatological framework. There is, therefore, a grand narrative of mission unfolding in the Bible that will ultimately follow the broad contours of creation → covenant → Incarnation → Cross → Resurrection → Pentecost → return of Christ → eschaton/New Creation. Missions must be understood as the driving *purpose* for this grand narrative, not as some optional auxiliary of it. In other words, the *missio dei* is the central message of the Bible. The Bible, like the *missio dei*, is the story of *God's redemptive, historical initiative on behalf of His creation*. Missions ultimately must derive its life from that source.

Chapter 5 will focus on the sending Father and seek to demonstrate how the well-known "Great Commission" texts in the New Testament must be seen within the larger context of the *missio dei* and the ministry of Jesus as the one sent by the Father.

— 5 —

The Sending Father
and the Sent Church

ANDREW WALLS TELLS THE STORY of an imaginary, scholarly, intergalactic time traveler who gets periodic grants to travel to planet Earth to study the Christian religion.[1] He studies Christianity in Jerusalem at 37 C.E., again at Nicea at 325 C.E, in Scotland in the seventh century, in London in the 1840s, and finally, in Nigeria in 1980. In his first-century trip to Earth, he finds that the early Christians are all Jews. In fact, they seem to be a "denomination" of Judaism with the particular belief that Jesus Christ is the Messiah, the fulfillment of the prior expectations of their own prophets. They are eager to share this good news with others.

Later, when the intergalactic traveler returns to Earth, he is like a fly on the wall at the great Council of Nicea in 325. The time-traveling professor is surprised to see that despite the diversity of this group, hardly any Jews are there at all. Christians now refer to Jesus as "Lord," and they are in a heated debate about the precise language used to describe the relationship of this Lord Jesus to God the Father. It is clearly an important issue to resolve since these delegates will be going back to many new followers of Jesus in many different places.

On the third trip, the traveler lands on the rocky coast of Scotland to observe Celtic monks "standing in ice-cold water up to their necks, reciting the psalms."[2] They are there in the Firth of Clyde calling the people

---

1. See Andrew Walls, "The Gospel as Prisoner and Liberator of Culture," in *The Missionary Movement in Christian History: Studies in the Transmission of Faith* (Maryknoll, NY: Orbis, 1996), 3–7.
2. Ibid.

to give up their worship of nature deities and find true joy in Jesus Christ. They are an austere group, and, interestingly, our observer notices that that these monks are using the formula for Christ that had been so hotly debated back in Nicea three hundred years earlier.

The spaceman's fourth trip brings him to Exeter Hall in London in the 1840s. He observes a large assembly hall of well-dressed people enthusiastically proposing that missionaries be sent to Africa with Bibles and cotton seeds. They are quoting verses from the Bible and calling on their government to stop the enslavement of a group of people known as Africans. Our traveler is surprised to see that most of those who are present have their own copies of the sacred Scriptures.

Finally, on his last journey, our traveler, who is now a full professor of Comparative Interplanetary Religions, lands in Lagos, Nigeria. He observes a group of Africans dancing in the streets on their way to church. They are inviting everyone they see to come and experience the healing power of Jesus Christ. One of the Africans claims to have seen a vision and another that he has been healed. All promise powerful preaching about Jesus Christ from this same sacred book that our traveler has observed.

The interesting point of this imaginary story is that even though these different groups might not even be able to fully recognize each other as Christians, they all share (from the long perspective of history) many profound similarities. These diverse groups are all proclaiming the ultimate significance of Jesus Christ. They all have a reverence for the Scriptures, which they regard as the Word of God. Finally, they all seem to be committed in their own way to sharing the message of Jesus Christ with as many people as they can. In other words, they are not merely Christians in some strict confessional sense; they are Christians whose very identity is linked to the ever-widening horizons of the church across new cultural boundaries.

This imaginary, long view of the church helps remind us that the church has its ultimate identity in the person and work of Jesus Christ and that our Lord has given us a missionary mandate. The entire church, not just a select group of professionals within it, is characterized by mission. It is fundamental to our very identity as Christians who proclaim that Jesus Christ is Lord. To put it another way, missions is more the mother of theology than the stepchild of theology. As Ben Meyer has commented, "Christianity has never been more itself, more consistent with Jesus and more evidently en route to its own future, than in the launching of the world mission."[3] The purpose of this chapter is to explore the final commission of Jesus Christ to his church and set it within the larger frame of the *missio dei*.

CLARIFICATIONS CONCERNING THE "GREAT COMMISSION(S)"

The common term "Great Commission" is a relatively late expression used to refer to the final commission of Jesus Christ to His disciples. For example, William Carey, widely regarded as the father of the modern missionary movement, never uses the expression "Great Commission" in his famous missions treatise known as *An Enquiry*. Its first appearance in print seems to be in the three-volume *History of the Church Mission Society* published in 1899.[4] The term often is identified specifically with Matthew 28:18–20 and, unfortunately, is frequently treated as an isolated pericope, separated from the rest of the gospel as well as the larger biblical context of the *missio dei*. It is beyond the scope of this study to fully explore the history of the interpretation of Matthew 28:18–20 in church history. However, suffice it to say, there is ample evidence to demonstrate that through much of church history, it was generally not quoted as a missionary text because it was thought to have been fulfilled already by the apostles who had originally received the commission. The text was largely used for other purposes, and its full import often was obscured by ecclesiastical controversies. A survey of its usage shows that it was far more likely to be cited as a text in support

---

3. As quoted in David Bosch, *Transforming Mission: Paradigm Shifts in Theology of Mission* (Maryknoll, NY: Orbis, 1991), 16. See Ben Meyer, *The Early Christians: Their World Mission and Self-Discovery* (Wilmington, DE: Michael Glazier, 1986), 206, cf. 18. Likewise, E. P. Sanders describes "the overwhelming impression . . . that Jesus started a movement which *came to see the Gentile mission as a logical extension of itself.*" See E. P. Sanders, *Jesus and Judaism* (Philadelphia: Fortress, 1985), 220 (italics in original). Sanders points out that no Christian group objected to the Gentile mission; the debate was over the terms and conditions of their entry.
4. The phrase "The Great Commission" appears as the first chapter title on page 3 and is used in the text on page 4. Interestingly, the phrase is used collectively to refer to all the gospel mandates and does not single out the Matthean version apart from the others. See Eugene Stock, *History of the Church Missionary Society*, vol. 1, "The Great Commission" (London: CMS, 1899), 3–4. In the 1895 publication of *A New Programme of Missions* by Luther Wishard, the phrase does not appear. He refers to the Matthew 28:18–20 text as the Lord's "gracious command" (p. 94). See Luther Wishard, *A New Programme of Missions* (New York: Revell, 1895), 94.

for the deity of Christ, the Trinity, or as the precise language to be used in baptismal formulas, than as the basis for any missionary mandate.[5]

The relatively scant treatment of this text as the basis for missions in earlier generations contrasts with the modern period, where it is quoted regularly and is the subject of countless books and articles. Today this final commission of Christ is commonly referred to in the most exalted terms, including phrases such as the "Great Commission," the "final Manifesto," the "climax" of Jesus' ministry, "the ticking clock for the end times," or "the most important concern of the gospel."[6] While the spotlight on this particular text has benefited the church, it has also caused misunderstandings about the nature of the missionary mandate to the church and how it is connected to the *missio dei*. It also has tended to isolate these particular texts from their natural connection to the gospels out of which they come. Therefore, it is important that several clarifications be made at the outset of this study.

The "Great Commission" Refers to Multiple Texts, Not a Single Text

First, the phrase "Great Commission" is used to designate an *entire range of texts* found in the New Testament, not simply the well-known passage found in Matthew 28:18–20. Each of the Gospels, as well as the book of Acts, records a dramatic pericope of commissioning to a group of gathered disciples. These texts are found in Matthew 28:18–20; Mark 16:14–18; Luke 24:44–49; John 20:19–23; and Acts 1:7–8. When we refer to these various passages, they can appropriately be called commissions or Great Commissions, in the plural. If we are referring to the larger theological and missiological mandate that collectively lies behind all of these commissions, then it is normal to speak of the Great Commission in the singular. However, this phrase should only be used as a broad reference to all the texts and the collective force of these passages, not just the Matthean version, as is commonly done.

---

5. For a survey of the history of the usage of Matthew 28:18–20, see John Jefferson Davis, "'Teaching Them to Observe All That I Have Commanded You': the History of the Interpretation of the 'Great Commission' and Implications for Marketplace Ministries," *Evanglical Review of Theology* 25 (2001): 65–80.

6. For these and several other quotations describing the closing pericope of Matthew's gospel, see Bosch, *Transforming Mission*, 57. The "ticking clock" phrase is drawn from a caricatured description of the text that is exposed by Christopher J. H. Wright in *The Mission of God* (Downers Grove, IL: IVP Academic, 2006), 35.

Postresurrection Sayings of Christ

Second, it is important to remember that these passages are all postresurrection sayings of Christ given at various times and places. The fact that these passages are all uttered by the risen Lord is, in itself, sufficient reason to refer to these commissions with the adjective *great,* especially given the narrow forty-day time frame and how little is recorded of the postresurrection discourses of Jesus.

The descriptor "great" gains even further credibility when we recognize how central it was to the teaching of Christ during the postresurrection period. It is not unusual for single events, miracles, or sayings of Christ to be commonly recorded in the Synoptic Gospels and, occasionally, in all four Gospels. However, this does not seem to be the case with the final commissions of Jesus Christ to His disciples. Not only is the language between the accounts remarkably distinct, but they are also set in diverse settings. This means that Jesus repeats various versions of the Great Commission in various places, with different emphases. Matthew's commission takes place in Galilee some weeks after the Resurrection. The setting of Mark's commission is difficult, if not impossible, to determine and is part of the larger textual difficulties that are present in the various endings to Mark's gospel. Nevertheless, the language of Mark's commission has distinctive language not shared by any of the other Gospels. Luke's and John's commissions both occur in Jerusalem on the very night after the Resurrection. Interestingly, although Luke's and John's commissions occur on the same night, there is not a single verbal overlap between the two, which means that they are distinct sayings of Christ. The commission in Acts takes place forty days after the Resurrection in Bethany, not in Jerusalem.

Reading the Texts in the Context of the Gospels

Third, the particularity of these various commissioning discourses demand that each be explored within the integrity and larger context of its own biblical setting. The gospel writers all place these commissioning texts in a position that serves as a climax to the gospel story that they are unfolding. The book of Acts places the commissioning text at the very beginning, not only to provide continuity with its previous companion volume (gospel of Luke), but also to provide a structural frame for the book. These texts are impoverished when they are taken out of that context and interpreted in isolation. The challenge is to make certain that each text is allowed to speak in its own distinctive voice, while at the same time seeing how they collectively serve the church and connect in their own way with the larger *missio dei*.

THE GREAT COMMISSION TEXTS

This section of the chapter will seek to examine each of the texts within their own setting as well as within the larger frame of the *missio dei*, especially as they represent an extension of the theme of the sending Father.

Matthew: Fulfilling the Abrahamic Promise
by Making Disciples of All Nations

Recognizing Matthew's commitment to a Christian mission to the Gentile nations of the world has not come easily, even among scholars of Matthew's gospel. One scholar expresses the difficulty of unraveling the Matthean paradox whereby "contradictory ideas [are] expressed side by side."[7] On the one hand, Matthew's gospel contains sayings of Jesus that are extremely particularistic to a Jewish audience and seem to explicitly restrict, limit, or even deny any mission to the Gentiles. On the other hand, some of the most dramatic sayings of Jesus that envision the early Jewish Christians bringing the gospel to every people group in the world are found in Matthew. However, by looking at Matthew's gospel as a whole, it will become evident that he enthusiastically embraces the Gentile mission, while insisting that it be understood as a natural extension of God's mission with Israel and not as a radical break from the Abrahamic tradition.

MATTHEW'S GOSPEL AND THE MISSION TO "ALL NATIONS"

We must begin by demonstrating how Matthew 28:18–20 fits within the larger context of Matthew's gospel. Some representative texts in Matthew's gospel will demonstrate that the final commission is fully consistent with, and flows out of, the larger message of the gospel.

Genealogy

Only Matthew and Luke contain genealogies of Jesus. Matthew's genealogy is unique in two major respects. First, Matthew structures it around three sets of fourteen generations: Abraham to David, David to the Exile, and the Exile

---

7. Kenzo Tagawa, "People and Community in the Gospel of Matthew," *New Testament Studies* 16 (1969–1970): 150.

to the birth of Christ. It is significant that Matthew traces Jesus' ancestry from Abraham and not Adam as in the Lukan version. In fact, the title of Jesus, "son of Abraham," which opens Matthew's gospel (1:1), is the only occurrence of this title in the New Testament. It reflects Abraham's position as the father of Israel and thus recalls the covenant in Genesis 12:1–3. Second, Matthew's genealogy includes four Gentile women: Tamar (1:3), Rahab (1:5), Ruth (1:5), and Bathsheba (1:6), whereas Luke's genealogy contains no mention of any women or Gentiles. Tamar and Rahab are Canaanites, Ruth is a Moabite, and Bathsheba is widely believed to be a Hittite. The inclusion of these names serves to remind Matthew's Jewish readers of two vital points. The inclusion of Ruth reminds readers that there are faithful, godly people who are part of the Gentile nations of the world. Even Tamar is declared in Genesis 38:26 to be more righteous than Judah. The inclusion of the Canaanite prostitute Rahab in the direct ancestry of the Messiah is a powerful testimony to the redemptive, transformative grace of God that extends to all nations, even those nations that were Israel's enemies.

Magi
The journey of the Gentile Magi from the East coming to offer gifts of gold, frankincense, and myrrh to Jesus is a powerful symbol of the nations of the world streaming to the Jewish Messiah. Their presence in the opening pages of Matthew's gospel recalls the prophecy of Isaiah that "nations will come to your light, and kings to the brightness of your dawn" (Isa. 60:3). The determination of the Magi is an inspiring picture of Gentiles who, at the risk of their own lives, faithfully submitted to divine revelation. Herod's cross-examination of the Magi about the exact time of the star's appearing (Matt. 2:7), his subsequent slaughter of all boys in the town up to two years old (2:16), and the note that Jesus was in a "house" (2:11) and not a stable suggest that the Magi appeared about a year after Jesus' birth. Matthew deliberately omits the birth narrative in favor of an account of Gentile foreigners who came to recognize and worship Israel's Messiah. Thus, Matthew frames his entire gospel with the nations streaming to Jesus (Magi) and the disciples streaming out to the nations (Great Commission).

Fleeing to Egypt
Immediately following the visit of the Magi, Matthew records the relocation of Joseph, Mary, and Jesus to Egypt (2:13–15). This is significant, of

course, as Jesus reenacts the Exodus, whereby the children of Israel came up out of Egypt (Hos. 11:1). However, it also represents "the transformation of Egypt from a symbol of oppression and bondage (Deut. 5:5, 15) to a haven and protector of Israel's messiah."[8] Egypt's role as a haven for the Messiah is not only theologically powerful, but it also helps to invigorate Israel's historical memory to the time long before their painful Egyptian bondage when Egypt provided a haven for Abraham (Gen. 12:10). It is a refreshing testimony to the power of the gospel to reconcile nations. Some scholars even believe that this pericope provided important support for the early Christian mission to Alexandria, Egypt.[9]

Inauguration of Jesus' Ministry

In Matthew's gospel, Jesus begins His ministry in Galilee, in "the area of Zebulun and Naphtali" (4:13). According to Matthew this was to fulfill the prophet Isaiah:

> Land of Zebulun and land of Naphtali, the way to the sea, along the Jordan, Galilee of the Gentiles—the people living in darkness have seen a great light; on those living in the land of the shadow of death a light has dawned. (Matt. 4:15–16, quoting Isa. 9:1–2)

Jesus begins His ministry in "Galilee of the Gentiles," and later, at the conclusion of his gospel, Matthew alone records Jesus and the angels directing the disciples back to Galilee (26:32; 28:7) in order to receive the final commission to "all nations" (28:18–20). In Matthew's gospel Jesus begins and ends His life and ministry "on the field," symbolized by Egypt and Galilee, not Jerusalem, the center of Judaism and revelation and the location of the temple.

God's Grace Beyond Israel in Matthew's Gospel

Matthew includes a wide selection of Christ's teachings that explicity demonstrate that Israel has no automatic claim to the kingdom, over against

---

8. James LaGrand, *The Earliest Christian Mission to "All Nations" in the Light of Matthew's Gospel* (Atlanta: Scholar's, 1995), 180.

9. See, for example, S. G. F. Brandon, "The Gospel of Matthew and the Origins of Alexandrian Christianity," in *The Fall of Jerusalem and the Christian Church: A Study of the Effects of the Jewish Overthrow of* A.D. *70 on Christianity* (London: SPCK, 1951), 217–48.

the unbelieving Gentiles. In the parable of the workers in the vineyard (Matt. 20:1–16), which is unique to Matthew's gospel, those who arrive in the vineyard late receive the same compensation as those who had "borne the burden of the work and the heat of the day" (v. 12). In the parable of the two sons (21:28–32), also found only in Matthew, it is the son who initially rebelled who is eventually commended for his obedience. Although the parable of the vineyard tenants (21:33–43) is found in the Synoptics, only Matthew includes Jesus' concluding application to Israel that "the kingdom of God will be taken away from you and given to a people who will produce its fruit" (21:43). In the parable of the wedding feast (22:1–14), those who were invited to the banquet were too preoccupied to come, so the servants were instructed to go out into the street corners to bring in those who had not been initially invited. Similar points can be observed in the parable of the ten virgins (25:1–13), the parable of the talents (25:14–30), and the parable of the sheep and the goats (25:31–46).

Matthew also includes accounts of Jesus healing non-Jews, including the servant of a Roman centurion (8:5–13) and the two demon-possessed men from the region of the Gadarenes (8:28–34). Clearly, Matthew is interested in pointing out how God's grace extends beyond the particularity of His covenant with Israel.

Sign of Jonah
In Matthew 12 Jesus is asked for a miraculous sign. His cryptic reply has puzzled Christians for generations. Jesus replied,

> A wicked and adulterous generation asks for a miraculous sign! But none will be given it except the sign of the prophet Jonah. For just as Jonah was three days and three nights in the belly of a huge fish, so the Son of Man will be three days and three nights in the heart of the earth. The men of Nineveh will stand up at the judgment with this generation and condemn it; for they repented at the preaching of Jonah, and now one [or something] greater than Jonah is here. (12:39–41)

Jonah's three days in the belly of the fish are compared to the three days Jesus will spend in the tomb. Just as Jonah was, so to speak, "raised from the dead" to preach the gospel to the Gentiles, so Jesus will be raised from the dead, and the gospel will be preached by the apostles to the Gentiles. It is important to note that this saying of Christ points out both Jonah's three days in the fish and the subsequent mission to the Gentiles that resulted in the salvation of Nineveh. Likewise, the parallel points not only to the resurrection of Jesus, but also to the subsequent proclamation of the gospel to the Gentiles who, like Nineveh of old, will respond in great numbers, astonishing the Jews.

Hard Sayings of Jesus

There are two passages in Matthew's gospel that are often cited in isolation to demonstrate that Jesus did not anticipate or embrace a Gentile mission. The first is found in Matthew 10, where Jesus sends out the Twelve on a mission with the instructions, "Do not go among the Gentiles or enter any town of the Samaritans. Go rather to the lost sheep of Israel" (10:5–6).

The second particularistic passage is found in Matthew 15, when Jesus withdraws to the region of Tyre and Sidon. When a Canaanite woman approaches Him and requests that He heal her daughter, He does not respond. When pressed by the disciples, Jesus tells them that He was "sent only to the lost sheep of Israel" (15:24). When the woman appeals to Jesus directly, He says to her, "It is not right to take the children's bread and toss it to their dogs" (15:26).

In reflecting on both these texts, it is vital that they be understood within the larger context of the ministry of Jesus. The mission of the Twelve appears to be restricted because the time was not fully ripe for a Gentile mission. Even the Apostle Paul, the undisputed Apostle of the Gentile mission, understood that the gospel was to the Jew first (Rom. 1:16). The church is never to forget that we were born out of the womb of Israel. We, the wild branches, have been grafted into *their* tree. When seen against the earlier pericope of Jesus' affirmation of the faith of the Gentile centurion, about whom Jesus said He had "not found anyone in Israel with such great faith" (8:10), coupled with the later pericope of the Gentile centurion who at the foot of the cross confesses, "Surely he was the Son of God!" (27:54), it is difficult to interpret Matthew as rejecting a universalistic message. Rather, it is an affirmation that Jesus comes first as the fulfillment of Jewish hopes and only in due course will the full Gentile mission be opened.

The Matthew 15 conversation between Jesus, the disciples, and the Canaanite woman is best understood if we hear it as a large, thoroughly theological conversation. It is significant to note that the woman addresses Jesus by His full Jewish title: "Lord, Son of David, have mercy One me" (15:22). Why would a Gentile woman from a foreign land address Him by His full, Jewish, messianic title, Son of David? Addressing Jesus by this exalted title, coupled with Jesus' very presence outside of Israel, drew attention "to the irregularity of a Gentile appeal for help from a Jewish Messiah."[10] This encounter, therefore, was an opportunity to raise the obvious theological question: Are Gentiles full recipients of Jewish promises? Her question is personal but, by extension, raises the larger question about the place of all non-Jews in the presence of Jesus of Nazareth.

Jesus' reply reveals that He was prepared to honor the covenantal priority of the Jews. The Jewish prophecies must first be fulfilled, then comes the Gentile mission. The comment about feeding the children first and then the dogs was not intended to insult her. "Dogs" here does not refer to wild, predatory, scavenging dogs but to working dogs with owners.[11] Jesus is pointing out that although both are fed and cared for, it is customary that one is fed before the other. It is a question of timing and the priority of order. However, the woman surprises Jesus when she cleverly replies, "Yes, Lord . . . but even the dogs eat the crumbs that fall from their masters' table" (15:27). Her insightful reply demonstrates to Jesus that she recognized that the Gentiles were *already* in the position of eating crumbs that fell from the Jewish table. For example, this is evident as far back as the ancient Ninevites and as recent as the Gentile centurion who received Jesus' blessing in Matthew 8:5–13. Her question raises the point that has been beneath the surface of Matthew's entire gospel. The Gentiles have always received crumbs that fell from the Jewish table, but is there anything greater breaking in? The Gentiles have been "under the table," but will they ever be seated "at the table" with Abraham, Isaac, and Jacob in the kingdom?

The woman is like someone you have invited to your home for a meal but shows up an hour early. As the host, you are surprised by your guest's early arrival, but once the knock at the door comes, you graciously receive your invited guest. In the same way, Jesus recognizes her faith. He hears her knock. He knows of the pending Gentile mission, and thereby

---

10. R. T. France, *The Gospel of Matthew*, New International Commentary on the New Testament (Grand Rapids: Eerdmans, 2007), 593.
11. John Nolland, *The Gospel of Matthew*, New International Greek Testament Commentary (Grand Rapids: Eerdmans, 2005), 634.

He grants her request; her daughter is healed. In the context of His healing ministry, Jesus already had declared that His healing of the sick was in fulfillment of the first Servant Song in Isaiah, which is quoted at length in Matthew 12:18–21, culminating in the declaration that "in his name the nations will put their hope." The foreign, Canaanite woman had put her hope in Jesus, and she would not go away disappointed. Rather than an embarrassing detractor from the Gentile mission, this text is actually a remarkable testimony to the certainty of the immanent Gentile mission.

Matthew's Apocalypse

In chapters 24 and 25, Matthew records the fifth and final major discourse in his gospel. This last discourse focuses on the end times. After discussing many of the tumultuous signs that will accompany the end, such as war, famines, earthquakes, false prophets, and the increase of wickedness, Jesus encourages His disciples to "stand firm to the end." Then, in verse 14, Jesus declares, "And this gospel of the kingdom will be preached in the whole world as a testimony to all nations, and then the end will come." The expanded reference to the gospel *of the kingdom* "marks the move from the ministry of Jesus to the post-resurrection ministry of the disciples."[12] Verse 14 is a statement of optimism about the final outcome, as Jesus reveals the full, universalistic mission of His church to "all nations." The lordship of Jesus Christ will be proclaimed to all nations. The universal preaching of the gospel should be seen, within the context of the chapter, as yet another sign of the end. It is not the final event that will *cause* the parousia, or return of Christ. The preaching of the gospel cannot "hasten the day" of Christ's return or "bring back the King" as has sometimes been invoked in missionary literature and hymnody. This would clearly violate the *missio dei*, which underscores God's initiative in revealing the "signs" that will accompany the end and the return of His Son. Nevertheless, the dramatic rise of preaching all over the world to thousands of new people groups is an important and dramatic "sign" of the approaching end when Christ will return.

MATTHEW'S GREAT COMMISSION

In light of this brief survey of these themes in Matthew's gospel, it should be clear that the final commissioning of Jesus to His disciples (28:18–20)

---

12. Ibid., 966.

flows naturally out of the larger context of this gospel. Jesus has returned to Galilee, where the mission began, marking a full circle and a sense of completion. Matthean scholar R. T. France rightfully observes that in the final commissioning of Christ to his disciples, "many of the most central themes of the gospel reach their resolution and culmination."[13]

Matthew 28:17 reveals a very human encounter as the eleven disciples are met by Jesus in Galilee. John Wenham argues that this is the largest of all Jesus' resurrection appearances and should be identified with Paul's statement that "he appeared to more than five hundred brethren at one time, most of whom are still alive" (1 Cor. 15:6 RSV). There is no other point in the forty-day period for a *chance* gathering of that size and Galilee was the strongest and most natural base for the church.[14] Those who gathered in Galilee worship the risen Lord, but some doubt (*distazō*), as they try to fully absorb the implications of the events of the last few weeks. This is an important theme in the Gospels, which are not shy about honestly reporting the initial doubts and fears of the disciples (Mark 16:8, 13; Luke 24:37–38; John 20:24–25). It underscores God's initiative in unfolding the Gentile mission.

Jesus addresses the disciples, saying, "All authority in heaven and on earth has been given to me" (Matt. 28:18). This is a widely neglected phrase in discussions concerning Matthew's commission. We are so eager to move on to the actual commission that we fail to see the important theological basis upon which the entire commission is built. The commission of verses 19–20 is built upon the foundation of a prior understanding of who Jesus *is* and what He has been given prior to this encounter in Galilee. The commission begins and ends with an affirmation of Jesus' presence, and the divine authority that entails. In other words, Jesus' *being* precedes the church's *doing,* a point too easily forgotten by a task-oriented church. Jesus is the recipient of all authority in heaven and on earth, quite separate from any human response or church-based initiative. Jesus' words are a clear allusion to Daniel 7, where the Son of Man is brought into the presence of the Ancient of Days. The prophet Daniel declares, "He was given authority, glory and sovereign power; all peoples, nations and people of every language worshipped him" (Dan. 7:14). It is this phrase that situates the sending of Jesus within the context of the *missio dei*. It is the Father

---

13. France, *The Gospel of Matthew*, 1107.
14. John Wenham, *Easter Enigma* (Eugene, OR: Wipf and Stock, 2005), 112–16.

who has bestowed authority and power and glory upon Jesus. It is the Father who has determined that all nations will ultimately worship Jesus Christ as Lord (Phil. 2:9–11), thus placing this commissioning within an eschatological context.

In Galilee, the eschatological worship of the nations is already breaking into the present order. The disciples are sent out as heralds of this good news. Thus, Jesus' sending of His disciples in verses 19 and 20 must be understood within the larger frame of the Father's action and initiative. This is why all the Great Commission passages must be seen within the larger conceptual frame of the sending Father.

In verses 19 and 20a Jesus says, "Go and make disciples of all nations, baptizing them in the name of the Father and of the Son and of the Holy Spirit, teaching them to obey everything I have commanded you." This part of the commission is organized around the central command to "make disciples" (*mathēteusate*), which is the only imperative found in the entire passage. In fact, this is the only time in his gospel that Matthew places the verb "to disciple" in the imperative. The command to "make disciples" is surrounded by three supporting participles: going, baptizing, and teaching. The participles are descriptive, assuming a church that, in the presence of the risen Lord, will be characterized by the ongoing actions of going, baptizing, and teaching. In the acts of going, baptizing, and teaching, Jesus expects His disciples to replicate among all nations the eschatological community known as the church.

The phrase *panta ta ethnē*, "all the nations" (i.e., ethnic groups), has received considerable attention in contemporary missions books. The focus on the precise meaning of this phrase is widely attributed to the writings of Donald McGavran (1897–1990) and Ralph Winter (b. 1924). Donald McGavran's *Bridges of God*, published in 1954, followed by his *Understanding Church Growth* in 1970, helped to revolutionize missionary thinking by turning the focus from *places* to *people groups*. In 1974, Ralph Winter gave a paper at the first Congress on World Evangelization held in Lausanne that is regarded as a turning point in contemporary missions. His paper was entitled "The Highest Priority: Cross-Cultural Evangelism." The paper emphasized the presence of thousands of people groups who were beyond the current reach of the church and would never be reached without some cross-cultural initiative. This focus on people groups, which will be explored in more detail in chapter 12, is based on the recognition that Jesus commands us in Matthew 28 to make disciples of "all nations."[15] The word *ethnē* refers to neither geography nor political entities; rather it indicates social and ethnic groupings of peoples. It is captured well by the phrase *people groups*. This is significant because it recalls the language found in the Abrahamic covenant, whereby God promises to extend a blessing to all the "extended families" or "ethnic groups" of the world.

It is also important to note that Jesus does not render the command with the individualistic emphasis of popular interpretation, "Make disciples of all the individuals within nations," but with the more daunting, holistic command to "make disciples of the nations." In other words, the entire notion of what constitutes our social and ethnic identity as peoples must be brought under the lordship of Jesus Christ. As Andrew Walls has pointed out, "National distinctives, the things that mark out each nation, the shared consciousness and shared traditions, and shared mental processes and patterns of relationships, are all within the scope of discipleship." Christ must become "visible within the very things which constitute nationality."[16] The Great Commission is more than a call to personal evangelism on a global scale. It is a call for Jesus' disciples to create "communities of obedience among the nations."[17] As the risen Lord, Jesus concludes the commission by promising His ongoing presence with the community, which is the distinguishing mark of His disciples (Matt. 28:20).

Mark: In the Midst of Suffering, Preach the Gospel to All Creation
THEMES IN MARK'S GOSPEL

Although Mark is the second gospel in the New Testament canon, it is widely regarded that it was written prior to Matthew's gospel. Therefore, Mark's gospel contains several of the themes regarding a universalistic mission that were carried over into Matthew's gospel and have already been explored, such as the parable of the vineyard tenants (Mark 12:1–12); the miniapocalypse of Mark 13, which, like Matthew, records that "the

---

15. If Jesus had wanted to emphasize geography or political units rather than peoples, there was a whole range of words He could have used, including *agros* (Mark 5:14; Luke 9:12; 23:26), *chōra* (Luke 2:8; 15:13), *apodēmeo* (Matt. 21:33; 25:14–15; Mark 12:1; Luke 15:13; 20:9), *basileia* (Matt. 4:17; 5:20; Mark 1:15; Luke 9:27; John 18:36), or *gē* (Matt. 6:19; 11:24; 24:35; Mark 4:28; 13:31; Luke 21:23; John 17:4). The use of *ethnē* does seem to point away from the traditional geographic and political state identities that have dominated missiological writings and discourse for centuries.
16. Walls, *The Missionary Movement in Christian History*, 27.
17. Wright, *The Mission of God*, 391.

gospel must first be preached to all nations" (Mark 13:10); Jesus' ministry in Gentile regions (Mark 7:24–30; 8:28–34), and the confession of faith by the Gentile centurion at the crucifixion of Christ (Mark 15:39). Mark also anticipates a worldwide mission when Jesus commends the woman who poured an alabaster jar of expensive perfume on His head. Jesus declares that "wherever the gospel is preached throughout the world, what she has done will also be told, in memory of her" (Mark 14:9).

All four Gospels record Jesus' cleansing of the temple (Matt. 21:12–13; Mark 11:15–17; Luke 19:45–46; John 2:13–16). However, Mark places more of an emphasis on the universal mission to the Gentiles in his record of the cleansing of the temple. Mark is the only one of the gospel writers who records the final phrase of the citation from Isaiah 56:7, "My house will be called a house of prayer *for all nations*."[18] It calls to mind that in its context Isaiah prophesied the divine welcome and favor that will come to the Gentiles who "bind themselves to the LORD" (Isa. 56:6). Isaiah's declaration that the temple would be "called a house of prayer for all nations" (56:7) is followed by the affirmation that not only will the Sovereign Lord gather the exiles of Israel, but He will also "gather still others to them besides those already gathered" (Isa. 56:8). As noted in chapter 4, the theme of the nations being gathered is a central theme in the original covenant to Abraham.

Mark's gospel is known for its emphasis on persecution and suffering. Many scholars believe that Mark was written during the time when Nero persecuted the church and famously blamed the Christians for the fire that swept through Rome in 64 C.E. Mark's gospel reminds us that mission occurs in the context of hostility and opposition.

MARK'S ANONYMOUS GREAT COMMISSION

The oldest manuscripts of Mark's gospel conclude at 16:8, which is, by all accounts, an unnatural and abrupt ending, both theologically and linguistically. The absence of a natural conclusion from the earliest manuscripts, coupled with the fact that both of the newer endings (16:9–20 or 16:9–10)

---

18. The omission by Matthew and Luke of the phrase "for all nations" is not generally regarded by New Testament scholars as an attempt to downplay the universal mission. Rather, the temple is regarded as a symbol of Israel, which is under God's judgment, rather than a natural place where the nations will be gathered. In this view, Christ Himself is the new Temple and, by extension, the church. See G. K. Beale, *The Temple and the Church's Mission* (Downers Grove, IL: InterVarsity Press, 2004), 169–200.

contain peculiarities of vocabulary and style that are uncharacteristic of Mark, raises serious doubts about whether the final commission as it appears in our received text is the original.[19] Some scholars are convinced that Mark 16:8 represents the original conclusion to Mark's gospel.[20] It is also possible that Mark's original ending has been lost and that the current ending(s) represents an attempt by the early church to restore the original account. It is worth noting that Mark does record Jesus' preparing His disciples for a postresurrection appearance. In Mark 14:28 Jesus says, "After I have risen, I will go ahead of you into Galilee." It seems odd, therefore, that Mark would omit any resurrection appearances at all.

Therefore, we have received an anonymous ending to Mark's gospel that includes a final commission from our Lord. The fact that the early church chose to restore the presumably lost ending underscores their understanding concerning the importance of the final commission as the proper culmination of the gospel. Therefore, while understanding this as a later addition, a few observations will be made about the text, with a special emphasis on those themes that are present in Mark's gospel.

First, the only imperative found in the passage is the word "proclaim" or "preach" (16:15). The passage commands the church to proclaim the good news to "all creation." This is particularly worth noting since proclamation

---

19. Neither ending is present, for example, in Sinaiticus or Vaticanus. The shorter ending to Mark's gospel is found in some Greek, Latin, Syriac, and Coptic manuscripts. It is as follows: "But they reported briefly to Peter and those with him all that they had been told. And after this, Jesus himself sent out by means of them, from east to west, the sacred and imperishable proclamation of eternal salvation." However, there are many words and phrases in the shorter ending that never appear in Mark's gospel, such as 'briefly" (*suntomōs*), "those around Peter" (*tois peri tou Petrou*), "told" (*exēggeilan*), "afterward" (*meta tauta*), "east" (*anatolēs*), "to" (*achri*), "west" (*duseōs*), "sent" (*exapesteilen*), "sacred" (*hieron*), "imperishable" (*aphtharton*), "proclamation" (*kērugma*), and "salvation" (*sōterias*).

20. If Mark 16:8 is the original conclusion, then the abrupt ending (the last word in the book would be the word "for") would represent a dramatic stylistic ending to emphasize a church on the move and under persecution with a deliberate attempt to not bring things to a natural, overly tidy, triumphalistic conclusion. Instead, it would emphasize the extreme vulnerability of the Christian church during the persecution of Nero. Matthew emphasizes Jesus' presence with His disciples; Mark emphasizes Jesus' absence—the bridegroom is absent (Mark 2:20), and, instead, we experience the presence of false prophets (13:5–6, 21–22). This would provide a heightened need for vigilance, a willingness to endure persecution, and the necessity of living in the expectation of the return of Christ. Luke's gospel emphasizes the ongoing presence and power of the Holy Spirit. Mark's gospel, in contrast, emphasizes the powerlessness of the church in the face of the powers aligned against it. The power of Christ and the final vindication of believers are anticipated only at the second coming of Christ (13:24–26). Until then, believers must persevere in the face of persecution (13:13).

and preaching is, in fact, a central theme in Mark's gospel. John preaches a baptism of repentance (1:4). Mark does not record any birth narrative but instead gives us our first glimpse of Jesus in Galilee "proclaiming the good news of God" (1:14). Mark also records Jesus "preaching in their synagogues" (1:39) and telling His disciples that they must go to nearby villages "so I can preach there also. That is why I have come" (1:38). Twice Mark records Jesus sending out His disciples to preach the gospel (3:14; 6:7–12). Thus, although we do not have the original commissioning of Jesus in Mark, the emphasis on preaching does flow out of a major theme in Mark's gospel.

Second, like Matthew's gospel, the text places the command within an eschatological context, warning that whoever believes "will be saved," whereas whoever does not believe "will be condemned" (16:16). Mark's entire gospel is set within an eschatological tension that is evident in his emphasis on the end of the world, the destruction of the temple, and the coming persecution of those who preach the gospel (13:1–27).

Finally, the text assumes that miraculous signs will accompany the worldwide preaching of the gospel, including driving out demons, speaking in tongues, laying hands on the sick for healing, and being unharmed by snakes or poisons. Mark's gospel, along with all the accounts of Jesus' ministry, emphasizes the miraculous ministry of Jesus. However, Mark is particularly interested in demonstrating that the miraculous ministry of Jesus is replicated in the lives of the disciples, through such works as casting out demons (3:15; 6:13) and healing the sick (6:13).

Looking at the anonymous ending as a whole, it is important to recognize that although the language is non-Markan, the central themes are all consistent with Mark's gospel. Mark understood the church as an eschatological community, empowered and equipped supernaturally by the risen Christ with a universal gospel to proclaim to the whole world. Thus, while we cannot know the precise words of Jesus as originally recorded by Mark, the overall message of Mark's anonymous conclusion is consistent with the church's self-understanding as an empowered community with a universal mission.

Luke-Acts: Holistic and Empowered Witnesses of God's Mighty Deeds
LUKE'S GOSPEL AND HOLISTIC, EMPOWERED WITNESS

It is important to reflect upon the two commissions given by Luke in Luke 24:45–49 and in Acts 1:7–8 within the larger setting of his writings, as well as within the larger context of the *missio dei.* The ongoing mission of those who follow Jesus is central to Luke's understanding of the church. This is particularly evident since he is the only gospel writer to write a companion volume, the book of Acts, which continues the story, demonstrating how the gospel continues to unfold after the Resurrection at Pentecost and in the ongoing witness of the church. David Bosch has correctly observed that "the principal manner in which Luke attempts to articulate his theology of mission is by writing not only one book, but two."[21] Luke's gospel testifies that the transformation of the church from a distinctive sect within Judaism to a movement that was increasingly Gentile has already occurred.

Luke addresses both his gospel and the book of Acts to a Roman official named Theophilus (Luke 1:3; Acts 1:1), and it is evident throughout both books that Luke has a predominantly Gentile audience in mind. Thus, Luke retells the gospel story in light of the growing Gentile presence in the church. He emphasizes Jesus' interactions with Gentiles, with women, with the poor, and with others, like tax collectors and Samaritans, who were marginalized. We will begin by exploring a few selected themes in Luke's gospel in order to set the final commissions in context. The focus here will be on Luke's gospel, with the opening commission of Acts as a bridge from the gospel to the book of Acts. Acts will be explored in more detail in chapter 14.

Jesus' Presentation at the Temple

Luke is the only gospel writer who records Jesus' presentation at the temple. The presentation and sacrifice on behalf of a child was a customary act of obedience to the Jewish Law as outlined in Leviticus 12. The surprise comes when Simeon, a devout and righteous Jew, is moved by the Holy Spirit to go into the temple courts and bless the child. His prayer of blessing, known as the *Nunc Dimittis*, is a powerful affirmation of the future universalistic mission to the Gentiles. Simeon declares that the Lord can now "dismiss [His] servant in peace" because his eyes have seen the salvation of the Lord (2:29–30). The infant Jesus is then declared to be "a light for revelation to the Gentiles and for glory to your people Israel" (2:32).

---

21. Bosch, *Transforming Mission*, 88.

John the Baptist's Ministry of Preparation

Not only do all four Gospels record the ministry of John the Baptist in preparing the way for the ministry of Jesus Christ, but they all also specifically cite Isaiah 40. However, Matthew, Mark, and John are quite succinct in recording Isaiah's prophecy, identifying John as "a voice of one calling in the desert, 'Prepare the way for the Lord, make straight paths for him'" (Matt. 3:3; Mark 1:3; cf. John 1:23), quoting from Isaiah 40:3.[22] However, only Luke quotes the entirety of Isaiah 40:3–5. This portion includes not only the familiar theme of valleys being filled in, mountains being made low, and crooked places being straightened but also the declaration that "all mankind will see God's salvation." Through this quotation, Luke confirms the declaration of Simeon about "revelation to the Gentiles," and anticipates the day when "all mankind" would see God's salvation.

Holistic Mission

Luke records that Jesus' ministry is inaugurated in Galilee, at the synagogue in Nazareth. Jesus takes the scroll of the prophet Isaiah and reads,

> The Spirit of the Lord is on me, because he has anointed me to preach good news to the poor. He has sent me to proclaim freedom for the prisoners and recovery of sight for the blind, to release the oppressed, to proclaim the year of the Lord's favor. (Luke 4:18–19, quoting Isa. 61:1–2)

Then, in dramatic fashion, Jesus declares, "Today this scripture is fulfilled in your hearing" (4:21). In this fashion, Luke sets the agenda for his understanding of Jesus' mission. With this one quotation, Jesus lays claim to a holistic vision that includes His liberating power in an economic context (the poor), a political context (prisoners and oppressed), and a physical context (the blind).[23] This concern for justice and a holistic perspective on salvation becomes a prominent theme in Luke's gospel. In Jesus' sermon on the plain, Luke records Jesus' statement, "Blessed are the poor" rather than the statement, "Blessed are the poor in spirit," as recorded by Mat-

---

22. It should be noted that when the Gospels quote Isaiah 40:3, they all make the change from Isaiah's general reference to "God" to a more explicit identification with Jesus as "Lord."

23. William J. Larkin Jr., "Mission in Luke," in *Mission in the New Testament: An Evangelical Approach*, ed. William J. Larkin Jr. and Joel F. Williams (Maryknoll, NY: Orbis, 1998), 159.

thew in Jesus' Sermon on the Mount. Luke would resist Western attempts to overly spiritualize Luke's emphasis on the poor and the downtrodden. Jesus' ministry really does represent good news for the economically poor. In passages unique to Luke's gospel, we read how He has "filled the hungry with good things but sent the rich away empty" (Luke 1:53). We hear how the poor man Lazarus rests secure in Abraham's bosom, while the rich man is in agony (Luke 16:19–31). In a passage he shares with the Synoptics, Luke records Jesus telling the rich young ruler to "sell everything you have and give to the poor" (18:22).

Luke frequently portrays Jesus in solidarity with the disenfranchised and outcasts of society, including women (13:10–17), tax collectors and sinners (5:29–31; 15:1–32; 19:1–10), and Samaritans (10:30–37; 17:11–19). Many of these texts are unique to Luke's gospel, such as Jesus' healing of the crippled woman, the parable of the good Samaritan, and the parable of the prodigal son. Luke alone records how Jesus healed ten lepers but only the Samaritan returned to give thanks (17:17).

While it is important not to spiritualize the concreteness of Jesus' mission in Luke, it also would be a mistake to drive an unnatural wedge between "gospel proclamation" and "social ministry." William Larkin Jr. makes the helpful observation that of the four infinitives Jesus quotes from Isaiah 61 at the inauguration of His ministry, three involve preaching: "the poor are evangelized (*euangelizomai*); the prisoners have release and the blind have recovery of sight proclaimed (*kērussō*) to them; and the year of the Lord's favor … is proclaimed (*kērussō*)."[24] Furthermore, the most frequent way Jesus releases prisoners from bondage in Luke's gospel is through demonic deliverance. In Luke's gospel, holistic ministry truly means holistic, encompassing the whole of life, both physical and spiritual. This is important to recall when we examine Jesus' commission at the end of Luke's gospel where we are called to be "witnesses of these things." Our witness must be understood from the broadest perspective.

Second Commissioning in Luke
One of the pivotal moments in Jesus' ministry as recorded in the Synoptic Gospels is the sending out of the Twelve, two by two, on a Galilean mission (Matt. 10:1–42; Mark 6:7–13; Luke 9:1–6). This mission takes place in Galilee

---

24. Ibid., 158.

and is clearly identified as a mission to the Jews (Matt. 10:5). The symbolism of the Twelve is quite obviously linked to the twelve tribes of Israel. Luke is the only gospel writer who records a *second* larger commissioning during the ministry of Jesus.[25] Luke 10:1 records that Jesus appointed "seventy-two [or seventy] others and sent them two by two ahead of him to every town and place where he was about to go." There is an important textual problem concerning the precise number of disciples who are sent out on this mission. Some manuscripts record seventy, others record seventy-two. The textual evidence is very evenly divided, which is why the discrepancy is reflected in modern translations of the Bible. The difficulty is linked entirely to the symbolism of the number. The significance of the number is widely believed to be symbolic of the nations of the world. After the great Flood (Gen. 6–9) and prior to God's covenant with Abraham (Gen. 12), there is a chapter that describes the diversification of the descendants of Noah (Gen. 10). This chapter is a rather lengthy list of names and, therefore, is often overlooked by contemporary Bible readers. However, it is an important chapter tradition-ally known as the Table of Nations. If you count the number of descendants ("nations") in the chapter, it comes to seventy. It is not necessary to insist that this is a comprehensive list of all the known nations of the world at that time. What is important is that this list *symbolizes* all the nations of the world. The discrepancy in the precise number arises between the Hebrew version of Genesis 10 and the Greek Septuagint version of Genesis 10, which was in wide use at the time of Christ. In the Septuagint there are some slight changes in the word divisions, which results in a list of seventy-two descendants in the Table of Nations, not seventy as in the Hebrew. Interestingly, because we have a textual discrepancy in the Lukan text, the obvious connection with Genesis 10 and the Table of Nations is highlighted. Thus, the number is used here to "anticipate the later mission to all the nations of the earth."[26]

An ongoing, universal mission is further anticipated by the opening words of Jesus' commission to the disciples: "The harvest is plentiful, but

---

25. Luke is also the only gospel writer who records Jesus sending "messengers" ahead of Him to a Samaritan village (9:51–56). However, since they were not welcomed, and Jesus and the disciples did not end up going there, it is not normally regarded as a separate mission.

26. John Nolland, *Luke 9:21–18:34*, Word Biblical Commentary, vol. 35b (Dallas: Word, 1993), 549. The textual discrepancy helps, for example, to effectively eliminate the alternative proposals that it represents the total number on the Sanhedrin, or the Septuagint, which, according to tradition, was translated by seventy scholars, or the seventy elders who receive the Spirit in Numbers 11:24–25.

the workers are few. Ask the Lord of the harvest, therefore, to send out workers into his harvest field" (10:2). The divine title, "Lord of the harvest," found only here and in Matthew 9:38, is very significant in placing this second commission within the larger context of the *missio dei*. "Lord of the harvest" is an ascription given by our Lord to *God the Father*. Jesus tells us to pray to the Lord of the harvest and ask *Him* to "send out workers." This places Jesus' ministry of sending within the larger context of the Lord of the harvest, who is the ultimate sender. This also anticipates that God the Father, as Lord of the harvest, initiates an ongoing mission of sending into the harvest field of the world, of which this mission is the firstfruits. Jesus is optimistic about the Gentile mission, even declaring that those in the Gentile region of Tyre and Sidon would be more responsive than those within Israel (10:13–14). Nevertheless, we are not given many details in Luke's gospel of the actual mission. We are only told that the seventy-two (or seventy) returned with joy, declaring that "even the demons submit to us in your name" (10:17), demonstrating the continuity between the ministry of Jesus and the ministry of the disciples.

Emphasis on the Holy Spirit
The structure of this Trinitarian missiology seeks to help those who are studying missions to conceptualize it within the context of the *missio dei*. In order to accomplish this, it is important to view all of missions within the framework of the Trinity. The Father is the sender, the Lord of the harvest; the incarnate Son is the model embodiment of mission in the world; and the Holy Spirit is the divine, empowering presence for all of mission. Therefore, in understanding the context of the commission in Luke's gospel, it is important to demonstrate the special emphasis he places on the ministry of the Holy Spirit, which finds full expression in the commissions, both in Luke and in the book of Acts, but is also present throughout his gospel.

First, more than any of the other gospel writers, Luke emphasizes various individuals being filled with the Holy Spirit, including John the Baptist (1:15), Mary (1:35), Elizabeth (1:41), Zechariah (1:67), Simeon (2:25), and Jesus Himself (3:22; 4:14, 18). Second, Luke, along with Matthew, anticipates persecution and opposition that will result in Jesus' disciples being "brought before governors and kings" (Matt. 10:18) or before "synagogues, rulers and authorities" (Luke 12:11). In either case, they need not prepare a defense because, Luke records, "the Holy Spirit will teach you at that time what you should say" (Luke 12:12).[27] It is in this context of persecution that Jesus also warns His disciples that "anyone who blasphemes against the Holy Spirit will not be forgiven" (Luke 12:10). Third, Luke joins with all the other Gospels in recording the words of John the Baptist that Jesus will "baptize . . . with the Holy Spirit" (Matt. 3:11; Mark 1:8; Luke 3:16; cf. John 1:33). However, only Luke connects this promise of John with the later descent of the Holy Spirit after the resurrection and ascension of Christ. Luke records, just prior to the ascension, Jesus' words, "For John baptized with water, but in a few days you will be baptized with the Holy Spirit" (Acts 1:5). The common theme in all these references is the identification of the Holy Spirit with the unfolding mission of God.

Universalistic Mission in Luke

Luke is widely known for his special interest in Gentiles. Not only does Luke record Jesus' ministry outside of ethnic Israel (Luke 8:26–39; 9:51–56), but he also puts a personal face on Gentiles who respond favorably to Christ. Some of these pericopes have already been explored in the context of Matthew's gospel, such as Jesus' encounter with the centurion, about whom He said that He had "not found such great faith even in Israel" (Luke 10:9; cf. Matt. 8:10). Matthew and Luke both portray Gentiles in Tyre and Sidon (Matt. 11:21–22; Luke 10:14) and the Ninevites in Syria (Matt. 12:41; Luke 11:29–32) as ones who will be judged more favorably than Israel on the day of judgment. Matthew and Luke both anticipate a Gentile ingathering whereby Gentiles "from east and west and north and south" will come and sit down at table with Abraham, Isaac, and Jacob in the kingdom (Luke 13:29; cf. Matt. 8:11). This is in contrast to many in Israel who will be "thrown out" (Luke 13:28).

However, there are several accounts reflecting this theme that are unique to Luke's gospel. Luke highlights the faith of "Naaman the Syrian" (4:27), the faith of the "widow in Zarephath in the region of Sidon" (4:26), and the faithfulness of the Samaritan in the parable of the good Samaritan (10:25–37). Luke is the only gospel writer who, in the parable of the wedding banquet, records a *second* call to the uninvited. In the first call, the servant

---

27. Matthew's gospel says, "It will not be you speaking, but the Spirit of your Father speaking through you" (Matt. 10:20).

brings in the "poor, crippled, the blind and the lame" (14:22). In the second call, the master sends his servant out again to "the roads and country lanes . . . so that my house will be full" (14:23). As noted above, Luke alone records the one thankful Samaritan, among the ten lepers who were healed, who returns to give thanks (17:11–19). Luke, writing to Gentiles, wants to emphasize the favorable response of the Gentiles to the ministry of Jesus. Indeed, Luke is the only gospel writer who prophetically presents the time between Christ's first and second comings as the "times of the Gentiles" (21:24).[28]

LUKE'S GREAT COMMISSION

In light of this brief overview of key themes in Luke's gospel, the final commissioning as recorded in Luke 24:46–49 and at the beginning of the book of Acts (1:7–8) will be considered.

Luke's takes place in Jerusalem on the night after the Resurrection and, therefore, is considerably earlier than Matthew's commission, which occurs in Galilee some weeks after the Resurrection.[29] The commission that appears in the book of Acts (1:7–8), in contrast, occurs last among all the other gospel commissions, taking place in Bethany just prior to Christ's ascension.[30] The unifying feature of both of the commissions recorded by Luke is the emphasis on the sovereignty of God in missions. The church's initiative and action can be seen only through the lens of the *missio dei*. This emphasis becomes evident in three main ways.

Luke's Commissions in the Context of God's Mission

First, Luke emphasizes the inability of the disciples to understand apart from God's prior action. Luke's gospel commission is preceded by Jesus' resurrection appearance to two of His followers on the road to Emmaus. They are all walking along together, but the text says, surprisingly, "They were kept from recognizing him" (24:16). It is not until Jesus breaks the bread that "their eyes were opened and they recognized him" (24:31). Luke

---

28. Larkin, "Mission in Luke," 165.

29. It should be noted, however, that one of the features of Luke's gospel is the collapse of all the final events into a single expression of an Easter narrative. Luke moves almost seamlessly from Easter to the Ascension, collapsing the forty-day period into a single, dramatic conclusion.

30. To reconcile the place of the Ascension with Luke's record in Acts, John Wenham suggests that the ascension of Christ takes place at the "Mount of Olives," which is "as far as the path to Bethany." It is at the summit of the Mount of Olives that Bethany is in view. See Wenham, *Easter Enigma*, 121.

emphasizes that their recognition was a result of an act of divine self-disclosure. This finds a remarkable parallel in the appearance to the apostles later that night. The disciples also did not recognize Him, thinking they saw a ghost (24:37). It is later when He "opened their minds so they could understand the Scriptures" (24:45) that they finally begin to understand. The same verb for "open" (*dianoigō* / διανοίγω) is used in 24:31, when the two on the road to Emmaus had their eyes opened, and in 24:45, when the disciples' minds were opened. The truth of the gospel is realized only in response to a prior divine self-disclosure. The use of this verb "open" (διανοίγω) to describe the opening of one's eyes, or mind, to understand the Scriptures, or Jesus' identity, is unique to Luke's gospel.[31] The only other occurrence of the word used in this way is also by Luke, when he records in Acts how God "opened" the heart of Lydia to respond to the message of Paul (Acts 16:14). This theme is also evident in Luke's commission in Acts. In Acts 1:7 Jesus says that it is not for us to know "the times or dates the Father has set by his own authority." The emphasis is on the action of God in unfolding His mission, in His time.

Second, Luke has a strong emphasis on the witness of the church as a fulfillment of (and in continuity with) the Old Testament. Jesus appears to His frightened disciples, shows them His hands and feet, and eats a piece of broiled fish in their presence, dispelling the notion that He was an apparition. Jesus then says, "This is what I told you while I was still with you: Everything must be fulfilled that is written about me in the Law of Moses, the Prophets and the Psalms" (Luke 24:44). This also finds a parallel in the earlier resurrection appearance on the road to Emmaus, when Jesus walked with two disciples. Jesus admonishes those two in a similar fashion, saying, "How foolish you are, and how slow of heart to believe all that the prophets have spoken! . . . And beginning with Moses and all the Prophets, he explained to them what was said in all the Scriptures concerning himself" (Luke 24:25, 27).

The fulfillment theme continues even within the content of the commissions. Indeed, one of the unique features of both of Luke's commissions is the absence of command forms, which are replaced with the language of fulfillment and God's prior action. In Luke's gospel, the future witness of the church is seen as a fulfillment of promises made in

---

31. I. Howard Marshall, *The Gospel of Luke*, New International Greek Text Commentary (Grand Rapids: Eerdmans, 1978), 905.

the Old Testament, just as the ministry of Christ was in fulfillment of the Scriptures. In Luke's gospel the commission begins with Jesus stating, "This is what is written" (24:46). Jesus then speaks of His life, as well as the church's witness, in the context of fulfillment.

> This is what is written: The Christ will suffer and rise from the dead on the third day, and repentance and forgiveness of sins will be preached in his name to all nations, beginning at Jerusalem. You are witnesses of these things. (24:46–47)

The disciples are portrayed as witnesses of God's action in fulfilling the promises of the Old Testament, most notably the Abrahamic covenant, among the nations of the world. The witness of the church is put solidly in the frame of God's mission and His action to fulfill His promises. In the commission in Acts, the witness of the disciples is portrayed as the action of God in and through them: "You will receive (λήμψεσθε) power . . . and you will be (ἔσεσθέ) my witnesses in Jerusalem, and in all Judea and Samaria, and to the ends of the earth" (Acts 1:8). This is prophetic language, which the church's later action will fulfill.

The third way that Luke places his commissions within the context of the larger frame of God's action is his emphasis on the inability of the disciples to engage in missions apart from the empowerment of the Holy Spirit. As noted, there is no command form that "sends" the disciples in either of Luke's commissions. Rather, it is the Holy Spirit who is sent. Instead of the expected command to *go*, Jesus tells the disciples to "stay in the city until you have been clothed with power from on high" (24:49). That same admonition given on the night after the Resurrection is recalled in the book of Acts: "Do not leave Jerusalem, but wait for the gift my Father promised, which you have heard me speak about. For John baptized with water, but in a few days you will be baptized with the Holy Spirit" (Acts 1:4–5). In Luke–Acts, the Holy Spirit is "the catalyst, the guiding and driving force of missions."[32]

Scope of the Commission in Luke–Acts
Luke's commission shares a common emphasis with Matthew's commission in that both have a universal scope. In Matthew's gospel the disciples

---

32. Bosch, *Transforming Mission*, 113.

were commanded to "make disciples of all nations." Luke's gospel envisions the preaching of repentance and forgiveness of sins "to all nations." As explored earlier, the word *ethnē* (nations) refers to people groups, indicating social and ethnic groupings of peoples, not the modern geopolitical "nation." This is important because it recalls the language of the Abrahamic covenant in Genesis 22:16–18.

The book of Acts is sometimes seen as a departure from the ethnic-oriented, "people-group" language of the Matthean and Lukan commissions. The phrase "in Jerusalem, and in all Judea and Samaria, and to the ends of the earth" (Acts 1:8) often is depicted as a geographic progression with Jerusalem at the center and the gospel spreading outward in ever-widening concentric circles until it eventually reaches the ends of the earth. However, as will be detailed in chapter 14, this is not the best understanding of the phrase. The missiological breakthrough in Antioch recorded in Acts 11:19–20 shows that it is not merely a *geographic* progression that the commission envisions but an *ethnic, cross-cultural* progression. The phrase "ends of the earth" in Acts 1:8 should be understood as an allusion to the second Servant Song explored in chapter 4, which concludes with the prophecy "that you may bring my salvation to the ends of the earth" (Isa. 49:6). The context of Isaiah's prophecy is the Messiah being a "light to the nations," and the language of "ends of the earth" is more a feature of Hebrew poetical parallelism than the introduction of a new, geographic frame. Missions, in both the Old and New Testament, is fundamentally about *peoples*, not *places*.

Witnesses of God's Mighty Deeds
The final major theme that emerges out of the commissions in Luke and Acts is the emphasis on the church as witnesses. The word *witness* (μαρτύς) is unique to the commissions in Luke and Acts. In fact, the church as a community of witnesses is one of the unifying themes that link the gospel of Luke with Acts (Luke 21:13; 24:48; Acts 1:8, 22; 2:32; 3:15; 5:32; 10:39, 41; 13:31; 22:15; 26:16). A witness is someone who testifies to what he or she has seen and heard. In the context of Luke and Acts, the witness of the apostles refers primarily to three things they had seen and experienced: the sufferings of Christ, His resurrection from the dead, and the offer of forgiveness in His name, which comes through repentance. Thus, the content of the "witness" recorded in Acts corresponds precisely to the three things spoken of by Christ in Luke's commission. Jesus said that

they would be "witnesses of these things" (Luke 24:48), and the book of Acts demonstrates their faithfulness in bearing witness to God's mighty deeds. However, the book of Acts also demonstrates that the mighty deeds of God do not stop at the Resurrection but continue on at Pentecost and in the unfolding *missio dei* in the life of the church. The church is the on-going witness to "all nations" of God's mighty deeds.

John: The Sending Sent One

John's gospel is written to persuade unbelievers to affirm the lordship of Jesus Christ and, therefore, is cast entirely in a missional framework. John writes, "These are written so that you may believe that Jesus is the Christ, the Son of God, and that by believing you may have life in his name" (John 20:31).[33] Our methodology with the Synoptic Gospels has been to highlight various themes within the gospel to demonstrate that a universal mission was central to the overall structure of the gospel. The purpose of this has been twofold. First, it keeps the Great Commission passages from being isolated from the larger gospel context out of which they arise, thereby avoiding the temptation toward proof-texting. Second, it demonstrates that the missionary mandate, and all the potential missions activities that flow from it, are closely tied to the larger framework of God's initiative in the *missio dei*.

This methodology could easily be followed in John's gospel as well. In fact, many of the best-known universalistic passages in the New Testament are found in John's gospel. For example, it is John who in his opening pro-logue declares that Jesus is "the true light that *gives light to every man* was coming into the world" (1:9, emphasis mine). It is John who records the verse that Martin Luther called the "gospel in miniature" and is probably the best-known verse in the New Testament: "For God *so loved the world* that he gave his one and only Son . . ." (3:16, emphasis mine). He is the one who records Jesus' revealing Himself as the Messiah to a Samaritan

---

33. For an exposition of this verse as central to our understanding the purpose of John's gospel, see D. A. Carson, "The Purpose of the Fourth Gospel: John 20:31 Reconsidered," *Journal of Biblical Literature* 106, no. 4 (1987): 639–51. Carson argues persuasively that John's gospel is not primarily addressed to Christians who are in dispute with their synagogue leaders but to unbelievers, primarily Hellenistic Jews, who do not yet know Jesus Christ. Even John 14–17, the least overtly evangelistic portion of the gospel, should be seen, argues Carson, as a testimony that John was not seeking converts with "superficial professions of faith" but those who grow, abide in Christ, and are discipled.

woman (4:21–26) and that many Samaritans "believed in him" (4:39). In a profoundly universalistic saying, John records Jesus saying, "I have other sheep that are not of this sheep pen" (10:16). Many more examples could be given. However, in examining John's gospel, I want to focus on one single theme that undergirds the entire gospel of John and is, in fact, the central theme out of which his Great Commission flows. The theme that we will examine is the sending Father.

THE SENDING FATHER IN JOHN'S GOSPEL

John's understanding of mission is primarily found in his use of the verb *to send* (*pempō* or *apostellō*). John's entire gospel is structured around the Father sending John the Baptist, sending Jesus, sending the Holy Spirit, and culminating in His sending of the church. The verb *to send* in John's gospel contains two ideas, one internal and one external. Internally, it "implies a personal relationship"; namely, that those who are sent are sent by somebody. Externally, it implies that the one who is sent is "sent for some purpose."[34] John the Baptist is sent as a witness to the arrival of the Messiah: "There came a man who was sent from God; his name was John" (1:6). John the Baptist speaks of both aspects of sending when he describes his mission:

> I would not have known him, except that the *one who sent me* to baptize with water told me, "The man on whom you see the Spirit come down and remain is he who will baptize with the Holy Spirit." I have seen and I testify that this is the Son of God. (John 1:33–34)

John sees himself as personally sent by God the Father, and his purpose is to testify, or bear witness, to the fact that Jesus is the Son of God. John was not the light, but "he came only as a witness to the light" (1:8). Ten times the gospel describes the purpose of John the Baptist's mission as one sent to bear witness to Christ (1:7 [2x], 8, 15, 19, 32, 34; 3:26, 28; 5:33).

When Jesus steps onto the historical stage in John's gospel, He uses the same language as John, declaring that He was sent by the Father. Like John the Baptist, Jesus uses the "sent" language in both its personal and missional sense. The intimacy between the Son and the Father and the sense of purpose and mission for which Jesus was sent are conveyed regularly in

---

34. James McPolin SJ, "Mission in the Fourth Gospel," *Irish Theological Quarterly* 36 (1969): 114.

John's gospel. The best way to fully grasp the centrality of this theme in John's gospel is to read through several examples at key moments in Jesus' ministry, all leading up to His final commission:

- "My food . . . is do the will of him who *sent me* and to finish his work" (4:34).
- "Whoever hears my word and believes him who *sent me* has eternal life" (5:24).
- "For I have come down from heaven not to do my will but to do the will of him who *sent me*" (6:38).
- "My teaching is not my own. It comes from him who *sent me*" (7:16).
- "I am not here on my own, but he who *sent me* is true" (7:28).
- "I am with you for only a short time, and then I go to the one who *sent me*" (7:33).
- "He who *sent me* is reliable, and what I have heard from him I tell to the world" (8:26).
- "The one who *sent me* is with me; he has not left me alone" (8:29).
- "As long as it is day, we must do the work of him who *sent me*" (9:4).
- "When a man believes in me, he does not believe in me only, but in the one who *sent me*. When he looks at me, he sees the one who *sent me*" (12:44–45).
- "Whoever accepts me accepts the one who *sent me*" (13:20).
- "They will treat you this way because of my name, for they do not know the One who *sent me*" (15:21).
- "Now I am going to him who *sent me*" (16:5).

JOHN'S GREAT COMMISSION

These texts all culminate in the Great Commission in John's gospel, found in John 20:21. Here is the last of forty occurrences of the title "sent one" as applied to Jesus in John's gospel.[35] The setting is identical to that of Luke's gospel, behind locked doors in Jerusalem the evening after the Resurrection. As with Luke's gospel, Jesus' first words of comfort to the disciples are, "Peace be with you!" followed by their examination of His hands and feet.

---

35. All the references are as follows: John 3:34; 4:34; 5:23–24, 30, 36–38; 6:29, 38, 44, 57; 7:16, 18, 28, 29, 33; 8:16, 18, 26, 29, 42; 9:4; 10:36; 11:42; 12:44, 45, 49; 13:16, 20; 14:24; 15:21; 16:5; 17:3, 8, 18, 21, 23, 25; and 20:21.

However, John alone records these words of commissioning to His disciples: "Peace be with you! As the Father has sent me, I am sending you" (20:21).

Jesus, as the sent one, now sends the church to continue the Father's mission in the world. There are three important features of Jesus' commission in John's gospel that are important to consider. First, the mission of the church is not a new development but a continuation of the ministry of Jesus as the ongoing expression of the Father's redemptive act of sending Jesus into the world. The Father's redemptive work is not finished with the ministry of Jesus but continues to unfold at Pentecost, in the life of the church, and ultimately in the New Creation. Earlier, Jesus had prepared the disciples for this final act of sending, most notably in the High Priestly Prayer when He prayed, "As you sent me into the world, I have sent them into the world" (17:18).[36] Jesus already had promised that His disciples would do even "greater things than these" (14:12). Now, in this postresurrection appearance, Jesus sends the disciples into the world, just as He was sent into the world.

Second, the mission of the church is clearly set within a Trinitarian framework in John's gospel. The Father is the sender. Jesus, as the sent one, sends the church. The Holy Spirit is imparted to the disciples for His presence, guidance, and empowerment of the mission. John records that Jesus breathes on them and says, "Receive the Holy Spirit" (20:22). Just as the Father breathed His Spirit into humankind at creation (Gen. 2:7), so now Jesus breathes the Holy Spirit on His disciples as a sign and seal of the New Creation. It is not necessary to drive a wedge between Easter and Pentecost, as some have, by making this only a symbolic or partial impartation of the Holy Spirit in light of the record in Acts 2. Both accounts are integral parts of the Easter event, which, for the gospel writers, is not a single day but an ongoing, grand reality in the life of the church.

Third, this commission forms the basis for the ongoing sending ministry of the church in missions today. Just as Jesus, who was sent into the world, becomes a sender, so we who have been sent into the world continue to reflect Jesus' ministry as we send out workers into the harvest field.[37] As Jesus said, "Whoever accepts anyone I send accepts

---

36. See also John 4:38.

37. The "as . . . so" construction is crucial to this understanding. As the Father has sent the Son, so the Son sends the church. As the Son sends the church, so the church sends future disciples into the world.

me; and whoever accepts me accepts the one who sent me" (John 13:20). Jesus was sent to announce the Father's forgiveness of sins for those who repent, as well as His righteous judgment on those who refuse to repent. In the same way, the church is given the ongoing authority to send workers into the field to announce the forgiveness that comes through repentance, as well as the Father's judgment on those who refuse to repent and believe (John 20:23).

CONCLUSION

This survey of the final commissions given by Jesus Christ and recorded in all four Gospels reveals that the Great Commission is actually multifaceted. Only by listening to the distinctive message of each do they collectively provide the theological basis for the wide range of redemptive works that the church engages in, which we call missions. Matthew emphasizes the role of discipleship and planting the church across ethnic and cultural boundaries among every people group in the world. Although we do not have the original words of Mark's commission, the received version is consistent with Mark's emphasis on perseverance in persecution and the central role of proclamation. Luke's commission emphasizes the importance of Spirit-empowered, holistic missions as we bear witness to the ongoing, mighty deeds of God. John's commission emphasizes the sending role of the church. Taken collectively, the commissions demonstrate the Father's initiative in missions. The Father imparts all authority to Jesus in Matthew's gospel. In Luke, the church fulfills only what the Father has promised. In John, the Father sends the Son, who, in turn, sends the church. Thus, all of the commissions are set within the larger context of the *missio dei* and God's original promise to Abraham that He would bless "all nations on earth" (Gen. 22:18).

Section B

Creation, Revelation, and the Human Response to God's Rule

— 6 —
A Trinitarian, "New Creation" Theology of Culture

ALTHOUGH THE WORD *CULTURE* has been described as one of the most "complex words in the English language,"[1] it hasn't stopped the word from becoming one of the most ubiquitous words in popular, Western discourse. If you listen carefully, you will hear the word used to describe a remarkably wide range of phenomena. Those who are not happy with the educational system often speak about a "culture of failure." Pacifists speak about promoting a "culture of peace." Those who think that Western society is too materialistic speak about a "consumer culture." Since 9/11 some have openly worried about the Western world becoming engulfed in a "culture of fear." Christian pastors exhort their congregations to "engage the culture."

The word *culture* can be used in surprisingly contradictory ways. Sometimes the word is used very broadly to describe entire blocks of civilization. For example, it is not unusual to hear people speak about "Asian culture" or "Western culture" in the singular as if each of these regions is inhabited by peoples who all share a single expression of culture. The rise of technology has even led some to describe the entire world as the dawning of a single "global culture." At other times, the word is used to describe very specific, particularized, and even exotic traits of a people. For example, cultural anthropologists speak about *com hen*, a cold rice dish flavored with clam juice and eaten in central Vietnam, as that particular people's "cultural food." With the rise of globalization, it seems

---

1. Terry Eagleton, *The Idea of Culture* (Malden, MA: Blackwell, 2000), 1.

that we are more aware than ever of our cultural diversity and new expressions like "multiculturalism," "cross-cultural," and "cultural sensitivity" are now commonplace. For some, the rise of multiculturalism is the most significant cultural development of our time. For others, multiculturalism simply means that they can walk within a block of their apartment and find pizza, Thai food, burritos, and sushi.

Interestingly, despite all the talk about culture, many Christians have never really thought about developing a *theology of culture*, and it is not unusual to find missions books and textbooks with dozens of references to culture but lacking any theological perspective on the concept. It is important to know if Christians have anything distinctive to contribute to a discussion about culture and to examine the impact these insights might have on our missiology. The purpose of this chapter, therefore, is to propose a theology of culture. We will begin by examining the classic book *Christ and Culture* by Richard Niebuhr, which was the most influential Christian reflection on culture written in the twentieth century. This will be followed by a critique of Niebuhr's presuppositions and methodology, followed by a proposal for a Trinitarian theology of culture for a post-Christendom world.

RICHARD NIEBUHR'S *CHRIST AND CULTURE*

Since its publication in 1951, H. Richard Niebuhr's landmark book, *Christ and Culture*, has remained the most influential book in shaping Christian thinking about culture.[2] Niebuhr defines culture as "the artificial, secondary environment which man superimposes on the natural. It comprises language, habits, ideas, beliefs, customs, social organization, inherited artifacts, technical processes, and values."[3] Niebuhr goes on to identify three defining marks of culture. First, he argues that culture is always *social*. It is concerned with the "organization of human beings," not with our private lives. Second, culture is described as a *human achievement*. By this Niebuhr means that it is not the result of biology or nature, but it is always the fruit of "human purposiveness and effort."[4] Finally, culture is always concerned with the *"temporal and material realization of values."*[5] Niebuhr correctly acknowledges that Christians have held a wide variety of positions in how

---

2. H. Richard Niebuhr, *Christ and Culture* (New York: Harper and Brothers, 1951).

3. Ibid., 32.

4. Ibid., 33.

5. Ibid., 36.

they have regarded culture, and the main thrust of his book is to explore five positions that have characterized the Christian response to culture.

In his classic typology, Niebuhr outlines five positions along a continuum in which the gospel and culture have historically related to one another. At one end of the spectrum, *"Christ against culture"* reflects a defensive posture that envisions the church's primary identity as resisting cultural accommodation. It is a picture of the church "in exile" as a subcultural movement in the midst of a fallen world. According to Niebuhr, this perspective on culture has been exemplified throughout history by such figures and movements as Tertullian, *The Rule of St. Benedict*, the Mennonites, and Leo Tolstoy. There is a distinct line that must separate the Christian gospel from sinful culture, "for it is in culture that sin chiefly resides."[6] On the other end of the spectrum, *"Christ of culture"* signifies an uncritical, accommodationist perspective on the relationship between gospel and culture. It is a picture of the church at the center of cultural life. Niebuhr says that those who hold this view "feel no great tension between church and world, the social laws and the Gospel, the workings of divine grace and human effort, the ethics of salvation and the ethics of social conservation or progress."[7] The tension between Christ and culture is erased because God's permeating presence is recognized in the midst of human culture and civilization. Niebuhr points out that this position has been observed most within contemporary, Protestant liberalism, which he aptly refers to with the Barthian phrase "Culture-Protestantism."[8]

Niebuhr goes on to present three mediating positions between these two extremes, which he collectively refers to as "the church of the center."[9] The *"Christ above culture"* position seeks to avoid both an uncritical accommodation to culture and a complete rejection of culture. This position criticizes the "Christ of culture" position because it fails to see how sin has permeated human institutions. However, it equally criticizes the "Christ against culture" view for not working hard to close the gap between Christ and culture. This third position, in contrast, adopts a synthesis approach,

---

6. Ibid., 52. It should be noted that several Anabaptist writers have objected to Niebuhr's categorizing Anabaptists as "Christ against culture." See, for example, Charles Scriven, *The Transformation of Culture* (Scottdale, PA: Herald, 1988).
7. Niebuhr, *Christ and Culture*, 83.
8. Ibid., 84.
9. Ibid., 116.

whereby the gospel elevates and validates the best of culture while rejecting that which is antithetical to the gospel. Niebuhr sees Clement of Alexandria as representative of this view, particularly in his view that a Christian must first be a "good man in accordance with the standard of a good culture." Christ builds on the foundation of commonly shared culture and "uses its best products as instruments in his work of bestowing on men what they cannot achieve by their own efforts."[10] This view finds its greatest adherent in Thomas Aquinas's medieval synthesis of faith and reason. For Thomas, the tension between Christ and culture is never answered with an "either-or" but always with a "both-and."

Niebuhr's fourth position, *Christ and culture in paradox*, understands culture as neutral, reflecting a deeper, fundamentally dualistic, tension between God and humanity. Sinful, fallen humanity produces corrupt cultural expressions within society. Redeemed humanity produces godly cultural expressions within society. The line is not so much drawn between the gospel and culture as it is drawn within the human heart. The conflict is between God and us. Niebuhr recognizes this perspective in Marcion, but it finds its greatest expression in Luther's theology of two kingdoms. God's kingdom is a kingdom of grace and mercy, whereas the kingdom of this world is a kingdom of wrath and severity. The Christian must always "affirm both in a single act of obedience."[11]

Finally, Niebuhr's *Christ the transformer of culture* typology is a "conversionist" approach to culture. This view understands that culture is a positive good. It does not accept the dichotomy of good culture and bad culture. Following Augustine, evil is the perversion of the good, and does not have its own fundamental reality. This position is distinguished by its positive attitude toward culture as a reflection of the doctrine of creation. The gospel optimistically stands as a transcultural or supracultural force that can redeem and transform culture, by extending God's kingdom into it and restoring culture back to God's original intent. This view is best represented by Augustine and, later, by John Calvin and his vision for the transformation of Geneva. Augustine, Calvin, and all those who embrace a "conversionist" approach to culture look "for the present permeation of all life by the gospel."[12]

---

10. Ibid., 127.
11. Ibid., 172.
12. Ibid., 217.

It is important to acknowledge our indebtedness to Richard Niebuhr. His book *Christ and Culture* has enjoyed an extraordinary readership over the years, across the whole theological spectrum. Niebuhr provided a reasonably transparent framework that has enabled generations of Christian students to reflect meaningfully and historically about culture and its relationship to the Christian gospel. However, there are some inherent problems with Niebuhr's understanding of culture, and his fivefold analysis. This chapter seeks to expose some of the problems with Niebuhr's traditional analysis and, in its place, recommend a Trinitarian model for understanding culture.

BEYOND *CHRIST AND CULTURE*

There are four basic difficulties with Niebuhr's understanding. *First, Niebuhr's understanding of culture was constructed on the foundation of secular anthropology.* When Niebuhr defines culture, he acknowledges that he can only give a "layman's definition" since he "cannot presume to enter into the issues raised by professional anthropologists." Indeed, when discussing culture, Niebuhr insists on providing a "definition of the phenomenon *without theological interpretation.*"[13] Because he understands culture as "the work of men's minds and hands," he inadvertently secularizes culture, creating an unbiblical dichotomy between human cultural activity and Christ. He refers to Christ and culture as "two complex realities" that are in "infinite dialogue."[14]

The secular foundation of Niebuhr's understanding of culture means that his entire method posits Christ and culture as two wholly separate entities or forces. However, God is the author of human culture and His ongoing sustenance of, and redemptive activity within, human culture is integral to a biblical view of God. This dichotomization creates serious theological difficulties that are never fully resolved by Niebuhr. The Incarnation and Pentecost, as well as God's ongoing redemptive acts in His church, all occur *within culture* and are fully *part of* culture. Christ does not exist as some abstract principle but "comes fully embodied and inculturated as a first century Mediterranean Jewish male."[15] To create a barrier between

---

13. Ibid., 30, emphasis mine.
14. Ibid., 39.
15. Amos Yong, "Culture," in *Dictionary of Mission Theology: Evangelical Foundations*, ed. John Corrie (Downers Grove, IL: InterVarsity Press, 2007), 85.

Christ and culture is to relegate God to the supracultural category, which may be acceptable to some Islamic theologians but can scarcely be accepted as a thoroughly Christian view. To bracket God from culture is an effective denial of the Incarnation, whereby Jesus stepped into our history—into human culture—as a particular man. In fact, it is a misunderstanding not only of the revelation of Christ but also of all revelation. The Christian view of revelation is that God has revealed Himself through all the particularities of language and culture. We do not affirm, as the Muslims do, a book of revelation that is untouched by human culture and experience.

To place God in a supracultural category also unduly separates the Holy Spirit from the church, which is being empowered to live out the gospel in real, historic settings. Niebuhr's theological input only emerges as historical reflections on the internal disagreements among Christians about how to be faithful to Christ while inhabiting the "world of values" constructed by human civilization. Thus, theology never informs Niebuhr's understanding of culture itself.

Second, *Niebuhr's entire perspective on culture assumes a Christendom framework.* This is the central criticism of Niebuhr offered by John Yoder in his "How H. Richard Niebuhr Reasoned," as well as by Craig Carter in his illuminating book, *Rethinking Christ and Culture: A Post-Christendom Perspective.*[16] Niebuhr wrote in the heyday of neoliberal Protestantism, when the Protestant church still dominated public life in America. He wrote before the fragmentation of Western culture, the breakup of the *corpus Christianum*, and the emergence of a dizzying array of "hyphenated theologies."[17] Carter points out that in Niebuhr's book, Christendom is taken for granted, and he "assumes that Christendom is real, permanent, and on the whole a good thing." Liberal Protestantism was at the zenith of its cultural influence, and it saw Niebuhr's book as a "justification of its cultural leadership, as well as a call for it to continue."[18]

---

16. John Yoder, "How H. Richard Niebuhr Reasoned: A Critique of Christ and Culture," in *Authentic Transformation: A New Vision of Christ and Culture,* ed. Glen H. Stassen (Nashville: Abingdon, 1996); Craig A. Carter, *Rethinking Christ and Culture: A Post-Christendom Perspective* (Grand Rapids: Brazos, 2006).

17. The phrase "hyphenated theologies" refers to the emergence of particularistic theologies (often denoted in their earliest expression as a hyphenated prefix to the word theology) that saw all theology as biased, such as feminist theology, black theology, dalit theology, minjung theology, liberation theology, etc.

18. Carter, *Rethinking Christ and Culture,* 56–57.

Niebuhr's book also appeared at the time when conservative Christians were eager to challenge the hegemony of Protestant liberalism in the public square and Roman Catholics were about to enter into a renewed engagement with society through Vatican II. Thus, most Christian traditions in North America were optimistic about the church's role in society and, therefore, could only read Niebuhr from the perspective of those who occupied an influential role at the center of public life. With the collapse of Christendom, the fragmentation of the Western church, and the emergence of a post-Christian West, Niebuhr's perspective is increasingly problematic as a viable way to engage the discussion in the twenty-first century.

Third, the *cogency of Niebuhr's argument requires a monocultural perspective and, therefore, is increasingly unpersuasive within the context of twenty-first-century multiculturalism.* Niebuhr lived at a time when most Americans still perceived their society in a homogenous way. The image of America as the great cultural "melting pot" had not yet given way to the image of the "tossed salad." Literature of the time unashamedly regarded America as a "promised land" that celebrated cultural assimilation (*e pluribus unum*), rather than encouraging people to retain their cultural particularities. The image of immigrants passing through Ellis Island under the shadow of the Statue of Liberty seeking a new beginning remains a treasured image in the American psyche. The civil rights movement in the United States (1954–1968) occurred *after* Niebuhr published *Christ and Culture*. Only then were Americans confronted with the troubling fact that many had been brought to these shores on slave ships and for them America was no promised land. In short, the United States of the 1950s was far less aware of the cultural diversity that was already present in its midst and had not yet experienced the dramatic rise in cultural diversity that emerged after the 1965 Immigration Reform Act, which dramatically changed ethnic diversity in North America.

The monoculturalism of Niebuhr is particularly evident in his discussion of culture. He begins by correctly pointing out that even though we need to understand culture as a general concept, it "appears only in particular forms." However, he goes on to say that a Christian in the West "cannot think about the problem save in western terms." This statement assumes that the West reflects a single cultural perspective out of which we all commonly understand and experience culture. Niebuhr envisions a world with many cultures, but none multicultural. He inhabits the center of what appears, from his perspective, to be a monocultural society. Niebuhr believes that cultural values are created and maintained by the single, dominant group that occupies the center of the culture. He says there is a "particular society or a particular class in that society which tends to regard itself as the center and source of value, seeking to achieve what is good for it, though justifying that endeavor by claiming for itself a special status as the representative of something universal."[19] When Niebuhr uses the word *culture,* he means an unarticulated but cherished notion of a particular high culture in which certain values in art, literature, and philosophy are promoted and protected by a dominant core on behalf of the rest. Today, this idea is not only considered too narrow an understanding of culture, but it is actually viewed as destructive because it deprives others the dignity of their own voice and values. Thus, Niebuhr's cultural analysis breaks down in a truly multicultural, postmodern society that is no longer dominated by a central set of commonly shared values.

Fourth, *Niebuhr's conception of culture is not set within an eschatological framework that sees the future as already breaking in to the present order.* Central to Jesus' message is the announcement of the inbreaking of God's kingdom: "The kingdom of God is near" (Mark 1:15). The inbreaking of God's rule has implications for the whole of human reality. In fact, nothing can finally be understood or explained apart from it. The rule of God is not merely a future event but one that already has begun to break into *this world.* Niebuhr never articulates an understanding of the Holy Spirit as God's empowering presence bringing the New Creation into the present order. Instead, his secularized view of culture, which puts God in a supracultural category, robs his entire project of the eschatological perspective that is so central to all Christian thinking. For example, Niebuhr says that "culture in all its forms and varieties is concerned with the temporal and material realization of values."[20] He goes on to acknowledge that even though not all values are purely materialistic, in a modern society they must be understood within the larger context of pluralism. Niebuhr says,

Among the many values the kingdom of God may be included—though scarcely as the one pearl of great price. Jesus Christ and God

---

19. Niebuhr, *Christ and Culture,* 36.
20. Ibid.

the Father, the gospel, the church, and eternal life may find places in the cultural complex, but only as elements in the great pluralism.[21]

When Niebuhr speaks of pluralism, he is not referring to ethnic, cultural diversity, as the word is sometimes used today. By pluralism, Niebuhr is referring to the tension between Christians, who live "under the authority of Christ," and those who only embrace "economic or biological interpretations of culture."[22] However, Niebuhr's understanding of culture insists that even this kind of pluralism ultimately must find common cause in the advancement of human self-realization, rather than any eschatological promise of the New Creation. Niebuhr says,

> It seems self-evident in culture that animals are to be domesticated or annihilated so far as these measures serve man's good, that God or the gods are to be worshiped so far as this is necessary or desirable for the sake of maintaining and advancing human life, that ideas and ideals are to be served for the sake of human self-realization.[23]

Thus, Niebuhr's only eschatology is an overly realized one within the rather narrow frame of human self-realization. This search for what is "good for man" is, for Niebuhr, the "dominant work of culture," rendering his project more utilitarian than fully biblical.[24]

In conclusion, a more biblical theology of culture is needed if we are to effectively negotiate the challenges of a postcolonial, post-Christendom context of multiculturalism. Unfortunately, the church on the whole has not provided a distinctively Christian perspective on culture, and the life of the church largely mirrors the wider cultural trends, accepting its unspoken assumptions in nearly every respect. A neglected or poorly conceived theology of culture also has had deleterious effects on missionary engagement, whether initiated by the West or by the Majority World. We will now propose an alternative model.

---

21. Ibid., 39.
22. Ibid., 38–39.
23. Ibid., 35.
24. Ibid. A humanitarian, utilitarian model of culture always seeks to avoid human pain. However, in the Christian worldview the redemptive nature of suffering and the importance of sharing in the suffering of others is central.

A TRINITARIAN VIEW OF CULTURE

In 1954, Alfred Krober and Clyde Kluckhohn, in their *Culture: A Critical Review of Concepts and Definitions,* identified 164 different definitions of culture. Today the number of published, distinctive definitions of culture has nearly doubled from the time of the 1954 survey. Clearly one of the challenges in understanding culture is that it, in the words of one writer, encompasses everything from "pig-farming to Picasso, from tilling the soil to splitting the atom."[25] Therefore, our development of a Trinitarian theology of culture must proceed carefully. We will develop the proposal in three stages. First, we will briefly examine the emergence of the modern notion of culture and how it has been expressed by anthropologists. Many important insights gained by the social sciences can assist us in our understanding of culture. Second, we will explore how a Christian perspective on culture overlaps with, and yet is distinguished from, those views. While learning from the social sciences, there are fundamental differences in the methodology and foundations of cultural anthropology, as it is understood as a discipline. We must be able to identify those differences and articulate precisely the distinctiveness of Christian understanding of culture. Finally, the broad outlines of a Trinitarian model will be explored, followed by a proposed "New Creation" model for cultural engagement.

Anthropological Understandings of Culture

The origin of the modern concept of culture often is traced back to the German thinker Johann Gottfried von Herder, a contemporary of Immanuel Kant. Even though he rarely used the word *culture,* Herder was fascinated with the "unalikeness of human societies" and "the sheer variety of human experience."[26] Although Herder began with an interest in capturing the genius, essence, or character of what it meant to be a German, he soon developed an almost mystical devotion to the principle of cultural diversity. He celebrated variety in all kinds of societies because he believed that human nature put "tendencies towards diversity in our hearts."[27] Herder is credited with pioneering the concept that there are features within societies that cause its members to "belong to themselves."

---

25. Eagleton, *The Idea of Culture,* 1.

26. Fred Inglis, *Culture* (Malden, MA: Polity, 2004), 11.

27. J. G. Herder, *Herder on Social and Political Culture,* trans. and ed. F. M. Barnard (Cambridge: Cambridge University Press, 1969), 186.

For Herder, every culture finds its identity through the shared experiences of the community, the *volk*. It is the *community* that determines the way people think, formulate values, clothe themselves, talk, develop aesthetic and moral sensibilities, and so forth.

For Herder, the concept of culture is closely tied to national identity or a particular civilization. A nation is like a large, extended family with a shared language and history. Since each expression of culture is intimately tied to the life of a particular people that exhibited a single "national character," he believed that each country should avoid "a wild mixing of various nationalities under one scepter."[28] Thus, despite his fascination with the particularities of cultural identity, Herder explicitly rejected the modern notion of multiculturalism. In short, he was enthusiastic about a culturally diverse *world* but not about a culturally diverse *society*.

The emergence of the word *culture* as a technical term to describe this shared community identity of thought and behavior is often attributed to the pioneer British anthropologist of the late nineteenth century Edward Tylor. In 1871 Tylor published a groundbreaking book entitled *Primitive Culture*, which defined culture and is still used as a starting point for many anthropologists today. He defined culture as,

> that complex whole which includes knowledge, belief, art, law, morals, custom, and any other capacities and habits acquired by man as a member of society.[29]

There are several dimensions of Tylor's understanding of culture that continue to influence contemporary anthropologists. First, culture is a *universal feature of human communities*. There are no communities without culture. There was a time when the word *culture* was used narrowly to refer to a particular "cultured" people with a refined appreciation for the arts and literature. The English word *culture* is derived from the Latin verb *colere* (to cultivate or instruct) and the noun *cultus* (cultivation or training), which tended to reinforce this narrow conception. This often created a false dichotomy between culture and nature that perceived some civilizations, or

---

28. Bhikhu Parekh, *Rethinking Multiculturalism: Cultural Diversity and Political Theory* (New York: Palgrave, 2000), 71.
29. Edward B. Tylor, *Primitive Culture*, vol. 1 (London: Murray, 1871), 1.

groups within particular societies, as cultured and others as primitive.[30] However, Tylor helped to establish the recognition that culture is a universal feature of all human communities.

Second, *cultures are differentiated from one another* because of differences in shared experiences, language, and history. No two cultures are identical. Anthropologists have disagreed about whether there are certain unifying cultural traits that are shared by all cultures, but virtually all have agreed that there are thousands of distinct, identifiable cultures in the world. Third, culture is *identified with learned behavioral patterns* and generally is not identified with our biological inheritance. Tylor's definition refers to "acquired habits" and is the basis for his important distinction between "biologically inherited and social acquired behaviors."[31] For example, a child born of Chinese parents but raised entirely in Nigeria by Nigerian parents would become inculturated into Nigerian society in a strikingly similar fashion as the indigenous Nigerians. Thus, the term *culture* seeks to capture the "complex whole," including everything that is not genetically transmissible.

Finally, every culture *is dynamic, adaptive, and changing*. Although culture is an overall stabilizing force in society, cultures are able to change and to adapt as its members adjust to new or perceived realities. Cultures are not all equally open to change, and certainly no two cultures change at the same pace. But because culture is bound up with human experience, newly acquired knowledge, social change, and, potentially, interactions with other cultures, then cultures are always subject to change and modification over time.

Anthropologists generally accept the broad "way of life" approach of Tylor, even if they continue to debate which elements within a culture are most determinative in shaping cultural identity. Some focus on historical processes, and others focus on the formation of mental perceptions, while still others focus on language or symbols.[32] Furthermore, some of Tylor's nineteenth-century views are widely rejected by anthropologists today,

---

30. For a helpful discussion on how the use of the term *culture* was broadened beyond the framework of "high" and "low" culture identified with particular classes, see John Frow, *Cultural Studies and Cultural Value* (Oxford: Clarendon, 1995).
31. John H. Bodley, *Cultural Anthropology: Tribes, States and the Global System* (Mountain View, CA: Mayfield, 1997), 9.
32. These different emphases are sometimes characterized with the three phrases "what they think, what they do, and the material artifacts they produce."

such as his belief that culture is a distinctively human phenomenon.[33] Nevertheless, the broad contours of Tylor's views continue to shape the discipline today.

Broadly speaking, Christian anthropologists have adopted an anthropological understanding of culture as a starting point for their own understanding of culture. For example, Paul Hiebert, a well-known Christian anthropologist, defines culture as,

> the more or less integrated system of ideas, feelings, and values and their associated patterns of behavior and products shared by a group of people who organize and regulate what they think, feel and do.[34]

This definition could easily find acceptance among many secular anthropologists. The methodology employed by many Christian missiologists is to use the social sciences as a common starting point and then modify it as needed when it comes into conflict with biblical norms. There is a long-standing and genuine debate among missiologists about the viability of this method, and fully exploring this debate goes beyond the scope of this chapter. [35] However, regardless of one's views about the relative compatibility between the disciplines of missiology and the social sciences, it is vital that we identify the four main areas in which the common anthropological understanding of culture stands in conflict with the Christian understanding.

Christian Perspectives on Culture

First, *Christians affirm that God is the source and sustainer of both physical and social culture.* By virtue of His triune reality, God is inherently relational, and human relationships, endowed by Him at creation, represent a reflection of His presence in creation itself. The Christian belief in the objective reality of God, who is beyond all human cultures and yet has

---

33. It has been demonstrated with reasonable certainty, for example, that some animals are able to communicate meaning, achieve goals despite opposition, and socialize their young into a larger collective identity.
34. Paul G. Hiebert, *Anthropological Insights for Missionaries* (Grand Rapids: Baker, 1985), 30.
35. For an overview of the debate, see Edward Rommen and Gary Corwin, eds., *Missiology and the Social Sciences: Contributions, Cautions and the Conclusions,* Evangelical Missiological Society series 4 (Pasadena, CA: William Carey Library, 1996).

chosen to reveal Himself in humans, who are created in His image, as well as within the particularities of culture remains a fundamental distinction between Christian anthropology and its secular counterpart.

Because the discipline of anthropology is limited to studying human beings within a closed natural system, God is generally denied, ignored, or treated as a fleeting projection of human social construction. For example, sociologist Donald Horne, in *The Public Culture*, invites his readers to embrace an "enlightened skepticism" whereby we "create 'realities' that divert our attention from the meaninglessness of existence."[36] Culture, for Horne, can never rise above the watermark of socially constructed frameworks because, he says plainly, "There is no supernatural."[37] Anthropologist Jeff Lewis concurs, arguing that Christianity, in particular, emerged because of its ability to provide "social consolation" for those who were subjugated and downtrodden.[38] Quite obviously, this perspective is fundamentally at odds with the Christian conception of reality.

Second, *Christians affirm the objective reality of sin, rooted in the doctrine of the Fall, which has both personal and collective implications for human society.* For Christians, human sinfulness, rooted in our common identity in Adam's rebellion, is a universal norm that has implications for every culture in the world. On the one hand, the Bible affirms the goodness of creation, validating the beauty and complexity of human cultures. On the other hand, the Bible also acknowledges the far-reaching effects of sin, which has alienated us not only from God but also from one another and from creation itself. Human cultures, therefore, are simultaneously a sign of God's creative design as well as a manifestation of human sin, which stands in opposition to God's rule.

Anthropologists, in contrast, are well known for having no doctrine of sin. Once God is reduced to a social construct, then there is no transcultural, metaphysical place to posit a doctrine of sin. Of course, this does not mean that anthropologists do not seek to understand the *meaning* that a belief in the creation-fall-redemption narrative may hold within a culture's wider religious construction. The point, however, is that the whole discussion is carefully kept within the subjective framework of a closed

---

36. Donald Horne, *The Public Culture* (London: Pluto, 1994), 25.
37. Ibid., 26.
38. Jeff Lewis, *Cultural Studies: The Basics* (London: Sage, 2002), 297.

system. Clifford Geertz, in his *The Interpretation of Cultures*, devotes considerable attention to exploring what he calls a "religious perspective" within cultures. However, for Geertz, this is merely another social construct that must be studied alongside a scientific perspective, an aesthetic perspective, or a commonsense perspective.[39]

Third, *Christians affirm that God has revealed Himself within the context of human culture.* God's revelation does not occur in a cultural vacuum apart from the particularities of culture. God has revealed Himself to men and women through the medium of human language and various cultural forms in specific cultural contexts. The biblical narratives emerged in the midst of a wide variety of cultures in the Mediterranean world. Abraham's call and identity occurred within and was shaped by the ancient cultures of Ur and Chaldea. Later, God revealed Himself to the descendents of Abraham in the midst of Egyptian culture. The Son of God became incarnate in Jesus of Nazareth, who was a full participant in the Jewish and Hellenistic cultures of the first century.

Revelation in Christianity has both an objective and a subjective dimension. Objectively, revelation represents God's free act of self-disclosure. God is the subject of revelation, and it occurs solely out of His gracious initiative. Revelation comes *to* us; it does not arise *from* us. In that sense, the revelation of God represents a transcultural message that originates outside of all cultures. However, revelation also has a subjective dimension. God's self-disclosure encounters us in the midst of particular events and comes through particular people who are fully embedded in human cultures. People appropriate and bear witness to God's revelation within specific cultural contexts. Even the most basic Christian affirmation, "Jesus is Lord," can be articulated only through the medium of some specific language spoken by someone within a particular cultural setting. Furthermore, the meaning of that affirmation must be applied and explored within all of the variegated realities of human culture. Thus, revelation is simultaneously an objective occurrence and a subjective experience. On the one hand, this means that God's free act of self-disclosure can be misunderstood and distorted by those to whom it is given. On the other hand, it also means that God's revelation perpetually stands as an objective basis for judging and/or affirming all cultures. John Calvin compared

---

39. Clifford Geertz, *The Interpretation of Cultures* (New York: Basic Books, 1973), 110.

revelation to those with poor eyesight receiving glasses that enable them to see God, the world, and themselves in a radically new manner.[40] Secular anthropologists deny the objective reality of divine self-disclosure, including both the revelation of Scripture and God's supreme revelation in the incarnation of Jesus Christ. This represents a fundamental line of demarcation separating a Christian anthropology from a secular one.

Fourth, *Christians affirm that a future, eschatological culture, known as the New Creation, already has broken into the present.* For Christians, the resurrection of Jesus Christ does not mark the end of the redemptive narrative but the starting point of a whole new order. Secular anthropologists can understand and accept the emergence of a first-century itinerant Jewish preacher who teaches a new ethic of love and self-sacrifice. There is an epistemological place in anthropology for new, even radical, teaching that attracts followers and changes how people think, behave, and perceive the world. However, the Christian claim reaches far beyond this. Christians claim that a new and future history already has begun to break into the present. There are no historical or cultural analogies for this, so it is beyond the remit of secular anthropological studies.

Jesus Christ, as the risen Lord, is the firstfruits of this New Creation. Those who are in Christ become partakers of, and participants in, the inbreaking of this eschatological reality, which has been inaugurated but not yet fully consummated. This is why Paul declares, "If anyone is in Christ, the New Creation has come" (2 Cor. 5:17 TNIV). Christians are distinctive in that we interpret culture within this larger eschatological framework. We are full participants in the culture of our birth and perhaps other adoptive cultures. However, we also can say with the apostle Paul that our "citizenship is in heaven" (Phil. 3:20). Paul was not merely referring to some future time after death when he would go to heaven. Paul understood that his future identity as a citizen of heaven already shaped and formed his present identity, which included, among other things, his citizenship in the Roman Empire (Acts 16:37–38; 22:27–28). However, it is also clear that this new reality has not been fully manifested. So, we continue to live simultaneously within the context of both realities.

These four realities of God, sin, revelation, and New Creation all have

---

40. John Calvin, *Institutes of the Christian Religion*, vol. 1 (1.6.1.), trans. Henry Beveridge (Grand Rapids: Eerdmans, 1957), 64.

dramatic implications for the formulation of a Christian anthropology. Nevertheless, there are innumerable insights from the discipline of secular anthropology that have greatly enriched missiological reflection. For example, our understanding of the dynamics of cross-cultural communication theory and cultural adaptation has been greatly enhanced by the insights of anthropology. Anthropologists have taught us valuable differences between egalitarian and kinship-based societies, which, in turn, have enabled Christian communicators to be far more effective than they otherwise would have been. Many more examples could be offered, and indeed chapters 11–13 will provide ample evidence of my indebtedness to the discipline of anthropology in a wide range of areas. My central concern is whether secular anthropology can really provide an adequate *foundation* for Christian anthropology to build upon, even if Christians make the necessary modifications along the way.

I think a more constructive way ahead is to establish a thoroughly *theological foundation* for anthropology and then, once that is established, freely bring into this biblical framework as many insights from secular anthropology as we deem beneficial. There is nothing wrong with "plundering the Egyptians" (Exod. 3:22; 12:36). I just want to make sure that the discipline of anthropology is hewing wood and carrying water for *us*, so that we Christians are not always struggling to steer clear of the fallacious presuppositions and parochialism inherent in the closed worldview of anthropology. This task is not easy, and it requires that the triune God and the *missio dei* be kept at the heart of our missiology, even in the midst of the most practical areas of missionary training and preparation. The remainder of this chapter will be devoted to sketching the broad outlines of a theology of culture that will provide the basis for thinking about anthropology from a Christian perspective.

A Trinitarian Framework for Forming a Theology of Culture

It is the presupposition of this book that we cannot properly understand the larger cosmos or the particular cultural realities in which we find ourselves apart from the triune God. The Trinity is not merely a metaphysical puzzle that concerns a few erudite theologians; it is the lens through which reality is finally understood and exposed. Ultimately, all reality is rooted in and flows forth from God Himself, even as Paul affirmed when he said, "In him we live and move and have our being" (Acts 17:28).

The historic difficulty Western Christians have faced in applying the Trinity to practical disciplines such as missiology is that our primary historical frame of reference concerning the Trinity is the ecumenical councils that first articulated the doctrine of the Trinity. The overriding concern of these councils was to explore whether or not Jesus Christ and, later, the Holy Spirit were God Himself or belonged "to some lower order of divine reality."[41] In short, the focus was on the ontology and inner reality of God's being, not on practical applications of the doctrine. The technical language that was required to separate the church from various heretical challenges (e.g., monophysitism, adoptionism, Arianism, etc.) has, at times, intimidated Christians from the ongoing theological work that fully applies the doctrine to the life and work of the church. When properly understood, the Trinity should be seen not merely as a conceptual grid through which we understand culture, but as God's own living and loving witness to our participation in His creation as members of particular cultures that have been endowed with His glory and presence.

THE FATHER AS THE SOURCE, REDEEMER, AND FINAL GOAL OF CULTURE

The biblical witness is framed by God's creation of the heavens and the earth (Gen. 1) and the account of the new heaven and the new earth (Rev. 21). Thus, all of human history and culture falls within the parameters of God's creative and sustaining acts. In the first creation, God sets the man and woman in the garden of Eden to work and care for it (Gen. 2:15). They are called to be "fruitful and increase in number" and to "fill the earth and subdue it" (1:28). All the features of culture are present in Eden in seed form, including language, symbols, communication, relationality, sedentization, domestication, and meaningful work. Later developments such as urbanization, industrialization, state formation, and even globalization are all complex extensions of this original culture. Paul later notes the significance of Eden in understanding human history when he says, "From one man he made all the nations, that they should inhabit the whole earth; and he marked out their appointed times in history and the boundaries of their lands" (Acts 17:26 TNIV).

Thus, Scripture views God as the author of human culture. God is not a cultural outsider who occasionally intervenes or interrupts the otherwise

---

41. Jaroslav Pelikan, *The Christian Tradition: A History of the Development of Doctrine*, vol. 1, *The Emergence of the Catholic Tradition (100–600)* (Chicago: University of Chicago Press, 1971), 173.

autonomous process of human history. Rather, Scripture presents God as intimately involved in the world. The psalmist declares, "The earth is the LORD's, and everything in it, the world, and all who live in it" (Ps. 24:1). Paul declares of God, "He has not left himself without testimony: He has shown kindness by giving you rain from heaven and crops in their seasons; he provides you with plenty of food and fills your hearts with joy" (Acts 14:17).

As noted above, sin distorts God's original plan and purpose for creation, and the effects of sin can be observed not only in individuals but also throughout all cultural systems. As René Padilla has observed,

> Man's problem in the world is not simply that he commits isolated sins or gives in to the temptation of particular vices. It is, rather, that he is imprisoned within a closed system of rebellion against God, a system that conditions him to absolutize the relative and to relativize the absolute, a system whose mechanism of self-sufficiency deprives him of eternal life and subjects him to the judgment of God.[42]

The result is that all of creation is "groaning" as it awaits liberation from its bondage. In short, not only individuals, but also the entire cosmos, are awaiting redemption. Central to our understanding of the *missio dei* is that God has taken the initiative to act on behalf of the redemption of the entire world. One of the dangers in post-Enlightenment thought that we explored in chapter 4 is the tendency to parochialize God's redemptive acts, seeing them only through the lens of the individual. However, as we explored in chapters 4 and 5, central to both the Abrahamic covenant and the Great Commission passages is the affirmation that God is on a mission to bless entire people groups (Gen. 12:3) and to disciple the nations (Matt. 28:18–20). The culmination of that promise finds its fulfillment in the New Creation.

As explored in chapter 5, God is a sending God. However, it should be clear that whether God the Father is sending prophets, Jesus Christ, the Holy Spirit, or His church into the world, His ultimate purpose is to draw entire peoples and cultures and, indeed, the entire cosmos into communion with His divine life. This is why human history climaxes in the full

---

42. C. Rene Padilla, "Evangelism and the World," in *Let the Earth Hear His Voice*, ed. J. D. Douglas (Minneapolis: World Wide, 1975), 120.

revelation of the New Creation. John captures a glimpse of the eschaton in his apocalyptic vision recorded in Revelation. John does not see disembodied souls or some generic gathering of the redeemed. Instead, he sees men and women "from every nation, tribe, people and language, standing before the throne and in front of the Lamb" (Rev. 7:9). In short, John sees men and women in all their cultural particularities. They take their place in the culture of the New Creation. The new heaven and the new earth are filled with God's glory. John tells us that the nations of the world will "walk by its light" and "the glory and the honor of the nations will be brought into it" (Rev. 21:23–26). Every culture in the world is ultimately validated, judged, and redeemed through the revelation of the New Creation.

THE SON'S EMBODIMENT IN HUMAN CULTURE
The Apostles' and Nicene Creeds move directly from the birth of Christ to His passion: The Apostles' Creed declares, "He was born of the virgin Mary and suffered under Pontius Pilate." Similarly, the Nicene Creed declares, "He came down from heaven and was incarnate from the Holy Spirit and the virgin Mary, and became man. He was crucified for us under Pontius Pilate, and suffered and was buried." In both of these historic creeds, the life of Jesus between His incarnation and His passion is curiously neglected. It is probably not surprising that a creed that is intended to focus on the most crucial elements of salvation history proceeds in this fashion. Indeed, some have even argued, incorrectly, that the Gospels are all essentially passion narratives with long introductions. However, the creeds should not lead us to the conclusion that the life of Jesus is not theologically important. From a missiological perspective, it is important to recognize the theological significance of the entire life of Jesus as a full participant in human culture.

We have demonstrated that a theology of culture must be related to the doctrines of creation and New Creation, which flow out of the Father's initiative. It is also essential that a theology of culture be properly related to a biblical Christology. In the face of numerous challenges attacking a real incarnation, the Council of Chalcedon in A.D. 451 issued a carefully worded position that continues to serve as the orthodox position on Christology.[43] On the one hand, Chalcedon insisted on two separate natures that

---

43. The full Chalcedonian statement is as follows: "Therefore, following the holy fathers, we all with one accord teach men to acknowledge one and the same Son, our Lord Jesus Christ, at

are not merged or suppressed by the union. Maintaining two separate natures allows biblical Christology to affirm the full, eternal deity of Christ without compromising an equally robust affirmation of a real, historical incarnation whereby the Son of God enters into specific history. Jesus is not a semidivine demigod. He is neither an exalted angel nor a divinized man. Chalcedon declares that Jesus is fully God and fully man, without compromise. On the other hand, Chalcedon insisted that the two separate natures were, in fact, united into one person. The council made it clear that the human nature of Christ did not possess an existence *independent from* the union with the divine person.[44]

Chalcedonian Christology has important implications for a theology of culture. This insistence on a true union of the divine and human natures into one person keeps the church from overly spiritualizing the Incarnation and disconnecting the Son of God from human experience. It guarantees a high view of creation and human culture. It also reminds us of the theological significance of Jesus' entire life, not just His birth and passion. Jesus' temptation and hunger in the wilderness (Matt. 4:1–2), His attendance at the wedding at Cana (John 2:1), and His enjoyment of a meal at the homes of Matthew (Matt. 9:10) and Zacchaeus (Luke 19:5) all become theologically significant.

There are two major implications drawn from the life of Jesus that are crucial for formulating a theology of culture. First, the life of Jesus as concretely revealed in real history is God the Father's *validation of the sanctity of human culture*. This should not be viewed as a kind of tangential

---

once complete in Godhead and complete in manhood, truly God and truly man, consisting also of a reasonable soul and body; of one substance (*homoousios*) with the Father as regards his Godhead, and at the same time of one substance with us as regards his manhood; like us in all respects, apart from sin; as regards his Godhead, begotten of the Father before the ages, but yet as regards his manhood begotten, for us men and for our salvation, of Mary the Virgin, the God bearer (Theotokos); one and the same Christ, Son, Lord, only-begotten, recognized in two natures, without confusion, without change, without division, without separation; the distinction of the natures in no way annulled by the union, but rather the characteristics of each nature being preserved and coming together to form one person and subsistence, not as parted and separated into two persons, but one and the same Son and only-begotten God the Word, Lord Jesus Christ; even as the prophets from earliest times spoke of him, and our Lord Jesus Christ himself taught us, and the creed of the Fathers has handed down to us" 451 A.D., Actio V. Mansi. (See Henry Bettenson, ed., *Documents of the Christian Church* [New York: Oxford University Press, 1977], 51–52.)

44. Paul Louis Metzger, *The Word of Christ and the World of Culture* (Grand Rapids: Eerdmans, 2003), 45.

application of the Incarnation but as central to our understanding of what Chalcedon meant by affirming the identity of Jesus as fully God and fully man. In the Incarnation, the Son of God's history intersects in specific ways with human history. There were those who wanted to assert an *anhypostasis*—a belief that Jesus took on humanity but not a specific human personality. However, as Andrew Walls has noted, "The incarnation is not just that God became a man, but that He became a *particular* man."[45] There is no generic incarnation. Jesus entered the history and culture of a particular group at a particular time. Jesus learned and spoke the languages of His time, and He fully entered into all the particularities of the Jewish culture in which He grew up. Jesus ate the same food as His contemporaries. He attended a wedding. He laughed and cried. He did not just walk on the vague sands of time; He walked on the real sands by the Sea of Galilee. Jesus is not like the passing, ephemeral avatars of Hinduism. Jesus fully steps into our history and becomes God the Father's supreme example of what it means to be fully human, to live in history and to participate in culture. The life of Jesus models for all cultures what it means to fully realize our true humanity. The Incarnation is, therefore, not only a revelation of *God* to humanity but also a revelation of *humanity* to humanity. In Jesus Christ we are learning what it means to be *fully human*. As Duane Friesen has said, "In Jesus we find God and our humanity most vividly illuminated."[46]

The life of Jesus not only affirms our humanity; it also encourages us to affirm the rich particularities of our cultural histories. In the modern period, there have been theologians who argued that because of the kerygmatic nature of the Gospels we can know nothing about the actual historical Jesus. Others have created an undue separation between real history (*historie*) and salvation history (*geschichte*). At times evangelicals also have spoken in ways that separate God from history, especially when assumptions are made that the gospel inhabits some acultural plane of existence or that the real significance of Jesus' work is found in heavenly transactions apart from history. However, in Jesus Christ, the Word and the world meet, time and eternity intersect, and transcendence and im-

---

45. Andrew F. Walls, *The Missionary Movement in Christian History: Studies in the Transmission of Faith* (Maryknoll, NY: Orbis, 1996), 27.

46. Duane K. Friesen, *Artists, Citizens and Philosophers: Seeking the Peace of the City* (Scottdale, PA: Herald, 2000), 109.

manence find common ground. The Incarnation, therefore, represents God's embrace of human culture.

Second, the life of Jesus as concretely revealed in Jesus of Nazareth provides *the basis for cultural critique.* The Chalcedonian insistence on the separation of the two natures provides the theological basis for a cultural critique. The Incarnation is the ultimate act of cultural translation. By translating deity into humanity, God enters into a fallen world without compromise. The very fact that God entered into human history protects us from complete ethical despair, even when we are reminded daily of the utter sinfulness of the world. Christ's very presence reminds us of the promise that "in your seed all the nations of the earth shall be blessed" (Gen. 22:18 NASB). This is why a biblical theology of culture must begin by affirming culture and rejecting all docetic, separationist views of culture, which do not make sufficient cultural space for the actual inbreaking of the New Creation into the present world. The true union of God and man in one person is the ultimate rebuke against the *secularization of culture.* Nevertheless, once that is said, we also must guard against an uncritical *divinization of culture,* which provides no basis for critique. The fact that Jesus had two distinct natures that were not merged means that the eternal God who transcends all human cultures enters into the cultural context of humanity without corruption or defilement. As John declares, "The Word became flesh and made his dwelling among us. We have seen his glory, the glory of the One and Only, who came from the Father, full of grace and truth" (John 1:14).

Every culture manifests examples of human alienation from God and antagonism toward His divine rule. The Holocaust in the heart of Christian Europe, the atrocities of Pol Pot and the Khmer Rouge in Buddhist Cambodia, the horrific ethnic genocides in Rwanda and the Balkans, and the acts of Islamic terrorism on 9/11 all provide ample testimony to the depth of evil in the world. However, the failure of culture lies not just in these examples of horrific evil, which from time to time are paraded across our television sets. There is an even deeper malady whereby cultural systems conspire to promote the commercialization of life, the disenfranchisement of the poor and the oppressed, and the cynical replacement of eternal values with the commoditization of modern existence.

Christianity recognizes that behind the world's rejection of God lie spiritual forces that are hostile to both God and humanity. "The whole world is under the control of the evil one" (1 John 5:19). The "god of this age has blinded the minds of unbelievers" (1 Cor. 4:4). As René Padilla has said, "Apart from faith, men are in subjection to the spirit of the age (the *zeit-geist*) controlled by the prince of the power of the air" (Eph. 2:2).[47] This is why Paul says that "our struggle is not against flesh and blood, but against the rulers, against the authorities, against the powers of this dark world and against the spiritual forces of evil in the heavenly realms" (Eph. 6:12).

In the context of post-Enlightenment Christendom, the struggle against evil was either personalized into the heart of each person or pushed outside of culture into an unseen ephemeral realm. A full realization of the evil in the various cultural structures, including, but not limited to, the erosion of the family, the rise of consumerism, the egoism of political power, the role of money, and the latest voices in philosophy and science, all give evidence that the "whole world is under the control of the evil one" (1 John 5:19).

Secular anthropology is incapable of recognizing the cultural significance of human and satanic rebellion against God. Since the discipline of missiology has, for the most part, been constructed on the foundation of secular anthropology, it is equally incapable of recognizing the scope and depth of the human rebellion that has become entrenched in every aspect of human cultures. Furthermore, because the discipline of anthropology operates within a closed system, there is no proper foundation upon which to think about an eschatological framework within which a Christian perspective on culture must be framed.

In summary, the carefully worded language of Chalcedon safeguards what Duane Friesen calls an "embodied" Christology. He correctly observes that "we need a Christology that can provide a vivid picture of a Christ who is not disembodied from cultural formation, but who is concrete enough to provide leverage for assessing how we should engage the particularities of culture."[48]

We now turn to the third and final component in the construction of a Trinitarian framework for a theology of culture.

THE HOLY SPIRIT AS THE AGENT OF THE NEW CREATION

Because secular anthropology operates within a closed system, it emphasizes that cultural change and development is a process with no end

---

47. Padilla, "Evangelism and the World," 119.
48. Friesen, *Artists, Citizens and Philosophers*, 109.

and no final purpose. Anthropologist Raymond Williams emphasizes this when he states that the cultural process "has no particular end . . . and can never be supposed at any time to have finally realized itself, to have become complete."[49] Building on this foundation has often hindered Christian anthropologists from recognizing the importance of placing our understanding of culture within an eschatological context. Yet, Karl Barth pointed out that a theology of culture should naturally emerge out of our eschatology.[50] Human history is moving toward an appointed end. Secular anthropologists such as Paul Lehman have argued that culture is an ongoing conversation among societies about what makes us human. To a point Christians can agree with this assessment, but we would insist that above the human project, God has acted and continues to act in history, and in the end He is the chief conversationalist.

In the Incarnation, Jesus Christ inaugurates the eschaton; the New Creation breaks into the present order. The New Creation represents the eschatological goal of all cultures. We tend to think of the eschaton as ushering in some kind of nonphysical world, but the New Creation is a completely new kind of world with an even more profound kind of physicality, a new cultural reality that is not subject to decay. The present creation and all the variegated expressions of culture are signposts pointing to the New Creation. N. T. Wright has observed that creation points to a world "which will be *more* physical, more solid, more utterly real, a whole in which the physical reality will wear its deepest meaning on its face, a world filled with the knowledge of God's glory as the waters cover the sea."[51] The New Creation should be understood as the inbreaking of a new and final culture. The New Creation is not ahistorical or beyond history; it is radically and profoundly historical. This puts all earthly cultural expressions in an eschatological context, simultaneously avoiding both the secularization and the divinization of human cultures.

At Pentecost, the Holy Spirit came as the agent of the New Creation. The Holy Spirit continues to summon us into all of the realities of the future order. The "explosion of joy" the church has experienced in the Easter

---

49. Quoted in T. J. Gorringe, *Furthering Humanity: A Theology of Culture* (Burlington, VT: Ashgate, 2004), 4.

50. Karl Barth, *Theology and Church: Shorter Writings 1920–1928*, trans. Louise Pettibone Smith (New York: Harper & Row, 1962), 337.

51. N. T. Wright, *Evil and the Justice of God* (London: SPCK, 2006), 75.

and Pentecost events sends us forth and empowers us to be witnesses of
the New Creation in the midst of a fallen world. The Spirit continues to
catechize the church into the life and ethic of the New Creation, so that we
ourselves are experiencing ongoing transformation. We learn to practice
what Miroslav Volf calls "exclusion and embrace." We increasingly learn
to identify evil in the world, name it, and separate from it. However, we
also increasingly learn how to practice "embrace" as we see signs of repentance in people and nations and the inbreaking of the New Creation.
Finally, because we believe in an inaugurated eschatology, not a fully realized one, we recognize that the world will continue its hostility toward
God's rule, and, therefore, we must be prepared to share in the sufferings
of Christ in this world as we eagerly await the full consummation of the
New Creation at the glorious return of Jesus Christ.

NEW CREATION MODEL OF CULTURE

Review and Critique of Other Models

In order to set the "New Creation" model in context, it is important to
understand how it contrasts with the traditional models provided in missions textbooks. Most books in this field follow some variation of one of
the following approaches.

CULTURE-A-ENCOUNTERS-CULTURE-B APPROACH

This approach conceptualizes the missionary encounter as essentially limited to the encounter between two different human cultures. For example,
a missionary from America goes to Senegal and lives there as a missionary.
The tension is between the norms of American culture and the norms of
Senegalese culture. The missionary, as the "gospel transmitter," is encouraged to adjust, adapt, and become, as much as possible, a cultural insider
with those who belong to the target culture. The missionary works hard
not to extract the Senegalese from their culture but to practice an identi-
ficationalist approach in order to establish a more receptive, empathetic
environment for the gospel to be received.

THREE-CULTURE APPROACH

This approach conceptualizes missions as an engagement among three
separate cultures. The first two are, as in the previous model, represented

by the gospel communicator and those in the target culture. However, this approach acknowledges that the biblical revelation represents a third cultural norm that becomes the standard of cultural evaluation. In this model, cultural forms, symbols, traditions, and practices are evaluated and measured against the Bible and upon that basis are either affirmed or rejected.

GOSPEL-BEYOND-ALL-CULTURE APPROACH

This approach downplays the importance of both the culture of the transmitter and the receptor culture. Instead, the main focus is on the gospel, which transcends any and every culture. The role of the missionary is to communicate the transcultural gospel into the new setting. The gospel does not have, nor does it seek, cultural embodiment since it transcends all cultures. A variation of this approach involves the acceptance of a particular, past cultural embodiment, which then becomes the standard for all other cultures to adopt. Once the particular language, liturgy, or doctrinal formulation of the idealized embodiment has been accepted, then the gospel has been successfully received and reproduced.

CRITIQUE OF THE APPROACHES

A critique of these three models first must be set within the context of an appreciation for what each model has to offer. Indeed, each model is built around a genuine truth. The first model correctly reminds us that we should enter into a culture as a humble learner, rather than extracting people from their cultural moorings. The second model properly admonishes us that a truly missionary encounter is about more than the meeting of two cultures. We need to reflect biblically on all the various expressions of culture we encounter. The third model insightfully reminds us that the gospel does, in fact, sit in judgment over every culture.

However, there are also sufficient problems with each of these models to necessitate an alternative model. We will begin with a critique of each of these models and then propose an alternative model. The first model, "culture A encounters culture B," never rises above what could be found in any secular textbook on cross-cultural communication.[52] Most of the

---

52. See, for example, James W. Neuliep, *Intercultural Communication: A Contextual Approach* (Thousand Oaks, CA: Sage, 2006). The basic understanding of culture outlined in this textbook would be broadly equivalent to what would be found in most standard Christian publications on the same theme.

principles in the various expressions of this model are perfectly valid, but do Christians have anything *else* to say about cross-cultural encounters? Are there not any distinctively Christian elements to communicating the gospel cross-culturally? The second problem with this model is that it emerges out of a nineteenth-century, monocultural conception that frames the tension between the "host" culture and the "target" culture. It speaks about American or Western culture in the singular, presupposing a certain conception of a particular dominant culture in America or the West, as well as a monolithic target culture. However, with the emergence of multiculturalism, which is increasingly a global phenomenon, it is difficult to speak about culture in this way.

The "three-culture" model fails to recognize that cultural expressions cannot be so easily categorized as "good" or "bad." This pick-and-choose approach seems plausible in a classroom setting, but once cultural engagements actually occur, it becomes increasingly problematic. First, it is nearly impossible for a cultural outsider to assess the meaning and significance of many expressions of a culture. Second, human sinfulness and the spiritual powers arrayed against God have left no part of culture untouched. Even cultural expressions that might be readily identified as "good" often become subtly distorted so that what, at creation, was declared "good" can easily become yet another object of false worship. Third, this model seems to only conceptualize individuals encountering other individuals within a culture, thus failing to recognize the influence of larger cultural systems and dynamics within which all of us participate.

The "gospel-beyond-culture" model fails to recognize that the gospel, like the Incarnation itself, must become embodied within culture. An acultural gospel cannot be inserted into a culture from some neutral vantage point. Those who communicate the gospel do so from within their own identity, and those who receive it do so from within their own identity. There is no neutral place that Christians inhabit. Furthermore, the gospel has never been embodied in some ideal way that can now be reproduced in new contexts. When this perspective is employed, it unwittingly becomes an expression of cultural imperialism, even if it idealizes a culture from the distant past.

Key Features of a New Creation Model

With these critiques in mind, there are several criteria that are essential for any alternative model. First, it must be theologically based, and reflect a distinctively Christian perspective. Cultural engagement must be fully grounded in and understood as a natural expression of Christian theology, particularly our understanding of Trinitarianism, creation, Christology, ecclesiology, and eschatology. Second, it must take sin and spiritual warfare seriously, while at the same time eagerly look for ways in which the New Creation may be breaking into the present order. Third, it must realize that the gospel becomes embodied within identifiable cultural particularities.

The broad outline of a "New Creation" model for understanding culture must be built on the Trinitarian framework that has already been set forth. Because God the Father is the source, redeemer, and final goal of culture, we are to celebrate the goodness of God's original design and intention for culture. As noted earlier, all expressions of human culture are framed by the Father's initiative in creation and the New Creation. Because God the Father is both the source and the final goal of all culture, we have placed this discussion within the redemptive initiative of God the Father. God the Father then sends God the Son as the historical embodiment of culture, providing the basis for both the affirmation of culture and the critique of culture. Finally, the Holy Spirit is the agent of the New Creation and is responsible for enabling and empowering the church to live out the realities of the New Creation in the present. The New Creation should be understood as a final culture, in which all of creation finds it ultimate meaning and purpose.

Building upon this foundation, several key components emerge in the New Creation model. First, as Christians, our *primary cultural identity is in the New Creation*. This does not disconnect us from either our home culture or our adopted culture, since we can see signs of the inbreaking of God's rule in every culture. We also recognize the depth of sin in every culture. This gives us a theological basis for rejecting the notion that there is any "Christian" culture that is bringing the gospel to any "non-Christian" culture. The New Creation perspective delivers us from the Christendom mind-set that so often promoted a sense of cultural superiority and triumphalism over the so-called "source" culture.

This also means that we must place the emphasis on cultural adaptation and assimilation, which is so heavily emphasized in missions training, within a larger context. Because of what Lamin Sanneh has rightly identified as the "Western guilt complex" regarding ourselves as cultural agents, we have felt acutely the need to distance ourselves from any possible scent of cultural triumphalism. Therefore, the overwhelming focus has been on the need for cultural adaptation to the target culture. However, as important as this advice is, we often have neglected to emphasize that our first allegiance is to be conformed to the image of Christ and to be ambassadors of the New Creation. The inbreaking of the New Creation into the present is inevitably a *countercultural* force, even though it ultimately serves to validate and to nurture the best in culture.

This "New Creation" model reestablishes the necessary *tension* between the universal realities of the New Creation and the cultural particularities within which we live. Andrew Walls has called this tension the "pilgrim principle" and the "indigenizing principle." The *pilgrim* principle emphasizes our identity in Jesus Christ and our rootedness in the eschatological realities of the New Creation. The *indigenizing* principle reminds us that the gospel really does penetrate the specific particularities of cultural life. The call to cultural adaptation is necessary, and we must always be on guard against cultural imperialism. However, we must recapture the courage to be agents of a prophetic imagination that envisions what is possible when any culture is brought under the lordship of Jesus Christ. Jesus is the model of cultural embodiment. As the second Adam, He was fully embodied within the particularities of culture. Yet, He was an agent of radical transformation as He called the world to repentance and inaugurated the realities of the New Creation into the present order. The witnessing church is a community defined by *metanoia* (repentance) and conversion, and we call all nations to repent and believe the good news because the kingdom of God is at hand (Mark 1:15). Jesus also awakens us to the realities of spiritual warfare, which stand opposed to the inbreaking of God's rule into the world.

Second, we recognize that *ultimate meaning can be found only in the triune God.* Clifford Geertz, one of the leading anthropologists of the twentieth century, observed that culture is ultimately about meaning. He defined culture, in part, as a "historically transmitted pattern of meanings."[53] Christians affirm that God has invested eternal meaning in culture. He is not merely saving individuals and plucking them out of culture. He is

---

53. Geertz, *Interpretation of Cultures,* 89. His full definition of culture is a "historically transmitted pattern of meanings embodied in symbols, a system of inherited conceptions expressed in symbolic forms by means of which people communicate, perpetuate, and develop their knowledge about and attitudes towards life."

calling the nations to repentance (Luke 24:47) and through His church He is discipling entire nations (Matt. 28:19). Christians participate in a "shared story," which is part of a larger grand narrative within the *missio dei,* that we summon all people and cultures to enter into. Through the agency of the Holy Spirit, the entire cosmos eventually will be brought into conformity with the rule and reign of Jesus Christ, to the eternal praise and glory of God the Father. We have a cultural mandate that is part and parcel of our evangelistic mandate. To "be saved" is far more than a legal statement about our justification before God; it is also an increasingly actualized reality as the fruits of the New Creation already begin to break into our present cultural existence. All the particularities of culture must find their ultimate meaning in the triune God. Rather than "picking and choosing" which parts of culture are good and which are bad, we recognize that all the particularities of culture are enhanced or destroyed or enlivened when they are brought under the lordship of Jesus Christ.

Third, the *church is the corporate, community witness to every culture of the New Creation.* We are called, as the church, to live out the future in the present. Even before Christian missionaries enter into a new "target" culture, we are *already participants* in two cultures. We are full participants in the culture(s) of our birth and we are, increasingly, experiencing and becoming partakers in the realities of the New Creation. These two cultures are not hermetically sealed off from one another but are in constant dialogue, with the culture of the New Creation always serving as the agent of cultural transformation. As we encounter new cultures, either because of cultural relocation or simply because of the realities of multiculturalism in our midst, we continue to reflect this ongoing dialogue between the culture of the New Creation and the various expressions of culture around us.

While we continue to affirm the necessity of personal transformation through the gospel, we also recognize that ultimately the reality of the New Creation in the present must become embodied in *communities.* Traditional models of culture continue to envision a nineteenth-century model of a solo missionary who shares the gospel with another individual. This new model recognizes that the gospel must become embodied in communities. It enables us to resist the overwhelming pressure to privatize the gospel and avoid the social and political ramifications inherent in following Christ *as a community* in the midst of a fallen world. This is why church planting must be central to our understanding of what it means to proclaim the gospel in the world. Only the church can embody God's original plan at creation. As Simon Chan has put it, the church is not merely an entity within the larger culture; it *is* a culture.[54] Tragically, the church is often neglected or completely ignored in our traditional understanding of culture. At best it is given only an *instrumental* role in preaching the gospel to a culture. But the church has a greater, *ontological* role in enabling creation to see its own final goal already embodied within a living community.

CONCLUSION

In summary, the New Creation model seeks to reposition our understanding of cultural engagement within a larger, Trinitarian framework. This has several distinct advantages. First, it keeps our discussion concerning culture within the context of the *missio dei*. Second, it places our understanding of human cultures within a theological, rather than a purely secular, framework. It is clear that the doctrines of creation, Christology, ecclesiology, and eschatology all have important contributions to our overall understanding of culture that should not be neglected. Finally, by relating the entire cultural process to the inbreaking of the New Creation, we are able to provide a vantage point from which to prophetically critique and enthusiastically celebrate as the gospel is embodied afresh in a potentially infinite number of new global contexts.

---

54. Simon Chan, *Liturgical Theology* (Downers Grove, IL: IVP Academic, 2006), 8.

— 7 —

An Evangelical Theology
of Religions

I RECALL WITH SOME FONDNESS my introductory typing class in high school back in 1974. Little did I realize when I took the class how much of my life would be spent typing on a keyboard. The typewriters in those days were manual machines that required considerable effort and timing to master. Learning to type normally begins with the "home row" keys, which represent the most frequently used letters in typing. The least used keys are positioned in more remote locations. One of the least used characters, stuck way up at the top of the keyboard above your left hand, was the @ sign. It was used only in the rarest of circumstances, and many of us wondered how it managed to find its way onto the keyboard at all. However, with the advent of e-mail, it quickly went from being the most neglected, somewhat exotic, symbol on the keyboard to its current status as one of the most often used symbols on the board.

This is analogous to the development of the relationship between Christianity and non-Christian religions. Within the long history of Christendom, other religions were remote and out of reach. Religious diversity in the world is ancient, of course. However, the awareness of Western Christians to other religions generally entered their consciousness only as exotic stories from distant lands. Suddenly, with the emergence of globalization, massive shifts in global immigration patterns, the rise of multiculturalism, the dramatic rise of Christianity in the heartlands of non-Christian faiths, and the events surrounding 9/11, the relationship between Christianity and other religions has become one of the most important issues dominating Christian discourse. Islamic mosques, Hindu temples, and Zen meditation centers are now found in nearly every major city in the Western world. With the collapse of Christendom and the rise of relativistic pluralism, postmodernity, and cultural diversity, we are awash in a sea of competing and conflicting truth claims.

Tragically, many seminary and divinity school programs have been slow to respond to this new situation. It is quite astonishing that theological students in the West will spend countless hours learning about the writings of a few well-known, now deceased, German theologians whose global devotees are actually quite small and yet completely ignore over one billion living, breathing Muslims who represent one of the most formidable challenges to the Christian gospel today. Many seminaries and divinity schools still do not require the study of any other religion besides Christianity as a part of their core curriculum. The study of other religions or the development of a theology of religions generally appears only as an elective course and, therefore, is still not considered essential for ministerial training in the twenty-first century.[1] Traditionally, such course work is directed either to those preparing for the mission field or for those interested in the academic study of religion. However, even a seminarian preparing to serve a pastorate in Kansas can no longer afford to ignore these issues. Indeed, it is increasingly evident that all who are interested in Christian leadership today must have a well-articulated, robust theology of religions as a normative part of their theological training.

The field of missiology has long understood the necessity of a theology of religions. However, I highlight this disconnect because it is important that theology become more missiological and missiology become more theological.[2] Today, missiology is serving as a major source of the global theological renewal, and missiology as a discipline is finally becoming more

---

1. For more on this, see my "Ministries for Which We Teach: A World Café Model," in *Revitalizing Practice: Collaborative Models for Theological Faculites,* ed. Malcolm L. Warford (New York: Peter Lang, 2008). I examined more than forty different M.Div. required curriculums across the theological spectrum of ATS membership schools.

2. I have argued this elsewhere in other publications. See, for example, Tennent, *Christianity at the Religious Roundtable: Evangelicalism in Conversation with Hinduism, Buddhism and Islam* (Grand Rapids: Baker Academic, 2002) and *Theology in the Context of World Christianity* (Grand Rapids: Zondervan, 2007).

grounded in theology.[3] These are positive and welcome developments. The purpose of this chapter, therefore, is to explore the broad outlines of an evangelical theology of religions that is relevant to ministry throughout the global context.

After discussing a few introductory matters, the chapter will fall into three major sections. First, the chapter will begin with an exploration of the four most widely held theologies of religion. Second, each of the four positions will be critiqued. Finally, the broad contours of an evangelical theology of religions will be proposed.

PRELIMINARY CONSIDERATIONS

There are two preliminary issues that must be explored at the outset of this study. First, what is the relationship between a theology of culture and a theology of religions? Second, within the context of a Trinitarian missiological framework, why is this theology of religions placed under the larger heading of God the Father?

Theology of Culture and Theology of Religions

Religion, as a common feature of human experience, does not *by necessity* exist outside of specific cultural settings. Among other things, religion involves ideas, symbols, feelings, values, and patterns of behavior. Therefore, religion, like all other expressions of human behavior, falls clearly within the parameters of how culture is defined and understood. So, from this vantage point, a theology of religions could be seen as a subset or particular consideration within a theology of culture. However, there are two reasons I have dedicated a separate chapter to the formation of a theology of religions. First, Christianity claims that the basis of the Christian proclamation is a transcultural source. God the Father is the source of all revelation, whether found in creation, the sending of Jesus Christ into the world, or the biblical texts. A similar claim is made, for example, by Muslims, who claim that the Qur'an has its source in Allah, who transcends all the particularities of Arabic or any other culture. This raises important issues concerning how we understand transcultural

---

3. I am reminded of Andrew Walls's insightful statement during my doctoral studies at the University of Edinburgh, when he said that "theological scholarship needs a renaissance of mission studies."

revelation coming into particular cultural contexts and creates the need for a separate treatment. Second, a whole body of literature has arisen in the last thirty years from within the theological community proposing various theologies of religion. This is quite distinct from the largely anthropological literature, which, for the most part, has dominated our understanding of and analysis of human cultures. To properly respond to this, a separate treatment is required, even though the two themes are related to one another.

Placement Within a Trinitarian Missiology

Biblical revelation makes two central claims about God the Father that are particularly important in placing a theology of religions at this point. First, God the Father is the ultimate source of creation and therefore the sovereign Lord over all that exists. Yahweh is not regarded merely as Israel's sovereign but as the ultimate ruler over all creation and everything in it. For example, Jeremiah proclaims, "Ah, Sovereign Lord, you have made the heavens and the earth by your great power and outstretched arm. Nothing is too hard for you" (Jer. 32:17). Similarly, the psalmist proclaims, "The earth is the Lord's, and everything in it, the world, and all who live in it" (Ps. 24:1). From a biblical perspective, there are no human cultures or societies that lay outside His sovereign rule. At its root Christianity is a declaration of the rule and reign of God. Everything within culture, including religions and their competing assertions affirming or denying God's existence, character, and work, must finally be accredited as true or exposed as false before the final tribunal of God the Father. Christianity as a religion is not above this verdict since all religions can either reflect the reign of God or join with larger cultural forces that stand in opposition to God's rule.

Second, God the Father is the source of all revelation. Revelation literally means an "unveiling" or "disclosure" of something previously hidden. In the Christian understanding, revelation comes as God's gift and is a freewill act of His self-disclosure. The Bible speaks of revelation not so much in a theoretical sense—as a doctrine of epistemology explaining how we *know* things—but in a more practical sense. God reveals truths about Himself and about humanity so that we might know Him and His saving purposes—in short, so that we might capture a glimpse of the *missio dei*.

Revelation occurs in a wide array of forms in creation, in historical acts, in the Incarnation, and in the Bible. In order to better understand revelation, many theologians have made the distinction between general or natural revelation and special revelation. General revelation represents those features of God's self-disclosure that are *universally accessible.* The two most prominent examples of general revelation are the created order (Ps. 19:1) and human conscience (Rom. 2:14–15), since both are shared by all humanity. Special revelation represents God's self-disclosure to particular people at particular times regarding His saving purposes. Special revelation is not universally accessible. Examples of special revelation would include such divine disclosures as the Jewish law, the incarnation of Jesus Christ, and the Bible.

The relationship between general and special revelation is crucial to developing a theology of religions. There are many different views among theologians about the relationship between general revelation and special revelation. On one end of the spectrum are those who believe that special revelation is nothing more than specific and particularized symbolism of the general revelation that is universally known. At the other end of the spectrum are those who emphasize that true knowledge is found only in Christ and the Scriptures and all other claims to knowledge are utterly false.[4] Later, we will explore my own view on this, but the point is that the centrality of revelation in the formulation of a theology of religions places the discussion within our larger understanding of God the Father as the source of all revelation.

THE CLASSIC PARADIGM—AND BEYOND

In 1982, Alan Race published *Christians and Religious Pluralism* in which he suggested that all theologies of religion operate within three basic paradigms known as pluralism, inclusivism, and exclusivism. This framework was later used and popularized by such well-known writers as the Roman Catholic Paul Knitter and the Protestant John Hick. Although the paradigm initially was used by pluralists, it quickly became used by writers across the theological spectrum, even if not all were happy with the precise language. Evangelicals emerged considerably later in the "theology of religions" discussion and have, in recent

---

4. Daniel L. Migliore, *Faith Seeking Understanding: An Introduction to Christian Theology*, 2nd ed. (Grand Rapids: Eerdmans, 2004), 30.

years, raised a number of concerns about the intent of the paradigm and, even more frequently, the adequacy of the language.[5]

In a more recent publication, Paul Knitter has changed the nomenclature for each of the positions, and he adds a fourth position along the spectrum.[6] He renames the exclusivist position the "replacement model," and the inclusivist position he calls the "fulfillment model." The most important difference for evangelicals is that Knitter has nuanced the "replacement" model by distinguishing between "total replacement," which he attributes primarily to fundamentalists, evangelicals, and Pentecostals, and "partial replacement," which he identifies with the new evangelicals, who, in his view, are more open to the idea of God's presence in other religions and hold a more robust view of general revelation. He cites, for example, Harold Netland, as an evangelical scholar who exemplifies the "partial replacement" model.[7] Knitter renames pluralism the "mutuality model" and identifies John Hick with this model. However, Knitter is surprisingly critical of Hick, citing the inherent relativism, the superficiality of analysis, and the reductionistic caricatures that result when one tries to discover common ground among the world's religions. Knitter suggests a fourth model, the "acceptance model," which draws primarily from postmodernism, George Lindbeck's postliberalism, and the idea of multiple salvations in the writings of Mark Heim.

Although I have tried to work within and modify the threefold paradigm, I think it is now necessary to acknowledge the growing influence of postmodern thought on these discussions. Therefore, we will move beyond the classic threefold paradigm and analyze four main views, as well as the long-needed distinctions within the evangelical view. For the sake of clarity, I will use in the headings both the traditional nomenclature and Knitter's more recent language. However, it should be acknowledged at the outset that these four paradigms do not represent precise positions but rather a wide variety of more nuanced views that fall along a broad spectrum.

---

5. Compare, for example, Harold Netland, *Dissonant Voices* (Grand Rapids: Eerdmans, 1991) with his later publication, *Encountering Religious Pluralism* (Downers Grove, IL: InterVarsity Press, 2001), especially, 47–54. See also Amos Yong, *Beyond the Impasse: Toward a Pneumatological Theology of Religions* (Grand Rapids: Baker Academic, 2003). I share many of these concerns. See Tennent, *Christianity at the Religious Roundtable.*

6. Paul F. Knitter, *Introducing Theologies of Religions* (Maryknoll, NY: Orbis, 2002).

7. Ibid., 41.

Exclusivism or the Replacement/Partial Replacement Model

The more conservative theologies of religions are generally grouped together in a category known as exclusivism or particularism.[8] An exclusivistic position affirms three nonnegotiables. First, exclusivists affirm the unique authority of Jesus Christ as the apex of revelation and the norm by which all other beliefs must be critiqued. Exclusivists draw on texts such as Acts 4:12 John 14:6 and 1 John 5:11–12 to show that Jesus is not just one of many lights in the religious cosmos; He is *the* light. Those who are without Christ are, to use the words of the apostle Paul, "without hope and without God in the world" (Eph. 2:12). Second, exclusivists affirm that the Christian faith is centered on the proclamation of the historical death and resurrection of Jesus Christ as the decisive event in human history (Acts 2:31–32). The Scriptures declare that "God was reconciling the world to himself in Christ" (2 Cor. 5:19) and "making peace through his blood, shed on the cross" (Col. 1:20). Third, it is believed that salvation comes through repentance and faith in Christ's work on the cross; thus, no one can be saved without an explicit act of repentance and faith based on the knowledge of Christ (John 3:16–18, 36; Mark 16:15–16).

The most well-known and uncompromising defense of the exclusivistic position was articulated by Hendrick Kraemer in his landmark book, *The Christian Message in a Non-Christian World.*[9] The book was written to stimulate discussion for the World Missionary Conference in Madras, India, in 1938. Kraemer's work has become a classic exposition of the exclusivist position. He advocated what he called a "radical discontinuity" between the Christian faith and the beliefs of all other religions. Kraemer refused to divide revelation into the categories of general and special, which he thought might allow for the possibility of revelation outside the proclamation of the Christian gospel.[10] For Kraemer, the incarnation of Jesus Christ represents the "decisive moment in world history."[11] Jesus Christ is the decisive rev-

---

8. Sometimes called restrictivism or Christocentric exclusivism.

9. Hendrick Kraemer, *The Christian Message in a Non-Christian World* (London: Edinburgh House, 1938).

10. Kraemer's disdain for general revelation is clearly influenced by Karl Barth. However, to borrow a metaphor from a letter A. G. Hogg wrote to Lesslie Newbigin in 1937, the Barthian bull pursued the matador of modernism into the china shop and disposed of him there at a destructive cost of many precious things. A proper view of general revelation is certainly one of the more unfortunate losses in Barth's neoorthodoxy.

11. Kraemer, *The Christian Message in a Non-Christian World,* 74.

elation of God that confronts the entire human race and stands over and against all other attempts by other religions or philosophies to "apprehend the totality of existence."[12] Kraemer's attack on what he calls "omnipresent relativism" includes dismantling anything that would chip away at the vast gulf that exists between God and the human race. This involves the complete separation of nature and grace, or reason and revelation.

A more contemporary exposition of the exclusivist position may be found in Ron Nash's *Is Jesus the Only Savior?*[13] Unlike Kraemer, Nash accepts the distinction between general and special revelation but argues that general revelation "performs the function of rendering man judicially accountable before God."[14] Nash exposes overly optimistic views of the salvific power of general revelation but does not clearly demonstrate how general revelation might assist or prepare one to receive special revelation.

As Paul Knitter has recognized, there are clearly those within the exclusivistic perspective who are not convinced that maintaining the three nonnegotiables necessitates a position of such radical discontinuity or a completely negative assessment of other religions. These views tend to be more optimistic about the role and function of general revelation. While acknowledging that there is no salvation in Hinduism, Buddhism, or Islam, and that general revelation is incapable of saving anyone, some exclusivists nevertheless believe that God provides truths about Himself and humanity through general revelation that are accessible to all and that some of these truths have been incorporated into the beliefs of other religions, providing points of continuity whenever there is a consistency with the biblical revelation. This view has been advocated by Gerald McDermott in *Can Evangelicals Learn from World Religions?* and by Harold Netland in *Encountering Religious Pluralism*.[15] This perspective does not see Christian truth as completely detached from truths that may be found through general revelation but nevertheless holds that other religions ultimately fall short and cannot provide salvation because they do not accept the centrality of Christ's revelation and His work on the cross. Furthermore, exclusivists insist that the

---

12. Ibid., 113.
13. Ronald Nash, *Is Jesus the Only Savior?* (Grand Rapids: Zondervan, 1994).
14. Ibid., 21. Nash is quoting Bruce Demarest, *General Revelation* (Grand Rapids: Zondervan, 1982), 69–70.
15. Gerald R. McDermott, *Can Evangelicals Learn from World Religions?* (Downers Grove, IL: InterVarsityPress, 2000); Netland, *Encountering Religious Pluralism*.

biblical message calls for an explicit act of repentance and faith in Christ that is obviously not part of the message or experience of non-Christian religions.[16]

Some who hold to the three nonnegotiables also have advocated a position known traditionally as fulfillment theology, which arose in the late nineteenth century, although the concept goes back as far as the second century with figures like Justin Martyr and his creative use of the *logos* concept. This use of the term *fulfillment* should not be confused with Knitter's more recent use of the term to describe inclusivism, which will be explored later. Unlike Kraemer, the governing purpose behind fulfillment theology is to demonstrate the continuity between human philosophies or religions and the supernatural religion of Christianity. While affirming the final revelation of Christ, fulfillment theologians saw God working through philosophy and non-Christian religions to prepare people to hear and respond to the gospel.

Fulfillment theology arose out of the nineteenth-century fascination with applying Darwinian ideas of evolution to science, sociology, religion, and ethics.[17] In the writings of Max Müller (1823–1900), the concept of fulfillment robbed Christianity of all claims to revelation, and the origins of religion were viewed as an expression of universal human experience.[18] All religions were arranged in stages from the lower religions to the higher, monotheistic religions, culminating in Christianity.

However, there were scholars as well as missionaries who adopted the fulfillment concept within an evangelical framework. The best-known scholar to do this was Monier Monier-Williams (1819–1899) at Oxford. Monier-Williams argued for the supremacy of historical Christianity as divinely revealed. He was convinced that in time all the other religions of the world would crumble as they came into contact with the truth of the Christian gospel. However, he developed a far more positive attitude toward the world religions, arguing that Christianity would not be

---

16. For a modern treatment of exclusivism, see John P. Newport, *Life's Ultimate Questions* (Dallas: Word, 1989). For a vigorous defense of exclusivism but one that ultimately leaves the fate of the unevangelized as a mystery known only to God, see Lesslie Newbigin, *The Gospel in a Pluralist Society* (Grand Rapids: Eerdmans, 1995).

17. Charles Darwin (1809–1882) published his landmark *On the Origin of Species by means of Natural Selection* in 1859. Later, Herbert Spencer (1820–1903) demonstrated how evolution should be applied to all areas of human existence.

18. See, for example, Max Müller, *Origin and Growth of Religion* (Varanasi, India: Indological Book House, 1964).

victorious because it *refuted* all religions but because it *fulfilled* them. He argued that all religions reveal universal, God-given instincts, desires, and aspirations that are met in the Christian gospel. The missionary community, particularly in India, where they were meeting stiff resistance from Hinduism, latched onto fulfillment ideas and began to explore them in earnest in the early years of the twentieth century.

The most notable and articulate expression of fulfillment thought came from missionaries working in India such as T. E. Slater (1840–1912), in his work *Higher Hinduism in Relation to Christianity*, and J. N. Farquhar (1861–1929), whose landmark book, *The Crown of Hinduism*, was published in 1913. Farquhar and Slater were two of the earliest scholars to produce major works that ambitiously set out to compare the doctrines of Hinduism with the doctrines in Christianity and demonstrate a fulfillment theme.[19] Farquhar sought to establish a nonconfrontational bridge for the Hindu to cross over to Christianity, arguing that all the notable features and aspirations within Hinduism find their highest expression and ultimate fulfillment in Christianity. He based the fulfillment theme on Christ's claim in Matthew 5:17 that He had not come to abolish or destroy but to fulfill.

The fulfillment motif among evangelicals was largely snuffed out with the publication of Kraemer's *The Christian Message in a Non-Christian World* in 1938, which reasserted a more rigid, uncompromising stance toward world religions. On the liberal side, the ongoing rise of rationalistic presuppositions further encouraged evangelicals to close ranks. However, the idea of a radical positive assessment of world religions without relinquishing the supremacy of Christianity found new expression in the second major attitude toward world religions, known as inclusivism.

Inclusivism or the New Fulfillment Model

Inclusivism affirms the first two of the three "nonnegotiable" positions held by the exclusivists. Thus, inclusivists affirm without qualification that Jesus Christ is the definitive and authoritative revelation of God. Furthermore,

---

19. See, J. N. Farquhar, *The Crown of Hinduism* (Oxford: Oxford University Press, 1913). This classic work was reprinted in 1971 by Oriental Books Reprint Corporation in New Delhi. See also T. E. Slater, *Higher Hinduism in Relation to Christianity* (London: E. Stock, 1903).

they affirm the centrality of Christ's work on the cross, without which no one can be saved. What makes the inclusivist position distinct from the exclusivists are their particular views regarding universal access to the gospel and the necessity of a personal knowledge of and response to Jesus Christ. The inclusivists argue from texts like John 3:16 and 2 Peter 3:9 that God's universal love for the world and His desire to save everyone implies that everyone must have *access* to salvation. Stuart Hackett, an advocate of inclusivism, makes the case for this in *The Reconstruction of the Christian Revelation Claim*, where he states that if every human being has been objectively provided redemption in Jesus Christ through the Cross, then "it must be possible for every human individual to become personally eligible to receive that provision."[20] In other words, universal provision demands universal access. Therefore, since the majority of people in the world do not have a viable access to the Christian message, the inclusivists believe that this access has been made available through general revelation, God's providential workings in history, and even other religions. They affirm that Christ's work on the cross is *ontologically* necessary for salvation but that it is not *epistemologically* necessary. In other words, you do not need to personally know about Christ to be the recipient of His work of grace on your behalf. Probably the best-known articulation of this view occurs in the Catholic Second Vatican Council document entitled *Constitution on the Church*, which declares,

> Those also can attain to everlasting salvation who, through no fault of their own, do not know the Gospel of Christ or his Church, yet sincerely seek God and moved by grace, strive by their deeds to do His will as it is known to them through the dictates of conscience.[21]

---

20. Stuart Hackett, *The Reconstruction of the Christian Revelation Claim* (Grand Rapids: Baker, 1984), 244.

21. *Lumen Gentium*, 16, as quoted in "Dialogue and Mission: Conflict or Convergence?" *International Review of Mission* 76, no. 299 (July 1986): 223. In another Vatican II statement, the *Constitution* declares that "since Christ died for all men, and since the ultimate vocation of man is in fact one, and divine, we ought to believe that the Holy Spirit in a manner known only to God offers to every man the possibility of being associated with his paschal mystery" (*Gaudium et Spes.*, 22). While Vatican II endorsed most of Rahner's theology of religions, it did not officially endorse the notion of an "anonymous Christian." So, there remains some differences between the inclusivism of Karl Rahner and the inclusivism of official Roman Catholic dogma.

Inclusivists generally point to examples of God working outside the covenant with Israel to show that faith, and even salvation, can be found among Gentiles. Biblical examples that are often cited include Melchizedek (Gen. 14), Rahab (Joshua 2), the Ninevites (Jonah 3), the Queen of Sheba (1 Kings 10), and Cornelius (Acts 10), among others.[22] Inclusivists also draw heavily from Paul's statements that God "has not left himself without testimony" (Acts 14:17) and that the Gentiles have "the requirements of the law written on their hearts" (Rom. 2:15). They interpret this witness as more than a *preparatio evangelica*—a preparation to receive and respond to the special revelation that follows. They see it as an independent salvific witness because Christ draws people to Himself not only explicitly through the Christian church, but also anonymously in countless hidden ways through creation, history, and the testimony of world religions. In short, salvific grace is mediated through general revelation, not just through special revelation.

The belief in universal access to the gospel and the expanded efficacy of general revelation has led inclusivists to make a distinction between a Christian and a believer. Both are saved through the completed work of Christ on the cross. However, the Christian has explicit knowledge of this, whereas the believer has only experienced Christ implicitly and does not even realize that he or she has been saved by Christ. The best-known proponent of inclusivism was the Roman Catholic theologian Karl Rahner, who called these implicit believers "anonymous Christians." Rahner taught that even though the non-Christian religions contain errors, God uses them as channels to mediate His grace and mercy and ultimately to apply the work of Christ.[23] The basis for the explicit-implicit or ontological-epistemological distinction is linked to the Jews themselves. Rahner argues that the be-

---

22. For a full treatment of the inclusivist position, see Clark Pinnock, *A Wideness in God's Mercy: The Finality of Jesus Christ in a World of Religions* (Grand Rapids: Zondervan, 1992), and John Sanders, *No Other Name: An Investigation into the Destiny of the Unevangelized* (Grand Rapids: Eerdmans, 1992).

23. Karl Rahner, "Christianity and the Non-Christian Religions," in *Christianity and Other Religions*, ed. John Hick and Brian Hebblethwaite (Philadelphia: Fortress, 1980). Rahner's most complete treatment can be found in volumes 5 and 6 of his 20-volume *Theological Investigations* (New York: Seabury, 1966–1983). Another, more accessible, defense of inclusivism may be found in E. Hillman's *The Wider Ecumenism: Anonymous Christianity and the Church* (London: Burns and Oates; New York: Herder and Herder, 1968). A well-known application of inclusivism specifically to the Hindu context may be found in R. Panikkar's *The Unknown Christ of Hinduism* (London: Darton, Longman and Todd, 1964).

lieving Jews of the Old Testament were reconciled to God through Christ, even though they could not possibly have known about Christ explicitly. Paul, for example, argues that Christ accompanied the Israelites during their wilderness wanderings (1 Cor. 10:4), even though they could not have been explicitly aware of it. By extension this is applied to peoples around the world, who, although they are living chronologically after Christ, are epistemologically living as if Christ had not yet come. It is these people, in particular, for whom the inclusivists want to hold out hope. Several leading Protestants have followed the new openness exhibited by Vatican II and with some qualifications have fully endorsed inclusivism. Two of the more prominent Protestants who advocate inclusivism are John Sanders, in *No Other Name*, and Clark Pinnock, in *A Wideness in God's Mercy*.

Pluralism or Mutuality Model

Pluralism rejects all three of the nonnegotiables held by exclusivists. Pluralists such as Paul Knitter, William Cantwell Smith, W. E. Hocking, and John Hick believe that the world's religions provide independent access to salvation. Conflicting truth claims are reconciled through relocating them from the level of objective, normative truth to subjective experience. John Hick, in *An Interpretation of Religion*, writes that world religions merely "embody different perceptions and conceptions of, and correspondingly different responses to, the Real from within the major variant ways of being human." He goes on to say that world religions all provide what he calls "soteriological spaces," or "ways along which men and women find salvation/liberation/ultimate fulfillment."[24] Christianity, then, is just one among many religions and has no unique claim as the final or authoritative truth. According to the pluralists, Christianity is not necessarily the most advanced religion, and it is not the fulfillment of other religions. In short, all claims to exclusivity have been surrendered through a process of radical relativization.

Pluralist Gordon Kaufman states candidly that exclusivistic views lead to idolatry and render it nearly impossible to take other faiths seriously.[25] Instead, he says, "We must find ways of relativizing and opening

---

24. John Hick, *An Interpretation of Religion* (New Haven: Yale University Press, 1989), 240.
25. Gordon Kaufman, "Religious Diversity, Historical Consciousness, and Christian Theology," in *The Myth of Christian Uniqueness*, ed. John Hick and Paul F. Knitter (Maryknoll, NY: Orbis, 1987), 5.

up our basic symbol system."[26] John Hick agrees, calling the claim of Christian exclusivity a "myth" that must be radically reconstructed into a statement of personal meaning, not historical fact. They argue that Christocentric views of Christians should be abandoned for a more globally oriented theocentric view that allows all religions to participate as equal players.[27]

Unlike exclusivists and inclusivists, pluralists do not accept the necessity of demonstrating biblical support for their view because that would cede to Christianity some kind of adjudicating role over other religions. The New Testament may be authoritative for Christians, but the Qur'an holds its own independent authority for Muslims, the Vedas for Hindus, and so forth. For the pluralists, the only universal standard of criteria rests in human experience, not in any particular sacred texts. This is in marked contrast to Kraemer and many of his followers, who tended to downplay general revelation altogether. Pluralists go to the opposite extreme and either deny special revelation outright or seriously degrade it to a kind of general revelation through universal religious consciousness.

Postmodern or Acceptance Model

As noted above, this fourth view traditionally has not appeared in the classic threefold paradigm of exclusivism, inclusivism, and pluralism. The acceptance model affirms the postmodern assertion that there are no universal truths and that it is arrogant to assert that such truths may exist. This view also, quite refreshingly, acknowledges that world religions really *are* fundamentally different from one another and we should quit trying to talk as if they were, on some deeper level, really all the same. According to George Lindbeck, each religion offers a total, comprehensive framework for understanding its view of reality, and any attempt to compare or find common ground is reductionistic.[28] In short, this model affirms the incommensurability of all religions.

Paul Knitter borrows Robert Frost's famous line, "good fences make good neighbors," as a metaphor for understanding the acceptance approach. Knitter says, "religions are to be good neighbors to each other.

---

26. Ibid.
27. See Hick and Knitter, eds., *The Myth of Christian Uniqueness*.
28. George Lindbeck, *Nature of Doctrine: Religion and Theology in a Postliberal Age* (Philadelphia: Westminster Press, 1984), 42.

Each religion has its own backyard. There is no 'commons' that all of them share. To be good neighbors, then, let each religion tend to its own backyard, keeping it clean and neat." When we talk with our "neighbors," we should do so over the back fence, "without trying to step into the other's yard in order to find what they might have in common."[29] The dialogue that plays such a central role in the pluralist/acceptance model is reduced to only "swapping stories" without searching for any commonly shared or universal truths. For Lindbeck, to say that "all religions recommend something which can be called 'love' . . . is a banality as uninteresting as the fact that all languages are spoken."[30]

Mark Heim, in *Salvations: Truth and Difference in Religions*,[31] takes the acceptance model to its logical conclusion. Heim argues that the postmodern perspective of the acceptance model means that we may really have multiple goals, multiple salvations, and multiple deities to which the various religions are related. Heim seeks to argue this point within the classic doctrine of the Trinity. Since Christians already affirm plurality in God, argues Heim, perhaps the plurality of religions can fit into the variety of relations that are in God, allowing for what he calls "permanently co-existing truths" and "parallel perfections."[32] Through the acceptance model, each practitioner can affirm the particularity and exclusivity of his or her own faith, for God does not reveal Himself generically but in the diversity of religious particularity. The classic pluralist metaphor of many paths up one mountain has been replaced in the acceptance model with many paths up many different mountains. Jesus, Buddha, Shiva, and Allah are all universal saviors, since none of them represents an exhaustive or exclusive revelation, but all reflect the infinite diversity of the Divine.

EVALUATION OF THE FOUR POSITIONS
Our evaluation will begin with a critique of the four positions as currently outlined and then explore some of the problems with the larger paradigm through which these positions are articulated.

---

29. Knitter, *Introducing Theologies of Religion*, 183.
30. Lindbeck, *Nature of Doctrine*, 42.
31. S. Mark Heim, *Salvations: Truth and Difference in Religions* (Maryknoll, NY: Orbis, 1995).
32. S. Mark Heim, *The Depth of Riches: A Trinitarian Theology of Religious Ends* (Grand Rapids: Eerdmans, 2001), 175.

Postmodern or Acceptance Model Evaluated

The acceptance model, on the surface, seems to come full circle back to the exclusivist position since it provides a way for Christians to reclaim the language of exclusivism and particularity. However, a closer examination reveals that although the language of particularity has been reclaimed, this masks several major deficiencies that are inherent in the acceptance model. First, *the model rejects objective revelation as the basis for truth by redefining truth as socially constructed narratives.* For example, this model simultaneously affirms the exclusive claims of Christianity and Islam and discourages us from contemplating that one set of claims may be right and the other wrong. Thus, they must *both* be right. However, a closer examination reveals that this claim is possible only through a radical redefinition of truth. For example, a central claim of Christianity is that God became incarnate in Jesus Christ (John 1:14). In Islam, such a claim is considered blasphemous, and to affirm it is to commit *shirk* (Surah 17:111; 19:35), the unforgivable sin (*kabirah*). Now, from the perspective of objective truth, either God did become incarnate in Jesus Christ, or He did not. The postmodern answer is to recast truth as a socially constructed metaphor. The word *truth* refers only to a rhetorical, imagined construct and cannot be applied to revelation as in the Christian use of the word. This is why this model cannot even explore the possibility of certain shared truths among religions. There is no shared truth to be known; all we have are individually constructed narratives, shared stories that float autonomously in the sea of religious discourse.

Second, *this model has a very weak view of history.* Some philosophies and religions do not necessitate a robust view of history. For example, a famous Zen Buddhist saying is, "If you should meet the Buddha on the road, you should kill him." The point of this rather shocking statement is that the historicity of the Buddha is not important. What matters is the teaching, or *dharma*, which he gave to the world. In contrast, Christianity (like Islam and Judaism) is constructed on specific historical events that are nonrepeatable and, therefore, unique. For example, Christians assert that the resurrection of Jesus Christ is an event that took place in real history. If Christ were not historically raised, then all the fervent devotion, earnest faith, and worship attributed to Jesus are instantly rendered vain and futile. This is why Paul declares, "If Christ has not been raised, your faith is futile; you are still in your sins" (1 Cor. 15:17). However, the acceptance model is based on a postmodern skepticism regarding history.

The actual historicity of the Incarnation or the Resurrection is regarded suspiciously as either unknown or unknowable.

One of the classic problems with postmodernism is that it creates worlds where everything is possible but nothing is certain. History, for the postmodern, is constantly mutable because it never rises above the watermark of an endless series of conjectures and biases. Therefore, the unique claims of religions are all allowed to coexist because none of them can either be denied or verified by history. George Lindbeck acknowledges the difficulty that this postmodern proposal poses for a Christian view of history. He says that it may be some time before Christians can accept his model because Christianity is "in the awkwardly intermediate stage of having once been culturally established but not yet clearly disestablished."[33] He means that Christianity has not yet been separated from history.

However, Christianity cannot be separated from history without ceasing to be Christianity. The apostolic faith is not only rooted in history, but it also proclaims a historical *telos*, an eschatological goal, to which all of history is moving. The eschaton is not *beyond* history but rather is the full manifestation of a new history that already has broken into the present.

Finally, *the antifoundationalist stance inherent in this model leads to an unbridled relativism.* With the twin collapse of truth and history, it becomes impossible to discover any basis for evaluating or adjudicating the various claims of the world's religions. How is someone to decide whether to be a Muslim, a Christian, a Satanist, or nothing at all? Even Lindbeck concedes that the choice is "purely irrational, a matter of arbitrary whim or blind faith."[34] He acknowledges the need to discover what he calls "universal norms of reasonableness," but he candidly admits that it is unlikely that any such norms can find mutual agreement among the plurality of faiths. The very fact that the advocates of the acceptance model are looking for such norms reveals that the ghost of the Enlightenment or, perhaps, latent Christendom, keeps them from believing their own message. The moment the "universal norms of reasonableness" are found, it would, by definition, mark the end of the acceptance model. It is a philosophical solvent that dissolves itself. Pluralists may accept multiple paths, but they at

---

33. Lindbeck, *Nature of Doctrine,* 134. Lindbeck makes it clear that the term *postmodern* or *post-revisionist* can be used instead of *postliberal* (p. 135).
34. Ibid., 130.

least still envision a *single* mountain and acknowledge that some religious movements exhibit qualities that are moving people *down* the mountain rather than up. For pluralists *many* religions does not necessarily mean *any* religion. However, the postmodernism of the acceptance model envisions, by its own account, an endless range of mountains, each independent of the other. We are left only with a radical form of relativism among multiple islands of religious autonomy.

Pluralism or Mutuality Model Evaluated

The pluralist position has numerous difficulties. First, *pluralism does not take seriously the actual claims and practices of those who practice the religions that are being considered.* Devout Muslims and Christians, for example, despite their differences, are equally disturbed by pluralism's attempt to relativize the particularities of their variant claims. Quite paternalistically, the pluralists claim to *see beyond* the actual beliefs and practices of religions to some deeper perspective that they have. According to the pluralists, those who actually follow these religions are largely unaware that the transcendent claims they have are actually only human projections and perceptions of their own humanity. However, what assurance do we have that the pluralists have found an Archimedean point from which they see all the other religions? Is not pluralism itself a particular stance, drawn from Enlightenment, Kantian philosophy?

Second, *the "God" of the pluralists is so vague that it cannot be known and is, in fact, unknowable.* The pluralist John Hick has forcefully called Christians to abandon a Christocentric view of reality. However, in its place he posits a theocentric center that is so vague that he cannot even use the word *God* to describe ultimate reality lest he offend non-theistic religions like Buddhism and Taoism, which his position insists that he regard with equality. The result is that Hick's "Real" (as he prefers to call the ultimate reality) is broad enough to encompass both the strict theism of Judaism and Islam and the atheism of Buddhism and Taoism. Hick's "Real" encompasses both the personal conception of God in Jesus Christ and the impersonal conception of God in the *nirguna* Brahman of Hinduism. The resultant fog gives us both a "God" and a "no-God" who is unknown and unknowable and about whom we can make no definitive statement because "the Real as it is in itself is never the direct object of religious experience. Rather, it is experienced by finite humankind in one of any number of historically and culturally conditioned manifestations."[35]

Third, *the pluralist position ultimately is based on the subjectivity of human experience, not on any objective truth claims.* Human experience is the final arbiter of all truth. Therefore, revelation as revelation is struck down. The deity of Christ, for example, is not an objective truth that calls for our response; rather, it is merely a subjective expression of what Jesus meant to His disciples, which may or may not affect or influence us because every human conceives of truth differently. For example, early in his writings Hick sought to define salvation vaguely as the "transformation from self-centeredness to Reality centeredness."[36] However, this definition of salvation came under the withering fire of feminist theologians, who argued that defining the lack of salvation as being self-focused and self-assertive is a characteristically male assessment. Females, they argue, find salvation by being more assertive and self-projecting. Hick conceded that female salvation may indeed be the opposite of male salvation.[37] This kind of unbridled subjectivity, which seeks to replace biblical theology based on the assurance of divine revelation with the ever-changing subjectivity of human experience, is, in my view, untenable. For the pluralist, religion is no longer about truth as truth but about filling a market niche. The question of truth is bracketed off by the pluralists. As George Sumner has observed, "The turban, the prayer wheel, and the mantra have all been rendered 'consumer preferences.'"[38]

Indeed, Clark Pinnock has gone so far as to say that the very term *pluralist* is an inaccurate label for this position. He points out that "a true pluralist would accept the differences of the various world religions and not try to fit them into a common essence. It would be better to call them relativists."[39]

Inclusivism or the New Fulfillment Model Evaluated
The inclusivist position is to be commended for its strong affirmation of the centrality of Jesus Christ and the indispensable nature of His death and

---

35. Netland, *Encountering Religious Pluralism*, 224.
36. John Hick, *A Christian Theology of Religions: The Rainbow of Faiths* (Louisville: Westminster John Knox, 1995), 18.
37. Hick, *An Interpretation of Religion*, 52.
38. George Sumner, *The First and the Last* (Grand Rapids: Eerdmans, 2004), 3.
39. Clark Pinnock, "Toward an Evangelical Theology of Religions," *Journal of the Evangelical Theological Society* 33, no. 3 (September 1990): 363, n. 12.

resurrection for salvation. Furthermore, inclusivism has keenly discerned how God has worked in the lives of those outside the boundaries of the covenant, such as Rahab and Naaman, along with many others. The more positive view of the relationship between general and special revelation is a welcome relief from the complete separation of nature and grace as seen in Kraemer. On this particular point, the inclusivists do not necessarily fall outside the parameters of Christian history and tradition. Indeed, Thomas Aquinas advocated a more open attitude toward general revelation with the dictum, *Gratia non tollit sed perficit naturam*, that is, grace does not abrogate but perfects nature. However, inclusivists have embraced additional views that are clearly at variance with historic Christian faith.

First, the inclusivist's attempt to drive a wedge between the ontological necessity of Christ's work and the epistemological response of repentance and faith cannot be sustained. Inclusivists can be very selective in their use of the biblical data. For example, they often quote the passage in 2 Peter 3:9 that says that God is "not wanting anyone to perish" but fail to quote the rest of the verse, which says God wants "everyone to come to repentance." God's universal salvific will is explicitly linked to human response. Inclusivists cite Paul's powerful statement about the universality of revelation in Romans 10:18, which says that the "voice" of revelation has "gone out into all the earth," but they fail to point out that this affirmation is in the context of Paul's declaration that "everyone who calls on the name of the Lord will be saved" (Rom. 10:13). Paul goes on to establish a chain that begins with the sending church and the preaching witness, leading to the one who hears, believes, and calls upon the name of the Lord (Rom. 10:14–15). The inclusivists want to separate the links of this chain and argue that the witnessing church is not necessary for believing, that is, implicit saving faith can be present apart from the explicit knowledge of Jesus Christ. However, if the inclusivist position were true, then it would diminish the importance of Christ's commission since it would mean that the non-Christian religions have brought more people to the feet of Christ (implicitly) than the witnessing church in the world.

Second, *for the inclusivists to argue that the object of all genuine faith is implicitly Christ shifts the emphasis from a personal response to Christ to the experience of faith regardless of the object of faith.* In this view, salvation comes equally to the Hindu who has faith in Krishna, or the Buddhist who has faith in the eighteenth vow of Amitaba Buddha, or the Christian who has faith in

Jesus Christ. Moving from the worship of Krishna to the worship of Christ does not involve a turning away from Krishna but merely a clarification that they were, indeed, worshipping Christ all along. As Paul Knitter says about inclusivism, "The purpose of the church is not to rescue people and put them on totally new roads, rather it is to burn away the fog and enable people to see more clearly and move more securely."[40]

However, in Acts 20:21 Paul says, "I have declared to both Jews and Greeks that they must turn to God in repentance and have faith in our Lord Jesus." What would the inclusivists have recommended to Wynfrith when he confronted the Frisian religion in A.D. 754? Would they have counseled Wynfrith to point out that the human sacrifices offered to Njord, the god of the earth, were actually only symbols or types of the Lamb of God? Was Thor really just another name for Jesus Christ?[41] This is not to deny that there are examples in the Old Testament of people who have faith outside the Jewish covenant, such as Jethro, Naaman, and Rahab; but the object of their faith is explicitly the God of Israel, not the indigenous gods they formerly worshipped. Paul's famous speech in Acts 17 should not be taken as the construction of a salvific natural theology but rather as Paul "picking up the inchoate longings of this exceptionally religious people and directing them to their proper object."[42]

Third, *the inclusivist position unduly separates soteriology from ecclesiology.* Inclusivism claims to be a "wider hope" answer to the question "Who can be saved?" However, the inclusivistic answer focuses on the earnest seeker quite apart from the church as the redemptive community that lives out, in community, the realities of the New Creation in the present. Only through dramatic theological reductionism can one equate biblical salvation in the New Testament to the individual destiny of a single seeker after God. Karl Rahner responded to this charge by arguing that the church and the sacraments become mysteriously embodied in the communities that gather at the temple or the mosque. Thus, Rahner does not just offer us anonymous *Christians;* he offers us anonymous communities, anonymous Scriptures, and anonymous sacraments. Rahner's solution may help to reunite soteriology with ecclesiology but only by robbing ecclesiology of

---

40. Knitter, *Introducing Theologies of Religions*, 74.

41. J. A. van Rooy, "Christ and the Religions: The Issues at Stake," *Missionalia* 13, no.1 (April 1985): 9.

42. L. T. Johnson, *The Acts of the Apostles*, Sacra Pagina (Collegeville, MN: Liturgical, 1992), 319.

any meaning, since, in the final analysis, Rahner cannot make a distinction between a Hindu or Islamic community and a Christian one.

Finally, *to call Hindus or Muslims or Buddhists "anonymous Christians" has long been regarded as an insult to those within these traditions.* It is a latent form of triumphalism to claim that you as an outsider have a better and deeper understanding of someone else's religious experience that trumps their own understanding of their actions and beliefs. It is patronizing to tell a devout Hindu who worships Krishna that he or she is really worshipping Christ but is temporarily in an epistemological gap. Could not the Buddhist or the Hindu respond that we as Christians are actually "anonymous Buddhists" or "anonymous Hindus"? Indeed, there are Buddhist and Muslim groups who have made that very claim.[43]

Exclusivism or the Replacement/Partial Replacement Models Evaluated

The strength of the exclusivist position is that it affirms the authority of Scripture, the unique centrality of Jesus Christ, and the indispensability of His death and resurrection. Furthermore, exclusivism takes seriously the call to repentance and the need to turn to Jesus Christ as the object of explicit faith. Exclusivism affirms the key tenets of the historic Christian proclamation as delivered to us in the ancient creedal formulations. The problem with exclusivism comes when, in a desire to protect the centrality of these truths, it overextends itself into several potential errors.

First, *in a desire to affirm the centrality of special revelation and the particular claims of Christ, exclusivism can fail to fully appreciate God's activity in the pre-Christian heart.* It is one thing to affirm that Jesus Christ is the apex of God's self-revelation; it is entirely another to say that Jesus Christ is the *only* revelation from God. Since all general revelation ultimately points to Christ, exclusivists need not be threatened by these pointers and signs God has placed in creation and in the human conscience that testify to Him. God is not passive or stingy in His self-revelation, but He has left "footprints" behind, whether in the awe-inspiring expanse of the universe, or in the recesses of a solitary heart groping after God, or in the depths

---

43. This claim is made by several Islamic groups in Indonesia as well as by the Hindu Ramakrishna, who claimed that all the religions of the world are contained within Hinduism.

of the reflective human mind as one explores many of the fundamental questions that have gripped philosophers and theologians throughout the ages. In this respect, the modified exclusivistic view that Knitter identifies as partial replacement is far better.

Second, *exclusivists sometimes have taken a defensive posture and been unwilling to honestly engage with the questions and objections of those from other religions.* The early Christians boldly proclaimed the gospel in a context of a dizzying array of cults, mystery religions, emperor worship, and more. The apostles surely would have found the defensiveness that often has characterized exclusivists as incomprehensible in light of our global mandate. Put simply, the match cannot be engaged if the players remain in the safety of the locker room. The creeds of historic Christianity are not bunkers behind which we hide; they are the basis for a global proclamation.

Third, *exclusivists have often unnecessarily bracketed off non-Christian religions and their sacred texts from the rest of culture.* This has inadvertently created a separation not only between general and special revelation but also between the doctrines of creation and soteriology. The result is what Enlightenment thinker Gotthold Lessing (1729–1781) has called the "ugly ditch" that separates the particularities of special revelation and history from the universal knowledge of God rooted in creation and human conscience. However, as I have demonstrated in an earlier publication, numerous truths from both general and special revelation have become incorporated into the actual texts and worldviews of other religions.[44]

THE CLASSIC AND EXPANDED PARADIGM REVISITED AND EVALUATED

Structural Problems

There are three major structural problems with the classic paradigm that are not sufficiently alleviated by Knitter's new nomenclature.

First, the positions within the paradigms have been primarily articulated within a *soteriological* framework. In other words, the various positions tend to be the answers to the questions "Who can be saved?" and

---

44. See, for example, my chapters "Hindu Sacred Texts in Pre-Christian Past" and "Is 'Salvation by Grace Through Faith' Unique to Christianity?" in *Theology in the Context of World Christianity*.

"What is the fate of the unevangelized?" Even though these are important questions, if they are asked in isolation, they become theologically reductionistic by separating the doctrine of salvation from the larger creational and eschatological framework from which the doctrine of salvation emerges in the Bible. Second, the positions within the paradigms have been understood as either validating or negating *particular religious traditions.* Exclusivists and inclusivists believe in the final supremacy of the Christian *religion*, whereas the pluralists and the postmodernists see the religions of the world on a more level playing field. This perspective is particularly evident in Paul Knitter's description of evangelicals within the total or partial replacement model (exclusivism). Knitter says that the replacement model is calling for a "kind of holy competition between the many religions. . . . Such competition is as natural, necessary, and helpful as it is in the business world. You're not going to sell your product effectively if you present it as 'just as good' as the next guy's. . . . So let the religions compete!"[45] However, the evangelical view is not to posit that Christianity *as a religion* is superior to all other religions. Rather, evangelicals assert that Jesus Christ is the apex of God's revelation. At times the Christian church has been faithful in proclaiming the good news of Jesus Christ. However, like any other religion, Christianity at times has been co-opted by cultural forces and become an expression of human rebellion like any other religion. It was Lesslie Newbigin who reminded us, based on Romans 3:2–3, that "it was the guardians of God's revelation who crucified the Son of God."[46]

Third, the traditional paradigm *emerges out of the Enlightenment project and completely ignores the Majority World church, which has a very different understanding and experience with religious pluralism.* The Enlightenment ushered in a skepticism regarding religious truth that continues to the present. The German philosopher Immanuel Kant (1724–1804) famously defined the Enlightenment as "the emergence of man from his self-incurred immaturity."[47] Kant attempted to construct a universal rational morality that would give rise to a natural religion. He rejected any claims of particularity based on special revelation, thereby

---

45. Knitter, *Introducing Theologies of Religions*, 31.
46. Lesslie Newbigin, *The Open Secret: An Introduction to the Theology of Mission*, rev. ed. (Grand Rapids: Eerdmans, 1995), 170.
47. N. J. Rengger, "Negative Dialect? The Two Modes of Critical Theory in World Politics," chap. 9 in Richard Wyn Jones, ed., *Critical Theory and World Politics* (London: Lynne Rienner, 2000), 92.

opening the doors to a radical kind of relativism regarding religion. Religion was seen as nothing more than a myriad of legitimate alternatives for explaining and interpreting the underlying natural religion that was part of the universal human experience. Rather than the mind being seen as the mirror that reflected the objective world, Kant introduced the subjective nature of all knowledge; so-called "reality" was nothing more than a construct of the mind. David Wells observes that it was Kant who initiated the breakdown "of the old distinction between subject and object."[48]

The Enlightenment perspective can be seen in the French philosopher Rene Descartes (1596–1650). Descartes believed that the only source of knowledge was logical deduction. His famous dictum, *cogito ergo sum* ("I think, therefore, I am"), demonstrates that knowledge for Descartes begins with a person as a thinking, doubting agent, not as the recipient of divine self-disclosure revealed in the Bible. As the Enlightenment progressed, the traditional Christian assertion of objectively received truth revealed propositionally and reliably in the Bible could no longer be countenanced.

This is to be contrasted with the rise of the Majority World church, which is taking place in the midst of religious pluralism as a descriptive fact. George Sumner is correct in observing that religious pluralism in the West has become the "presenting symptom for a wider epistemological illness in western Christianity."[49] In contrast, religious pluralism in the Majority World is closer to the context of the first century. Global Christianity, as a rule, is more theologically conservative, less individualistic, and has far more experience interacting with the actual devoted practitioners of major world religions than most Western scholars. Having worked in Asia for twenty years, I have observed that, for the most part, despite living in a context of religious pluralism, Majority World Christians do not view religions as "comparable religious artifacts" but rather as an actual stimulus to the proclamation of Jesus Christ.[50]

Amos Yong's Pneumatological Approach
An alternative approach to the classic paradigm from a conservative perspective has been proposed by Pentecostal theologian Amos Yong from

---

48. David Wells, *God in the Wasteland: The Reality of Truth in a World of Fading Dreams* (Grand Rapids: Eerdmans, 1994), 104.
49. Sumner, *The First and the Last*, 5.
50. Ibid., 3.

Regent University. Yong, in his books *Discerning the Spirit(s)*, *Beyond the Impasse,* and *Hospitality and the Other,* has proposed an approach that can be understood broadly as a pneumatological theology of religions. Yong begins by observing that the way pluralists have framed a theology of religions as a subset of a generic doctrine of God is overly optimistic. Likewise, framing a theology of religions as a subset of the doctrine of soteriology is unnecessarily pessimistic. Furthermore, Yong argues that any theology of religions that is framed by Christological categories may position us quite well *defensively* to mute the claims of other religions, but it is less effective in a more *offensive* engagement that acknowledges that the particularity of the "Word made flesh" (John 1:14) must be balanced by the universality of the "Spirit poured-out-on-all flesh" (Acts 2:17). Instead, Yong proposes a theology of religions framed around pneumatology. Yong is convinced that neglect of the doctrine of the Spirit in Western theology has led to an overly negative perception of the Spirit's work in non-Christian faiths. In contrast, Yong invokes Irenaeus's metaphorical reference to the Son and the Spirit as the "two hands of the Father."[51] Yong explores how we might discern how the "hand" of the Spirit may have extended God's presence and activity in non-Christian religions.

Yong proposes a threefold criteria (divine presence, divine absence, and divine activity) that can enable the church to discern God's presence and work or reject the demonic or destructive. In his more recent writings, Yong emphasizes that the Spirit enables Christians to embody the "hospitality of God" by helping us to interact positively as hosts in a religiously plural world. Recalling the multiplicity of tongues on the day of Pentecost, Yong reminds us that even if the religious "other" speaks in a religiously foreign tongue, the Spirit may enable us to understand and discern His presence and work within the other religions.

The strength of Yong's proposal is that his pneumatologial approach places the discussion within a much larger theological framework. The Spirit's work in creation allows Yong to embrace a more robust view of general revelation. He cites examples from patristic writers such as Irenaeus, Clement, and Justin Martyr to demonstrate that the early church fathers framed their theology of religions within a much larger framework than the classic paradigm. Yong's pneumatological approach also allows him to ask bigger questions in

---

51. Yong, *Beyond the Impasse,* 43.

seeking to discern God's work in human culture, including the religious narratives of people who are created in the image of God.

Despite these positive developments, Yong's proposal has three main weaknesses. First, it is not sufficiently Christocentric. Yong's original intention was to propose a more thoroughgoing Trinitarian theology of religions that uses pneumatology as a *starting point*. Yong points out that "any Christian theology of religions that begins pneumatologically must ultimately include and confront the Christological moment."[52] At the start of his proposal, he agrees to "bracket, at least temporarily, the soteriological question."[53] However, as his project develops, it seems that he never fully returns to the centrality of Christology and soteriology. In fact, Yong speaks of Christology imposing "categorical constraints" on his theology of religions.[54] While Yong surely assumes Christology, he is not explicit enough to protect his theology from subjectivism. In the end,, Yong's thesis stands or falls on the development of a trustworthy set of criteria that can empower the church to discern the presence of the Holy Spirit from the presence of demonic and destructive spirits, which may be present in the life and thought of the adherents of non-Christian faiths. Unfortunately, his threefold criteria are too ambiguous to provide the assurance that such an ambitious project demands. Even Yong concedes that "discerning the spirits will always be inherently ambiguous."[55] Yong also concedes, rightly, that no religious activity can be so neatly categorized as divine, human, or demonic.[56]

Second, his proposal still does not provide a way to move beyond a dialogue between reified religious traditions and structures. As will be demonstrated later, an evangelical theology of religions must demonstrate that the tension is between Christ and all religions. It cannot be a proposal that, despite all its generosity, inevitably exudes the presumptuous sense that evangelicals believe in the superiority of the Christian *religion*.

Third, Yong's proposal, like the classic paradigm, does not sufficiently take into account the very different ways religious pluralism is understood and experienced within the global church. Yong remains determined to find a new theology of religions that will enable evangelicals to have a

---

52. Ibid., 103.
53. Ibid., 29.
54. Ibid., 167.
55. Ibid., 159–160.
56. Ibid., 167.

voice within the larger Enlightenment project. However, in light of the dramatic shift in the center of Christian gravity, it is no longer sufficient to only address such a narrow Western audience.

An Evangelical Theology of Religions

The proposal I am setting forth begins by reviewing five standards or benchmarks that any evangelical theology of religions must meet. After the standards have been explored, I will demonstrate one example of how an evangelical theology of religions might be constructed in a way that is consistent with these five standards.

Five Standards in the Formulation of an Evangelical Theology of Religions

Being Attentive to Our Nomenclature

First, labels or nomenclature for various positions must be understood both descriptively and performatively. This means that any descriptive words or phrases used to describe a position should be accurate and acceptable to those who adhere to the position being named. Unfortunately, positions within interreligious dialogue often have been caricatured. An honest engagement with the actual positions is needed. Furthermore, the positions should not just describe what we believe in some static way but should also reflect our actions and our lives in relationship to those who belong to non-Christian religions. In other words, a theology of religions must have an ethical and relational orientation, not merely a descriptive and doctrinal one.

Maintaining a Trinitarian Frame with Christological Focus

Second, a theology of religions must be part of a larger Trinitarian theology. There have been quite a few scholars who have proposed their theology of religions within a Trinitarian framework, but it is important that it also be Christocentric. In the final analysis, Christology provides the only truly objective basis for evaluating truth claims, whether those claims emerge from within Christianity (intrareligious dialogue) or in response to normative claims from other religions (interreligious dialogue).

Proclaiming Biblical Truth

Third, an evangelical theology of religions must proclaim biblical truth. In recent years, increasing numbers of evangelicals have lost confidence in the exclusivity of the gospel message. Indeed, the very word *exclusivism* is avoided because of various negative associations with the word. Furthermore, we have become increasingly accommodating to the relativistic mood of the culture. Although, as this proposal will reveal, I do not suggest retaining the word *exclusvisim*. My choice is not motivated by an attempt to lessen the "scandal of particularity" but to create a nomenclature that is more appropriate without sanding down the rough edges of the gospel message.

We must recognize that we are now proclaiming the gospel within a context where relativity is not merely a theoretical proposal but a moral postulate. One of the most amazing casualties in the contemporary emergence of interreligious dialogue is the absence of the word *truth,* as articulated within a biblical understanding of revelation. Today, the tension is increasingly not between truth and falsehood but between tolerance and intolerance. As explored in chapter 1, evangelicals have not negotiated the transition from the center of cultural life to the margins very well. Therefore, while being fully engaged in global realities, we need to reclaim the language of truth, even if from a position of exile.

PLACING THE DISCUSSION WITHIN A LARGER THEOLOGICAL SETTING
Fourth, an evangelical theology of religions must be placed within a larger biblical and theological context. This should not be understood to downplay the importance of the three nonnegotiables (uniqueness of Jesus Christ, centrality of His death and resurrection, and the need for an explicit response of repentance and faith) affirmed in the traditional exclusivistic position. However, these nonnegotiables must be articulated within the larger context of the doctrines of creation, revelation (general and special), anthropology, the Trinity, Christology, pneumatology, ecclesiology, and, importantly, eschatology. This also will keep our theology of religions from being either too individualistic or theologically reductionistic.

RECOGNIZING THE GLOBAL DIMENSION OF RELIGIOUS PLURALISM
AND WORLD CHRISTIANITY
Fifth, an evangelical theology of religions must be articulated within the context of different understandings and perceptions of religious pluralism that are present in the world today. In the West, globalization, immigration, and the collapse of Christendom have given rise to a particular form of modern, religious pluralism that is decidedly relativistic. Religious

pluralism is not merely a descriptive fact of our world; it is a "conflict of normative interests."[57] Religious pluralism in the West is generally committed to making all religious discussions a subset of anthropology, which is consistent with the Enlightenment project. While the post-modern paradigm rejects the Enlightenment's reliance upon reason and the notion of inevitable progress, it just as emphatically rejects the notion of revelation. However, in the Majority World, religious pluralism is more of a *descriptive* fact. Christians in the Majority World are accustomed to living side by side with actual practitioners of non-Christian religions, and they have been able to articulate the normative primacy of Christ in the midst of this pluralistic milieu. Any theology of religions today must be articulated from the perspective of the global church, not the dwindling community of Enlightenment scholarship.

Building a Theology of Religions on the Restated Classic Paradigm

An evangelical theology of religions need not abandon the widely used classic paradigm, although allowing a fourth position to reflect a post-modern perspective, as Knitter has proposed, is a helpful and important addition to the paradigm. It remains important to use the classic or the modified paradigm since this paradigm remains the starting point of how the discussion has been framed. However, "the paradigm" needs to be revised. We will begin by looking at the nomenclature of the paradigm as a whole. In keeping with the first standard, we will suggest more descriptive terminology, as well as seek to explore what we can learn from the performative practices of each of the positions. Then, we will focus just on the traditional evangelical view and demonstrate how the remaining principles will help to strength an evangelical theology of religions.

First, an evangelical theology of religions should *embrace more precise and descriptive terms while at the same time recognizing what we can learn from the performative practice of each position in the actual give-and-take of interreligious encounter.* In keeping with the first principle, I propose changes in the way each of the positions within the paradigm are described. In doing so, I earnestly seek to create a phrase that is not only more descriptively accurate, but also one that adherents of that position can recognize and affirm as their own. Thus, exclusivism should be

---

57. Jerome Paul Soneson, *Pragmatism and Pluralism* (Minneapolis: Fortress, 1993), 137.

renamed *revelatory particularism*. The word *revelatory* stresses the importance of revelation (both in Scripture and in Jesus Christ) in the evangelical view. An evangelical theology of religions can never relinquish the
normative nature of biblical revelation or the final primacy of Jesus Christ.
The word *particularism* emphasizes the primacy of Jesus Christ and is
more precise than the word *exclusivistic,* which is understood by some
to mean that we are intent on excluding people, when the intended focus
is on the exclusivity and primacy of Jesus Christ. The word *particularism*
also protects the evangelical view from proposals that are Christocentric
but become untethered from the historicity of the Incarnation in favor of
a cosmic Christ, which in practice often becomes disconnected from the
apostolic proclamation concerning Jesus Christ.

Inclusivism should be known as *universal inclusivism*. This emphasizes the universal scope that lies at the heart of inclusivism's claim,
trumping even the epistemological need to personally respond to the
gospel message. Inclusivism has the performative function of reminding
all of us that God's revelation extends beyond the propositions of biblical
revelation. The Reformer John Calvin pointed out that God Himself "has
endued all men with some idea of his Godhead, the memory of which he
constantly renews and occasionally enlarges."[58] In this context, the Reformer refers to the "sense of the Divine" (*sensus divinitatis*) and the universal "germ of religion" (*semen religionis*). Likewise, Augustine, in his
Confessions, speaks of the "loving memory" of God that lies latent even
in unbelievers.[59] While we must be careful not to allow general revelation
to swallow up special revelation, we must not relinquish the basic truth
that there is a continuity between the two and that even in the encounter
with other religions, God has not left Himself without a witness.

Pluralism should be renamed *dialogic pluralism*, reflecting the performative interest in engaging the religious other with openness and humility.
Evangelicals sometimes have been too wary of interreligious dialogue and
have taken an overly defensive posture in engaging the honest questions
and objections from those in non-Christian religions. Evangelical writer
Gerald McDermott, in *Can Evangelicals Learn from World Religions?*

---

58. John Calvin, *Institutes of the Christian Religion,* vol. 1 (1.3.1), trans. Henry Beveridge (Grand
Rapids: Eerdmans, 1957), 43.
59. Augusine, *Confessions* (7.17.23), trans., Henry Chadwick, Oxford World's Classics (New York:
Oxford University Press, 1998), 128.

has ably demonstrated that there are many things we can learn from the honest encounter with practitioners of world religions.

Finally, the postmodern "acceptance" model of Knitter should be renamed *narrative postmodernism*. While much of the postmodern worldview is incompatible with biblical revelation, the performative emphasis on narrative is very helpful. Evangelicals often have equated the biblical message with a short list of doctrinal propositions, unnecessarily separating our proclamation about Christ from the myriad of ways in which the gospel intersects our lives. We must take the individual religious narratives of those we encounter very seriously, even as we seek to connect them to the larger metanarrative of the gospel.

In short, an evangelical theology of religions should be able to embrace the positive performative qualities of each position. We should embrace the "hospitality" of openness, which is characterized by pluralists. We should learn from the inclusivists' eagerness to see that the *missio dei* transcends the particularities of the church's work of mission and witness in the world. We should take notice of the importance of biblical and personal narrative in the way we communicate the gospel.

The remaining four principles will be applied to the evangelical position renamed as revelatory particularism.

Second, *revelatory particularism should be articulated within a Trinitarian context*. This application of the second standard reminds us that the Christian gospel is unintelligible apart from the doctrine of the Trinity, since the doctrine of the Trinity is both the foundation and the goal of all Christian theologizing. This is the most practical way to keep all interreligious and intrareligious discussions within a broad theological frame that represents the fullness of the Christian proclamation.

God the Father is the source of all revelation. This connects particularism with the doctrine of creation and helps to maintain a robust view of general revelation. We can affirm that every religion, in various ways, contains "the silent work of God."[60] They reflect God's activity in the human heart and the human quest for God. Religions also reflect our unending attempts to flee from God, even in the guise of religious activity. As Calvin Shenk has observed, human religion reflects both "cries for help and ef-

---

60. J. H. Bavinck, *The Church Between Temple and Mosque: A Study of the Relationship Between the Christian Faith and Other Religions* (Grand Rapids: Eerdmans, 1966), 200.

forts of self-justification."[61] The Reformers insightfully applied the "law and gospel" theme to other religions by noting that other religions can serve one of the classic purposes of "law"; namely, they can create such despair and unanswered questions in the life of the adherent that he or she comes to the gospel of God's grace.[62]

God the Holy Spirit, as the agent of the New Creation, helps to place revelatory particularism within an eschatological context. For Christians, salvation is far more than the doctrine of justification. Salvation involves becoming full participants in the New Creation, which is already breaking into the present order. As we explored in chapter 6, this touches upon every aspect of culture.

Finally, at the heart of Trinitarianism is Jesus Christ, who is the apex of God's revelation and the ultimate standard by which all is judged. Rather than comparing and contrasting Christianity with other religions, we measure all religions, including Christianity, against the revelation of Jesus Christ, who is the embodiment of the New Creation. This is why it is important that an evangelical theology of religions be both Trinitarian and Christocentric.

This has important implications for the practice of interreligious dialogue, which often compares doctrines or experiences between two religions. For example, if a Hindu and a Christian are in a dialogue about the doctrine of karma, the only intelligible response from a Christian would be to relate the doctrine of karma to the Christian proclamation of the grace found in Jesus Christ. If a Muslim and a Christian are in a dialogue comparing Qur'anic and biblical views of revelation, it would only be a form of theological reductionism if the Christian did not point out that, for the Christian, the greatest form of revelation is embodied and personal in Jesus Christ. In short, the Trinity, and Jesus Christ in particular, is the hub around which all the doctrinal spokes of the Christian proclamation are held together. The particularity of Christ is crucial because Christianity always has claimed that there has been a very specific

---

61. Calvin E. Shenk, *Who Do You Say That I Am? Christians Encounter Other Religions* (Scottdale, PA: Herald, 1997), 75.

62. Terry Tiessen, following the work of Mariasuasai Dhavamony, makes the observation that cosmic religions focus on the revelation of God in creation, ethical religions reflect that the divine absolute makes Himself known in the human conscience, and salvific religions are a response to the awareness of the Fall and the need for salvation. See Terry Tiessen, "God's Work of Grace in the Context of the Religions," Διδασκαλια 18, no. 1 (Winter 2007): 167–168.

historical intervention by God, which is an "irruption of the timeless into time, by taking on of flesh by the Godhead."[63] God who is always "subject," never "object," has voluntarily placed Himself into the place of "object" for a while, to be seen, touched, and observed. Therefore, Christ represents the ultimate revelation of the whole Trinity. Jesus' life and ministry was empowered by God the Holy Spirit, and Jesus declared, "Anyone who has seen me has seen the Father" (John 14:9).

Third, *revelatory particularism embraces a canonical principle that asserts that the Bible is central to our understanding of God's self-disclosure.* God addresses fallen humanity not only in the Word made flesh but also in the Word that has been inscripturated into the biblical text. Revelatory particularists affirm without qualification that "all Scripture is God-breathed" and therefore "useful for teaching, rebuking, correcting and training in righteousness" (2 Tim. 3:16). The third principle insists that all insights from general revelation, or the particular claims of other religions, must be tested against the biblical revelation and against the person and work of Jesus Christ. Firm belief in personal and propositional revelation is the only sure way to deliver us from the abyss of relativism, endless human speculations, or, worse, the notion that religions are nothing more than pragmatic, consumer preferences in a global religious marketplace. As noted earlier, it is not enough to simply state that revelatory particularists affirm the three nonnegotiables. An evangelical theology of religions must be articulated within the larger frame of the entire canonical witness. Furthermore, we should always remember that the gospel is good news to be proclaimed. We are called to be witnesses of Jesus Christ, even in the context of interreligious dialogue.

Fourth, *revelatory particularism positions an evangelical theology of religions within the context of the missio dei.* In keeping with the fourth principle, it is only through the lens of the *missio dei* that a theology of religions can be fully related to the whole frame of biblical theology. Central to the *missio dei* is the understanding that through speech and actions, God is on a mission to redeem and bless all nations. In that sense, Kevin Vanhoozer is correct when he argues that God's self-disclosure is fundamentally theo-dramatic. In other words, revelation does not come down separate from human culture and context, as in Islam. Instead, God

---

63. Richard Holloway, *Signs of Glory* (London: Darton, Longman and Todd, 1982), 5.

enters into and interacts with human narratives and thereby is set within a *dramatic, missional* context.

The gospel is the greatest drama ever conceived. The divine theodrama begins with creation and the human response to God's rule, which we call the Fall. God responds to the Fall by initiating a redemptive covenant with Abraham, which includes a commitment to bless all nations. The theater of God's self-disclosure is the stage of human history, which Calvin referred to as the *theatrum gloriae Dei* (theater of the glory of God).[64] God Himself is the primary actor, in creation, in redemption, and in the New Creation. God acts and God speaks, and human history, including religious history and narratives, is the response to God's actions and words. God's deliverance of Israel from Egypt represents on a small scale what God intends to do with the entire human race on a deeper level. Vanhoozer points out that as the divine drama unfolded, there were many dramatic tensions that made it difficult to discern how God would keep His promise to Abraham and bless all nations. The death and resurrection of Christ represents the resolution of the tensions.[65] Sin and death are defeated, the New Creation is inaugurated, and the Spirit is sent to continue unfolding the drama of God's redemptive plan. An evangelical theology of religions should always be set forth within the larger context of the drama of the *missio dei*.

Finally, *revelatory particularism should be both evangelical and catholic.* Evangelical means being committed to the centrality of Christ, historic Christian orthodoxy, and the urgency to proclaim the gospel in word and deed, calling the world to repentance and faith. Evangelical faith helps us to remember the center of the gospel. However, we are catholic in the sense that we share a unity with all members of the body of Christ throughout the world. A robust commitment to ecumenism strengthens the whole church as long as it is bounded by the centrality of Christ and the principle of canonicity. We believe that "the *one* gospel is best understood in dialogue with the *many* saints."[66] The fifth standard reminds us that the entire global church brings different experiences and perspective on how to articulate the Christian faith within the context

---

64. Calvin, *Institutes of the Christian Religion* (1.14.20 and 2.6.1), 156, 293.
65. Kevin J. Vanhoozer, *The Drama of Doctrine: A Canonical-Linguistic Approach to Christian Theology* (Louisville: Westminster John Knox, 2005), 42.
66. Ibid., 30.

of religious pluralism without being hampered by the governing philosophical assumptions of the Enlightenment. The emergence of the global church represents a unique opportunity to recover biblical catholicity, which, as the Apostles' Creed reminds us, is one of the marks of the true church.

CONCLUSION

Retaining the classic paradigm with these modifications allows us to continue to engage in interreligious discussions within a commonly understood paradigm. However, the more precise nomenclature of the four positions, coupled with the broad outline on how to build upon the position of revelatory particularism, will help to invigorate evangelical involvement in interreligious dialogue, clarify our public witness in the midst of religious pluralism, and enable us to remain in consonance with the witness of the global church throughout history and around the world.

PART THREE

GOD THE SON:
THE REDEMPTIVE EMBODIMENT
OF THE *MISSIO DEI*

Section A

Missions History as a
Reflection of the Incarnation

— 8 —

Turning Points in the History of Missions before 1792

OVID, IN HIS *METAMORPHOSES*, is one of the earliest writers to record the ancient myth of Narcissus. According to Ovid, after his encounter with Echo, Narcissus fled to a river, where he knelt down to drink. However, as he was about to drink, he caught sight of his own reflection in the water and fell in love. Whenever he tried to drink from the river, the reflection was disturbed. So Narcissus refused to drink, and he gazed longingly at his own reflection until he died.

The myth of Narcissus has been used by modern writers and artists as varied as Keats, Dostoevsky, Freud, and even Bob Dylan to highlight the destructive nature of narcissism. Today, mirrors are among the most common objects in the world. They can be used in telescopes to bring distant images closer or in carnivals to make us laugh at our own caricatures. Mirrors are used every day by people all over the world to help with personal grooming.

According to Webster's dictionary, a mirror is a smooth surface with spectral qualities. In other words, a good mirror is one that is able to reflect an image with clarity and precision. From a theological perspective, the earliest and most important mirror is found in the original creation account. We are told that God created man and woman in His image. That is, we were designed to be a reflection, or mirror, of God in the created order. After the Fall, the mirror of God's image in us became distorted and fuzzy. It is in the Incarnation that God enters into our history in Jesus Christ. It is in Christ that we see God the Father perfectly imaged. Jesus represents the perfect representation of God in human flesh.

Missions history can be conceptualized as a mirror, or image reflector. Just as God in Jesus Christ entered history in order to show us what God is like, so the church is to embody and reflect the very presence of God in the world. In short, missions history is a reflection of the Incarnation. The role of the church is not just to bring a particular message but to *embody* the message as we image the Incarnation and foreshadow the coming New Creation. Undoubtedly, numerous examples can be cited where we have distorted God's intention for the church in the world. Like the distorted mirrors at carnivals, we have sometimes reflected only a crude caricature of Jesus Christ in the world. However, God in His providence has chosen and sent the church into the world to bear witness to His glory and the salvation that is found in Jesus Christ.

It is vital that anyone who senses God's call to be a missionary or who aspires to study missiology has a firm grasp of the historical sweep of missions history. Missions history should not be confused with church history. In chapter 1, we explored the important distinction between *church* history and *Christian* history. Church history inevitably is related to a particular group of Christians who share a particular geographic or confessional heritage. Writing Christian history is far more difficult, since it seeks to look at the experience of the entire global church. The telling of *missions* history has suffered similar problems as observed with church history. There are four tendencies that have at times plagued the church's understanding of missions history.

First, we often suffer from *historical myopia*, that is, we tend to neglect Christian movements that took place more than a few hundred years ago. This is why many Protestants seem to think that missions began in the eighteenth century with William Carey. Second, we have been guilty of *denominational parochialism*, which sees the history of missions only through the lens of whatever sector of the Christian church we happen to belong to. This leads many to think about missions only within the parameters of, for example, what the Lutherans or the Southern Baptists have done, thereby losing the important vantage point of world Christianity and diminishing our broader perspective on the *missio dei*. Third, missions history is seen as moving in a *singular direction*. Missions is conceptualized as a movement that extends from the West to the non-Western world. This is what we referred to in chapter 1 as the "West-reaches-the-rest" paradigm. We do not see ourselves as the recipients of missionary initiative, and we are often ignorant of important missionary initiatives from the Majority World. Finally, there is often an *antihistorical mood* that has affected some in the church and is manifested in various ways. For example, there is the attitude that history is boring and irrelevant because what "really matters" is what is happening right now. Also, in reaction to sectarian denominationalism, some speak about going to an unreached people group and preaching the gospel "just like they did in the book of Acts." They do not seem to realize that, for better or for worse, over two thousand years of Christian history have shaped or formed how the overwhelming majority of non-Christians view the Christian message. We cannot pretend that history doesn't exist and jump directly from the first century to the twenty-first century. The gospel comes to all of us *through* history, not *around* history.

Chapters 8, 9, and 10 are not intended to summarize the complex breadth of missions history. Missions history involves innumerable initiatives from all over the world, the most important of which are probably known only to God. Instead, the purpose of these chapters is to identify key snapshots or major turning points in the history of missions. Given the broad sweep of history, we can capture only a few tiny glimpses, which hopefully will give a *perspective* on history that is valuable and helpful.

This chapter will highlight seven key turning points in the history of missions prior to 1792, the year that traditionally marks the beginning of modern missions. These seven are chosen out of thousands of potential choices because of their importance in forming our understanding of the dynamics of the world Christian movement. The general method that will be followed is to briefly highlight the historical period and then identify why this event is so crucial to our understanding of Christian missions.

Unnamed Disciples from Cyprus and Cyrene

Our study begins, quite necessarily, in the years immediately following Christ's commission and the emergence of the Gentile mission. It is tempting to focus this first highlight on the apostle Paul, the reputed "apostle to the Gentiles" (Rom. 11:13: Gal. 2:8) and probably the greatest missionary in the history of the church. However, I have chosen to focus on a small group of unnamed disciples from Cyprus and Cyrene, who were the first to address the gospel to Gentiles who had no prior identity with Judaism.[1] These early missionaries preached the gospel to Gentiles *prior to* Paul's first missionary journey. They were used by God to foster arguably the most important missiological breakthrough in the entire book of Acts.

It is sometimes easy to forget that the Christian movement began as a messianic movement within a relatively small segment of first-century Judaism. These early Jewish Christians worshipped Jesus *Christ*, the Jewish Messiah. The cultural and linguistic translatability of the gospel, which we celebrate today, lay only in seed form. Jesus had commanded His disciples to "make disciples of all nations." By the internal logic of the gospel, if Jesus is who He claims to be, then His significance reaches far beyond the walls of Judaism. However, this truth remained untested. Jesus fulfilled Jewish expectations and Jewish prophecies, but was He also the answer to the deepest longings of Gentiles? Was the gospel "good news" to the pagan as well? The earliest major test occurred around A.D. 37 in the city of Antioch, just a few years after the resurrection of Christ.

The book of Acts records that a great persecution broke out against the church in connection with the martyrdom of Stephen (Acts 8:1). This persecution caused a scattering of believers from its base in Jerusalem to such faraway places as Phoenicia, Cyprus, and Antioch. Acts records that these scattered believers went around "telling the message only to Jews" (11:19). However, Acts 11:20 records, "Some of them, however, men from Cyprus and Cyrene, went to Antioch and began to speak to Greeks also, telling them the good news about the Lord Jesus." The Lord blessed these early missionaries and "a great number of people believed and turned to the Lord" (Acts 11:21). This is the origin of the church at Antioch, which some years later would be the sending church for the apostle Paul's great missionary journeys (Acts 13:1–3).

There are three very important observations that should be made in reflecting on this early missiological breakthrough among the Gentiles. First, *the encounter between these unnamed Jewish believers and the pagan*

---

1. The emphasis on "prior identity" is, of course, to acknowledge that God-fearers like Cornelius and the Ethiopian Eunuch were becoming Christians. However, these Gentiles already had identified themselves with the Jewish hope.

Gentiles of Antioch was precipitated by the persecution that broke out in Jerusalem. While it is not good to overly romanticize persecution, it is nevertheless important to see that God has used persecution throughout mission history to advance the *missio dei*.

Second, *we do not even know the names of these believers*. We only know that they were "men from Cyprus and Cyrene." These men were not apostles. They were not part of the inner circle of Peter, James, and John in Jerusalem. They occupied the *margins* of the fledgling Christian movement. After the dramatic Gentile breakthrough occurred in Antioch, "news of this reached the ears of the church at Jerusalem" (Acts 11:22). The church leadership was in Jerusalem, while the front edge of God's work was taking place in Antioch. Throughout the history of missions, we discover that God often takes initiatives at the margins, not always at the center of the Christian movement.

Third, *it is the Gentile breakthrough in Antioch that led to the famous Jerusalem Council recorded in Acts 15.* As long as the number of Gentiles remained small, the Jews had ways of accommodating Gentiles within a larger Jewish movement that retained Jewish identity. However, the growth of the Gentile movement forced the Jerusalem Council to meet in A.D. 49. The council was not, as is sometimes thought, a meeting of Jewish leaders to decide whether Gentiles could become followers of Christ. On the contrary, by the time of the council no one could deny the large number of Gentiles who were coming to the Lord Jesus. The council met only to debate the *terms* of the Gentile entry into the church. Would Gentiles be asked to submit to the "yoke of the Torah," or could they be accommodated on *their own cultural terms*. The decision of the Council of Jerusalem was in favor of *one* body of Christ but *multiple* cultures and lifestyles within the broad parameters of Christian morality. In short, the church embraced the cultural translatability of the gospel, opening the door to a potentially infinite number of cultural expressions that could all be authentically Christian. Excepting any ethnic Jews who are following Christ and reading this book, every Christian who is reading these pages is indebted to these earliest unnamed Christians who crossed that first cultural boundary with the good news of Jesus. We are Christians because someone followed in the footsteps of these "men from Cyprus and Cyrene" who preached the gospel to pagan Gentiles, "telling them the good news about the Lord Jesus."

ST. THOMAS PREACHES THE GOSPEL IN INDIA

In chapter 5 we examined the Great Commission passages that culminate the gospel accounts. John records those powerful words of commission by Jesus to His disciples, "As the Father has sent me, I am sending you" (John 20:21). However, John records that Thomas was not with them that evening (20:24). When Thomas heard about the appearance, he famously declared that unless he saw the nail-scarred hands of Jesus and put his finger into them and into Jesus' sword-pierced side, he would not believe (20:25). Because of this declaration, Thomas has become known as "Doubting Thomas." It seems that the church has sometimes forgotten that one week later when Thomas himself saw the risen Lord, he made the most powerful declaration of the deity of Christ found in any of the Gospels: "My Lord and my God! (20:28).

Although there are important traditions surrounding the ministries of all the apostles, we will focus our second highlight on the St. Thomas mission to India, which has been called by mission historian Samuel Moffett one of the "the oldest and strongest traditions in church history."[2] The earliest record of the mission of Thomas to India is found in the apocryphal *Acts of Thomas,* which was written around the turn of the third century. The *Acts of Thomas* records a dramatic moment, when the eleven apostles all gathered in Jerusalem and divided the known world into various regions. They then cast lots to determine where each of them would go. India fell to Thomas. According to the account, Thomas objected, saying that because of his "weakness of the flesh" he could not travel. However, Christ appeared to him in a vision and promised to be with him. Thomas eventually traveled by ship along one of the well-established trade routes to India, arriving in A.D. 52. He preached the gospel in various locations in India and finally suffered martyrdom and was buried near modern-day Chennai.

Although the *Acts of Thomas* as a whole is generally regarded as apocryphal and gives an overly romanticized view of Thomas, many scholars accept the basic historical nucleus of the account. The Western tradition has a number of corroborating references in other writers such as Ephraim, Gregory of Nazianzus, Ambrose, and Jerome.[3] There is also archaeological evidence from India, as well as an independent Indian tradition, that

2. Samuel Moffett, *A History of Christianity in Asia: Beginnings to 1500,* vol. 1 (Maryknoll, NY: Orbis, 2001), 25.
3. For a full discussion of the St. Thomas tradition, see Ian Gillman and Hans-Joachim Klimkeit, *Christians in Asia Before 1500* (Surrey, UK: Curzon, 1999), 166–73.

chronicles precise numbers of people healed from various diseases and maladies and detailed accounts of those who were converted, including what caste they were from. These sources also give a rich description of the circumstances around the martyrdom of Thomas. According to the Indian tradition, Thomas's martyrdom occurred on the third day of the month of Karkadakam (July) in A.D. 72, approximately six years after tradition tells us that the apostle Paul was martyred. Thomas met a group of high-caste Brahmins who were on their way to sacrifice at the temple of the goddess Kali. They tried to get Thomas to participate in the sacrifice, and, upon his refusal, they "pierced him with a lance."[4]

The specific details of these traditional accounts, about which we cannot speak with certainty, are not nearly as important as the core historical claim that Thomas brought the gospel to India in the first century. This vignette from mission history is important for our study for three reasons. First, *the Thomas tradition highlights the multidirectional mission of the early church.* This tradition represents the oldest documented account of the church in Asia beyond the borders of the Roman Empire. Even though Christianity was born in Asia, Samuel Moffett points out that because first-century Palestine was governed by Rome, it was "drawn into western church history."[5] Paul's missionary journeys, as recorded in Acts, detail the movement of the gospel farther into the West. There is no parallel account to the book of Acts that tells the story of the gospel's advance into the East. Therefore, very few Christians who read the book of Acts realize that at about the same time as Acts 19 records the apostle Paul preaching in Ephesus, the apostle Thomas was preaching the gospel in India. The book of Acts is not intended to give us a comprehensive picture of the entire early Gentile mission but rather highlights the spread of the gospel to the seat of the Roman Empire. It is important for students of mission to realize that from the beginning the spread of the gospel was multidirectional.

Second, the tradition of Thomas also underscores the importance of *recognizing the multiple layers of Christian tradition that are often present in Asian Christianity.* The apostolic tradition of Thomas is but the first of a series of initiatives into India. Thomas is followed by the arrival of

4. Mathias Mundadan, *History of Christianity in India: Beginnings to 1572*, vol. 1 (Bangalore: Theological Publications in India, 1984), 31–32.
5. Moffett, *A History of Christianity in Asia*, 25.

Thomas of Cana and Syriac Christians, who brought an Eastern liturgy in the fourth century. This is followed years later by major Roman Catholic initiatives, beginning with the arrival of Francis Xavier in 1542. Later, India receives Protestant missionaries with the arrival of the Lutheran missionaries Ziegenbalg and Plutschau in 1706. These are all examples of distinct traditions, all of which coexist in India to the present day. Diverse expressions of Christianity arrived at different times in different parts of India, and they all interacted in various ways, not only with the Hindu traditions, but also with the various Christian traditions as well.

Third, the presence of Christianity in ancient India also highlights the *difficulties in speaking without qualification of Hinduism as the "indigenous" religion of India.* Some accounts of Christianity in India leave the impression that Christianity in India is a movement that coincides with the British colonial presence there. It should be remembered, however, that the early religious forms of what is today known as Hinduism came from migrating Aryans who originated outside of India. There are many people groups in India who were Christians for centuries before the British presence was established. For example, in 1653 an event known as the oath of the Coonan cross took place among St. Thomas Christians in southwest India. Indian leaders took an oath, vowing to never become Roman Catholic because their indigenous faith was Eastern Orthodox Christianity.

In conclusion, the Thomas tradition reminds us that although the apostle Thomas may have come to believe in the resurrection of Jesus Christ a week after the other apostles, he went on to become one of the greatest cross-cultural missionaries of the first century.

THE TALE OF TWO MONKS, ALOPEN AND AUGUSTINE

The third historical highlight juxtaposes two missionary initiatives precipitated by two groups of monks during the seventh century, in two completely different parts of the world. The first story is associated with the papacy of Pope Gregory the Great. Gregory is hailed by Roman Catholic Christians as one of the great missionary popes. According to the Benedictine historian Venerable Bede (672–735), Gregory encountered several young, blonde-haired, blue-eyed boys being sold in the slave market. He inquired as to their ethnic origin, and upon hearing that they were Angles, he famously replied, *"non Angli, sed Angeli,"* that is, "They are not Angles but angels." This led to his dispatch St. Augustine of Canterbury on a mission to the Anglo-Saxon kingdoms in 596. Despite significant reluctance, Augustine, along with forty monks, arrived in 597 and was warmly received by King Ethelbert of Kent, who was married to a Christian princess named Bertha from Gaul. Over the next year, not only the King but approximately ten thousand Saxons also were baptized. However, Augustine became deeply concerned about the superficial nature of their conversion and also about a wide range of customs these new believers were bringing into the church. The reply of Pope Gregory the Great in A.D. 601 has become one of the classic mission letters in history.

The most important part of the letter is as follows:

> The heathen temples of these people need not be destroyed, only the idols which are to be found in them . . . If the temples are well built, it is a good idea to detach them from the service of the devil, and to adapt them for the worship of the true God . . . And since the people are accustomed, when they assemble for sacrifice, to kill many oxen in sacrifice to the devils, it seems reasonable to appoint a festival for the people by way of exchange. The people must learn to slay their cattle not in honor of the devil, but in honor of God and for their own food; when they have eaten and are full, then they must render thanks to the giver of all good things. If we allow them these outward joys, they are more likely to find their way to the true inner joy . . . It is doubtless impossible to cut off all abuses at once from rough hearts, just as the man who sets out to climb a high mountain does not advance by leaps and bounds, but goes upward step by step and pace by pace.[6]

This letter gives us a remarkable insight into a very early period of Christian missions. It demonstrates how the challenges of contextualization, the force of the gospel's translatability, and the pastoral needs of new believers are as old as the gospel itself.

However, before we reflect further on this early seventh-century letter, we need to travel from England in the West to China in the East. In 1623, some workmen digging near the city of Xián, the ancient capital of the

---

6. Norman E. Thomas, ed., *Classic Texts in Mission and World Christianity* (Maryknoll, NY: Orbis, 2003), 22.

T'ang dynasty, uncovered a massive limestone monument over nine feet high. At the top of the monument was carved a cross rising out of a lotus blossom. The inscription beneath tells the story of the Nestorian mission to China headed up by a monk named Alopen in A.D. 635. The following is a selection from the inscription on the Nestorian monument.

> Fulfilling the old law as it was declared by the twenty-four Sages, He (the Messiah) taught how to rule both families and kingdoms according to His own great Plan. Establishing His New Teaching of Nonassertion which operates silently through the Holy Spirit, another Person of the Trinity, He formed in humanity the capacity for well-doing through the Right Faith. Setting up the standard of the eight cardinal virtues, He purged away the dust from human nature and perfected a true character. . . . He brought Life to Light and abolished Death . . . He swept away the abodes of darkness. All the evil devices of the devil were thereupon defeated and destroyed. He then took an oar in the Vessel of Mercy and ascended to the Palace of Light. . . . The Great Means of Conversion (or leavening, i.e., transformation) were widely extended, and the sealed Gate of the Blessed Life was unlocked . . . His law is to bathe with water and the Spirit, and thus to cleanse from all vain delusions . . . His ministers carry the Cross with them as a Sign. They travel about wherever the sun shines and try to reunite those that are beyond the pale (i.e., those that are lost).[7]

It is fascinating that the arrival of Augustine of Canterbury to the Saxons and the arrival of Alopen to the Chinese court are separated by less than forty years. Our general familiarity with the Western missionary expansion often eclipses the remarkable expansion of the gospel along the silk route by Nestorian missionaries. This is particularly true of the Nestorian Christians because of the condemnation of Nestorius at the Council of Ephesus in A.D. 431. Nestorius and his followers were uncomfortable with expressions like "God was crucified," and "God suffered," and references to Mary as the "mother of God." This led to conflicts over the precise

---

7. Ibid., 11–12. For the complete text of the Xi'an Stele with a full analysis, see Jean-Pierre Charbonnier, *Christians in China* (San Francisco: Ignatius, 2007), 21–38.

way to describe the relationship between the humanity and the deity of Christ and how each relates to His nature and His person. This eventually led to a split that expelled the Nestorians, who are known in the East as the Assyrian Church of the East. Once expelled, the Nestorians became great missionaries, traveling to distant places with the gospel. Today, it is widely accepted that those early missionaries were largely orthodox, even if they objected to the precise wording of what eventually became the Chalcedonian formulation of A.D. 451.

There are two important lessons to be drawn from the work of these two bands of monks, led by Augustine and Alopen. *First, we should observe the deep commitment of these early missionaries to the cultural translatability of the gospel.* The letter from Gregory the Great and the monument to the Nestorian mission both demonstrate deep reflection concerning the contextualization of the gospel. Gregory the Great's letter establishes three principles of contextualization that continue to guide missionaries today. First, he establishes the principle of *adaptation* in relation to cultural forms. He tells Augustine not to destroy the well-built temples but simply to cleanse them of the idols that are found inside. The pagan temples then could be adopted and used as places of Christian worship. Second, he establishes the principle of *exchange* in relation to pagan practices. Gregory the Great wisely understands that it is not sufficient to simply condemn the pagan sacrifices, which play such a central role in the religious life of the Saxons. He instructs Augustine to tell the new believers to give up their pagan sacrifices and to provide an alternative Christian ritual that allows them to sacrifice their animals in praise to God. Christians may disagree about whether this was good advice, but it is important to recognize the principle that is involved and the situation, which countless missionaries have faced over the centuries. Finally, Gregory sets forth the principle of *gradual transformation*. He realizes that the Saxon community will not be transformed overnight, so he encourages Augustine to allow time for the Holy Spirit to work in the lives of the new believers. It may be several generations before the Saxons are discipled into full-orbed faith and practice.

The Nestorian monument demonstrates that the Nestorians did not impose a Western gospel on the Chinese and insist that it be stated in precisely the same way they had learned the gospel. The T'ang dynasty was a period when Confucianism and Buddhism were both thriving. The Nestorian missionaries related the truths of the gospel in a way that drew heavily from the current religious understanding of the Chinese. Yet, despite the use of language and terms that sound strange to Western ears, one cannot help but discern in reading the entire inscription that the Nestorian monks were equally committed to communicating the Christian gospel.

Second, as noted with the apostle Thomas's mission to India, *we should recognize the antiquity of Christianity in Asia*. Later, Roman Catholic and Protestant missionaries arrived in China and discovered that the message of the gospel had *already preceded them*. This is an important reminder of the relationship of the *missio dei* to the missionary agent. Missionaries sometimes have mistakenly seen their role as "bringing the gospel" to a particular people group. However, one of the important lessons of the *missio dei* is to recognize God's primary agency in the missionary task. The missionaries did not bring the gospel to China; God brought the missionaries to China. After the dramatic conversion of the Saxons, Augustine inquired about a suitable location to build a church. To the surprise of Augustine, Queen Bertha brought him to the ruins of a Christian church, which had been constructed centuries earlier. It is thought that the gospel's first entrance into England probably came through unnamed soldiers of the Roman Empire who had been converted. The gospel spreads not just through the officially commissioned missionaries, but also through countless ordinary believers who, wherever they go, bear witness to the good news of Jesus Christ.

RAYMOND LULL AND THE CHALLENGE OF ISLAM

It is difficult for us to fully grasp how the rapid spread of Islam beginning in the seventh century affected the psyche of the average Christian in the Middle Ages.[8] Muhammad died in A.D. 632. Within four years Islamic armies had captured Damascus and Antioch. By 638 they had laid siege to Jerusalem and captured it in only four months. This soon was followed by the fall of Caesarea (640) and Alexandria (642). Islamic armies eventually crossed over into Europe and captured most of Spain and would have penetrated even deeper into Europe if they had not been stopped by Charles Martel at the Battle of Tours in A.D. 732. However, Islam continued to spread into North and East Africa and deep into Asia. Within a

---

8. The Middle Ages generally refers to the period between the papacy of Gregory the Great and the capture of Constantinople by Muslims in 1453. Others extend the Middle Ages until the inauguration of the Portuguese and Spanish voyages of discovery.

few centuries, the Islamic Empire stretched from Spain in the West, across North Africa, the Middle East, and portions of central Asia. Although the Byzantine Empire did not officially fall until the Muslims sacked Constantinople in 1453, the threat of Islam was an ongoing source of anxiety and speculation throughout the entire Middle Ages.

The Christian response to the rise of Islam is remembered mostly as a series of military campaigns launched by Western Christendom against Islam known as the Crusades. The seven campaigns that are generally identified as the "Crusades" took place between 1095 and 1250. The reasons for the Crusades were complex and intertwined, ranging from a desire to safeguard pilgrims to the Holy Land, to the search for new sources of wealth, to the need to strengthen the waning power of the papacy. However, the central long-term objective was to defeat the Islamic armies and to retake the Holy Land, thereby reclaiming lost territories for Christendom. From both a military and a spiritual perspective, the Crusades were a total failure. Indeed, the negative memory of the Crusades continues to inform Islamic attitudes about Christianity, even to the present day.

It is important to realize, however, that the Crusades are not the *only* story of the Christian response to Islam during the Middle Ages. The fourth historical focus highlights the life and ministry of Raymond Lull (1232–1315), known as the Father of Islamic Apologetics. Lull was born during one of the most remarkable and tumultuous times in history. During his lifetime, Spain was being liberated from Islamic domination. Within the first few decades of his life, he witnessed the rise of the Ottoman Turks, the dismal failure of the seventh crusade, and the founding of the first college of Oxford University.

By his own account, Lull was a licentious young man and, even after marriage, engaged in several adulterous relationships. He was a well-known poet and skilled musician in the Christian court of Aragon, where he grew up. However, after a dramatic vision of Christ, Lull was powerfully converted in his early thirties and became a dedicated follower of Christ.[9] He was deeply disturbed by the hateful and militaristic attitude of Christians toward Muslims that was prevalent in his day. He was dismayed to realize that no Christian writer was responding to the philosophical challenges that had been posed by the famous Islamic philosophers Ibn Sina

---

9. Lull tells the story of his conversion in his book, *The Tree of Love,* trans. Edgar Allison Peers (London: SPCK, 1926).

(Avicenna, 980–1037) and Ibn Rushd (Averroes, 1126–1198). Lull decided to dedicate his life to finding a way to effectively communicate the gospel to Muslims.

With nearly three hundred published works, Lull's writings are vast, covering political theory, poetry, mathematics, science, philosophy, and theology.[10] Early on in his writings, Lull recognized the need to develop a Christian apologetic that specifically and directly responded to Islamic misunderstandings and objections to Christianity. Lull spent nine years learning Arabic and carefully studying Islamic philosophy and theology. Eventually he developed a multivolume, Trinitarian apologetic, known as *Ars Generalis Ultima* (The Ultimate General Art), which answered Islamic objections to Christianity and advocated a method for talking to Muslims that is sometimes known as the Lullian method. Lull was convinced that the military confrontation represented by the Crusades was a mistake. Rather, he believed that Muslims should be addressed in love, not hate, and by the force of logic, not the instruments of war.

Lull also recognized the need to train and mobilize an entire new movement of monks who would go into the Muslim world as missionaries. Lull called on the pope and the princes of Christendom to establish monasteries for the study of Arabic and other languages spoken by Islamic peoples in order to train monks in his "method" and send them out to turn the Islamic world to Christ. Lull wrote,

> I see many knights going to the Holy Land in the expectation of conquering it by force or arms; but instead of accomplishing this object, they are in the end all swept away themselves. Therefore, it is my belief that the conquest of the Holy Land should be attempted in no other way than as Christ and his apostles undertook to accomplish it; by love, by prayer, by tears, and by the offering up of our own lives. It seems that the possession of the Holy Sepulchre can be better secured by the force of preaching than by the force of arms, therefore let monks march forth as holy knights . . . and proclaim to the infidels the truth of His passion.[11]

10. For a sampling of Lull's writings, see Anthony Bonner, ed., *Doctor Illuminatus. A Ramon Lull Reader* (Princeton, NJ: Princeton University Press, 1985).
11. Augustus Neander, *General History of the Christian Religion and Church*, trans. Joseph Torrey (Boston: Crocker and Brewster, 1854), 191.

Lull eventually secured the support for this plan from Pope John XXI. Lull insisted that everyone trained in his method be *committed to Christian martyrdom*. Given the ongoing conflicts with Islam in his day, this was a sober realization by Lull of the inherent dangers in any Islamic mission. Lull made at least four missionary journeys to Islamic North Africa. He was able to present his apologetic defense of Christianity to Muslim leaders. However, he also suffered expulsions, abuse, and long imprisonments. Finally, when he was in his eighties, he preached to a gathering of Muslims in Algiers and was stoned. Early biographers are divided about whether he died as a result of the stoning and was brought back to Spain where he is buried, or whether he was severely injured and died a year later back in Spain.

Lull is important in the history of missions for several reasons. First, *Lull was ahead of his time in his recognition of the long-term ill effects of the Christendom-sponsored military confrontations with Islam.* In his *Treatise on the Manner of Converting the Infidels* (1292), he unequivocally denounced the Crusades as a bitter failure. In our own day, the Western world is, once again, involved in a protracted, military struggle with Islam. In the midst of the "war on terror," the Christian community must redouble its efforts to find ways to communicate the good news of Jesus Christ in love.

Second, *Lull understood the role of apologetics in the Christian mission and the need to respond to objections that were posed.* Even though some of Lull's arguments in the *Ars Generalis Ultima* are inconsistent and not always even fully coherent, he profoundly understood the importance of developing an apologetic that considers the particular issues that are important in Islam.

Finally, *Lull was committed to missions mobilization.* The most successful missionaries in history are those who were also good mobilizers, multiplying their life and vision into others. Lull recognized that the religious, cultural, and theological structures of Islam could not be responded to by a few Christians but needed the attention and focused effort of tens of thousands of Christians.

Lull's ministry and scholarship have given him many titles, including *Doctor Illuminatus*, Father of Islamic Apologetics, and Father of Islamic Missions. However, perhaps his most important and enduring title is that of the apostle of love in an age of hate.

FROM PADROADO (1493) TO PROPAGANDA FIDE (1622)

This fifth historical snapshot is not focused on one particular individual but on a very influential period in the history of Roman Catholic missions. When Columbus returned to Spain from his famous voyage to the New World, his ship was blown off course, and he landed in Lisbon, Portugal. King John II saw this as an opportunity to claim that all the territorial discoveries made by Columbus belonged to Portugal. A Western route to Asia was considered vital to bypass Islamic powers, which controlled the traditional routes to the East. King Ferdinand and Queen Isabella of Spain sent ambassadors to Rome to resolve the conflict. On May 4, 1493, Pope Alexander VI issued a papal bull that created a line of demarcation that ran longitudinally "one hundred leagues toward the west and south" from the Azores and Cape Verde Islands. This line down the Atlantic, known as the Padroado, essentially granted special patronage to Spain in the West and to Portugal to the East. A year later, the line was moved 370 degrees west, granting Portugal a foothold in the New World and allowing it to colonize Brazil, which explains why Portuguese is the language spoken in Brazil. Pope Alexander VI was a secular and nepotistic pope who was more interested in amassing wealth and power than in extending the gospel. Nevertheless, the Padroado had important implications for world evangelization and our understanding of the legacy of the modern-day missions movement.

The Padroado raises important questions about the relationship of Christian missions and colonization. It is commonly believed that missions were but the vanguard of colonial imperialism and colonialism, which in turn operated under the guise of divine sanction. Today, churches often carry a strong sense of guilt about the whole missionary enterprise, largely because missions has "acquired the unsavory odor of collusion with the colonial powers" and become associated with imperialism and forced conversions.[12] However, Yale historian Lamin Sanneh, in *Translating the Message: The Missionary Impact on Culture*, has argued that we should be careful not to accept this sweeping judgment too uncritically. Sanneh argues that there are two distinct impulses that have operated throughout the history of Christian missions, including during

---

12. Lamin Sanneh, *Translating the Message: The Missionary Impact on Culture* (Maryknoll, NY: Orbis, 1989), 88.

the colonial expansion. He summarizes these two impulses as "missions as translation" and "missions as cultural diffusion." The former is the missionary impulse that learns the local languages and seeks the successful indigenization of the gospel. The latter is the impulse that imposes a foreign language and merely replicates Western cultural religious forms. Sanneh argues that while both have been present, missions as translation has been the "dominant mode of operation."[13]

Roman Catholic missionaries operating under the Padroado found themselves in constant conflict with the secular authorities. For example, when the authorities issued an injunction that all religious instruction was to take place in the Castilian language, the missionaries refused to cooperate. The missionary movement and the colonial movement coincided in time, but they were two distinct movements. Of course, there are examples of embarrassing entanglements when missionaries were co-opted by the secular authorities and pursued mission as "cultural diffusion." However, we should resist the reductionism that paints all missionaries with this one brush. To illustrate this point, I have chosen two missionaries who represent a counterbalance to the view that sixteenth-century missions was nothing more than "imperialism by prayer."

Bartolomé de las Casas (1484–1566) immigrated to the island of Hispaniola in the Caribbean in 1502. Upon his arrival he was shocked by the cruel treatment of the Indians by the colonial authorities. He eventually was ordained as a Dominican priest and became a fierce critic of Spanish colonial practices. The governor of Hispaniola, Nicolas de Ovando, had introduced a system of encomiendas, which gave Spanish settlers Indians as slaves, ostensibly in return for Christian instruction. Las Casas carefully documented the atrocities of the conquistadors and was instrumental in not only getting laws passed to protect the rights of indigenous peoples, but also in stimulating an important theological debate about Christian attitudes toward human rights. Las Casas articulated a doctrine of natural human rights that was well ahead of his time, earning him the title "Protector of the Indians" in 1516.

Alessandro Valignano was born into an Italian noble family and joined the Society of Jesus (Jesuits) in 1566. In 1573 he was appointed director of all the Jesuit work in the East, and he is considered the architect of the Jesuit mission to Asia. He made regular trips to India and China,

---

13. Ibid., 90.

but particularly to Japan (1579–82; 1590–92; 1598–1603). It was through his observation of Christianity in Japan that he first articulated the Jesuit missiology in his *Il Ceremoniale per I Missionari del Giapponne*, published in 1581. In the policy, Valignano established a number of important principles that continue to inform missionary work today, including the following examples. First, he distinguished between European culture and the essentials of the Christian faith. Second, because of tensions between Spain and Portugal during the post-Padroado period, he pointed out the inevitable problems when the state is given sovereignty over missionary work. He argued for a necessary independence from Portugal in the missionary work in Asia. Third, he rejected the conquistador principle, which had undergirded the Crusades and supported the use of military action to gain former Christian lands that had been seized by Muslims. Fourth, he encouraged his missionaries, wherever possible, to affirm Japanese cultural practices and even encouraged the ordination of Japanese priests.[14]

As time progressed and new churches began to emerge, the missionaries were increasingly vocal about their discontent concerning their dependence on colonial powers who clearly had only their own economic interest in view. The defeat of the Spanish Armada in 1588 marked the end of Spanish political and military hegemony in Europe. As Spanish and Portugese power waned, the papacy decided to regain a more central role over the missionary work of the church. Pope Gregory XV had chosen the name Gregory because, as we saw earlier, the name Gregory was associated with an interest in missionary outreach. Gregory XV established a special arm of the church dedicated solely to organizing and overseeing the missionary outreach of the Roman Catholic Church. This special department is known as the *Sacred Congregation of the Propaganda Fide*, in essence, a holy department to oversee the propagation of the faith.[15]

---

14. Stephen Neill, *A History of Christian Missions* (Baltimore: Penguin, 1964), 157–158. Missions historian Samuel Moffett points out that Valignano's insistence on missionaries learning to speak Japanese and the importance of ordaining Japanese as priests went against the views of Francisco Cabral, who was the resident superior of the Japanese mission. This demonstrates the wisdom and persistence of Valignano despite opposition, even by his senior mission colleagues. See Samuel Moffett, *A History of Christianity in Asia: 1500–1900*, vol. 2 (Maryknoll, NY: Orbis, 2005), 77–78.

15. The Sacred Congregation of the Propaganda Fide should not be confused with the Society for the Propagation of the Faith, which was founded in 1822 by Pauline-Marie Jaricot in Lyons, France, and is one of the four modern Pontifical mission societies.

The declaration was made by the pope on January 6, 1622 as follows:

> In the Name of Christ. In the year 1622 after His birth, on January
> 6th, our Holy Father in Christ, Gregory XV by divine providence
> Pope, in the conviction that the most notable duty of his pastoral
> office is the dissemination of the Christian faith, through which
> men may be brought to the knowledge and adoration of the true
> God, constituted a congregation of thirteen cardinals and two
> prelates, with a secretary, to whom he entrusted and commanded
> the care for the propagation of the faith.[16]

The first secretary of the *Propaganda* was Francesco Ingoli. He set
vital precedents for missionary mobilization and strategy, which are still
important today. Prior to the *Propaganda Fide,* missionaries were often
sent to distant lands without any plans or strategy. The new department
in the Vatican helped to coordinate and reflect on the overall missions
strategy of the church.

This period of Roman Catholic missions is important for three reasons. First, contrary to many prevailing assumptions, *many of the Roman
Catholic missionaries were sensitive to the challenges of contextualization.*
These early missionaries reflected deeply on how the gospel might best
take root in a new culture. Many of the missionaries resisted the colonial
patrons of power and were far more committed to "mission by translation"
than is sometimes assumed.

Second, this period represents *an important advance in the fledgling
field of missiology,* especially in the area of research and missiological
training. The *Propaganda Fide* devoted considerable resources in order
to gain accurate information about the status of Christianity around the
world and the particular problems each field posed. The congregation
created the position of vicars apostolic, who was directly accountable to
Rome and did not have to go through either Spain or Portugal. A special
training center known as the *Société des Missions Étrangères* was established in France for training Roman Catholic missionaries.

Finally, *the Roman Catholic missionaries had an enormous influence
on many of the later Protestant missionaries to Asia.* For example, Hudson

---

16. Neill, *History of Christian Missions,* 178.

Taylor drew many positive lessons from the Roman Catholic Jesuit missionaries, such as Matteo Ricci (1552–1610), who had preceded him in China.

COUNT NICOLAS VON ZINZENDORF
AND THE MORAVIAN MISSION

Popular missionary literature often cites William Carey as the father of the modern Protestant missionary movement. In chapter 9 we will explore why Carey's role is so pivotal in the history of modern missions. However, it is important to recognize that an entire Protestant missionary movement occurred *prior* to William Carey.

The Moravian missionary movement arose out of a seventeenth and eighteenth-century movement known as Pietism. Pietism was a renewal movement that emphasized personal devotion, Bible study, sermons, and the role of the laity. Many of the key themes of Pietism are found in Philip Jacob Spener's classic work, *Pia Desideria* (Pious Desires) published in 1675.[17] The full extent and far-ranging influences of Pietism on Christianity are beyond the scope of this chapter. However, it is important to note that the sixteenth-century Protestant Reformation did not produce any missionaries.[18] It was the advent of Pietism two centuries later that produced the first Protestant missionaries, Bartholomew Ziegenbalg and Henry Plutschau, who went to India in 1705 through the Danish-Halle mission. However, the Moravians and the mobilization efforts of Count Nicolas von Zinzendorf will be the focus of this historical spotlight because the Moravians represent the first major Protestant missionary *movement*.

Count Nicolas von Zinzendorf (1700–1760) grew up under the influence of Pietism. Most of his early years were spent in Halle, Germany, under the influence of August Francke, one of the great figures of early Pietism. In 1722, Zinzendorf, a wealthy German nobleman, purchased a large estate in Berthelsdorf (eastern Germany), which he allowed to be used as a refuge for Christians from Bohemia and Moravia (present-day Czech Republic) who were fleeing persecution from the established church.

---

17. Philip Jacob Spener, *Pia Desideria* (Philadelphia: Fortress, 1964). Spener lived from 1635 to 1705.
18. John Calvin did attempt to send missionaries to Brazil to serve as chaplains to the French colonists. However, they are not generally accepted as the first missionaries because they were not admitted into the country, and they were not seeking to carry the gospel across cultural lines.

Although the Moravian Church did not become a separate denomination until the 1740s, it has roots in the fourteenth-century Hussite movement associated with the dissenter John Hus. Often cited as a pre-Reformation Protestant, John Hus was one of the earliest critics of the abuses present in Roman Catholicism at that time. Hus's followers eventually formed a movement known as the Unity of the Brethren (*Unitas Fratrum*), which continued as an early "Protestant" movement. However, the movement often was persecuted and existed primarily underground. In 1722 the Brethren took refuge at Zinzendorf's estate. The number of refugees eventually grew to over three hundred, including some dissenting German Pietists who also joined the Brethren. They named the place where this community formed Herrnhut, meaning, "The Lord's Watch."

On August 13, 1727 the community received a powerful outpouring of the Holy Spirit, causing a dramatic revival among the Brethren. Many who were there described it as a Pentecost-like event that brought a powerful sense of unity, prayerfulness, spiritual fervor, and renewed dedication to Jesus Christ. Within a few years the *Unitas Fratrum*, now known as Moravians, were to become a major force for world evangelization under the guidance, itinerancy, and mobilization of Zinzendorf, who in 1737 was consecrated as the bishop of the church. The Moravians eventually sent hundreds of missionaries all over the world, including the Caribbean, North and South America, the Arctic, Africa, the Middle East, and India.

There are several vital lessons we can learn from this first Protestant missionary movement. First, *the Moravians were deeply committed to pray for the evangelization of the world*. The dramatic move of God in their midst on August 13, 1727, was so profound that they continued taking turns in maintaining a prayer vigil. The Moravians focused their "prayer wall" on the evangelization of the world. This prayer vigil was maintained twenty-four hours a day, seven days a week, for over one hundred years! We must remember that many decades later when famous pioneer missionaries such as William Carey and Adoniram and Ann Judson arrived in India and Burma respectively, this prayer meeting was still going on. The entire "great century" of Protestant missions was birthed out of the fervent prayers of the Moravians at Herrnhut. There is no better way to situate all missionary endeavors and mobilizations in the *missio dei* than through a commitment to prayer.

Second, the Moravians were the first modern group of Christians to fully recognize that *the missionary enterprise was the primary work of all Christians*, not just a few selected specialists. Because of their history of persecution and displacement as refugees, the Moravians were accustomed to adversity and travel. Therefore, they made excellent missionaries. Charles Robinson's classic summary of the Moravian mission underscores this point,

> Within twenty years of the commencement of their missionary work the Moravian Brethren had started more missions than Anglicans and Protestants had started during the two preceding centuries. Their marvelous success was largely due to the fact that from the first they recognized that the evangelization of the world was the most pressing of all the obligations that rested upon the Christian church, and that the carrying out of this obligation was the "common affair" of the community.[19]

Theologically, this commitment to full mobilization was possible only because of the Moravian ecclesiology, which emphasized the central role of the laity, downplayed denominational affiliation, and refused to associate the church with the state, as was the common practice in Europe at that time. Zinzendorf's commitment to mobilize the entire movement also made him a forerunner in encouraging female preachers, evangelists, church planters, catechists, and pastors. The pietistic Moravian mission was like a traveling monastic order, but rather than a celibate clergy, they were sending out entire families as models of Christian community.

Third, *the Moravians were self-supporting missionaries*. Long before the twentieth-century notion of professional "tentmakers" came into vogue, the Moravians understood that a professionalized missionary force would require extensive financial and logistical support to maintain. To support full-time professional missionaries would require up to 90 percent of the church to remain home in order to generate sufficient disposable income to support the missionaries. Instead, the Moravians opted for a lay mission force that would be completely self-supporting through the practice of their own trades. Stephen Neill observes that one of the

---

19. Charles Robinson, *History of Christian Missions* (Edinburgh: T & T Clark, 1915), 49–50.

distinguishing qualities of the Moravian missionaries was that they were "simple people, peasants and artisans."[20]

The first Moravian missionary sent out from Herrnhut is representative of many who followed. Leonhard Dober (1706–1766) had traveled 315 miles on foot to get to Herrnhut, arriving in 1725. He was, by trade, a potter, as his father had been before him. While at Herrnhut he experienced the spiritual awakening that took place in 1727. Like many of the Brethren, he loved music and served the community by directing the choir and composing hymns, revealing the ongoing influence of Pietism in the community. Later, Zinzendorf introduced to the community a former African slave known as Anton who had become a Christian. The slave challenged the community to send missionaries to work with African slaves. After a sleepless night in prayer, Dober committed himself to become a missionary to African slaves. On August 21, 1732, Dober was sent from Herrnhut to the malaria-infested island of St. Thomas in the Caribbean, where he ministered to African slaves. He was sent out (along with a carpenter named David Nitschmann) and charged to support himself by his own hands. Dober went on to have a long and distinguished career as a missionary, general elder, and later, bishop of the Moravian Church.

Finally, the Moravians were known *to send missionaries to difficult places to work among marginalized peoples.* The work among slaves on St. Thomas is representative of the Moravian commitment to the margins of society. Because the Moravians were themselves a marginalized and persecuted community, they had a special burden for other displaced and suffering peoples. This commitment often came at great sacrifice. For example, of the eighteen missionaries who were eventually sent from Herrnhut to work with the slaves on St. Thomas, half died within the first six months.

While the Moravian Church has never been large, it has exerted an influence well beyond its size. Influential Christian leaders such as John Wesley and William Carey have all paid tribute to the formative role the Moravians played in their spiritual formation. There are many surprising personal and literary associations that connect the Moravian mission with the missionary work of the Puritans of New England.[21] As the first Protes-

---

20. Neill, *History of Christian Missions,* 237.
21. For example, the correspondence of Cotton Mather, the leader of Boston Puritanism, with August Francke, who was at the heart of the pietistic missionary movement, and with Ziegenbalg, the first Protestant missionary, is sometimes ignored. Other personal encounters, such

tant missionary movement, the Moravians continue to inspire and inform all later endeavors that seek to follow in their footsteps.

THE ODD ORIGINS OF KOREAN CHRISTIANITY

Despite being one of the last countries in Asia to receive the Christian message, Korea has one of the most fascinating and unusual origins of any church in the world. The history of "The Hermit Kingdom" has been marked by numerous invasions and periods of isolation from outside contact. Korea often was invaded because it was considered a "stepping stone to the conquest of China."[22] One of the most important invasions of Korea took place in 1592, when the Japanese army of Toyotomi Hideyoshi sent nine army divisions to crush Korea.[23] Many Koreans were taken back to Japanese prison camps, where they met Jesuit priests, who were permitted to work in Japan at that time.

Japan often is thought of as a place completely closed and isolated from the gospel. It is true that between the Great Edict of Annihilation issued in 1614 by Ieyasu until the arrival of the gunships of Matthew Perry in 1853, Japan was completely isolated from any outside contact, and thousands of Christians were martyred during those years.[24] However, prior to 1614, there were times of considerable freedom for Jesuits to work in Japan, and many Japanese came to Christ during this time. According to Samuel Moffett, in 1595–1596 there were 137 Jesuit missionaries in Japan. By 1609 they had over 220,000 Christians under their care in Japan. By the time of the Great Edict of Annihilation, Moffett estimates that the number of Christians in Japan was between 300,000 and 500,000.[25] However, what sometimes is not recognized is the contact these Christians had with Koreans being held in Japanese prison camps. For example, one of the Jesuit missionaries, Father Fróis (1532–1597), working under the auspices

---

as Gilbert Tennent's meeting with Count Nicolas Von Zinzendorf in New York, provide an important clue to the interconnectedness of these missionary thrusts. For more on the connections between pietistic and Puritan missions, see Ernst Benz, "Pietist and Puritan Sources of Early Protestant World Missions," in *Christianity and Missions, 1450–1800*, ed. J. S. Cummins (Brookfield, VT: Ashgate, 1997), 315–42.

22. Moffett, *A History of Christianity in Asia: 1500–1900*, 143.

23. Ibid., 144.

24. The Jesuits were ordered to leave the country in 1587, but due to the careful negotiation of Alessandro Valignano, the Jesuits were permitted to stay as long as they agreed not to involve themselves in any political affairs.

25. Moffett, *History of Christianity in Asia: Beginnings to 1500*, 95.

of Portugal, reported in 1596 that there were at least three hundred Koreans being held by the Japanese in Nagasaki alone. Interestingly, there are no known Christians in Korea at this time, but Koreans were becoming Christians in Japanese prison camps. In fact, the presence of Korean Christians in Japanese prison camps is confirmed during the persecution following the 1614 Edict. Japanese records indicate hundreds of Korean prisoners who were put to death for their faith along with the Japanese. Because Korea was closed to outside missionaries, it became necessary to work with expatriate Koreans who were being held in Japan. It is ironic that Koreans already were being martyred for their faith even before there were any known Christians in Korea.[26]

Other influences came to Korea via China. Around 1770 the Korean ambassador to China, Chong tu-won, brought back to Korea Matteo Ricci's *Tianzhu* or *True Doctrine of the Lord of Heaven*.[27] This and other works gradually trickled in from China during these years. One young Korean scholar known as Yi Pyok was part of an intellectual movement known as the Shilhak school (School of Practical Learning). The Shilhak school was a neo-Confucian movement that sought to return to the practicality of Confucian thought over against a more philosophical trend. The Shilhak scholars were interested in learning from the Western world and were open to studying thinking from outside of Korea. In 1783 these scholars asked Yi Sang-Hung (Lee Seung-Hun), the son of the ambassador, if, while he was at the imperial court, he could visit the Catholic missionaries in China and learn all he could about Christianity. The twenty-seven-year-old Yi was instructed by the Jesuits and baptized in Beijing prior to his return to Korea. When Yi returned to Korea in 1784, now with the baptismal name Peter Lee Seung-Hun, he brought with him Christian literature from China, which he distributed to the Shilhak scholars. They decided that Christianity would be beneficial to Korea because it established authority based on merit, not based on birth, and because the basic ethics of Christianity were not in

---

26. One Spanish Jesuit priest, Gregorio de Cespedes (1551–1611), was permitted to serve Japanese Christians in Korea, but he was not permitted to have any contact with Koreans. The only Koreans he probably ever met were Korean prisoners of war being sent back to Japan to be sold as slaves. Nevertheless, Gregorio de Cespedes is the first known Westerner to set foot on Korean soil.

27. According to Moffett, the earliest mention of a Christian book in Korea was by Confucianist scholar Yi Syu-Kwang (d. 1627), who gives a summary of Matteo Ricci's *The True Meaning of the Lord of Heaven* (T'ien-chu Shih-i). See Moffett, *History of Christianity in Asia: 1500–1900*, 146.

major conflict with Confucian ethics. Peter Lee baptized a Korean believer, Lee Pyok, and renamed him "John-Baptist." Together they started to baptize others and ordain priests. This marks the beginning of Roman Catholic missionaries being permitted to spread the gospel in Korea.

There are three important observations about the emergence of Korean Christianity that are crucial to our understanding of the emergence of global Christianity. First, *Korea is one of the few countries in the world where the church was born outside the country through expatriates who were being held as prisoners.* Second, *the first missionaries to Korea were not foreign missionaries but Koreans themselves who had come to Christ outside of Korea and returned as indigenous propagators of the gospel.* Third, *one of the earliest documentations of the Christian message was from Chinese Christian documents, rather than literature that explained the gospel in Western terminology.* Since Korea has become one of the most Christianized countries in Asia and today is the home of the largest Christian churches in the world, it is important to recall the unusual origins of Korean Christianity, which was birthed through indigenous expressions of faith. If the *missio dei* is best understood as the arrival of the gospel prior to the missionaries, then the Korean church represents one of the foremost examples.

CONCLUSION

These seven snapshots of missionary activity prior to 1792 provide only a few brief glimpses into some of the remarkable turning points in the history of missions. All the lessons that have been highlighted collectively underscore the importance of viewing missions through the lens of the *missio dei*. Missions history is about God keeping His promise to Abraham to bless all nations. The Incarnation is the embodiment of that blessing and is the greatest example of God's commitment to all nations on earth. Every missionary endeavor since the coming of Christ has been an attempt, however imperfectly, to reflect the incarnation of God in Jesus Christ. Missions history, when rightly understood, is diminished when it is seen only through the lens of human agency and plans or through the parochialism of a particular denominational effort. Ultimately, all missions should be an expression of the *mission dei*.

— 9 —
The "Great Century" of Missions, 1792–1910

THE ANCIENT GREEKS HAD two different words for time. The first word, *chronos*, is the source of our word *chronology*. It refers to ordinary "clock time," which is measured in history and is marked when someone says, for example, the Battle of Hastings took place in 1066.[1] The other word for time is *kairos*, which has a more qualitative, and not merely quantitative, dimension to it. It refers to a specially appointed time, an opportune moment, or the right timing. Jesus, for example, calls us to recognize the "signs of the *times*" (Matt. 16:3). When He announces the inbreaking of the kingdom of God, He says, "The *time* has come . . . the kingdom of God is near" (Mark 1:15). In both of these examples, Jesus uses the word *kairos*, indicating that he is not merely referring to a point of chronology but to a decisive moment in the history of God's purposes in the world.

The well-known twentieth-century theologian Paul Tillich emphasizes the importance of the word *kairos* in formulating a Christian view of history. Tillich argues that *kairos* moments have "occurred again and again in the history of the church."[2] In his day, the critical challenge of the

---

1. Delling says that the dominant understanding of *chronos* is "span of time." See G. Delling, "χρονος," *Theological Dictionary of the New Testament*, ed. G. Kittel, vol. 9 (Grand Rapids: Eerdmans, 1974), 591.
2. Paul Tillich, *Systematic Theology*, vol. 3 (Chicago: University of Chicago Press, 1963), 394. For a fuller treatment of this theme, see Paul Tillich, *Kairos: Zur Geisteslage und Geisteswendung* (Darmstadt, Germany: Otto Reichl Verlag, 1926).

time was how the church responded to the rise of Nazism. As a German Christian, Tillich saw firsthand how the "time" of the Nazis was rising up against the ultimate "*kairos*" of Jesus Christ. Tillich makes the observation that the only way to recognize a *kairos* moment is when it is tested against what he calls the "great *kairos*" of all time, the Incarnation. All of history is a struggle between what Tillich calls "demonically distorted experiences of *kairos*," which lead "inescapably to self-destruction," and the "great *kairos*" of Christ, which, through the Incarnation, has inaugurated the New Creation. Even though the inbreaking of God's kingdom is an ever-present reality in history, we realize that not all periods of history are the same. Tillich observes that "history does not move in an equal rhythm but is a dynamic force moving through cataracts and quiet stretches . . . the kingdom of God is always present, but the experience of its history-shaking power is not."[3] *Kairos* moments are, in fact, rare, and the "great *kairos*" of Jesus Christ is, of course, a completely unique event in human history.

This distinction between *chronos* and *kairos* is important as we continue in these historical reflections. In chapter 8 we pointed out that missions history is about much more than just being able to chronologically tabulate all the things that have happened in history. Instead, we sought to highlight seven key moments in early missions history in order to gain some perspective as we move into the modern period.

This chapter will focus on the remarkable period between 1792 and 1910, which, in my view, represents one of these *kairos* periods in the history of the church.[4] The period spans from the publication of *An Enquiry* by William Carey to the 1910 conference in Edinburgh, which is regarded as the world's first global missionary conference.[5] During that period, which is roughly coterminous with the nineteenth century, more new Christians emerged from a wider number of new people groups than at any previous time in the history of the church. Never before had so many

---

3. Tillich, *Systematic Theology*, vol. 3, 396.
4. This period roughly corresponds historically to the period from the outbreak of the French Revolution in 1789 to the beginning of the First World War in 1914. This was a "European" century, both in global affairs and in the witness of the church throughout the world.
5. The full title of Carey's landmark book is *An Enquiry into the Obligations of Christians to Use Means for the Conversion of the Heathens: In Which the Religious State of the Different Nations of the World, the Success of Former Undertakings, and the Practicability of Further Undertakings, Are Considered.*

Christians moved to so many vast and remote parts of the globe and communicated the gospel across so many cultural boundaries.[6]

Looking back from our perspective, we can see even more clearly what a *kairos* moment it was for the Western church. The twentieth century would witness the surprising and dramatic decline of the Western church and the equally surprising and dramatic rise of the church in the Majority World. The seeds planted in the nineteenth century are bearing remarkable fruit in the twenty-first century. Who would have believed that in such a short time, the English-speaking world, which for a period was the center of global missionary sending, would now be *receiving missionaries* from the new vibrant centers of African, Asian, and Latin American Christianity, which had been the object of missionary work during the nineteenth century? It is thrilling to see those who received the gospel now bringing the gospel back to the West and reminding the West of that which has been largely forgotten. There is an African proverb that comes from the Akan in southern Ghana: "The mother feeds the baby daughter before she has teeth, so that the daughter will feed the mother when she loses her teeth."[7] Perhaps there is a lesson here for us. This chapter is not intended to celebrate a period of Western hegemony in missions *per se* but to recognize a particular *kairos* period in history that helped to bring the entire church to where it is today.

In chapter 8 we acknowledged the impossibility of writing even a cursory summary of the history of missions. I am reminded of Stephen Neill's comment in the preface to his superb volume on missions history in which he acknowledged the difficulty of reducing the entire history of Christian missions to a single volume. Neill said that he was able to do it only because he made the "resolute determination to omit!"[8] Likewise, our purpose is not to convey a vast, detailed account of this remarkable period, which the imminent church historian Kenneth Scott Latourette called the "Great Century." Rather, our purpose is to highlight some key themes or trends that can help to establish a framework for seeing the big picture—the *missio dei*—which unfolded during this remarkable *kairos* moment in the history of world Christi-

---

6. Kenneth Scott Latourette, *A History of the Expansion of Christianity*, vol. 6 of *The Great Century: North Africa and Asia* (Grand Rapids: Zondervan, 1970), 443.

7. Diane B. Stinton, *Jesus of Africa: Voices of Contemporary African Christology* (Maryknoll, NY: Orbis, 2004), 252.

8. Stephen Neill, *A History of Christian Missions* (Baltimore: Penguin, 1964), 9.

anity. We will focus on Protestant missions because, by comparison to other sectors of the church, this was a time of particular vibrancy for the missionary outreach of Protestantism. Rather than focusing on key people, this chapter will focus on five defining themes that give shape and force to the *kairos* of the "Great Century."

HOLY "SUBVERSION": THE BIRTH OF THE PROTESTANT MISSIONARY SOCIETY

One of the perplexing curiosities in the history of missions is why William Carey became known as the "Father of Modern Missions." Occasionally you will read or hear statements that Carey was the first missionary of the modern period or that he was the first Protestant or even the first Baptist missionary. However, none of these statements are true. We already have examined the remarkable Moravian missionary movement, which preceded Carey by six decades and sent missionaries all over the world, including India. The first Baptist missionary (and the first missionary from the United States) was the African-American George Liele, the Baptist pastor of the first African Church of Savannah, who was able to purchase his own freedom and then went to Kingston, Jamaica, in 1783 as a missionary to African slaves. By the time Carey left for India, Liele already had planted the African Baptist Church of Kingston with more than five hundred members.[9]

Even those who know the chronology of missions history still sometimes cite Carey as the "father" because of the length of his ministry in India (forty-one years), because of his commitment to Bible translation, or because he was an English speaker. However, when Carey arrived in India in November 1793, the German Protestant missionary Friedrich Schwartz already was in the forty-third of what would eventually be forty-eight years of ministry in India. Furthermore, the first Protestant missionaries, Ziegenbalg and Plutschau, translated the New Testament into Tamil by 1715, less than a decade after their arrival in India. There were several

---

9. Timothy C. Tennent, "Adoniram Judson and the Mission Societies of the Great Century," *American Baptist Evangelicals Journal* 11, no. 3 (Summer 2003): 20–24. For more on George Liele (1750–1828), see Clement Gayle, *George Liele: Pioneer Missionary of Jamaica* (Kingston, Jamaica: Jamaica Baptist Union, 1982), and E. A. Holmes, "George Liele: Negro Slavery's Prophet of Deliverance," *Baptist Quarterly* 20 (October 1964): 340–51. Liele's mission work also dispels the widely held belief that Adoniram and Ann Judson were the first missionaries from America to leave the country and to go to a foreign field.

well-known English-speaking missionaries before Carey, including John Eliot (1604–1690) and David Brainerd (1718–1747). In short, looking at the pure chronology of missions, it is difficult to see why Carey is considered the "first" or the "father" of modern missions. However, this is why missions history must be seen not simply through the lens of *chronos* but also through the lens of *kairos*.

William Carey *can* be referred to as the Father of Modern Missions, but not because of any of the reasons that are normally offered. William Carey is the father of modern missions because he stepped into a *kairos* moment, which stimulated the founding of dozens of new voluntary missionary *societies* and propelled hundreds of new missionaries out onto the field in what became the largest missions mobilization in history. However, to fully appreciate the role of the voluntary mission society in the "Great Century," we must reflect on the early life of Carey and the developments that led him to found the Baptist Missionary Society in 1792.

William Carey was born in England on August 17, 1761. There was little in his early life that would have given any indication of the dramatic way in which God would use Carey. He was from a very poor family from a tiny village. He had a skin disease that prevented long exposure to the sun, so he became a cobbler. He belonged to the Particular Baptists, widely despised at the time for being religious nonconformists.[10] In every way, economically, socially, and religiously, Carey represented someone at the margins of his society. However, in the providence of God, Carey had become a Christian and had become ordained as a pastor of a small Baptist church. We first get a glimpse into the zeal of Carey when he challenged his fellow ministers to dedicate one of their monthly meetings to the question, "Does the commission given by our Lord Jesus Christ to His disciples still apply to us today?" This discussion eventually led Carey to write and publish in 1792 an eighty-seven-page book, which has been called the most influential missionary tract ever written in English. A close examination of the title of the book is very important. Carey called his book, *An Enquiry into the Obligation of Christians to Use Means for the Conversion of the Heathen*. It was not unusual at that time for books to

---

10. The Particular Baptists, unlike the General Baptists, believed in limited atonement, i.e., that Christ died only for the elect. The Particular Baptists, over time, became associated with hyper-Calvinism, which helps to explain the reluctance of Carey's ministerial peers to accept his missionary vision.

have long, descriptive titles, rather than the shorter, often more oblique, titles that are given to books today.

The title of Carey's treatise falls into three major parts. The first part, *An Enquiry into the Obligation of Christians*, reveals the historical and theological obstacles Carey faced in becoming a missionary. Theologically, hyper-Calvinism had persuaded many to believe that the conversion of the world would be done by the Lord apart from any human agency, such as the witnessing church. Historically, it was widely believed that the original apostles already had "fulfilled" the Great Commission by going out to the entire world. Carey devoted considerable time in his tract dispelling these misunderstandings. The latter part of the title, *For the Conversion of the Heathens*, reveals Carey's firm commitment to the gospel of Jesus Christ and the need for all peoples to hear and to respond. Calling those who do not believe the gospel *heathens* sounds pejorative and insulting to modern ears. However, in that time period, *heathen* served as a generic, descriptive word for people who had never heard the gospel, and it did not carry the connotations it carries today.[11] Carey included in his book a number of detailed charts that showed where the non-Christians were located in the world, their approximate number, and their current religion, if any.

It is the *middle* of the three parts of the book's title that has been the most neglected, and yet it is arguably the most important. It is the phrase *to use means*. In this tiny phrase lies the remarkable genius of William Carey and, fascinatingly, the reason why he is known today as the Father of Modern Missions.

Andrew Walls observes that Carey's phrase "to use means" points to the "responsibility of Christians. . . . to *seek the appropriate instrument*, to accomplish a task which God has laid upon them."[12] In other words, some *structure* was needed that would allow Protestants to support missionaries. The Roman Catholics have a long history of allowing a wide range of alliances, known as sodalities, which could focus on and address specific needs, including youth ministry, missions, charitable work, and so forth. In chapter 8 we examined how, for example, the pope set up the *Propa-*

---

11. The term was not normally applied to monotheistic, non-Christian peoples, such as Jews and Muslims. Even within the *Enquiry*, Carey distinguishes between "pagans" and "Mahometans."
12. Andrew Walls, "Missionary Societies and the Fortunate Subversion of the Church," in *The Missionary Movement in Christian History: Studies in the Transmission of Faith* (Maryknoll, NY: Orbis, 1996), 244, emphasis mine.

ganda Fide to create a structure through which missionaries could be sent to the field, policies and strategy could be developed, and oversight could be given. Today, many people admire and are acquainted with Mother Teresa's Missionaries of Charity, which is a sodality dedicated to serving the poorest of the poor and now operates in over one hundred different countries. The Reformers did not carry over the idea of sodalities into the ecclesiology of the Reformation. Therefore, the reasons why Protestants did not send any missionaries out for the first two hundred years were not only *theological* but also profoundly *structural*.

Although Carey's *Enquiry* is filled with solid theology and history, this is not the source of the radical nature of Carey's proposal. For example, the sixteenth-century theologian Adrian Saravia already had made most of the same theological and historical arguments Carey made in the late eighteenth century. The problem with Protestant missions, as Andrew Walls has observed, was "the simple fact that the Church as then organized, whether episcopal, or presbyterian, or congregational, could not effectively operate missions overseas."[13] There simply was no structure. "It became clear that there were things—and not small things—but big things, things like the evangelization of the world, which were beyond the capacities" of the static ecclesiastical structures of the time.[14]

Carey, as a Protestant, had no ecclesiastical structures to look to for guidance. So, he proposed a mission society based largely upon the model of secular trading societies, which were being organized for commercial purposes. Carey writes as follows,

> Suppose a company of serious Christians, ministers and private persons, were to form themselves into a society, and make a number of rules respecting the regulation of the plan, and the persons who are to be employed as missionaries, the means of defraying the expense, etc., etc.[15]

Here was a very secular structure—quite untheological on the surface, which was, in fact, one of the most important theological developments in

---

13. Ibid., 246.
14. Ibid., 247.
15. William Carey, *An Enquiry into Obligations to Use Means for the Conversion of the Heathens* (London: Carey Kingsgate, 1961), 82.

Protestantism. It is even more amazing that Protestants had never really thought about the *theological* implications of the Reformation ecclesiology, which did not have the flexibility to allow for voluntary, mostly lay, associations that could focus on specific tasks. Andrew Walls continues, "There never was a *theology* of the voluntary society. The voluntary society is one of God's theological jokes, whereby he makes tender mockery of his people when they take themselves too seriously."[16] The church leadership was as opposed to the missionary movement as the structure was resistant to the missionary enterprise. However, gradually these lay associations not only generated recruits to become missionaries but also eventually generated considerable amounts of money to provide for their support. A new kind of structure was emerging among Protestant churches, which was inadvertently creating a new power base. The mission society represented a kind of "holy subversion" of a recalcitrant church. The implications this had for lay ministry, for enabling women to exercise their gifts cross-culturally, and for achieving specific, Christian goals in faraway places were enormous.

Within a few short years of Carey's proposal to create a mission society, over a dozen new mission societies began to spring up on both sides of the Atlantic. The birth of the mission society created a new sodality structure that would enable thousands of people to relocate cross-culturally for full-time mission service. William Carey is a stellar example of missionary service, but this is not why he is known as the "Father of Modern Missions." Carey is known as the "Father of Modern Missions" because he proposed that the church "use means" to reach the world, namely, to create a new structure that could make possible the response of obedience. Many Christians had been inspired by Jonathan Edwards's call forty years earlier to engage in a concert of prayer for the evangelization of the world. Many others were deeply moved by reading the journal of David Brainerd and encountering his burden for the lost. But at some point this inspiration had to translate into some kind of organizational structure that made obedience possible. The Baptist Missionary Society, the London Missionary Society, the Church Missionary Society, the Religious Tract Society, the British and Foreign Bible Society, the American Board of Commissioners for Foreign Missions, and the American Baptist Missionary Board are just

---

16. Walls, *The Missionary Movement in Christian History*, 246.

a few of the early societies that helped to launch this remarkably vibrant period of Protestant missions.[17]

The mission society structure not only served to *launch* the "Great Century," it also continued to serve as the practical engine for missionary mobilization throughout the period. It proved to be a flexible structure that could accommodate changing times and new vision. For example, in 1853, right in the middle of the "Great Century," Hudson Taylor went to China under a mission society known as the China Evangelization Society. After a few years in China, Taylor became deeply burdened by the neglect of interior China as well as the need to mobilize a whole new generation of missionaries. The mission societies at the time drew mostly from the educated, privileged classes of people, who were reluctant to go into the rural, malaria-infested interior of China. Taylor envisioned a new kind of mission society that would draw from working-class laborers, even those who were not formally educated. He wanted to run the mission from the field, which would mean not having a supporting church structure back home but relying upon people who would live by faith and trust God for their financial needs. Furthermore, he wanted to dedicate these new missionaries to work in the interior parts of China. Thus, in 1865 Taylor established the China Inland Mission.[18] The success of this mission was so dramatic that by 1895 Taylor was overseeing 641 new missionaries, more than the entire Protestant missionary force when he first arrived in China. More importantly, Taylor had proven that the mission society structure could be adapted to completely new methods of mobilization. The result was another large wave of new mission societies such as North Africa Mission (1881),[19] Africa Inland Mission (1895), and Sudan Interior Mission (1898), which modeled new ways of mobilizing missionaries, were interdenominational, and were dedicated to going where other missionaries had not gone before.

Today, when a student walks into my office and tells me he or she is interested in becoming a missionary, I have at my fingertips a catalog

---

17. The explosive growth of mission societies spread throughout Europe, beginning with the Berlin Society in Germany and the Basel Mission in Switzerland. Within just a few years, there were mission societies in every country of Western Europe. Stephen Neill writes that by the end of the century "almost every denomination" had some kind of mission society through which they sent or supported missionaries. See Neill, *History of Christian Missions,* 252.
18. Today the China Inland Mission is known as OMF, Overseas Missionary Fellowship.
19. The North Africa Mission is today known as AWM, Arab World Ministries.

of all the mission agencies in North America, many of which have very specific and focused ministries. The catalog is more than six hundred pages long, listing hundreds of mission organizations.[20] The mission societies collectively made the "Great Century" possible and continue to be the greatest resource for missions mobilization in the world.[21] Looking back, Carey's call to "use means" was a spark that ignited one of the great *kairos* moments in the history of the church, the birth of the Protestant missionary society.

THE WORD MADE TEXT: VERNACULAR BIBLE TRANSLATIONS

Christianity is the only world religion whose primary source documents are in a language other than the language of the founder of the religion. This is unheard of among world religions. Muhammad spoke Arabic, and the Qur'ān is in Arabic; the Brahmin priests in India spoke Sanskrit, and the Upanishads are in Sanskrit. Jesus spoke Aramaic, and yet the primary documents that record Christ's teachings are not in Aramaic but in Koine Greek, the language of Gentile Hellenism. This is a remarkable testimony to the translatability of the Christian message that has been enshrined in our most sacred texts. Christians affirm that the gospel releases its power even as it is made intelligible and announced in specific, local contexts in a myriad of new languages. Lamin Sanneh argues that translating the gospel from the words of Aramaic and Hebrew into Greek simultaneously relativized the Jewish roots *and* destigmatized the Gentile cultures.[22] In other words, the gospel emerged out of and is nourished by its roots in Judaism, but it can be expressed in language and thought forms that are alien to the original context. This means the gospel can be expressed with new language forms, while retaining its transforming power. Thus, translating the Bible into a vernacular language is an important *theological assertion* about the translatability of the Christian gospel. This is in contrast with the Muslims, who maintain the Qur'ān is untranslatable and the Word of Allah can be conveyed only in Arabic. Likewise, Hindu priests traditionally have

---

20. Dotsey Welliver and Minnette Northcutt, eds., *Mission Handbook: U.S. and Canadian Protestant Ministries Overseas*, 2004–2006 (Wheaton, IL: Emis, 2004).

21. A more detailed analysis of the theology of the mission society will be explored in chapter 15.

22. Lamin Sanneh, *Translating the Message: The Missionary Impact on Culture* (Maryknoll, NY: Orbis Books, 1989), 1.

taught that the mantras of ancient Hinduism lose their power when they are uttered in a vernacular language.

Tragically, the theological importance of the translatability of the Word of God has not always been recognized by the church. In the late fourth century, Pope Damascus I charged Jerome with revising some of the older Latin translations. Jerome eventually retranslated the entire Bible into Latin, mostly utilizing Greek manuscripts. Jerome's Latin Vulgate became the officially authorized version of the Bible for the Roman Catholic Church. The church resisted vernacular translations and eventually developed the attitude that the only three languages into which the Bible could be translated were the three languages of the inscription placed on the cross of Christ (Hebrew, Greek, and Latin; see John 19:20). With the plethora of various translations available today, it is difficult for some Christians to imagine how William Tyndale (1494–1536), who was the first to complete a full translation of the Bible into English from the original languages, had to do so in secret, smuggling the Bibles into England and Scotland from Germany. When Tyndale's New Testament was published, Cardinal Wolsey condemned the work and called for Tyndale's arrest. He was eventually arrested, imprisoned, tried for heresy, and burned at the stake for his effort.

One of the most important victories of the Reformation was reestablishing the principle of the linguistic translatability of the Bible. Martin Luther's translation of the Bible into German (1522–1534) was not only a major literary landmark in the history of the German language but also a vital theological statement on behalf of the whole church. It set the stage for what would, in time, become a dramatic rise in vernacular Bible translations by Protestant missionaries. Roman Catholic missionaries, such as Alessandro Valignano, whom we highlighted in chapter 8, promoted indigenous language learning and even produced vernacular catechisms. However, the translation of the Bible into vernacular languages became one of the most important distinguishing features of Protestant missionary work.

The emergence of the New Testament in Tamil illustrates the significance Protestants placed on vernacular Bible translation. The Roman Catholic missionaries preceded the Protestants in India by many centuries yet never produced a single vernacular Bible translation. One of the most famous Jesuit missionaries to work among the Tamil in South India was Robert de Nobili (1577–1656). De Nobili arrived one hundred years before the first Protestant missionaries came to India. He was the first European to learn Sanskrit and became an expert in the Tamil language, including the intricacies of Tamil poetic forms. De Nobili was also deeply committed to contextualization, completely adapting himself to the lifestyle, clothing, diet, and teaching methods of the Brahminical priests of that time. Yet, de Nobili never translated the New Testament into Tamil. In contrast, this became the first item of importance for the first Protestant missionaries, Bartholomew Ziegenbalg and Henry Plutschau. They arrived in India in 1706, and Ziegenbalg was able to publish the Tamil New Testament by 1715, accomplishing in less than ten years what the Roman Catholics had failed to do in the previous two centuries.

Ziegenbalg's Tamil New Testament represented the firstfruits of hundreds of new translations by Protestant missionaries. William Carey dedicated himself almost exclusively to Bible translation. In November of 1821 the American Missionary Register included an update on the translation work of the Serampore mission of which Carey was a part. It reported that Carey had completed the entire Bible in five separate Indian languages, Bengali, Sanskrit, Hindi, Oriya, and Marathi. It also reported the New Testament had been translated into fifteen other languages and portions of the Bible into six more.[23] Toward the end of Carey's long ministry in India, he wrote a letter to Robert Ralston on December 31, 1827, in which he confirmed his commitment to Bible translation. Carey wrote,

> The translation of the Sacred Scriptures into the languages of the East, is the work which has from the commencement of the Mission most of all occupied my time and attention, and I bless God that this work has, in several successive editions, been so corrected, that I can leave it to the Indian churches, so far as regards the leading and principle languages of the country, with some degree of confidence.[24]

The commitment to Bible translation is one of the major hallmarks of the "Great Century" of missions. A few more examples will help to illus-

---

23. American Missionary Register (November 1821). A similar report was published in the *Boston Recorder* on Saturday, December 8, 1821 (no. 50, vol. 12).

24. William Carey to Robert Ralston, later published in the *Boston Recorder and Religious Telegraph* on Friday, July 4, 1828 (no. 27, vol. XIII).

trate the trend. Robert Morrison (1782–1834) arrived in China (Canton) in 1807. By 1823 the entire Bible was published in Chinese. Adoniram Judson (1788–1850), the famous American pioneer missionary, went to Burma in 1812 and translated the entire Bible into Burmese by 1834. The commitment to Bible translation extended even to languages most people in the West had never heard of. For example, Robert Moffatt (1795–1883) dedicated over forty years of his life (1826–1870) to the people of Kuruman (modern-day Botswana) and translated the entire Bible into Sechuana between 1840 and 1857. These are but a few examples of what collectively amounted to a dramatic rise in the availability of vernacular Bible translations. During the "Great Century" alone, over four hundred new language groups received either the New Testament or the entire Bible in their language. This commitment to Bible translation continues to the present day. Currently, the New Testament or entire Bible is available in 1,573 languages.[25] At least one book of the Bible has been translated in an additional 853 languages.[26]

An evaluation of Protestant missionary efforts during the 1792–1910 period must recognize, to use Sanneh's words, that "their translation work made mother tongues the centerpiece of mission." Undoubtedly, the most important legacy of this emphasis was that millions of people now could read or hear the Word of God in their own language. William Tyndale's determination to help the "boy who drives the plow" to know the Bible is a vision that the collective work of thousands of missionaries has helped to fulfill.[27] This basic goal represents the central evangelical concern that led missionaries to give their lives to Bible translation. However, there are many other important benefits these missionaries were affirming through the act of Bible translation, perhaps unknowingly. First, Bible translation became a powerful tool of cultural affirmation and indigenous identity. Bible translation stirred ethnic consciousness, providing a linguistic base that nurtured nationalism and empowered local cultural agents. Translation, as it turns out, was about much more than language, since language itself is a vital expression of cultural identity. The stereotypical view many

---

25. According to Wycliffe Bible Translators, of the 1,573 languages, 429 have the complete Bible and 1,144 have the New Testament and 853 have at least one book of the Bible.
26. For a full breakdown of statistics related to Bible translation, see www.wycliffe.org.
27. Elizabeth Kirkland Cahill, "A Bible for the Plowboy: Tyndale at the New York Public Library," *Commonweal* 124, no. 7 (1997): 19–20.

secularists have of missionaries is that of people who arrive on the mission field uninvited and unannounced and then proceed to "destroy the culture" through the imposition of Western cultural values. In actuality, the missionary commitment to vernacular language translation meant that the missionaries were often (even unknowingly) agents of cultural preservation and local empowerment.

Second, Bible translation is the greatest testimony to "mission as translation" rather than "mission as cultural diffusion." If a missionary simply imposes foreign religious forms expressed through a language foreign to the people, then the missionary remains the instructor and the primary agent of change. However, if the missionary is committed to a Bible in the vernacular language, then the indigenous agents are the experts, and the missionary becomes the learner.

Third, the linguistic translatability of the Scripture provides the foundation for the full cultural and theological translatability of the Christian message. In other words, once the Word is made text in a vernacular language, then this naturally leads to the witness of a new believing community who are members of a particular culture, which is no longer tied to the original culture that transmitted the gospel message. These new Christians can now apply the Bible to their own particular challenges and opportunities without having to go through a foreign missionary as an intermediary. Eventually, as indigenous churches emerge, they are then able to formulate their own theological framework for understanding and reproducing the biblical message. None of this would be possible if missionaries had rejected the linguistic translatability of the Bible and instead opted for some form of cultural diffusion.

The legacy of Bible translation cannot be heralded as the triumph of any one person or denomination. Instead, the Reformation brought about a theological correction, which, as it turned out, unleashed one of the great, *kairos* periods in the history of the church. The Protestant commitment to Bible translation led to hundreds of new translations, which provided the basis for indigenous expressions of Christianity all over the world.

PERPETUATING PERPETUA: THE LEGACY OF WOMEN MISSIONARIES

Vibia Perpetua, who was martyred in Carthage in A.D. 203, is probably the most famous female martyr of the early church. After her arrest, she was imprisoned, where she recorded an account of her sufferings, the pressures on her to renounce her faith (even from her own father), and several dramatic visions she had leading up to her martyrdom. The actual martyrdom of Perpetua is added at the end of her account by some eye-witnesses. Perpetua's account, known as the *The Passion of Perpetua and Felicitas,* is considered important for church history in a way that goes beyond the historical accounting of early Christian martyrdom. First, the account is a treasure because it is widely regarded as the earliest writing by a female Christian in the history of the church. Perpetua tells her own story in her own way. A glimpse into the inner life of an early Christian female who is facing martyrdom is extraordinary, particularly since Perpetua shares things that are unique to the experience of being a female. For example, Perpetua was a twenty-two-year-old woman who was still nursing her newborn child at the time of her arrest. She describes in detail the emotional anguish of separation, as well as the rather intimate record of the pain in her breasts because her child was not receiving the breast milk.[28] The whole account reminds us of the wonderful particularity that is present in a female perspective. Reading Perpetua's account is also a reminder of how often women in the church have been "seen as adjuncts to men, rather than as historical protagonists in their own right."[29]

Second, Perpetua is a poignant symbol of the cost of discipleship, even in the face of family members and others who encouraged her to offer a sacrifice to the gods and return to her responsibilities as a wife and mother. The story is even more remarkable in that the well-educated and aristocratic Perpetua is being martyred side by side with the slave girl Felicitas. Felicitas was pregnant at the time of her arrest and gave birth while being held in prison. Perpetua and Felicitas were put into the arena to be tortured and finally sent to the executioner to be beheaded. One comes away from the story of Perpetua and Felicitas with a profound appreciation for their deep love of Jesus Christ, which transcends the social and cultural boundaries that normally would separate two such women.

Finally, Perpetua is from North Africa, which at the time was the emerging heartland of Christian faith. Perpetua lived during one of those

---

28. The authorities eventually allow her to see, and nurse, her child while she is awaiting trial.
29. Fiona Bowie, "Reclaiming Women's Presence," in *Women and Missions: Past and Present: Anthropological and Historical Perceptions,* ed. Fiona Bowie, Deborah Kirkwood, and Shirley Ardener (Providence: Berg, 1993), 1.

remarkable *kairos* moments when the collapsing Roman Empire struggled and lashed out against the rising tide of Christian faith. Today, Islamic North Africa is once again one of the great mission fields of the world. Christians are again being persecuted and martyred in North Africa, even in the midst of a small but growing church there. We are reminded of the ebb and flow in the tide of history.

The memory of Perpetua is embedded into the life fabric of the church, and in many ways the female missionaries who have offered up their lives for the sake of the gospel perpetuate her legacy. The role of women in missions is a complex story that defies easy generalizations. On the one hand, the work of missions, like almost all expressions of Christian ministry in the nineteenth century, was focused on male agency. Valentine Cunningham once remarked concerning the practice and outlook of the London Missionary Society that the word *missionary* was "a male noun which denotes a male actor, male action and male spheres of service."[30] Mission historiography of the "Great Century" too often has been silent about the work of women, and only in the last thirty years has this omission begun to be addressed. On the other hand, the mission field opened up ministry opportunities for women that would have been scarcely imaginable in the very countries that sent the women out. Mission work was also one of the few occupations in the nineteenth century that would foster worldwide travel by women.[31] Once on the mission field, women were serving as evangelists, teachers, catechists, administrators, and even church planters.

Making broad generalizations about the role of women in missions is difficult because the experience of women on the mission field was so diverse. Protestant women served as missionaries with the English Anglicans, the Dutch Reformed, the Swiss Pietists, the Norwegian Lutherans, and the American Baptists, to name a few. These groups all have very different views about clerical authority and the role of women, as well as a variety of attitudes about marriage and social and cultural practices that impact women's roles on the mission field. Nevertheless, if we focus on the role of Protestant women in missions over the entire period from 1792–1910, there are several broad trends that can be observed. We will

---

30. Ibid.

31. It is important to remember that even nineteenth-century "secular" occupations such as being a soldier or an explorer were not options for women.

examine these trends under three headings, Mobilization and Support, Professional Employees, and Pioneer Missionaries.

Mobilization and Support

As noted earlier, the birth of the Protestant missionary society created a separate structure (sodality), which was distinct from the traditional, fixed power base of church governance in the nineteenth century. Leadership in the mission society was not restricted to ordained clergy. Andrew Walls argues that the voluntary mission society was the first structure in Protestantism that "made the laymen of real significance above the parish or congregational level."[32] This had enormous implications for women in ministry. Even though the formal structure of the society had male leadership, women were often the lifeblood of the society in organizing meetings, recruiting missionaries, raising funds, mobilizing prayer, and in time, teaching about missions.

In the earliest period, women went to the field as the wives of the commissioned missionaries. For example, when the American Board sent its first five missionaries out in 1812, two of the missionaries, Adoniram Judson and Samuel Newell, were already married. However, upon arriving on the field, the women became deeply involved in the mission. For example, Ann Judson became proficient in the language and organized a group of Burmese women who met together weekly for prayer and Bible study. Later, when Ann was back in the United States on furlough, she wrote the inspiring history of the Burmese mission, which became instrumental in recruiting new missionaries. However, during this phase, women were not regarded as missionaries in their own right.

Professional Employees

As the work of missions grew, there were many new kinds of professional positions that needed to be filled. For example, nurses and teachers were needed for mission hospitals and schools. In Roman Catholic missions, these roles traditionally had been filled by special orders of missionary nuns. Protestant missions, in contrast, were extremely reluctant to send out single women as missionaries. As we will see later, this attitude continued until 1865. The solution was the recruitment of the wives of missionaries to fill certain specialized roles. This is an important development, because

---

32. Walls, *The Missionary Movement in Christian History*, 249.

for the first time women now had official, salaried roles within the mission that were not directly related to the work of their husbands.

Pioneer Missionaries

The year 1865, right at the heart of the "Great Century," is often cited as a watershed in the history of women in missions. This is the year that Hudson Taylor founded the China Inland Mission. This mission represented a dramatic shift in missionary recruitment and service, with important implications for women. As a Brethren, Taylor did not believe in ordination and therefore was eager to mobilize as many lay missionaries as possible. Taylor was the first Protestant leader of a mission to directly recruit women as full missionaries in their own right. Because the China Inland Mission was a "faith mission," there were no financial support concerns, which had often hindered the denominational efforts from recognizing women as full-fledged missionaries. Mission historian Rhonda Semple highlights the watershed change represented by Hudson Taylor when she writes that, at least when it came to missionary recruitment in the CIM, "the differentiation between male and female candidates and between single and married female workers did not exist."[33] Single women received the same training as the men. The women were not just permitted to preach, they were expected to.[34] Drawing from working-class peoples, men and women who were prepared to live by faith and face new challenges became part of the missions ethos from the beginning. Taylor founded the CIM while on furlough in England and returned in 1865 with the first fifteen missionary recruits, seven of whom were single women.

Many of the new "faith" mission societies that had been inspired by Taylor's CIM also actively recruited women as full-fledged missionaries. Mission organizations such as the North Africa Mission, the Gospel Missionary Union, and the Algiers Mission Band all mobilized more women than men for cross-cultural service. In fact, Lilas Trotter, the well-known artist-missionary to the Islamic world, was the founder of the Algiers Mission Band, making her the first Protestant woman to found and lead a mission society.

---

33. Rhonda Anne Semple, *Missionary Women: Gender, Professionalism and the Victorian Idea of Christian Mission* (Rochester: Boydell, 2003), 55.

34. Klaus Fiedler, *The Story of Faith Missions: From Hudson Taylor to the Present* (Irvine, CA: Regnum Books, 1994), 292.

Taylor's pioneering effort to mobilize and send out single, female missionaries was followed by the earlier mainstream societies. For example, in 1866 the London Missionary Society authorized an auxiliary organization known as the Ladies' Board "to examine and train women candidates and to help place them in their fields of work."[35] In the same year, the Society for Propagating the Gospel (SPG) set up an auxiliary structure known as the Ladies Association, which was also created solely for the purpose of recruiting female missionaries. An advertising pamphlet used later by the SPG to recruit women gives several reasons why women are needed on the mission field. The pamphlet, quite naturally, pointed out the need for "professional qualifications . . . especially in medicine, nursing and teaching." However, in an early foreshadowing of what is today called "friendship evangelism," the SPG also stressed the relational skills of women. The pamphlet states that "in the work of evangelism women are needed abroad not only as district visitors, but as *friends*—the importance of friendship with educated women must be emphasized, especially in China, Japan, India, etc."[36] These auxiliary societies were soon followed by mission societies solely dedicated to mobilizing women. By the end of the nineteenth century, "there were more than forty women's mission societies in the United States alone," and by 1910, the end of the "Great Century," the number of women outnumbered the men in Protestant missions.[37]

Few women embodied the new possibilities for the single, female pioneer missionary like Charlotte "Lottie" Moon (1840–1912), sometimes called the "patron saint" of Baptist missions. Lottie and her sister were teachers in a school for girls in Cartersville, Georgia. When the door opened for single women to become missionaries, Lottie applied, was accepted, and arrived in China in 1873 as a Southern Baptist missionary. After twelve years in China serving in fairly traditional roles, Lottie decided to move from Tengzhou to the interior city of Pingtu, over one hundred miles away, and start her own work. This was the first time a single female had ever started a new mission work in China. Moon eventually saw hundreds of Chinese come to the Lord, and her ministry led to the establishment of over thirty new

35. Semple, *Missionary Women*, 20.
36. Deborah Kirkwood, "Protestant Missionary Women," in *Women and Missions* (Oxford, England: Berg, 1994), 1, emphasis in original.
37. Ruth A. Tucker, *From Jerusalem to Irian Jaya: A Biographical History of Christian Missions* (Grand Rapids: Zondervan, 1983), 288.

Chinese churches. Over the next twenty years, thousands of new believers were baptized, making Pingtu the "greatest evangelistic center ... in all China" for the Southern Baptists. Moon worked tirelessly, spending several months each year doing evangelism in villages and devoting the rest of her time to training new missionaries and writing influential articles and opinion pieces, which were published in Southern Baptist mission magazines back in the United States. She encouraged Southern Baptist women to organize mission societies to fund and recruit more missionaries. In 1887, Moon wrote to the *Foreign Mission Journal* and proposed that the Sunday before Christmas be set aside for a special offering for missions. This annual offering, today known as the Lottie Moon Christmas Offering, remains the largest single annual offering for missions in history, with the annual amount today exceeding twenty million dollars.

Like Perpetua of long ago, Lottie gave her life for the sake of the gospel. At the end of her life, it was discovered that she had been giving her food rations to Chinese Christians who were suffering during a famine that was sweeping across China at that time. Doctors discovered that her sacrifice had led to extreme malnourishment, and she was placed on board a ship to return home so she could receive medical care. However, she died on Christmas Eve in 1912, while still aboard the ship. The first Christmas offering enabled three new missionaries to come to China. Today, her life story, along with the Christmas offering, have helped to inspire, recruit, and support thousands of new missionaries. Furthermore, men and women alike continue to be inspired by her dedication and sacrifice. Although Lottie Moon was only four feet, three inches tall, she has cast a long and influential shadow on the entire modern missionary movement.

INDIGENOUS INGENUITY:
CHURCH PLANTING IN THE "GREAT CENTURY"

The Christendom model of Christianity, which nurtured an established state church, has become one of the enduring legacies of European Christianity. However, one of the stark lessons of missions history in the "Great Century" is that the Christendom model was not reproducible outside of Europe. During the previous centuries, the Jesuits, inspired by Thomas More's *Utopia*, had managed to reproduce a Latin American version of Christendom but only because of massive European immigration into the region. A new kind of ecclesiology had to be envisioned once Protestant missionaries began to arrive in China, Japan, India, the Middle East, and Africa.

In chapter 8, we explored how Protestant missions was born out of the efforts of pietistic nonconformists, like the Moravians and the Baptists, who stressed individual conversion and an ecclesiology that was free from the state, which they viewed, quite understandably, with suspicion. Even when the established churches of Europe and the mainline Protestant churches of the United States began to engage in missions, the earliest mission societies, such as the American Board of Commissioners for Foreign Missions (ABCFM) and the Church Missionary Society (CMS), were voluntary societies with free associations.[38] The on-the-ground realities of the mission field stimulated important advances in Protestant ecclesiology.

No two people helped the Anglican and Protestant churches to think more about the missiology that lay beneath their mission-sending fervor than the two towering missionary statesmen of the nineteenth century, Rufus Anderson (1796–1880) of the ABCFM and Henry Venn (1796–1873) of the CMS. Anderson and Venn affirmed the need for people without Christ to hear the gospel and the importance of individual conversion. However, they also wisely understood that in the long run conversions would not last, nor would the missions movement succeed, unless there was an emphasis on indigenous church planting. Venn and Anderson were voluminous writers, in correspondence with hundreds of missionaries and responsible for dozens of policy manuals. They were also controversial figures with a host of critics. It was farsighted but considered radical for Rufus Anderson to write that missionaries should "not attempt the transfer of the religious denominations of Christendom, full-grown and with all their peculiarities into heathen lands; at least, until the new-born churches shall have had time to acquire a good degree of discriminative and self-governing power."[39] Instead, he was an early champion of what he termed an "indigenous church."

Venn and Anderson went on to develop an emphasis on church planting that would result in churches that would be, in their famous

---

38. Although the ABCFM and the CMS served the Congregationalists and Anglicans respectively, they became more closely identified with specific denominational work only after the growing diversification of other mission-sending societies. The "free association" was limited to those who practiced paedobaptism.
39. R. Pierce Beaver, ed., *To Advance the Gospel: Selections from the Writings of Rufus Anderson* (Grand Rapids: Eerdmans, 1967), 139.

axiom, "self-governing, self-supporting and self-extending."[40] This "three-self" concept continues to inform missiology today and is still widely used as a benchmark for measuring church indigeneity, although the phrase "self-extending" was later amended to "self-propagating."[41] This policy encouraged self-determination regarding ecclesiastical structures and discouraged reliance upon foreign funds. Venn and Anderson were both convinced that reliance on foreign missionaries and foreign funding hindered the long-term growth of the indigenous church. Therefore, they were committed to training and ordaining indigenous pastors who would be supported by the new Christians.[42] As early as 1841, Anderson made the case (which has been repeated often in our time) that the cost of supporting twenty-five missionary families from America was the same amount needed to "educate a thousand natives and support two hundred as pastors."[43]

Following in the footsteps of Alessandro Valignano, Venn and Anderson were the first *Protestant* missionary statesmen, and their writings and extensive policy guidelines were highly influential since dozens of mission societies adopted their policies and read their work.

The growing commitment to plant churches on the mission field (not just evangelize), coupled with the dizzying array of Protestant groups who were involved in missions, over time led to a stunning variety of churches planted on the mission field. Some of the new churches were intentionally planted as a "daughter" church, which remained financially and ecclesiologically dependent on the "mother" church in the West. Other new churches were organized into some kind of new national association

---

40. Timothy Yates, *Christian Mission in the Twentieth Century* (New York: Cambridge University Press, 1994), 35.
41. Current missiologists often speak of the need to add a fourth or fifth "self," usually including self-theologizing and self-missionizing. Other missiologists, including myself, have been critical of the three-self benchmarks. However, there is no doubt that the concept has had an important legacy in missiology and has been widely used to strengthen the case for indigenous churches.
42. Paul Harris argues that Anderson's motivation was more to save money by not having to fund native pastors than a commitment to autonomous indigenous leadership. While, as a mission administrator, Anderson does regularly emphasize the economic benefits of his missiology, it is, in my view, impossible to read Anderson's writings without a deep admiration for his genuine interest in the progress of the gospel around the world. See Paul Harris, "Denominationalism and Democracy: Ecclesiastical Issues Underlying Rufus Anderson's Three-Self Program," in *North American Foreign Missions, 1810–1914*, ed. Wilbert R. Shenk (Grand Rapids: Eerdmans, 2006), 61–85.
43. Ibid., 66.

with varying levels of dependence and association (theologically or organizationally) with the ecclesiology of the sending body. Still other new Christian movements organized themselves into indigenous churches that were organizationally autonomous from the church of the missionary. An analysis of the details of the explosive growth of churches and denominations during the "Great Century" would be nearly impossible. However, to capture a small sense of the sheer scale of the new church planting efforts, missiologists David Barrett and Todd Johnson have documented 1,488 separate denominations or church movements that emerged between 1792 and 1910.[44] This represents hundreds of thousands of new Christians throughout every inhabited continent.

An examination of where Christians were located in 1792 and in 1910 is very revealing. While the dramatic growth of Christianity in the Majority World took place in the twentieth century, the nineteenth century planted the seeds for that growth, without which we would not be celebrating the shift in the center of global Christianity, as explored in chapter 1. In 1792, 98 percent of all Protestant Christians lived in the Western world.[45] By the end of the nineteenth century, small but vibrant groups of Christians were found in many countries all around the world. The 176,000 Christians in Nigeria in 1900 or the 92,000 Christians in Tanzania may seem tiny by today's standards of Christianity in Africa, since today Nigeria has over 64 million Christians and Tanzania has 20 million, but the point is that the church was planted and planted widely. Of course, Christianity did not always grow and prosper in the wake of the missionary labors of the "Great Century." Morocco, for example, had over 30,000 Christians at the end of the nineteenth century, but since that time the number of Christians in Morocco has continued to decline as a percentage of overall population.[46]

Nevertheless, looking back on the whole sweep of the "Great Century," one must recognize that it represented a truly *kairos* moment for church planting around the world. Never before in history had so many new expressions of the church emerged in so many places. If the linguistic

---

44. David B. Barrett and Todd M. Johnson, eds., *World Christian Trends, AD 30–AD 2200: Interpreting the Annual Christian Megacensus* (Pasadena, CA: William Carey Library, 2001), 24–33, 390–92.

45. Ibid., 331.

46. All statistics taken from World Christian Database, www.worldchristiandatabase.org (accessed May 2008).

translatability of the gospel, expressed through Bible translation, was the seed, then the cultural translatability of the gospel, expressed through the emergence of indigenous churches, was the fruit.

GLOBAL COLLABORATION:
THE BIRTH OF "WORLD CHRISTIANITY"

The fifth and final theme that helps to capture the *kairos* of the "Great Century" is the first World Missionary Conference, which was held in Edinburgh, Scotland, June 14–23, 1910. This conference is widely regarded as the most important missionary conference in the twentieth century, and it stands as one of the great landmarks of missions history. Two major international conferences held in September 2010 in Edinburgh and in October 2010 in South Africa, both to mark the centenary of the 1910 conference, only serve to highlight the ongoing significance of the 1910 conference in the history of missions.

The climate that led to the Edinburgh conference in 1910 can best be summed up by the publication of John Mott's *The Evangelization of the World in This Generation*.[47] John Mott (1865–1955) was an indefatigable missions mobilizer, having founded and chaired the Student Volunteer Movement from 1888 to 1920, as well as serving as the traveling secretary of the YMCA (1888–1915). Thousands of students came through these movements and joined the ranks of the mission societies to serve cross-culturally. Over the course of his work, Mott traveled nearly two million miles, gaining a great deal of firsthand knowledge about the work of missions around the world. Mott became convinced that with better coordination and strategic thinking, the entire world could be evangelized in one generation.[48] This led

---

47. John Mott, *The Evangelization of the World in This Generation*, 3rd ed. (London: Student Volunteer Missionary Union, 1903). The actual phrase "the evangelization of the world in this generation," which in 1889 became the slogan or "watchword" of the Student Volunteer Movement, is attributed to A. T. Pierson (1837–1911), a well-known pastor of Clarendon Street Baptist Church, missions mobilizer, prolific writer, and president of Boston Missionary Training Institute, forerunner of Gordon College and Gordon-Conwell Theological Seminary.

48. Readers who may not have been exposed to missiology may need to be reminded that the word *evangelized* only refers to giving people *access* to the gospel, not that any have necessarily responded to the gospel message, or that the church is viable. This will be discussed in more detail in chapter 12. It has been said that John Mott was the most traveled person in the history of the world at that time. See Yates, *Christian Mission in the Twentieth Century*, 17, and Basil Matthews, *John R Mott, World Citizen* (New York: Harper and Brothers, 1934). Mott won the Nobel Peace Prize in 1946 for his humanitarian work around the world.

to the publication of Mott's book in 1900, which sparked a wave of optimism about "fulfilling" the Great Commission in that generation.[49] The book also highlighted the need for greater cooperation among the many mission agencies and more strategic thinking about the entire missionary enterprise. People became increasingly aware of the need for more information about the current state of Christianity around the world and for more collaboration in overcoming the remaining obstacles to world evangelization.

There had already been two major conferences, in London in 1888 and in New York in 1900, which had received delegates from a wide range of mission societies in order to share "missionary intelligence" about the world and to reflect together on mission policies and practices. However, despite the size and success of the New York conference, many of the leaders decided that a more representative conference was needed, one that was not intended as an inspirational rally for the faithful but as a working conference that focused exclusively on the opportunities and challenges of doing missions in the non-Christian world.[50] The organizing committee's stated aim for the Edinburgh 1910 conference was to sponsor "a united effort to subject the plans and methods of the whole missionary enterprise to searching investigation and to coordinate missionary experience from all parts of the world."[51] John R. Mott was named the chair of the event. Mott described the 1910 World Missionary Conference as "the first attempt at a systematic and careful study of the missionary problems of the world."[52]

From the perspective of the twenty-first century, it would be easy to dismiss the conference as overly audacious in calling itself a "World" missionary conference. From today's perspective the delegates would be too

49. David Bosch sums up the missionary mood of the time as "pragmatic, purposeful, activist, impatient, self-confident, single-minded, and triumphant." See David Bosch, *Transforming Mission: Paradigm Shifts in Theology of Mission* (Maryknoll, NY: Orbis, 1991), 336.

50. The Ecumenical Missionary Conference in New York attracted between 170,000 and 200,000 people, making it, at that time, the largest gathering in American religious history. However, it was a popular gathering, including addresses from President McKinley and the then governor of New York, Theodore Roosevelt. Former president Benjamin Harrison was the honorary chair of the event.

51. Cited by Keith Clements, *Faith on the Frontiers: A Life of J. H. Oldham* (Edinburgh: T & T Clark; Geneva: World Council of Churches, 1999), 77. A similar statement can be found in Ashley Carus-Wilson, "A World Parliament on Missions: The Meaning and Methods of the Edinburgh Conference of 1910," *The Quiver* 45 (1910): 632.

52. As quoted in Andrew Walls, *The Cross-Cultural Process in Christian History* (Maryknoll, NY: Orbis, 2002), 59.

white, too Western, too Protestant, and far too triumphalistic. After all, although the conference did bring together 1,400 delegates, the vast majority of them were British or American. There were no Roman Catholic or Eastern Orthodox present as official delegates, although several attended as observers.[53] Furthermore, out of the 1,400 delegates, there were only seventeen from the Majority World. As for the optimistic, triumphalism of the conference, we must remember that the "Great Century" was characterized by extreme optimism, which pervaded the entire Western world until the advent of the two world wars.

However, from the perspective of the early twentieth century, it was meticulously planned to be the most globally representative event in history. Rather than inviting delegates from churches, with their potential endless theological debates and ecclesiastical divisions, the invitations went out to every known mission society that was working with non-Christian peoples.[54] The societies were invited to send delegates based on a strict proportionality to the size and scope of the work of the missions organization. Thus, although the ethnic origin of most of the delegates was of European descent, they came, quite literally, from all over the world, bringing extensive, firsthand experience of the mission field.

Because the World Missionary Conference in Edinburgh had formal and informal opportunities for delegates to meet and discuss the situation in the global church, it is a mistake to gauge the breadth of the conference by those who gave the plenary addresses. It was a true working, consultative conference, and the impact and perspective of those from the Majority World was enormous. In fact, at the close of the conference, an official letter was drafted from the delegates to "the members of the Christian Church in non-Christian Lands." The letter spoke of the delegates, saying that "none have been more helpful in our deliberations then members from your own Churches." In addition to the input from the Majority World delegates, the collective, firsthand, cross-cultural experience among delegates was unparalleled for its time. W. H. T. Gairdner,

---

53. There is the famous comment by one of the Roman Catholic observers of the Edinburgh conference who was asked what it felt like to be a Roman Catholic in the midst of such a large gathering of Protestants. He replied, "We are like a few uneasy lions thrown into the den of the Protestants."

54. At the time, there were a number of "mission" societies that were conducting a wide range of ministries among the poor in the evangelized world.

a 1910 delegate and the author of a firsthand account of the conference, declared that the conference was a "true World conference" because the delegates have come "from every point of the compass to this ancient city ... representing so many races, nations, tongues, traditions, ranks and professions."[55] From our perspective, this statement seems hyperbolic, but it does give an insight into the ethos of the conference and how it was experienced by those who attended.

The conference was organized thematically, with each day of the conference centered on one of the following themes:

1. Carrying the Gospel to all the Non-Christian World
2. The Church in the Mission Field
3. Education in Relation to the Christianization of National Life
4. Missionary Message in Relation to the Non-Christian World
5. The Preparation of Missionaries
6. The Home Base of Missions
7. Missions and Governments
8. Cooperation and the Promotion of Unity

These eight themes shed light on what were considered the most important issues and concerns of the day.[56] Themes one, four, and six highlight how dramatically the world has changed in the last century. In 1910 it seemed entirely plausible to divide the world into the "Christian" and "non-Christian" spheres, with the West representing the "Christian" world, and the Majority World the "non-Christian" world. In 1910, the "home base" of missions undoubtedly was the Western world. Today, such assumptions are no longer tenable. Theme two (the Church in the Mission Field) reflects the hunger for accurate information about the state of the church in the Majority World. Themes three and five reveal the long-term value of education in Protestant missions. Themes four and seven highlight the

---

55. W. H. T. Gairdner, *Edinburgh 1910: An Account and Interpretation of the World Missionary Conference* (Edinburgh: Oliphant, Anderson and Ferrier, 1910), 48–49.
56. As a point of comparison, the Edinburgh 2010 centenary event was, by design, structured much like the Edinburgh 1910 event. However, the themes studied were: Foundations for Missions, Christian Mission Among Other Faiths, Mission and Postmodernity, Mission and Power, Forms of Missionary Engagement, Theological Education and Formation, Christian Communities in Contemporary Contexts, Mission and Unity—Ecclesiology and Mission, and Mission Spirituality and Authentic Discipleship.

importance of understanding the challenges and issues raised by followers of Hinduism, Buddhism, and Islam, as well as the political contexts into which religion is embedded, and which so dramatically influence the missionary encounter. The last theme highlights the need for cooperation and collaboration as we collectively understand our shared roles in participating in God's *missio dei*.

The 1910 Edinburgh World Missionary Conference concluded with the realization, quite insightfully, that "God is the ultimate Home Base of missions." It is *His* work through *His* church. Mott concluded, saying, "God has been silently and peacefully doing His work, but He has infinitely greater designs than these. It is not in His will that the influences set forth by Him shall cease this night. Rather shall they course out through us to the very ends of the earth."[57]

From the perspective of 2010, looking back on the 1910 World Missionary Conference in Edinburgh, there are several key features that capture the legacy of the conference. First, Edinburgh 1910 initiated an entirely new structure and constituency for reflecting on Christianity in the world. By focusing on delegates from the mission societies rather than the churches themselves, the conference was able to bring together people who were personally engaged in missionary work and who understood the challenges that faced the church at that time. Because it was a "working" conference rather than a motivational or inspirational event, the delegates were required to read and prepare a considerable amount of material before arriving at the conference. Therefore, those who came were prepared for a serious engagement of important issues.

Second, Edinburgh 1910 "marked, if not the birth, the genuine renaissance of mission studies."[58] The conference gave impetus to a whole range of scholarly work, which could be beneficially applied to missions. For example, empirical studies that could provide reliable information, trends, and statistics began to be used. One of the reports to the conference was a "Statistical Atlas of Christian Missions," which was the forerunner of today's *World Christian Encyclopedia* and *Atlas of Global Christianity*.[59] Several important journals, such as the *International Review of Missions*

---

57. Gairdner, *Edinburgh 1910*, 259, 267.
58. Walls, *The Cross-Cultural Process in Christian History*, 61.
59. David Barrett, George T. Kurian, and Todd Johnson, eds., *World Christian Encyclopedia: A Comparative Survey of Churches and Religions in the Modern World*, 2nd ed. (New York: Oxford

(IRM) and *The Muslim World*, were started in the wake of the conference.[60] The IRM represented the first international, ecumenical missiological journal. *The Muslim World* marked an important application of mission practice and theory to the particular challenges of Islam.

Finally, over the course of the ten-day conference, there was a growing realization and recognition that Christianity was a truly worldwide movement. Edinburgh is widely regarded as the beginning of the ecumenical movement, which gave birth to such influential global movements as the International Missionary Council and the Lausanne movement. In the well-known words of Archbishop William Temple, the emergence of the global church became "the great new fact of our time." Andrew Walls echoed this sentiment when he said that "it was at Edinburgh that western Christianity, at least Protestant western Christianity, first caught a clear sight of a church that would be bigger than itself."[61] Never again could the Western church think honestly about the Christian movement in isolation from vibrant currents of indigenous Christianity around the world. Edinburgh 1910 was truly a *kairos* moment in the history of world Christianity. It is one of the great ironies of history that at a conference held in the heart of old Europe, the church, for the first time, captured a glimpse of a Christianity that would be global and post-Western.

CONCLUSION

This chapter has highlighted five key themes: the birth of the Protestant missionary society, the commitment to Bible translation in vernacular languages, the emerging role of women in missions, the importance of church planting, and the growing awareness of global Christianity. None of these themes, by itself, can capture the vibrancy of the "Great Century." However, collectively, they mark the defining themes and some of the remarkable contours of the Christian church between 1792 and 1910, which stands as one of the great *kairos* periods in the history of world missions.

University Press, 2001), and T. M. Johnson, K. R. Ross, and S. S. K. Lee, eds., *Atlas of Global Christianity* (Edinburgh: Edinburgh University Press, forthcoming).

60. Both journals were founded in 1912, the latter originally as *The Moslem World*, later changed to *The Muslim World*.

61. Walls, *The Cross-Cultural Process in Christian History*, 61.

— 10 —

The Flowering of World Christianity, 1910–Present

MOST OF US HAVE become accustomed to seeing a wide range of new translations and specialty Bibles that are now widely available. The days when the King James "Authorized Version" was the only Bible for English speakers has been eclipsed by dozens of new translations, paraphrases, study Bibles, and special focus Bibles. In addition to translations like the Revised Standard Version, the New American Standard Bible, the New International Version, and the New English Bible, we can now read translations and paraphrased Bibles especially for children,[1] for youth,[2] for feminists,[3] for Southerners,[4] and so forth. So, perhaps it is not too much to ask the reader to imagine another remarkable and unusual kind of Bible. Rather than a Bible that is in only one language, imagine a Bible that has the amazing ability to reflect the languages Christians around the world speak, in the actual proportion to how they are globally represented.

If this Bible had been held by a Christian who was attending the World Missionary Conference in Edinburgh in 1910, the vast majority of the Bible would be in English and a few other Western European languages. However, if that same Bible were to be opened one century later, in 2010, it

---

1. *The Children's Bible in 365 Stories* (Oxford, England: Lion Children's Books, 1995).
2. *The Youth Bible* (Nashville: Word, 2002).
3. *The Inclusive New Testament* (Hyattsville, MD: AltaMira, Priests for Equality, 1996).
4. See Clarence Jordan, *Cotton Patch Version of Matthew and John, Cotton Patch Version of Luke and Acts, Cotton Patch Version of Hebrews and General Epistles* (El Monte, CA: New Win, 1970–1997).

would be a vastly different Bible. You would read this imaginary Bible in Spanish from Genesis 1 all the way through the third chapter of Joshua, since Spanish now represents the most spoken language of world Christianity. The Bible would then become English and continue in English from Joshua 4 all the way to 1 Kings 6. Then, quite surprisingly, the Bible would become Chinese from 1 Kings 6 through 2 Chronicles 14. The language changes then would start to appear more regularly, including major sections of the New Testament in Korean, Hindi, and Swahili. By the time you reached Revelation, the Bible would be changing languages almost every verse and then every word, until all of the 2,251 languages spoken by Christians around the world would find their place in this imaginary Bible. I don't know how useful this Bible would be, but it would dramatically illustrate the central theme of this chapter, namely, the emergence of vibrant Christianity in many different and diverse parts of the world. The global expansion of the church of Jesus Christ is widely regarded as the single most important development in the history of the church of the twentieth century.

In chapter 1, we examined some of the broad demographics of world Christianity as a way of setting the context for why we need to rethink how we talk about and engage in global missions in the twenty-first century. The purpose of this chapter is to cast a historical light on the emergence and flowering of Christianity as a world movement. As was the case with missions prior to 1792 (chapter 8) and from 1792 to 1910 (chapter 9), a full survey of the period from 1910 to the present is not possible in a single chapter without reducing the period to an almost mindless barrage of statistics and data. Therefore, to capture something of the grandeur and spirit of twentieth-century missions, we will focus on seven brief stories or vignettes of world Christianity. These representative stories are taken from Africa, Latin America, the Middle East, three parts of Asia, and Europe. The following stories will be examined: (1) the growth of Pentecostalism in Latin America, (2) the African Independent Churches in sub-Saharan Africa, (3) Muslims who are following Christ in the mosque, (4) South Indian missionaries to Hindus in North India, (5) non-registered "house-church" movements in China, (6) the Korean missionary movement, and (7) vibrant European churches emerging out of post-Christian Europe. Each story is illustrative of the much larger story of global Christianity.

PENTECOSTALISM IN LATIN AMERICA

Our first story of global Christianity focuses on Latin American Pentecostalism as representative of a larger global phenomenon in world Christianity. There are several aspects of this story that underscore its importance in understanding global Christianity today.

Growth of Global Pentecostalism

First, Pentecostalism is the fastest growing Christian movement in history, and with over half a billion adherents, it is second only to Roman Catholicism as the largest single block of Christian identity.[5] Roman Catholic missionaries began to arrive in Latin America in the late fifteenth century after the Padroado. Over the next few centuries, Latin America became one of the most thoroughly Roman Catholic regions in the world. Protestant missionaries did not arrive until the late nineteenth century, and Pentecostalism did not come to Latin America until the early decades of the twentieth century. Yet, after only seventy-five years in Central and South America, Pentecostals make up "three-quarters of all Latin American Protestants."[6] This is important because the vast majority of what is called "Protestant," or "independent" or "indigenous," growth in Latin America is made up of Pentecostals. As early as 1962 *Time* magazine declared Pentecostalism to be the "fastest growing church in the western Hemisphere."[7] Reflecting on the growth of Latin American Protestantism, which is growing three times faster than the population, David Stoll predicts that "by 2010 evangelicals will be a third of the population" of Latin America, and the vast majority of these evangelicals will be Pentecostal Christians.[8] Even Roman Catholic

---

5. David B. Barrett, George T. Kurian, and Todd M. Johnson, eds., *World Christian Encyclopedia: A Comparative Survey of Churches and Religions in the Modern World*, 2nd ed. (New York: Oxford University Press, 2001), 4; Teresa Watanabe, "Global Convention Testifies to Pentecostalism's Revival," *Los Angeles Times*, May 31, 2001. In 2008, the World Christian Database cited 565,053,091 "renewalists" and 1,093,065,563 Roman Catholics. See also Philip Jenkins, *The Next Christendom: The Coming of Global Christianity* (Oxford: Oxford University Press, 2002), 8: "Since there were only a handful of Pentecostals in 1900, and several hundred million today, is it not reasonable to identify this as perhaps the most successful social movement of the past century? According to current projections, the number of Pentecostal believers should surpass the one billion mark before 2050."

6. Everett A. Wilson, "Latin American Pentecostals — Their Potential for Ecumenical Dialogue," *Pneuma: the Journal of the Society of Pentecostal Studies* 9, no. 1 (Spring 1987): 86.

7. *Time* 2 November (1962): 56.

8. David Stoll, "A Protestant Reformation in Latin America?" *Christian Century* 107, no. 1 (1990): 45.

journalist Penny Lernoux observed that "every hour four hundred Latin Americans convert" to Protestantism. It is not uncommon to hear the criticism that Pentecostalism is "a mile wide and an inch deep." While this is an important concern, we cannot ignore the vibrant life of this new branch of Christianity in Latin America, which is almost without parallel and exceeds the growth rate of Protestantism in Central Europe during the time of the Reformation.[9] This transformation deserves our attention.

Pentecostalism and Christendom
Second, the story of Latin American Pentecostalism is a helpful contemporary example of the breakup of the Christendom arrangement that has dominated the Latin American religious and political landscape since the sixteenth century. For centuries evangelism in Latin America meant a process of general acculturation, whereby people were Christianized and incorporated into "a monocultural Christendom in which they were subject to Christian authorities, both ecclesiastical and civil."[10] The once secure Roman Catholic hegemony over Latin America is passing away, particularly in countries like Brazil, Chile, and Guatemala.[11] Several countries in Latin America already have more Pentecostal pastors than Roman Catholic priests.[12] By 2010 the evangelicals, mostly of Pentecostal persuasion, will outnumber the Roman Catholics in some countries.[13]

However, Latin America is not merely the story of the rise of Pentecostalism and the decline of Roman Catholicism, or the intrusion of Pentecostals into Roman Catholic territory. As with the European Reformation, this new reformation has also stimulated vitality in the

---

9. Russell Watson, "Latin America: John Paul Goes to War," *Newsweek* (February 12, 1996), 39. See also, C. Peter Wagner, "The Greatest Church Growth Is Beyond Our Shores," *Christianity Today* 28, no. 8 (1984): 27–28. Wagner estimates that the growth rate of Protestantism (mostly Pentecostal) is three times the rate of population. It is estimated that about 8,000 are being baptized every day with over 100 million on the continent. See also David Stoll, *Is Latin America Turning Protestant? The Politics of Evangelical Growth* (Los Angeles: University of California Press, 1990), xiv.

10. John F. Gorski, "How the Catholic Church in Latin America Became Missionary," *International Bulletin of Missionary Research* 27, no. 2 (April 2003): 60.

11. Stoll, "A Protestant Reformation in Latin America?" 46. Stoll provides a chart showing 1985 percentages of evangelicals in Brazil (15.95%), Chile (21.57%) and Guatemala (18.92%). He then extrapolates to predict the potential evangelical population in 2010.

12. Stoll, *Is Latin America Turning Protestant?* 6. In Brazil, for example, Stoll cites that there are 13,000 Roman Catholic priests and 17,000 ordained Protestant pastors and 13,000 non-ordained ones.

13. Allan Anderson, *An Introduction to Pentecostalism* (Cambridge: Cambridge University Press, 2004), 63.

Roman Catholic Church, resulting in a renewed emphasis on evangelism and mission. As Roman Catholic missiologist John Gorski has noted, "Evangelization in the specific sense of announcing the Gospel to enable a personal encounter with the living Christ, leading to conversion and discipleship, became a conscious concern of the Catholic Church only within the past half century."[14] The point is, the Reformation has finally arrived in Latin America! Just as the sixteenth-century Protestant Reformation in Europe challenged and helped to foster the emergence of a new branch of Christianity and to bring reformation to the established church of its day, so today the Pentecostals in Latin America are bringing along the emergence of new Christian movements and the renewal of Roman Catholicism, as well as theological discussions that mirror many of the broad contours of the Protestant Reformation in Europe.

However, this is not merely a repeat of the European Reformation or a delayed extension of it. The Latin American struggle has its own unique features, particularly in the emphasis on the Holy Spirit, which had not been a prominent feature of the European Reformation. Latin American Pentecostalism also is influenced by modern forces of globalization. The single, all-embracing system of religious life in the region has been replaced by a new religious marketplace and the democratization of religious choice. This "third force"[15] of Christianity is bringing "*la renovación*" to Christians throughout the region and, in the process, transforming the religious landscape.

Pentecostal Influence on Theological Discourse
Third, the theology of Latin American Pentecostals brings several important challenges to traditional evangelical discourse in Europe and North

---

14. Gorski, "How the Catholic Church in Latin America Became Missionary," 60.
15. The expression "third force" was coined by Henry P. Van Dusen in 1958 to describe the new wave of missionary activity coming out of Pentecostal Christianity. See Henry P. Van Dusen, "The Third Force in Christendom," *Life* (June 9, 1958): 113–24. The first wave was Roman Catholicism; the second wave was Protestantism. It is interesting to note that Eastern Orthodoxy is omitted, despite its vigorous and inspiring missionary work in the nineteenth century. Furthermore, according to Walter Hollenweger, the charismatic movement also has swept through portions of the Eastern Orthodox Church. See Walter Hollenweger, *Pentecostalism: Origins and Developments Worldwide* (Peabody, MA: Hendrickson, 1997), 154. Todd Johnson documents 3,300,000 Eastern Orthodox Christians who would identify themselves as part of the charismatic renewal and an additional 628,000 who are part of the neocharismatic renewal. See Todd M. Johnson, "Three Waves of Christian Renewal: A 100–Year Snapshot," *International Bulletin of Missionary Research* 30, no. 2 (April 2006): 76.

America concerning the work of the Holy Spirit in the world and in the lives of believers, which is of particular importance to the theme of this study. Latin Americans long have insisted that traditional European and North American theologies of the Spirit were too static and disconnected from the suffering and economic hardships of the peoples of Latin America. Furthermore, Pentecostals have felt that many of the mainstream North American theologies were overly preoccupied with theoretical issues and, in the process, lost the evangelistic urgency needed to evangelize the world.

It has taken a long time for North American historians and theologians to take seriously either the global Pentecostal movement or any critique it might offer to our own theology. As late as 1968 William McLoughlin contributed a chapter to *Religion in America* entitled, "Is There a Third Force in Christendom?" where he dismissed the Pentecostal movement as a passing "effluvia." He predicted that "the pietistic upthrust by fringe-sect dissenters and come-outers does not in itself constitute the creation of a significant new religious movement in Christendom." He went on to say that Pentecostalism does "not constitute a dynamic new force capable of replacing or seriously threatening the old order."[16] What McLoughlin failed to realize is that the very thing he predicted would not happen had, in fact, *already happened!* By 1968 the global shift, while yet unrecognized, already had occurred, and Christendom as McLoughlin knew it was already being dismantled. The shift happened swiftly and dramatically because at the same time that Pentecostals around the world were in the process of rediscovering the vibrancy of historic Christian faith, the mainline churches were largely abandoning it, losing members by the millions and thereby accelerating their move to the sidelines of American religious life.[17] As Andrew Walls has noted, "One has to go back many centuries to find such a huge recession in one part of the world paralleled by such a huge simultaneous accession in another."[18] It is our turn to humbly admit that we have much to learn from this dramatic and global work of God among our Pentecostal brothers and sisters in Latin America.

---

16. William G. McLoughlin and Robert Bellah, eds., *Religion in America* (Boston: Houghton Mifflin, 1968), 47.

17. C. Peter Wagner has pointed out that "theological liberalism shows the highest negative correlation with growth." C. Peter Wagner, *Church Growth and the Whole Gospel* (San Francisco: Harper and Row, 1981), 196.

18. Andrew F. Walls, "Eusebius Tries Again: Reconceiving the Study of Christian History," *International Bulletin of Missionary Research* 24, no. 3 (July 2000): 105.

THE AFRICAN INDEPENDENT CHURCHES
IN SUB-SAHARAN AFRICA

The demise of Western colonialism in Africa occurred at such a rapid pace
that it surprised both the colonizers and the colonized, as much of Africa regained its independence during the short years between 1958 and
1964.[19] The broad expectation at the time was that the demise of colonialism would bring about a rapid decline in Christianity, since many Africans associated Christianity as the religion of their former colonizers.
However, the last half of the twentieth century turned out to be the genesis
of an entirely new Christian awakening in Africa. For example, in the last
three decades of the twentieth century, the overall percentage of African
Christians rose from around 25 percent of the population to about 46
percent of the population, which amounts to 8.4 million new Christians
every year (23,000 per day).[20] The dramatic growth of the church in Africa
stands as a living contradiction to what Philip Jenkins calls the "modern
mythology," which asserts that Christianity was "exported to a passive or
reluctant Third World."[21]

Much of this Christian awakening in Africa remains securely within
the Roman Catholic, Anglican, and Protestant churches, which remained
after the end of colonization. For example, as recently as 1955 the Roman
Catholic Church cited only 16 million members on the entire African
continent, compared with over 150 million Roman Catholics in Africa
today. It is estimated that by 2025 this number will blossom to around 230
million.[22] Similar growth has been cited among Anglicans in Africa. For
example, the number of Anglicans in Nigeria alone is now approaching
the number of Anglicans in England, the traditional heartland of Angli-

---

19. Elizabeth Isichei, *A History of Christianity in Africa* (Grand Rapids: Eerdmans, 1995), 323.
    Earlier independence occurred in Egypt (1952), Tunisia, Morocco, Sudan (1956), and Ghana
    (1957). Guinea gained independence in 1958, followed quickly by Cameroon, Congo-Brazza-
    ville, Gabun, Chad, Central African Republic, Togo, Ivory Coast, Cahoney, Upper Volta, Niger,
    Nigeria, Senegal, Mali, Madagascar, Somalia, Mauretania, and Congo-Leopoldville, all in 1960.
    The year 1958 is chosen as the beginning of this remarkable period because that is the year of
    the First Conference of Independent African States, which took place in Accra, Ghana. For more
    on this conference, see *A History of Christianity in Asia, Africa and Latin America, 1450–1990*,
    ed. Klaus Koschorke, Frieder Ludwig, and Mariano Delgado (Grand Rapids: Eerdmans, 2007),
    245–246.
20. Jenkins, *The Next Christendom*, 56.
21. Ibid., 53.
22. Ibid., 58.

canism.[23] The shifting center of gravity within Anglicanism has important implications for the future of the worldwide Anglican communion and has been regularly cited, for example, in the recent struggles within the Episcopalian Church in the United States, where churches opposed to departures from historic orthodoxy have separated from their Episcopalian bishop and submitted to the authority of an African bishop. Protestantism also has grown substantially in Africa. For example, between 1970 and 2005 the Methodists in Nigeria grew from 80,000 to over 2 million. As a point of comparison, it should be noted that during that same time period, the Methodists in the United Kingdom lost over half of their entire membership (2 million to 996,000) and the United Methodist Church in the United States lost 6 million members, dropping from 14 million down to 8 million members.[24]

However, I have chosen to focus on the burgeoning growth of the independent, or indigenous, African churches, beginning in the first decades of the twentieth century. While indigenous Christian movements in Africa encompass a wide variety of churches, they are often spoken of collectively as the AIC, which is an acronym for African Independent Churches or, alternatively, African Indigenous or African Instituted Churches. There is no single movement known as AIC. Rather, this is a broad term representing over 60 million churches, which belong to over 10,000 distinct African denominations or smaller movements. Harold Turner once defined the AIC as "a church which has been founded in Africa, by Africans, and primarily for Africans."[25] However, this description belies the more important observation that collectively, the AIC represents vital new theological and ecclesiastical developments within African Christianity, which will have a tremendous influence on the future of Christianity all over the world. Andrew Walls once said that "what happens within the African churches in the next generation will determine the whole shape of church history for centuries to come." Therefore, the "sort of theology which is more characteristic of Christianity in the twenty-first century may well depend on what has happened in the minds

---

23. The World Christian Database cites 18,500,000 Anglicans in the Anglican Church of Nigeria and 24,300,000 in the Church of England. If one compares attendance in services of worship, Anglicanism in Nigeria dwarfs that of the Church of England.
24. World Christian Database, www.worldchristiandatabase.org (accessed May 12, 2007).
25. Harold Turner, *Religious Innovation in Africa* (Boston: G. K. Hall, 1979), 92.

of African Christians."[26] If African Christianity does indeed become the most representative Christianity of the twenty-first century, then this particular story must be known and understood.

To grasp the magnitude of this movement, we will first explore what is meant by "indigenous" churches (as well as some of the other terms that are used to describe these churches) and why they have arisen. Then, we will examine some of the broader ways in which the AIC is identified within the larger fabric of global Christianity.

The Rise of the AIC

An indigenous church is an expression of Christianity that has either a weak or nonexistent link to historic, organized expressions of Catholic, Orthodox, or Protestant manifestations of Christianity and is generally marked by ethno-specific or cultural aspects that emphasize the local or regional particularity of the church.

The first AIC in the modern period were established in Sierra Leone in West Africa. In 1787 Freetown was founded as a colony for freed slaves and "recaptives," who had been rescued from slave ships on the high seas and brought to Freetown. Tens of thousands of former slaves eventually settled there, speaking as many as 117 different languages.[27] With so many different cultures and languages in such close proximity, Freetown was probably one of the most culturally diverse cities in the world at that time. The Church Missionary Society (CMS) developed extensive mission work in Sierra Leone and, under the leadership of Henry Venn, made two decisions that became important milestones in the emergence of indigenous Christianity in Africa. First, the CMS founded the Fourah Bay College in Freetown, which offered the first Western-style higher education in all of West Africa. The Fourah Bay College became known as the "Athens of Africa" and was an important center for training future African leaders. For example, the first student who enrolled at the college was Samuel Adjai Crowther (1808–1891), who eventually became the first African Anglican bishop in history and an influential missionary in the Niger territories.

---

26. Andrew F. Walls, "Towards an Understanding of Africa's Place in Christian History," in *Religion in a Pluralistic Society,* ed. J. S. Pobee (Leiden: E. J. Brill, 1976), 183.

27. Stephen Neill, *A History of Christian Missions* (Baltimore: Penguin, 1964), 304.

Second, in 1861, as part of Henry Venn's vision for the "euthanasia of missions," the CMS founded the Native Pastorate, later renamed the Sierra Leone Church, as a "self-governing" church.[28] The emergence of an African independent church in Sierra Leone inspired dozens of African movements to secede and form independent churches. However, the overall numbers remained relatively small until the emergence of African nationalism and political independence.[29] Today, the number of African Christians who are part of an independent Christian movement is estimated between 40 million and 86 million worldwide.[30]

In an attempt to share resources, promote theological training among their clergy, and have their voices heard by the Western churches, the independent churches of Africa for a number of decades tried to join various conciliar bodies. However, after repeated denials, the independent churches of Africa began to form their own conciliar bodies. In 1978 the first continent-wide conciliar body was formed, the Organization of African Independent Churches, known as the OAIC. This organization was founded in Cairo through the work of Bishop Markos of the Coptic Orthodox Church of Egypt. The Coptic Church played a central role in the formation of the OAIC because it is widely regarded as one of the earliest African churches with no ties to colonization. Later, in 1985, the OAIC was registered by the Kenyan government as an international body to serve the entire African church. The "I" in the acronym was changed from "independent" to "instituted" to emphasize that these churches were founded and led by Africans but did not want to be independent from the global church. It was not until 1998 that the OAIC was finally invited to become an associate council of the World Council of Churches as well as an official council within the All

---

28. Isichei, *A History of Christianity in Africa*, 164.
29. In 1910 at the time of the Edinburgh conference, the number of Africans who belonged to independent churches was probably not more than 100,000. However, as independence spread, the numbers swelled into the millions. By 1968, David Barrett estimates that the number was close to 6 million.
30. David Barrett and Todd Johnson, "Annual Statistical Table on Global Mission: 2001," *International Bulletin of Missionary Research* 25, no. 1 (2001): 24. World Christian Database cites the following breakdown of independents in Africa: Eastern Africa, 20,038,967; Western Africa, 30,419,745; Middle Africa, 16,108,130; Northern Africa, 392,859; and Southern Africa, 19,817,290 for a total of 86,776,981. A lower figure of 60 million is cited in Lawford Imunde and Dr. T. John Padwick, "Advancing Legal Empowerment of the Poor: The Role and Perspective of the African Independent Churches," Organisation for African Instituted Churches (OAIC) document. http://www.wcrp.org/files/AICs%20and%20Legal%20empowerment.FINAL_.doc (accessed January 2008).

Africa Conference of Churches. Because some of these movements were actually initiated by Western missionaries but became fully indigenous later, some prefer to speak of the AIC as African *indigenous* churches. The different usages of the acronym AIC highlight the diversity and complexity of this emerging face of African Christianity.

Causes in the Emergence of the AIC

There are three main reasons the AIC have emerged, although not all three of these apply equally to all AIC. First, the rise of nationalism in the postcolonial period stimulated the need for churches that were established or led by Africans. Some of the AIC are highly structured and hierarchical movements, whereas others are more informal and lay oriented. Nevertheless, all of the AIC emphasize the importance of African leadership within their respective movements. Second, AIC churches seek to reflect African cultural forms and take pride in their African identity and heritage. In some cases earnest attempts were made to accommodate traditional African practices and customs. In other cases, as we observed in Gregory the Great's advice to Augustine, alternative Christian practices were set in place to help separate Africans from what were regarded as unbiblical customs and practices. In both cases these churches demonstrate their awareness of the indigenous context.

Finally, the AIC generally emphasize doctrinal themes or practices they feel were neglected or misunderstood in the various expressions of Christianity that had been imported into Africa from the West. These themes often include a greater emphasis on personal holiness and the role of the Holy Spirit in the Christian life. Many churches within the large AIC movement point out that Western missionaries did not take the spirit world or demons seriously enough. They often point out how the ministry of Jesus was characterized by supernatural healing and demonic deliverance, whereas the missionaries largely interpreted disease in a scientific and rationalistic way and relied more on hospitals than on prayer.[31] Others feel that greater doctrinal clarity was needed on a wide range of other issues as well, including marriage (especially polygamy) and gender issues, the Christian response to poverty, and the environment.

---

31. Isichei, *A History of Christianity in Africa*, 254.

Broad Categories of AIC

Because of the size and varying emphases of these indigenous movements, it is not easy to generalize about the AIC. The movements can be variously described as pietistic, legalistic, fundamentalist, liturgical, messianic, or Pentecostal, to name a few. Allan Anderson, a leading expert on the AIC, has characterized them with the word *pluriformity,* seeking to capture the notion of their diversity, while maintaining their unity as participants in an identifiable Africanness. Generally speaking, the AIC have three major expressions known as *nationalistic* or *Ethiopian* churches, *Zionist* or *Spirit* churches, and, finally, *prophetic or messianic* churches.[32]

The first scholar to categorize the various expressions of the AIC was Bengt Sundkler, in his landmark book *Bantu Prophets in South Africa,* published in 1948. Sundkler's research identified two main types of AIC, which he called "Ethiopian" and "Zionist."[33] This distinction, later adopted by scholars such as Marthinus Daneel, broadly distinguished the movements by whether or not they emphasized the ongoing role of prophecy and the revelation of the Holy Spirit.[34] However the growth and diversity within the Zionist movements eventually led later scholars, such as Adrian Hastings and, more recently, Philip Jenkins, to recognize a third distinction, known as "prophetic" or "messianic" churches.[35] It would be a mistake to make absolute distinctions between these groups, since they have all influenced each other, and indeed some AIC have intentionally sought to creatively combine various aspects of these movements. As each of these movements is explored, the reader should view them as tendencies or broad characteristics rather than strict lines of institutional separation.

---

32. These are broad categories. A more detailed analysis can be found in the World Christian Database, which examines the AIC under thirteen separate headings: cell-based networks, healing networks, independent apostolic, independent charismatic, independent deliverance, independent full gospel, independent neocharismatic, independent Pentecostal, independent spiritual, neocharismatic with mixed traditions, African oneness Pentecostal, African radio/TV believers, and African word of faith/prosperity.

33. Bengt Sundkler, *Bantu Prophets in South Africa* (London: Lutterworth, 1948), 38, 47f, 53. Sundkler acknowledges in his research that the "Zionist" churches go by a wide variety of names, including Zion, Apostolic, Pentecostal, and Faith.

34. Marthinus Daneel, *Old and New in Southern Shona Independent Churches,* vol. 1 (The Hague: Mouton, 1971), 285.

35. Adrian Hastings, *The Church in Africa, 1450–1950* (Oxford: Clarendon, 1994), 478–87 (Varieties of Ethiopianism), 499–504 (Rise of Zionism), 505–18 (Harrists, Kimbanguists, and Aladura). Also, as early as 1979, Hastings spoke of "prophetic" and "healing" churches. See Adrian Hastings, *A History of African Christianity 1950–1975* (New York: Cambridge University Press, 1979), 68. See Jenkins, *The Next Christendom,* 52.

NATIONALISTIC OR ETHIOPIAN CHURCHES

The nationalistic churches, sometimes referred to as Ethiopian churches, were formed as a specific response to the colonial presence in Africa. The term *Ethiopian* comes from a late nineteenth-century movement, in which African Christians broke from the Anglican and Methodist churches in protest against segregation by white missionaries and the lack of African leadership within the church. *Ethiopian* was chosen not only because Ethiopia had successfully resisted Western colonization, but also because the conversion of the Ethiopian eunuch in Acts 8:26–40 demonstrates that Africans received the gospel even before the Europeans, which does not occur until the conversion of Lydia in Acts 16:11–15. The movement chose Psalm 68:31 as its theme verse: "Ethiopia shall stretch forth its hands unto God."[36] These churches did not substantially change the theology, liturgy, or polity of the mission churches, which were mostly Anglican and Methodist. However, the Ethiopian churches were committed to a self-governing African church with African leadership. They were also more openly committed to political agitation as a means to free Africans from the vestiges of colonial or Western control.[37] Once Sundkler identified Ethiopian churches as those that were nonprophetic and more politically activistic, then the meaning of the term gradually broadened to include a wide range of churches that are not, strictly speaking, part of the original "Ethiopian" secessions.

One example of an Ethiopian church is the Ethiopian Catholic Church in Zion, founded in 1904 by James Brander. In 1892 Brander united with the original Ethiopian church founded by Mangena Mokone when he left the Anglican church. The church decided to seek recognition and possible funding for theological education by affiliating with the African Methodist Episcopal Church (AMEC) in the United States. However, Brander eventually became disillusioned with the AMEC and on April 3, 1904 forty-five worshippers officially started the new Ethiopian Catholic Church in Zion in Pretoria, South Africa. The church was very liturgical and largely mirrored the Anglican and

---

36. Sundler, *Bantu Prophets in South Africa*, 39. The reference to "Ethiopia" in the text of Psalm 68:31 is taken from the King James Bible, which was used by the English-speaking missionaries.

37. Anglican Bishop Samuel Adjai Crowther died in 1891 and was not replaced by an African diocesan bishop. By 1925, there were still no African disocesan bishops in any mission church and no African clergy were being appointed to any prominent churches. This was widely perceived by African Christians to be a reassertion of white control in the churches and helped to fuel separatistic, Ethiopian movements. The first African Roman Catholic diocesan bishop did not appear until 1939, when Victor Mukasa was appointed in Buganda, located today in south central Uganda.

Methodist heritage of most of its membership. Eventually many new completely independent Ethiopian churches sprang up and, increasingly, became more vocal about their resistance to the European presence in South Africa.

The most important legacy is not so much the organizational or doctrinal distinctives of these churches, but their influence on major political organizations that eventually brought an end to colonization. This is particularly evident in their challenges to apartheid in South Africa. Hennie Pretorius and Lizo Jafta, in *Christianity in South Africa: A Political, Social and Cultural History,* document at least seven political organizations in South Africa in which AIC Ethiopians had prominent roles, including what would become known as the ANC, the first national political organization for Africans in South Africa.[38] The Ethiopian churches also have been cited as having a significant influence on the Jamaican Marcus Garvey and his "Back to Africa" movement, as well as the Rastafarian movement.[39]

Zionist or Spirit Churches

The Zionist, or Spirit, churches are identified by their strong emphasis on the presence and power of the Holy Spirit. In the early research on this movement, Sundkler called these churches "Zionist" because "the leaders and followers of these churches refer to themselves as *ama-Ziyoni*, or Zionists."[40] Their services are characterized by exuberant worship, which often uses African songs, indigenous rhythms, and liturgy. These churches are known for strong preaching and effective use of personal testimony as a part of the worship service.

Surprisingly, Zionist churches did not originate in Africa but "grew ultimately from charismatic sects in late nineteenth-century North America, which practiced faith-healing and speaking in tongues."[41] The use of the word *Zion* is a spiritual reference not only to Mount Zion in Jerusalem, but also to Zion City, Illinois, which is regarded as the fountainhead of the American charismatic movement.[42] In 1910, at the same time the World Missionary

38. Hennie Pretorius and Lizo Jafta, "A Branch Springs Out: African Initiated Churches," in *Christianity in South Africa: A Political, Social and Cultural History,* ed. Richard Elphick and T. Davenport (Berkeley: University of California Press, 1998), 211–26.

39. William Spencer, *Dread Jesus* (London: SPCK, 1999), 18, 30, 74–75, 136–37.

40. Sundkler, *Bantu Prophets in South Africa,* 54.

41. Jenkins, *The Next Christendom,* 52.

42. Zion City, Illinois, was founded by John Alexander Dowie in 1896 as a theocracy. It was very influential in early Pentecostalism and, from the beginning, had important ties to Africa.

Conference was being held in Edinburgh, Engenas Barnabas Lekganyane was receiving a vision from God that led him to establish the Zion Christian Church (ZCC) in South Africa. The ZCC is characterized by an emphasis on divine healing, purification rites, dietary taboos, dancing in the Spirit, speaking in tongues, and prophecy. However, within ten years the Zionist movement had split into numerous branches, finding its greatest strength among the Zulu and Swazi, where "it would become almost the national religion."[43] Globally it claims as many as 12 million followers, making it larger than the combined strength of the United Methodist and Presbyterian Church (USA) in the United States.[44]

MESSIANIC OR PROPHETIC CHURCHES

The messianic, or prophetic, churches often share the emphasis on the Holy Spirit observed in the Zionist churches but are distinctive in that they are formed around a dominant personality or prophet figure. In contrast, the Zionistic churches are mostly led by Pentecostal ministers rather than prophet figures.[45] In the messianic churches, the founders or leaders are often attributed special powers, prophetic gifts, or even a mediatory role between the members and Christ. Over time these churches tend to become increasingly hierarchical and can be legalistic, with long lists of taboos. The worship in the prophetic churches is quite similar to other Pentecostal movements around the world. Probably the most noticeable difference with other examples of global Pentecostalism is that many of the members of prophetic churches wear white robes or white clothing to church as a sign of their separation from the world.

There are a number of prominent African Christian movements of this type, three of which will be briefly noted.

The Liberian William Wade Harris (1865–1929) received a vision from the archangel Gabriel, calling him to preach the gospel. Walking barefoot, wearing a long white robe, and carrying only a cross, a Bible, and a bowl for baptism, Harris preached in West Africa from 1913 to 1915, along the coast of what is today known as Liberia, Cote d'Ivoire, and Ghana. He called people to give up their fetishes, denounce the evil spirits, and

---

43. Hastings, The Church in Africa, 1450–1950, 501.

44. Ibid. In its annual Easter conference at Pietersburg, the ZCC attracts up to 2 million worshippers, making it one of the largest annual gatherings of Christians on earth.

45. Ibid., 502.

be baptized. It is estimated that Harris baptized between 100,000 and 120,000 new Christians in a year.[46] Harris did not intend to establish a separate church and actually encouraged his followers to wait for the missionaries to arrive and to join the mission churches. However, many "Harrist" churches, including the *Eglisa Harrisiste* and the Church of the Twelve Disciples, sprang up, especially among the uneducated villagers, and they continue to thrive.

Just a few years after Harris's famous preaching campaign, Simon Kimbangu (1889–1951) received a vision in 1918, calling him to be a prophet and a healer to the Congo.[47] Kimbangu's vision took place at the same time a flu pandemic was sweeping central Africa, which "made the limitations of both western and traditional medicine painfully apparent."[48] Healings began to take place through the ministry of Kimbangu, and by 1921 great crowds began to flock to his home in N'Kamba. The scale of the crowds, coupled with false rumors that Kimbangu had told his followers not to pay taxes and that he had seen a vision of the overthrow of white rule, caused such alarm among the Belgian authorities that they arrested Kimbangu and sentenced him to death. Due to the intervention of Baptist missionaries who knew the claims to be false, his sentence was eventually commuted, although he spent the rest of his life in prison.

The early followers of Kimbangu were Baptists and, despite rumors to the contrary, were not opposed to either the mission churches or the Belgian colonial authorities. However, once the movement was forced into hiding and his followers were forced to scatter, they inadvertently became traveling evangelists, causing the movement to grow enormously. A number of new prophets arose, which broadened the movement into an indigenous church quite distinct from the mission churches. Some of the prophets were largely orthodox in their theology, whereas others operated like the traditional spirit-animated prophets known as *ngunza*, which were part of the Congo culture. Some of these *ngunza*-type prophets claimed to speak in the spirit of Kimbangu or believed that they had access to secret teachings of Jesus that were not known to other Christians. Many within the larger Kimbanguist movement, as well as the official Church of Jesus Christ of the Prophet Simon Kimbangu, which

---

46. Isichei, *A History of Christianity in Africa*, 285.
47. Kimbangu was from what is known today as the Democratic Republic of Congo (formerly Belgian Congo and Zaire).
48. Isichei, *A History of Christianity in Africa*, 199.

was legalized in 1959, still regard Simon Kimbangu as an African savior. Today, the entire movement claims about eight million members.

A final example of the prophet-inspired churches are the Aladura churches, found prominently in Nigeria. In 1920, just a few years after Simon Kimbangu's ministry began, reports began to emerge of prophets appearing among the Yoruba in Nigeria. One of these prophets, Joseph Sadre, had started a prayer group known as the Precious Stone Society and was advocating Pentecostal theology and practice. They rejected the use of Western medicine and insisted on the power of prayer. Other prophets, such as Moses Orimolade, Joseph Babalola, and Josiah Ositelu, arose in response to visions from God and began to preach on prayer, fasting, and the importance of spiritual warfare. These prophets helped to initiate thousands of prayer groups. This prayer movement initially took place within the Anglican church, but the participants eventually met with such opposition that they left Anglicanism and began to form their own churches.

These churches became known as *aladura* churches, which is a Yoruba word meaning "praying people." Today there are many Aladura churches, including the Church of the Cherubim and Seraphim, Christ Apostolic Church, the Church of the Lord (Aladura), and the Holy Assembly of Christ from Heaven.[49] These churches are becoming increasingly important in our understanding of changes in European Christianity, since there are now more than three thousand of these congregations in the United Kingdom.[50]

It should be noted that these prophetic movements all sprang up in the years immediately following the World Missionary Conference in Edinburgh and, over the next century, dramatically altered the religious landscape in Africa. Even this brief survey should make it clear that the sheer size and diversity of the AIC means that it is not possible to generalize about the theology and practice of indigenous churches in Africa. Many of these churches reflect biblical orthodoxy, are Christocentric, and have a high regard for the Scriptures. In reflecting on these movements, it is important to remember that sometimes what are cited as heretical practices by Western writers are either neutral cultural expressions of Christianity or the resto-

---

49. Ibid., 283–84.

50. T. Jack Thompson, "African Independent Churches in Britain: An Introductory Survey," in *New Religions and the New Europe,* ed. Robert Towler (Aarhus, Denmark: Aarhus University Press, 1995), 224–31.

ration of certain features of biblical Christianity that have been neglected by some Western expressions of Christianity. Of course there are plenty of examples of quasi-orthodox and heretical beliefs, practices, or tendencies that have been incorporated into various expressions of African Christianity. However, we can no longer afford to ignore the voices and experiences of African Christians, since Africa will soon become the most Christian continent on earth.

MUSLIMS WHO ARE FOLLOWING CHRIST IN THE MOSQUE

When reflecting on the emergence of global Christianity, there is a natural tendency to focus exclusively on the large megamovements comprising millions of new followers of Christ. However, it is important to remember that all of these large movements started as small, marginalized events, which at the time were not appreciated or recognized for their significance. For example, looking back over the twentieth century, probably the single most dramatic development in the church was the emergence of global Pentecostalism, which, along with charismatic and neocharismatic movements, now comprises 600 million people worldwide.[51] However, at the 1910 World Missionary Conference in Edinburgh, it received virtually no attention at all, even though dramatic movements of the Holy Spirit already had taken place in Wales (1904–1905), Azusa Street in the United States (1906–1909), India (1906), Korea (1907), China (1908), and Africa (Ivory Coast, Ghana, and Nigeria, 1908–1914).

Thus, it is important to be attentive to movements that may be quite small numerically but represent important, strategic breakthroughs and that could become major developments in the world Christian movement. For this reason the focus of the third story of global Christianity will be a small but important Christian movement that is quietly occurring in the Islamic world.

---

51. Barrett, Kurian, and Johnson, *World Christian Encyclopedia*, 4. Barrett, Kurian, and Johnson cite 523,777,994 in 2000, but with more than an 8 percent growth rate Pentecostals and charismatics will have 811,551,594 adherents by 2025. In this context, classical Pentecostalism refers to the emergence of new denominations and Christian movements defined in some way by Pentecostal theology. Charismatic and neocharismatic refers to various waves of renewal that occurred within—and stayed within—the older, established churches. For more on the emergence of global Pentecostalism, see Harvey Cox, *Fire from Heaven: The Rise of Pentecostal Spirituality and the Reshaping of Religion in the Twenty-first Century* (Reading, MA: Addison-Wesley, 1995), and Walter Hollenweger, *Pentecostalism: Origins and Developments Worldwide* (Peabody, MA: Hendrickson, 1997).

The Islamic world has long been considered one of the most challenging places for Christian witness. This is partly because of distorted understandings of Christians and the Christian gospel found throughout the Islamic world. For example, Robby Butler tells the story of a Kuwaiti Muslim who was asked what he knew about Christians and Christianity. He replied that a Christian is someone who promotes immorality, pornography, and sexually oriented television programs like *Sex in the City*, *Desperate Housewives*, and so on. Butler goes on to comment that "for a Muslim to say that he has become a Christian is to communicate that he has launched into a secret life of immorality."[52] In short, Butler discovered that becoming a Christian is perceived by Muslims as entering a prayerless, apostate community.[53] Yet, despite these perceptions about Christianity, Muslims generally hold very positive views of Jesus Christ since the Qur'ān teaches that Christ had a miraculous birth, was a miracle worker, and was a prophet without sin.[54]

These positive views of Christ alongside such embarrassing perceptions regarding words like *Christian, church,* and *Christianity* within the Muslim community have led some Muslims who have become followers of Jesus to remain in the mosque rather than unite with any Christian church.[55] For example, *Mission Frontiers* highlighted a missionary couple named Alejandro and Bertha Ortiz, who have nurtured several of these "Jesus mosques" in the African country of Benin. They claim that in another Muslim nation there are over 100,000 Muslims who worship Jesus as *Isa* in Islamic mosques.[56]

This marked association of the Christian message with Western culture has led to more vigorous attempts to appropriately contextualize the Christian message for Muslims and Hindus. There has been a sin-

---

52. Robby Butler, "Unlocking Islam," *Mission Frontiers* 13, no. 1 (January–March 1991): 24.
53. Ibid.
54. See Surah 19:15–22; Surah 3:49–50. Christ is given at least fourteen major titles in the Qur'ān, including Messiah, Servant of God, Prophet, Messenger, the Word, a Sign, etc. For a full exploration of Qur'anic teachings concerning Christ, see chapter 7 of my book *Christianity at the Religious Roundtable: Evangelicalism in Conversation with Hinduism, Buddhism and Islam* (Grand Rapids: Baker Academic, 2002).
55. Rafique Uddin, "Contextualized Worship and Witness," in *Muslims and Christians on the Emmaus Road*, ed. J. Dudley Woodberry (Monrovia, CA: MARC, 1989), 269–72; Barry Yeoman, "The Stealth Crusade," *Mother Jones* (May/June 2002): 48.
56. Erich Bridges, "Of 'Jesus Mosques' and Muslim Christians," *Mission Frontiers* 19, nos. 7–10 (July–October 1997): 19. See also, "A Different Kind of Mosque," *Mission Frontiers* 19, nos. 7–10 (July–October 1997): 20–21. For security purposes, this chapter will not cite specific Islamic countries in North Africa and the Middle East where these movements are taking place.

cere and necessary effort to be more self-critical about our comparative failure to penetrate the Islamic contexts with the gospel. Gradually it has become clear that many Muslims who seem resistant to the gospel are actually not rejecting the gospel *per se* but Westernized forms, distortions, and misunderstandings of Christianity, which Muslims find repugnant, as noted in the examples above. This realization has given rise to vigorous attempts to envision and implement more contextually appropriate methods for communicating Christ to Muslims without unnecessary foreign baggage.

The best-known summary of the spectrum of Muslim background believers (known as MBBs) found in the Islamic world was published by John Travis in 1988 and has become the standard reference point for discussing contextualization in the Islamic context.[57] The spectrum is known as the C1 to C6 Spectrum, although the last point on the spectrum, C6, is a special category of persecuted, secret believers and will not be discussed in this chapter. The C stands for Christ-centered communities.[58] The various numbers reflect differences based on three main areas: the language of worship, the cultural and religious forms that are used in both their public life and in their worship, and, finally, their self-identity as Muslims or Christians.

C-1 refers to a "traditional church using outsider language," that is, a language other than that used by the Muslim population. This is a church that, for example, worships in English, uses pews, and follows a Western liturgy.

C-2 refers to a "traditional church using insider language," that is, a church that worships in the language of the Muslim population, such as Arabic or Turkish, but otherwise is the same as a C-1 church. Travis argues that the majority of churches in the Islamic world are either C-1 or C-2, but only a fraction of MBBs have united with churches of either type.[59]

---

57. John Travis, "The C1 to C6 Spectrum," *Evangelical Missions Quarterly* 34, no. 4 (1998): 407–8. John Travis is a pseudonym. See also Phil Parshall, "Danger! New Directions in Contextualization," *Evangelical Missions Quarterly* 34, no. 4 (1998): 404–6, 409–10, and Mark Williams, "Aspects of High-Spectrum Contextualization in Ministries to Muslims," *Journal of Asian Mission* 5, no. 1 (2003).

58. In the introductory article, Phil Parshall refers to the C as referring to "Cross-Cultural Church-Planting Spectrums." However, it is important in my later analysis of this spectrum to note that John Travis in both the text of his explanation and the article heading indicates that the C stands for "Christ-centered communities." This is confirmed in the numerous citations of the Travis scale throughout the literature.

59. Travis, "The C1 to C6 Spectrum," 407.

C-3 refers to "contextualized Christ-centered communities using insider language and religiously neutral cultural forms." These churches not only adopt the language of the surrounding Islamic community, but they also embrace nonreligious cultural forms such as folk music, dress, and artwork. Nevertheless, a C-3 church intentionally seeks to filter out any religious forms that are specifically associated with Islam, such as keeping the fast of Ramadan.

C-4 refers to "contextualized Christ-centered communities using insider language and biblically permissible cultural and Islamic forms." These churches are like C-3, except that Islamic cultural and religious forms are adopted as long as they are not explicitly forbidden in Scripture. For example, using Islamic terms for God (*Allah*), prayer (*salat*), and the Gospels (*injil*) would all be accepted in a C-4 context. Likewise, a C-4 church embraces outward practices normally considered symbols of Islamic faithfulness, such as avoiding pork, abstaining from alcohol, removing shoes when coming to worship, or fasting during Ramadan. C-4 believers normally do not identify themselves with the term *Christian* but refer to themselves as "followers of *Isa al-Masih*" (Jesus the Messiah) or as members of the *Isaya Umma* (Community of Jesus) or use similar expressions.[60] Despite the intentional contextualization, these followers of *Isa* are not regarded by those in the Islamic community as being Muslims.

C-5 refers to "Christ-centered communities of 'Messianic Muslims' who have accepted Jesus as Lord and Savior." These followers of *Isa* remain legally and socially within Islam, refer to themselves as Muslims, and are, in fact, regarded by the Muslim community as Muslims. Features of Islamic theology that are clearly incompatible with biblical faith are rejected or cleverly reinterpreted if possible. Approximately half of these C-5 believers continue to attend the mosque, even if they also attend small gatherings of other C-5 believers.[61] Sometimes these gatherings are referred to in missionary writings as "Jesus mosques."[62] Furthermore, these Christ-loving Muslims who remain fully embedded in the Islamic community and continue to attend the mosque are often referred to as being part of an "insider movement."[63] These insider movements have generated consider-

---

60. *Isa* is the Arabic word for Jesus. *Umma* is the Arabic word for community.
61. Parshall, "Danger! New Directions in Contextualization," 406.
62. See, for example, Bridges, "Of 'Jesus Mosques' and Muslim Christians," 19.
63. See, for example, *Mission Frontiers* 27, no. 5 (Sept.– Oct., 2005), which devoted the entire issue to insider movements. Also, the 2005 Conference of the International Society for Frontier

able discussion in missiological circles in recent years, and articles have even begun to appear in nonmission journals and popular magazines.[64]

In earlier publications I have analyzed and offered some serious critiques of many of the historical, biblical, theological, and ethical arguments that have been cited in support of these "insider movements" known as C-5.[65] Nevertheless, despite my concerns, it is clear that Muslims are encountering Christ in dreams and visions and are coming to Christ in ways that are unprecedented in the history of the church's work among Islamic peoples. The C-4 church movements are demonstrating that they are able to nurture a dynamic faith in the lives of Muslim background believers in a way that is true to the Christian gospel yet minimizes unnecessary cultural disruptions. I see C-5 as a temporary, transitional bridge over which some Muslims will be able to cross into more explicit Christian identity.

It is difficult to predict from this vantage point whether or not the quiet emergence of C-4 and C-5 gatherings in the Muslim world are the firstfruits of a long-awaited movement to Christ in the Islamic world. There could be tens of thousands of people who belong to Islam in a public, formal sense who gradually, over a period of years, realize that their most important identity is no longer as a "Muslim" but that their truest identity is with Jesus Christ and with all the people of God throughout the world and back in time who also know, serve, and follow Jesus Christ as Lord. If so, these C-4 and C-5 movements may someday be seen as a powerful testimony to the *missio dei* being extended into the Islamic world.

SOUTH INDIAN MISSIONARIES TO NORTH INDIA

When we think of missionaries, we often think about Westerners traveling to faraway countries to preach the gospel and plant churches. One of the most important developments in the history of modern missions

---

Missiology was dedicated to the theme, "Insider Movements: Doing Church Where There Is No Church."

64. See, for example Frank Decker's article, "When 'Christian' Does Not Translate," which appeared in the United Methodist renewal journal, *Good News Magazine* (May/June 2005), or Barry Yeoman's article entitled, "The Stealth Crusade," which appeared in *Mother Jones* (May/June 2002).

65. For my historical concerns, see "The Challenge of Churchless Christianity," *International Bulletin of Missionary Research* 29, no. 4 (October 2005): 171–77. For my biblical, theological, and ethical critique, see, "Followers of Jesus (*Isa*) in Islamic Mosques: A Closer Examination of C-5 'high spectrum' Contextualization," *International Journal of Frontier Missions* 23, no. 3 (Fall 2006): 101–15. See, also, chapter 8 of my *Theology in the Context of World Christianity* (Grand Rapids: Zondervan, 2007), 193–220.

has been the emergence of growing numbers of missionaries from Latin America, Africa, and Asia. This fourth vignette of world Christianity focuses on Indian missionaries from South India who are crossing cultural and linguistic barriers to bring the gospel to North India.

In chapter 8 we explored the early roots of Christianity in India through the apostle Thomas, who arrived in India in A.D. 52 and, according to tradition, started seven churches. These churches remained small and culturally isolated in India until the arrival of a group of traders led by a wealthy Syrian merchant named Thomas of Cana. They settled in Kerala around the year A.D. 345 and were influential in getting these Mar Thoma,[66] or St. Thomas Christians, to adopt a Syriac liturgy and come under the authority of the Eastern Orthodox Patriarch in Antioch. When the Roman Catholic missionaries arrived in the late fifteenth century, a long struggle between the East and the West began over the loyalty of the St. Thomas Christians. Many became Roman Catholic, but most remained loyal to the Syrian Orthodox tradition.[67]

Despite nearly two millennia of Christian presence in southwest India, the Bible had never been translated into Malayalam, the language of Kerala, and these Christians showed no interest in evangelizing even their own nearest Hindu neighbors. In short, it was a form of cultural Christianity and functioned like a separate "Christian caste" within the larger Hindu milieu. This changed in 1806 with the visit of an Anglican, Rev. Claudius Buchannan, who was the vice-provost of the college of Fort William in Calcutta. Buchannan hoped for a union between the Anglicans and the Syrian Orthodox in India, and he envisioned the day when these Christians could be spiritually renewed and mobilized to reach all of India. He met with the leaders of the Syrian church and secured their agreement to translate the Bible into Malayalam and had some initial, although naïve, discussions about possible union. This led to the establishment of a CMS mission in Kerala.

---

66. *Marthoma* is Aramaic for St. Thomas.

67. The tension between the West and the East has a long and checkered history in southwest India. One of the most memorable events is known as the Pledge of the Crooked Cross (Coonan Kurisu Satyam), when thousands pledged to not become Roman Catholic. However, of the 20,000 who remained Eastern Orthodox, approximately 400 became Roman Catholic. The *padroado* seriously hurt Roman Catholic work in India, since the Portuguese failed to appoint bishops to oversee Kerala. For example, the seat of Cochin was kept vacant from 1778 to 1818. The vicars apostolic, whom the pope appointed to circumvent the Portuguese, were ignored and resisted by the Portuguese authorities in India. Furthermore, there had not been any attempt by the Roman Catholics to train indigenous clergy. Even by the mid-nineteenth century there were more than twenty bishops in India, all European.

A school was established, and in 1816 Benjamin Bailey and his wife arrived and were given the responsibility of translating the Bible into Malayalam. At that time there were no dictionaries or grammars available, and the New Testament translation that was produced in 1829 was criticized as being difficult to read and overly reliant upon Sanskrit words. However, the five thousand copies that were printed quickly sold out, revealing the hunger for God's Word. In 1839 a German missionary and philologist named Herman Gundert (1814–1893) arrived in Kerala under the auspices of the Basel mission. Gundert compiled the first Malayalam dictionary and grammar and eventually produced a well-received translation of the Bible. Indian historian Stephen Neill has argued that "perhaps no single event contributed more to the renewal of life among the Thomas Christians" than the translation of the Bible into Malayalam.[68] This highlights one of the great legacies of the "Great Century," namely, the translation of the Bible into the vernacular.

The availability of the Bible in Malayalam stimulated a number of renewal movements, which awakened many within the Syrian tradition. One of the most important occurred in 1859 and was led by Abraham Malpān (1796–1843), known as the "Martin Luther of the East." Malpān was the professor of Syriac at the CMS college in Kottayam. He had been deeply influenced by the Anglican missionaries and their regard for the Bible. This led Malpān to lead a group of reformers within the Syrian Orthodox Church in Kerala to "test all things by the Bible" and to reject any customs or ceremonies that were not authorized by Scripture. The "Ninety-five-Theses moment" came on the eve of the Maramom festival, when Malpān seized an image of a saint that was used in the well-known (and lucrative) festival and threw it into a well, stirring up rage among the pilgrims. He then presented a manifesto of twenty-three corrupt practices in the faith and life of the church that he considered unbiblical. He advocated many mainstream evangelical principles, including the authority of Scripture and justification by faith alone. The reformers were expelled, Malpān was excommunicated, and they eventually formed an independent church known as the Mar Thoma Church of Malabar, under the leadership of a sympathetic bishop known as Mar Thomas Athanasius.[69]

---

68. Stephen Neill, *A History of Christianity in India, 1707–1858* (New York: Cambridge University Press, 1985), 243. The entire Bible became available in 1841.

69. Neill, *A History of Christian Missions*, 271. The church was originally known as Naveekarnna Sabha, later changed to the Mar Thoma Church of Malabar. For a full account of the

The evangelical emphasis on preaching, justification by faith, and the authority of Scripture over the years led to at least thirty distinct reform movements, including the Malankara Mar Thoma Church, the St. Thomas Evangelical Church of India, and the Indian Pentecostal Church.[70] In the twentieth century, a number of these groups began to send missionaries to the largely unreached Hindu populations of North India. This missionary movement has largely gone unnoticed by missiologists because of a general failure to fully appreciate the cross-cultural barriers *within* India, and missiologists generally have recognized only those who left India as missionaries. However, for a South Indian to relocate to North India involves all of the language learning and cultural adaptation that traditional pioneer missionary work often necessitates. If a missionary is defined as someone who crosses a cultural barrier to communicate the gospel (rather than as one who leaves his or her country), then India is second only to the United States in the number of missionaries sent out, with 41,064 Indians crossing cultural boundaries with the gospel within India, just behind the 44,384 fully supported missionaries from the United States.[71]

Rather than explore this movement in broad terms, I would like to focus on one example of a ministry in North India I have had the privilege of observing for the last twenty years. Our focus will be on the ministry of *Bharat Susamachar Samiti,* founded by George Chavanikamannil in 1987.[72] George Chavanikamannil was born in Kerala in 1948 and grew up in the Syrian Orthodox Church. While in college he was exposed to evangelical teachings and was called to be a missionary to North India. Although he immigrated to the United States to receive theological training and then worked for World Vision, he never forgot his call to North India. He eventually decided to return to India and relocate to North India as a missionary. One day, he took out a calculator and, after a few calculations, determined that even if he were

---

"reformation" of Abraham Malpān, see M. M. Thomas, *Towards an Evangelical Social Gospel: A New Look at the Reformation of Abraham Malpān* (Madras: CLS, 1977).

70. K. E. Abraham, who was instrumental in the founding of the IPC, grew up in the Syrian Orthodox Jacobite Church.

71. For the estimate of U.S. full-time missionaries, see Linda J. Weber and Dotsey Welliver, eds., *Mission Handbook: U.S. and Canadian Protestant Ministries Overseas, 2007–2009* (Wheaton, IL: EMIS, 2007), 13. The estimate of Indian missionaries is from Patrick Johnstone, Robyn Johnstone, and Jason Mandryk, *Operation World, When We Pray God Works* (Carlisle, England: Paternoster Lifestyle, 2001), 895–901.

72. *Bharat Susamachar Samiti* is Hindi for Good News for India Society. The organization also has a supporting organization based in the United States called Good News for India.

to preach to 5,000 people every day, it would take him nearly three centuries to preach the gospel to everyone in India. He realized the importance of multiplying laborers for the harvest, based on Jesus' words that "the harvest is plentiful but the workers are few" in Matthew 9:37. Therefore, he decided to start a training school to equip hundreds of new laborers for the task.

The New Theological College was officially opened in 1989 and over the last twenty years has equipped and trained hundreds of Indians, from both north and south, to plant churches in North India. A sister organization, known as Christian Evangelistic Assemblies (CEA) also was founded to help coordinate and support graduates who focused on church planting. In less than two decades, graduates working through the CEA have planted over five hundred churches in North India, mostly among Hindu background believers. The central training center in Dehra Dun, Uttarchand, in North India is supported by ten regional training centers strategically located across North India for the purposes of discipleship, ongoing training, and supervision. The church-planting ministry also has invested considerable resources in practical development in India, including schools, orphanages, literacy centers, job training, and a wide range of other ministries. This ministry, along with dozens of other similar ministries founded by South Indians, is having a dramatic impact on the growth of Christianity in what is known as the "Hindi belt," long considered one of the most challenging mission fields in the world.

THE NON-REGISTERED HOUSE-CHURCH MOVEMENT IN CHINA

Three Self Patriotic Movement
October 1, 1949, marks the victory of the Communists in China under the leadership of Mao Zedong (Tse-tung) and the emergence of the People's Republic of China. In the first year of Communist rule, thousands of foreign missionaries were forced out of China. It is estimated that in 1949 there were approximately four million Christians in the entirety of China.[73] The new Communist leadership declared their unequivocal opposition to

---

73. The estimated numbers are 3,274,740 Roman Catholics and 936,000 Protestants. See David Aikman, *Jesus in Beijing: How Christianity Is Transforming China and Changing the Global Balance of Power* (Washington, DC: Regnery, 2003), 52.

all theistic religions, insisting instead on the worship of the state, especially the personality cult of Mao Zedong, known simply as Chairman Mao.

In 1951 the Communist Party set up the Religious Affairs Bureau to oversee and supervise what it anticipated to be the final death throes of theistic religion in China. When the rapid demise of religion did not occur, the Chinese government opted for a policy of draconian control. The Protestant churches were controlled through an official government body, which eventually became known as the Three Self Patriotic Movement (TSPM).[74] The TSPM closed the majority of churches and forced all pastors in China to acknowledge that Christianity in China had largely been used as a force for imperialism and Western aggression against China. The TSPM claimed that the legacy of Protestant missions in China was a church divided hopelessly into a multitude of denominations. The TSPM ostensibly sought to unite the church under a single "patriotic" banner. Any pastor who refused to sign a statement of patriotic loyalty to China, which included a denunciation of all expressions of Protestantism other than those registered by the TSPM and controlled by the Religious Affairs Bureau, would face imprisonment, beating, and public shaming. Roman Catholic Christians likewise were persecuted and controlled through a similar organization known as the Catholic Patriotic Association (CPA), which is also part of the Religious Affairs Bureau. However, since the Roman Catholic bishops were forced by the government to reject papal authority, they were excommunicated by Pope Pius XII in 1957.[75]

During the Cultural Revolution (1966–1976), Chairman Mao stepped up the official hostility toward Christianity by promoting the destruction of church buildings, the confiscation of church property, and the disenfranchisement of all public expressions of faith. This was a part of his campaign against what he called the "Four Olds": old ideas, old culture, old customs, and old habits. The triumphalistic attitude of Communist

---

74. The best collection of primary source materials concerning the TSPM can be found in Wallace Merwin and Francis Jones, eds., *Documents of the Three-Self Movement: Source Materials for the Study of the Protestant Church in Communist China* (New York: National Council of Churches, 1963). For a historical overview of the rise of the TSPM, see Richard C. Bush Jr. *Religion in Communist China* (Nashville: Abingdon, 1970), 170–208.

75. There are millions of Roman Catholics who refused to join the CPA and opted instead to worship in underground churches. They continue to quietly confess loyalty to Rome and respect for papal authority. The Communist government also set up a third "patriotic" arm of religion under the RAB for Muslims, known as the Chinese Patriotic Islamic Association.

leaders, who maintained that Christianity would perish in China, was reflected in the headline of the *South China Morning Post* in August of 1966, which proudly declared, "Christianity in Shangai Comes to an End."[76] As it turned out, this was hardly the case.

Throughout these early decades of Communist rule in China, God raised up a number of prominent Chinese dissidents, such as Wang Mingdao (1900–1991), Allen Yuan (1914–2005), and Moses Xie (b. 1918), who remained faithful to the gospel and steadfastly refused to register with the TSPM. Each of these men spent at least two decades in prison and were repeatedly intimidated, beaten, and interrogated by Chinese authorities because of their faith in Jesus Christ. Other famous dissidents who spent decades in prison were Watchman Nee (1903–1972) and Samuel Lamb (b. 1925). These leaders also opposed the politicization of the church and wrote many Christian books, pamphlets, and hymns, which helped to foster and nurture networks of non-registered house churches completely independent of the TSPM.[77]

At the time of the 1949 Communist revolution, there were less than one million Protestants in China. After the Cultural Revolution ended, the Religious Affairs Bureau again permitted properly registered churches to meet publicly. In 1980 the China Christian Council was formed as a service organization of the TSPM to facilitate social concerns, the printing of Bibles, and theological education.[78] Today the TSPM churches "serve about 15 million Protestant believers" and the CPA claims to have "6 million registered Catholics."[79] However, despite a few brief respites of openness, the hostility

---

76. As quoted in Tony Lambert, *The Resurrection of the Chinese Church* (Wheaton, IL: Harold Shaw, 1994), 9.
77. Watchman Nee founded a network of house churches known as the Little Flock. Watchman Nee published many books, including, *The Normal Christian Life, The Spiritual Man,* and *Christ the Sum of All Spiritual Things.* Samuel Lamb is the pastor of a famous house church in Guangzhou, which is responsible for thousands of Chinese coming to Christ. Lamb also distributed his sermons through a cassette tape ministry and produced many pamphlets and hymns to spread the gospel. Because he managed to openly operate a non-registered church and to receive foreign guests, he is credited for encouraging thousands of others to start house churches. For a survey of some of the major independent, house-church movements, both before and after the rise of the Communists, see Alan Hunter and Kim-Kwong Chan, *Protestantism in Contemporary China* (Cambridge: Cambridge University Press, 1993), 119–23.
78. G. Thompson Brown, *Christianity in the People's Republic of China* (Atlanta: John Knox, 1986), 172.
79. Aikman, *Jesus in Beijing,* 7, 137. Bishop K. H. Ting, who retired in December 1996, served as the head of the TSPM and the China Christian Council (CCC) for many years. The TSPM and CCC now have separate leadership under Luo Guanzong and Cao Shengjie respectively.

of the Chinese government to Christianity continues. The more significant and dramatic growth of the Chinese church has occurred in the non-registered house churches in the country. Ironically, the government's forced separation of the Chinese church from outside associations actually helped to further stimulate indigenous Christianity, which was not associated with or dependent on foreign funds, personnel, or initiatives. The result was an explosion of the independent, non-registered churches in China, which appear to be impacting almost every segment of Chinese society. While estimates vary, there are probably over 90 million Christians in China today, making it one of the fastest growing churches in the world.[80] From these new Chinese Christians, mostly found in non-registered churches, a remarkable missionary thrust is emerging.

Back to Jerusalem Movement

Peter Wagner predicted that "by the year 2025 China will be sending out more foreign missionaries to other countries than any other nation."[81] This bold prediction was based on two realities: first, the dramatic growth of the Chinese church; and, second, a growing conviction of tens of thousands of Chinese Christians that God has sovereignly called them to play a central role in global evangelization. This development surprisingly contrasts to other parts of the world, where any manner of a missionary vision lagged behind the initial phase of evangelism and church planting for generations.

This missionary movement among Chinese Christians is known informally as the "Back to Jerusalem Movement" (BTJM). The origins of the BTJM have been traced to a movement of God in 1942–1943 at the Northwest Bible Institute in Shaanxi Province.[82] Mark Ma, the vice principal of the institute, and several students began to be burdened for the Muslim people groups who are located in the province of Xinjiang in northwest China. Soon Mark Ma and the other students began to sense that Xinjiang was not only a mission field but also a potential training ground for a major missionary initiative back across the ancient Silk Route, directly into the

---

80. Barrett, Kurian, and Johnson, *World Christian Encyclopedia*, 191. David Aikman estimates 80 million. See *Jesus in Beijing*, 7.

81. As quoted by Charles R. Powell, "Spiritual Awakening in China Today: Out from, and Returning to, Jerusalem, vol. 1" (D.Min. diss., Gordon-Conwell Theological Seminary, 2003), 197.

82. Ibid., 23.

heart of the Islamic countries of central Asia. The Chinese province of Xinjiang borders the central Asian Islamic countries of Kazakhstan, Kyrgyzstan, Tajikistan, Afghanistan, and Pakistan. After prayer and fasting, Mark Ma received a direct call from God to "bring to completion the commission to preach the gospel to all the world."[83] Ma understood that the broad sweep of the missionary movement had moved from Jerusalem to Antioch to Western Europe to North America and eventually arrived in China at port cities like Shanghai, Macau, and Guangzhou on the eastern and southern coast of China. The Lord impressed upon Ma and the others that, to complete the circle, the gospel should continue into northwestern China, across central Asia, and on to Jerusalem, where the Great Commission was first given. A contemporary Chinese leader expressed this vision as follows:

> We believe that the farthest the gospel can travel from Jerusalem is to circle the entire globe and come all the way back to where it started—Jerusalem! When the fire of the gospel completes its circuit of the whole globe, the Lord Jesus will return! *"For the earth will be filled with the knowledge of the glory of the Lord, as the waters cover the sea"* (Hab. 2:14).[84]

These Chinese believers probably were aware that the gospel also had spread eastward and had, in fact, first arrived in China through Nestorian missionaries via central Asia across the Silk Route. However there are several observations that place this missionary vision in its proper context. First, the dominant thrust of the missionary movement in history was *primarily* a westward expanse, as the "center of gravity" map in chapter 1 clearly demonstrates. Second, the modern missionary movement to China, both Roman Catholic and Protestant, arrived in eastern and southeastern China, not western or northwestern China. Finally, the churches that had been planted by Nestorian missionaries along the Silk Route had all but disappeared after the rise of Islam in the seventh century.

The movement was originally called the Preach Everywhere Gospel Band (*Bian Chuan Fuyin Tuan*), but in May of 1946 it was formally

---

83. Ibid., 25.
84. Ibid., 20.

organized as the Back to Jerusalem Evangelistic Band.[85] A few Chinese Christians began to capture the Back to Jerusalem vision, and gradually the movement specifically targeted all the Islamic countries in central Asia and North Africa, culminating with the Jews in Palestine itself. In fact, Mark Ma himself claims that the Lord spoke to him, saying that the "hardest field of labor is my own people the Jews . . . it is not that their hearts are especially hard, but I have kept for the Chinese church a portion of [the] inheritance."[86]

Several of these early pioneers began to make their way toward Xinjiang to start learning the language and culture of that part of China.[87] However, this coincided with the political upheaval in China that culminated in the Communist rise to power in 1949. The Communists, who relentlessly opposed all missionary activity, forcibly imprisoned several of the pioneers and forced the movement underground. Probably the most important of these early pioneers was a man named Simon Zhao, who survived over forty years of imprisonment in Xinjiang. Zhao was able to "keep alive the original Back to Jerusalem vision and impart it to the current leadership of China's house church networks."[88] The vision has now spread to a number of these networks, and the early 1990s brought a dynamic rekindling of the Back to Jerusalem vision.

What has become increasingly clear over the last twenty years of the rekindled movement is that the BTJM is not a structured, defined, organized movement operating under a single bureaucratic umbrella. Instead, BTJM is more of a vision statement that many Chinese Christians throughout the world have identified with, and yet it provides no formal connection among its adherents. Nevertheless, the collective force of this growing missionary movement from China may well be one of the most important stories in the history of twenty-first century missions.

---

85. Aikman, *Jesus in Beijing*, 196–197. Aikman argues that the name "Back to Jerusalem Evangelistic Band" was decided by Ma as early as May 1942. The year 1946 represents the official adoption of the name and the acceptance of a formal mission statement by the group.

86. Paul Hattaway, *Back to Jerusalem* (Carlisle, UK: Piquant; Waynesboro, GA: Authentic Media, 2003), 26.

87. China has fifty-six different nationalities and several hundred minority groups, even though 92 percent of China are Han and an additional 3 percent have been assimilated into the Han.

88. Aikman, *Jesus in Beijing*, 200. Simon Zhao died in Henan Pronvince on December 7, 2001 at eighty-three years old.

THE KOREAN MISSIONARY MOVEMENT

Despite the relatively late origin of Christianity in Korea, as explored in chapter 8, Korean Christianity has experienced remarkable growth. In fact, South Korea is widely regarded as the home of the modern church growth movement, which is exemplified by the remarkable story of the Yoido Full Gospel Church founded by Dr. David Cho. Begun in 1958 with only five people in a small living room, the church now claims over 700,000 members, making it easily the largest church in the world. Today, there are more than 15 million Christians in South Korea alone, belonging to around 47,000 churches, making it one of the most important centers of Asian Christianity.[89] The focus of this vignette will be the modern Korean missionary movement, which has distinguished itself as one of the fastest growing national missionary movements in the world.

The Korea Research Institute for Missions (KRIM) has conducted regular studies of the Korean missionary movement. In 1979 it reported 93 Koreans who were involved in overseas missions. This number has steadily increased to 1,178 serving in 1989, and 8,103 in 2000. By 2006, there were 14,905 Korean missionaries serving with 174 different mission agencies, representing a 106–fold increase in only twenty-seven years.[90] Korean missionaries are now in 168 different countries, mostly in Asia (47 percent), especially China, Philippines, and Japan, with less than 6 percent serving in Latin America and less than 8 percent in Africa, although the trend in recent years has been toward a more fully global presence of Korean missionaries.[91] Currently, about one thousand new missionaries are sent out

---

89. Soo-il Chai, "*Missio Dei*—Its Development and Limitations in Korea," *International Review of Missions* 92, no. 367 (2003): 538.

90. Steve Sang-Cheol Moon, "The Protestant Missionary Movement in Korea: Current Growth and Development," International Bulletin of Missionary Research 32, no. 2 (April 2008): 59. See also Moon's "The Recent Korean Missionary Movement: A Record of Growth, and More Growth Needed," International Bulletin of Missionary Research 27, no. 1 (January 2003): 11. See also the same author's "The Acts of Koreans: A Research Report on Korean Missionary Movement," found at www.krim.org. Moon estimates that by 2006, 39.1% of these missionaries were focused on church planting and 21.5% in discipleship. The remainder was focused on educational ministries (9.2%), theological education (5%), itinerant evangelism (4.4%), social welfare (4.3%), community development (4%), medical work (3.5%), business (3.4%), Bible translation (2.9%), and other (2.7%). The ten most prominent mission sending agencies in Korea are currently as follows: Global Missionary Society, University Bible Fellowship, Tonghap Presbyterian Mission Board, Methodist Mission Board, Assembly of God Mission Board, Campus Mission International, Global Missionary Fellowship, Baptist Mission Board, Holiness Church Mission Board, and Youth with a Mission.

91. Moon, "The Protestant Missionary Movement in Korea," 59.

by South Korea each year, leading Andrew Walls to call Korea the "missionary phenomenon of the century."[92]

Korean missionaries sometimes have been criticized for being overly preoccupied with numbers and conveying a sense of triumphalism because of the success of church growth in Korea. Others have pointed out a resistance to collaborate with non-Koreans and an unwillingness to serve with international mission agencies, rather than agencies founded and directed from Korea. However, these observations often are based on a lack of appreciation for the youthfulness of the Korean missions movement. An examination of the organizations Korean missionaries have been working with over the last twenty years reveals that the trend among Korean missionaries is clearly toward *more* collaboration, not less. Furthermore, the number of Koreans working for international mission agencies not run by or based in Korea is also on the rise. Finally, Korean missionaries have demonstrated the ability to learn, adapt, and, when necessary, ask for forgiveness.

For example, in July 2007, media around the world carried the story of three Korean missionaries and twenty short-term workers from Korea who were abducted by the Taliban in Afghanistan, who held them hostage for forty-three days and killed two of the Koreans. In the aftermath, although condemning the abductors, many were critical of the missionaries because they had not demonstrated the necessary caution when operating in an Islamic context. In response, the Korean church responded by holding a prayer meeting of repentance and issued a statement apologizing for mistakes the Korean missionaries had made.[93]

Looking at the movement as a whole, Andrew Walls probably reflects the best overall assessment when he writes, "The great missionary nation is now Korea; in every continent there are Korean missionaries by the hundreds, in coming years we can expect hundreds more, preaching from Tashkent to Timbuktu, and reaching where westerners have long been unable to tread."[94] Indeed, the story of twenty-first-century missions

---

92. Andrew F. Walls, *The Cross-Cultural Process in Christian History* (Maryknoll, NY: Orbis, 2002), 64. Korea still ranks behind the United States, which supports 44,384 full-time missionaries. However, Moon's claim that Korea represents the second largest missionary sending force in the world does not take into consideration the missionary movement *within* India, which, as noted earlier, is currently estimated at over 41,000.

93. Sarah Pulliam, "In the Aftermath of a Kidnapping: The South Korean Missionary Movement Seeks to Mature Without Losing Its Zeal," *Christianity Today* 51, no. 11 (2007): 64–65.

94. Walls, *The Cross-Cultural Process in Christian History*, 45.

can no longer be told without considering the increasingly global witness of Korean Christians.

POST-CHRISTENDOM VIBRANCY IN EUROPEAN CHRISTIANITY

In *The Next Christendom*, Philip Jenkins adapts the old adage about Russia to Christianity, when he says, "Christianity is never as weak as it appears, nor as strong as it appears."[95] This adage is certainly true of European Christianity. One might be tempted to think that with the rise of the Majority World church, the collapse of old Christendom, and the emergence of a post-Christian climate in Europe, the two words *Christianity* and *Europe* might begin to sound like an odd oxymoron. This is further underscored by the fact that, according to *World Christian Trends*, the top ten people groups most resistant to the gospel are now all found in Western Europe.[96] Timothy Ash has gone so far as to describe Europe as "the most secular continent on earth," a development that would "make Voltaire proud."[97]

However, there are two pictures in Europe that must be understood to complete these seven vignettes of twenty-first-century world Christianity.[98] The first is the rise of vibrant immigrant churches in Europe, which are transforming the face of Christianity within Europe and giving rise to a post-Western Christianity right in the heart of Europe. The second picture is ministers and priests in the older churches who are remaining faithful in the midst of the transition from Christendom to post-Christendom.

The Rise of Immigrant Churches in Western Europe

One of the most important differences between the missionaries coming from North America and those that are sent from the Majority World is

---

95. Jenkins, *The Next Christendom*, 220.
96. Todd Johnson and David Barrett lay out an extensive case for how to statistically measure responsiveness. See David B. Barrett and Todd M. Johnson, eds., *World Christian Trends, AD 30—AD 2200: Interpreting the Annual Christian Megacensus* (Pasadena, CA: William Carey Library, 2001), part 26, "Georesponse," 773–78. In part 11 (Listings) they list the ten most responsive and the most resistant people groups (see secs. 137–38). Remarkably, the top ten most responsive people groups in the world are all located in China and India. In contrast, all ten of the most resistant peoples are located in Europe (see p. 404).
97. Timothy Garton Ash, "Christian Europe, RIP," *Guardian* (April 29, 2005), accessed at http://www.guardian.co.uk/theguardian/2005/apr/29/guardianweekly.guardianweekly1.
98. While these seven vignettes are designed to take "snapshots" of Christianity around the world outside of North America, many of the dynamics in Europe can be applied to peoples of European descent around the world, including in North America.

the latter's focus on Europe. The majority of North American mission agencies are focused on the traditionally unreached people groups of the world, especially those within the so-called 10/40 Window.[99] In contrast, missionaries from Africa and Asia have demonstrated a sustained interest in planting churches in North America and Europe.

We do not normally think about the heartlands of old Christendom as a place for new church plants. In fact, if one drives through any major city in Western Europe, it is not difficult to find large church buildings that have been closed because of dwindling, elderly congregations who were no longer able to sustain the enormous cost of keeping up such large facilities.[100] In Denmark, for example, even though 83 percent of the population are nominally affiliated with the Lutheran state church, only 1 to 2 percent attend with any regularity.[101] The Church of Scotland, which is the official state church in Scotland, now has less than 500,000 members in the entire country. In 2005, George Carey, the former Archbishop of Canterbury, gave an address entitled, "A Faith for a Confused and Challenging Time," in which he said that if the Church of England were a human being, "the last rites would be administered at any moment."[102] These statements and statistics are now commonplace. However, if you live in Europe, perhaps the most obvious sign of these troubles is seeing how so many of these churches have been transformed into housing flats, theaters, public halls, and businesses. For example, just below the historic castle in Edinburgh, at the top of the Royal Mile, is the site of the former Church of Scotland Assembly Hall and the former home of the Highland Church of Scotland. Its spire towers over

---

99. The "ten-forty window" is an expression first articulated by Luis Bush in 1989 to describe the region of the Eastern hemisphere from ten degrees latitude north to forty degrees north where the majority of unreached people groups reside. The "window" stretches across North Africa, the Middle East, and Central Asia to the Far East.

100. The Church of England has a special Redundant Church Division to help facilitate the number of church closures and determine if demolition, sale, or preservation should be pursued. Likewise, there is a nonprofit charity in Scotland called the Scottish Redundant Church Trust, which helps to preserve churches that have been closed for public worship but are considered important historic landmarks.

101. Philip Jenkins, *God's Continent: Christianity, Islam, and Europe's Religious Crisis* (New York: Oxford University Press, 2007), 49.

102. Address given in October 2005 and accessed at http://www.glcarey.co.uk/Speeches /2005/ BeaconsDay1.html. The comment also was reported in the *Telegraph* by Danny Kruger, "There's Plenty of Life Left in the Churches," *Telegraph* (October 13, 2005). See http://www. telegraph.co.uk/opinion/main.jhtml?xml=/opinion/2005/10/13/do1302.xml&sSheet=/ opinion/2005/10/13/ixopinion.html.

Edinburgh and is the highest point in the city. Today, however, the church is closed, and it is now the center for the annual Edinburgh cultural festival. Hundreds of examples like this could be cited all across the United Kingdom and throughout Western Europe.

It comes as a surprise, therefore, to realize that in the midst of the dramatic decline of the old state churches, there is a remarkable growth in the immigrant churches, which often occurs under the radar of all of these dismal statistics. Philip Jenkins estimates that there are now approximately 1,500 missionaries from 50 nations working in the United Kingdom alone.[103] The amazing stories of these "new" missionaries make for fascinating reading. We often think of missionary biographies that focus on Western missionaries in remote, tribal areas. The story of Marilyn Lazlo in the jungles of Papua New Guinea or of Amy Carmichael rescuing orphan girls from a life of temple prostitution in India fall within the comfortable parameters of what we have heretofore known as the classic "missionary biography." It is more difficult to envision new twenty-first-century missionary biographies of, for example, African missionaries planting churches in the urban West. Yet, the story of African, Brazilian, and Korean missionaries coming to Europe is the new unfolding missionary story.

One of these missionaries, a Nigerian named Matthew Ashimolowo, founded the Kingsway International Christian Centre (KICC) in London in 1992 with only a few hundred members. Today, their main place of worship, known as the Miracle Centre, has a seating capacity of 5,000 worshippers (twice the seating capacity of Westminister Abbey) with seven services each Sunday. KICC has approximately 12,000 in attendance each week and is widely cited as one of the largest churches in Europe.

The Aladura churches, highlighted earlier in our exploration of the AIC, have caught a missionary vision and are now sending missionaries and planting churches all over the world. For example, the Redeemed Christian Church of God (RCCG) was founded in Nigeria in 1952 by Josia Olufemi Akindayomi, who was originally a member of the Cherubim and Seraphim Aladura Church. The church spread dramatically and, as a missionary church, began to draw Aladura Christians from around the world. One of the RCCG churches, known as the Jesus House in London, was planted in 1994, yet it

---

103. Jenkins, *God's Continent*, 89.

already claims to have over 2,500 in weekly attendance. The RCCG now has churches in the United Kingdom, Germany, France, and the United States.

Because of their facility in English and French, African missionaries prefer to go to their former colonizers with the gospel. However, African missionaries are now found in every country of Western Europe. The AIC first arrived in Germany in 1974, but today claim over two hundred new church plants in many of the major cities of Germany. The Church of Jesus Christ of the Prophet Simon Kimbangu has churches in Spain, Portugal, France, Germany, Belgium, Switzerland, and England.[104]

The African churches represent the largest and most visible segment of the "new Christians" of Europe. However, similar stories on a smaller scale can be found among the growing Indian, Chinese, Brazilian, Filipino, and Korean churches in Europe, to name a few. These new churches represent the new face of European Christianity. No longer can glib statements be made about the decline of Christianity in Europe without clarifying that we are referring to what is sometimes called the "old-stock white" peoples of Europe. The growing immigrant populations are not part of this decline but are increasingly building vibrant new churches.

Keeping the Faith in Europe

To simply characterize Europe as teeming with vibrant immigrant churches that are growing alongside dying historic churches would be a gross exaggeration for two reasons. First, there are signs that the second and third generation members of the immigrant churches are beginning to move into the religious mainstream. In 2005 John Sentamu, a Ugandan, was installed as the Archbishop of York, widely regarded as the second most important Anglican bishopric, behind only the Archbishop of Canterbury. In his installation address, he declared that the time had come for the church to "learn the faith afresh from the Christians of Africa and Asia." In Kiev the Nigerian pastor Sunday Adelja pastors a Pentecostal congregation of 30,000 members, who are overwhelmingly white. [105]

Second, it is important to look beyond statistics (either of growth or decline) in an assessment of the health of the church. I have had the privilege of living in Europe from 1995 to 1998 and again for six months in 2008.

---

104. Ibid., 88.
105. Ibid.

During the years we lived in Scotland, we moved several times and always sought to attend a church within walking distance of our home. I had the privilege of sitting under the ministries of a number of faithful pastors such as Kevin Scott in Edinburgh, Peter Gardner in Pathhead, Mark Nicholas in Gorebridge, and Kenneth Baird in North Leith. None of these men pastor large churches, and all are serving denominations (Church of Scotland and the Scottish Episcopal Church) that are, statistically speaking, in serious decline. Yet, each of these men is faithfully preaching the gospel each week. They are quietly conducting Alpha courses, holding Bible studies, and sharing the gospel in their respective parishes. Certainly one of the most enduring lessons of the crucifixion of Christ is that God often does His most profound work under the cloak of failure.

Furthermore, all the statistics about the decline of the *state* churches in Europe often fail to point out the rise of the independent churches in Europe. There are Baptist, Pentecostal, and interdenominational churches all across Europe, many with growing and thriving congregations, drawing from both traditional and immigrant communities. In Edinburgh, for example, among the largest congregations in the city are the nondenominational Carrubbers Christian Centre, originally a D. L. Moody mission dating back to 1858, and Charlotte Chapel, an independent Baptist church located in the heart of the city. These churches are demonstrating how to be faithful to Jesus Christ in the midst of a cultural exile, in which the church is often regarded as an outdated icon of the past. They are learning to be missionaries in the midst of the crumbling ruins of Christendom and the emerging "mission field" of Europe. They have the prophetic vision to see the shallowness of Europe's great experiment with secularism and take the long view that the gospel always retains the power to raise up better hearers.

CONCLUSION

These seven portraits of twenty-first-century world Christianity offer a few important glimpses into the unfolding *missio dei* of our time. Many of the most important stories will not be fully known until the full revelation of the New Creation. Until then, we "see but a poor reflection" (1 Cor. 13:12). However, the few glimpses we are able to discern reveal that the global church of Jesus Christ is beginning to reflect that great eschatological vision of the apostle John in which he sees men and women from every nation, tribe, people, and language worshipping the Lamb, our Lord Jesus Christ.

Cross-Cultural Communication as a Reflection of the Incarnation

— 11 —

The Incarnation and the Translatability of the Gospel

DURING THE WORLD WAR II Battle of the Bulge, quite a few German infiltrators tried to slip across into Allied-controlled territory dressed in American uniforms. It was not always easy to determine whether they were Americans or not, so the American armed forces used a very old method called a "shibboleth" to identify true Americans. They asked anyone suspected of being an infiltrator who had won the World Series the previous year. If they didn't know, they were immediately arrested as an enemy combatant. The word *shibboleth* is a Hebrew word meaning "stream." Its modern English usage derives from a story in the Old Testament. After the men of Gilead defeated the Ephramites in battle, it was nearly impossible to determine who the Ephramites were, so many of them were sneaking back across the river to safety. However, the Gileadites knew that the Ephramite dialect made it nearly impossible for them to pronounce the "sh" sound, so the Gileadites stood guard at the fords of the river and when someone asked to pass over, he would be asked to say the word *shibboleth,* or "stream," in order to be allowed safe passage. Those who said "*sibboleth*" rather than "*shibboleth*" were put to death.[1]

Today, the word *shibboleth* refers to any kind of linguistic password that serves to identify a member of the "in" group. To violate a shibboleth automatically brands one as an outsider. Over the centuries, Christians often have produced shibboleths to determine who was a true member

---

1. See Judges 12:5–6.

of the church. One of the earliest was the sign of the fish, which was used by Christians during the time of persecution to make sure that their meetings were not being infiltrated by government informants. The Greek word for fish, *ikthus* (ιχφύς), was used as a password, a shibboleth, which only true Christians would know was also an acronym for "Jesus Christ, God's Son, Savior."

There is nothing inherently wrong with shibboleths, because it is essential for any movement to define its boundaries and clearly articulate the core values that serve to shape and form its identity.[2] The difficulty is that the way we talk about and frame our shibboleths are often shaped by the particular historical context out of which those discussions emerge. For example, a Christian from India who fully affirms the absolute and final authority of Scripture but was not privy to the heated discussions among American evangelicals over the authority of Scripture during the 1980s may not understand the nuances that gradually came to be attached to words like *inerrancy* and *infallability*. Likewise, incest and child pornography are horrific evils, which evangelicals, like all Christians, condemn, but neither of these became a shibboleth because they did not create the defining tensions between *cultural* values (the freedom to choose versus the sanctity of life) that abortion brought to the surface.

This background underscores the special challenges that are inherent when the gospel is proclaimed in a new cultural context. As we shall explore, communicating the gospel is far more challenging than just getting people to repeat, and affirm, the various shibboleths that have defined our own Christian identity. The gospel message is universal, and its transforming power is applicable to any and every culture on earth. There is not a single person or ethnic group on earth for whom the gospel is not good news for salvation. How this gospel has been effectively communicated to various cultures throughout history, however, has not been universally constant. The reason for this will become clear, especially as we explore missionary communication through the lens of the Incarnation.

God is the ultimate universal constant. However, when God chose to communicate Himself to humanity, He did so within the context and variegated nuances of human language and culture. He revealed Himself to

---

2. For a recent statement of evangelical faith, see the Evangelical manifesto found at www .anevangelicalmanifesto.com.

Abraham and spoke through the prophets in specific languages and in ways that were culturally understandable for the intended receptors. Likewise, God's greatest self-revelation, namely, the Incarnation, took place within all of the particularities of a specific time and culture. To borrow Andrew Walls's phrase, in the Incarnation, God became "at home in specific segments of social reality."[3] Without ceasing to be God, Jesus fully entered into the frame of reference of a first-century Jew. The Incarnation is the ultimate example of what we call the *translatability of the gospel*. In this context, the translatability of the gospel refers to *the ability of the gospel to be articulated, received, appropriated, and reproduced into a potentially infinite number of cultural contexts*. Jesus embodies the good news and, in the Incarnation, that good news became wonderfully present in a specific setting.

At the heart of any *bona fide* missionary preparation is learning to effectively communicate the gospel into a new cultural context. We need to understand how to re-present Christ within the context of new "segments of social reality." Looking back over the missions history explored in the previous three chapters, we can observe that, indeed, the gospel has been effectively communicated to observant Jews, Greek-speaking Hellenists, invading "barbarians," Irish ascetics, German peasants, Victorian elites, white-robed Nigerians, and Indian mystics, to name a few. This should encourage us, for it demonstrates that the translatability of the Christian gospel is not just a theoretical hope but a descriptive fact. The church is already the most ethnically, culturally, and linguistically diverse movement on the planet. This chapter seeks to explore the translatability of the gospel through the understanding that the Incarnation provides the foundation for any theology of missionary communication.

While modern communication theory is vitally important in the preparation of missionaries and should be incorporated at various points, it is important that training in missionary communication be built upon a *theological foundation*. This chapter will provide this foundation by examining three important lessons that can be learned from the Incarnation regarding missionary communication. Each theme will be introduced and then used as the basis for exploring key features of effective missionary communication.

---

3. Andrew F. Walls, *The Missionary Movement in Christian History: Studies in the Transmission of Faith* (Maryknoll, NY: Orbis, 1996), xvii.

LESSON #1: MISSIONARY COMMUNICATION AS A RETRANSLATION AND REDISCOVERY OF THE INCARNATION OF CHRIST

Effective missionary communication begins by remembering that the primary task of any missionary is to communicate Jesus Christ. Just as the Incarnation represents God's act of translating Himself into specific humanity, so effective missionary communication is fundamentally a re-translation of Christ into a new setting. It is easy to confuse the cherished language we use to speak about Christ with Christ Himself. However, a simple illustration will demonstrate that we cannot equate the two. When John the Baptist sought to identify the significance of Jesus to his hearers, he declared, "Behold, the Lamb of God who takes away the sin of the world" (John 1:29 NASB). This statement is absolutely true and inspired but, quite frankly, is intelligible only if the hearer first understands the Passover, the Jewish sacrificial system, and what the word *sin* means. If an understanding of these concepts is lacking, then the statement is no less true, but it fails to communicate the intended meaning.

One might go so far as to say that in the ears of an observant Jew, John's statement is one of the most brilliant affirmations of Jesus that could be uttered. The phrase "Lamb of God" beautifully recalls both the Passover and the sacrificial system, embodying the rich, redemptive concepts of divine deliverance and blood sacrifice in a single phrase. To borrow a memorable phrase from Fleming Rutledge, these concepts were as familiar to observant Jews as television commercials are familiar to modern Americans.[4] However, in the ears of a pagan Hellenist who knew very little, if anything, about the Passover or the Jewish sacrificial system and had a deficient understanding of sin, John the Baptist's affirmation communicated very little, if anything, about Jesus Christ.

Three Possible Solutions

When faced with this dilemma, the early Christians had three options, and these same three options continue to confront gospel communicators today. The first was to conclude that the significance of Jesus Christ was limited to Jews. For the Jews, Jesus Christ was the perfect fulfillment of their messianic expectations, the hope of their prophets, and the

---

4. Fleming Rutledge, *The Undoing of Death* (Grand Rapids: Eerdmans, 2002), 61.

culmination of all that defined them as the people of God. So perhaps Jesus was "good news" only for *them*. This is what I call the *Ebionite solution*, so named after that small sect of first-century Jewish Christians who rejected any Gentile mission, arguing that the Scriptures taught that the Messiah only fulfilled and met Jewish hopes and expectations.[5] By extension, today the Ebionite solution describes any group who insists that all others must discover the significance of Jesus within a certain source culture and linguistic framework.

The second option, which had the support of many, was to first orient the Gentiles to Judaism—thoroughly ground them in Jewish customs, language, laws, and expectations—so that then they would gradually be able to comprehend the messianic significance of Jesus. This is known as the *Judaizer solution*, sometimes referred to more generally today as the *monocultural solution* or, in Lamin Sanneh's phrase, *mission by diffusion*.[6] The Gentiles would be able to understand and appreciate the significance of Jesus only insofar as they accommodated themselves to Jewish language, history, and culture. It is analogous to someone being given a potted plant that is thought to thrive only if kept in the original soil; in other words, it is untransplantable. The idea of transplanting the plant into new soil is considered too risky. In this view, the gospel could grow and flourish only in Jewish soil. The gospel may be good news for the world, but it could be experienced only by passing through the cultural doorway of Judaism.

The third option, and by far the riskiest, was for the communicators of the good news of Jesus Christ to enter into the cultural, linguistic, and social framework of the target group and explain the gospel through whatever terms and concepts were already present in, and understood by, the target group. This is known as the *multicultural solution*, or *mission by translation*. The early church, at the Jerusalem Council recorded in Acts 15, opted for this third option. This was difficult for some to accept because it inevitably meant the abandonment (at least temporarily) of certain cherished shibboleths, which had defined the early church as long as it was predominantly composed of people who were following Jesus within the larger context of their Jewish identity. It was not easy to find new ways

---

5. For the Ebionites, any "God-fearing" Gentile presence in the church was only to fill out the number of Jews who had rejected the Messiah.
6. Lamin Sanneh, *Translating the Message: The Missionary Impact on Culture* (Maryknoll, NY: Orbis, 1989), 29.

to communicate Jesus when such rich terms as *Messiah* and *Lamb of God* and *Son of David* continued to be so meaningful in their own discovery and ongoing experience of the significance of Jesus Christ. Yet, right in the pages of the New Testament, we see the early communicators of the gospel adapting their language to communicate the significance and meaning of Jesus in fresh and understandable ways to the new Gentile hearers.

Examples of the Multicultural Solution: Mission by Translation
We will now examine several examples from the preaching and teaching of the early church to Gentiles in order to demonstrate that they sought to communicate the gospel within the intellectual and linguistic framework of their hearers, rather than insisting that the Gentiles discover Jesus within the existing framework of Judaism.

JESUS AS MESSIAH—JESUS AS LORD

For the early Jewish believers, the most effective and descriptive way to speak of Jesus was as "Messiah" (Hebrew) or "Christ" (Greek), meaning the Anointed One. The title was shorthand for all the Jewish hopes and expectations. However, this image (while completely true) was insufficient to fully capture what the Gentiles were finding in Jesus. For the Gentiles, to call Jesus the Messiah would have been merely mimicking what Peter said of Jesus, "You are the Messiah, the Son of the living God" (Matt. 16:16 TNIV). By affirming it, they might have passed the shibboleth test, but they would not really have embraced the full significance of Jesus since they did not share the Jewish prophetic hopes for a coming Messiah. The title *Messiah*, as rich as it was, simply did not carry much meaning for a Gentile.

The strategic solution emerges rather subtly in the New Testament. We discover it in the message of those unnamed disciples from Cyprus and Cyrene recorded in Acts 11. Those unnamed disciples are credited as the first to address the gospel to Gentiles who had no prior identity with Judaism. The pivotal moment came in Acts 11:20, when Luke records that they began "to speak to Greeks also, telling them the good news about the Lord Jesus." It is a very important transition from preaching Jesus *Christ* to preaching the *Lord* Jesus. Although these early Christian disciples were Jews, they realized that the title *Messiah* would not be comprehended as good news for a pagan Greek. Instead, they utilized the title *kurios*, which, although richly used in the biblical tradition, was the word Hellenistic pagans gave to their cult deities. Having little, if any, knowledge of the He-brew usage of the word *Lord,* the Gentiles hearers would more likely have associated it with *kyrios Sarapis* or *kyrios Adonis,* rather than the Lord of biblical revelation.[7] Andrew Walls points out that surely some of the brethren must have "recoiled at the syncretistic possibilities." However, Walls goes on to say that even this "daring act of metaphysical translation" succeeded because they were prepared to give the new concept "explana-tion, qualification, supplementation, and definition as the identity of Jesus was explored in terms of Hellenistic language and thought."[8]

The example of these early disciples is followed by the apostle Paul. In the book of Acts, Paul continues to preach *to Jews* that Jesus is the Messiah (Acts 9:22; 17:3; 18:5), while avoiding this title in his preaching *to Gentiles.* Instead, following the lead of those earlier Jewish missionaries, he also pro-claims the "Lord Jesus" to Gentiles (Acts 13:48–49; 16:31; 19:5, 17; 20:21).[9]

JEWISH SCRIPTURES AND PAGAN SOURCES

The second example is taken from Acts 17:16–34, which records Paul's visit to Athens, where he is invited to the Areopagus to preach. His audi-ence is Greek, not Jewish. Thus, rather than drawing from the cherished and inspired Jewish Scriptures with which Paul was so familiar, he instead quotes from the Athenians' own Greek poets. In verse 28 Paul quotes from the seventh-century B.C. Cretan poet Epimenides, when he declares, "In him we live and move and have our being." In the same verse Paul goes on to say, "As some of your own poets have said, 'We are his offspring,'" a quotation from the Cilician poet Aratus.[10]

Epimenides and Aratus were pagan poets committed to the worship of false gods. Epimenides' poem, cited in Acts 17, consists of words on the lips of Minos, Zeus's son, and was given in praise of Zeus. Minos declares,

---

7. *Kyrios Sarapis* was the Greco-Egyptian deity of the sun. He eventually was regarded as lord of healing and fertility, and his worship was prominent throughout the Mediterranean world.

8. Andrew F. Walls, "Old Athens and New Jerusalem: Some Signposts for Christian Scholarship in the Early History of Mission Studies," *International Bulletin of Missionary Research* 21, no. 4 (October 1997): 148.

9. By the time of Paul's letters, the term *Christ* was widely used (Paul uses it 270 times) by Gen-tiles. But, as Larry Hurtado points out, this word as used by Gentile Christians was a *name* for Jesus rather than a Jewish *title.* See Larry Hurtado, *Lord Jesus Christ* (Grand Rapids: Eerdmans, 2003), 99.

10. The quote appears in Aratus's *Phaenomena,* as well as in Cleanthes (331–233 B.C.) in his *Hymn to Zeus.*

"But thou art not dead; thou livest and abidest forever, *for in thee we live and move and have our being.*"[11] Paul clearly rejected that Zeus was alive and "abidest forever," but he boldly applied it to the Lord Jesus, calling on pagans to reach out and receive God's grace in their lives.

The original quote from Aratus was also in honor of Zeus. The original line of the poem is as follows: "It is with Zeus that every one of us in every way has to do, *for we are also his offspring.*"[12] However, Paul used the quote to demonstrate that the entire human race is under the rule of the living God of biblical revelation and that He is calling the whole world to account and will judge the world by and through the Lord Jesus (Acts 17:28–31). This is the basic pattern of Paul, whether he is quoting from the sacred Jewish Scriptures or from a pagan source. He imports the text out of its original context and reorients it within a new, distinctively Christian setting.

Now, applying this to the present, what would happen if the apostle Paul were preaching, not in Athens, but in modern-day India? Let us imagine Paul preaching the gospel to Hindus in India rather than to Hellenistic pagans in the Roman Empire. What if we found Paul standing in the holy city of Varanasi on the banks of the Ganges River rather than on top of Mars Hill in Athens? In some ways the scene would be very familiar to Paul. If you are standing on top of Mars Hill, the most imposing visual site is the massive Parthenon, the great temple of the goddess Athena, which is immediately to the southeast of Mars Hill. Likewise, if Paul were in Varanasi and stood on the banks of the Ganges River, the most imposing visual site would be the great Kashi Vishwanath Temple of Lord Shiva, the god of the Ganges River.[13] It is believed that the Ganges River flows from Shiva's hair and that anyone who dips in these sacred waters will have their sins washed away. For centuries Hindus have made the long and arduous pilgrimage to this city, considered the holiest city in India, and, like Athens, one of the oldest cities on earth.

Scripture records that in Athens Paul saw dozens of altars with inscriptions to various gods and goddesses, including one with the inscription, "TO AN UNKNOWN GOD" (Acts 17:23). Likewise, if Paul were in Varanasi

---

11. Richard N. Longenecker, "Acts," in *The Expositor's Bible Commentary*, ed. Frank E. Gaebelein (Grand Rapids: Zondervan, 1981), 9:476, italics mine, to emphasize the portion Paul quotes.
12. Ibid. Italics mine, to emphasize the portion Paul quotes.
13. Kashi is the ancient name of modern-day Varanasi, a city the British called Benares. Vishwanath means "Lord of All."

and walked along the banks of the Ganges, he would see hundreds of shrines and temples and altars to various gods and goddesses in the Hindu pantheon. While in Athens, Paul got into a dispute with a group of Epicurean and Stoic philosophers, two of the major intellectual schools of that time (17:18). If Paul were to stay long in Varanasi, he would soon find himself in a dispute with philosophers who teach at the famous Benares Hindu University. Followers of the great philosophers Sankara and Ramanuja still debate the nature of God, the reality of the world, and the best path to salvation. Finally, Paul's Hindu audience in Varanasi would be just as ignorant of Jewish promises and prophets found in the Old Testament as were those "men of Athens" who heard Paul's message on Mars Hill.

In such a situation, would it not be just as unlikely for the apostle Paul to try to reach Hindus with the gospel by quoting foreign Jewish prophets about whom they know nothing? If Paul were to walk around Varanasi for long, he would notice that the Hindus, like the Athenians, are very religious. They take great pride in the outward religious displays of sacrifice, self-denial, pilgrimage, and so forth. One of the most important messages for a Hindu is that outward ritual and outward religiosity have no benefit, because God looks into our hearts. Paul might quote the well-known text from 1 Samuel 16:7, "The LORD does not look at the things man looks at. Man looks at the outward appearance, but the LORD looks at the heart." But then, to corroborate this text, I can certainly see the apostle Paul going on to say, "For even as your own poet Tukārām has said, 'The shell of the coconut is hard, but the inside is excellent. In accordance with this, remember, that purity inside is what we aim at . . . the value of a thing depends on its inner qualities.'"[14]

Quoting Tukārām in such a context does not give an exalted or inspired status to Tukārām's poem any more than Paul's quotation of Epimenides' poem *Cretica* gave it any kind of special status. Yet it serves as a powerful indigenous corroboration of the biblical text that brings the message of Jesus Christ into the Hindu worldview, rather than insisting that they relate to Christ as a stranger.

---

14. J. N. Fraser and K. B. Marathe, *The Poems of Tukārām*, vol. 111 (Madras: Christian Literature Society, 1909), 197, as quoted in Aiyadurai Jesudasen Appassamy and E. H. Waller, *Temple Bells: Readings from Hindu Religious Literature* (Mysore, India: Student Christian Movement, 1930), 84. Tukārām was a seventeenth-century Marati poet-saint from Maharashtra. Tukārām was a devotee of the god Krishna, and his poems are filled with love and adoration to Krishna. They are used as sacred texts in the *bhakti* tradition of Hinduism.

JESUS IS THE "LOGOS" OF GOD

The third example that demonstrates that the earliest Christian writers and preachers used the thought forms of the target group in order to communicate the gospel is found in the apostle John. In the opening prologue of his gospel, John declares Jesus to be the *logos,* or "Word." The word *logos* had many recognizable associations in the ancient world, as it had a rich philosophical application dating back to Heraclitus (535–475 B.C.E.) and had been used in a variety of ways in the writings of Platonists and Stoics. It is sometimes translated as "active reason," or the "animating principle" that undergirds the entire universe.[15] John's contemporaries would have understood *logos* as a philosophical term referring to a rational capacity or "generative principle" that is present in all of nature. In the first century, *logos* was regarded as the principle that creates the world, gives it order, and extends its animating power through all matter.[16]

To put it in perspective for modern readers, it might be helpful to recognize that because the term *logos* referred to an impersonal, all-pervading force or animating principle, its semantic starting point was actually closer to a Hindu worldview than to orthodox Judaism or Christianity. In short, it is not as natural a starting point for Christian proclamation as it might appear to a modern reader who simply reads the words in English, "In the beginning was the Word, and the Word was with God, and the Word was God" (John 1:1).

In the prologue to his gospel, John ingeniously uses the philosophical term *logos* as his starting point, but he connects it with the divine, spoken word that in Genesis brings the whole created order into being. John is very careful to properly reorient the term to make it consistent with biblical revelation when he declares, "The *logos became flesh* and dwelt among us" (John 1:14). In its secular usage, the *logos* could not possibly *become flesh.* By declaring that the *logos,* or Word, became flesh, John is making a claim for a real-flesh, historically rooted, incarnation. In fact, it is this phrase, *sarx egeneto* ("became flesh"), which was translated into Latin as *incarnates,* which is the source of our English word *incarnation.* By

---

15. For a full discussion of the development and usage of the term *logos,* see H. Kleinknecht, "The Logos in the Greek and Hellenistic World," *Theological Dictionary of the New Testament,* vol. 4, ed. G. Kittel (Grand Rapids: Eerdmans, 1967), 77–91. It is the principle that creates the world, i.e., that orders and constitutes it, which makes it. It is the animating power that extends throughout all matter.

16. Ibid., 84–85.

reorienting the *logos* principle to the creation account in Genesis and the real incarnation of Jesus Christ, John is not identifying Jesus with the Stoic or Platonic principle, but rather, he is using it as a *starting point*, a contextual bridge, to call the Gentile hearer into a Christian worldview.

Dangers Inherent in Translatability

We noted earlier how the early Christian decision to opt for multicultural translatability rather than the Ebionite or Judaizer solution carries with it the wonderful possibility of the gospel becoming planted in the native soil of every culture. However, it also opens up the door to potential dangers when Christ is "mistranslated." For example, several contemporary applications of John's *logos* Christology have failed to appreciate the importance of John rooting the *logos* in the historic incarnation of Christ with the phrase "the *logos* became flesh." Writers such as John Hick and Raimondo Panikkar have unduly separated verse 1 from verse 14 and thus promoted a disembodied Christ—Christ apart from the flesh—as a template for religious pluralism. Once the *logos* is reconceived as an abstract notion, then it can be placed inoffensively into almost any conceivable religious structure.[17] However, to separate John 1:1 from 1:14 is to unduly separate the Jesus of history from the Christ of faith, which undermines the very doctrine of the Incarnation. In contrast, John effectively models the translatability of the gospel, demonstrating how it can be done in a way that is sensitive to the context and yet remains true to Jesus Christ and the historic Christian gospel.

A "Both-And," Not an "Either-Or," Proposition

These three examples cited from some of the earliest communicators of the gospel help us to understand the missiological significance of the Incarnation. The Incarnation provides the ultimate example of the universal being translated into the particular. The examples provided in this chapter

---

17. See John Hick, *The Metaphor of God Incarnate* (London: SCM, 1993), and Raimundo Panikkar, *The Unknown Christ of Hinduism* (London: Darton, Longman and Todd, 1964). Hick argues that the Incarnation is but a "mythic story [which] expresses the significance of a point in history where we can see human life lived in faithful response to God and see God's nature reflected in that human response . . . To the extent that a man or a woman is to God what one's own hand is to oneself, to that extent God is 'incarnate' in that human life . . . In Jesus we see a man living in a startling degree of awareness of God and of response to God's presence" (pp. 105, 106). This is a "mistranslation" of the gospel, effectively ending in a denial of, rather than a proclamation of, the incarnation of God in Jesus Christ.

demonstrate that the early church effectively learned to re-present Christ in new ways.

It is important to recognize that the hard work of finding new ways to speak about Christ does not in any way diminish the earlier language that members of other (or earlier) communities have used to celebrate the ultimate significance of Jesus Christ. To proclaim, as John did, that Jesus is the *logos* of God is a bold attempt to make a contextually appropriate connection about the meaning of Christ to someone whose primary frame of reference is the Greek world. However, it in no way diminishes the truth that Jesus is the "Lamb of God." Christians in every generation are not asked to abandon earlier language, even as they discover new ways of speaking about Christ. This is because when someone comes to Christ, that person takes on what missiologists refer to as a new "adoptive past." This means that in Christ we become connected, through the global church around the world and back through time, with others, not part of our culture and language, who also have discovered the ultimate significance of Jesus Christ. Even though I am not a Jew and I grew up in a large urban area, I have come to appreciate the significance of Jesus as the "Lamb of God," although I will probably never be able to hear it with quite the depth of understanding of one of those early Jewish Christians. In the same way, when Africans celebrate Jesus as the "Proto-Ancestor" or "Supreme Ancestor" who fulfills all of their expectations and hopes, which only dimly had been reflected in their pre-Christian practice of ancestor veneration, my own view of Christ is enlarged, not diminished, even if I can only appreciate it from a distance.[18] Thus, translatability always works in two directions. Christ is translated into the new context, and then as the meaning and significance of Christ is received and appropriated in the new setting, we experience the blessed reflex of having our own view of Jesus enlarged.

Naturally, each generation is tempted to think that their own particular insights into Christ are normative and represent the last word for each succeeding generation, but the discovery of new insights continues as each new group hears and responds to the gospel. Jaroslav Pelikan, in his *Jesus Through the Centuries*,[19] has carefully documented

18. For a full evaluation of Christ as "Supreme Ancestor" or "Proto-Ancestor," see chapter 5 in my *Theology in the Context of World Christianity* (Grand Rapids: Zondervan, 2007), 105–34.
19. Jaroslav Pelikan, *Jesus Through the Centuries: His Place in the History of Culture* (New Haven: Yale University Press, 1985).

how different generations have responded to the question, "Who is Jesus Christ?" He documents eighteen different portraits of Christ over the centuries. However, more portraits of Christ are yet to be celebrated. On the Day of Pentecost, all of those gathered heard the wonders of God in their "own language." God speaks in the vernacular. Kwame Bediako insightfully reminds us that Pentecost is not just a *sociological* event but a *theological* statement demonstrating God's ongoing commitment to translate the good news of Jesus Christ into the heart language of every culture in the world.

This first theme establishes that the gospel must be communicated within the frame of reference of the target group. This calls for cultural identification, rather than extracting people out of their cultural moorings and insisting that they can discover Christ only on *our* cultural terms. This principle is consistent with the theology of culture explored in chapter 6. It is also one of the fundamental lessons of the Incarnation.

To apply this principle, let us return to our original example of John the Baptist's declaration that Jesus is the "Lamb of God who takes away the sin of the world." We have already explored how the phrase "Lamb of God" would need considerable explanation before any meaning could be communicated. Alternative expressions may need to be used to communicate the person or mission of Jesus more clearly. Wherever possible, it is preferable to use concepts that already have a home in the biblical record or a firm place in Christian theology such as "Savior" or "Deliverer." However, sometimes new understandings of Jesus, such as "Chief Ancestor" in Africa, "everlasting guru" in India, or chüng-tzu (the ideal man who embodies all the Confucian ideals) in China, have been used in ways that were consistent with the biblical record and yet drew upon indigenous ideals that were already present. It should be clear that this is for appropriate communication of the significance of Jesus and is not being suggested as a principle for Bible translation or permanent replacement of established biblical imagery.

Any proposed title for Christ must be tested by the Scriptures and the apostolic witness to Jesus, since the Word of God provides divine revelation about Jesus Christ and the inerrant record of the actual eye and ear witnesses to Him. Many of the images that have emerged over the centuries reflect genuine and helpful insights about the Lord Jesus Christ. However, as with all metaphors, each also holds the potential to lead astray (as in the application of *logos* theology by Hick and Panikkar) without constant vigilance and clarification. Yet, even those reflections about Christ that have stood the test of Scripture and time cannot be used to declare a moratorium on new reflections and discoveries. If the gospel had stayed contained within the single ethnicity of Judaism, we would not have benefited from the insights of the Hellenistic Christians. In the same way, as the gospel has been translated into cultures found in China, India, Japan, Africa, Korea, and other places, we have gained more and more insights into the beauty and reality of Jesus Christ.

The second part of the phrase, "who takes away the sin of the world," highlights the universal need to communicate the concept of sin in the target culture. Anthropologists occasionally comment that there are many cultures with no concept of sin. For example, anthropologist Roger Keesing decries the legacy of missionaries by saying, "The concept of sin must rank with smallpox among our most damaging exports."[20] However, comments like this only serve to illustrate a misunderstanding regarding the meaning of the concepts that are translated "sin" in the Bible.

In contemporary usage the word *sin* is generally used as a category to describe what religion (or God) condemns but society does not act to pass legislation against. So, for example, adultery might be regarded as a sin, but murder is regarded as a crime. In other words, the word *sin* has taken on a rather narrow theological meaning. However, the semantic range of the word *sin* in the Bible is much broader than that. In fact, the Bible uses what we would call "secular" words to convey the notion of sin. For example, in Hebrew the word *chata* means "missing the mark" and originally referred to missing an intended target with a stone thrown from a sling. However, the Bible uses the word to describe someone who "misses the mark" of God's holiness. The Hebrew word *avar* means "to cross over" and was originally used in the literal sense of crossing over a line, but the Bible applies it to someone who violates the law or command of God and "crosses over" a moral boundary. Other words, such as *awah,* meaning "to bend or twist," were adapted in a similar fashion. So, while it is true that some cultures do not have a distinct word for sin that exclusively refers to a transgression against God, every culture has words that can easily be adapted to communicate the idea of sin.

The Christian anthropologist Robert Priest discovered in fieldwork

---

20. Roger Keesing, *Cultural Anthropology: A Contemporary Perspective* (New York: Holt, Rinehart, and Winston, 1981), 40.

among the Aguarana-Jivaro of Peru that they had a wide variety of vocabulary that could be used to capture the notion of sin, such as *pegkegchau,* meaning something ugly or deformed; *tsuwat,* meaning something filthy; *antuchu,* meaning someone who refuses to listen; and *tudau,* meaning someone who has been engaged in a wide variety of cultural transgressions, including adultery, wife beating, or preparing a bad meal. Robert Priest demonstrates how each of these words can be used to convey the biblical notion of sin as a moral transgression against God.[21] However, engaging in this kind of effective communication of the gospel takes considerable time and patience, which brings us to the second lesson from the Incarnation regarding effective missionary communication.

LESSON #2: MISSIONARY COMMUNICATION AS A RESPONSE TO INDIGENOUS QUESTIONS

One of the most challenging aspects of being a missionary is learning to see the world through the eyes of those we are seeking to reach with the gospel. This is why language learning and cultural adaptation is such an important and indispensable feature in the life of a missionary. One of the abiding values of language acquisition is developing the capacity to listen well. Most missionary training programs focus almost entirely on teaching missionaries what to *say,* with very little emphasis on learning how to listen well. However, as anyone who has been a missionary knows, learning to listen well is one of the important components of effective communication. Before we can share the gospel with people effectively, we must understand them and their worldview.

There are two important lessons we can draw from the Incarnation in respect to the role of listening. First, Jesus spent thirty years growing up and living in the culture of His birth before He began to teach and proclaim the kingdom of God. Even though Jesus was the Son of God, there was no replacement for growing up in the culture and becoming a cultural insider. Second, the only glimpse we have of Jesus between His birth and His baptism, which inaugurates His public ministry, is as a twelve-year-old boy in the temple. In that brief glimpse into Jesus as a young person, we do

---

21. I am indebted to Robert Priest for his insights on this. See his "Christian Theology, Sin, and Anthropology," in *Explorations in Anthropology and Theology,* ed. Frank A. Salamone and Walter Randolph Adams (New York: University Press of America, 1997), 23–37.

not find Him preaching to anyone or teaching the elders. Rather, we find Him *listening* and asking questions. Luke 2:46 records, "After three days they found him in the temple courts, sitting among the teachers, listening to them and asking them questions."

When we arrive in a new culture, we are tempted to move quickly to share the gospel and in the process make the assumption that the target culture has all the same questions we had, questions to which we can provide "answers," based on our understanding of the gospel. However whenever the gospel crosses new cultural frontiers, new questions are raised in the encounter for which we may have no ready answer. What we call theology is the result of all our most important questions being posed to the text of Scripture and reflecting on how the Bible addresses or answers those questions. An examination of any systematic theology textbook will quickly reveal that it is not a systematic summary of all that the Bible teaches about everything. Rather, it is a summary of those questions we have posed and that were important in our own reception of the gospel. For example, despite the fact that the Bible addresses issues like demonic bondage and food sacrificed to idols, the many questions that might naturally arise from such texts are generally not found in theology textbooks in the West, because they were not at the forefront of Western experience or perceived concerns. One of the by-products of the long sojourn of the gospel in Western culture is the false assumption that all potential questions have been canvassed and answered and that there are fundamentally no new questions to be answered. Thus, Christian theology becomes static within certain fixed categories.[22]

Questions Hindus Ask Christians

One of the most enlightening experiences in my own life has been the opportunity to work with Indian missionaries over a period of twenty years. A few years ago I conducted a survey of several hundred church planters who are all working as missionaries among Hindus in North India. I wanted to find out what questions were most often asked by Hindus who first encountered the gospel and a Christian missionary. The results of this survey were stunning.[23] It demonstrated quite conclusively that Hindus

---

22. For more on this, see my *Theology in the Context of World Christianity*.
23. I chose the top fifteen questions most asked by Hindus and wrote replies to them, which were eventually published in Hindi and in English under the titles *Your Questions—Our Answers* and *Āpke Savāl, Hamāre Jvāb*.

have a whole range of questions our missionary training program in North India (where I have taught since 1989) was not adequately preparing students to respond to. It is not unusual for theological training programs throughout the Majority World to follow Western training models and even to use Western textbooks or translations of Western books to train and equip students. As helpful as these programs are, they often fail to address a range of issues that are crucial to effective communication of the gospel, because they follow training models and texts that were designed and framed for Western use.

A few examples from the survey will help to demonstrate this problem. First, Hindu views of karma make it exceedingly difficult for a Hindu to comprehend that Jesus' death on the cross could have any impact (beyond a mere moral example) on someone living today. Any program that seeks to train Indians to work with Hindus must clearly demonstrate the differences between the Hindu doctrine of karma and the Christian doctrine of grace.

Second, Hindus are not particularly troubled, as a Muslim would be, when Christians claim that Jesus is God in the flesh, since this is a widely accepted concept within Hinduism. It is the *uniqueness* of the Incarnation, not the *fact* of it, that is a challenge to Hindus. Furthermore, Hindus find it difficult to understand how Christians can claim that Jesus is the supreme example of humanity while lacking a wife or children, since all of the most revered gods in Hinduism have wives and children.

Third, Hindus view religion in cultural terms and assume that there are many paths to God that have been given to each culture. They do not see the value of accepting a "foreign God" over their own national gods. Many Hindus do not even believe it is possible to "change" your religion.

Finally, Hindus are deeply disturbed by the fact that Christians eat meat, especially since most Hindus believe that Jesus was a vegetarian. These few examples illustrate important issues that anyone working among Hindus must be prepared to respond to but would, in all likelihood, not be addressed in a typical Western-oriented training program.

All the questions in my survey arose from listening carefully to questions about (and objections to) Christianity held by Hindus living in North India. If a similar survey were done among Muslims in North Africa, folk Buddhists in Thailand, or secular postmoderns in North America, for example, the questions and stumbling blocks would be profoundly different. The point is, we cannot assume that traditional Western textbooks on theology, pastoral training, evangelism, and so forth are adequate for the challenge of effective global witness or are always culturally transferable. There is no replacement for getting to know a particular culture, listening carefully to their questions, and reading Scripture afresh in light of the culture and its questions.

Questions Christians Ask

Listening to the questions of non-Christians is only half of the listening exercise. It is also vitally important to listen to the questions of *Christians* who are members of the target culture. In some cases, there may not be any indigenous Christians, so this will have to wait until the first believers begin to respond to the gospel and encounter biblical teaching. Over the years, I have asked my Indian students who were studying to be missionaries to write down and submit to me their own questions, which have arisen from their experience or from reading Scripture, for which they need more understanding. Having collected these questions over many years, it has helped to shape and give direction to the content of what I teach when training Indian missionaries.

The questions most often posed by Indian Christians fall into four general categories. I will briefly mention each of the categories and provide an example or two from each one.

First, many questions revolve around dress and ornamentation. In India, religious communities often are identified by their dress, particular markings, or ornamentation they wear. Thus, Indians often ask, for example, if people from a Sikh background who come to Christ should be asked to remove their turban. Likewise, it is customary for married Hindu women to wear jewelry (usually nose or earrings and wrist or ankle bangles) and to apply a red powder, known as *sindoor*, in the part of their hair as a sign that they are married. Christians often insist that female believers from a Hindu background remove all jewelry and discontinue wearing *sindoor* in their hair. However, this sends the unintended message to the Hindu community that the woman is now in a state of mourning (no ornamentation) and that she is no longer devoted to her husband (no *sindoor*).[24]

---

24. While there is no need for Hindu background believers to discontinue wearing jewelry, we encourage that it be used modestly, in keeping with 1 Peter 3:1–4. In my view, there is no need to discourage the application of sindoor since it is primarily a cultural sign of one's married state (like wearing a wedding band in the West). However, there are some Hindu women who burn

Likewise, Sikhs who remove the turban are often thought to have forsaken their Sikh culture and heritage, not simply to have embraced Christianity.

A second category of questions revolves around the celebration of various national festivals. India celebrates a wide range of festivals, some of which are clearly in honor of Hindu deities, such as Janmashtami (birthday of Krishna) and Ganesh Chaturti (celebrating the life and exploits of Ganesh). Others are widely regarded as more cultural, such as Holi (celebrating the end of winter) and Devali (festival of lights), though even these are often mixed with various Hindu associations. Can Christians continue to celebrate these holidays?[25]

A third category of questions revolves around the use of various names and terminology. Hindu background believers often wonder how much of their former religious vocabulary can or should be carried over into their newfound Christian faith. Hinduism is full of language for God, devotion, worship, prayer, and so on. It is also customary for Hindu parents to name their children after a Hindu god or goddess. Throughout India you meet men named Krishna, Ram, or Shivraj and women named Lakshmi, Parvati, or Radha. Christians often ask if a person named after a Hindu god or goddess should receive a new "Christian" name at baptism.[26]

A fourth category relates to food. Should Christians exercise their freedom to eat meat, or should they refrain for the sake of their Hindu friends? Should Christians eat food that is given to them by their Hindu neighbors, even if it has been sacrificed to idols (*prasad*)? These questions are identical to the questions the Corinthian believers addressed to Paul in the first century, but they are rarely discussed in traditional ministerial preparation in the West.

---

incense to Hindu gods as a part of the morning application of the sindoor. If this is the case, then this act of worship should be either separated from the application of sindoor or be transformed into a daily prayer to God, asking Him to bless the marriage and keep the wife faithful to her vows.

25. We counsel Indian Christians to continue to participate in those festivals that are largely *cultural* and thereby deflect the common criticism of Hindus against Christians that they are not patriotic.

26. Unless it is a matter of personal conscience, we encourage Indians to keep the names given to them at birth. Not only will this help them in their witness to Hindus, but there is also ample biblical evidence that Christians in a similar situation in the first century kept their names. For example, an examination of Christians Paul greets in Romans 16 includes people named Hermes, Olympas, Narcissus, and so forth (16:11–15). The shift from Paul's use of his Hebrew name (Saul) to his Greek name (Paul) does not occur at his conversion or baptism as is sometimes erroneously thought. Rather, Paul uses his Greek name when his ministry begins to be focused on Gentiles. Thus, he actually uses a name that more fully identifies with his target culture.

These questions arise specifically out of an Indian context and cannot be applied to other contexts. For example, Christians from certain regions of Africa sometimes ask if it is appropriate for women to preach or take Communion during their menstrual cycle. They want to know what they should do if they come to Christ already having three wives. Should they divorce two of them? Christians from an Islamic background in North Africa or the Middle East often ask if they should continue to keep their head covered when they pray or fast during Ramadan, as they did when they were Muslims. All of these questions require fresh theological and missiological reflection.

I recommend that missionaries keep a file of all the questions they are asked by Christians and non-Christians alike. Over time, certain patterns will begin to emerge, which will reveal key points to emphasize when communicating the gospel and training new believers. It is vital that we discover what *their* fundamental questions are and engage in the necessary biblical and theological reflection that is required whenever the gospel crosses new cultural boundaries.

LESSON #3: MISSIONARY COMMUNICATION AS A PROCLAMATION OF THE KINGDOM OF GOD AMONG THE KINGDOMS OF THIS WORLD

The third and final lesson from the Incarnation focuses on Jesus' announcement of the kingdom of God. "The time has come. . . . the kingdom of God is near. Repent and believe the good news!" (Mark 1:15). These are the first words of Jesus' public ministry, as recorded in Mark's gospel. The kingdom of God is widely regarded as the central message of Jesus and is probably the most succinct single phrase summarizing the gospel of Jesus Christ. The gospel is about the inbreaking of God's rule, the decisive defeating of the powers of evil arrayed against us, and the inauguration of the New Creation. All of these great truths lie in seed form in the simple phrase, the kingdom of God. No sharing of the gospel can be considered adequate apart from an understanding of the kingdom of God. Therefore, learning how Jesus *communicated* the kingdom of God is the third lesson from the Incarnation.

Announcing the Kingdom

First, Jesus comes and "announces," or "proclaims," the good news of God's inbreaking reign. The Incarnation represents a divine invasion into the present evil order. The gospel represents a decisive inbreaking of good news. In today's pluralistic environment, the exclusive claims of the gospel and the uniqueness of Jesus Christ sound odd, and it is easy for Christians to lose their courage to proclaim the gospel. However, the gospel of Jesus Christ proclaims decisive acts of God in real history. To domesticate these events into some generic spiritual message that can be amalgamated with other world religions or to make it a version of American's self-help gospel beneath a thin veneer of Christian language is a denial of the reign of God. The kingdom of God encompasses the origin, purpose, and final destiny of the entire universe. As Lesslie Newbigin has said, "We are not dealing with a local and temporary disturbance in the current of cosmic happenings, but with the source and goal of the cosmos."[27] It is not merely about human happiness but about the unfolding of the *missio dei*. The good news of Christ's ministry, teaching, death, and resurrection is the way God the Father chose to fulfill His promise to Abraham to bless all nations (Gen. 12:3). We should proclaim this good news with boldness and confidence.

Communicating the Kingdom

Second, one of the biggest surprises in reading the Gospels is that Jesus never explicitly defines the kingdom of God. If we are looking for a lexical, dictionary-type definition of the phrase, we will be disappointed. Instead, Jesus links the concept of the kingdom of God to existing concepts and gradually uses that to build an understanding of the kingdom of God. Jesus compared the kingdom of God (or heaven) to a wide range of common images, including a man scattering seed, a tiny mustard seed, yeast a woman uses in baking bread, a treasure hidden in the field, a fisherman's net, a man who brought treasures out of his storehouse, and so forth.

Using insights from contemporary communication theory, we can gain a deeper appreciation for this practice. Communication theorists teach that integral to the universal feature of cultural learning and language acquisition is developing thousands of "anchors of reality" known as paradigms. For example, after being exposed to dozens of examples of things known as "trees," we eventually develop a paradigm known as "tree" and learn to distinguish between what can appropriately be called a "tree" and what is not a "tree." Eventually the word *tree* becomes a fixed

---

27. Lesslie Newbigin, *The Open Secret: An Introduction to the Theology of Mission*, rev. ed. (Grand Rapids: Eerdmans, 1995), 30.

point of knowledge. A similar process takes place with thousands of other words, concepts, and values.

When a new paradigm is introduced, it is often necessary to relate it to an existing paradigm. In fact, research demonstrates that whenever we are exposed to a new potential "anchor of reality," we seek to understand it by relating it to something we already know. The New Testament regularly models this in communicating the gospel. The apostle Paul, following the example of Jesus, often related new Christian doctrines to existing paradigms of knowledge or association within the culture. For example, the word *church* simply means a "public assembly." However, Paul fills out its meaning by comparing the church to a human body with many members, controlled by the head, Jesus Christ (1 Cor. 12:27; Eph. 1:10, 22–23). Paul also relates the church to a building, with the apostolic teaching forming the foundation and Jesus Christ as the "cornerstone" who holds it all together (1 Cor. 3:9; Eph. 2:20). Paul compares the persecuted church with the Roman procession of prisoners after they return home from a victorious battle (1 Cor. 4:9; 2 Cor. 2:14). We can recall similar examples in the earlier teaching of Jesus, when Jesus compared Himself to a "vine" (John 15:1–5) or a "gate" (John 10:7) or a "shepherd" (John 10:11, 14) or other paradigms that were familiar to His hearers.

The Kingdom of God in Context: Contextualization and Translatability
Third, Jesus addresses the good news of God's reign to the specific contexts of the time and culture in which He lived. The kingdom of God was not declared as a mere theoretical concept or only a vague, future reality. In Jesus Christ the good news of God's rule and the New Creation was already breaking in. The kingdom of God was addressed to specific situations—to prostitutes, tax collectors, self-righteous Pharisees, religious leaders, political rulers, and so forth. In today's nomenclature, we would say that Jesus' message of the kingdom was *contextualized* such that the Word of God was addressed to a specific audience. The message of the kingdom of God is universal and transcends all cultures, but it can only become manifest in the lives and experience of particular communities. The universal gospel must become particularized in specific settings. This particularization is widely referred to today as contextualization, a term that needs further exploration.

Very few words have risen to such prominence in discussions about communicating the gospel as the word *contextualization*. It is important that we understand the meaning and history of the word, as well as the usefulness and limitations of the term. The word *contextualization* first appeared in missions literature in 1972 in a Theological Education by Extension (TEE) document expressing legitimate concerns about traditional models of theological education.[28] While the term was new, it built upon a number of earlier words such as *accommodation, inculturation,* and *indigenization,* which play an important role in today's use of the word *contextualization.*

ACCOMMODATION

The word *accommodation* emerged out of the missionary practice of the Roman Catholic Church. In particular, *accommodation* refers to a series of strategic experiments led by Jesuit missionaries during the sixteenth to eighteenth centuries to use indigenous terminology and cultural practices in presenting the Christian faith. The most famous examples are Matteo Ricci's use of the Chinese word *T'ien* (heaven) for God and his adaptation of ancestor veneration as a symbol of family cohesion rather than worship. The ensuing controversy over these accommodations eventually led to the famous Rites Controversy.[29] In India, Robert de Nobili became famous for "accommodating" the Brahminical lifestyle in his mission to the high-caste Brahmins. DeNobili dressed, ate, and lived like a Brahmin and did not insist that high-caste Hindus who became followers of Christ change their caste practices.

INCULTURATION

The word *inculturation* (adapted from the anthropological word *enculturation*) began to be used by Roman Catholic missionaries in the twentieth century to refer to the process through which *cultural insiders* who have become Christians adapt, assimilate, and apply the gospel to their own cultural context. Accommodation emphasized strategic decisions made by the missionaries (who were cultural outsiders) about what aspects of

---

28. *Ministry in Context: The Third Mandate Programme of the Theological Education Fund, 1970–1977* (Bromley, England: Theological Education Fund, 1972), 139–45, as cited by David Hesselgrave and Edward Rommen, *Contextualization: Meanings, Methods and Models* (Pasadena, CA: William Carey Library, 2000), 28.

29. The Rites Controversy refers to a major debate within Roman Catholicism between 1630 and 1742 (although the controversy was revisited in the twentieth century) about how much missionaries were allowed to accommodate ancestor and emperor veneration in their adaptation of the gospel in light of Chinese social customs and expectations.

the target culture *they* (or church authorities) were willing to adapt or accept. This new term shifts the emphasis to the indigenous church. The word *inculturation* acknowledges that in the final analysis it is the Christians in the target culture who ultimately must render judgments about what areas of the culture can be accommodated and what areas of the culture must be challenged and transformed by the gospel.

INDIGENIZATION

Finally, the term *indigenization* was borrowed from its earlier usage as a political and sociological term and brought into missions discussions in the 1970s, around the same time as the word *contextualization*.[30] Indigenization refers to the process through which existing cultural and social practices can be infused with new Christian meaning. Used in this way, both accommodation and inculturation can be cited as *examples* of indigenization, the former through missionary initiative, the latter through the initiative of Christians in the target culture. In practice, however, both accommodation and inculturation tended to focus only on the effective communication and reception of the gospel message, whereas indigenization often is used to refer to the signs of a healthy, indigenous church. In this connection, the term *indigenization* is often used in contrast to the term *Westernization*. Once a missionary-planted church had indigenous leadership or became self-supporting, then it was said that "indigenization" had taken place.

Helpful Contributions of Contextualization
Although each of these terms contributed to our understanding of the process that occurs when the gospel crosses cultural boundaries, it gradually became evident that each of the terms also had limitations. The word *accommodation* completely neglected the active role of the receptors in the communication process. The word *inculturation* focused on indigenous Christians but seemed to be regarded by Western Christians as a process limited to the mission field. Any changes from the Western patterns of Christian doctrine and practice often were regarded as exceptional, even exotic, adaptations by the indigenous Christians. Given enough time, it was thought they would

---

30. The emergence of new terminology is the result of discussions in North America prompted by the rise of liberation theology in Latin America, which claimed to correct biases that were present in North American theology.

eventually conform to the practices of Western Christianity. There was little appreciation that Western Christianity also had received and adapted the gospel through a long inculturation process or that there might be valuable insights in the experience, faith, and practice of indigenous churches that could help to renew or revitalize Western Christianity.

The term *indigenization* is still in wide use today, but some have felt that the Christian use of the term, like *inculturation,* was almost exclusively in reference to the mission field. It did not help that it was regularly contrasted with *Westernization.* Finally, many felt that just because a church had an indigenous pastor or was self-supporting did not necessarily mean that the church could be declared indigenous. A term with a broader, more global, application was needed. The use of the word *contextualization* in the TEE report by Shoki Coe provided the needed word, and the term very quickly became widely used by theologians and missionaries across the theological spectrum. The most valuable contribution of the word *contextualization* was its broadening of the discussion beyond the content of theology or the reactive adaptation to isolated cultural forms. Advocates of contextualization called for a fresh examination of all aspects of church life and experience, including church architecture, worship styles, indigenous music, preaching practices, church governance, evangelistic methods, and so forth. Furthermore, the term is as readily used by emergent and missional churches in the West as it is by missionaries working among people groups who are receiving the gospel for the very first time.

There is no single definition of contextualization that everyone agrees on. However, broadly speaking, the term stresses the importance of "formulating, presenting and practicing the Christian faith in such a way that is relevant to the cultural context of the target group in terms of conceptualization, expression and application; yet maintaining theological coherence, biblical integrity and theoretical consistency."[31] The historic deposit of the gospel is unchanging, but contextualization acknowledges the need to "translate" the message into forms that are meaningful and applicable to peoples in their separate cultural settings in such a way that the original message and impact of the gospel is communicated.[32]

---

31. Enoch Wan, "Critiquing the Method of the Traditional Western Theology and Calling for Sino-Theology," *Chinese Around the World* (November 1999): 13.
32. David Hesselgrave, *Communicating Christ Cross-Culturally,* 2nd ed., (Grand Rapids: Zondervan, 1991) 143–144.

On the whole, the word *contextualization* has served missiological studies in some positive ways.[33] However, because of the widespread use, misuse, and varying applications of the term in contemporary theological and missiological literature, there are important clarifications that must be made if the term is to continue to serve the church well. I will begin by pointing out two positive features of the term, followed by a critique of what I regard as misunderstandings or misapplications of the term.

First, *the term highlights the importance of addressing specific contexts with the gospel.* Contextualization represents an ongoing check against two dangerous attitudes about the gospel, which have, on occasion, prevailed in the church. There have been those who have viewed the gospel through a monocultural lens and felt that the only way to reproduce the gospel was to extract people from their own culture and introduce them to the gospel through the language, experience, and perspective of the source culture. We already have noted that the early Christians in Acts 15 opted against this approach. Occasionally, this lesson has been forgotten, and the emphasis on contextualization helps to remind the church of its original commitment to a multicultural stance.

There are others who speak as if the gospel resides in some acultural or transcultural plane of existence, hermetically sealed off from history and culture. However, as noted in chapter 6, in the incarnation of Jesus Christ, the Word and the world meet, time and eternity intersect, and transcendence and immanence find common ground. The commitment to contextualization, therefore, keeps the gospel from being separated from real history. The truths of the gospel are unchanging and not culturally determined, but those truths cannot be experienced, celebrated, or communicated without being culturally embodied. All gospel communication, including the New Testament itself, is a contextual event. Even a concept as simple as "Jesus is Lord" must be communicated in a particular language to some particular cultural setting. Contextualization, therefore, assures that the objective and subjective dimensions of revelation are not allowed to drift apart.

Second, the term *contextualization refers to the positive goal of the universal good news of Jesus Christ being authentically experienced in the*

---

33. For a fuller treatment of the meaning and uses of the word *contextualization,* see "Contextualization" in Dean Gilliland, *Evangelical Dictionary of World Missions,* ed. A. Scott Moreau (Grand Rapids: Baker, 2000), 225–27.

particularities of a local context. It is important to remember that contextualization always must begin by being faithful to the original biblical context and authorial intent of the biblical message. Contextualization is achieved only if the gospel of Jesus Christ is received, assimilated, and reproduced in a way that is consistent with the apostolic witness to Jesus Christ as revealed in Scripture. Contextualization also involves a growing awareness of our own cultural setting and how our own perception of the gospel inevitably has blindspots that new cultural embodiments of the gospel may shed light upon.

One of the most valuable guides in understanding contextualization is the study of church (Christian) history and global Christianity. As we become increasingly identified with the church throughout time (history) and space (around the world), we begin to see with greater clarity the common faith that is shared by all Christians. It is easy to focus on all the differences between Christians around the world and throughout history. However, there is also a deeper unity that unites all authentic Christians in every age, affirmations that have been held *semper ubique ab omnibus* ("always, everywhere, by everyone"). Many of these great truths have been expressed doctrinally in historic creeds such as the Nicene Creed. However, the shared faith of Christians cannot always be packaged so neatly in theological language. It also involves a spiritual unity that acknowledges our catholicity because we are all members of the body of Christ and share a common union with Jesus Christ expressed through vibrant faith, holy living, shared sacraments, and a burden to bear witness unto Him in authentic ways throughout the whole world. We must never forget that a new Christian not only *has* faith, but he or she also is brought *into* a common faith. Thus, contextualization must be sensitive to multiple cultural contexts and continually learn to identify authentic expressions of Christian faithfulness.

Critique of Contextualization

The widespread use of the word *contextualization* has led inevitably to various abuses of the term. It is important to candidly identity these abuses if the term is to continue to be useful in missiology.

First, *unfortunately the term has become identified with the increasing fragmentation of theological discourse.* Sometimes so-called "contextualized" theologies have reinforced the notion that there is no universal core gospel message and that meaning is culturally determined. The term *contextualization* originally emerged in theological discussions as a response to the rise of liberation theology in Latin America, which did, in fact, shed light on several glaring weaknesses in "traditional" North American theological discourse. However, this was soon followed by a range of contextualized theologies, such as the feminist theology of Rosemary Radford Ruether (b. 1936) and the black theology of James Cone (b. 1938).[34] This, coupled with the rise of post-modernism, has led to the growing fragmentation of theological discourse today. There has been a dangerous tendency toward using contextualization to justify a potentially infinite number of niche theologies.

Today, some have used contextualization to promote the idea that just as Latinos have liberation theology, Koreans should have a *ming jung* theology, women a feminist theology, blacks a black theology, Indians a *dalit* theology, and so forth. However, every authentic theology must not only celebrate the insights of its own particularity but also *reflect the catholicity shared by all Christians everywhere*. As Andrew Walls has said, "The Lord of hosts is not a territorial Baal."[35] If Jesus is truly Lord, then He is Lord of us all; we are all members of the same body. Contextualization always should promote the mutual edification of the entire church and not be used to create hermetically sealed spheres of discourse, which neglect our shared apostolic faith and only celebrate our points of divergence.

Second, *contextualization sometimes is used as a vague synonym for cultural particularity*. It is not unusual to hear even missiologists speak of a certain proposal as being "overly contextualized" or "undercontextualized," based upon how much emphasis is placed on cultural particularity. Others occasionally speak of "high" or "low" contextualization. However, these uses fail to recognize that contextualization always refers to a positive goal. If, for example, some particular strategy places too much emphasis on cultural particularity at the expense of some universal core element of the gospel, then it is appropriate to call it syncretistic, but not "overly contextualized." If a missionary is unduly tied to his or her own cultural embodiment of Christianity and unwilling to enter into the

---

34. Rosemary Radford Ruether, *New Woman, New Earth: Sexist Ideologies and Human Liberation* (New York: Seabury, 1975); James Cone, *Black Theology and Black Power* (Maryknoll, NY: Orbis, 1969, 1999).

35. Andrew F. Walls, "Eusebius Tries Again: Reconceiving the Study of Christian History," *International Bulletin of Missionary Research* 24, no. 3 (July 2000): 107.

framework of the target culture, it would be appropriate to identify him or her as ethnocentric, but not as "undercontextualized." Contextualization should always refer to the *positive goal* and should be spoken of in reference to both the universality of the gospel message and the ways in which that message has been effectively communicated and understood in various cultural settings.

Third, contextualization sometimes has served as a shibboleth "code word," which provides amnesty for any kind of experimentation that helps to identify with the target culture. As noted earlier, it is essential that the starting point of contextualization is the biblical text. If the focus is only on making accommodations to the target culture in order to alleviate anything that might be considered offensive, then we have missed contextualization by a wide mark. We must never forget that it is the inbreaking realities of the New Creation that all cultures are summoned to. The New Creation is the final norm to which all creation must finally be transformed and conformed. Culture is not the norm to which the gospel must conform. Some, for example, have advocated that contextualization in the Islamic context means downplaying the deity of Christ or, among postmoderns, downplaying the doctrine of sin or the call to repentance. However, this demonstrates a denial of Christ, contempt for the gospel, and an insult to the multitude of Christians over the centuries who have given their lives for the faithful proclamation of the gospel.

Contextualization is never about producing a domesticated version of the gospel. Contextualization is not about making the gospel acceptable in the ears of the target culture. It is not enough to simply be committed to "where people are" and knowing "where the culture is." We also must have a concomitant conviction about where the culture *should be* under the influence of the inbreaking New Creation. Contextualization demands that we point out how the gospel stands in judgment against the idolatry that is inevitably present in every culture. Contextualization is about effectively communicating *the gospel*, not simply effective communication in some generic sense.

In conclusion, the word *contextualization* has suffered considerable misuse in recent years. It has been used to support the relativistic notion that one special interest group or one person's interpretation of Scripture is as good as the other. It has been used to provide sanction for idolatrous entertainment-oriented churches in North America. Does misuse of the word mean that we should abandon the word completely? Perhaps we should, although in principle it is important to fight for the proper use of words, even if they are regularly abused. Nevertheless, I advocate using the word *translatability* instead of the word *contextualization*. In the context of missiology, Lamin Sanneh, among others, has pioneered the broader use of the word *translatability* to include not merely linguistics, but also the entire process of the faithful transmission of the gospel across new cultural frontiers.[36]

Translatability

There are three distinct advantages to using the language of "translation." First, it immediately brings to mind the idea of Bible translation, which seeks to move faithfully from the sacred text to the target language. That is an important paradigm, which serves as the basis for extending the analogy to include the faithful transmission of the Christian gospel. Indeed, it is difficult to even conceptualize the word *translation* without thinking of both the source and the target. This is one of the ongoing problems with the word *contextualization,* which focuses only on the target context. In contrast, the word *translatability* reminds us that we must always remain faithful to *both* the apostolic message and the particularities of the target culture.

Second, because the term *translatability* is an extension of the primary idea of Bible translation, there is little doubt about the priority of the biblical message. In Bible translation it would be unthinkable to change the translation to a new meaning, which was not in the original text, simply because the resulting verse might offend members of the culture. Yet, on the other hand, as with any Bible translation, only members of the target culture can finally render the verdict on whether a particular translation effectively communicates, or re-presents, the gospel in an effective way or not.

Finally, using the language of translation serves as an ongoing reminder of the necessary boundaries to translatability. Bible translators undertake their work with the greatest care because they must be constantly vigilant against the possibility of a mistranslation of a biblical text. In the same way, mistranslation is also possible in the process of communicating the gospel. The Word of God is the final arbiter in the communication

---

36. Sanneh, *Translating the Message.*

process. There is an overwhelming pressure today to sacrifice the gospel at the altar of the "market," which treats the recipients of the gospel as consumers who must be satisfied by giving them what they want to hear rather than the unpopular message of repentance and a crucified Savior. However, if missionary practice and strategy become "market-driven," then the objective reference point of the triune God and His self-revelation will be lost to a democratizing spirit with no normative standards beyond majority opinion. Thus, translatability is a valuable theological principle, which, alongside the careful use of contextualization, can serve an important function in helping the church to be faithful to the gospel as we cross new cultural frontiers.

CONCLUSION

This chapter has demonstrated that the Incarnation provides the theological foundation for effective missionary communication. It serves as the model for all the ways that we seek to contextualize or translate the universal gospel message into a potentially infinite number of particular settings. There is indeed much to be gained from insights from anthropology, ethnography, and communication theory. However, if the whole of the missionary enterprise is to be properly rooted in the *missio dei*, it is essential that the foundation arise out of the missional and incarnational heart of the triune God.

— 12 —
Access and Reproducibility in Missions Strategy

IN JULY 1974 OVER TWO THOUSAND delegates sat in a large auditorium and listened to Ralph Winter's address entitled, "The Priority of Cross-Cultural Evangelism." The occasion was the closing plenary address of the International Congress on World Evangelization held in Lausanne, Switzerland. The ten-day conference already had featured a number of well-known and respected Christian leaders of the day, including Billy Graham, Francis Schaeffer, Malcolm Muggeridge, Samuel Escobar, and John Stott. The end of the conference was at hand, and, while the delegates representing over 150 nations realized that this was a historic conference, they were understandably tired and ready to begin their long journeys home. Little did the delegates realize as they listened to this rather technical address by Winter that one of the most momentous shifts in the history of modern missions thinking was being articulated. Looking back from the perspective of the twenty-first century, it is not an exaggeration to say that one cannot speak about modern missions strategy without referencing this address given by Ralph Winter in Lausanne. The year 1974, and this address in particular, has become the dividing line representing a fundamental shift in how Christian leaders and missionaries think about the missionary task.

What was it in this address that unleashed so much creative new thinking about missions? It is the purpose of this chapter to reflect on the address and the subsequent changes it stimulated in modern missions practice. However, if it could be summarized in a single sentence, the 1974 conference in Lausanne was the time when missions strategists stopped thinking about missions as "places" and began to think about missions as "peoples." This shift from geography to ethnography may seem small, but it opened up fresh ways for the church to understand the disparities in the world in terms of access to the gospel. This, in turn, resulted in major changes in missions strategy and the deployment of missionaries. It dramatically reshaped what is meant by the term *mission field*. As this chapter will demonstrate, many of the insights of 1974 are even more relevant today because of globalization and the increased scale and pace of immigration. Many new terms and phrases, including *people group, unreached peoples, access and viability,* and *near-neighbor versus cross-cultural evangelism,* entered the lexicon of missiologists.

From a theological perspective, all discussion concerning access to the gospel arises appropriately from the doctrine of the Incarnation. At the heart of the Incarnation lies the Father's commitment to take the initiative and enable both Jew and Gentile to have access to the good news of God's redemption in Jesus Christ. Ephesians 2:18 declares that "through him we both have access to the Father by one Spirit." This verse provides insight into the triune God's activity in the *missio dei*. The specific context of the verse is what Andrew Walls calls the "Ephesians Moment," whereby both Jew and Gentile have access to salvation and a common reconciliation with God and one another. Thus, a vigorous missiological discussion concerning which people groups have access to the gospel and which do not is a natural extension of the Incarnation.

LAUSANNE 1974

Ralph Winter's Defining Moment
In order to place Winter's address at Lausanne in context, it is important to briefly review his larger place as one of the most innovative missiologists of the twentieth century. Ralph Winter was born in 1924. After receiving his doctorate at Cornell University, he served as a missionary with a Mayan tribe in Guatemala from 1956 to 1966. While in Guatemala, Winter realized how difficult it was for pastors in remote areas to receive theological education. Thus, Winter became instrumental in founding Theological Education by Extension (TEE), a pioneering program of distance education that has revolutionized theological education around the world. In 1968 Winter joined the faculty of Fuller Theological

Seminary, where he taught missions for the next decade and interacted with hundreds of students from around the world. Winter gradually recognized that existing missions organizations (and the missions strategy upon which they were based) would never be able to reach most of the world's peoples who did not currently have any church or gospel witness. Winter saw the need for new thinking and greater collaboration among missions organizations. This led him to found the United States Center for World Mission in 1976, which has become the base for dozens of missions organizations, and affiliate partnerships with hundreds of others, all focused on strategy, mobilization, and training for effective cross-cultural missions.

Winter went on to found William Carey International University, which offers masters and Ph.D. degrees in international development through an innovative distance education model. Seeing the difficulty of getting missions books published through traditional publishers, Winter founded the William Carey Library for the publication and dissemination of missions books. Hundreds of publications, including the influential *Operation World* prayer guide for global missions, have contributed significantly to a deeper understanding of missions.

His interest in promoting academic reflection on missions also led him to found the International Society for Frontier Missiologists and to cofound the American Society of Missiology. Winter also has been on the forefront of important missiological journals and missions resources, including *Frontiers, Global Prayer Digest,* and the *International Journal of Frontier Missiology.*[1] His ongoing interest in providing more grassroots understanding of missions led Winter to start the Perspectives on the World Christian Movement, a lay program in missions training, which is conducted in churches across the country and has over eighty thousand graduates.

In recalling Ralph Winter's remarkable career as a missionary, mobilizer, and missions strategist, I am reminded of a well-known saying that the entire career of a famous photographer sometimes comes down to a single, defining photograph. For example, Associated Press photographer Joe Rosenthal took thousands of pictures in his career, but he will always be known for his 1945 Pulitzer Prize winning shot of six soldiers raising the American flag at Iwo Jima. Likewise, Steve McCurry took many photographs, but his defining

---

1. IJFM was formerly known as *International Journal of Frontier Missions.*

moment came when he captured the young Afghan girl with the haunting green eyes, who appeared on the front cover of *National Geographic* in June of 1985. In the same way, despite the many achievements of Ralph Winter's remarkable career, I think his address at Lausanne will go down in missions history as the defining moment of his career.

1974 Lausanne Address

By 1974 there were many in the church who were quite enthusiastic upon realizing that, for the first time in history, there were identifiable Christians located in every country in the world. The church was no longer confined to the West and a few isolated pockets around the world; it was now a *bona fide* global movement. If the Great Commission was conceptualized as essentially a "geographic" challenge, then the job was virtually accomplished. Across the country most mainline churches, long the backbone of the Western missionary movement, were dramatically downsizing their mission force, and many were calling for a complete moratorium on missions.

It was at Lausanne that Ralph Winter played the spoiler with hard, new facts about thousands of ethnic groups or "people groups" with no accessibility to the Christian gospel.[2] Winter pointed out that the Bible does not primarily conceptualize the world in the geopolitical terms with which we have become so accustomed. Instead, the Bible conceptualizes the world as populated by ethnic blocks, which are defined culturally and linguistically, not by modern political boundaries. Winter pointed out, for example, that even though the Nagas in northeast India are almost all Christians, this does not have an appreciable impact on hundreds of other cultural groups who, although they also live in India, remain behind cultural and linguistic barriers that would prevent them from being reached by even the most vigorous Naga evangelists, apart from a cross-cultural initiative. Winter insisted that we have to measure access to the gospel, not in terms of *geographic* distance, but in terms of *cultural* distance. This represented a major paradigm shift in the way people understood the missiological challenge of global evangelism.

As noted in our exegesis of the Great Commission passages in chapter 5, the shift from conceptualizing the Great Commission as a "geographic"

---

2. The entire text of Ralph Winter's address, including the paper sent to all the delegates in advance of the congress, as well as the actual address given by Winter at Lausanne, is available at www.lausanne.org/documents.

challenge focused on political countries to conceptualizing it as a "cultural" challenge focused on ethnic groups is supported in the language Jesus used. If Jesus had wanted to emphasize geography, there are a number of words, such as *basilea* (kingdom), *chōra* (territory, region), and *agros* (country), He could have used. However, Matthew's gospel uses the word *ethnos* (nation), referring to *ethnic* groups, not geopolitical units. Because modern English usage frequently obscures the distinction between a "country" and a "nation," the biblical emphasis on *peoples* is also frequently lost. However, there is an enormous difference between Jesus commanding us to "make disciples" in 238 distinct political units, which we call "countries," and His commanding us to "make disciples" in over twenty-four thousand distinct ethnic groups in the world.

Winter referred to all "near culture" evangelism as E-1, whereas cross-cultural evangelism is E-2 or, in the case of major cross-cultural barriers, E-3. The letter *E* represents evangelism, and the numbers represent the increasing cultural distance between the evangelist and the targeted people. Winter relates the taxonomy of E-1, E-2, and E-3 to the command of Christ in Acts 1:8 that we are to be His witnesses in Jerusalem and Judea, Samaria, and to the ends of the earth. Jerusalem is E-1 evangelism, a Jew sharing the gospel with another Jew, and by extension represents all the normal activity we refer to as evangelism with our culturally near neighbors. In E-1 evangelism there is no linguistic or cultural barrier to cross. However, "Samaria" represents E-2 evangelism, since there is a cultural gap between Jews and Samaritans. Finally, "the ends of the earth" represents E-3 evangelism and, by extension, evangelization of any people group that requires a major cross-cultural initiative.

Winter devoted considerable time in his Lausanne address demonstrating that the terms used in Acts 1:8 do not primarily represent a geographic progression but a cultural and ethnic progression. Indeed, if they represent a geographic framework, then there is no explanation for the important emphasis made in Acts 11 on the early Christian witness to the *Greeks* in Samaria as opposed to those who preached to their fellow *Jews* in Samaria.

The shocking news Winter delivered at Lausanne was that even if the entire Christian world would be mobilized for effective E-1 evangelism, there would be nearly 2 billion people who would still have no access to the Christian gospel, because they can be reached only by a cross-cultural initiative.

POST-1974 ANALYSIS OF PEOPLE GROUPS

The address by Ralph Winter caused a dramatic shift in missiological thinking of the time, especially among evangelicals, who were the dominant participants in the 1974 congress. In the years following the Lausanne conference, more detailed ethnographic study was done to identify how many ethnic groups or people groups had viable, reproducing churches, which could reach their remaining populations with E-1 evangelism. Further study was conducted to determine how many people groups did not currently have any access to the gospel or did not have sufficient numbers of Christians to constitute a viable church, able to reproduce itself through E-1 evangelism without outside assistance. In order to do this, it was necessary to carefully define exactly what was meant by a "people group." Once that was determined, further consensus was needed to define what it meant for a people group to be declared "reached" or "unreached." Other questions inevitably arose: At what point could missionaries declare a church "viable" and able to reproduce itself without outside assistance? What about countries that have a high percentage of nominal Christians? Is there a way to determine what percentage of Christians in a given people group is committed to sharing their faith with another person?

Statistics on People Groups

The original statistics provided by Ralph Winter in 1974 were, by his own admission, based on very rough estimates, since the fields of ethnography and religious demographics were still in their infancy at that time. However, today there are three separate organizations that produce empirical data and analysis to help Christians better understand the current status of global evangelism and church planting.[3] Therefore, rather than examine the original statistics offered by Winter, we will look at the latest statistics and definitions currently utilized by the three groups involved in producing this data.

---

3. In addition to these three groups, there is also the linguistic data provided by SIL, which, while not focused on evangelism, response to the gospel, or church planting, provides important research related to the 6,912 living languages in the world. Since one of the central criteria for defining a people group is linguistic, this research continues to assist missiologists. See www .ethnologue.com. Ethnologue is an extension of the work of SIL, the linguistic arm of the Wycliffe Bible Translators.

JOSHUA PROJECT

The first group, affiliated with the United States Center for World Mission, is known as the Joshua Project.[4] The Joshua Project has adopted the definition of a people group that was agreed upon by a Lausanne working group in 1982. A people group is defined as "the largest group within which the Gospel can spread as a church planting movement without encountering barriers of understanding or acceptance." The Joshua Project has focused primarily on linguistics as the most basic division between peoples. According to the Joshua Project, there are currently 16,304 people groups in the world. Of that number, 6,748 are considered unreached, representing 2.68 billion people.

INTERNATIONAL MISSIONS BOARD

The second group that provides statistics is the International Missions Board (IMB), which oversees the extensive missions work of the Southern Baptist Church.[5] The IMB identifies 11,571 people groups in the world. Of that number, 6,450 are considered unreached. The IMB defines a people group as "an *ethnolinguistic group* with a common self-identity that is shared by the various members." The IMB also cites the Lausanne definition as an additional definition. However, the distinctive contribution of the IMB definition of a people group is the emphasis on "self-identity." When does an "us" group begin to see another group as a "them" group?

WORLD CHRISTIAN DATABASE

The third research organization dedicated to researching people groups is the Center for the Study of Global Christianity located at Gordon-Conwell Theological Seminary.[6] This research group publishes the *World Christian Encyclopedia,* as well as the annual table of statistics for the *International Bulletin of Missionary Research.* While the Joshua Project focuses primarily on linguistics and ethnicity in determining the number of people groups, the center at Gordon-Conwell includes more factors, such as caste identity, historical enmity between groups, and other cultural and behavioral differences that may keep the group from being sufficiently unified to be the target of a single-people movement to Christ. This information is

---

4. http://www.joshuaproject.net.
5. http://imb.org/globalresearch/.
6. http://worldchristiandatabase.org/wcd/.

compiled in a database known as the World Christian Database (WCD). Currently, the WCD identifies 13,611 distinct people groups in the world.

Different Ways of Thinking About "People Groups"

Rather than viewing the different numbers of identifiable people groups that are cited as a problem to be solved, it is more helpful to understand the usefulness of different kinds of analysis regarding people groups. Those organizations committed to Bible translation are primarily interested in linguistic differences between people groups. Those involved in making broad, strategic decisions concerning church planting need the broadest analysis possible, which includes not only linguistics but also religious and cultural factors. Those involved in local evangelism need to know even more detailed information about the potential receptivity of various groups, not only to the gospel, but also to any message that might be brought by a near-culture neighbor. Thus, some analysis necessitates "lumping" many people groups together, whereas this is not helpful in other kinds of analysis. Rather than promoting one methodology over another, it is more helpful to see that each has its own usefulness, depending on the questions being asked or the nature of the strategic planning. These differences are reflected in widely used terms such as *megaclusters, sociolinguistic peoples,* and *unimax peoples.* Each of these three terms will be briefly explained.

MEGACLUSTERS

One method of analyzing people groups seeks to avoid what at times can be seemingly endless ways of dividing groups into smaller and smaller units. This method seeks to look at the world in terms of major ethnolinguistic clusters of peoples. The terminology varies among "megacluster," "affinity group," and "megapeople," but the controlling idea is to seek to analyze the remaining task of world missions in terms of the viability of the church within major blocks of peoples. The most basic grouping places all of the most unreached people groups into the following twelve blocks: African Sahel, Cushitic, Arab World, Iranian, Turkic, South Asian, Southeast Asian, Tibetan, East Asian, Malay, Eurasian, and Jewish.[7] It should be noted at the

---

7. Ralph Winter and Bruce Koch, "Finishing the Task: The Unreached Peoples Challenge," *International Journal of Mission Frontiers* (June 2000): 24. It should be noted that although Winter and Koch establish that there are twelve affinity groups, they mistakenly list only eleven, omitting "Jewish" from the list.

outset that these are ethnographic terms and have no necessary relationship to particular geographic regions of the world. These affinity blocks are
found in pockets in many urban cities in the West, for example, as well as
in their geographic sphere of origin. So, for example, Arab World Ministries is committed to promoting ministry among Arab peoples, regardless
of where they may be located in the world. This basic twelve-block analysis
can be helpful in identifying broad strategic commitments.

The Center for the Study of Global Christianity places the 13,611 identified people groups into 621 larger blocks known as "megapeoples." Even
though this is a much larger number than the twelve major blocks noted
earlier, this is more representative of how the term *megacluster* is generally
used. The World Christian Database defines a "megapeople" as a group in
excess of 100 million who share a common mother language.

There are three advantages to this kind of "big picture" analysis. First,
it helps to identify broad, global trends in receptivity or resistance to the
gospel. Second, it fosters collaboration among various missions agencies
that may be working in a related people group. Third, it is a way of acknowledging that if a people movement started in a related group, it has
important implications for near-culture peoples.

Related to this is the idea of focusing church-planting efforts on certain
"gateway cities." A gateway city is a large urban area with significant cultural
influence on a larger sphere of people groups or, alternatively, throughout the
entire megasphere. So, for example, if a people movement to Christ started
among Turkish Muslims in Istanbul, it could potentially have an enormous
impact on all Turkish people groups. The AD 2000 and Beyond movement
has identified one hundred gateway cities within the 10/40 Window. The
biblical support for a gateway city is drawn from the missionary practice of
the apostle Paul, which focused on key strategic cities, which, once reached,
would be better equipped to reach related people groups, rather than starting
new movements in every single people group.

ETHNOLINGUISTIC PEOPLES

A second method for classifying people groups is based on identifying
a group's own markers of cultural identity and distinctiveness. This approach acknowledges that even if a group shares a similar language (as in
the megacluster analysis), there may be historical or cultural barriers that
cause a group to see itself (or to be seen by others) as a separate group.

Thus, since the gospel tends to be most naturally shared within one's own cultural sphere (E-1 evangelism), it may be necessary to initiate hundreds of separate church-planting movements within a single megasphere. This requires a more detailed analysis of separate people groups.

UNIMAX PEOPLES

A third and final method for classifying people groups is called the "un-imax" approach. This method seeks to establish a comprehensive list of all people groups where no cultural or linguistic or social or ethnic barriers exist at all. This method maximizes the number of people groups. In India, for example, even if a group shares a common culture, nationality, ethnicity, and language, there may be important caste barriers that make it nearly impossible for a church-planting movement in the group to significantly influence others who may be a part of the same ethnolinguistic group. The major criticism of the unimax concept is that because it tends to focus on what divides people rather than on what unites them, it can foster an interminable fragmentation of smaller and smaller subgroupings. For example, based on the unimax concept, some have argued that prostitutes, truck drivers, people who live in nursing homes, or homosexuals should all be treated as distinct people groups.

While this kind of detailed focus would be problematic for a healthy church-planting strategy, it does highlight the realities of local evangelism. For example, one of my Indian students was instrumental in starting a church among a Dalit people of Saharanpur in North India. The people are in a caste known as Chamars. These Dalit (outcaste) peoples were mainly used in scavenging dead carcasses of animals. When they began to come to Christ, they were not able to effectively witness to people right in the same town where they lived, although they shared a similar ethnic and linguistic background. Rather, they traveled to a dozen other villages and shared the gospel with members of their own caste. This is an important evangelistic principle, which has given rise to what is known as the homogeneous unit (HU) principle.[8] The HU principle states that people tend to share the gospel with people who are part of their own group. There is a natural ten-

---

8. In my own missiology, I think it is helpful to distinguish between a HU (which is the smallest unit of natural evangelistic sharing) and a people group, which is the maximum size of a group before a significant barrier is reached that fundamentally hinders the communication of the gospel.

dency to not cross cultural boundaries with the gospel, as well as to resist receiving the gospel from someone from the other side of a cultural barrier. It should be noted that the HU principle, when properly understood, was never intended to be a prescriptive reality of what the church should look like but merely a descriptive reality for what most naturally happens.

All three of these approaches have helped to serve the larger cause of missions. The megacluster approach helps on the larger strategic level. The ethnolinguistic approach is particularly helpful in knowing where to initiate church-planting movements. The unimax approach is vital for understanding how evangelism often takes place once the church is started within a particular group.

What Is an "Unreached" People Group?

JOSHUA PROJECT'S PROGRESS SCALE

The Joshua Project defines an unreached people group by what is known as the "five-percent rule." The basic idea is that if the number of Christians within a people group is 5 percent or less, then it is considered unreached. This means that there must be more than 50,000 Christians for every million people in a given group for it to be classified as reached. However, the Joshua Project also insists that there must be at least 2 percent (20,000 per million) or more Christians who are identifiably "evangelical" within the 5 percent if the group is to be considered reached.[9] Eventually, the Joshua Project recognized that the terms *reached* and *unreached* did not provide sufficient clarity on the overall spectrum of the progress of a people group toward having a healthy, reproducing, viable church. The Joshua Project has adopted the following four positions on a "progress scale": (1) unreached/least reached, (2) formative/nominal, (3) emerging church, and (4) growing church. Each of these four positions is further divided into at least two stages, and each is marked by a number that is linked to each group (see figure 12.1). On the whole, the Joshua Project scale is helpful, particularly in highlighting that the progress of a people group from no knowledge of the

---

9. The Joshua Project defines an evangelical by four beliefs: 1. The Lord Jesus Christ is the sole source of salvation, which comes through faith in Him. 2. Personal faith and conversion with regeneration by the Holy Spirit. 3. A recognition of the inspired Word of God as the only basis for faith and living. 4. A commitment to biblical preaching and evangelism that brings others to faith in Christ.

gospel to a mature, reproducing church is a spectrum that transcends the simplistic categories of reached and unreached.

Figure 12.1. Joshua Project's Progress Scale		
Category	**Level**	**Level Description**
Unreached/Least Reached	1.0	Status data unavailable; in regions with no known access to the gospel
	1.1	Less than 5% Christian
	1.2	Less than 5% Christian, but evangelicals between 0.01% and 2%
Formative/Nominal Church	2.0	Status data unavailable; in regions that have access to the gospel
	2.1	Cultural/nominal "adherents" greater than 5%
	2.2	Cultural/nominal "adherents" greater than 5% plus evangelical presence between 0.01% and 2%
Emerging Church	3.1	Evangelical Christians between 2% and 5%; presence of evangelical churches
	3.2	Evangelical Christians greater than 5%; growing number of churches
Growing Church	4.1	Evangelical Christians greater than 10%; One evangelical per 10,000 people
	4.2	Evangelical Christians greater than 15%; One evangelical per 15,000 people

The most striking weakness of the Joshua Project taxonomy is linking the term *evangelical* so prominently to the long-term status of a viable church. The open acknowledgment of the presence of nominal or cultural Christianity is important, but it could be taken to imply that evangelicalism as a modern movement is the only viable or reproducible form of Christian faith. Since many other Christian movements affirm the historic Christian confessions and have demonstrated their commitment to nurturing and replicating faith, it might be more helpful to refer to "historic" or "orthodox" Christians and avoid the use of the term *evangelical,* especially since so many new emergent, Pentecostal, and charismatic groups do not consider themselves evangelical.

THE IMB'S GLOBAL STATUS OF EVANGELICAL CHRISTIANITY

The IMB of the Southern Baptist Church defines an unreached people group by using only the second part of the Joshua Project's criteria, namely, a group is considered unreached if less than 2 percent of the population are evangelical Christians.[10] This explains why using the Joshua Project's criteria, 41 percent of the world's people groups are unreached, whereas using the IMB criteria, 56 percent of the world's people groups are un-reached. The IMB makes a further distinction between an "unreached" group and an "unengaged" group. A group is considered "unengaged" if there is currently no church-planting effort in that particular people group.[11] Currently the IMB estimates that of the 6,512 unreached people groups, there are approximately 3,498 that remain unengaged.

The major strength of the IMB analysis is that it conceptualizes missions within the larger framework of helping to foster church-planting movements within new people groups.

Out of this commitment, the IMB has established the Global Status of Evangelical Christianity Model, commonly known as the GSEC Model. This model seeks to measure three factors: first, the extent to which a people group is evangelical; second, whether the group has access to the gospel; and, third, the status of church planting within the group.

The use of the word *access* in the IMB analysis is significant, because it highlights the important, though subtle, distinction between *response* to the gospel and *accessibility* to the gospel. Although the IMB uses the language of access, the taxonomies used by both the Joshua Project and the IMB are focused on *response* to the gospel, which is measured in specific percentages of Christians (or evangelical Christians), those who identify

---

10. The IMB Web site defines an evangelical Christian as follows: an evangelical Christian is a person who believes that Jesus Christ is the sole source of salvation through faith in Him, has personal faith and conversion with regeneration by the Holy Spirit, recognizes the inspired Word of God as the only basis for faith and Christian living, and is committed to biblical preaching and evangelism that brings others to faith in Jesus Christ.
11. The Joshua Project's list is linked with the Adopt-a-People Campaign, which enables Christian groups to "adopt" a people. However, the IMB does not consider a group "engaged" unless there is an actual church-planting effort at work among the people.

themselves as followers of Jesus Christ. However, access to the gospel does not necessarily translate into response to the gospel. This is particularly important when analyzing Christianity in regions of the world that have a history of Christendom. Accessibility to the gospel is quite high in Western Europe, for example, even though the percentage of those responding to the gospel is falling dramatically. Therefore, missiologists often make the distinction between "reached" and "evangelized." The term *evangelized* refers to access to the gospel, whereas the term *reached* refers to a certain percentage of a people group who have responded to the gospel.

The IMB, like the Joshua Project, has seen the need to further understand the overall resistance to or movement toward Christ within a group in a way that goes beyond simply using the language of "reached" or "unreached." Therefore, the Global Research Division of the IMB has established an eight-point scale to identify where people are in their movement from unreached to a viable, reproducing church. The numbers 0–3 are all subcategories of "unreached" peoples, and the numbers 4–6 are all subcategories of "reached." The last category refers to people groups where insufficient information is available to make a determination. The scale is known as the Global Status of Evangelical Christianity (see figure 12.2).

Figure 12.2. Global Status of Evangelical Christianity, IMB	
Status Level	**Description**
0	No evangelical Christians or churches or access to the gospel
1	Less than 2% evangelical, no active church-planting efforts in the previous two years, but with some access to the gospel
2	Less than 2% evangelical, but with a church-planting effort that has "engaged" the people group
3	Less than 2% evangelical, but with widespread church-planting efforts
4	Greater than or equal to 2% evangelical Christians
5	Greater than or equal to 5% evangelical Christians
6	Greater than or equal to 10% evangelical Christians
7	Unknown status of Christianity

THE WORLD CHRISTIAN DATABASE

The distinction between "reached" and "evangelized" is an integral feature of the World Christian Database (WCD), which does not describe people groups as either "reached" or "unreached" but focuses entirely on accessibility to the gospel, regardless of response. The WCD classifies the 3,611 people groups they identify into three broad categories known as "World A," World B," and "World C." World A refers to 223 megapeople groups with over one million members, of whom over 50 percent have no access to the gospel. World B refers to 138 megapeople groups, among whom evangelized persons number over 50 percent but Christians who have responded to the gospel is less than 60 percent. World C refers to 260 megapeople groups where over 60 percent of the population identify themselves as Christians. Essentially, World A refers to those with no access to the gospel, World B to those with access but have not responded to the gospel, and World C to those who have access and have responded to the gospel.

The WCD defines access as "an indigenous community of believing Christians with adequate numbers and resources to evangelize their own people group without needing outside, cross-cultural assistance."[12]

Further Development in Winter's Original Nomenclature

Ralph Winter's original E-1, E-2, and E-3 scale focused on measuring the cultural distance between the missionary and the targeted people group. In its original presentation, it did not specifically address the distinction between "reached" and "evangelized" or "unreached" and "unevangelized." However, the research that took place in the wake of the International Congress at Lausanne in 1974 stimulated two important developments in Winter's nomenclature. The first was the addition of a fourth category, known as E-0, to acknowledge the presence of nominal Christians who may already belong, in a formal sense, to the church but had not responded to the gospel. The second development was the acknowledgment that the cultural distance between the missionary and the target group was still being conceptualized. This assumed that the missionaries all shared a common cultural starting point and did not take into consideration that there might be viable churches that were

---

12. World Christian Database, glossary; www.worldchristiandatabase.org.

culturally nearer to the unreached group than the church represented by a Western missionary agent. This led to the development of the P-scale, representing the distance a given people group is from another viable church.[13] In short, the E-scale measures the cultural distance between the missionary and the targeted people group, whereas the P-scale measures the cultural distance between the targeted people group and the nearest viable church. The former starts with the missionary; the latter starts with the people group.

P-0 represents nominal Christians who identify themselves as Christians but may not have responded personally to the gospel message. P-1 represents non-Christians who do not consider themselves Christians but live in a people group that contains a viable church. P-0 and P-1, like E-0 and E-1, represent the evangelistic mandate, since no cross-cultural effort is required for a person to hear the gospel and become incorporated into an already present indigenous church. P-2 and P-3, like E-2 and E-3, represent increasing cultural distances. However, as noted, the P-scale measures the cultural distance from the people group to a viable church, whereas the E-scale measures the cultural distance from the missionary agent to the targeted people group, as follows (see figure 12.3).

Figure 12.3. Measuring Cultural Distance

E-Scale				P-Scale			
Missionary Agent		Church					
E-0	E-1	E-2	E-3	P-3	P-2	P-1	P-0
same culture		different culture	very different culture	very different culture	different culture	same culture	

There are several important advantages to the E-scale and P-scale over the taxonomies used by the Joshua Project, the IMB, or the WCD. The E/P-scale is the only scale that places cultural distance at the center

---

13. See Winter and Koch, "Finishing the Task: The Unreached Peoples Challenge," 15–24. Please note that after September 2006 and the vol. 23:3 issue, the journal known as the *International Journal of Frontier Missions* was renamed the *International Journal of Frontier Missiology*.

and interprets it in relation to a potential missionary movement, rather than only analyzing percentages of people who have responded to or have access to the gospel. The "unreached" and "unengaged" distinction used by the IMB shows whether a people group is "engaged" but is silent about both the cultural distance that separates the missionary agent from the "engaged" group and whether there are any culturally near Christians who might more effectively be mobilized as missionary agents. The second value of the E/P-scale is that it is better suited for global collaboration. For example, if the cultural distance in the E-scale is higher than the cultural distance in the P-scale, then there is inevitably a waste of effort that needs to be corrected. In other words, why should the Western church train and mobilize missionaries to cross large cultural gaps (e.g., E-3 situations), if the people group being targeted is culturally close to another viable church (e.g., a P-1 or P-2 situation)? Rather than sending pioneer missionaries from the West, it may be more strategic if missionaries were sent to mobilize a viable, but not yet mobilized, church that is culturally nearer the targeted group. Having spent twenty years helping to mobilize South Indian Christians who are culturally closer to North Indian Christians than I am, I know the value of the multiplication of laborers, which is possible when we think beyond the West as the sole source of missionary agents.[14]

If too many missionaries are being mobilized to reach those peoples who are already reached—that is, missionaries are doing cross-cultural evangelism when local evangelism could or should be mobilized—then large numbers of people will remain unreached, because, in effect, the missionaries are going to the wrong people groups. This is not merely a theoretical problem. This continues to be the dominant theme of Western missionary mobilization. In fact, Ralph Winter has argued that 97.6 percent of all missionaries are working among reached peoples and only 2.4 percent are working among the unreached.[15] This remains one of the most formidable challenges in contemporary missionary mobilization.

---

14. This should not be taken in a way that implies that there are not significant cultural, historical, and linguistic barriers between North and South Indians. The point is that the gap is less than a Western missionary would face. Furthermore, this underscores the truth that lies behind the Lausanne mission statement: "The whole church, bringing the whole gospel, to the whole world." Every church on every continent should be a sending and a receiving church.

15. Winter and Koch, "Finishing the Task: the Unreached Peoples Challenge," 22.

SHIFTS IN MOBILIZATION

One of the greatest needs in missions today is a fundamental shift in missionary mobilization. Therefore, this missiology proposes three principles that should guide missionary mobilization in the twenty-first century.

Principle #1: The Priority of the "Access" and "Viability" Criteria[16]

THE IMPORTANCE OF ACCESS AND VIABILITY

The most basic principle of missionary mobilization is that priority should be given to those people groups with no current access to the gospel. If we use a socio-linguistic definition of a people group, which is widely regarded as the best measurement for church-planting strategy, then there are between 6,512 and 6,748 people groups that currently have no access or insufficient access to the gospel. Approximately half of these unreached people groups have never even had the opportunity to respond to the gospel. Reaching these peoples is beset with significant cultural, political, geographic, and religious barriers. However, many of these barriers are significantly lowered if we think more globally about mobilization, rather than assuming that Western missionaries must be mobilized to reach the remaining unreached people groups.

Why is it that the church continues to ignore the issue of access in the mobilization of missionaries? There are two main reasons. First, there remains the lingering notion that stimulating evangelistic activity in as many places in the world as possible will inevitably (or at least potentially) lead to the evangelization of the world. However, what would happen if all the Christians in the world were mobilized as evangelists and they witnessed effectively to every single person they knew? The good news is that there would be over 3 billion new Christians, including over a billion nominal Christians and over 2 billion non-Christians who would come to Christ. However, there would still be nearly 2 billion (1.9 billion or 32.8 percent of the world) who would not have heard the good news of Jesus Christ.

This highlights the vital difference between evangelism and missions. Evangelism refers to same-culture witness and can reach only E-0 (P-0)

---

16. There are actually four criteria I use with churches and missions organizations to help evaluate their strategic investments of finances and personnel. The four are as follows: access, viability, reproducibility, and sustainability. However, in this chapter the latter two are incorporated in the way the first principle is developed.

and E-1 (P-1) groups. In contrast, missions refers to *cross-cultural witness* and is the only way to reach people who have no near-neighbor Christians who can evangelize them. Therefore, missionary mobilization should focus on sending missionaries either to where there are no Christians or to where the church is not yet viable. Instead, the Western church often raises enormous funds and invests in expensive training programs in order to equip someone to travel to a distant point of the globe only to work in areas where the church is already viable.

Second, it is important to establish at the outset that it is the responsibility of the local church, wherever it is in the world, to evangelize their near neighbors (E-0 and E-1). There remains the lingering notion in both the Western church, and throughout many parts of the Majority World, that evangelism *and* cross-cultural missions are the work of the Western church. This has resulted in thousands of Western missionaries being deployed to do work that should be done by local Christians. If there is no local church, then, obviously, evangelism is not possible; it is a viable mission field. However, once the local church is established and viable, then it is an improper use of resources to send cross-cultural missionaries to do their E-1 evangelism for them. This robs the local church of its responsibility to share the gospel and be faithful witnesses to Christ where they are. Sending cross-cultural missionaries to people groups where there is already a viable church promotes lethargy in the indigenous church and fosters unhealthy dependency relationships.

Once the global church becomes committed to prioritizing their mobilization to focus on those with no access, then it becomes crucial to determine when a church is viable and no longer requires missionary assistance. The Center for the Study of Global Christianity defines a viable church as "an ethnolinguistic group or indigenous community of believing Christians with adequate numbers and resources to evangelize their own people group without needing outside cross-cultural assistance."[17] But how do we know when a church has adequate "numbers" and "resources"? As noted earlier, the Joshua Project and the IMB both link viability to specific percentages of Christians. But is there any empirical evidence that once the aggregate number of Christians crosses the "reached" threshold of 5 percent (or 2 percent evangelical) that there is, therefore, a viable church? In

---

17. World Christian Database, glossary of terms, www.worldchristiandatabase.org.

the nineteenth century, Henry Venn spoke of the necessary "euthanasia" of missions, once an indigenous church had become self-supporting, self-governing, and self-propagating. Are the three-self criteria still a valid way to measure viability?

There is some merit to linking the 5 percent or 2 percent rule to identifiable markers such as Henry Venn's three-self criteria. The difficulty with the three-self criteria is that they tend to celebrate independence as a goal. If the tension is between "independence" and "dependence," then independence is a desirable goal. The goal of increasing independence is an appropriate goal for a young person who is growing up and needs to be encouraged to grow into his or her own distinctive identity. From a nineteenth-century perspective, when much of the Majority World church was, comparatively speaking, in its infancy, then the goal of independence seemed entirely appropriate. However, today there is a growing need for greater collaboration and mutual dependence on the strengths of each sector of the church. The three-self conceptualization of viability does not envision a healthy *inter*dependence between grown-up, mutually respectful, national bodies of believers. However, the growing maturity of the global church, and the need for the mutual edification of each part of the church, call for a new kind of measurement of church viability.

The "Three Belongings" Test of Access and Viability

The access and viability proposal this missiology advocates is called the "Three Belongings" test. It does not focus primarily on independence (as with the three-self model) but on identifying true signs of *belonging*. We begin by asking, "What does it mean to belong to, and participate as a vital member of, the body of Christ?" The three-self model envisions a time when local Christians are no longer dependent on other parts of the church. However, the biblical metaphor of the body of Christ emphasizes an ongoing *inter*dependence as a sign of health. No part of the body should ever say to any other part, "I have no need of you" (1 Cor. 12:21).

Ekklēsia Test

Therefore, the first test asks how many Christians in a particular people-group belong to *gathered expressions of the church*. This is the *ekklēsia test* of belonging. The "2-percent" or "5-percent" criterion of viability used by the IMB and the Joshua Project envisions a certain percentage of people within a people group who have experienced genuine conversion. However, these percentages do not necessarily require that these Christians be incorporated into an expression of the church. The *ekklēsia test* links conversion with community. It doesn't matter how many Christians may be present in a particular group; we must ask what percentage are active participants in the church. An active participant is defined as one who attends some gathered community of believers two or more times per month. If more than 96 percent of a people group are not active participants in a church, then this group should be considered unreached and placed on a high priority list for the development and implementation of a strategy that will result in effective church planting. There is no need to proceed with the other two tests of belonging.

This test has enormous implications for many Western European people groups that have a high percentage of nominal Christian affiliation but only a tiny percentage of Christians who regularly participate in any kind of gathered community of believers. The current methodology for identifying unreached people groups, whether the Joshua Project, the IMB, or the World Christian Database, all declare (statistically speaking) that Europe is the most Christian continent on the planet. It is clear that the time has come for an analysis that makes a distinction between Christian affiliation and actual participation in a gathered fellowship.

Of course, insistence on a "gathered fellowship" does not necessarily require visible churches with their own buildings and public visibility, as is customary in many parts of the world. Many of the early Christians met quietly in homes or even in the catacombs, but they understood that being a Christian did mean meeting regularly together. Christians have always gathered to celebrate in words, songs, and formal actions their common faith in Jesus Christ. There can be no viability without Christian community. Where two or more *are gathered*, Christ is present (Matt. 18:20). It is the presence of the risen Christ that ultimately attests to our viability, so it can never be enough simply to count individual Christians or, as in the case of many parts of Western Europe, to point to vast numbers of nominal Christians as a testimony that a people group is "reached."

Apostolic Test

The second test of belonging probes further into what it means to belong to Christ. It is not only important that new believers be connected to a fellowship of other Christians; it is also important that the church itself remains connected to the apostolic message. Thus, this second test is known as the *apostolic test*. Do the churches that are present in the people group affirm and proclaim historic Christian orthodoxy? This is a broad doctrinal test to make certain that if a person is united with a church there can be a reasonable expectation that the person will be nurtured within a community that is faithful to Christ and the Christian gospel. While being faithful to Christ is always *more* than any doctrinal expression, it is certainly never *less* than that.

Two of the most faithful doctrinal tests can be found in the Apostles' and the Nicene Creeds. The advantage of these creeds is twofold. First, they provide succinct summaries of the substance of the Christian faith. Second, the Apostles' and Nicene Creeds historically have been affirmed by every major branch of the Christian church.[18] This allows for the deepest kind of Christian identity, which resonates throughout the history of the church, both East and West, while at the same time avoiding Christian sectarianism and a competitive, denominationally oriented witness.[19] If 4 percent or more of the entire population of a people group belong to churches that affirm historic Christian orthodoxy, then that group should no longer be regarded as unreached. The focus should shift to the mobilization of those Christians for (what is for them) E-1 evangelism.

Some argue that these creedal affirmations are products of Western reflection and are increasingly irrelevant in this new era of global Christianity. However, all Christians in all cultures and throughout every age are beneficiaries of the work and reflection done by our brothers and sisters who have preceded us. Mark Hatcher, in his work among Korean Christians, has demonstrated how the ancient creeds of the church can become very meaningful if explored in the context of Bible study and communicated with the use of concrete images and narrative structures.[20] The creeds continue to provide a rich resource for a deeper ecumenism, which is fully orthodox while at the same time transcends denominational sectarianism.

---

18. I am referring to the earliest Nicene Creed, as formulated in 325.
19. For more on this, see my "The Church: What Are Its Boundaries?" *American Baptist Evangelicals Journal* 9, nos. 1–2 (March and June 2001): 3–9.
20. Mark J. Hatcher, "Contextualizing the Creed Through Structured Bible Study," *Missiology: An International Review* 26, no. 3 (July 1998): 315–28. See also Chrisopher R. Seitz, ed., *Nicene Christianity: The Future for a New Ecumenism* (Grand Rapids: Brazos, 2001).

Reproducibility Test

The third and final test of belonging examines the vibrancy of the church. There are churches that affirm the right doctrines in a formal sense but whose level of Christian outreach and vibrancy are quite low. One of the signs of the health and vibrancy of any living organism is its reproducibility. This third test is the *reproducibility test*. Is the church growing and reproducing itself through witness and evangelism? All churches, even vibrant ones, do not grow at the same pace, but all should show signs of growth and reproducibility. If no new church plants have occurred in a people group over a five-year period, even if the number of Christians in the people group is as high as 10 percent, it is a clear sign that even though the people group is reached, the church is still not yet viable and needs further assistance, discipleship, or training.

These three tests, the *ekklēsia*, the apostolic, and the reproducibility tests, together demonstrate what it means to belong to Christ and be a full and vibrant member of His body.

Principle #2: The Priority of Church Planting

The second major principle of missionary mobilization is the prioritization of church planting in all mission strategy. We already have seen how this begins with our analysis of the world in terms of access to the *church* and the viability of the *church*, rather than simply tallying up the aggregate numbers of believers. First, and more fundamentally, the emphasis on church planting requires a shift in the way in which missions, and the goal of missions, is broadly conceptualized.

Protestant theology has tended to equate the doctrine of salvation with the doctrine of justification. Biblically, the doctrine of salvation does include justification, but it also includes the doctrines of sanctification and our final glorification.[21] This is why Scripture speaks of salvation in all three tenses: you *were* saved (justification), you are *being* saved (sanctification), and you *will be* saved (glorification).[22] A theological reductionism that equates salvation with justification is so common in popular Protestant writings that we

---

21. Louis Berkhof, for example, states, "God does not impart the fullness of His salvation to the sinner in a single act." It is only by distinguishing between God's "judicial" acts and His "recreative" acts that we can properly discuss the fullness of God's plan of salvation for us. Louis Berkhof, *Systematic Theology* (Grand Rapids: Eerdmans, 1941), 416.
22. See, for example, Ephesians. 2:5; 1 Corinthians 1:18; 3:15.

often fail to recognize how this influences our discussions regarding missionary work. For example, it often gives rise to a minimalistic, individualistic emphasis, which downplays the role of the church in the final goal of missions. We often are preoccupied with what is the absolute bottom-line minimum an individual has to know or believe in order to be justified. Of course, when the issue is framed in this way, very little is required. After all, the thief on the cross had no opportunity to be a part of any local fellowship of believers, and his theological knowledge must have been quite low. What about the Philippian jailer or Lydia and her household? I think everyone can agree, as Dean Gilliland has correctly pointed out, that the Holy Spirit can still be active "in poorly informed" believers.[23] The emphasis on numerical growth in evangelism and missions has tended to focus on a minimalistic view of salvation, rather than the long-term viabililty and reproducibility of the church. The goal of missions should always be conceptualized as a viable, reproducible community of believers, regardless of the particular emphases of the work to which we are called.

Second, a focus on church planting provides a necessary corrective to popular missions practice, which has tended to emphasize the faith of the individual rather than the collective faith of the community of believers. We are much more comfortable speaking about the faith of *individuals* than we are about the faith of the *church*. When Jude says, "I had to write and urge you to contend for the faith that was once for all entrusted to the saints" (Jude 3), both the words "you" and "saints" are in the plural. In that great chapter on the resurrection in 1 Corinthians, Paul declares, "This is what we preach, and this is what you (plural) believed" (1 Cor. 15:11). Paul saw his preaching in continuity with the apostolic preaching (*we* preach), and he declares this to the church (you, plural). It is important to recognize that Paul says "this is what you believed," even though the context of the passage reveals that there were *individuals* in the church who did not, at least on this point, believe along with the church. The way the question is framed tends to produce a particular answer. If you ask, "What is the minimal core confession of the *church* regarding salvation?" then the bar is raised, and we find the church far more articulate about the core of salvific faith.

---

23. Dean Gilliland, "Context Is Critical in 'Islampur' Case," *Evangelical Missions Quarterly* 34, no. 4 (October 1998): 417.

As noted earlier, the Apostles' Creed and the Nicene Creed are examples of the early church's attempt to put down into a short list the most basic theological propositions that unite the *church* in a common faith. The church did this even though they also must have realized, as we do today, that there are many justified *individuals* who neither understand, nor fully believe, every single article of faith in these documents. The gap between the faith of the historic church and the faith of many of the individuals in the church is why these truths are confessed week after week in the churches. It is essential that the faith of the church be reinforced on all those who claim to be followers of Christ.

Third, a focus on church planting helps us to avoid the modern trap of putting the "personal" and the "propositional" at odds with one another. For example, some want to emphasize that a personal relationship with Jesus Christ is all that matters; others want to make sure that certain historic propositions are affirmed. This latter group is accused of placing too much emphasis on defending the written words of Scripture and certain doctrinal formulations (rather than Jesus Christ). They are asked, "What is the value of confessing a mountain of creeds and doctrinal formulations if, at root, we do not have a personal relationship with Jesus Christ?" They, in turn, respond by insisting that the only way we know anything about God that is distinctively and properly called *Christian* is because God has spoken to humanity in a free act of self-disclosure. In obedience to this revelation, God's servants have faithfully recorded these words in the Bible. Without the Bible, they argue, how can we distinguish between the personal faith of a Muslim and the personal faith of a Christian?

Thus, we are put in the unenviable position of being forced to choose between God revealing Himself and God revealing truths about Himself. The missionary movement is one of the most promising ways in which the doctrines of soteriology and ecclesiology can be properly brought together. The further the doctrine of salvation is allowed to drift away from the church toward individualism, the more likely a missions organization will downplay the particulars of specific doctrinal formulations, because the focus is on the individual's personal relationship with Christ. Also, it is far more likely that this organization will tend to equate the doctrine of salvation with the doctrine of justification. On the other hand, the closer the doctrine of salvation is tethered to the life of the church through time (history) and space (around the world), the more likely it is that a missions organization will emphasize our common faith and the importance of even a brand-new believer realizing the faith he or she is being united with. A new convert not only *has* faith; he or she is brought *into* a common faith.

Missionary strategy today must have a more long-term view of salvation, even while emphasizing the importance of the initial acts of repentance and conversion. It is also important to remember that even if a new convert is the only known Christian in a particular region or village, the believer should be made to understand from the outset his or her connection to other Christians, or followers of Jesus, who share a common faith.[24]

Finally, it is important to recognize that the focus on church planting should not be construed in a way that downplays or marginalizes ministries devoted to social action, relief and development, or justice. On the contrary, the calling of the church is to bear witness to the inbreaking of God's reign in every segment of life and culture. It is often overlooked that the *church* is called to bear witness to these new realties. Therefore, church planting is the most effective long-term strategy for raising up an *indigenous witness* for the inbreaking of God's reign. If, for example, we are burdened by the vast number of homeless or orphaned children in Delhi or Bangkok, then one of the most effective long-term solutions is to establish indigenous churches in Delhi and Bangkok. I have seen this process work quite well in India, where church plants very quickly began to see opportunities all around them to bear witness to Christ. I have seen very new church plants in India move within a few short years to the establishment of orphanages, schools, sewing centers, literacy instruction, and relief work.

Principle #3: *The Priority of Collaboration with the Global Church*
The third and final priority that will influence missions mobilization in the twenty-first century is collaboration with the global church. Jesus Himself has summoned the church to be His body in the world, and only the global church can fully reflect the embodiment of the Incarnation.

---

24. This explains why parachurch organizations that focus on *evangelism* often have very different views on this issue compared to church-planting organizations. This is clearly seen, for example, in the article by David Garrison, entitled, "Church Planting Movements vs. Insider Movements," which points out the need to connect the evangelistic energy of parachurch sodalities with new dynamic models of church planting. See David Garrison, "Church Planting Movements vs. Insider Movements: Missiological Realities vs. Mythiological Speculations," International Journal of Frontier Missions 21, no. 4 (Winter 2004): 151–54.

This theme will be explored by first placing the twenty-first century in a larger historical context.

HISTORICAL CONTEXT

The nineteenth-century missionary movement can be summarized as a "mission to the world." The emphasis was the mobilization of Western missionaries to cross geographic boundaries outside of the Western world in order to plant churches and to bear witness to Christ. The world outside the West was conceptualized primarily as a world without Christians. There were very few Christians or churches in the Majority World with which one could collaborate in a common commitment to evangelism and church planting.

The twentieth-century missionary movement witnessed the dramatic emergence of the Majority World church. It was during the twentieth century that the number of Christians in the Majority World surpassed the number in the traditional Christian heartlands of the West. Missionary bodies increasingly became aware that they had not only a mission to the "world" but also a mission to the wider global church. The majority of twentieth-century missionary activity was focused on strengthening the national churches throughout the Majority World. This can be summarized as a "mission to the church." As we saw in chapter 1, in the latter half of the twentieth century, many mainline churches declared a moratorium on missions and believed that the remaining work could be done by the national churches.

Ralph Winter's address on the vast numbers of hidden, unreached people groups helped to stimulate a fresh wave of missionary work among unreached people groups in the last quarter of the century. This was an important reminder that a "mission-to-the-church" paradigm must be seen to build up and supplement, not replace, a "mission-to-the-world" paradigm. Indeed, the important transition from conceptualizing missions as a broad, geographic challenge to seeing the full complexities of the ethnic challenge allows the "mission to the world" and the "mission to the church" to flourish. Once we conceptualize that missions is about *peoples*, not *places*, then an unreached people group may exist in close proximity to near-culture viable churches in the same geographic region. This is increasingly important in identifying church-planting opportunities among immigrant communities in urban areas around the world.

TWENTY-FIRST-CENTURY STRATEGY

The twenty-first-century missionary movement must recognize, not only the presence of Majority World Christians and the dramatic rise of indigenous churches, but also the emergence of multiple missionary-sending movements from various sectors of the Majority World. Missions organizations must develop collaborative relationships with other mission-sending bodies around the world as we work together toward the goal of viable, reproducing churches in every people group in the world. This can be summarized as "mission to mission."[25] Most missionaries are now sent by churches or mission organizations located in the Majority World. Thus, twenty-first-century strategy requires a deep commitment to global collaboration. There are several particular ways this will be important.

First, missionary strategy will increasingly discover that for a Western missionary, his or her E-scale number will be higher than the P-scale number of the targeted group. Therefore, this will require greater efforts in collaborating with viable churches that are culturally and linguistically closer to the targeted group.

Second, the new global realities highlight the need to "think outside the box" when it comes to the emphasis on the 10/40 window. The call for Western churches to prioritize the sending of missionaries to the peoples of the 10/40 window still perceives Western agents as the world's missionaries. However, in the twenty-first-century one of the most strategic ways to reach Muslims in North Africa (who live in the 10/40 Window) may be to relocate to Brazil (outside the 10/40 Window) to help train Brazilian missionaries who can, in turn, relocate into the Islamic world as missionaries.

Third, Western denominationally based, mission organizations will have to develop a missionary vision that extends beyond the identity of their particular denominational body. The larger trend will be toward looser, strategic relationships with indigenous church movements. Churches in the West will need to learn to work cooperatively to help encourage and stimulate church-planting movements that do not have any formal

---

25. I am grateful to Richard Showalter, my former student and currently president of Eastern Mennonite Missions, for the helpful phrases "mission to the world," "mission to the church," and "mission to mission," as a way of conceptualizing changes. See Richard Showalter, "Bands and Bonds: Authentic Missionary Practice for the Twenty-First Century" (D.Min. diss., Gordon-Conwell Theological Seminary, 2004).

connection with any Western denomination. More importantly, the vast majority of missionary activity will be *initiated* by movements within the Majority World. In the past the word *partnership* generally meant a missionary initiative from the Western world, which is planned and financed by the West but uses national workers in the implementation of the plan. This frequently turned out to be more of a *sponsorship model* than a true *partnership model*. However, with the dramatic rise of the global church, as well as the increasing vitality of many economies in the Majority World, the twenty-first century promises to be more profoundly collaborative. Churches from around the world will be taking the initiative in missionary planning and global engagement.

DOES COLLABORATION FOSTER DEPENDENCY?

A call for greater, global collaboration is seen by some as an unwarranted extension of the long and painful history of the mission churches developing an unhealthy dependency upon the Western church for financial resources. Frequently, it is those who continue to embrace the "three-self" benchmarks of indigenization (which conceptualizes healthy churches as those that are completely independent from the "mother" church) who find the emphasis on collaboration disturbing. Thus, one must ask, "Does collaboration foster unhealthy dependency?"

Before we address that question, it is important to candidly acknowledge that unhealthy dependency relationships often have occurred between the younger and the more established churches. Glenn Schwartz, director of World Mission Associates, has written extensively about the debilitating effects of unhealthy dependency. In his book, *When Charity Destroys Dignity*, Schwartz documents several examples of unhealthy dependency relationships that have developed between churches in East Africa and well-meaning churches in the West who, through generosity, were unknowingly causing long-term harm to the very churches in Africa they were seeking to help.[26] Similar concerns have been raised by Jonathan Bonk in his *Missions and Money*, which introduced the phrase "doing harm by doing good" into the missionary lexicon.[27]

---

26. Glenn J. Schwartz, *When Charity Destroys Dignity: Overcoming Unhealthy Dependency in the Christian Movement* (Lancaster, PA: World Mission Associates, 2007).
27. Jonathan J. Bonk, *Missions and Money: Revised and Expanded* (Maryknoll, NY: Orbis, 2006).

However, there are also numerous examples of how generous financial investments from the Western world have borne long-term fruit on the mission field, stimulating and supporting remarkable, healthy ministries. After Bosnia was devastated by the Serbs in the 1990s, the generosity of Western Christians helped to rebuild churches and Bible schools and greatly helped the growth and leadership development of the small but growing national church in Bosnia. One instrumental leader who helped to raise money to assist the Bosnian church during those war-torn years is John Rowell, who has documented his experience in his book, *Magnify Your Vision for the Small Church*. More recently, Rowell has written *To Give or Not to Give*, which sets forth his understanding of how Western funds can be used strategically to promote effective missions work. Rather than seeing Western funding as a dependency problem, Rowell calls for a missiological "Marshall Plan," which dramatically increases the amount of money given by Western churches to support the work of global missions around the world.[28]

The fact that Glenn Schwartz and John Rowell could both produce major books on the same subject in the same year and come to two completely opposite conclusions demonstrates the complex and contextual nature of each situation. There is a big difference between a missionary whose primary context is a stable, even if poor, country and one serving in a country that has been completely devastated by war. Sometimes the differences have to do with the people themselves. Having been intimately involved with ministries in North India for over twenty years, I have observed both unhealthy dependency as well as strategic synergy. Over the years I have developed a few guiding principles that have helped to maximize strategic synergy and minimize unhealthy dependency when a Western church or missions organization is involved financially in a poorer country.

The first principle is to *develop economically sustainable mission structures*. Jonathan Bonk has observed that in the first twenty centuries of Christian missions the overwhelming trend is that typically the gospel has flowed from people with greater economic means to those with lesser economic means. Although this trend is finally changing with the retreat of Christianity in the West and the rise of Majority World missionaries,

---

28. John Rowell, *To Give or Not to Give* (Tyrone, GA: Authentic, 2007).

this has been the dominant historical pattern.[29] The temptation is to build organizations and structures that are consistent with the home culture and therefore are unsustainable without the perpetual investment of Western funding. It is unethical to establish an elaborate, administratively top-heavy organization with buildings and staffing that are expensive to maintain and then expect the local Christians to pick up the full tab once it is established. Instead, everything should be organized and constructed from the start in a way that reflects indigenous patterns of long-term sustainability.

The second principle is to *discern the difference between the kind of investments that often produce dependency and those that do not.* In my observation, there is a major difference between Western involvement in supporting a local church and in supporting a training center such as a Bible college or seminary. I have been involved in theological education for many years, as a student, a teacher, and an administrator, in both India and North America. Very few of the 253 schools accredited by the Association of Theological Schools (ATS) could be considered self-supporting. One of the main functions of a college or seminary president is to strengthen *external* constituencies through vigorous fund-raising. Even large seminaries cannot sustain themselves through tuition and the yields gained from their modest endowments. Residential theological education is expensive. If Western seminaries are not self-supporting, then why should we expect seminaries or Bible colleges in economically developing countries to be self-supporting? My experience has been that investments in these kinds of institutions often can be healthy and strategic.

In contrast, I have found that Western financial support of *local churches*, whether it be helping to meet the monthly budget or supporting the pastor's monthly salary, almost always has a deleterious effect on the long-term health of the church. Similar problems exist in some of the programs that encourage ongoing individual child sponsorship from a distant, faceless donor, which is often destructive to the normal responsibilities of families, relatives, and local communities. One of Glenn Schwartz's cardinal rules for avoiding dependency is that no foreign funds be used in

---

29. Bonk, *Missions and Money: Revised and Expanded*, 82. For further reflection on case studies of mission initiative from the "margins" of the Global South, see Samuel Escobar, "Mission from the Margins to the Margins: Two Case Studies from Latin America," *Missiology: An International Review* 26, no. 1 (January 1998): 87–95.

the development or sustenance of local churches.[30] From my perspective, this is wise counsel. Nothing drains a church's incentive to give than the knowledge that some outside source is paying the bills. Nothing robs a church of its dignity and sense of indigenous ownership of a ministry than the knowledge that some outside source is paying the bills. It is important that pastors all over the world teach their congregations about the importance of stewardship and sacrificial giving, rather than allow a culture of dependence on outside help to gain a footing.

Another important difference I have observed is between a single offering or short-term support in response to a *particular crisis* and long-term support for the normal work and ministry of the church. If our brothers and sisters in another part of the world have experienced a famine or an earthquake or the devastation of war, it is entirely appropriate to extend financial support. The apostle Paul raised money from the church in Corinth to help the Christians in Jerusalem, who were suffering from a famine. Even Glenn Schwartz, the leading voice against dependency, approvingly cites the gift of an East African church to the home mission in Scotland when they became aware of a surge in homeless children in Edinburgh, Scotland. Schwartz does not express concern that this gift may create an unhealthy dependence of the Church of Scotland on the Presbyterian Church in East Africa. A onetime gift of generosity to meet specific, short-term needs is often a sign of a healthy sense of solidarity with the worldwide church, not a sign of an unhealthy dependency relationship.

While the dangers of dependence are genuine, the entire discussion often is framed in a way that presupposes the dominance of the Western church as the "mother" church who is concerned that her children grow up to be mature, independent adults. In today's global context, interdependence and collaboration are the hallmarks of twenty-first-century missions. It is also important to recognize that there are different kinds of abundance, as well as different kinds of scarcity, throughout the global church. Whereas one part of the body may be rich in *financial* resources, another part may be rich with a sense of *community*. Each part of the body has gifts and resources that should be freely shared with other members of the body. Western Christians desperately need to realize how much we

---

30. Schwartz, *When Charity Destroys Dignity*, 28.

need the generosity of the global church. We need to be refreshed by their evangelistic fervor, their personal piety, and their vision for transformation. The Majority World can benefit from the organizational, educational, and financial resources we have, if they are invested wisely and in a true spirit of partnership and global collaboration. While both the Western church and the Majority World church mutually bless one another, I cannot help but think that the oxygen-deprived Western church has the most to gain. What we do not want to encourage are global ecclesiastical silos that are not encouraged to enrich one another through sharing the gifts God has given to each of us according to His pleasure and purpose. If mature, godly discernment is exercised, global collaboration can flourish without creating unwanted and unhealthy dependency relationships.

CONCLUSION

The Incarnation makes the good news of God's redemptive love accessible. God, in Christ, relocates into our frame of reference and makes the in-breaking of God's rule intelligible in culturally understandable ways, summoning all cultures to the new realities of the kingdom of God. The themes of this chapter have been raised in order to help the church to better reflect the Incarnation as we seek to make the gospel accessible to every people group and as we nurture viable, reproducing churches in every people group in the world.

— 13 —

Reflecting the Incarnation
in Holistic Missions

PHILIP YANCEY, IN HIS BEST-SELLING BOOK *The Jesus I Never Knew*, chronicles his slow realization that the Jesus he met in Sunday school was not the same Jesus he met in the pages of the New Testament. Yancey recalls a poster of Jesus displayed on the wall of his Sunday school class, which portrayed Jesus serenely standing in a pastoral setting in the midst of children with a small, sleeping lamb in His arms.[1] I too vividly remember that very picture of Jesus, as it must have been displayed on the walls of Sunday schools across the country. The Jesus portrayed in Sunday school and children's sermons is often, Yancey comments, "a Mister Rogers before the age of children's television."[2] He is kind, gentle, reassuring, otherworldly, and, most of all, very nice. However, at some point it dawned on Yancey that no government in the world would execute Mister Rogers.

During the turbulent 60s and 70s there were other, more shocking, posters of Jesus that emerged, including Jesus as a revolutionary, holding an AK-47, or as a long-haired antiestablishment figure standing in opposition to corrupt governments. Certainly these posters simultaneously remind us of both the compelling complexity of Jesus Christ and the ongoing temptation to domesticate the Jesus of the New Testament, reshaping Him

---

1. Philip Yancey, *The Jesus I Never Knew* (Grand Rapids: Zondervan, 1995), 13.
2. Ibid.

into our image. In recent years, Dan Brown's *The Da Vinci Code* sought to convey that the Jesus who has been proclaimed by Christians is nothing more than a Jesus who has been deceitfully marketed by the Roman Catholic Church to protect the power and influence of the church. For Brown, Jesus is nothing more than a product of religious consciousness. It seems that the crucified and risen Christ of history continues to be a foolish scandal and a "stumbling block" to those who find their "nice" or "regal" or "stained-glass" Jesus contradicted by the vulnerability of the Crucifixion, the boldness of His claims, or the divisive and prophetic figure portrayed by the actual eye and ear witnesses of His life and ministry, as recorded in the New Testament.

THE "EVANGELISM" VERSUS "SOCIAL ACTION" DEBATE

Two Paradigms

Few areas of contemporary Christianity have reflected the tension between a domesticated Christ of our imaginations and the actual Jesus of the New Testament than the debate about the relationship between "evangelism" and "social action." Starkly put, the word *evangelism* in this context refers to the proclamation of the good news that through the death and resurrection of Jesus Christ sinful people can be forgiven and reconciled to God. Thus, the church's primary mission is to proclaim this good news, calling people to repentance and personal faith in Jesus Christ. An obvious biblical example of this is found in the well-known sermon by Peter on the Day of Pentecost recorded in Acts. Peter proclaimed the centrality of Jesus' death and resurrection to a large gathering in Jerusalem. Upon hearing this good news, Acts records that the people were "cut to the heart" and asked what they should do. Peter replied, "Repent and be baptized, every one of you, in the name of Jesus Christ for the forgiveness of sins" (Acts 2:38). In response, about three thousand people repented, were baptized, and became Christians. This account, along with similar passages, represents the classic "evangelistic paradigm." For many, it is similar to one of the large evangelistic campaigns of Billy Graham, who for sixty years faithfully stood before crowds all over the world, proclaimed the good news of Jesus Christ, called people to repentance, and witnessed an overwhelming response not unlike what took place after Peter's sermon recorded in Acts.

This evangelistic paradigm need not be expressed only in large, formal gatherings. It could be reflected in sharing the gospel with a friend over a cup of tea or during an Alpha course.[3]

The phrase *social action* refers to the church's cultural mandate to express God's love practically through tangible acts of compassion and justice for the poor, the homeless, the sick, and the disenfranchised. The resulting "social action/social justice paradigm" is a powerful testimony of God's love and compassion for the whole person. A frequently quoted passage in support of the social action paradigm is the parable of the sheep and the goats told by Jesus and recorded in Matthew 25. The parable portrays Jesus as the exalted "Son of Man" of Daniel's prophetic vision, who judges the nations. At the final judgment, Jesus receives those who were engaged in social action in His name. He declares, "For I was hungry and you gave me something to eat, I was thirsty and you gave me something to drink, I was a stranger and you invited me in, I needed clothes and you clothed me, I was sick and you looked after me, I was in prison and you came to visit me" (Matt. 25:35–36). Those Jesus commends do not recall seeing Jesus hungry, or thirsty, or in prison, and so on. However, Jesus replies that "whatever you did for one of the least of these brothers of mine, you did for me" (25:40).[4] The parable highlights the vital importance of social compassion and clearly makes the connection between our eschatological salvation and the practical ways we have loved and served Jesus through our service to a needy world. Evangelical writer Jim Wallis recalls a beautiful prayer offered by an elderly African-American woman just before the start of a new day at a food kitchen in a poverty-stricken region of Washington, D.C. With a long line of homeless and needy people lined up outside waiting to come in, she prayed, "Lord, we know that you'll be comin' through this line today. So help us to treat you well."[5]

For many, Mother Teresa's lifelong work among the poor and homeless on the streets of Calcutta epitomizes the social action/social justice

---

3. Alpha refers to a popular ten-week course that introduces people to the Christian faith in a relaxed, relational atmosphere. Alpha was founded by Charles Marnham in London and eventually spread to over 150 countries. Over 11 million people have participated in Alpha courses around the world.
4. The identification between how we treat the poor and our attitude toward God is an Old Testament theme. Proverbs 17:5 says, "He who mocks the poor insults his Maker" (RSV). Conversely, "He who is kind to the needy honors [God]" (Prov. 14:31 RSV). This theme is also prominent throughout the Old Testament Law.
5. Jim Wallis, *The Soul of Politics* (New York: Harvest Books, 1995), 59.

paradigm. Some who emphasize the importance of social action point out the need to not only compassionately respond to the innumerable manifestations of human need in the world, such as hunger and homelessness, but also to address the structural, root causes, which often conspire to disenfranchise the most vulnerable in society. This has led to the distinction between "relief" work and "development" work. The term *relief* refers to immediate assistance to those in need, whereas *development* focuses on the larger, structural and systemic causes of poverty. Relief is generally perceived as a short-term provision to victims in an acute state of crisis who cannot wait until the larger, structural issues are addressed. In contrast, development is a more lengthy process that enables chronically vulnerable individuals, households, and communities to achieve greater self-reliance in meeting their own needs. This might be achieved, for example, through better investments of capital into a community, which expands productivity, or through changing an economic, political, or social policy that is recognized as detrimental to the poor and powerless. Because relief work primarily focuses on "microsolutions," it is most often found in the presence of those who are most needy—helping children orphaned by the AIDS pandemic, serving in a soup kitchen in an inner-city ghetto, or visiting prisoners in a local prison. Because development work primarily focuses on "macrosolutions," it is most often seen in the presence of the most powerful in society—working with politicians and policy makers, raising awareness among powerful lobbyists, preparing position papers for Washington "think tanks," meeting with officials from the World Bank, and so forth. In practice, many organizations are committed to both and devote considerable resources to addressing both short-term relief and long-term development.[6]

Christian Angst About Evangelism and Social Action

A historical view of the Christian church reveals that Roman Catholics, Anglicans, Orthodox, Protestants, Pentecostals, and independent indigenous churches have all demonstrated, in a wide variety of ways, their commitment to *both* evangelism and social action.[7] It is true that

---

6. An examination of the membership of the Association of Evangelical Relief and Development Organizations (www.aerdo.net) reveals the commitment to both relief and development.

7. Pentecostalism is sometimes portrayed as committed to aggressive evangelism while lacking a theology of social concern. However, even though a theology of social action that is distinctively

evangelical, Pentecostal, and independent Christians are sometimes caricatured as being committed to *only* evangelism, and other Christian bodies are caricatured as being committed *only* to justice and social action. However, the difference is often one of emphasis and definition of what it means to evangelize, rather than discreet spheres of commitment. The tension between the two is perhaps most profoundly observed among evangelical Christians, but the tension is present throughout the church around the world and across history. For the sake of clarity, this chapter will focus on how the tension has manifested itself among evangelicals, but similar observations could be made about other branches of the global church.

It is difficult to find evangelicals who do not acknowledge the importance of social action. Evangelical Christians have a long and distinguished record of establishing schools, hospitals, orphanages, soup kitchens, and so forth. Evangelicals also have been at the forefront of major structural changes in society, which resulted in the establishment of child labor laws and the abolition of slavery. Evangelicals, along with Roman Catholics and others, continue to speak out today against legislation that promotes a culture of death due to the unrestricted availability of abortion.

An examination of signed evangelical statements regarding the importance of social action can be found in the 1966 Wheaton Declaration and the World Congress on Evangelism in Berlin, also in 1966, as well as the Chicago Declaration of Evangelical Social Concern in 1973 and the 1974 Lausanne Covenant put out by the International Congress on World Evangelization. The Lausanne gathering was intended to be a focus on the *how* of global evangelism, but voices from the Majority World reminded the congress that the more profound question was answering *what* evangelism entailed, namely, the need to address not merely the spiritual condition of the world but also the social and political realities that trapped people in poverty and oppression. The result was a more profound understanding of the necessity for an evangelical commitment to social action. For example, article five of the Lausanne Covenant is dedicated solely to this issue. It is representative of the earlier statements and, for those who

---

Pentecostal in its orientation has emerged only in recent years, Pentecostals have generally had an impressive commitment to the poor and disenfranchised. See Veli-Matti Karkkainen, "Are Pentecostals Oblivious to Social Justice? Theological and Ecumenical Perspectives," *Missiology: An International Review* 29, no. 4 (October 2001): 417–31.

may not be familiar with this portion of the Lausanne Covenant, deserves to be quoted in full.

> We affirm that God is both the Creator and the Judge of all men. We therefore should share his concern for justice and reconciliation throughout human society and for the liberation of men and women from every kind of oppression. Because men and women are made in the image of God, every person, regardless of race, religion, colour, culture, class, sex or age, has an intrinsic dignity because of which he or she should be respected and served, not exploited. Here too we express penitence both for our neglect and for having sometimes regarded evangelism and social concern as mutually exclusive. Although reconciliation with other people is not reconciliation with God, nor is social action evangelism, nor is political liberation salvation, nevertheless we affirm that evangelism and socio-political involvement are both part of our Christian duty. For both are necessary expressions of our doctrines of God and man, our love for our neighbour and our obedience to Jesus Christ. The message of salvation implies also a message of judgment upon every form of alienation, oppression and discrimination, and we should not be afraid to denounce evil and injustice wherever they exist. When people receive Christ they are born again into his kingdom and must seek not only to exhibit but also to spread its righteousness in the midst of an unrighteous world. The salvation we claim should be transforming us in the totality of our personal and social responsibilities. Faith without works is dead.[8]

There are three key features of this statement that deserve to be highlighted. First, it properly places social action in a theological context, linking it to the doctrines of God, reconciliation, righteousness, and the fact that all men and women are created in the image of God. Second, the statement affirms that evangelism and social action are not "mutually exclusive," thereby laying the groundwork for an integrated view of how the person and work of Christ are reflected in the life and witness of the church.

---

8. The Lausanne Covenant, http://www.lausanne.org/lausanne-1974/lausanne-covenant.html (accessed November 10, 2008).

Finally, at the heart of the statement is an expression of *metanoia,* or repentance, for the church's failure to live consistently with the biblical witness to social action and the struggle for justice on behalf of the oppressed.

The angst for evangelical Christians, and to varying degrees other Christian bodies, has been our understanding of what it means for evangelism and social concern to not be "mutually exclusive." As James Gustafson has observed, although the Lausanne statement "advocated that both evangelism and social action are part of Christian duty, thus implying that the results of evangelism should impact society, the nature of that relationship was not spelled out."[9] In other words, there continues to be broad differences on how we should express the *relationship* between evangelism and social action. Some evangelicals see relief and development as a *bridge* to evangelism. Others conceptualize relief and development as a natural *consequence* of evangelism. Still others try to see the two as *complementary* partners. In any case, they are broadly understood as vitally important, but distinct, ministries of the church. Evangelism is understood narrowly as an explicit presentation of the gospel, and social action is viewed as serving a supporting role of bearing witness to the gospel or, at times, as a tool that leads to a greater acceptance of the gospel message. Sometimes social action is portrayed in ways that convey the idea that it is a form of stealth evangelism or a strategic kind of tactic that has no lasting merit unless it culminates in evangelism. Once evangelism and social action are conceptualized as two separate spheres, it is inevitable that evangelism is given a priority over social action, and various explanations are required to demonstrate how social action leads to, culminates in, or arises out of evangelism and church planting.

The missionary movement, as with Christians in general, has reflected this tension. Missionaries have demonstrated a profound commitment to social action but have been ambivalent about the relationship between social action and evangelism and, therefore, have felt the need to justify how their ministries of compassion lead to evangelism. It is important, therefore, that the relationship between the two are clearly understood by those in missiological training and flow out of a proper biblical and theological framework.

---

9. James W. Gustafson, "The Integration of Development and Evangelism," *Missiology: An International Review* 26, no. 2 (April 1998): 132.

BIBLICAL/THEOLOGICAL FOUNDATIONS

Old Testament

The Old Testament identifies three qualities that exemplify a healthy community: justice (*mishpat*), kindness/faithfulness (*hesed*), and compassion (*rahamim*). The test of all three is demonstrated in how the people of God treat four groups of people—widows, orphans, immigrants, and the poor. These four groups are identified because they were powerless and therefore vulnerable to injustice, cruelty, and a general lack of concern. In the ancient world, if a woman with children lost her husband due to illness or war, it was very difficult for her to survive. Similarly, when children became "fatherless" or lost both of their parents, they were vulnerable to poverty and exploitation. The third group is often translated as "alien" or "sojourner," but it clearly corresponds to the modern usage of the word *immigrant*. Immigrants have no natural connections with the community. They speak with an accent, look different, and are not familiar with many of the customs and protocols of the people. In short, they are regarded as outsiders, making it more difficult to become full participants in the society. Therefore, they require special protection.

Throughout the Old Testament, God's righteous character is exemplified through His care for the poor, the weak, and the powerless. The psalmist praises Yahweh because He is "a father to the fatherless, a defender of widows" (Ps. 68:5). Even before the Hebrews entered the Promised Land, God prepared His people (through the giving of the Law) to understand the implications of what it meant to live in a covenant relationship with Him. Because He was a holy and righteous God, they were called to be a holy and righteous people. One of the primary ways they were to manifest this was in the way they treated widows, orphans (or fatherless), immigrants, and the poor. In the Law, Yahweh declares, "Do not mistreat an alien or oppress him, for you were aliens in Egypt. Do not take advantage of a widow or an orphan" (Exod. 22:21–22). This theme is repeated in every major portion of the Old Testament. In the Psalms the Lord stands as the righteous Judge who will judge His people if they do not "defend the cause of the weak and fatherless; maintain the rights of the poor and oppressed [and] rescue the weak and needy" (Ps. 82:3–4). The prophets regularly remind the Israelites of God's heart for the most vulnerable. Jeremiah declares, "Do no wrong or violence to the alien, the fatherless or the widow" (Jer. 22:3). When Israel is being sent into exile, Isaiah declares that one of the reasons is because of their disregard for the poor and needy in their midst. Isaiah declares a woe on those who "deprive the poor of their rights and withhold justice from the oppressed of my people, making widows their prey and robbing the fatherless" (Isa. 10:2).

To return to the distinction between relief and development or between social action on the microlevel versus social justice on the macrolevel, both are recognized within the structure of Old Testament Law. For example, on the personal level, landowners are commanded to leave some grain standing at the edge of the field, some olives on the trees, and some grapes on the vine during the harvest. The widows, orphans, and immigrants are allowed to glean from that produce (Lev. 19:9–10; 23:22; Deut. 24:19–21). If an owner realizes that a sheaf of grain had been left in the field, he is commanded not to go back and get it but to leave it "for the alien, the fatherless and the widow." If someone takes a material object such as a garment as collateral for a loan, it must be returned before sundown because, "his cloak is the only covering he has for his body" (Exod. 22:27). In fact, the Law even instructs people to not go unannounced into a debtor's house to get the collateral item but to wait outside and allow the debtor to bring it out, thereby preserving the debtor's dignity (Deut. 24:10–11).[10]

On the structural level, it is incumbent on a righteous king to care for those most vulnerable in society. Proverbs 29:14 reminds the people that "if a king judges the poor with equity his throne will be established forever" (RSV). The Law stipulates that they were not to deny justice to the poor when they brought a lawsuit (Exod. 23:2). They are called to be on guard against judges who might be inclined to take a bribe from the wealthy. Yahweh declares, "You are to have the same law for the alien and the native-born" (Lev. 24:22; cf. Exod. 12:49). Isaiah declares "woe" on "those who make unjust laws, to those who issue oppressive decrees" (Isa. 10:1). In Jeremiah, the political leadership is rebuked for not defending the poor against oppression. King Jehoiakim is judged for not defending the "cause of the poor and needy" as his father had done. After all, Yahweh declares, "Is that not what it means to know me?" (Jer. 22:16).

The failure of Israel to obey and to embody the ideals of justice (*mishpat*), faithfulness (*hesed*), and compassion (*rahamim*) must be seen

---

10. Bruce Malchow, "Social Justice in the Israelite Law Codes," *Word and World* 4, no. 3 (Summer 1984): 302.

together with the Jewish messianic expectation that God would send a deliverer who would establish God's justice and inaugurate His *shalom* (peace) on the earth. In other words, social justice is not merely something that the people of God do, or fail to do; it is ultimately a new order that comes through God's initiative. Peace and justice are themes that are partially and sporadically realized in the present but eschatologically assured. The prophets, in particular, highlight the expectation that the Messiah will come to defend the cause of the poor and helpless. Isaiah envisions the day when the Messiah will come and "preach good news to the poor" (Isa. 61:1). Malachi declares that the Messiah will come to testify against "those who defraud laborers of their wages, who oppress the widows and the fatherless, and deprive aliens of justice, but do not fear me" (Mal. 3:5).

In conclusion, the Old Testament roots the concern for the helpless and vulnerable first and foremost in the character and initiative of God. Our concern for the poor, the immigrant, the orphan, and the widow is a reflection of His righteousness in the world. Richard Patterson sums this up well when he comments that "throughout the Old Testament, the cause of the widow, the orphan, and the poor is particularly enjoined upon Israel as befitting a redeemed people who are entrusted with the character and standards of their Redeemer."[11]

New Testament: Luke-Acts

Jesus was born into the lower rank of society among a people group who were widely despised and marginalized. The New Testament emphasizes the humble beginnings of Jesus. He was born in a stable to a young peasant girl, dedicated through the sacrifice of two young pigeons because His parents couldn't afford a lamb, and raised as a carpenter in Nazareth, a town that is never mentioned in the Old Testament. Nathanael summed up the general attitude about the backwardness of Jesus' hometown when he, upon hearing that Jesus was from Nazareth, exclaimed, "Nazareth! Can anything good come from there?" (John 1:46). It is out of this context that the Messiah emerges.

While each of the gospel writers distinctively demonstrates Jesus' identification with the poor and other marginalized groups, it is Luke who

---

11. Richard Patterson, "The Widow, Orphan, and the Poor in the Old Testament and in Extra-Biblical Literature," *Bibliotheca Sacra* 130, no. 519 (July–September 1973): 232.

makes this theme the centerpiece of his gospel. Therefore, this overview will primarily focus on the Luke-Acts narrative. As early as the *Magnificat,* we hear Mary declaring that "he has brought down rulers from their thrones but has lifted up the humble. He has filled the hungry with good things but has sent the rich away empty" (Luke 1:52–53). The Messiah will inaugurate a radical transformation with implications for the entire political, social, and religious norms of the day. This theme continues to unfold in Luke's gospel. In that unforgettable day in the synagogue at the beginning of Jesus' public ministry, He takes the scroll of Isaiah and announces that His messianic presence will be good news to the poor, the captive, the blind, and the oppressed. He reads those words from Isaiah 61, beginning, "He has anointed me to preach good news to the poor" (Luke 4:18). And after reading the entire passage, He declares, "Today this scripture is fulfilled in your hearing" (Luke 4:21).

Luke's gospel also records Jesus' words, "Blessed are you who are poor, for yours is the kingdom of God. Blessed are you who hunger now, for you will be satisfied. Blessed are you who weep now, for you will laugh" (Luke 6:20–21). Each of the blessings has a corresponding woe on the rich, the well fed, and those who laugh (vv. 24–25). Jesus comes to inaugurate the new order, the great reversal the prophets anticipated.

Some have argued that Matthew's version, "Blessed are the poor *in spirit*" places a tension between Matthew and Luke, with the former emphasizing *spiritual* poverty. However, most scholars recognize that it is wrong to overly spiritualize Matthew's account, or to regard Luke as failing to recognize that spiritual poverty is the greatest expression of human need. David Bosch points out that the words poor (*ptōchos*) and rich (*plousios*) are comprehensive terms that involve "the whole identity of a person" and the "entire orientation of their lives."[12]

The rich young ruler and Zacchaeus, highlighted by Luke, are *both* materially rich *and* spiritually bankrupt. Their differing responses to the summons of Jesus highlight the broad, comprehensive way the inbreaking of the kingdom of God is understood by the writers of the New Testament. It is not uncommon for those who are materially wealthy to be blind to their deeper spiritual poverty, as the Lukan parables of the rich fool (Luke

---

12. David Bosch, *Transforming Mission: Paradigm Shifts in Theology of Mission* (Maryknoll, NY: Orbis, 1996), 99.

12:16–21) and the rich man and Lazarus (Luke 16:19–31) illustrate. Yet there were followers of Jesus who were rich, such as Joseph of Arimathea (Matt. 27:57), and there is certainly no evidence that all poor people, then or now, recognize their need for salvation. Thus, contemporary attempts to draw a bold distinction between physical and spiritual poverty are unwarranted, especially if it becomes a foil for neglecting those in physical need. Luke's gospel moves in the opposite direction, often portraying the close relationship between the two. The poor widow may have put only two small coins into the temple treasury, but in the estimation of Jesus, she had "put in more than all the others," signifying the depth of her *spiritual* offering to God (Luke 21:1–4).

All the Gospels highlight the healing ministry of Jesus as an integral part of His announcement of the kingdom of God. There is no wall of separation between the physical and the spiritual in His ministry, since His preaching and His healing are both signs of the inbreaking kingdom. Likewise, in Luke's gospel when Jesus sends out the Twelve (Luke 9:1–6) and, later, the seventy-two (Luke 10:1–16), they are sent out to preach the kingdom of God *and* to heal the sick.

Evidence of a broader, more comprehensive, understanding of the "poor" in Luke's gospel is also seen in that Jesus' identification with the poor is set within a larger, eschatological context. Good news is already being announced to the poor. The inbreaking of God's rule has been inaugurated. The future realities of the great reversal have been set into motion. Luke records the time when Jesus was invited to dine with a prominent Pharisee. Jesus told His host that the next time he threw a luncheon or a dinner he should not invite his friends, relatives, and rich neighbors. Instead, Jesus said, "Invite the poor, the crippled, the lame, the blind, and you will be blessed" (Luke 14:13–14). Jesus is not only giving advice on a practical way to serve the poor; He is also bearing witness to the future, eschatological banquet, when God sits down at table fellowship with the humble and poor of this world.

Luke's emphasis on understanding God's work within an eschatological framework continues in the book of Acts. In Acts, the formerly excluded religious outsiders, the Gentiles, take center stage. Through the ministry of the apostles, the blind see (9:1–18), the lame walk (3:1–10; 14:8–10), the prison doors are opened (5:19; 16:26), the dead are raised (20:7–12), and the poor receive the abundance of the church's generosity (24:17). The nations are called to repentance and faith and are summoned to submit to the kingship of Jesus Christ. Acts portrays a church that has been sent out into the world to bear witness to all these future realities in the midst of the present unrepentant, corrupt world. The church lives out its witness in the ongoing tension between the "already" and the "not yet." We know that there will be no poor, homeless, or fatherless in the New Creation. But in the present order, we still hear the cries of the poor. The homeless still await the Jubilee year, when all debts will be canceled. Those most vulnerable are still being neglected. Approximately thirty-five thousand children die every day because of a lack of clean water and basic nutrition, which, to drive home the point, is equal to 350 infants and children being placed in one hundred jumbo jets and having one crash every fourteen minutes, and repeating this all over again every single day.[13] The nations still rage and plot in vain against the Lord and His Anointed One (Acts 4:25–26). The cross is still a stumbling block, and the gospel message seems foolish by the standards of the wisdom of this age. Nevertheless, we continue to bear witness to the cross and to God's compassion as we await the final consummation, when "every knee [shall] bow . . . and every tongue confess that Jesus Christ is Lord" (Phil. 2:10–11). We continue to proclaim the gospel through word and deed until the full revelation of the New Creation, when "he will wipe every tear from their eyes" and "there will be no more death or mourning or crying or pain, for the old order of things has passed away" (Rev. 21:4).

Theological Implications for Missions Practice

There are three important theological implications for missions practice that arise out of this biblical reflection. First, *we must recognize the fundamental unity between word and deed.* From the vantage point of the Incarnation and the New Creation, it is clear that evangelism and social action can be separated only in the rarified air of theological discourse, not in the actual engagement of the church in the world. In the Incarnation, God's word and God's deed are one. Matthew's gospel, in particular, demonstrates this unity by emphasizing how the full stature of Jesus' ministry is recognized in His threefold ministry of teaching, preaching, and healing. In rapid fashion Matthew brings the reader through a breathtaking array

---

13. Wallis, *The Soul of Politics*, 71.

of pericopes, which give us a broad perspective on the full ministry of Jesus. At the conclusion of chapter 9, Matthew provides a brief summary statement of Jesus' ministry: "Jesus went through all the towns and villages, teaching in their synagogues, preaching the good news of the kingdom and healing every disease and sickness" (Matt. 9:35).

Jesus' ministry was characterized by teaching, preaching, and healing. Those were the signs of the inbreaking of God's rule in Jesus Christ.

Matthew then tells us that Jesus saw the crowds and was filled with compassion because they were "harassed and helpless, like sheep without a shepherd" (Matt. 9:36). Then, He said to His disciples, "The harvest is plentiful but the workers are few" (v. 37). Here the disciples move from being passive learners to being active participants in the ministry of Jesus. The compassion of Jesus for the overwhelming needs of the world becomes the springboard for the very first commissioning of His disciples: "The harvest is plentiful but the workers are few. Ask the Lord of the harvest, therefore, to send out workers into his harvest field" (vv. 37–38). Jesus then sends the Twelve out on a mission to "the lost sheep of Israel." This is clearly a training mission, preparing them for the more expansive, global mission that culminates Matthew's gospel and, in due course, thrusts these very disciples out to new people groups in Africa, Asia, and Europe. However, at this point Matthew is very intentional about showing that the disciples' ministry is to reflect the ministry of Jesus. Jesus says to the Twelve, "As you go, preach this message: 'The kingdom of heaven is near.' Heal the sick, raise the dead, cleanse those who have leprosy, drive out demons. Freely you have received, freely give" (10:7–8). In other words, their ministry is to express the same kind of unity between word and deed that they had observed in the life and witness of Jesus Christ.

The theological tension between evangelism and social action is fundamentally about the relationship between word and deed in the ministry of the church. This has been an ongoing struggle in the church, as we have sought to adequately reflect the full measure of Jesus' life and ministry in the world. On the one hand, Scripture teaches us through precept and example of the central and abiding importance of proclamation. Paul says to the Corinthians, "We preach Christ crucified: a stumbling block to Jews and foolishness to Gentiles, but to those whom God has called, both Jews and Greeks, Christ the power of God and the wisdom of God" (1 Cor. 1:23–24). Paul tells the church at Rome that the unbelieving world will not be saved apart from the public preaching of the gospel. He says, "How, then, can they call on the one they have not believed in? And how can they believe in the one of whom they have not heard? And how can they hear without someone preaching to them? And how can they preach unless they are sent?" (Rom. 10:14–15). The proclamation of the Word is central to our identity as the church. If the church ever ceases to call the world to repentance and faith solely in the crucified and risen Lord Jesus Christ, then we cease to be faithful to Christ and the apostolic message.

On the other hand, Scripture also warns us against the perils of a "dead faith." James asks, "What good is it, my brothers, if a man claims to have faith but has no deeds? Can such faith save him? Suppose a brother or sister is without clothes and daily food. If one of you says to him, 'Go, I wish you well; keep warm and well fed,' but does nothing about his physical needs, what good is it? In the same way, faith by itself, if it is not accompanied by action, is dead" (James 2:14–17). James explicitly connects the witness of the church with the signs of righteousness in the Old Testament when he says, "Religion that God our Father accepts as pure and faultless is this: to look after orphans and widows in their distress and to keep oneself from being polluted by the world" (James 1:27). The church took their social responsibility seriously, as evidenced by the dispute that broke out in the church concerning the daily distribution of relief for widows in need. The Greek-speaking believers charged that their widows were being neglected in the daily distribution of relief in favor of the widows who spoke Aramaic. The apostles resolved this dispute by appointing the first seven deacons, who were responsible for distributing the relief with equity (Acts 6:1–7).[14]

From the earliest days, word and deed were united in the New Testament's understanding of the life and witness of the church. The apostle Paul, the great preacher, teacher, and church planter, worked tirelessly in raising money for those in distress in Jerusalem due to famine and persecution (Acts 24:17; Rom. 15:25–29; 1 Cor. 16:1–4). Early in his ministry, Paul met with the apostles to discuss the gospel of grace and the propriety of extending the gospel to Gentiles. He comments that they reached an agreement but concludes by saying, "All

---

14. Relief for the widows was not a mere institutional response to the crisis of widowhood in the ancient world. Paul argued that widows should first be cared for by the generosity and love of their own extended families and should remain on the church's list only if they were over sixty years old and had no one in their family who was able to provide assistance (1 Tim. 5:3–10).

they asked was that we should continue to remember the poor, the very thing I was eager to do" (Gal. 2:10). In short, it is a caricature of Paul's ministry to see him as committed only to the preaching of the word and planting churches. Paul's ministry reflects the ministry of Jesus in his commitment to preaching, teaching, and healing.

The world needs the full ministry of the church if it is to "hear" the gospel. This is symbolized by two of the postresurrection appearances of Jesus. In Luke 24 the risen Lord walks side by side on the road to Emmaus with two distressed disciples. Although He spoke many words to them and "explained to them what was said in all the Scriptures concerning himself" (24:27), they were not able to recognize Him. It was only later, as they sat at the table and He broke the bread, that "their eyes were opened and they recognized him" (24:31). In contrast, when the risen Lord appeared to Mary Magdalene in John 20, He spoke only one word, "Mary," and she instantly recognized Him (20:16). Despite our many words, some only recognize Jesus in our deeds, whereas others recognize Him in the spoken word. We must not allow the ministries of word and deed to become unduly separated one from another. Evangelism and social action are not separate tasks of the church, they are a unified reflection of the holistic ministry of Jesus. If a Christian group is involved in a ministry of compassion and are asked to give a reason for the hope within them, and they are not able to articulate the necessity of faith in Jesus Christ, then their works, however sincere, will not bear long-term fruit. Likewise, if a ministry committed to preaching and evangelism does not demonstrate compassion toward those who are suffering and disenfranchised, then it is not an expression of living faith that honors the full ministry of Jesus Christ.

Tite Tienou at the Wheaton Consultation in 1983 summed it up well when he said,

> Social transformation is part of the message of and a natural outgrowth of evangelism. . . . but it will likely not take place through a dead evangelism: evangelism will likely not result in social transformation unless the church and Christian community witness by their lifestyles that they have been transformed. If we really mean business let us deflate our empty words and inflate our actions.[15]

---

15. Quoted in Gustafson, "The Integration of Development and Evangelism," 132.

The church cannot claim to be faithful to Christ unless and until we reflect His ministry of preaching, teaching, and healing.

Second, *we must resist the incessant individualism that does not make room for varying gifts and graces within the body of Christ*. Much of the unwarranted tension between evangelism and social action arises because of Western individualism, which fails to appreciate the larger, corporate witness of the church. In chapter 5 we examined each of the Great Commission passages given by the risen Lord and discovered four vital ministries that are integral to our corporate faithfulness to Christ and to the gospel. Matthew emphasized the role of discipleship, Mark emphasized the role of proclamation, Luke emphasized the role of witnessing, and John emphasized the role of sending. The ministry of sending is reflected in all the ministries that focus on mobilizing and supporting laborers for the harvest. The ministry of witnessing broadly reflects the full range of ways in which Christians bear witness to the *missio dei*. The ministry of proclamation emphasizes the centrality of preaching in the life of the church. Finally, the ministry of discipleship reminds us of the importance of church planting and the necessity of helping newly evangelized believers to become incorporated into the life of the church and to learn to exercise their varying gifts of ministry.

Why would the evangelist in North Africa say to the one who has given his life to teaching in a Bible college in the Philippines, "I have no need of you, because evangelism is the most important ministry in the church." Can those involved in bearing witness to Christ through ministries of compassion say to the evangelist, "We have no need of you"? Why would missionaries out in the field, whether evangelists or church planters or those committed to social action, say to those who stay behind and mobilize support that they are not essential for the overall ministry of the church in the world? Only collectively, as each group exercises its gifts, can the full measure of Christ's ministry of preaching, teaching, and healing be reflected in the world.

Having taught in a training school in India for many years, as well as at Gordon-Conwell in the United States, I have observed firsthand how God calls men and women to very different kinds of ministries, each with its own emphasis and purpose. If isolated from the others, none of these ministries reflects the full measure of Christ's ministry. However, collectively, as each member of the body exercises his or her gifts, we can reflect faithfulness to Christ. Many remember the tragic death of Diana, Princess of Wales, in 1997. Only five days after her death, Mother Teresa died. Nonstop coverage of the last moments of Diana's life and the ensuing analysis and, finally, the funeral were carried on live television in the West for a number of days, with only brief references to Mother Teresa. In contrast, for several days India broadcast a similar kind of coverage, focusing on Mother Teresa's life and ministry and, finally, her funeral. Across the subcontinent of India, there was a period of greater openness to the preaching of the gospel because of the widespread appreciation for the sacrificial ministry of Mother Teresa. Her lifelong commitment to bearing witness to Christ's love for the helpless on the streets of Calcutta created a reservoir of goodwill toward Christianity, which opened doors for our evangelists, who were evangelizing and planting churches.

Third, *all authentic ministry must be lived out within the context of the missio dei.* The modern debate about evangelism and social action is intelligible only if one conceptualizes the two as separate tasks the church has been called to. As long as the two are viewed as separate tasks, then the resultant language of "linking" and "bridging" and "consequence of" encourages the continual bifurcation in our understanding of the mission of the church. This is further exacerbated through the structural separation of evangelistic and church-planting mission agencies and relief and development agencies in contemporary mission practice. This creates the notion that the missions agencies are involved in "spiritual" work, whereas Christian relief and development agencies are engaged in "socioeconomic" or secular work.[16] However, the fundamental truth is that God, through the *missio dei*, is acting redemptively in the world through His church.

Understanding evangelism through the lens of the *missio dei* broadens our understanding of evangelism, so that we may embrace the fullness of what it means to obey Jesus' command to "disciple the nations." It is not merely about discipling *individuals*; it is about our summoning the *entire culture* to the inbreaking realities of the New Creation. Evangelism is the permeation of the whole gospel into every aspect of a culture and demonstrating, through word and deed, what it means to be "in Christ." Evangelism is not just about our "doing"; it is fundamentally about our "being." The church is to be a community of health, demon-

---

16. Ibid.

strating through our words and actions the qualities of justice (*mishpat*), kindness/faithfulness (*hesed*), and compassion (*rahamim*).

Our understanding of relief and development, likewise, has become overly secularized. Because many governments and nongovernmental organizations are involved in relief and development, we can easily forget that the widely used secular indicators of health are insufficient for Christians, who should have a more holistic understanding of poverty, which includes the ultimate poverty of being separated from Christ. The economic models of this world focus on self-interest and independence, rather than the kind of mutual interdependence that is central to God's vision for redeemed humanity. Secularized social action fails to understand that inner-city youths killing other youths is not simply a crime problem but is fundamentally a spiritual problem—a longing for the true *shalom* of God. The church is not just sponsoring another welfare program. We are summoning men and women to the community of the New Creation. Furthermore, secular development concepts fail to appreciate the profound poverty in the affluent world, which is manifested in the loneliness, isolation, fragmented families, and spiritual indifference that plague even our wealthiest communities.

A biblical understanding of relief and development can be properly united to a more robust conception of evangelism only if the ministries of the whole church are understood in an eschatological perspective. Evangelism and social action are signs of the New Creation, which is being ushered in through the *missio dei*. Seen in a larger eschatological framework, biblical faith is related to social conversion; personal conversion to the cries of the poor; theological reflection to the care for the environment; core religious values to new economic priorities; the call of community to racial and gender justice; morality to foreign policy; and spirituality to politics.[17] All of the future realities of the New Creation are breaking into the present order. We are not simply offering "help" to the poor from our places of security, isolation, and privilege. We minister out of a profound sense of rememberance. In Exodus 23:9 the Lord says to His people, "Do not oppress an alien; you yourselves know how it feels to be aliens, because you were aliens in Egypt." We remember that we, too, were once in bondage. We remember that we, too, once knew nothing of the glorious riches to which we have become heirs through the extrava-

---

17. Wallis, *The Soul of Politics*, 47.

gant generosity of God's grace. We see in the faces of the immigrant, the homeless, and the spiritually downtrodden our own faces. Only in the gospel can the dividing wall of hostility be broken down. Only through the work of Christ can we transcend the barriers of "us" and "them" and discover our shared place in the new humanity, as we increasingly realize the fruits of the New Creation.

CONCLUSION: HOPE FOR THE TWENTY-FIRST CENTURY

In conclusion, the world Christian movement is in a profoundly different position than it was a century ago. Today, the majority of Christians live in countries that are dominated by economic poverty, political powerlessness, and religious pluralism. The shifting demographics of the church to the southern continents has placed most Christians in close proximity to profound social needs and long-standing religious diversity. Their witness to the gospel has brought the social implications of the gospel into new prominence, helping to eclipse the Western tendency toward the compartmentalization of life. The emergence of a post-Western Christianity has finally liberated Christianity from what Kwame Bediako calls the "western possessiveness of it."[18] The result is that a paradigm of evangelism that is focused on "saving souls" while closing our eyes and ears to human need is no longer tenable. For centuries most of the church has looked upon a world of need from the upper-side perspective of privilege and power. Today, most of the church reads the Bible from the "lower-side" perspective of poverty and powerlessness. In this respect, we may finally have come full circle to a global situation that is far closer to the vibrancy and holistic perspective of the first-century Christians.

---

18. Kwame Bediako, *Christianity in Africa: The Renewal of a Non-Western Religion* (Maryknoll, NY: Orbis, 1995), 122.

PART FOUR

GOD THE HOLY SPIRIT:
THE EMPOWERING PRESENCE
OF THE *MISSIO DEI*

Section A

Empowering the Church to Embody the Presence of the Future

— 14 —
The Holy Spirit, the Book of Acts, and the *Missio Dei*

JOHN MBITI TELLS THE STORY of one of the first Africans to go to Europe to study for the ministry. He learned German, Latin, Greek, and Hebrew and studied the writings of Bultmann, Barth, Küng, and Niebuhr, among others. He carefully studied church history, systematic theology, homiletics, and biblical exegesis. Eventually he was awarded a master's degree and returned to Africa. The relatives and neighbors in his home village were excited to celebrate his newly acquired knowledge (he was the first from his village to ever receive a higher theological degree), and upon his return, they planned a large celebration to welcome him home. However, during the festival the man's older sister suddenly shrieked and fell to the ground. Everyone gathered around her and called her brother to come and help. He came and insisted that she be taken immediately to the hospital. They reminded him that the hospital was over fifty miles away. Someone else pointed out that she was possessed by a demon and the hospital would not be able to help her anyway. The village chief insisted that since the man had studied the Bible and theology for all these years, he should be able to help her himself.

Despite his great learning, Mbiti concluded, the man was not able to help his sister because "Bultmann has demythologized demon possession."[1] Mbiti acknowledges that the story is fictional, and it certainly caricatures

---

1. To read the full story, see John Mbiti, "Theological Impotence and the Universality of the Church," in *Mission Trends, No. 3: Third World Theologies*, ed. Gerald Anderson and Thomas Stransky (New York: Paulist; Grand Rapids: Eerdmans, 1976), 6–8.

the broad spectrum of Western Christianity, but it is still important that we listen to this story because it gives an important insight into how Western Christianity is *perceived* and the very real disconnect that many sense between the practice of Christianity in the West and what we observe about the church in the book of Acts.

One of the abiding concerns that has given rise to this book is that churches and mission agencies have increasingly taken their cue from the *business* world rather than from biblical models rooted in Scripture and arising out of theological reflection. The result has been the rise of consumer-driven churches and missions agencies, all striving to compete for market share. In this environment, consumer satisfaction trumps theology, the social sciences trump missiology, and pragmatism trumps biblical reflection. Of course, the whole enterprise is often unashamedly sprinkled with Christian jargon to give it a thin veneer of theological and biblical plausibility. However, we might begin to suspect something is wrong when we soberly realize that the vast majority of the programs and ministries in many of our Christian organizations and churches would continue on unabated even if the Holy Spirit did not show up. It is startling, then, to read the book of Acts and realize that the whole church seems to be scrambling to keep up with the unfolding and empowering work of the Holy Spirit! This section seeks to demonstrate that the Holy Spirit is the empowering presence of the *missio dei* in the book of Acts, and the church is summoned to participate in His work in the world. This chapter focuses on the book of Acts and offers some perspective on the work and ministry of the Holy Spirit. The following chapters in this fourth section of the book seek to demonstrate what this might practically mean for churches, mission agencies, and missionaries on the field.

There are several questions this chapter seeks to answer. First, what role does the Holy Spirit play in the life and ministry of the early church? An examination of this question will help to demonstrate the growing prominence of the Holy Spirit in the life and experience of the church after Pentecost. Second, we must explore in what way the apostolic church as portrayed in Acts is intended to be a model for the church today. Does Acts function *descriptively*, giving us an accurate historical record of what happened without necessarily saying that the practice and experience of the first century is what it should be in the twenty-first century? Or does Acts function *prescriptively*, giving us a positive model for the church of all times, cultures, and ages to emulate? If it is the former, then the church in the book of Acts is more like a "seed" out of which the twenty-first century church grows, and looking back, it may be difficult to see the continuity between the acorn of the apostolic church and the oak of today. If it is the latter, then the church in the book of Acts is more like a blueprint the contemporary church should emulate and follow as closely as possible. Finally, what particular role does the third person of the Trinity play in the unfolding of the *missio dei* and in fulfilling God's promise to Abraham?

THE HOLY SPIRIT IN THE LIFE
AND EXPERIENCE OF THE EARLY CHURCH

In chapter 2 we explored how the modern church often has privatized salvation and given the church a mere *instrumental* role, effectively conceding that the gospel story was completed at the Cross and the Resurrection. From this perspective, the church's role—and therefore the work of missions—is merely to look back and tell the world what happened at the Cross and the Resurrection. Of course, the Cross and the Resurrection always must remain central to the church's proclamation.[2] However, it is important to recognize that the gospel does not stop at the Cross and the Resurrection but continues to unfold in God's ongoing initiatives at Pentecost and the subsequent ministry of the third person of the Trinity in the life of the church.

Luke portrays the coming of the Holy Spirit on the Day of Pentecost as another kind of divine invasion, as an extension of the Incarnation through the abiding and empowering presence of the Holy Spirit. The Holy Spirit is not merely an impersonal force or a *donum superadditum* (i.e., a spiritual add-on). Rather, the Holy Spirit is the authoritative, empowering presence of the living God, "another self-revealing extension of his person and vitality into history."[3] God's actions in salvation history continue to unfold in the world. The Holy Spirit is the ongoing reminder that God does not just exercise imperial authority *over* the world but an executive authority to act *in* the world.[4]

---

2. It should be noted that an emphasis on pneumatology should not erode our Christology, since the Holy Spirit functions as the chief witness to Jesus Christ.
3. Max Turner, "The 'Spirit of Prophecy' as the Power of Israel's Restoration and Witness," in *Witness to the Gospel: The Theology of Acts*, ed. I. Howard Marshall and David Peterson (Grand Rapids: Eerdmans, 1998), 329.
4. John A. Studebaker Jr., *The Lord Is the Spirit: The Authority of the Holy Spirit in Contemporary Theology and Church Practice* (Eugene, OR: Pickwick, 2008), 7.

There are three major themes that summarize the purpose and work of the Holy Spirit in the life of the early church.

First, *the Holy Spirit empowers the church for a global mission*. Just prior to the Ascension, Jesus tells His disciples to wait until they have been "baptized with the Holy Spirit" (Acts 1:5). Jesus goes on to say, "You will receive power when the Holy Spirit comes on you; and you will be my witnesses in Jerusalem, in all Judea and Samaria, and to the ends of the earth" (1:8). Ten days later, when the Day of Pentecost dawns, we find a small group of Jesus' followers praying in Jerusalem. The Holy Spirit dramatically descends in a violent wind and with fire, two of the central images of the presence of God in the Old Testament. The fire immediately calls to mind Yahweh's appearance to Moses in "flames of fire" at the burning bush (Exod. 3:2), the pillar of fire that protected and guided the Israelites in the wilderness (Exod. 13:21–22), and Yahweh's descent onto Mount Sinai in fire at the giving of the Law (Exod. 19:18). Pentecost is, after all, the time when the Israelites celebrated the giving of the Law. The wind recalls the breath of God, which gave life at creation (Gen. 2:7), or the manifest presence of God to the prophets (1 Kings 19:11–12; Ezek. 1:4; Nah. 1:3).

The disciples begin to "speak in other tongues" as the Spirit enables them (Acts 2:4). This manifestation should be understood as more than a mere *sociological* event that enables foreign visitors who were in Jerusalem for the feasts of Passover and Pentecost to hear the gospel in their own language (Acts 2:6–12). Rather, it was a *theological* statement whereby God takes the initiative to overturn the chaos of Babel, which symbolized the global rebellion against God (Gen. 11:1–9), and in its place empowers the church for a global mission of redemption to the ends of the earth. At Pentecost, the birthday of the church, a small group of Jewish followers of Jesus are baptized into the reality of the infinite translatability of the gospel for every language and culture.[5] In the theology of Luke, the empowerment of the Holy Spirit for global mission is linked to the infinite translatability of the Christian gospel.

Second, *the Holy Spirit endues the church with God's authority*. In responding to some Pentecostal exegetes who emphasize the role of the Holy Spirit only in empowering believers for witness, Max Turner makes the

---

5. I am indebted to Kwame Bediako for pointing out that language is not merely a vehicle of communication but the central way we give expression to our culture. To use the words of John Pobee, language carries the "weight of culture."

observation that several of the key manifestations of the Holy Spirit in the book of Acts are not linked to an empowerment-for-witness theme.[6] In several texts people are filled with the Holy Spirit to give service or direction to the church. For example, in Acts 6 the seven deacons are filled with the Holy Spirit to serve the church (6:1–7). Similarly, in Paul's farewell to the elders at Ephesus, he acknowledges that it was the Holy Spirit who had appointed them as overseers of the church (20:28). In Acts 11:27–28, Agabus is filled with the Holy Spirit to inform the church that a severe famine will spread over the entire Roman world. In Acts 15 the Holy Spirit directs the church in their decision regarding the terms through which Gentile believers were to be admitted into the church (15:28). The Holy Spirit extends the judgment of God on both the church and on the unbelieving world (5:3, 9; 13:9–12). Thus, the Holy Spirit serves not only to empower the church to witness but also is the "teacher of the church" and the "executor of Christ's will in the world" (John 15:26; 16:14–15).[7] The Holy Spirit conveys revelation to the church by communicating to the church the will of God, thereby helping to bring the church under the authority of Christ. The early church regularly confesses that it is the Holy Spirit who inspired the biblical authors and, thereby, delivered to the church the Word of God (Acts 1:16; 4:25).

Third, *the Holy Spirit extends the inbreaking of the New Creation through the powerful manifestation of signs and wonders and holiness of life.* On the Day of Pentecost, Peter declares that the coming of the Holy Spirit fulfilled Joel's prophecy, which declared that God would "show wonders in the heaven above and signs on the earth below" (Acts 2:19). The ministry of the early church reflected the ministry of Jesus Christ in the emphasis on the proclamation of the Word through preaching and teaching, and in the ongoing ways in which the realities of the New Creation continued to break into the present order through signs and wonders and holy living. Luke records that "everyone was filled with awe, and many wonders and miraculous signs were done by the apostles" (2:43). The manifestation of signs and wonders was not limited to the apostles but also was evidenced in the ministry of Stephen (6:8) and Philip (8:6, 13).

The signs and wonders were understood to accompany the preaching of the Word to provide divine confirmation of God's presence working

---

6. Turner, "The 'Spirit of Prophecy,'" 341.
7. Studebaker, *The Lord Is the Spirit*, 12, 19.

through the church, bringing a unity of word and deed. For example, in Acts 4:30–31 the church prayed, "'Stretch out your hand to heal and perform miraculous signs and wonders through the name of your holy servant Jesus.' After they prayed, the place where they were meeting was shaken. And they were all filled with the Holy Spirit and spoke the word of God boldly." Later, Luke records that in the ministry of Paul and Barnabus in Iconium they "spent considerable time there, speaking boldly for the Lord, who confirmed the message of his grace by enabling them to do miraculous signs and wonders" (14:3).

The Spirit's role in extending the inbreaking of the New Creation is not limited to an evangelistic or missional context. Joel Green has pointed out that in Luke's writings the reception of the Spirit in the life of the believer is an integral aspect of his understanding of salvation.[8] It is not an extra add-on reserved for a dedicated few. When Peter preaches, he declares to the entire assembly that if they believe, they "will receive the gift of the Holy Spirit" (Acts 2:38). Peter goes on to assure them that this promise is not only for those who hear him, but also for their children and "for all who are far off—for all whom the Lord our God will call" (2:39). The same Spirit who empowers us for witness is the one who empowers us for holy living. The same Spirit who transforms the unbelieving nations of the world is the one who transforms our hearts, teaching us to say "no" to sin and to embrace the righteousness of Jesus Christ.[9]

ACTS AS DESCRIPTIVE HISTORY
OR PRESCRIPTIVE MODEL?

We explored three key themes in our overview of the person and role of the Holy Spirit in Acts: the Spirit empowers the church for global mission, endues the church with divine authority, and extends the inbreaking of the

---

8. Green argues that there are four aspects of Luke's understanding of salvation: (1) Incorporation and participation in the Christocentric community of God's people, (2) rescue from our enemies, (3) forgiveness of sins, and (4) reception of the Holy Spirit. See Joel Green, "Salvation to the End of the Earth (Acts 13:47): God as Saviour in the Acts of the Apostles," in *Witness to the Gospel: The Theology of Acts* (Grand Rapids: Eerdmans, 1998), 90–95.

9. The twin roles of the Holy Spirit as an agent of holiness and the one who empowers for witness is seen in the Methodist and the Keswick roots of Pentecostalism. Wesley emphasized the role of the Spirit as the sanctifier. In contrast, Keswick pneumatology emphasized that the Holy Spirit empowers the believer for witness, service, and evangelism. In the New Testament, the Holy Spirit transforms both the inner life *and* our external witness.

New Creation through signs and wonders and the manifestation of holiness in the life of the church. We now come to our second key question. Is the work of the Holy Spirit in Acts intended to be historically *descriptive* or missiologically *prescriptive*? To put it plainly, is it appropriate for the twenty-first-century church to expect visions from God in the ongoing direction of His mission? Should those who preach across new cultural and social boundaries pray that the Holy Spirit confirm their preaching through the inbreaking of signs and wonders? If so, then why is this supernatural dimension seemingly absent from so many churches? Now that the church has the Scriptures, do we still need the kind of supernatural intervention characterized by the Holy Spirit's interaction with the early church in Acts? Another way of getting at the question is to ask in what way Acts serves as a *history* of the early church and in what way it serves as a *theological treatise* reflecting the early church's missiology. If Acts is primarily a historical work, can missiology, pneumatology, theology, and ecclesiology be drawn out in ways analogous to how doctrine is derived from the apostolic letters or John's apocalypse?

Since none of these questions are new, it is important that we begin with a historical overview of the development of pneumatology in the West, which has shaped the context of how we in the West have approached these questions. Second, we will explore how the emergence of Pentecostalism and the rise of the Majority World church in the twentieth century have influenced the church's understanding of the Holy Spirit and its interpretation of Acts. Finally, we will explore how this might impact contemporary missiological thinking, strategy, and praxis.

Historical Development of Pneumatology

Jaraslav Pelikan, in his survey of the development of Christian doctrine, points out that the doctrine of the Trinity represents the apex of doctrinal development in the early church. Pelikan writes, "In this dogma the church vindicated the monotheism that had been at issue in its conflicts with Judaism." Jesus Christ, the Redeemer, did "not belong to some lower order of divine reality, but was God himself."[10] Jesus fully shares in the essence of the Father (*homoousios*, not *homoiousios*). Likewise, the Holy Spirit shares

---

10. Jaraslav Pelikan, *The Emergence of the Catholic Tradition* (100–600), vol. 1 of *The Christian Tradition: A History of the Development of Doctrine* (Chicago: University of Chicago Press, 1971), 172–173.

fully in the divine essence, since the Scriptures give Him both the titles and the prerogatives of deity. The church affirmed one God (one *ousia*), in three eternal personal distinctions (three *hypostases*).

However, the relative paucity of biblical references to the deity of the Holy Spirit as compared with the deity of Jesus Christ meant that it took quite some time for a full-orbed Trinitarian theology to develop. In fact, for some time there was a fairly strong Spirit-Christology, which did not acknowledge the Holy Spirit as a third person of the Trinity. Even as late as 380, Gregory of Nazianzus conceded that "of the wise men among ourselves, some have conceived of him (the Holy Spirit) as an activity, some as a creature, some as God; and some have been uncertain what to call him . . . and therefore they neither worship him nor treat him with dishonor, but take up a neutral position."[11]

This ambiguity and neutrality is reflected in the Apostles' Creed (which is probably based on the earlier second-century Roman Creed) and the original Nicene Creed of A.D. 325, which simply states, "We believe in the Holy Spirit," without further commentary. In 381, a second ecumenical council met in Constantinople. The further deliberations on the Holy Spirit led the council to amplify and clarify the faith of the Nicene Creed so that it unequivocally declared the deity of the Holy Spirit.[12] The Niceno-Constantinopolitan Creed declares, "We believe in the Holy Spirit, the Lord and Giver of Life, who proceedeth from the Father, who with the Father and the Son together is worshipped and glorified, who spoke by the prophets."[13]

Even though the deity of the Holy Spirit was resolved by A.D. 381, discussions about the exact nature and relations of the Trinity continued for almost a century.[14] All of this had a profound effect on theological dis-

---

11. Ibid., 213.
12. The first ecumenical council (Nicea, 325) had been preoccupied with responding to various challenges to the deity of Jesus Christ and therefore was not in a position to consider the deity of the Holy Spirit. The deity of the Father, Son, and Holy Spirit, which was affirmed in A.D. 381, implies the Trinity, although the full doctrine of the Trinity was not officially reaffirmed until the fifth ecumenical council in Constantinople in A.D. 553.
13. Philip Schaff and Henry Wace, eds., *The Seven Ecumenical Councils*, vol. 14 of *Nicene and Post-Nicene Fathers* (Peabody, MA: Hendrickson, 1999), 163. It should be noted that the phrase "and the Son" (*filioque*) was not inserted after the phrase "who proceedeth from the father" until the year 447 at the Synod of Toledo in Spain. The Eastern church does not accept the addition of this phrase.
14. Acknowledgment of the deity of the Holy Spirit must not be confused with a full affirmation of the Trinity. The Trinity was officially reaffirmed at the fifth ecumenical council in Constantinople in A.D. 553. As late as A.D. 380, Gregory of Nazianzus conceded that "to be only slightly

course in the Western tradition concerning the Holy Spirit. Because the ecumenical discussions about the Holy Spirit were focused primarily on the deity of the Holy Spirit and His relationship within the Trinity, there was a serious neglect of a full development of His work. Indeed, William Menzies points out that "the ancient church from the second century through the ninth century was almost totally preoccupied with questions pertaining to the identity of Jesus Christ, so that what was said of the Holy Spirit was largely an appendage to theology, and was limited largely to ontology, the Being of God within his inter-trinitarian relationships."[15] That remained largely unchanged in medieval scholarship.

The Reformation's emphasis on the authority of Scripture, ecclesiology, and Christology are clearly reflected in the post-Reformation attempt to systematize the theological deposit of the Reformers. However, as was the case during the patristic period, this meant that a full development of the doctrine of the Holy Spirit was delayed and several vital aspects of the person and work of the Holy Spirit were neglected in post-Reformation Protestant theology in the West.

Over time, several major theological traditions developed that either denied completely or extremely limited the active role of the Holy Spirit in miracles, divine healing, demonic deliverance, prophecy, tongues speaking, and other elements that later would become central features of the Pentecostal doctrine of the Holy Spirit. This tendency is evident in many expressions of Reformed theology, as well as the later nineteenth-century dispensationalism, although the precise lines of their argumentation against the exercise of the gifts of the Holy Spirit today are quite different from one another.

Space does not permit an analysis and evaluation of each of the systems of thought and their defense of the cessationist position. Indeed, there are many different forms and degrees of cessationism. Some would go so far as to deny all subjective forms of guidance, such as claims that the Lord was leading one to do something or that the Holy Spirit had helped one to understand a particular passage of Scripture. Others are, practically speaking, partial cessationists, opposing the exercise of certain gifts such as prophecy

---

in error (about the Holy Spirit) was to be orthodox." See Pelikan, *The Emergence of the Catholic Tradition,* 213.

15. William W. Menzies, "The Holy Spirit in Christian Theology," in *Perspectives on Evangelical Theology,* ed. Kenneth Kantzer and Stanley Gundry (Grand Rapids: Baker, 1979), 67.

and tongues but functioning as continuationists when it comes to praying for the sick or believing that the Holy Spirit can directly speak to someone.

There are also different ideas as to the original purpose of these supernatural gifts. Some argue that the apostolic miracles served to grant authority to the ministers in the church, whereas others claim they were given only to attest to His Word. There are also different ideas as to exactly when and why these gifts stopped. For example, some argue that the gifts ceased after the canon of Scripture was completed, while others say it was when the last apostle died. Still others insist that the exercise of spiritual gifts died out gradually over the first four centuries until the official persecution ceased and Christianity was granted full legal status in the Roman Empire. Some argue that while the gifts are not a normal part of the life of the church, they might still be manifested by God in extraordinary situations. But regardless of which of these schemes are followed, the point is that theological reflection in the West gradually became dominated by a range of theological systems that denied that the full exercise of the supernatural gifts of the Holy Spirit was a normative, much less essential, part of the church's *ongoing* life and witness in the world.

B. B. Warfield, the great nineteenth-century Princeton theologian, is one of the best-known and influential representatives of the cessationist viewpoint. In his book *Counterfeit Miracles*, Warfield argues that the diffusion of miraculous gifts by the Holy Spirit was confined to the apostolic church and "they necessarily passed away with it." He insists that "the theologians of the post-Reformation era, a very clear-headed body of men, taught with great distinctiveness that the charismata ceased with the Apostolic age."[16]

---

16. B. B. Warfield, *Counterfeit Miracles* (New York: Charles Scribner's Sons, 1918), 6. Warfield's view is that the miracles ceased with the last person upon whom the apostles conferred the working of miracles through the imposition of their hands, explaining the gradual decline of miracles (p. 23). It should be noted that Warfield specifically uses A. J. Gordon's *The Ministry of Healing*, or *Miracles of Cure in All Ages*, as the best book representing his opponent's position. See pp. 159–60. Gordon taught, for example, that "it is still the duty and privilege of believers to receive the Holy Spirit by a conscious, definite act of appropriating faith, just as they received Jesus Christ. . . . To say that in receiving Christ we necessarily received in the same act the gift of the Spirit, seems to confound what the Scriptures make distinct. For it is as sinners that we accept Christ for our justification, but it is as sons that we accept the Spirit for our sanctification... logically and chronologically the gift of the Spirit is subsequent to repentance." See A. J. Gordon, *The Ministry of the Spirit* (Philadelphia: American Baptist Publication Society, 1894), 76–77. A century earlier, Jonathan Edwards taught that the gifts of prophecy, tongues, and revelations would cease and "vanish away" when the church reached maturity. Edwards did not accept the supernatural gifts as valid for today, and he explicitly stated that he did not expect, or desire, a

This Princeton theological tradition[17] influenced a large part of the Reformed tradition and subsequent systematic theologies in the West. A typical example can be found in Louis Berkhof's *Systematic Theology*, a classic text in Reformed theology still in use today. Berkhof devotes significant attention in part 1 (Doctrine of God) of his theology to defending the deity, personality, and prerogatives of the Holy Spirit within the larger setting of his defense of the doctrine of the Trinity. Later, in part 4 (Doctrine of the Application of the Work of Redemption), Berkhof discusses the work of the Holy Spirit in applying the work of Christ into our lives (i.e., regeneration) and in personal holiness (i.e., sanctification). In part 5 (Doctrine of the Church), Berkhof is silent about the role of the Holy Spirit in empowering the church for witness and global missions.

In summary, traditional Western understanding of pneumatology is adequate in its treatment of the Spirit's place in the Trinity and His role in soteriology, but it is often silent about many of the key elements present in the book of Acts, including the baptism of the Holy Spirit, divine healing, speaking in tongues, the role of the Holy Spirit in the mission of the church, and so forth. In fact, many of the older Western systematic theologies did not even develop the person and work of the Holy Spirit as a separate category of study but rather developed their theology of the Holy Spirit as subsets under the doctrine of God and soteriology.[18] However, in the closing decades of the twentieth century, the renewed emphasis on the Trinity and the rise of Pentecostalism resulted in an increasing interest in the work of the Holy Spirit. We will now explore how the emergence of Pentecostalism and the rise of the Majority World church have influenced Western pneumatology and missions practice.

Pentecostalism and the Rise of the Majority World Church

In chapter 1, we explored seven megatrends that are shaping twenty-first-century missions. Two of the trends are the rise of global Christianity and the increasing numbers of Christians who are not identified with the

---

restoration of these miraculous gifts in the latter days prior to the inauguration of the millennium. See C. C. Goen, ed., *The Distinguishing Marks*, vol. 4 of *Works of Jonathan Edwards* (New Haven: Yale University Press, 1972), 280–281.

17. The Princeton theology refers to the period when great theologians such as Archibald Alexander, Charles Hodge, A. A. Hodge, and B. B. Warfield taught at Princeton Theological Seminary.

18. See, for example, Henry C. Thiessen, *Lectures in Systematic Theology*, rev. ed. (Grand Rapids: Eerdmans, 1979).

traditional tripartite identification of Roman Catholic, Eastern Orthodox, and Protestant branches of Christianity. Both of these trends are seen in the rise of Pentecostalism, which now comprises a global force of half a billion adherents, making it one of the most dramatic shifts in Christian alignment in history.

Pentecostalism traces its origins to a series of revival movements that simultaneously emerged in the first decade of the twentieth century. In the United States, Pentecostalism traces its origin to a black preacher named William Seymour from Louisiana, who came to Los Angeles teaching that God was restoring the first-century apostolic church. This included a fresh visitation of Pentecost in which believers could be baptized in the Holy Spirit, speak in unknown tongues, be empowered for witness, and live a holy life.

Seymour had first learned this message from the former Methodist preacher turned healing evangelist from Kansas, Charles Parham (1873–1929). Seymour fervently believed that the time of God's visitation had come to Los Angeles. What are now known as the Azusa Street revivals began on Sunday, April 15, 1906, when Jenny Evans Moore spoke in tongues at the conclusion of the service at the Azusa Street Mission. News about this move of the Holy Spirit spread throughout Los Angeles. A few days later, the front page of the *Los Angeles Daily Times* contained the extended headline: "Weird Babble of Tongues, New Sect of Fanatics Breaking Loose, Wild Scene Last Night on Azusa Street, Gurgle of Wordless Talk by a Sister."[19] This was the first public announcement that something dramatic was happening on Azusa Street.

The revival lasted from April 1906 through the early months of 1909 and drew tens of thousands of people from all over the world, who came to witness the outpouring of the Holy Spirit during one of the three daily services. Over the three-year period, the Azusa Street Mission could hardly contain the crowds, as thousands found redemption in Jesus Christ and experienced what was known as a "second Pentecost." It is not surprising that when Seymour began to publish a newspaper to help spread his teachings in September 1906, his lead article in the inaugural edition was entitled "Pentecost Has Come!"

Similar revivals, independent of the Azusa Street meetings, included the famous Welsh revival that lasted from September 1904 to June 1905

---

19. "Weird Babble of Tongues," *Los Angeles Daily Times* April 18, 1906, 1.

and witnessed over ten thousand people come to Christ. A few years later, revivals broke out in Korea, several of which occurred in what is today North Korea, including Wonsan and Pyongyang. These Korean revivals became known as the "Korean Pentecost."[20]

The evangelistic and missionary fervor that burst forth from these revivals helped to spark new waves of Pentecostalism around the world. For example, Welsh missionaries working in India, fresh from the revivals in Wales, witnessed dramatic Pentecostal revivals in the Kashi Hills of Northeast India. In 1906, another revival broke out near Pune, India, at the Mukti Mission of the famous Brahmin convert to Christianity, Pandita Ramabai. Similar revival movements occurred in China, as well as several countries of Africa, including the Ivory Coast, Ghana, and Nigeria.

Pentecostal scholar Allan Anderson points out that the Azusa Street revival "turned a fairly localized and insignificant new Christian sect into an international movement that sent workers to more than twenty-five nations in only two years."[21] Similar evangelistic and cross-cultural initiatives occurred out of the other revivals. If Pentecostalism is, as the title of Harvey Cox's landmark book declares, a "fire from heaven," then it is a fire that has spread around the world.[22]

One of the affirmations that unites all Pentecostals is the belief that the practice and exercise of spiritual gifts as exhibited in the book of Acts should be *normative* for the church today. Pentecostalism is fundamentally a renewal movement, seeking to challenge blind spots in the Western development of pneumatology, which focused on the person of the Holy Spirit and neglected a proper understanding of His work. We will first explore three ways in which Pentecostalism has influenced Christianity in general and then examine the specific ways it has impacted missions practice.

First, Pentecostals believe that the full range of gifts and miraculous manifestations of the Spirit present in the New Testament are available for

---

20. Allan Anderson, *An Introduction to Pentecostalism* (Cambridge: Cambridge University Press, 2004), 37.
21. Allan Anderson, "To All Points of the Compass: The Azusa Street Revival and Global Pentecostalism," *Enrichment Journal*, online journal of the General Council of the Assemblies of God, http://enrichmentjournal.ag.org/200602/200602_164_AllPoints.cfm.
22. Harvey Cox, *Fire from Heaven: The Rise of Pentecostal Spirituality and the Reshaping of Religion in the Twenty-first Century* (Reading, MA: Addison Wesley, 1995).

believers today. Pentecostals reject any notion that Acts is merely descriptive and no longer applicable to believers today. They reject the idea that the gifts of the Holy Spirit are either limited to the first century or passed away with the apostles. This view is perhaps summed up best by one of the early pioneers of Pentecostalism, the itinerant evangelist Aimee Semple McPherson, who once asked, "Is Jesus Christ the Great I Am? or is He the Great I Was?"[23] Pentecostals believe that the Holy Spirit continues to make available to the church the full range of Jesus' miraculous ministry, as well as the apostolic signs and wonders explored earlier. Pentecostals understand that if someone is demon possessed, then having the demon cast out in the name of Jesus is still part of the good news and the practical extension of Christ's triumphant victory over the principalities and powers (Col. 2:14–15; Eph. 6:12). In other words, if the Holy Spirit is alive and real, then He must have the power and the means to extend his Dynamic life in real and concrete ways into the lives of those who are suffering. If God raised the dead in the first century, why can't He do it in the twenty-first century?

Second, Pentecostalism has unleashed a renewed emphasis on the practice of worship. Pentecostals are known for less formalized and expressive forms of worship, including lifting hands, dancing, shouting, and clapping. While this should not eclipse the rich heritage of theologically sound hymnology or liturgical worship, one cannot help but observe that many of the forms of worship around the world have dramatically changed since the advent of Pentecostalism, which has stimulated deep reflection about the nature and practice of worship.

Third, because Pentecostals believe that they are living in the last days before the return of Christ, they are marked by a special urgency to evangelize the world. The effective evangelism exhibited by Pentecostals also can be attributed to their distinctive pneumatology, which is not encumbered by the truncated pneumatology that is so prevalent in North American theologies. The Holy Spirit is not only a full person of the Godhead, a member of the Trinity; He not only inspired the Holy Scriptures and regenerates us; but He also empowers us for effective evangelism.

---

23. Aimee Semple McPherson, from her Divine Healing Sermons, as quoted in Cecil M. Robeck Jr., "Pentecostals and Apostolic Faith: Implications for Ecumenism," *Pneuma: The Journal of the Society for Pentecostal Studies* 9 (Spring 1987): 64.

Pentecostals are convinced that the Holy Spirit confirms the preaching of the gospel and the declaration of the resurrection of Jesus through the giving of signs and wonders, just as He did through those unlearned fisherman and tax collectors who were His first apostles.

Influence on Missions Practice

These new emphases within Pentecostalism, coupled with the extraordinary growth of the movement around the world, have had a profound effect on Christianity as a global force, including the practice of missions in several key ways.

BIRTH OF "GOBAL CHRISTIANITY"

First, Pentecostalism had led the way in the rise of what is now known as "global Christianity." The Pentecostals were among the first to understand the global implications of transcending the traditional denominational divides that have characterized Protestant identity for centuries. Because Pentecostalism did not have its origin in a single church tradition or geographic region, it was birthed in diversity. Modern-day Pentecostalism can be traced to classical Pentecostal denominations, as well as to indigenous revivals erupting on five different continents. A second wave of Pentecostalism has swept through mainline Protestant, Roman Catholic, and Eastern Orthodox churches. This diverse background forced Pentecostals to embrace unity in spiritual terms, rather than in structural or doctrinal terms. This is why the word *Pentecostal* is frequently used both as an adjective and a noun in a way that is not generally found with terms such as *Lutheran* or *Methodist*. People can consider themselves to be Pentecostal Roman Catholics or Pentecostal Methodists without fear of contradiction. In fact, one of the most dynamic Pentecostal movements in Chile emerged within the Methodist Church under the leadership of an American Methodist missionary named Willis Hoover.[24] This spiritual basis for unity means that a Pentecostal can "have true ecumenism or genuine *koinōnia* with all Christians who have a personal relationship with God."[25] Discovering this "common spiritual center" is, according to

---

24. See Willis C. Hoover, *History of the Pentecostal Revival in Chile* (Santiago, Chile: Imprenta Eben-Ezer, 2000).
25. Robeck, "Pentecostals and the Apostolic Faith," 65.

Karl-Wilhelm Westmeier, the reason that Pentecostalism has been able to
work across denominational lines.[26]

   Because Pentecostals see themselves as reviving the apostolic faith rather
than breaking off from or emerging out of any existing movements, it allows
them, even if naïvely, to provide a basis for ecumenism around their common
commitment to the biblical witness in Scripture and their shared experience
of the Holy Spirit. Though most Pentecostals deride the word *ecumenical*
and, quite frankly, have exhibited as much sectarianism and theological
controversy as any other Christian group, it is nevertheless remarkable to
see how Pentecostalism actually has contributed positively to ecumenism.
The Pentecostals learned the principle of *sola scriptura* from the Reformation
but then used it as a basis for celebrating a supernatural, apostolic faith that
predated the historical divisiveness of denominationalism. The result was a
new basis for cooperation and collaboration in missions, which facilitated
the rapid spread of Christianity around the world. The growth of the global
church in the wake of Pentecostal witness was so profound that Henry Van
Dusen coined the expression "Third Force" to describe it.[27]

EMPHASIS ON THEOPRAXIS OVER FORMAL THEOLOGY

Second, Pentecostals tend to focus outwardly on evangelism and missions rather than inwardly on either defending themselves against their
critics or expending a lot of energy on defining their own identity. In the
formative stages of Pentecostalism, the movement held a distrust of academic scholarship, which they called a "tragedy, whose fruit is empty
churches . . . the result of our 'theologizing to death.'"[28] Of course, Pentecostals were recipients of centuries of serious theological reflection in the
church upon which their faith depended. Nevertheless, this has not been
sufficiently acknowledged because Pentecostals see themselves as a return

---

26. Karl-Wilhelm Westmeier, *Protestant Pentecostalism in Latin America* (London: Associated
   University Presses, 1999), 19. This is also celebrated in Matthew Marostica's chapter entitled,
   "The Defeat of Denominational Culture in the Argentine Evangelical Movement," in *Latin
   American Religion in Motion*, ed. Christian Smith and Joshua Prokopy (New York and London:
   Routledge, 1999), 148–72.

27. Henry P. Van Dusen, "The Third Force in Christendom," *Life* (June 9, 1958): 113–24. The first
   wave refers to Roman Catholic missions; the second wave refers to Protestant missions. It is
   interesting to note that Eastern Orthodoxy is overlooked by Van Dusen, despite their vigorous
   and inspiring missionary work in the nineteenth century.

28. Walter Hollenweger, *Pentecostalism: Origins and Developments Worldwide* (Peabody, MA: Hendrickson, 1997), 194.

to the first century and the original apostolic faith and practice. Although this anti-intellectualism among Pentecostals has changed significantly in recent years, it is still true that Pentecostals are more interested in theo-*praxis* than theology in the formal sense. Pentecostalism is, at root, an evangelistic-missions movement.

Because of the emphasis on evangelism and missions within Pentecostalism, the movement continues to provide an important check against the tendency for theology to lose its missional focus and become too rationalistic and theoretical. Our tendency toward a cerebral-oriented scholasticism must learn to appreciate and benefit from the counterbalance of the Pentecostal orientation toward a heart-oriented praxis that fully embraces a supernatural worldview.

In the past, when missionaries arrived with their modified Enlightenment worldview and their restricted, truncated pneumatology, they did not know what to say when someone claimed that a drought was caused by God's judgment, or when concerned parents came and asked the missionary to cast out the demon tormenting their daughter, or when someone claimed to have received a vision to preach the gospel in a new region. Sadly, the missionary often had no training or categories to respond to such worldviews. They inhabited a Christianized version of a two-tiered universe, whereas they were working among people who lived in what Paul Hiebert insightfully calls the world of the "excluded middle."[29] The only category the missionaries had was a term like *superstition,* which they frequently resorted to in order to explain these spiritualized explanations of what surely had its basis, they reasoned, in naturalistic explanations. These missionaries were evangelical in their theology, but when it came to pneumatology applied to real-life praxis, they were functional deists. This is why Lesslie Newbigin argued that Western missionaries were one of the greatest forces of secularization in history.[30]

In contrast, Pentecostalism emerged among uneducated peoples who were the least influenced by the Enlightenment worldview. Furthermore, their personal experience with the Holy Spirit gave them reason to believe that the same Holy Spirit who acted supernaturally in the lives and

---

29. Paul G. Hiebert, *Anthropological Reflections on Missiological Issues* (Grand Rapids: Baker, 1994), 189–201.
30. Lesslie Newbigin, *Honest Religion for Secular Man* (Philadelphia: Westminster, 1966), as cited in Hiebert, *Anthropological Reflections,* 197.

witness of the apostles is active today in similar ways. The result of this conviction has been the emergence of a global Pentecostal pneumatology that *anticipated* God's ongoing intervention in the world through miraculous healings, prophetic guidance to the church, demonic deliverance from evil, and an empowered witness to the world. In short, the Holy Spirit continues to usher in the firstfruits of the New Creation into the fallen world. Many of the future realities of the kingdom are now fully available to all believers through the person and work of the Holy Spirit.

God used the seventeenth-century pietistic movement to balance out the tendency toward an overly cerebral scholasticism in post-Reformation Protestant theology in Europe. Pietism became unconsciously ecumenical as it quietly spread its influence through most of European Protestantism. Today, there is no formal denomination that has emerged from Pietism, but there is hardly a Protestant movement in the world that has not in some way been influenced by Pietism.

Today, God is using the Pentecostals in the same way. Indeed, one of the neglected stories of global Pentecostalism is not so much how they have grown as distinct, identifiable Pentecostal groups but how deeply they have influenced so much of the faith and practice of non-Pentecostals around the world. The Pentecostal sense of the immediacy of God's presence and power has struck a responsive chord in Christians everywhere and has helped to stimulate fresh evangelistic and missional activity.[31] It is also a wonderful reminder of how crucial it is that the *noetic* principle in theology (reflection, reason, propositional statements, etc.) always must be balanced by the *ontic* principle (immediacy of God's presence, personal experience with God, etc.).[32] If either of these tendencies is allowed to run unchecked, the church falls into error.

Beyond the HU Principle in Missions Strategy

Finally, Pentecostals have provided an important counterbalance to the strong emphasis on reaching unreached people groups on the basis of

---

31. Roman Catholic missiologist John Gorski has noted that "evangelization in the specific sense of announcing the gospel to enable a personal encounter with the living Christ, leading to conversion and discipleship, became a conscious concern of the Catholic church only within the past half century." This was stimulated by the presence of Pentecostals in Latin America. See John F. Gorski, "How the Catholic Church in Latin America Became Missionary," *International Bulletin of Missionary Research* 27, no. 2 (April 2003): 60.

32. Paul A. Pommerville, *The Third Force in Missions* (Peabody, MA: Hendrickson, 1985), 68.

Donald McGavran's homogeneous unit (HU) principle, which has dominated both the church growth movement and evangelical missions since
1974.[33] According to McGavran, a homogeneous unit refers to "a section of
society in which all the members have some characteristic in common."[34]
The homogeneous unit principle focused on identifying particular peoples
who shared a common cultural, linguistic, and social identity and stimulating a "people movement" within this particular ethnic group. The whole
basis for the HU principle was the proven sociological fact that people
prefer to not cross social and ethnic barriers when becoming Christians.
Furthermore, people prefer to worship with people who are culturally like
themselves.[35] This is the principle that drives the church growth movement
to focus, for example, on young, middle-class, unchurched professionals
in building megachurches. This is the same principle used by mission
organizations, for example, when they target a particular caste group in
India to evangelize. Over the last thirty years, the focus on people groups
has become the "holy grail" of evangelical missions, and undoubtedly,
there are tens of millions of new Christians in the world today because
of the effective application of this principle. But the Pentecostals, by and
large, have been reluctant to embrace this principle in their evangelism
and mission work. The Azusa Street Mission was, from the start, a multi-
racial event that transcended the normal social and ethnic barriers. Pentecostalism and neo-Pentecostalism demonstrated over and over again the
power of the Pentecostal message to penetrate high church Anglicans as
well as poor, uneducated laborers and then bring them together in a way
that confounds the dynamics of proven sociological expectations.

Pentecostals have modeled on a global scale what happened to Peter and
Cornelius in Acts 10, which I alluded to in chapter 3. The two men were
completely separated, both theologically and culturally. One was an uncir-
cumcised Gentile, the other a Law-abiding Jew. In short, they were certainly
not part of the same "homogeneous unit." They were not even able to share

---

33. As highlighted in chapter 12, 1974 is the year when Dr. Ralph Winter delivered his now famous
paper at the first Lausanne Congress on World Evangelization, entitled, "The Highest Priority:
Cross-Cultural Evangelism." This date is used to mark the shift in mission practice from a focus
on places to a focus on peoples.

34. Donald McGavran, *Understanding Church Growth*, rev. ed. (Grand Rapids: Eerdmans, 1990),
69.

35. This is the basis for the well-known saying that 11:00 a.m. is the most segregated hour in
America.

table fellowship and certainly could not stand in the presence of God together. However, once the Holy Spirit came on the whole household (Acts 10:44), everything changed. Peter and Cornelius had a new basis for unity through the power of the Holy Spirit, who sovereignly yoked them to one another and to Christ. We normally read Acts 10 as the story of Cornelius's conversion, but a more reflective reading reveals that both men were transformed. Cornelius became a full member of the body of Christ, and Peter had his truncated view of God enlarged and transformed. He now understood that God was a missionary God with a heart for the whole world. The Pentecostals may make evangelicals uncomfortable with their comparative disinterest in formal theology, but they also have the capacity to transform our understanding of God in many positive ways.

In conclusion, the growth of Pentecostalism, neo-Pentecostalism, Charismatic and neo-charismatic movements globally now exceeds 600 million Christians. This has had a dramatic impact on our understanding of pneumatology and missions practice. Increasingly, missions practice around the world understands the book of Acts not only as an accurate *description* of the Holy Spirit's work through the early church, but also as a *prescriptive* paradigm that should guide the church's practice today.

THE ROLE OF THE HOLY SPIRIT IN DIRECTING AND UNFOLDING THE *MISSIO DEI*

The third and final key question this chapter seeks to address is how the person and work of the Holy Spirit relates to the *missio dei*. The ethnic and geographic movement of the book of Acts from Jerusalem to Judea and Samaria and to the "ends of the earth" provides an important testimony to the larger global mission to which the church has been called. It reminds us of God's promise and initiative in Genesis 12 to bless all the nations on earth. The witness and growth of the church, therefore, must be seen through the larger frame of God's initiative and action in the *missio dei*.

Many of the key missiological turning points in Acts are precipitated by supernatural visions, including the conversion of Saul of Tarsus (9:3–6), Ananias's obedience (9:10–16), Cornelius's conversion (10:3–6), Peter's obedience (10:9–20), and the direction of Paul's missionary journeys (16:9), giving testimony to the Holy Spirit's role as the director of God's mission in and through the life and witness of the church.

Through visions, words of revelation, and signs and wonders, the Holy

Spirit leads the church, not only in effective evangelism and witness, but also into a deeper understanding of the *missio dei*, often in ways that surprised the early Jewish Christians by challenging many of their attitudes and pre-existing ideas about God's work. Because of the reputation of Saul of Tarsus as an enemy of the church, Ananias was reluctant to go to him, but he did so in direct response to a vision (Acts 9:10–19). Later, a God-fearing Gentile named Cornelius sent for Peter in response to another vision (10:1–8). As an observant Jew, Peter was clearly uncomfortable going into Cornelius's home and went only in response to a vision (10:9–20) and the direct action of the Holy Spirit speaking to him. Luke records that "while Peter was still thinking about the vision, the Spirit said to him, 'Simon, three men are looking for you. So get up and go downstairs. Do not hesitate to go with them, for I have sent them'" (10:19–20). The Holy Spirit took the initiative in the Gentile mission and is portrayed as the central actor in both speaking and sending.

Acts 13 records the sending out of Paul and his companions on the first of several church-planting initiatives, widely known today as the missionary journeys of Paul.[36] Paul and Barnabus were senior leaders in the church at Antioch. Barnabus had been sent from the Jerusalem church to Antioch in order to help strengthen the young church. Barnabus had recruited Paul to help him in the work there (11:25–26). During the next year, Paul and Barnabus devoted themselves fully to teaching and discipling the new believers. Later, while the church was worshipping and fasting, "the Holy Spirit said, 'Set apart for me Barnabus and Saul for the work to which I have called them'" (13:2). The church obeyed and became the sending church for the apostle Paul, evidenced not only through the laying on of hands to commission them (13:3), but also through the eventual return of the missionaries to Antioch, where they "gathered the church together and reported all that God had done through them" (14:27).[37] However,

---

36. I prefer to call them "church-planting initiatives" rather than missionary journeys to clarify the common misconception that Paul is rapidly traveling from town to town on an extended evangelistic campaign. Paul's ministry of church planting takes place over a thirteen-year period. It is beyond the scope of this work to explore each of Paul's journeys. Acts records three major church-planting initiatives (13:1–14:28; 15:36–18:22; 18:23–21:17). Some scholars argue that other textual and historical evidence indicates that Paul went on a fourth mission, perhaps to Spain, between his first and second imprisonments in Rome.

37. See, also, Acts 18:22, when Paul returned to Antioch after the second journey. His third journey, however, ended in Jerusalem, not Antioch. Acts records that Paul reported about his ministry among the Gentiles to the "pillars" of the church in Jerusalem.

seen through the lens of the *missio dei*, it is clear that Antioch's role as the sending church is clearly subordinate to the prior sending agency of the Holy Spirit.[38]

The Holy Spirit not only initiated, called, and sent the missionaries into the Gentile mission, He also continued to direct the mission on the field. For example, during the second missionary journey, Paul's missionary band is "kept by the Holy Spirit from preaching the word in the province of Asia" (Acts 16:6). When they come to the border of Mysia and try to enter Bithynia, the "Spirit of Jesus would not allow them to" (16:7). The text does not tell us precisely *how* the Holy Spirit prevented their northward journey, nor are we told *why* turning to the west (toward Europe) was given priority. Nevertheless, the band turns to the west and travels to Troas on the coast, when once again the Holy Spirit intervenes by giving Paul a vision of a "man of Macedonia" who stood before Paul and begged him to "come over to Macedonia and help us" (16:9). It is this vision that caused Paul and his companions to cross the Aegean Sea into Europe. A woman named Lydia, a dealer in purple cloth, was the first to respond to the gospel in Europe, when "the Lord opened her heart to respond to Paul's message" (16:14). Lydia represents the firstfruits of a great spiritual harvest in Europe.

The unfolding story of Acts is certainly about the obedience of the early church to the Great Commission of Christ. However, it is also the story of the ongoing initiatives of God the Father through the Holy Spirit to direct and guide His church to extend the *missio dei* and fulfill His promise to Abraham. The Holy Spirit is still the agent of initiating, calling, sending, and directing the unfolding of the *missio dei* as He was in the life of the early church.

CONCLUSION

This chapter began by examining the role of the Holy Spirit in the life and witness of the early church, as recorded in Acts. We then demonstrated how the slow development of a full and robust pneumatology caused the church to neglect a proper emphasis on the work of the Holy Spirit in the church and in our global witness in the world. An embarrassing gap

---

38. This is not to diminish the doctrine of ecclesiology in mission sending but rather to emphasize the importance of conceptualizing the church's role within the larger context of the *missio dei*. This will be discussed in more detail in chapter 15.

developed between the church in Acts and the life and practice of many churches around the world.

During the twentieth century, the Pentecostal movement served to re-awaken the church to the normative aspect of the Holy Spirit's activity in the church and in our witness in the world. Ultimately the Spirit is the central agent in the ongoing unfolding of the *missio dei*, enabling the church to experience the realities of the New Creation in the present. Of course, there have been glaring inconsistencies and theological problems within Pentecostalism, as with any Christian movement. If, in this chapter, I have neglected the "mote" in the Pentecostal eye, it is only because I am so painfully aware of the "beam" in my own eye. In other words, I maintain that despite its problems, Pentecostalism remains an important corrective to the blind spots in the pneumatology and practice that have dominated the West for centuries. As Samuel Escobar has wisely stated, evangelical Protestantism emphasized the "continuity in truth by the Word," whereas Pentecostalism has emphasized the "continuity in life by the Spirit."[39] To be faithful to Christ in the twenty-first century, the church desperately needs the dynamic union of both.

---

39. Samuel Escobar, "A Missiological Approach to Latin American Protestantism," *International Review of Mission* 87, no. 345 (April 1998): 172.

— 15 —

The Church as the Embodiment of the New Creation

AFTER WORLD WAR II, the Communists designed Nowa Huta on the outskirts of Krakow, Poland, to be "a living monument to Communist utopianism."[1] From the start, it was designed to be a worker's paradise, embodying all the lofty ideals of atheistic communism. It was designed to be a massive, industrial city that would draw peasants and working-class people to the area, since they embodied the proletariat ideal of Marxist ideology. The massive steel plants and towering apartment complexes were built around a central public square, which was dominated by a bronze statue of Lenin. In 1954 when the Lenin Steelworks was officially opened, Nowa Huta was touted as the showpiece for the communist vision of the future. There was only one problem with the new city. There was no church. The communist designers had assumed that everyone who lived there and worked in the steel factories would be enlightened atheists. However, the steel workers wanted a church. The authorities dismissed their backward thinking and told them that there was no place for such superstitious nonsense in the new order of communism.

The authorities did not realize that Nowa Huta had been built in the jurisdiction of a little known Polish bishop named Karol Wojtyla. The young bishop and others repeatedly applied for permits to construct a church but were always denied. Eventually, they took two rugged beams and made a

---

1. Charles Colson, *The Body: Being Light in Darkness* (Dallas: Word, 1992), 201. The name *Nowa Huta* means "New Steelworks" or "New Foundry."

rough cross and placed it at the center of the city and held open-air worship services. The authorities would tear down the cross and disperse the crowds with water cannons. Yet, each night the cross kept reappearing, and the crowds kept growing. Karol Wojtyla, along with other priests, gave sermons in the open air, sometimes in unbearable heat, freezing rain, or snow. Nevertheless, the faithful kept on meeting and praying and believing. Twenty years after the first permit was denied, a permit was finally granted to build a church at the site of the protests. A year later, Bishop Karol Wojtyla was elected Pope John Paul II.

The pope's visit back to Nowa Huta in 1979, along with his frank denunciation of atheistic communism and well-articulated moral vision, is widely attributed as the catalyst that led to the fall of communism in Poland. Ten years later, the famous statue of Lenin in Nowa Huta was torn down, marking the end of communism in Poland. Looking back on this dramatic history, the Christians of Nowa Huta recall that it was in those evening gatherings beneath the wooden cross, lining up for Communion in the face of the relentless propaganda and wrath of the government, that they realized the true nature of the church. The identity of the church transcended any building or institution. There had always been a church in Nowa Huta. It was composed of men and women worshipping Jesus Christ, even while facing the scorn of this world. The church is the community of Christ, which embodies hope in a world of despair.

This story helps to highlight the importance of a proper understanding of ecclesiology. Because Protestantism was born out of a reaction to abuses that were present in the institutional church of the medieval period, there has always been a healthy recognition within Protestantism that the church can become co-opted by sin. The notion of "*ecclesia semper reformanda debet*," that is, the church always needs reformation, is an important principle within Protestantism. The church in every generation must listen afresh to the Word of God and be summoned afresh to the gospel of Jesus Christ and to the new realities the church has been called to embody. However, the Protestant emphases on the fallibility of the church, the necessity of personal conversion, and the free exercise of conscience at times have exposed our vulnerability to a weak ecclesiology. Protestant ecclesiology tends to be functional, instrumental, and pragmatic, leaving us without a proper ontological, theological, and historical grounding for ecclesiology. This has had important implications for the missionary movement. The purpose of this chapter is to explore the role of ecclesiology in twenty-first-century missions.

FOCUSING THE ISSUE

Ecclesiology lies at the heart of many of the most pressing issues in contemporary missiology. Whether we are discussing the breakup of Christendom in Latin America, church dependency in Africa, church planting among Hindus in North India, or the rise of churchless Christianity among Muslims, all of these issues require prior reflection on ecclesiology. Yet, ecclesiology has lagged far behind other branches of theology in missionary writings. Since the nineteenth century, Protestant missions strategy often has been conceptualized around the priority of evangelizing individuals rather than planting churches, which bring together the nucleus of a new community of believers. If church planting was emphasized, it often was thought of in formal structural and organizational terms. It was assumed that the entire administrative and ecclesial framework or structure of the sending church could be transplanted seamlessly into the new culture. New believers were discouraged from establishing their own church movements, and the cross-cultural implications of church organization and indigenous leadership development received scant attention.

On the sending side of missions, the role of the specialized parachurch missions agency grew more and more dominant. Beginning in the nineteenth century, the church witnessed the dramatic rise of specialized missions organizations, which focused on a wide array of ministries ranging from Bible translation, to street evangelism, to medical missions, to church-planting ministries.[2] Many of these organizations were interdenominational and drew from a wide spectrum of Christian traditions. Because these parachurch agencies were not sponsored by any single denomination, they were generally organized as "faith" missions. This meant that the missionaries were responsible for raising their own financial and prayer support. Often this was done by missionaries speaking in dozens of churches and raising support from individuals and churches

---

2. David B. Barrett, Todd M. Johnson, and Peter F. Crossing, "Missiometrics 2008: Reality Checks for Christian World Communions," *International Bulletin of Missionary Research* 32, no. 1 (January 2008): 27–30. The growth is reflected in the income of parachurch organizations, which has grown from 1 billion in 1900 to 20 billion in 1970 to 240 billion in 2008, and is projected to rise to 570 billion by 2025.

across the country. Through this method, hundreds of new missionaries were enabled to serve in missions, even though they may never have been formally sent out by any single church. Instead, they were sent, trained, and supervised by an independent, parachurch mission agency.

By the dawn of the twenty-first century, there was a renewed emphasis on the role of the local church in sending out and supporting missionaries. Books such as *Loving the Church, Blessing the Nations* appeared, which demonstrated new ways churches could network together for global missions independent of the traditional missions-sending agencies.[3] This, in turn, has caused both churches and mission agencies to reflect more deeply about ecclesiology. This chapter will focus on the doctrine of ecclesiology, particularly as it applies to the relationship between the local church and the specialized mission agencies in the work of missions.

Two Structures of God's Redemptive Mission

The Church

It was in the pluralistic environment of Caesarea Philippi that Jesus first used the word *church* to describe the community of those who follow Him. Jesus said to Peter, "I tell you that you are Peter, and on this rock I will build my church" (Matt. 16:18). Many have been surprised by Jesus' use of the word *church* to describe this newly emerging community within Judaism. The word was not drawn from the rich vocabulary of the Old Testament, or from Jesus' religious background in Judaism. Instead, the word *church* (*ekklēsia*) was a secular word used by Greeks to refer to a public assembly. *Ekklēsia* was a common term used in Greek cities for assembling citizens together, often to render decisions related to public affairs.[4] The words *synagogue (sunagōgē)* and *congregation (qahal)* were the more common words used by Jews to describe their religious gatherings for prayer, worship, and exhortation. Jesus could have called His followers into a new synagogue or some other adaptation of a preexisting Jewish term. Instead, Jesus used a word that implied a public gathering for *everyone,* Jew and Gentile. The word *church* thrusts us into the *public* arena. The followers of Jesus could have avoided persecution by remaining within Judaism, which enjoyed a protected status as a *cultus*

---

3. George Miley, *Loving the Church, Blessing the Nations* (Carlise, UK: Authentic Media, 1969).
4. Henry George Liddell and Robert Scott, *A Greek-English Lexicon* (Oxford: Clarendon, 1996), 509.

privatus (private cult) within the empire. The word *synagogue* referred to a religious community that had withdrawn from the world, whereas the word *church* refers to a public gathering of people at the center of society.

Lesslie Newbigin, in *The Open Secret*, comments on the use of the word *church* when he says, "The community that confesses that Jesus is Lord has been, from the beginning, a movement launched into the public life of humankind. The Greco-Roman world in which the New Testament was written was full of societies offering to those who wished to join a way of personal salvation through religious teaching and practice."[5] These private cults, known as *cultus privatus*, were in contrast to the only officially sanctioned *public* cult, *cultus publicus*, which was the Roman Empire itself, under the sovereign lordship of Caesar. However, using the word *church* meant that the followers of Christ could not avail themselves of this option. They "could not be a society offering personal salvation for those who cared to avail themselves of its teaching and practice."[6] Instead, the followers of Christ boldly claimed that the message of the gospel was for *all peoples*. By using the word *church,* God was, in effect, summoning the entire world to a public assembly (*ekklēsia*), which would proclaim that Jesus is Lord. It was a direct challenge to the public cult of the empire, claiming that Caesar was not Lord. Instead, "Jesus is Lord" became the first creed of the early church (1 Cor. 12:3).

This "public" understanding of the church stands in opposition to the modern reinterpretation of Christianity as a "private cult." It is quite common to hear Christians say that the controlling idea of the word *church* is that it refers to those whom God has "called out" of the world. While it is true that Christians are to reject the lusts, ambitions, and idolatries of this world (1 John 2:15–17), we have not been called *out* of the world but *into* the world. The church, through the Holy Spirit, is part of the ongoing invasion of the age to come into the present age; the New Creation is already transforming the old creation. In Jesus' high priestly prayer, He specifically prays, "My prayer is not that you take them out of the world but that you protect them from the evil one. They are not of the world, even as I am not of it. . . . As you sent me into the world, I have sent them into the world" (John 17:15–16, 18). The church has been summoned by Christ into a new community, and we are

---

5. Lesslie Newbigin, *The Open Secret: An Introduction to the Theology of Mission* (Grand Rapids: Eerdmans, 1995), 16.
6. Ibid.

called to go out into the world as His public witnesses. It is the *public* witness of the gospel that is the primary feature of the use of the word *church*. Thus, the word *church* is more about calling the church into the world than out of it.

The Western church was caught off guard by the rapid collapse of Christendom and the dramatic rise of religious diversity and pluralism. The primary response has been to retreat into the safety of a privatized faith, a *cultus privatus*, which makes Christianity just another method or path of personal salvation that does not make any broader claims that challenge the truth claims of alternative spiritualities, religious practices, or world religions. Postmodernism with its loss of meaning, history, and objective truth finds it particularly difficult to reclaim this ground. We have become reasonably comfortable with telling people that Christianity is meaningful *for us*, but it seems arrogant and triumphalistic to insist that the gospel is publicly summoning the entire world to repentance and faith in Jesus Christ. Most churches in the West, with some notable exceptions, were not prepared for the robust catechesis and discipleship that was required to retool the church to face the simultaneous rise of pluralism and postmodernism. However, the privatization of the gospel is a *mistranslation* of the gospel of Jesus Christ.

Since much of the emerging Majority World church is embedded in a context of religious pluralism and public persecution, we have much to learn from our brothers and sisters around the world about how to be faithful to our public witness in the midst of an unbelieving and, at times, even hostile context. Western missionaries must not go out and reproduce privatized versions of Christianity, rather they must commit to discipleship for an engaged public witness. Ironically, the rise of pluralism and the post-Christendom retreat of Christianity in the West may provide the best training ground for producing a more effective and robust missionary force from the Western world, arising out of a strong sense of what it means to be the church of Jesus Christ in the world.

The Mission Society
Chapter 1 recounted how the World Council of Churches called for a moratorium on missions in 1972. The mainline churches in the West responded by cutting funding for missions and bringing missionaries home. Some missionaries continued on in administrative and social work, but the work of evangelism and church planting was largely discredited. The result was a precipitous decline of missionaries sent out from mainline, Western

churches. However, the retreat of the global witness of the Western church did not mark the demise of the missionary movement from the West.[7] Indeed, the number of missionaries from the West (as a percentage of population) declined only slightly throughout the moratorium on missions.[8] The main reason was a steady restructuring of how missionaries were mobilized, trained, and sent out. The numbers sent out by mainline denominational sending agencies did decline sharply. However, the latter part of the twentieth century saw the rise of dozens of new, independent "faith" mission-sending agencies. They are now responsible for mobilizing and sending more missionaries from the Western world than any other source. The result is that we now have two major structures for sending out missionaries: the institutional church (through their own sending mechanisms) and the independent mission agency. Is this emergence of independent mission-sending societies a sign of the church's vitality or a sign of ecclesiastical neglect? Are these two structures biblical, and, if so, what is the relationship between the two? We will begin with a biblical and theological reflection on whether two separate structures can be supported by the New Testament.

THE CHURCH AT ANTIOCH AND PAUL'S MISSIONARY BAND

There are several reasons why the church at Antioch is one of the most significant churches in the New Testament. First, it is in Antioch that the first predominately Gentile church emerges. Greeks in Antioch received the gospel and "a great number of people believed and turned to the Lord" (Acts 11:21). In fact, it was the predominance of Gentiles in the church of Antioch that made it increasingly problematic to continue conceptualizing the church as a messianic movement within Judaism. Therefore, it is in Antioch that the disciples are first called *Christians* (11:26). Second, the church at Antioch is a discipled church. Paul and Barnabus spent a year discipling the new believers in Antioch (11:26), and in the opening verses of chapter 13, we discover that the church has recognized "prophets and teachers" in addition to the apostolic and pastoral leadership of Paul and Barnabus (13:1). Third, the church at

---

7. We have explored how during this time the Majority World churches became increasingly involved in missions. However, the point of this chapter is to examine the way mission mobilization has been restructured in the West and the implications this has for ecclesiology.

8. David B. Barrett, George T. Kurian, and Todd M. Johnson, eds., *World Christian Encyclopedia: A Comparative Survey of Churches and Religions in the Modern World* (New York: Oxford University Press, 1982), 803 and (2nd ed., 2001), 843.

Antioch is a diverse, multiethnic church. Not only is the church membership made up of Jews and Gentiles, but the leadership also is multiethnic, as indicated by the diverse list of five prophets and teachers in Antioch (Acts 13:1). Simeon was probably an African, because Luke tells us that he was called "Niger" by those who knew him. Lucius was a common Gentile name in the Roman world. Quite likely he was one of the Greeks who initially responded to the gospel in Acts 11 and was now a prophet and teacher in the church. Manaen was a foster brother to Herod Antipas, the youngest son of Herod the Great who ruled during the lifetime of Jesus. Paul and Barnabus are the most prominent names in the list but are named without any special distinction along with the others. Finally, it is the church at Antioch that is the sending church for Paul and his companions in all three of their missionary journeys. Thus, the church at Antioch gives important clues to the relationship between the church and the missionary enterprise.

There are two vital observations about the relationship of the church at Antioch and the missionary bands led by Paul.

Two Distinct Structures

First, Paul's missionary band *is a distinct structure from the local church*. Acts 13:2 records that the Holy Spirit spoke to the church, presumably through a prophetic utterance given by one of the prophets who was assembled during their gathered worship, and directed them to set apart Paul and Barnabus for the work to which He had called them. After more prayer and fasting, the two were commissioned through the laying on of hands and were sent out (13:3). This is the origin of the first traveling band of Christian missionaries. Thus, there are two distinct redemptive structures. The church of Antioch is a New Testament example of a local church and is "the prototype of all subsequent fellowships where old and young, male and female, are gathered together as normal biological families in aggregate" for worship, preaching, fellowship, and the sacraments.[9] Paul's missionary band, in contrast, involves a *secondary* commitment beyond membership in the local church. Furthermore, the missionary band was dedicated to one particular task, namely, evangelization leading to the planting of a new

---

9. Ralph D. Winter, "The Two Structures of God's Redemptive Mission," in *Perspectives on the World Christian Movement,* ed. Ralph D. Winter and Steven C. Hawthorne (Pasadena, CA: William Carey Library, 1999), 221.

church. There are many pastoral and ministerial obligations such as visiting the sick and caring for widows that are integral aspects of the life of a healthy church but are not essential to an itinerant missionary band. Paul's missionary band is a prototype "of all subsequent missionary endeavors organized out of committed, experienced workers who affiliate themselves through a second decision beyond membership in the first structure."[10]

Accountability to the Church

Second, *Paul's missionary band was accountable to the church at Antioch and to the senior leaders of the entire Christian movement, who were based in Jerusalem.*

Even though Paul is considered an apostle, it is a misreading of Acts to view Paul and his missionary band as an autonomous group of itinerant missionaries without any accountability to the church. Luke's record of Paul's return to Antioch at the conclusion of his first missionary church-planting journey clearly demonstrates that Paul understood that he had been commissioned by the church at Antioch for the work and that he was, therefore, accountable to report back to them. Luke records the end of the first journey as follows:

> From Attalia they sailed back to Antioch, where they had been committed to the grace of God for the work they had now completed. On arriving there, they gathered the church together and reported all that God had done through them and how he had opened the door of faith to the Gentiles. And they stayed there a long time with the disciples. (Acts 14:26–27)

Likewise, Paul returned to Antioch after his second missionary journey (18:22).

At the conclusion of Paul's third missionary journey, he does not return to Antioch but returns to Jerusalem and meets with the senior leadership of the church. Paul previously had met with the elders in Jerusalem and records in Galatians 2:2, "I . . . set before them [the elders] the gospel that I preach among the Gentiles." He goes on to say that he did this with the elders privately "for fear that I was running or had run my race in vain."

---

10. Ibid.

Paul submitted his ministry to the senior leaders in Jerusalem. Some years later, Paul ended his third missionary journey in Jerusalem. Luke, who was a member of the missionary band, records their arrival as follows:

> When we arrived at Jerusalem, the brothers received us warmly. The next day Paul and the rest of us went to see James, and all the elders were present. Paul greeted them and reported in detail what God had done among the Gentiles through his ministry. (Acts 21:17–19)

Accountability is an integral feature of all Christian ministry in the New Testament. So, though the New Testament provides evidence of two separate structures, they are not "separate-but-equal" entities. Rather, the secondary structure exists for the sole purpose of serving the church, and it is, in the final analysis, accountable to it.

Modality/Sodality

Ralph Winter has pointed out that the two redemptive structures of local church and missionary band function as modalities and sodalities respectively. A *modality* is a structured organization with diverse responsibilities and includes men and women of all ages. In contrast, a *sodality* involves a secondary commitment beyond membership in the modality, and membership is generally restricted in some way. Sodalities normally have a much narrower focus. For example, the United States, or any state government, is a *modality*. To be born in the United States, or a particular state, automatically entitles you to citizenship and certain privileges, which embrace men and women of all ages. As a modality, the government is responsible for a wide array of tasks, ranging from education, to national defense, to paving roads. In contrast, a local hardware store, or even a chain of hardware stores, is an example of a *sodality*. For example, True Value Hardware is a private company based in Chicago, which has thousands of hardware stores across the country. It is a sodality because Americans are not naturally a part of the True Value Hardware company. Those who are have made a secondary commitment to work on behalf of the company. Furthermore, there are countless tasks True Value Hardware is not responsible for because, as a private enterprise, it is able to focus on one specific task, namely, providing hardware to its customers.

In a similar way, churches are modalities. Christians of all ages and genders belong to churches. It is the most basic organization to which all Christians belong in a way that is roughly analogous to the idea that all citizens in this country belong to the United States. Churches are responsible for everything Christ has called His people to do, to reflect and extend the inbreaking of His rule. Churches must preach the gospel, care for the elderly, catechize children, administer sacraments, disciple new believers, exercise church discipline, and much, much more. As a modality, a church cannot decide to neglect most of these responsibilities and specialize in just one. Modalities, by definition, always carry a broad range of responsibilities that are essential to their existence. A government is not faithful if it neglects all of its other duties and focuses solely on paving roads, even if it produces the finest paved roads in the world. Likewise, a church is not being faithful if it neglects all of its other duties and focuses solely on caring for the elderly, as important as that is.

A mission organization, on the other hand, is a sodality. Christians who belong to the church make a secondary commitment to join an organization with a particular focus. Wycliffe Bible Translators is an example of a sodality. The church, as a modality, has the broad responsibility of making sure that the Bible is translated into every language on earth. However, with the church's wide range of other responsibilities and the level of expertise that is required for this particular task, it can easily be neglected. The average congregation, however committed, is generally unable to organize the resources and personnel necessary for Bible translation. However, a sodality like Wycliffe can focus on that particular task and organize a team of dedicated professionals who are committed and gifted for this particular work. As a sodality, Wycliffe cannot be criticized for not administering sacraments or caring for the elderly any more than one could criticize True Value Hardware for not repairing a bridge or paving a road. The reason is that a modality and a sodality represent two fundamentally distinct structures.

In my view, there is sufficient evidence to indicate that Paul's missionary band functioned as a sodality, whereas the church of Antioch, like any other local church, functioned as a modality. If so, then this provides the biblical basis for the existence of specialized missions organizations. However, not all Christian sodalities are the same. There are some, like Wycliffe Bible Translators or Youth with a Mission (YWAM), that function independently from any particular denomination and are not directly accountable to any specific modality. There are others, such as Mission to the World of the Presbyterian Church of America and the International Mission Board of the Southern Baptists, that are directly accountable to a specific denominational modality. Therefore, even if one accepts the biblical basis for two distinct structures, we must address the question of accountability and how sodalities are related to modalities.

To accomplish this, it is important to place the discussion into a larger historical frame and examine how modalities and sodalities have functioned throughout history.

Two Structures in Historical Perspective

Emergence of Modality and Sodality Structures in Roman Catholicism
The local church modality, wherever it exists in the world, is normally made up of men and women, married and single, youth and children, young and old. The vast majority of the people in the congregation are occupied with their education, working, families, and, in general, the wide variety of necessary labor that is essential for life. Early on, Christians recognized that the long-term vitality of the church, as well as the extension of the church across new cultural, social, and linguistic barriers, required a secondary group of people who were not bound by the normal responsibilities of life. Religious orders developed, which called people to a life completely consecrated to God, marked by vows of poverty, chastity, and obedience. These religious orders functioned as sodalities. Belonging to a religious order was never intended to be a general expectation of the entire church but a special, *voluntary* commitment for a few who felt led by God to dedicate themselves completely to Christian service. The vows were considered necessary in order to free these Christians from the heavy, time-consuming obligations of property, work, and family.

Broadly speaking, these specialized religious orders emerged historically for two main reasons. First, they emerged as a way to reenergize a church that had fallen to a low spiritual ebb. God frequently uses groups of dedicated Christians who have united themselves together in a common witness in order to call the larger church back to faithfulness and to become better hearers of the gospel. Second, religious orders emerged out of a vitalized church that wanted to extend the gospel across new cultural boundaries. Special people were needed who were able to devote themselves full-time to arduous travel, language acquisition, cultural adaptation, and so forth. Thus, the religious orders emerged both for internal spiritual renewal and for missionary outreach. Those who belonged to these religious orders were not part of the ordinary hierarchy of the church, unless they were also ordained priests. Instead, they had their own governance structure and followed their own rule of conduct such as the Rule of St. Benedict, the Rule of St. Francis, or the Rule of St. Augustine. The Rule of St. Benedict, for example, is the most widely used rule in the Western monastic tradition.[11]

The Benedictine order emerged in the sixth century as a counter to the growing nominalism in the church. Over the centuries, the Benedictines have been an important model for purity and holiness in the midst of a church hierarchy that at times has become corrupted with secular power and wealth.

Some of the best-known religious orders, such as the Franciscans, Dominicans, and Jesuits, all trace their origin to the need for spiritual renewal. The Dominicans were founded as a preaching order in France in the thirteenth century.[12] The growing urbanization of European society posed new problems and created the need for a group of dedicated preachers who were theologically trained to counter heresies and were able to preach in the vernacular. The Franciscans were founded by St. Francis of Assisi in the thirteenth century to counter the growth of heresy and secularism in the church. St. Francis's humility and freedom from earthly possessions has been an inspiration to Christians all over the world. The Jesuits were founded by Ignatius Loyola as the Society of Jesus in the sixteenth century to address many of the corruptions that been brought to light during the Protestant Reformation. Jesuit priests belong to a worldwide apostolic society and are known for their commitment to scholarship, theological reflection, and missionary commitment. Ignatius Loyola sent Jesuits out as missionaries around Europe to evangelize and to begin new schools, colleges, and seminaries.

The Dominicans, Franciscans, and Jesuits are not, technically speaking, monastic orders but *mendicant* orders.[13] This means that these communities

---

11. Other orders, such as the Cistercians and the Trappists, have adopted the Rule of St. Benedict.

12. The Dominicans are known as the Order of Preachers, using the initials O.P. to designate those in the order. They are also known as Blackfriars because of the black capes they wear over their habits. This is in contrast to the Greyfriars (Franciscans) and the Whitefriars (Carmelites).

13. The word *mendicant* means "openhanded" and refers to their practice of begging for their sustenance. Most individuals within the monastic communities had no personal wealth but all was held in common by the community, whereas the mendicant orders eschewed the accumulation of wealth, both individually and corporately.

were not cloistered behind walls for contemplation but were sent out into the community as teachers and exhorters. Mendicants were not assigned to one particular monastery or convent but were free to move around, as needed, from place to place.[14] Sometimes they are called friars, rather than monks, to emphasize the public nature of their work in the world. The word *friar* comes from the word *brother* and was used to refer to those who publicly begged for alms for their support, since the mendicant orders embrace both personal and collective poverty. The mendicant orders have not only monks and nuns, but also a "third order" of laypeople who continue in their normal life and work but commit themselves to holy living and service to the church. The mendicant orders created a powerful force of renewal in the church, as well as workers to assist in the public ministry of the church in the world. It is, therefore, misleading to draw a firm line between the contemplative and activistic traditions since even traditionally stationary, contemplative orders had long histories of mobilization for missionary purposes. Likewise, the mendicant orders that were committed to public ministry became powerful resources for renewal within the church.

In chapter 8 we explored how Gregory the Great mobilized a group of Benedictine monks under the leadership of Augustine of Canterbury to evangelize and plant churches among several people groups in what is now England. Peripatetic monks were instrumental in bringing the gospel to a number of remote areas of Europe, including Scotland and Ireland. Missions history resounds with well-known missionary monks such as St. Aidan, St. Columba, and St. Patrick, who brought the gospel to new people groups in Northumbria (northwest England), Scotland, and Ireland, respectively. The stereotypical perception of monks as those who have fled the world and live cloistered lives of isolation must be countered by an appreciation of the remarkable evangelistic and missionary vitality of these communities.

Thus, from the fourth century onward, we see that the church developed two distinct structures. The first structure, the local church, was centered on a relatively small, defined geographic area known as a parish and its members enjoyed the oversight of a local pastor. Several parishes collectively formed a diocese, which was, in turn, under the authority of a bishop. The second structure was a more flexible and autonomous structure, known as a

---

14. The word *monastery* is generally used to refer to communities of monks, whereas a *convent* generally refers to communities of nuns.

monastery or a community of mendicants, whose members enjoyed the oversight of an abbot or vicar and lived under a particular order. One structure
formed around the local church, the parish, the diocese, and the bishop. The
second structure was far more flexible but required a secondary commitment
beyond the local church and was generally focused on a particular task such
as education, scholarship, helping the elderly, sick, and poor, or evangelism.
This second structure formed around a monastery or convent, which brought
together monks or nuns who lived under a common rule and submitted to
the direction of an abbot they elected. The mendicant orders swore allegiance
directly to the pope and were not under the authority of any bishop.

The Roman Catholic Church has functioned with these two structures
for centuries. At times there were tensions between the two structures, so
that the bishop and the abbot, the diocese and the monastery, the local
church and the mendicants developed rivalries and sometimes failed to
trust or appreciate each other. However, overall the two structures have
been extremely beneficial, enabling the church to do things it otherwise
could never have done. A local church or even a diocesan bishop may have
had a deep burden to help famine victims in Africa or to evangelize and
plant a church in an unreached people group, but the localized nature
of the church created a logistical and structural challenge. The religious
orders provided the structure, the organization, and the men and women
who were prepared to sacrifice to extend the church's ministry in various
ways. In short, the two structures nurtured and helped one another.

The Emergence of Modality and Sodality Structures in Protestantism
The Protestant Reformers decided not to establish monastic, mendicant,
or other associated orders and societies within the newly emerging Protestant churches of the sixteenth century. Even though Luther rediscovered
the gospel as an Augustinian monk, he nevertheless ended up completely
dismantling all of the traditional sodality structures of the church. In order
to understand why this was done, we must first explore how the Protestant
Reformation represented an important shift in the doctrine of the church,
which initially made it difficult to sustain a secondary sodality structure.

ROMAN CATHOLIC AND PROTESTANT UNDERSTANDING OF THE CHURCH
The Protestant Reformation in the sixteenth century often is thought of
as primarily a struggle over soteriology. In other words, at the heart of

the Reformation was a struggle about the terms through which God saves us in Jesus Christ, especially the relationship between faith and works. The five "*solas*" of the Reformation are widely regarded as summarizing the key themes of the Reformation: *sola Scriptura, sola fide, sola gratia, solo Christo, and Soli Deo Gloria* (Scripture alone, faith alone, grace alone, Christ alone, for the glory of God alone). These five themes continue to serve as valuable confessions of Protestant identity. However, it is also important to note the absence of the *church* in the five *solas*. One could argue, of course, that the church is *presupposed* or *assumed* by all five, since it is only the church that can make these confessions. However, for many, these five confessions find their primary locus in the heart of an *individual* who trusts in God's Word as revealed in Scripture and has placed his or her personal faith in Jesus Christ by the grace of God. Central to the Reformation is the belief in the priesthood of all believers. God's salvation is mediated directly to the believer through Jesus Christ. This affirmation reveals that the Reformation was as much about *ecclesiology* as it was about soteriology.

In contrast, the traditional Roman Catholic understanding of salvation establishes a firm link between the doctrine of salvation and the doctrine of the church. The well-known phrase *Extra Ecclesiam Nulla Salus* (outside the church there is no salvation) is the classic summary of the Roman Catholic view. The phrase was first coined by Cyprian of Carthage who, in his *On the Unity of the Church*, argued that the doctrine was based on Jesus' words "unless you eat my body and drink my blood, you have no part of me."[15] The doctrine was more fully articulated by Pope Innocent III at the Fourth Lateran Council in 1215 and by Pope Boniface VIII in 1302, who identified salvation with being sacramentally connected to Christ through the church. Thus, to not be receiving the sacraments is to cut yourself off from Christ. To invoke a favorite metaphor, the church is like an ark. It is the vessel God has provided to save us from judgment. Those who get into the ark are saved; those who do not are lost.[16] From the traditional Catholic perspective, one's salvation is linked to corporate participation in the

---

15. See The Epistles of St. Cyprian of Carthage, Epistle 72, par. 21 in *The Ante-Nicene Fathers*, ed. Alexander Roberts and James Donaldson, vol. 5 (Peabody, MA: Hendrickson, 1999), 384, 421–29. See also St. Cyprian of Carthage, Treatise 1.
16. Cyprian of Carthage, Epistle 74, part. 15 in *Ante-Nicene Fathers*, ed. Roberts and Donaldson, vol. 5, 394.

life and faith of the church.[17] The Eastern Orthodox Church has a similar perspective.

The Reformation represented a crisis of ecclesiology, since the emergence of a separate branch of Christianity seemed to be an affront to the catholicity of the church. As far back as Cyprian, the church fathers interpreted the church's unity as not merely mystical or invisible but episcopal. Cyprian not only gave us the phrase *Extra Ecclesiam Nulla Salus* but also the statement that "he cannot have God for his father who has not the church for his mother."[18] In the Roman Catholic view, the apostolic authority of the church was conveyed and continues through the episcopal laying on of hands from St. Peter to the present pope. The Reformation, therefore, represented a fracturing of the outward, visible unity of the Roman Catholic Church. It was a challenge to their episcopal authority and thereby was viewed as schismatic and a destruction of the Nicene marks of oneness, apostolicity, and catholicity.

Luther responded with a rearticulation of ecclesiology that was not as tied to the structure and sacraments of a particular church organization but rather to the mystical communion of the saints, which transcends all particular ecclesiastical organizations. The church is apostolic, not because of an episcopal chain of the laying on of hands, but when and only when, it teaches what the apostles taught—thus *sola scriptura*. If the apostolic message is proclaimed, then the church is apostolic, and it shares in the mystical oneness and catholicity, which are the marks of the true church. Luther, in his *On the Councils and the Churches*, defines the true church as the *sancta, catholica, Christiana*—a Christian, holy people. Luther goes on to explicitly argue that when the Nicene Creed speaks of one holy, catholic, apostolic church,

---

17. I emphasize "traditional" because in the post–Vatican II era of Roman Catholicism, this issue has been revisited, especially through the writings of Karl Rahner, who espoused implicit Christianity, which is, as explored in chapter 7 of this book, untethered from either baptism or membership in any visible church. Vatican II decreed that "those who, through no fault of their own, do not know the Gospel of Christ or his Church, but who nevertheless seek God with a sincere heart, and, moved by grace, try in their actions to do his will as they know it through the dictates of their conscience—those too may achieve eternal salvation" (see The Dogmatic Constitution on the Church of the Second Vatican Council; Lumen Gentium, par. 16. See www.usccb.org/catechism/text. See article 9, "I Believe in the Holy Catholic Church." This is the official Web site of the U.S. Conference on Catholic Bishops).

18. See The Treatises of Cyprian, *The Unity of the Catholic Church,* 6, in *The Ante-Nicene Fathers,* ed. Roberts and Donaldson, vol. 5, 423.

it means one, holy, catholic apostolic *people*.[19] The emphasis, he argued, has always been on the people of God, not the organizational structure to which they belonged. This is why Luther did not like the German word *Kirche* for church but preferred the word *Gemeinde*, "community." Therefore, for Luther, this true, organic church has both a visible and an invisible nature. The visible church contains both unredeemed sinners and those who are saints by God's divine work. The invisible church, in contrast, consists of all true believers throughout time and space, and its composition and number is known only to God.[20] Thus, the Reformation emphasized the spiritual and invisible, rather than institutional and episcopal, nature of the church.

This new understanding of ecclesiology made it extraordinarily difficult to maintain separate sodality structures for several reasons. First, the emphasis on the priesthood of all believers was inherently more individualistic and democratic and therefore placed less emphasis on elaborate, multilayered ecclesiastical structures. As noted earlier, the sodality structures were accountable to either an abbot or directly to the pope. Yet, unlike the office of bishop, Protestants did not recognize the offices of abbot or pope, since neither was prescribed in the New Testament. Therefore, it became difficult to

---

19. Hugh T. Kerr, ed., *A Compend of Luther's Theology* (Philadelphia: Westminster Press, 1966), 124–125.

20. Luther's concept of the invisible church was widely accepted in Protestant ecclesiology as reflected in the Scottish Confession of Faith in 1560, for example, which states, "This Kirk is invisible, knawen onelie to God, quha alane knawis whome he hes chosen; and comprehends as weill the Elect that be departed, commonlie called the Kirk Triumphant, and they that zit live and fecht against sinne and Sathan as sall live hereafter" (Scottish Confession of Faith, 1560, article XVI). The language also appears in the Irish Articles of Religion of 1615, which states, "Because this Church consisteth of all those, and those alone, which are elected by God unto salvation, and regenerated by the power of his Spirit, the number of whom is known only unto God himself: therefore it is called the *Catholic* or universal, and the *Invisible* Church (Irish Articles of Religion, 1615, line 68, emphasis original). The language also is enshrined in the Westminster Confession of Faith, 1647, which states, "The catholic or universal Church, *which is invisible,* consists of the whole number of the elect, that have been, are, or shall be gathered into one, under Christ the lead thereof; and is the spouse, the body, the fullness of him that filleth all in all. The *visible Church,* which is also catholic or universal under the gospel (not confined to one nation as before under the law) consists of all those, throughout the world, that profess the true religion, and of their children; and is the kingdom of the Lord Jesus Christ, the house and family of God, out of which there is no ordinary possibility of salvation" (Westminster Confession of Faith, 1657, chapter XXV "Of the Church" article 1, 2, emphasis mine). The Savoy Declaration of 1658 (see chapter XXVI, articles I and II) and the Baptist Confession of 1688 (see chapter XXVI, line 1) also accept this distinction. This is particularly notable in that the Baptist Confession largely accepts much of the Westminster Confession but undertakes a major rewrite of the section on the church. However, the invisible/visible distinction is preserved in both confessions.

maintain the sodality structures that were so directly related to and accountable to these offices. Second, while Jesus clearly and explicitly founded the
church, there is no comparable and explicit statement of Jesus founding any
separate sodality structures. Even though we have argued that a secondary
structure is implied in Paul's missionary band sent out by the church of Antioch, it is not explicitly set forth in the New Testament with the same kind of
clarity and ongoing intentionality as the church. The sodalities seem to flow
out of the church as a way of serving the church, rather than having the kind
of ontological purpose the church carries in the larger *missio dei*.

THE GREAT GAP: 1517 TO 1793

The dismantling of the sodality structures made it exceedingly difficult
for Protestants to extend their message beyond the walls of Christendom.
The fact that nearly two hundred years passed from the birth of the Reformation to the sending of the first Protestant missionaries indicates, in
my view, both theological and structural problems within Protestantism.

Theologically, the Reformers were hindered by two views that ad-
versely affected their ability to engage in cross-cultural missions. First,
many of the key texts in the New Testament related to the cross-cultural
witness of the gospel had become obscured by ecclesiastical and doctrinal controversies. For example, the Great Commission as recorded
in Matthew 28:18–20 was, throughout the patristic period, quoted primarily in support of the deity of Christ, the doctrine of the Trinity, and
the precise language used in baptizing someone.[21] In other words, Matthew 28:18–20 was reflected on *doctrinally* but not *missiologically*. This
continued in the writings of the Reformers. For example, Martin Luther
quotes or alludes to Matthew 28:16–20 a total of fifty-one times in his
writings.[22] "Three citations relate to the papacy,[23] three to the nature of

---

21. The words of Jesus, "All authority in heaven and on earth has been given to me," were used to
    support the deity of Christ. The phrase "baptizing them in the name of the Father and of the Son
    and of the Holy Spirit" was quoted in support of the doctrine of the Trinity as well as a baptismal
    formula. For more on the history of the interpretation of Matthew 28:18–20, see David Bosch,
    "The Structure of Mission: An Exposition of Matthew 28:16–20," in *Exploring Church Growth*,
    ed. Wilbert R. Shenk (Grand Rapids: Eerdmans, 1983), 218–48. See, also, David Bosch, *Trans-
    forming Mission: Paradigm Shifts in Theology of Mission* (Maryknoll, NY: Orbis, 1991), 56, 57.
22. See Jaroslav Pelikan and Helmut T. Lehman, eds., *Luther's Works*, 55 vols. (St. Louis: Concordia,
    1959–1986). The Scripture index that accompanies *Luther's Works* will assist the reader in easily
    locating every usage of the text by Luther. The following citations are all taken from this collection.
23. 2:99; 35:148; 41:33.

priesthood and ordination,[24] fourteen to controversies concerning baptism and the Anabaptists,[25] five to the presence of Christ in the Lord's Supper,[26] one to the doctrine of the Trinity,[27] five to the nature of a true Apostle,[28] thirteen to the nature of the true church and its teaching,[29] two to the enduring nature of the Word of God,[30] and five related to various other topics."[31]

Elsewhere in his writings, Luther does recognize the importance of Christians going to those who have not heard. For example, Luther says that Christians must bear witness to those to whom "Christ has not been proclaimed … so that they, too, may be brought to the spiritual kingdom of Christ."[32] In his commentary on Psalm 117, Luther reflects on the opening phrase, "Praise the LORD, all you nations." He points out that the nations of the world cannot praise the Lord unless they first hear His Word. Luther goes on to say, "If they are to hear His Word, the preachers must be sent to proclaim God's Word to them."[33] However, these references arise out of Luther's commentaries on the Old Testament and are never connected with, or rooted in, any of the Great Commission mandates found in the New Testament.

The second theological perspective that influenced many of the Reformers was the belief that the Great Commission passages already had been fulfilled during the lifetime of the apostles. This is why Luther does not read such well-known passages as Matthew 28:18–20 missiologically. He accepted the widely held view that the apostles already had brought the gospel to the ends of the earth and, therefore, that the original *missiological* force of the text no longer applied to Christians today. In other words, it was widely believed that the Great Commission had already been

---

24. 36:111; 38:196; 38:212.

25. 3:104; 8:81ff; 23:78; 35:91; 38:24; 38:27; 38:87; 38:198; 40:245; 40:252; 51:320; 51:376; 54:55; 54:113.

26. 30:38; 34:74–75; 36:351; 37:331; 38:161.

27. 12:288.

28. 13:272; 34:74–75; 36:351; 37:331; 38:161.

29. 13:19; 13:49; 15:350; 41:196; 41:481; 41:581; 41:107; 41:132; 41:148; 41:155; 41:202; 46:222; 47:117.

30. 17:309; 17:374.

31. 6:311 (comfort in affliction); 6:128 (nature of true worship); 20:338 (the day of judgment); 28:262 (secret will of God); 51:308 (prayer and faith). I am indebted to my colleague Jack Davis and his careful research on this topic as found in John Jefferson Davis, "'teaching Them to Observe All That I Have Commanded You': The History of the Interpretation of the 'Great Commission' and Implications for Marketplace Ministries," *Evangelical Review of Theology* 25, no.1 (January 2007): 65–80.

32. John Warwick Montgomery, "Luther and Missions," *Evangelical Missions Quarterly* 3, no. 4 (1967): 197. Primary source: Weimar Ausgabe, 16, 215ff.

33. Martin Luther, "Selected Psalms III," in *Luther's Works*, ed. Pelikan and Lehman, 14:9.

fulfilled. This is why the text was used for other doctrinal purposes, which seemed to ignore the primary thrust of the text. The belief that the apostles already had brought the gospel to the ends of the earth was based on the idea that every national church was legitimized through its apostolic origin. There are a considerable number of national churches around the world that hold to a tradition that their origin can be traced back to a first-century apostolic visit. In addition, there was an important Syriac tradition that claimed that after Jesus gave the Great Commission mandates, the apostles all gathered together in Jerusalem and cast lots, thereby "dividing the regions of the world, that each one of us might go to the region which fell to his lot, and to the nation to which the Lord had sent him."[34]

These theological perspectives tended to obscure the central missiological thrust of the New Testament mandates. For example, commenting on 1 Corinthians 12:28, John Calvin makes a distinction between the office of an apostle and that of a pastor. Calvin argues that the apostles were appointed by God to spread the gospel "throughout the whole world," whereas pastors were not given such a mandate but instead were to look after the churches committed to their charge.[35] The Lutheran theologian Johann Gerhard (1582–1637) did not recognize any mandate for the universal preaching of the gospel around the world since, in his view, the apostles had already obeyed the command.

There were notable dissenting voices that challenged this mainstream view. The most important were the Dutch theologian Adrianus Saravia (1531–1613) and Erasmus of Rotterdam (1466–1536). Adrianus Saravia argued that the final commissions by Jesus were still in effect and invoked a line of argumentation very similar to that which would be used by William Carey two centuries later in his *Enquiry*, which helped to stir the fires of missions throughout the Protestant world. Erasmus's careful exegesis of Matthew 28:18–20 was instrumental in helping the Anabaptists to rediscover the missiological implications of the text in their own time.[36] However, these voices were in the minority, and on the whole the Great Commission mandates were not read missiologically.

34. David Aune, ed., *The Westminster Dictionary of New Testament and Early Christian Literature and Rhetoric* (Louisville: Westminister John Knox, 2003), 21. See "Acts of the Holy Apostle Thomas," in *The Ante-Nicene Fathers*, ed. Roberts and Donaldson, vol. 8, 535.

35. John Calvin, *The Epistles of Paul the Apostle to the Corinthians*, trans. John W. Fraser (Grand Rapids: Eerdmans, 1960), 270–271.

36. See Abraham Friesen, *Erasmus, the Anabaptists, and the Great Commission* (Grand Rapids: Eerdmans, 1998).

In addition to these theological challenges, there was an even more important *structural* problem within Protestantism. It is this problem that serves as the central theme of this chapter. Even if the Reformers were convinced that all men and women needed to respond to the gospel of Jesus Christ, there were no sodality structures available to support the sending out of Protestant missionaries across cultural boundaries. As Andrew Walls has noted, "The simple fact was that the Church as then organized, whether Episcopal, or Presbyterian, or Congregational could not effectively operate mission overseas."[37] The reason was that the Protestant churches had dismantled all the sodality structures of Roman Catholicism, leaving them with no structures to support a cross-cultural missionary endeavor. This is why we argued in chapter 9 that the birth of the Protestant missionary society was one of the most momentous *kairos* moments in the history of missions. William Carey is considered the father of the modern missionary movement, not only because he carefully set forth a *theology* of missionary activity, but also because he set up a *secondary structure*, a missionary society—a sodality—which provided the means that enabled men and women to effectively serve as missionaries. Since there was no Protestant precedent for such a society, Carey modeled it after secular trading societies. Thus, as noted in chapter 9, Carey wrote,

> Suppose a company of serious Christians, ministers and private persons, were to form themselves into a society, and make a number of rules respecting the regulation of the plan, and the persons who are to be employed as missionaries, the means of defraying the expense, etc., etc.[38]

So, even though there were Protestant missionaries prior to Carey, it was Carey who set forth a new *structure,* which enabled the mainstream church to enter into and engage in cross-cultural missions in a way that was unprecedented in the Protestant churches. Indeed, one of the great ironies in the life of the church is that modality structures like the local church are often resistant to sodality structures, but sodality structures are the most effective

---

37. Andrew F. Walls, *The Missionary Movement in Christian History: Studies in the Transmission of Faith* (Maryknoll, NY: Orbis, 1996), 246.
38. William Carey, *An Enquiry into Obligations to Use Means for the Conversion of the Heathens* (London: Carey Kingsgate, 1961), 82.

means for establishing new modalities. Furthermore, the local church modality is the most effective place to give birth to new sodalities. It was the birth of the voluntary mission society that enabled the church to recognize that there were "things—not small things, but big things, like the evangelization of the world—which were beyond the capacities" of the local church without supportive sodality structures.[39] The nineteenth century witnessed dramatic growth in the number of mission societies, most belonging to the new "faith missions" movement modeled on the China Inland Mission of Hudson Taylor. The result was the largest mass mobilization of Christians to bear witness to Christ in new, frontier cross-cultural settings in history.

The Relationship Between Modality and Sodality in Contemporary Context

The preceding biblical and historical survey has demonstrated three things. First, the local church and the mission society represent two distinct structures. Second, these voluntary associations (sodalities) have a long history of serving the church, both in stimulating spiritual renewal and fostering cross-cultural outreach. Third, the relationship between these two structures often has been murky at best and sometimes even beset with antagonism and mistrust between the two.

The relationship between modalities and sodalities could be dramatically clarified and improved if a few key principles are followed. First, *there must be mutual appreciation for the importance of both structures*. On the one hand, the church of Antioch had to appreciate that they were unable to extend their influence apart from the willingness of a small group of dedicated people to leave behind the responsibilities and obligations inherent in property, work, and family in order to devote themselves wholeheartedly to this ministry. On the other hand, Paul's missionary band was birthed out of the local church (Acts 13:1), was an extension of it, and was fully accountable to it. In short, Paul's missionary band existed for the sole purpose of serving the church. It stimulated new expressions of church modalities. Indeed, apart from the church, the very existence and purpose of an itinerant missionary band would be rendered meaningless.

The fruits of this mutual appreciation will benefit both modality and sodality. Churches must learn to appreciate the flexibility, mobility, and focus

---

39. Walls, *The Missionary Movement in Christian History,* 247.

that often characterize effective sodalities. Likewise, mission societies must learn to appreciate the stability, wisdom, and perspective that mark Christ's holy church. Sodalities are in a constant state of change and adaptation. Like an orchestra with a diversity of instruments all playing variations on a common theme, so monasteries, mendicant orders, and mission societies are all diverse variations of the voluntary society. In the future, entirely new sodality structures may emerge, which will be suited to the conditions and peculiar challenges of that time. Yet, throughout all times and ages, the church will always be the gathered community of God's people, living out the realities of the future in the present. Unlike societies and organizations that are constantly changing and adapting to the times, the church never needs to fear change or becoming out-of-date. The true church of Jesus Christ is always living out the *future* in the present. In that sense, sodalities are fixed in time and are therefore constantly changing with the times, whereas the church is fixed in the future and is the one voice in society that is summoning everyone forward to that great eschatological *fact* of Jesus Christ.

Second, *sodalities must always be held accountable to the church.* This was clearly observed in the relationship of Paul's missionary band to the church at Antioch and to the apostolic leadership in Jerusalem. There is simply no biblical precedent for an *autonomous* sodality untethered from the church or one that claims only a vague "spiritual" connection. This principle does not represent a major challenge for the vast number of mission sodalities, which are formal extensions of denominations or affiliated networks of churches. Because of the hierarchical nature of Roman Catholicism, all of their sodalities are ultimately brought under the accountability of the larger church.[40] In Protestantism, this typically occurs within each separate denomination or affiliated network. For example, Mission to the World is the missionary sending arm (in essence, the sodality) that has been officially sanctioned by the Presbyterian Church of America (PCA) to mobilize, send out, and support missionaries who have been called by God out of their congregations. All of these missionaries are accountable to the PCA. Likewise, the Assemblies of God World Missions is the supporting

---

40. Because of the focus and purpose of this chapter, it was not possible to also develop the way sodalities have functioned within Eastern Orthodoxy. However, there are many similarities with Roman Catholicism. For example, the Arab Orthodoxy Society is a charitable organization that brings relief and development to those in need in Jerusalem. It is supported by, and accountable to, the Greek Orthodox Church.

sodality of the Assemblies of God, the largest Pentecostal denomination in the United States. Their mission structure currently has mobilized over two thousand Assemblies of God missionaries to serve in hundreds of different cross-cultural settings. Every one of these missionaries is directly accountable to the leadership, oversight, and direction of the Assemblies of God Church. There are hundreds of examples of mission sodalities that function in this way, under some denominational oversight.

However, there are an increasing number of mission societies that have been founded as interdenominational or independent mission boards, which draw their "secondary commitment" workers from a broad range of churches and denominations. Although these organizations are frequently held accountable to an independent board of directors made up of mature Christian leaders, they are, strictly speaking, autonomous from any church. Because these mission boards are not formally or organizationally connected to the church, they frequently adopt their own statement of faith to demonstrate their commitment to historic orthodoxy or some particular distinctive that helps prospective applicants to know what general theological orientation the organization is drawing candidates from. It is not unusual to see on the Web sites of independent mission boards certain code words such as *evangelical, baptistic, Pentecostal, Reformed,* or *ecumenical,* which not only help to guide those who are interested in applying but also help the organization to foster a harmonious climate by bringing people together with shared values and a common perspective.

The dilemma is whether having an independent oversight board whose members are drawn *from* the church sufficiently satisfies the principle of accountability *to* the church. On the one hand, it is not prudent to overly spiritualize an organization's connection with the invisible church by saying that we are all accountable to God. Many well-intentioned mission organizations and ministries have sprung up over the years that were conceived with great vision and energy but lacked any tangible form of accountability. Unfortunately, the result often has been disastrous. On the other hand, there are a number of vital organizations that are well governed by wise and godly men and women that *could not exist* if they were directly associated and legally accountable to the institutional church. For example, Wycliffe Bible Translators, along with their partner organization, SIL International, would not be permitted to work in many countries if they had a formal connection with the church.

The best solution is for all independent sodalities to make a threefold commitment. First, they must all be governed by an independent board made up of godly, well-respected Christian leaders who, in turn, are accountable to the church. Second, these organizations must clearly communicate that their ultimate purpose is to serve the church and to assist in the mobilization of men and women from the church into the mission field. Third, these organizations must insist that all of their individual members produce, as a part of their application process, a signed statement from the leadership of a local church that they are members in good standing and that they are going to be held accountable to that church in some regular and definable way. With these safeguards in place, there can be reasonable assurance that a proper and healthy relationship between the sodality and the modality will be maintained. Many of the finest independent sodalities have modeled all three of these commitments. For example, Arab World Ministries is governed by an independent board, and it insists that all of its members belong to and be sent out by a local church. Furthermore, their Web site clearly indicates that they exist to serve the church.[41] In this way, the functional and flexible nature of sodalities can continue to thrive, while always acknowledging the permanent and ontological nature of the church of Jesus Christ.

CONCLUSION

This chapter has sought to examine the relationship between biblical ecclesiology and the emergence of various voluntary associations, parachurch ministries, and mission organizations that serve the church. Only the modality of the church infused with the Holy Spirit can embody the full realities of the New Creation in the present age. Sodalities exist only to further this goal. It has been argued that sodality structures are biblical and have historically served and assisted in the effective mobilization of the church in a wide variety of ways. However, it is essential that these organizations be held accountable to godly Christian leadership and that the individual members of the various societies be sent out from, and be held accountable to, a local church.

---

41. See http://awm.gospelcom.net/splash/index.php. The AWM Web site states the following: "We're convinced that the local church is God's primary plan for world evangelization. It's our honor to facilitate in any way whatever God is calling your church to do in the Arab world."

Missionaries as Agents of Suffering and Heralds of the New Creation

— 16 —
The Suffering, Advancing Church

IT WAS WITH CONSIDERABLE TREPIDATION that, as a young teacher, I faced my first class of all Indian students. It was 1987, and I had traveled to North India to teach a course entitled "Principles of Biblical Hermeneutics." Approximately fifty evangelists, pastors, and students had registered in advance for the course, although considerably more showed up hoping to be a part of the class. On the very first day, as I stood lecturing to the class, I could not help but notice a young man sitting near the front who appeared to have been severely beaten in the not-too-distant past. During a break in the class, I found out that his name was Ashwin Kumar, and over the next few weeks, we became friends.[1]

Ashwin was a twenty-one-year-old evangelist who had tried to bring the gospel to several villages in a remote part of North India, but he had been met with repeated hostility. On one occasion, villagers had taken his Bible, torn it into pieces, and thrown it into the ditch filled with muddy brown waters from the recent monsoon rains. They threatened him, warning him to never come back to that village. However, Ashwin kept insisting that he must return because he had good news for them. Finally, on another visit the villagers seized his bicycle and destroyed it and began to beat Ashwin with such severity that when they threw him out onto the road just outside the village, they presumed him to be dead. He probably would have died were it not for a person who was walking along the road (whom he had never

---

1. Although the story is true, I have changed the name of the evangelist and have not revealed the exact location of these villages in order to protect the man's identity, which, if known, could potentially expose him to harm.

met), who saw his condition and like the Good Samaritan of Jesus' parable lifted Ashwin up, gave him water to drink, and bandaged his wounds. This had happened just a few weeks prior to the start of this class I was teaching.

After Ashwin completed his training program, he returned with renewed energy to preach the gospel to the people of that very village, where he had been persecuted. I cannot tell you the joy that was mine when, a year and a half later, Ashwin sent me a photograph of himself standing waist deep in a river, baptizing the first twenty Christians from that village. I have had the privilege of knowing Ashwin Kumar for over twenty years now, and I visit with him almost every year. He continues to have a thriving and growing ministry in what is widely regarded as one of the most resistant people groups in India. Ashwin will be the first to tell you that the persecution that he faced strengthened his faith, steeled his determination, and even helped to soften the hearts of those who would later believe, when they saw how he continued to love them despite their hostility and brutality.

In many ways, this account reflects a certain positive trajectory often found in stories concerning persecution. The story develops along the following lines. In obedience to Christ's command, people go to an unreached people group and preach the gospel. They meet with severe resistance, being severely beaten or even killed for their testimony. However, over time, God honors His suffering servants, and the church advances, reflecting the well-known words of Tertullian that "the blood of Christians" becomes the "seed" of the church.[2] A new church emerges and serves as a visible testimony to the faithfulness and perseverance of those who brought the gospel in the midst of such a torrent of opposition.

However, not all persecution stories turn out this way. There are numerous examples in which the blood of martyrs has not appeared to result in the growth of the church. Some of the most moving and thought-provoking accounts of persecution and martyrdom can be found in the writings of the Japanese novelist Shusaku Endo. As a Roman Catholic writer, he has spent most of his literary life wrestling with the presence or absence of God in the lives of those who are being persecuted or are suffering unjustly. He finds Jesus' cry of dereliction, "My God, My God, why have you

---

2. Tertullian, *Apology*, chapter 50, in *The Ante-Nicene Fathers*, ed. Alexander Roberts and James Donaldson, vol. 3 (Peabody, MA: Hendrickson, 1999), 55. The exact quote is "The oftener we are mown down by you, the more in number we grow; the blood of Christians is the seed."

forsaken me?" echoed in the experience of many Christians who faced persecution and martyrdom and seemed only to experience God's silence.

For example, Endo's novel *Silence* is set in Japan in the late sixteenth and early seventeenth centuries, when Japanese Catholics and European priests were being tortured and forced to apostatize if they wished to save the lives of their fellow priests. Endo tells the story of a young Portuguese priest named Sebastian Rodrigues, who travels to Japan from Macao to confirm the seemingly impossible news that his mentor, Father Christovao Ferreira, has apostatized. Rodriques arrives full of faith and vigor but gradually comes face-to-face with the shallowness of his own faith and the shocking brutality of what suffering Christians are facing in Japan. The novel's title *Silence* is a reminder of how Rodriques's own simplistic answers were swallowed up by the awful silence of God in the face of one of the most intense periods of persecution the church has ever faced. The priests cried out to God from their narrow prison cells, even as they heard the screams of their fellow priests and Japanese Christians being tortured. One of Endo's characters declares, "I cannot bear the monotonous sound of the dark sea gnawing at the shore. Behind the depressing silence of this sea, the silence of God. . . . the feeling that while men raise their voices in anguish God remains with folded arms, silent."[3] A reoccurring image in the book is that of the missionaries becoming mired down in the "swamp of Japan."

The persecution and struggles that the Christians and priests endured and that are captured by Endo's novel are based on real events. In 1587 the Japanese feudal ruler (*daimyo*) Hideyoshi overturned the previous patronage of Christians, which had been extended under the leadership of Nobunaga. This was later followed by the Great Edict of Annihilation in 1614 by the powerful shogun Ideyasu. This persecution continued from 1614 until the arrival of Commodore Perry in 1853, marking one of the most prolonged periods of persecution in the history of the church. Throughout the period the church became increasingly marginalized and greatly reduced in size. Even to this day, despite centuries of missionary effort, the percentage of Japanese Christians is not much higher than it was in 1587, when the patronage the Japanese authorities had extended to Christians came to an end.[4]

---

3. Shusaku Endo, *Silence*, trans. William Johnston (New York: Taplinger, 1980), 61.
4. According to the World Christian Database, at the end of the patronage period, approximately 2 percent of Japan identified with Christianity. The current percentage of Japanese Christians is 2.28 percent. See Colin McEvedy and Richard Jones, *Atlas of World Population History* (New

The purpose of this chapter is to explore the role of persecution and suffering within the larger context of the *missio dei*. As agents and heralds of the New Creation, missionaries frequently face intense opposition, persecution, and even martyrdom. In the face of such opposition, can we be assured, as Tertullian declared, that the blood of the martyrs is the seed of the church? What is the relationship, if any, between suffering and the advancement of God's rule in the world? Can those who are preparing for missionary service learn to think more reflectively about persecution, beyond inspiring anecdoctal stories and mind-boggling statistics? Tragically, most missions training, especially coming from Western authors, has not included persecution as a theme for reflection, or, if it has, it has not been understood within a larger theological framework. Now that we stand at the end of the long legacy of Christendom, it is vital that Western Christians be given a more robust theological and missiological framework to help us understand persecution better. Likewise, the decades ahead will almost certainly be increasingly difficult for our brothers and sisters in the Majority World, who are facing heightened opposition, particularly from Islamic and Hindu fundamentalists.

We cannot ignore persecution or fail to incorporate it into our overall theological framework for understanding God's work. Central to the work of the Holy Spirit is not only assisting the church in embodying the in-breaking realities of the New Creation but also helping us to understand the victory of Christ in the midst of the opposition we face as we live our lives in the present evil age. We will begin by exposing some of the major *misunderstandings* about persecution that often have prevailed in the church. Then, a comprehensive framework for understanding persecution within the context of the *missio dei* will be explored.

FIVE PREVAILING PERSPECTIVES ON PERSECUTION

Charles Tieszen, in *Re-Examining Religious Persecution*, has carefully surveyed a representative sampling of the published literature on persecution.[5]

York: Penguin, 1978), 181, chart. See also David B. Barrett, George T. Kurian, and Todd Johnson, eds., *World Christian Encyclopedia: A Comparative Survey of Churches and Religions in the Modern World*, 2nd ed. (New York: Oxford University Press, 2001), 415.

5. Charles L. Tieszen, *Re-Examining Religious Persecution: Constructing a Theological Framework for Understanding Persecution* (Kempton Park, Johannesburg: AcadSA, 2008), 17–35. While I do not adopt the same nomenclature for the five views as Tieszen, I remain indebted to him for his survey of the literature and his isolation of the five distinctive views. Tieszen's five views are:

Tieszen identifies five representative viewpoints regarding persecution, which dominate the literature, whether written by Western or Majority World authors. It should be noted at the outset that there is a certain degree of truth in all five of these perspectives. However, if taken in isolation, each one actually serves to inhibit the development of a comprehensive theological framework for understanding persecution. The five most widely held views regarding persecution will now be explored.

Impending Parousia: Persecution as a Sign of the End Times

There are a number of writers who identify persecution as one of the leading signs of the end times and the imminent return of Jesus Christ. Reports of persecution from around the world are the "birth pains," which in time will bring forth the Great Tribulation, a period of intense persecution. A steady stream of popular end-times books have been published in recent years, such as Hal Lindsey's *The Late Great Planet Earth*,[6] and the *Left Behind*[7] series by Tim LaHaye and Jerry Jenkins. All of these best-selling books reinforce the idea that persecution is associated with the Great Tribulation. In these writings, persecution is interpreted primarily as an eschatological event. This is further supported by the teaching that Christians will be spared from the Great Tribulation through a "pretribulation" rapture, since, in their view, God would not allow His children to undergo such an intense period of persecution.

This perspective tends to diminish the significance of suffering throughout church history and, in particular, the fact that God *already* has permitted His church to suffer the worst kinds of torture and cruelty imaginable in the cause of Christ. While it is true that one of the signs of the coming Parousia is increased persecution, this should not be seen in isolation from the general recognition that Christians throughout the ages have experienced persecution.

Eschatological Experience, Isolated Historical Experience, Experience of Majority World Christianity, Suffering in General, and Martyrdom.

6. Hal Lindsey, *The Late Great Planet Earth*, 25th ed. (Grand Rapids: Zondervan, 1998). The first edition was published in 1970.

7. Tim LaHaye and Jerry Jenkins, *Left Behind* (Carol Stream, IL: Tyndale, 1996). This is the first novel of a popular sixteen-book series, which concludes with *Kingdom Come*. The entire series is known, collectively, as the *Left Behind* Series. The series has sold over 65 million copies.

Early Church Perils: Persecution Before Constantine's Edict of Toleration

A second view is a tendency to think of persecution as an experience of only the Christians who lived in the pre-Christendom world prior to Constantine's Edict of Toleration in A.D. 313. Most students of church history study the state-sponsored persecution under Roman emperors such as Nero, Valerian, and Diocletian. However, because church history is normally seen only through the lens of the Western church, most Christians are ignorant of the historical fact that the end of persecution in the West was the beginning of a new wave of persecution against Christians in the East, who were living in Persia. Samuel Moffett observes that it was the political threat of Rome, more than the religious intolerance of Persia's Zoroastrianism, that sparked this new wave of persecution. The Persians interpreted the new peace with Christians in the Roman Empire as a potential threat to Persia, since the Christians potentially were a "fifth column" of Roman hegemony in Persia. As long as Christians were considered an enemy to Rome, they were regarded as friends of Persia, but the emergence of Christendom caused the Persian ruler Shapur II o regard Christians with suspicion. It is ironic, therefore, that the conversion of Constantine to Christianity was the catalyst for the great persecution that broke out against Christians in Persia between 340 and 401.[8]

Yet, the great persecution under Shapur II is largely unknown by Western students of church history because, even today, it is primarily the Western trajectory of church history that is followed, while the history of Eastern Christianity is largely ignored. Therefore, there is a widespread view, held even by seminary graduates, that the fourth century marks the end of religious persecution, until, perhaps, the contemporary period. This perspective tends to ignore both the reality of persecution among Majority World Christians and the ongoing experience of persecution throughout the history of the church.

Majority World Problem: Persecution as an Experience Only for Others

A third view that dominates a considerable body of persecution literature is that persecution occurs in the Majority World, especially in the

---

8. Samuel Moffett, *A History of Christianity in Asia*, vol. 1, *Beginnings to 1500* (Maryknoll, NY: Orbis, 1998), 137.

Middle East, Eastern Europe, and Asia. A number of writers consistently make the point that the Western world knows very little about persecution, while stories abound of ongoing persecution in the Majority World. In February 1988 a consultation was held in Hong Kong under the theme, "The Church in the Midst of Suffering." Although the title of the conference implied a more global view, the papers from the conference were published under the title, *Christian Suffering in Asia*.[9] The book highlights numerous case studies of persecution throughout Asia but fails to recognize persecution as a global phenomenon. If the consultation were entitled "The *Asian* Church in the Midst of Suffering," then one might expect the focus to be exclusively on Asia. However, the conference inadvertently reinforced the stereotype that persecution is a normal part of the experience of Asian Christians but is not part of the experience of Western Christianity.

Richard Wurmbrand is probably the most recognized name among Christians who have devoted their lives to helping the persecuted church. Wurmbrand spent fourteen years in prison in Romania, where he was tortured for his faith in Christ. After his release from prison, Wurmbrand became the "voice of the underground church." His newsletter, *The Voice of the Martyrs*, has become a major source of information about the persecuted church and has widely popularized the idea that persecution is limited to the "closed" countries, which do not enjoy the religious freedom of the Western world.

Brother Andrew, another popular writer, became a household name in Christian circles after the publication of his book *God's Smuggler*, which highlighted his experience smuggling Bibles into the former Soviet Union. Brother Andrew, in his "How Should Christians Regard Persecution?" argues that "suffering has already come, gradually or suddenly, upon half of the world—and that includes half of the church of Christ, half of the Body of Christ."[10] In this view, persecution is the normal, daily experience of Majority World Christians, but it has not yet come into the Western world.

Scott Cunningham concludes a lengthy study of persecution in Luke-Acts by stating that Luke's theology of persecution should bring "reassur-

---

9. Bong Rin Ro, ed., *Christian Suffering in Asia* (Taichung, Taiwan: Asia Theological Association, 1989).

10. Brother Andrew, "How Should Christians Regard Persecution?" in *Destined to Suffer? African Christians Face the Future,* ed. Brother Andrew (Orange, CA: Open Doors, 1979), 17.

ance" to Majority World Christians, who are being persecuted, whereas it is troubling to Western believers, who live in a land where Christianity has become "culturally acceptable" and who thus "know nothing" of the experience of persecution.[11] Cunningham goes on to pose the question, "What would Luke say concerning the *lack* of persecution in the West?"[12]

These writers continue to embrace a Christendom perspective on Western Christianity and either downplay or completely ignore persecution in the Western world, which, although it may take different forms than in more openly hostile environments, is nevertheless a real and significant part of the experience of Christians around the world.

Daily Pinpricks: Persecution as an Explanation for Every Difficulty

A fourth view tends to identify any and all difficulties faced by believers as persecution. This perspective tends to blur the distinction between the general suffering (or even mundane inconveniences) of believers and the genuine persecution endured by others. This view equates persecution with the general effects of the Fall, which all believers are daily subjected to. One author has argued, for example, that even an experience such as having an accident or having your car stolen should be regarded as persecution. Furthermore, when this same author chose to live among the poor and discovered that he was treated as a "second-class" citizen, this was regarded as a form of "persecution."[13] The theological rationale for this broad interpretation of persecution is the recognition that among the greatest weapons from the "arsenal of evil" are the "little things" that disrupt our lives and our ministries. Therefore, anything that impedes the smooth service of God's children in advancing God's rule and reign must be a form of persecution.[14] This view does avoid the pitfalls of the other views through its recognition that persecution is something that affects all Christians, in all parts of the world, throughout all time. However, it accomplishes this through a dramatic redefinition of the word *persecution* to include even mild forms of suffering or even inconvenience.

---

11. Scott Cunningham, *Through Many Tribulations: The Theology of Persecution in Luke-Acts* (Sheffield, England: Sheffield Academic, 1997), 342.

12. Ibid.

13. Aida Besancon Spencer and William David Spencer, *Joy Through the Night* (Downers Grove, IL: InterVarsity Press, 1991), 76–78.

14. Ibid., 78.

Preferential Piety: Persecution Limited to Specially Chosen Martyrs

Finally, there is a view that resides at the opposite end of the spectrum from the previous view. In this view, one can speak of persecution only if the suffering the believer endures eventually leads to his or her martyrdom. Most students of church history learn the remarkable stories of the early Christian martyrs. Well-known early martyrs such as Stephen (d. 35), Polycarp (d. 156), Justin Martyr (d. 165), Perpetua (d. 203), and Cyprian (d. 258), among others, form a special group of Christians who made the ultimate sacrifice in the cause of Christ. In this fifth view, only suffering that ultimately leads to death qualifies as religious persecution. In this view, the words *persecuted* and *martyred* are used interchangeably. This is based on Jesus' command for us to take up our cross and follow Him and the promise that whoever loses his life for Jesus' sake will find it (Matt. 10:38; 16:24; Mark 8:34). Since the cross was an instrument of death, Jesus' words are interpreted to mean that the highest calling is to follow Jesus in martyrdom, losing one's life for His sake.

While there is no doubt that those who have given their lives for the sake of the gospel are recipients of religious persecution, this view tends to minimize the real persecution of believers who may have been beaten or harassed because of their faithfulness to the gospel but have not actually been put to death. Well-known books such as Foxe's *Book of Martyrs* have created a special reverence for those who have been martyred for their faith. Some, arguing from Revelation 20:4, have taught that there will be a special eschatological reward for those who are martyred, which will not be given to other Christians. Roman Catholicism has a long history of giving special honor to those who were martyred. For example, in Roman Catholicism, a person who was martyred can be saved, even if the person had not been baptized because he or she has been "baptized by blood." This view is based on 1 John 5:6, which declares that Jesus "came by water and blood." This is interpreted as a reference to His baptism in water and His later crucifixion on the cross. The special provision of being "baptized by blood" did not apply even to those who had received severe beatings because of their faith but applied only to those whose sufferings led to martyrdom.

It is appropriate for the church to honor those who have been martyred. Nevertheless, this should not obscure the experience of hundreds of thousands of Christians each year who are subjected to hostile actions because of their faith in Jesus Christ but do not end up as martyrs. Luke alone records Jesus adding the word "daily" (*kath hemeran*) to the phrase "take up his cross" (Luke 9:23), implying not only the daily possibility of martyrdom but also the ongoing perseverance that is required in the face of persecution and rejection, which, in Luke's view, is part and parcel of the daily exercise of discipleship that applies to all believers everywhere. We need a larger perspective on persecution, which includes martyrs but also looks at a wider range of Christian experiences in the face of hostility.

This survey of the five most prominent views demonstrates deficiencies that have hindered the development of a comprehensive theological framework for thinking about persecution. Thus, we will set forth a working definition of persecution and then develop the key elements that should constitute a theology of persecution.

DEFINING CHRISTIAN PERSECUTION

In this book, Christian persecution refers to *various kinds of hostile acts or unjust discriminations by individuals or groups, including both religious and political representatives, which are primarily in response to someone's Christian beliefs or actions and can be found throughout the history and experience of the church.* There are four aspects of this definition that need further clarification. First, the scope and focus of this chapter requires a focus on *Christian* persecution, even while acknowledging that all religious groups can document examples of religious persecution.[15]

Second, persecution refers to acts, not merely attitudes or prejudices, and is primarily a response to someone's Christian beliefs or actions. This does not mean that those who are perpetuating religious persecution always recognize it as religiously motivated. However, it must be religiously motivated, lest all general forms of suffering or hardship end up becoming classified as persecution.

---

15. It is in the long-term interest of Christians to promote religious freedom and toleration for all religions. Our advocacy for freedom of Christian expression is often directly linked with the larger question of religious freedom in general. The Lausanne Covenant calls upon national leaders "to guarantee freedom of thought and conscience, and freedom to practice and propagate religion in accordance with the will of God and as set forth in The Universal Declaration of Human Rights" (See Lausanne Covenant, article 13). I fully affirm this statement. Nevertheless, there are particular theological truths related to Christian persecution that do not apply to the broader discussion, so the focus of this chapter will be on Christian persecution.

Third, persecution sometimes comes from individuals who act informally and independently from the larger society, but persecution also may arise from groups who are acting in some official or authorized capacity. In either case, we must candidly acknowledge that a considerable amount of persecution, arising from both individuals and larger, authorized actions, has come from Roman Catholic or Protestant groups who have become enshrined with political power. The persecution of Protestants by Roman Catholics in Latin America and the persecution of Catholics in Northern Ireland by Protestant groups are just two notable examples.[16]

During the twentieth century, Roman Catholic and Protestant groups became increasingly aware of religious persecution in general and the importance of opposing all religiously motivated persecution. Roman Catholic and Protestant leaders have been widely supportive of the United Nations Universal Declaration of Human Rights, adopted in 1948.[17] Furthermore, in 1996 the National Association of Evangelicals adopted a "Statement of Conscience," which expresses "our deep concern for the re-

---

16. Prior to Vatican II the official Roman Catholic position regarding religious freedom was enshrined in the "thesis-hypothesis" arrangement. This is the classic view within Christendom. The standard "thesis" was the understanding that the Roman Catholic Church stands as the privileged partner with the civil authorities. The church actively supports the government, and, in turn, the government provides protection and legal standing to Roman Catholicism. However, the "hypothesis" arrangement acknowledged that there were some political states that were confessionally neutral, such as the United States, or were confessionally non-Roman Catholic, such as the United Kingdom with the official Church of England (Anglican) and the Church of Scotland (Presbyterian), for example. The Roman Catholic Church viewed these as unacceptable but tolerated them on a temporary basis until the church could officially turn them from an "hypothesis" to a "thesis" arrangement. See Peter Kuzmic, "To Suffer with Our Lord: Christian Responses to Religious Persecution," *Brandywine Review of Faith and International Affairs* 2, no. 3 (Winter 2004–2005): 36–37. The Italian Cardinal Alfredo Ottaviani exemplified this view by stating that all other Christian churches, as well as other religions, were full of error. He argued that since "error has no right to exist," the church is under no obligation to support non-Roman Catholic arrangements. It was American Jesuits such as John Courtney Murray who argued that the separation of church and state could be a positive arrangement and that the debate should not focus on the negative judicial view that "error has no right" but on a positive moral view that "*persons* have rights." Once this shift occurred, it opened the door to freedom of conscience and religious liberty, which eventually became enshrined in the Vatican II Declaration of Religious Freedom, which unequivocally declared that "the human person has a right to religious freedom."

17. The United Nations Universal Declaration of Human Rights states in article 18 that "everyone has the right to freedom of thought, conscience and religion; this right includes the freedom to change his religion or belief, and freedom, either alone or in community with others and in public or private, to manifest his religion or belief in teaching, practice, worship and observance." For a full text of the document, see www.ung.org/Overview/rights.html.

ligious freedom of fellow believers, as well as people of every faith." While the statement focuses primarily on Christian persecution, it unequivocally endorses religious freedom for men and women of all religious persuasions. Thus, the collapse of Christendom, coupled with changing perspectives on religious liberty, has dramatically reduced persecution that arises from any official actions of the church.

Finally, the definition advocated here acknowledges that persecution is part of the ongoing experience of the church throughout its history and in every part of the world. Our response to, and perseverance in, persecution is integral to the work of the Holy Spirit in and through the church of all ages. As we shall see, it is part of our training as disciples of Jesus Christ. This separates this definition from most of the popular understandings of persecution and reminds us that persecution is part of the inherent nature of the church. All Christians who are truly united to Christ will suffer persecution.

THEOLOGICAL FRAMEWORK
FOR UNDERSTANDING PERSECUTION

John Piper's classic book on missions, *Let the Nations Be Glad!* is one of the few missions books that includes a chapter on persecution. Chapter 3 is entitled, "The Supremacy of God in Missions Through Suffering." Piper shares many inspiring stories about how God uses persecution to further His purposes and then gives six "reasons why God appoints suffering for his servants."[18] Although Piper tends to focus on stories similar to Ashwin Kumar's, which I narrated at the beginning of the chapter, rather than on the more disturbing experiences such as that of the Jesuits working in Japan, his theological analysis nevertheless remains sound and helpful. The most valuable feature of Piper's book is that he reminds us all of the need to set forth a comprehensive theological framework that places the entire missionary enterprise, including persecution, within the larger framework of the supremacy and sovereignty of God.

In my understanding, there are three key elements that establish the place of persecution within our overall understanding of the *missio dei*: the nature of the church, our identity with Christ, and what it means to

---

18. John Piper, *Let the Nations Be Glad! The Supremacy of God in Missions* (Grand Rapids: Baker, 1993).

be heralds of the New Creation in the midst of the "not yet." Each of these will now be explored.

Persecution and the Nature of the Church

First, persecution must be placed within the larger context of our understanding of the nature of the church. The church is the body of Christ and therefore participates in His suffering. In Matthew 11:12 Jesus says that "from the days of John the Baptist until now the kingdom of heaven suffers violence, and violent men take it by force" (NASB). Interestingly, the NIV translates the same verse as follows: "From the days of John the Baptist until now, the kingdom of heaven has been forcefully advancing, and forceful men lay hold of it." The two very different translations are based on the translation of the single Greek word, *biazomai*. The word *biazo* undoubtedly denotes some forceful action, but the *omai* ending is identical for both the passive and the middle voice.[19] In other words, it is unclear whether *biazomai* denotes a church that is on the receiving end of some forceful action ("suffers violence") or the church itself is acting forcefully ("forcefully advances"). The ambiguity itself is instructive, for the larger context of the verse indicates that the church advances in the context of suffering.

In the context, Jesus points to parallels between His own ministry and that of John the Baptist. John was a great prophet and herald of the kingdom, yet he had been imprisoned and was soon to be beheaded for his testimony (Matt. 11:2; 14:1–12). Likewise, Jesus Himself faced intense opposition from the religious authorities, even though He came announcing good news. Even as Jesus made His slow but certain "progress towards the passion," the blind were receiving sight, the lame were walking, the deaf were hearing, and the dead were being raised (11:5).[20] Jesus is establishing the theological perspective that not only would He be persecuted, but all those who are part of His body likewise will suffer violence. The kingdom of God forcefully advances insofar as the people of God are prepared to suffer violence. The two are linked, though we may not always see or personally experience the

---

19. William F. Arndt and F. Wilbur Gingrich, *A Greek-English Lexion of the New Testament*, 2nd ed., adaptation and translation of Walter Bauer's 4th ed. (Chicago: University of Chicago Press, 1979), 140–141.
20. The phrase "progress towards the passion" is taken from H. Conzelmann, *The Theology of St. Luke*, trans. G. Buswell (Philadelphia: Fortress, 1982), 63.

connection. Nevertheless, even the worst kind of persecution occurs within the larger context of the ongoing inbreaking of God's rule and reign in the world. The mission of God is always moving toward its divinely appointed eschatological goal, but it unfolds, as did the ministry of Jesus, within the more immediate context of suffering and persecution.

All members of Christ's church should not only expect persecution but also regard it as a *normative* expectation. Jesus declares, "All men will hate you because of me" (Matt. 10:22). Therefore, as the apostle Peter reminds us, we should "not be surprised" when we face painful trials and suffer, "as though something strange were happening to [us]" (1 Peter 4:12). Persecution is a normative, not exceptional or extraordinary, feature of the church's existence in the world. It is central in the Holy Spirit's work of making effective followers of Christ in the world. Without persecution, we would have neither the perseverance nor the discipline to be His ambassadors.

Martin Luther correctly observed that suffering should rightly take its place as one of the true marks of the church, along with the traditional affirmations of oneness, holiness, catholicity, and apostolicity.[21] This true sign of the church emerges as an extension of the prophetic ministry of God's people in the world. Just as the Old Testament prophets suffered persecution and rejection as heralds of God's word, so the church should expect to be rejected as the bearer of God's word. Jesus told His church to rejoice when persecuted, "for in the same way they persecuted the prophets who were before you" (Matt. 5:12).

The Gospel writers emphasized that Jesus' martyrdom and death took place in Jerusalem, since Jerusalem is the traditional place where the prophets met their death, even though it was the seat of Jewish religious authority and power. We are reminded that the bastions of religious power often stand opposed to the gospel and its messengers. Only with the welcome collapse of Christendom can the church finally reclaim its prophetic role in society. This requires a significant theological adjustment for many Christians, who are accustomed to a theology of power and success rather than a theology of suffering and the cross. We should no longer ask *where* Christians are being persecuted in the world, since we should presuppose that *all* Christians are persecuted. Rather, we should ask *how* persecution is

---

21. Douglas John Hall, *God and Human Suffering: An Exercise in the Theology of the Cross* (Minneapolis: Augsburg, 1986), 123–24.

being manifested in this particular place among these particular Christians. The precise forms or manifestations of persecution will be dramatically different among Christians living under Islamic *sharia* law, which strictly forbids conversion, as opposed to a society such as the United Kingdom, which purportedly guarantees freedom of religious expression. Under *sharia* law someone can be put to death for receiving Christian baptism. However, in the West, we should not underestimate the power of the subtle persecution that gives Christians the "freedom" to affirm a domesticated gospel as long as we do not prophetically challenge the citadels of power.

The true church, throughout time and around the world, is always a community of both hope and suffering. Because we are heralds of the New Creation, the Holy Spirit enables and empowers the church to persevere as we represent and embody the future hope of final consummation. However, because the world desperately wants to cling to the old order of sin and human pride, the church will always be a community of suffering, recalling the words of the apostle Paul, "Everyone who wants to live a godly life in Christ Jesus will be persecuted" (2 Tim. 3:12).

Persecution and Our Identification with Christ

The church is marked by suffering because of our identity with Christ. Jesus said, "If they persecuted me, they will persecute you also" (John 15:20). The church participates in the suffering of Christ in the world. Only once we emerge from what Douglas Hall calls the "Constantinian captivity" of the faith, which has bound the church to expectations of power and privilege are we then able to encounter afresh the central symbol of the Christian faith, the cross.[22] A theology of triumphalism can then be replaced by a theology of the cross.

Of all the Gospel writers, it is Luke, in his extended narrative of Luke-Acts, who provides the clearest exposition of how suffering inevitably arises out of our identification with Christ. Luke prepares his readers to anticipate that the inbreaking of God's reign will face resistance and that the opposition to Jesus will continue on in the life of His disciples. Luke develops this by demonstrating the continuity between the persecution of Jesus and the persecution of Jesus' followers, as embodied in the church. The Holy Spirit helps the church to "take up our cross daily" (Luke 9:23) and learn daily

---

22. Ibid., 104.

what it means to fully identify with Christ. This identification with Christ in the context of persecution will be developed under three themes: Jesus and the church as divider, Jesus and the church as suffering servant, and Jesus and the church as participants in God's sovereign purposes.

JESUS AND THE CHURCH AS DIVIDER

Early in Luke's gospel, while Jesus is still an infant, Simeon holds Him in his arms and declares that Jesus will be "a light for revelation to the Gentiles" (2:32). Yet, this good news for the world is tempered by Simeon's prophecy that it will be a message that divides Israel. Simeon goes on to say that Jesus is "destined to cause the falling and rising of many in Israel, and to be a sign that will be spoken against" (2:34). In Luke 12 Jesus asks, "Do you think that I came to bring peace on earth? No, I tell you, but division. For now on there will be five in one family divided against each other, three against two and two against three" (12:51–52).

Luke's gospel repeatedly demonstrates how Israel becomes divided over the ministry of Jesus. Luke records Jesus' inaugural message in the synagogue in Nazareth, when He quotes Isaiah 61, which brings together the prophetic and messianic nature of Jesus' ministry. Jesus goes on to explicitly identify Himself as a prophet when He declares that "no prophet is accepted in his hometown" (4:24). Like the prophets, Jesus' message is divisive. Initially, they "all spoke well of him and were amazed at the gracious words that came from his lips" (4:22). However, upon hearing more of Jesus' prophetic message, their attitude changes, and only a few verses later they violently react to the teaching of Jesus: "All the people in the synagogue were furious when they heard this. They got up, drove him out of the town, and took him to the brow of the hill . . . in order to throw him down the cliff" (4:28–29).

Luke includes this account to demonstrate that "the rejection of Jesus by his own people confirms the identity of Jesus as a prophet."[23] The encounter in Nazareth anticipates on a small scale the later and more significant rejection of Jesus by many (but not all) in Israel. The person and teaching of Jesus divides people in general, although the deepest cleavage is between the "positive response of the crowds and the negative response of the Jewish leadership," particularly the Pharisees and the Sadducees.[24]

---

23. Cunningham, *Through Many Tribulations*, 61.
24. Ibid., 56.

Just as the person and message of Jesus divided people, so that same division continues through the lives of the heralds who bear the message of Jesus into the world. In Acts, Luke records how the forces arrayed against Jesus continue their opposition to Jesus' followers. The religious and political rulers are arresting and placing the heralds of the kingdom into jail (4:3; 16:23), beating them (5:40; 16:23), and putting them to death (7:58–59), even as the good news is announced (2:38–39; 19:8), the blind see, the lame walk (3:6–8; 9:33–34; 14:9–10), and the dead are raised (9:40; 20:10). On the one hand, when Paul and Barnabus are in Iconium, they speak "boldly for the Lord," and He confirms the message by "enabling them to do miraculous signs and wonders" (14:3). Yet, on the other hand, the "people of the city were divided" (14:4). The good news spread, even as the people plot to "mistreat them and to stone them" (14:5). Those who receive the good news hold the apostles and the name of Jesus in "high esteem," even while the religious authorities cover their ears and put God's servant to death (7:57–58), just as they had put God's Son to death.

Jesus and the Church as Suffering Servant

Luke portrays the entire ministry of Jesus within the larger context of suffering and rejection.[25] Jesus is not only the fulfillment of the perfect prophet, priest, and king but also the fulfillment of the Suffering Servant motif. Luke records Jesus' explicit prediction that His public ministry will culminate in His untimely death. Jesus tells His disciples, "The Son of Man must suffer many things and be rejected by the elders, chief priests and the teachers of the law, and he must be killed and on the third day be raised to life" (9:22). Later, Jesus tells His disciples that the Jewish leaders will accomplish this through handing Him over "to the Gentiles," who will "mock him, insult him, spit on him, flog him and kill him" (18:32). However, as before, He assures them that the gospel advances through suffering when He declares that "on the third day he will rise again" (18:33).

Jesus makes clear to His disciples that they also will suffer and be rejected because of their identity with Him: "Blessed are you when men hate you, when they exclude you and insult you and reject your name as evil, because of the Son of Man" (Luke 6:22). When Jesus sends out the Twelve in Luke 9 and, later, the seventy in Luke 10, He prepares them for rejection

---

25. Luke 5:35; 9:22, 9:43b–45; 11:29; 12:50; 13:31–35; 17:25; 18:31–33; 20:9–18; 22:19–22; 24:6–7.

and persecution. In the first commission, Jesus acknowledges that people will "not welcome you" (9:5). Later, in the larger commissioning, Jesus tells them that He is sending them out like "lambs among wolves" (10:3).

The heralds of the kingdom must be prepared, not only to suffer because of their identity with Jesus, but also to expect the same kind of treatment Jesus received. Jesus reminds us that the servant is not greater than the master (John 13:16; 15:20). We should expect persecution. In fact, it is persecution that authenticates us as truly followers of Jesus. This is why persecution cannot be isolated to any particular period in church history, group of people, or geographic region.

In the book of Acts, Luke shows the continuity between the ministry of Jesus and the ministry of His disciples. Just as Jesus' ministry is summarized as being "powerful in word and deed" (Luke 24:19), so the disciples are portrayed as proclaimers of the gospel and powerful in deed, healing the sick, casting out demons, and raising the dead. However, this is coupled with the expectation that they also will share in the sufferings of Christ.[26] In Acts 5 the Sanhedrin has Peter and the other apostles flogged, and they order them to not speak in the name of Jesus anymore. The text declares that the apostles "left the Sanhedrin, rejoicing because they had been counted worthy of suffering disgrace for the Name" (5:41). In Acts, Luke specifically recalls Simeon's prophecy that Jesus will be a sign that will be "spoken against," when he revisits the phrase in Acts 28:22 to describe the Jewish leaders who declared that people everywhere were "talking against" the emerging Christian movement.

JESUS AND THE CHURCH AS PARTICIPANTS IN GOD'S SOVEREIGN PURPOSES
The third and final way the Luke-Acts narrative seeks to demonstrate our identity with Christ and His suffering is through placing suffering in the larger context of God's sovereign purpose, or the *missio dei*. Luke's narrative identifies various temporal agents who "cause" the suffering of Christ, particularly the elders, the chief priests, the teachers of the law (Luke 9:22), the "hands of men" (9:44), Jerusalem (13:34), "this generation" (17:25), Gentiles (18:32), Judas (22:22), and "sinful men" (24:7).

---

26. Luke seeks to demonstrate the connection between Jesus' glory and His suffering. For example, Luke intentionally identifies Jesus' exalted title "Son of Man" from Daniel 7:13–14 with suffering and rejection. See Luke 9:22, 44; 17:24–25; 18:31; 22:22; and 24:7.

However, all of these are placed within the larger context of God's sovereign purposes. God's sovereign plan is accomplished through human agency. Behind the schemes and plots of sinful humanity and religious zealots lies the guiding hand of God, as Peter reminds his hearers that Jesus "was handed over to you by God's set purpose and foreknowledge" (Acts 2:23).

There are two key ways Luke communicates this. First, he emphasizes the notion of necessity, that Christ *must* suffer, be rejected and, ultimately be put to death.[27] Second, Luke emphasizes that the passion of Christ occurs in *fulfillment* of the Scriptures. In Luke 9:22 Jesus introduces His impending passion by declaring, "The Son of Man *must* suffer many things." He tells His disciples that the Son of Man will someday be revealed in His full glory and power, but before that happens, "he *must* suffer many things and be rejected by this generation" (17:25). Jesus declares that He *must* go to Jerusalem because, "surely no prophet can die outside of Jerusalem" (13:33). And in His first postresurrection appearance in Luke's gospel, Jesus asks the two disciples on the road to Emmaus, "Did not the Christ *have to suffer these things* and then enter his glory?" (24:26).

Jesus also portrays His persecution as a *fulfillment* of Scripture. Jesus assures His disciples that He is going to Jerusalem so that "everything that is written by the prophets about the Son of Man will be fulfilled" (Luke 18:31).[28] Jesus identifies the "stone the builders rejected" of Psalm 118:22 with Himself (Luke 20:17). Similarly, Jesus quotes Isaiah 53:12, "he was numbered with the transgressors," and says, "This must be fulfilled in me. Yes, what is written about me is reaching its fulfillment" (Luke 22:37). After His resurrection, the angel tells the women to remember the words of Jesus that "the Son of Man must be delivered into the hands of sinful men, be crucified and on the third day be raised again" (24:7). Jesus, as the risen Lord, chastises His disciples for being so "slow of heart to believe all that the prophets have spoken!" (24:25). Finally, as we saw in chapter 5 of this book, Luke is the only gospel writer who introduces his Great Commission as a fulfillment of Scripture: "This is what is written: The Christ will suffer and rise from the dead on the third day, and repentance and forgiveness of

---

27. This theme is portrayed in Luke through the use of "*dei*" (9:22; 13:33; 17:25) and the use of the divine passive (9:44).

28. It should be noted that the parallel sayings of Jesus found in Matthew 20:18–19 and Mark 10:33–34 do not include the reference to His passion being a fulfillment of prophetic expectation.

sins will be preached in his name to all nations, beginning at Jerusalem"
(24:46–47).

The persecution, suffering, and eventually death of Christ are portrayed as fulfilling God's sovereign plan. In the same way, although the
suffering and persecution of the church takes place through the agency of
a sinful world, it too is part of the larger, unfolding plan of God's sovereign purpose for His church. In the face of persecutors, the disciples are
told not to fear "those who kill the body and after that can do no more"
(Luke 12:4), because human history is moving toward that point, in God's
own plan, when He will vindicate His servants and judge the unbelieving
world. In Luke 21:12–19, Jesus prepares His disciples to face persecution,
declaring, "They will lay hands on you and persecute you. They will deliver
you to synagogues and prisons, and you will be brought before kings and
governors, and all on account of my name" (21:12). Luke is quite intentional in his later narrative in Acts in demonstrating that this is precisely
what happens to those who herald the gospel and identify with the name
of Jesus. This is particularly true for Peter, Stephen, and Paul, who exemplify Jesus' expectation of what all future followers of Jesus should expect.

Luke demonstrates how Peter, Stephen, and Paul, in particular, suffer
for the sake of the gospel, but through that suffering the gospel continues
to spread and the signs of the inbreaking of the New Creation abound. The
religious authorities put Peter and John into prison, even as many heard
the good news and the church "grew to about five thousand" (Acts 4:3–4).
Stephen is martyred for his faith, but the forced scattering of the disciples
from Jerusalem becomes the primary stimulus for the gospel's spread, over
time, from the Jewish center in Jerusalem to the Gentile center in Antioch.
Saul of Tarsus is an ardent persecutor of the church, and yet he is called and
appointed as a witness of the gospel to the Gentiles. When the Lord speaks
to Ananias in a vision and instructs him to go and pray for Saul of Tarsus,
Ananias initially objects because of the well-circulated stories of Saul's ani-
mosity toward the church. However, the Lord says to Ananias, "Go! This
man is my chosen instrument to carry my name before the Gentiles and
their kings and before the people of Israel. *I will show him how much he
must suffer for my name*" (Acts 9:15–16, emphasis mine). The ministry of
the apostle Paul is marked simultaneously by a supernatural witness of the
Spirit, extending God's sovereign purposes among the Gentiles, as well as
intense opposition and persecution (Acts 9:29; 13:50; 14:19; 16:22–23; 17:13;

18:12; 20:23; 21:13, 30–31; 22:24; 23:10–14; 28:16). As in the life of Jesus, God's sovereign purposes are fulfilled within the context of suffering. The life and ministry of the church reflect the life and ministry of Jesus.

Persecution Because We Are Heralds of the New Creation Living in the "Not Yet"

Central to the overall theological argument of this book is the recognition that all missionary activity must be placed within the larger context of the *missio dei*. Missionaries are heralds of the New Creation, announcing and embodying in the midst of a fallen world the inbreaking of the future realities of God's rule. Precisely because we are heralds of a kingdom that has been inaugurated but not fully consummated, we live in the constant tension between the "already" and the "not yet" of God's rule. Because missionaries live out their lives among people groups who do not initially know or recognize the rule of God, they must expect opposition and suffering. A "gospel" that only proclaims prosperity and comfort is *not* the Christian gospel but a caricature of the gospel that fails to recognize that the Spirit bears witness through the church in the context of suffering.

Our inability to live theologically in the "not yet" arises (particularly in Western theology) because of a rigid, Enlightenment-initiated, dualism, which unduly separates God and the world, including God and His church. This has caused the church to interpret suffering and persecution as times when the "real presence" of Christ is absent from His church. Pentecostalism may have helped to restore a proper view of God's ongoing involvement in the life of the world and the church through miracles and signs and wonders. However, Pentecostalism has been far slower in recognizing God's presence and participation in and through our *sufferings*.

The Holy Spirit helps us to see that the sufferings of Christ continue as an ongoing reality in and through the life and witness of the church. In other words, it is not the church that suffers while God is silent and unmoved from the distant portals of heaven. Rather, *Christ* is suffering in and through the suffering of the church. The apostle Peter says, "Rejoice that you *participate in the sufferings of Christ*, so that you may be overjoyed when his glory is revealed" (1 Peter 4:13, emphasis mine). When Saul of Tarsus, the angry persecutor, is confronted by the risen Lord on the road to Damascus, Christ says to him, "Saul, Saul, why do you persecute *me*?" (Acts 9:4; cf. 22:7; 26:14). To persecute the church is to persecute Christ, because of His divine presence in the church. Jaroslav Pelikan argues that it is this single statement of the risen Lord to Paul that gave birth to the later Pauline phrase the "body of Christ" in reference to the church (Rom. 12:5; 1 Cor. 12:27; Eph. 1:23; 4:12; Col. 1:24; 2:19).[29]

Paul himself would later write that "the sufferings of Christ flow over into our lives" (2 Cor. 1:5), indicating that our present suffering is understood as the overflow of the sufferings of Christ in His body, the church. Yet, this is integral to what it means to "know Christ." We cannot know the "power of his resurrection," Paul assures us, unless we are prepared to enter into the "fellowship of sharing in his sufferings" (Phil. 3:10).

Paul declares to the church at Colosse, "I rejoice in what was suffered for you, and I fill up in my flesh what is still lacking in regard to Christ's afflictions, for the sake of his body, which is the church" (Col. 1:24). There are three questions that immediately arise from this text. First, how can Paul rejoice in his sufferings? Second, how can Paul suffer *for the church*, especially the church at Colosse, whom he had never even met? Third, how can we possibly speak of anything lacking in the afflictions and sufferings of Christ? First, Paul rejoices in suffering for the same reason that the apostles left the Sanhedrin "rejoicing because they had been counted worthy of suffering disgrace for the Name" (Acts 5:41). Their suffering authenticated their identity with Christ, and that is always a source of rejoicing. In the Old Testament, it is the righteous who are afflicted (Pss. 12:5; 31:7); so, for the Christian, persecution is a sign that we share in the righteousness of Christ. In addition, Paul rejoices because, for him, it is a testimony to the inbreaking of the gospel among the Gentiles. Paul understands that his calling as a missionary to preach the gospel across new frontiers (Rom. 15:20) is united to his calling to suffering. As missionaries, we should rejoice in our sufferings, because this is part of the inevitable response to the extension of God's rule and the inbreaking of the New Creation into the present age.

Second, as an apostolic minister to the Gentiles, Paul understands his ministry as *representing* the larger body of Christ. Paul's missionary

---

29. Jaroslav Pelikan, *Acts* (Grand Rapids: Brazos, 2005), 123. This question by the risen Lord, argues Pelikan, marks Saul as "the successor of those who had tormented Jesus Christ in his passion" and marks "the church as the successor of Christ in his passion." Paul supposed that he was attacking "the miserable adherents of a wretched fringe movement," but ultimately he realizes that the target of his rage and violence was Jesus Christ Himself.

work, including his suffering on behalf of the gospel, is an extension of the church's larger witness and work in the world. Therefore, Paul sees all of his sufferings to be "for the sake of" the body of Christ, the church. The church at Colosse, as with any other church, is a beneficiary of the sacrifice, commitment, and sufferings of those who give their lives heralding the gospel and announcing the inbreaking of God's rule.

F. F. Bruce observes that Paul's conception of representative suffering on behalf of the larger body of Christ is derived from Isaiah's Suffering Servant motif. Israel as a nation was called to be God's servant and to bear the sufferings of the righteous. However, Israel was a disobedient servant. Therefore, the Suffering Servant was ultimately fulfilled in the person of Jesus Christ. In the face of stiff persecution and opposition by the Jews, Paul quotes Isaiah 49:6 when he launches his ministry among the Gentiles (Acts 13:47). Not only does the light of Christ continue to be extended through His obedient servants, but His servants also are called upon to continue bearing the sufferings of Christ on behalf of the people of God.[30]

From our perspective, even though we have never met William Carey, Hudson Taylor, Lottie Moon, Gladys Alyward, or Deitrich Bonhoeffer, we should all recognize that they suffered "for our sake" and that the whole body of Christ is strengthened through their sacrifice. As missionaries we are not ultimately serving a particular denomination, mission board, or theological agenda. Rather, we are serving the church of Jesus Christ, the body of Christ, which exists back through time and around the world. We represent Christ and His body in all our sufferings.

Third, Peter O'Brien makes a convincing case that Paul's reference to filling up in his flesh "what is still lacking in regard to Christ's afflictions" is most likely an apocalyptic conception concerning suffering, which will precede the ushering in of the kingdom.[31] Jewish apocalyptic writing supports the idea that just before the entrance of the coming age and the rule

---

30. E. K. Simpson and F. F. Bruce, *The Epistles to the Ephesians and Colossians,* The New International Commentary on the New Testament (Grand Rapids: Eerdmans, 1982), 215–216.

31. Peter T. O'Brien, *Colossians, Philemon,* Word Biblical Commentary, vol. 44 (Waco: Word, 1982), 78. O'Brien surveys four other alternative explanations: (1) Something is lacking in the vicarious sufferings of Christ that must be supplied by the apostle Paul; (2) it is merely a reference to Paul suffering "for the sake of" Christ; (3) Paul's sufferings actually resemble the sufferings of Christ, or were similar in terms of their level of distress; (4) Paul's sufferings are in mystical union with Christ. The view advocated by O'Brien and adopted in this work has the strongest supporting evidence.

of God's anointed Messiah, there will be a period of increased persecution and suffering that will be endured by the people of God.

Christians came to realize that in Jesus Christ, God's Messiah already had come. However, rather than the expected full, immediate, and cataclysmic consummation of the kingdom, God inaugurated the kingdom in Jesus Christ but left the full consummation of His kingly rule for a future time. The age to come has already broken in, even while the present age continues to exert its presence and influence. Because we live in the tension between the "already" and the "not yet," this means that the entire history of the church occurs within the context of the "last days." Thus, the heightened persecution that was once a particular expectation for the end of time has become *normative* for the church. The Holy Spirit enables us to live in these in-between times. This should not be understood in such a way as to preclude an even more intense period of persecution just prior to the return of Christ. Rather, it provides a theological framework for understanding persecution as normative, even if there are particular prolonged periods of heightened opposition to the inbreaking of God's rule.

The apostle Paul anticipates that there is a certain measure of affliction that must be endured by the church before the final and full revelation of God's glorious reign. When Jesus spoke of persecution against the church, He said, "If the Lord had not cut short those days, no one would survive. But for the sake of the elect, whom he has chosen, he has shortened them" (Mark 13:20). There is a limit to how much God will allow the church to suffer. More to the point, there is a limit to how much God will allow His Anointed One, Jesus Christ, to suffer. Christ has inaugurated the anticipated "messianic woes," but the full extent of the overflow of Christ's sufferings in and through the church has not yet reached its limit. That which is "still lacking" in Christ's afflictions refers to the suffering that Christ, through His church, must continue to endure until the full extent has been reached and the kingdom is consummated.

Paul's sufferings are "filling up what was lacking of a predetermined measure of afflictions which the righteous must endure."[32] Paul's suffering, therefore, reduces the tribulations for other believers since the more sufferings "he personally absorbed, as he went about preaching the gospel,

---

32. Ibid., 80.

the less would remain for his fellow Christians to endure."[33] We do not know when the full measure of suffering will be reached. However, in light of the history of persecution against the church, we do know that each day we, as the people of God, move closer to that point. Until that time, the whole creation "is groaning as in the pains of childbirth" in expectation of the full revelation of God's rule in the world (Rom. 8:22). Paul is so certain about the final outcome of this epic struggle, he declares, "I consider that our present sufferings are not worth comparing with the glory that will be revealed in us" (Rom. 8:18).

CONCLUSION

This chapter has provided a theological framework that places persecution and suffering within the larger context of the *missio dei*. Within this context, it is clear that persecution should not be viewed as an unfortunate bane in the life of the church or something that is experienced only by certain groups of Christians in history or only in a few parts of the world. Rather, persecution serves four main purposes within the *missio dei*. First, persecution authenticates our identity as disciples of Jesus Christ. We have observed that the New Testament develops this identity theologically in several ways. To begin with, the church stands in continuity with the prophetic stream of the Old Testament, of which Jesus is the ultimate fulfillment. Furthermore, the church continues to embody Christ's presence in the world; therefore, the rejection of God's Anointed One continues on in the lives of those who herald the gospel. Finally, the afflictions and sufferings of Christ continue to "overflow" in and through His body, the church.

Second, persecution is a normative part of training the church in discipleship and nurturing perseverance as we await the full consummation of the rule and reign of God. Paul openly tells the Corinthians about "hardships . . . in the province of Asia," which he endured. But he goes on to say that "this happened that we might not rely on ourselves but on God, who raises the dead" (2 Cor. 1:8–9). Persecution is one of the ways in which God keeps the church from drifting into triumphalism and the inevitable nominalism that emerges when the church is trapped in the "Constantinian captivity," which binds the church to false expectations of power and privilege rather than a theology of the cross.

---

33. Ibid.

Third, persecution provides a context for the effective witness of the church. The major new frontier of Gentile evangelism and church planting, including that which was initiated in Antioch, as well as the later ministry of the apostle Paul, arises in response to persecution.[34] Jesus tells His followers to expect to be handed over to authorities, who will beat them and flog them (Matt. 10:17). On account of His name, the followers of Jesus will be "brought before governors and kings *as witnesses to them and to the Gentiles*" (10:18, emphasis mine). However, Jesus admonishes us not to worry about what to say or how to say it, for "you will be given what to say" because "it will not be you speaking, but the Spirit of your Father speaking through you" (10:19–20). In Luke's gospel Jesus says, "I will give you words and wisdom that none of your adversaries will be able to resist or contradict" (Luke 21:15). The testimony of Acts demonstrates that this is precisely what happened through the persecution and witness of the early church.

Fourth, persecution is the normative expectation of a church living in the reality of the "not yet," as we wait patiently for the full measure of suffering before the final consummation of the kingdom of God. This places all suffering within the larger context of God's sovereign plan for all believers everywhere. Just as Jesus said that He *must* suffer, and that His passion is in *fulfillment* of the Scriptures, so the church must suffer in order to fulfill God's sovereign purpose and plan for His church. Seen in this light, persecution becomes an integral part of the divine triumph, which is being manifested in Jesus Christ. We may, like Ashwin Kumar, see with our own eyes in this life the divine vindication of His faithful, suffering servants. Alternatively, like the Jesuits, we may have to share in the sufferings of Christ and, like Jesus, stand silent before our accusers and wait until the eschaton to see the full revelation of God's victory. Either way, we hold fast to what Jesus said in the Upper Room Discourse the night before He would be martyred for His faithful witness: "In this world you will have trouble. But take heart! I have overcome the world" (John 16:33).

---

34. Scott Cunningham makes the point that in the Gospels the general point is that persecution will be a "testimony" in reference to future judgment, i.e., used as evidence against those who opposed the spread of the gospel. However, he points out that in the Luke-Acts narrative persecution is developed more positively as achieving the opposite effect, i.e., not squelching the gospel but helping in its dissemination. See Cunningham, *Through Many Tribulations*, 135.

— *Conclusion* —

The Church as the Reflection
of the Trinity in the World

THERE HAS BEEN CONSIDERABLE SPECULATION over the years among *Titanic* enthusiasts over what caused the mighty ship to sink on its maiden voyage. Some have argued that the tragic accident was caused by a faulty rudder. Others have insisted that it was ultimately caused by poor communications, or the angle at which the ship hit the iceberg. However, a recent study of scientists has concluded that the best explanation for the disaster was something far more mundane—second-rate rivets.

In the book *What Really Sank the Titanic: New Forensic Discoveries*, Jennifer McCarty and Timothy Foecke argue that the vessel's manufacturer, Harland and Wolff, was under so much pressure to secure sufficient quantities of iron to make the rivets for the vessel that it made some crucial compromises.[1] The White Star Line company, which owned the *Titanic,* was in competition with another company, named Cunard, in an age when the construction of luxury ocean liners by Belfast shipyard workers translated into child labor, exhausting work schedules to meet deadlines, and enormous pressure to cut corners. McCarty and Foecke argue that in the rush to get the *Titanic* afloat first, the White Star Line ended up with a vessel that looked impressive but was made with substandard materials. At the time of the *Titanic's* construction, there was a shortage of quality iron. According to records, managers turned a deaf ear

---

1. Jennifer McCarty and Timothy Foecke, *What Really Sank the Titanic: New Forensic Discoveries* (New York: Citadel, 2008).

to numerous objections about the potential hazard of using substandard rivets. Everything was sacrificed to keep the *Titanic* on schedule.

Forty-nine rivets have now been recovered from the wreckage, and a forensic analysis revealed that they indeed contained high levels of slag, making the iron brittle. These tests reveal that the rivets used in constructing the *Titanic* were, in fact, substandard and did not meet the design specifications. The *Titanic* could have struck an iceberg and stayed afloat even if as many as four of its sealed compartments were flooded. Instead, so many rivets popped along the starboard side of the ship that five compartments ended up flooding, sending more than fifteen-hundred people to their deaths.

This story is a powerful reminder of the importance of not forgetting the most basic fundamentals when building a big project. In the scale and grandeur of a project like the *Titanic,* with hardwood dance floors, hanging chandeliers, and solid brass faucets, it was all too easy to ignore the importance of a lowly rivet. This book has been about constructing a missiology, with special attention given to the fundamental building blocks that are essential to producing healthy missions movements. Therefore, we will begin by summarizing the key argument of the book and the four theological building blocks upon which this missiology is constructed. This will be followed by an examination of a case study taken from contemporary missions discourse in order to demonstrate how a Trinitarian theology rooted in the *missio dei* might shed light on one of the pressing missiological issues of our day.

SUMMARY OF KEY ARGUMENT

Missions is a complex and multifaceted enterprise that requires special attentiveness to the proper foundation. This book has argued that the missiology upon which much of contemporary missions is based requires a fresh reconceptualization of its basic theological foundations. Like the *Titanic* of old, we cannot take comfort in how large, how global, or how impressive our missionary structures are if we have not attended to the basic structural fundamentals that hold the entire enterprise together. In chapter 1, I quoted the well-known comment by Hendrick Kraemer, "the church is always in a state of crisis; its greatest shortcoming is that we are only occasionally aware of it."[2] The crisis of our time is embodied in the

---

2. As quoted by David Bosch, *Transforming Mission: Paradigm Shifts in Theology of Mission* (Maryknoll, NY: Orbis, 1991), 2.

forces of relativism, pragmatism, and institutional parochialism, which have hindered the emergence of a healthy, robust missiology. Over time, the missionary enterprise gradually has become oriented to a myriad of independent organizations and denominational efforts that are pragmatically driven and not understood within the larger context of God's initiative. Social science assumptions often trump biblical ecclesiology, financial exigencies frequently govern strategic planning, and relativism silences the missions impulse in many churches.

We live in a post-Christendom, increasingly postmodern world, and the assumptions that produced a normative Christian plausibility structure have collapsed. The resulting fragmentation has left the church unclear about its mission. Some have advocated a retreat to a privatized faith, which leaves the pluralistic relativism of the new reigning plausibility structure unchallenged. Others have insisted that we continue with business as usual and regard the massive cultural shifts as passing effluvia, of which we will soon see the other side. Still others have called for a radical reinterpretation of the Christian faith that embraces a postmodern epistemology.

In addition to these theological and epistemological challenges, we are also living in the midst of a dramatic shift in the center of Christian gravity, with the emergence of millions of new, vibrant Christians throughout many sectors of the Majority World. Latin American Pentecostalism, African initiated churches, hundreds of thousands of new unregistered house churches in China, dynamic and energized Korean and Indian missionary movements—these are the new players in the world Christian movement. Therefore, we in the West need to pause, take a breath, and accept a brief interlude—a *selah*—that will enable us to reconfigure and reconceptualize missions in a more theologically and biblically robust way. Thus, we will review the key fundamentals upon which this missiology has been constructed.

FOUR FUNDAMENTALS IN MISSIOLOGY

The Missio Dei
The starting point of missions must be the *missio dei*. Missions must first and foremost be about what God is doing in the world, not what we are doing. Missions must step back from the competitive, pragmatic, market-driven impulses, which tempt us to think about missions in

anthropocentric or institutional ways. Instead, missions must be conceptualized within the larger framework of God's redemptive plan, not ancillary actions of the church for self-aggrandizement through institutional expansion, even on a global scale. If we are honest, we must recognize that much of our missionary activity is overly preoccupied with human plans and institutionally driven strategies built largely upon the foundation of the social sciences. While acknowledging the abiding value of the insights of the social sciences, and even insights from the business world, we nevertheless insist that missions cannot be built upon or constructed in this fashion without, in the long run, producing missionary movements that have fundamental design flaws. The "nuts and bolts" of missions must be theologically driven.

The *missio dei* is a shorthand way of linking the sovereign, prior action of God to the life, ministry, and work of the church. Before we can speak of the church *doing* missions, we must first see God as the God of mission. Everything must be founded on the prior nature, character, and initiative of God. Even the Great Commission, arguably the greatest example of a church called to action, in Matthew's expression of it, begins with an affirmation of who God *is*: "All authority in heaven and on earth has been given to me" (Matt. 28:18). Missions begins with who God is; only then can it be cast as specific duties or responsibilities of the church in the world. Only when we capture a glimpse of the sovereign glory of God can we properly respond to the imperatives that are given to Christ's holy church.

In most standard mission textbooks, this is accomplished through a section typically entitled, "The Biblical/Theological Foundations for Missions." However, this biblical/theological section often remains disconnected from a missiology that, on the whole, is not articulated from a theological framework that informs and enlivens the entire work. Sometimes biblical texts are cited to provide justification for actions that already have been determined to be right and proper. And sometimes a multitude of strategies, presuppositions, and actions are enjoined on the church without demonstrating how they are related to the theological foundations that were set forth earlier. In the world of Christendom, this flaw was not as detectable or as glaring since the vast majority of those who studied missions were already convinced about the task set before the church, and they were supported by a church that accepted the missions imperative. Furthermore, since the vast majority of missions initiatives emanated from the Western world, there were few alternative perspectives to offer the necessary critique. However, such a consensus no longer exists in the West. Furthermore, with the rise of the Majority World church, the gospel often is taking root and flourishing on the periphery of societies that are built on very different foundations. We sometimes forget how, in the first century, the gospel flourished and spread in a context of so-cial, religious, and political hostility. The best way forward is to return to the basic foundation of the *missio dei*, which serves as the starting point of all missions, whether East or West, whether from places still living in the shadow of Christendom, or from a region that is dominated by non-Christian religions or ideologies.

The Triune God

This missiology has attempted to place missions within the life and activity of the triune God in the world. In chapter 4 we explored how God the Fa-ther is the providential source and goal of all missions. Missions begins with God the Father's initiative in calling Abraham out of idolatry to follow the one true God. Without the covenantal action of God's prior initiative to Abraham, there would be no Incarnation, no inbreaking of the New Creation, and certainly no missions. Missions therefore is placed securely within the context of revelation and response. God reveals His sovereign purposes, and the church responds in acts of faithful obedience to His un-folding plan. Scripture faithfully records countless examples of God's rev-elation to His people of His saving purposes, which include all peoples on earth. Once we capture a vision of God's action in and through history, we are buoyed by the certainty of God's victory as the sovereign Lord of the universe. We can no longer say, as is often said, that the church is one gen-eration from extinction. God has announced that He will be known. We may envision ourselves as beleaguered and marginalized, but He always has "seven thousand" who "have not bowed down to Baal" (1 Kings 19:18).

There is nothing in the universe more durable than the people of God. Of course, this is not linked to any particular institutional manifestation, polity, or denomination of the church, but to the historic expression of Christian faithfulness through time. God is building His church, and the gates of hell shall not prevail against it. Thomas Oden, in *The Rebirth of Orthodoxy,* has commented, "While grace does not coerce belief, neither does it bat zero in any given ecclesial season."[3] In every generation we can boldly proclaim that the triune God of biblical revelation has not left Himself without a witness. This truth is not based, ultimately, on our obedience but on God's faithfulness, which calls forth an obedient response from those He has called.

GOD THE FATHER

The Great Commission texts in the New Testament do not represent a new departure but stand in continuity with God's past actions, beginning with His covenant with Abraham to bless all nations (Gen. 12:3). We should not speak of the sending church unless and until we first understand God the Father as the Sender. The Father sent His Son into the world, and the church becomes the ongoing reflection of the triune God in the world. We recognize that there are principalities and powers that stand in opposition to God's rule. This opposition is not a mere theoretical reality unattached from the world, but it manifests itself in particular cultural forces and attitudes that must be countered and responded to by the people of God. Therefore, we establish a biblical basis for a theology of culture and a theology of religions. God the Father is the ultimate reference point for the church in understanding the source and goal of all missionary activity.

GOD THE SON

Through the incarnation of Jesus Christ, we see the redemptive embodiment of God's mission in the world. God the Father sends God the Son into the world to embody the New Creation and to demonstrate how to engage an unbelieving world with truth and grace (John 1:14, 17). Throughout history, and despite periods of glaring unfaithfulness, the true church has reflected that embodiment, concretizing God's presence through specific acts of incarnational obedience. The Incarnation, therefore, provides the theological basis for how we understand issues of access, reproducibility, and holism in missions.

The Incarnation was initiated by God the Father in order to provide a means through which sinful humanity might regain access to God. In the same way, God sends the church as a reflection of the Incarnation in the world in order to assist people in gaining clearer access to the gospel.

---

3. Thomas Oden, *The Rebirth of Orthodoxy* (New York: HarperSanFrancisco, 2003), 45.

The Incarnation is the ultimate "translation" of deity into humanity. God takes on human flesh and demonstrates how we are to live in this world. The church mirrors the Incarnation by embodying and reproducing the presence of Christ through gathered congregations around the world. Finally, in the Incarnation we experience the full scope of God's compassion for the human race. God is determined not only to reverse the curse of death but also to redeem every aspect of human life and dignity that has been robbed by the Fall and the entrance of human sin into the world. The church mirrors this holistic compassion of God by recognizing that whether we are expositing a passage from the Bible from a pulpit or serving mashed potatoes to the homeless in a food kitchen, we are, in our own way, reflecting the love of Christ for the whole person. An individualistic view of missions often seeks to rank certain kinds of ministries as "more important" or "more biblical" or "more influential" than other kinds of ministries. However, Paul reminds us "the body is not made up of one part but of many" (1 Cor. 12:14). Paul exhorts us to remember that "those parts of the body that seem to be weaker are indispensable, and the parts that we think are less honorable we treat with special honor" (1 Cor. 12:22–23). All the individual acts of obedience represent a "yes" to God's rule and, collectively, point to the great "YES" of Jesus Christ, who is the ultimate embodiment of God's rule and reign.[4]

GOD THE HOLY SPIRIT

The Holy Spirit is the empowering presence of the *missio dei*. The church is not only nourished by the memory of the Incarnation, but we also are empowered by the presence of the risen Lord in the church, which is made manifest to us and the world through the empowering presence of the Holy Spirit. The gospel and God's initiatives do not stop at the Cross and the Resurrection but continue at Pentecost and in the life and witness of the church. The Holy Spirit enables and empowers the church to extend God's mission into the world.

The Holy Spirit also helps the church to understand missions within a larger eschatological context. The incarnation, the public ministry, and the

---

4. The church should not forget the important lessons of the past regarding holistic ministry. It is important to honor the contribution of every member of the body, which, collectively, reflects the full ministry of Christ to the whole person. However, Christians must be vigilant not to allow the church's ministry as a collective to become overly weighted toward social ministries and neglect the explicit call to repentance and faith in Christ.

death and resurrection of Jesus Christ represent the "firstfruits" of the New Creation (1 Cor. 15:20). In Christ, the rule and reign of God the Father is breaking into the present evil order. The Holy Spirit empowers the entire church to live out the future realities of the New Creation in the present. Missions must always be understood fundamentally as an extension of the life and purposes of the triune God, acting in and through His church.

The New Creation

Once missions is rooted in the mission of the triune God, it is placed within an eschatological context. God the Father is the Lord of creation. We were created to worship Him and live under His sovereign rule. Due to Adam's rebellion and our persistent confirmation of that rebellion in our own lives, we are participants in a fallen creation, no longer experiencing the full majesty of God's righteous rule and reign in the world. The Incarnation represents a dramatic divine initiative to reverse the curse of the Fall and to purchase our redemption; it is the inbreaking of the rule and reign of God. The kingdom of God, or rule of God, has been inaugurated, even though we still await its final consummation. Missions is about extending the claims and realities of the New Creation into the present order. As Christians we live in the "already/not-yet" tension. In Jesus Christ the kingdom of God *already* has broken into the present evil order, but we do *not yet* experience the end of human hostility toward God. At the heart of missions is the announcement of God's reign. We are ambassadors of the New Creation. Through the witness of the faithful church, Christ continues to summon men and women to repent and believe the good news of the gospel. Missions summons people not merely to "make a decision" to follow Christ but also to enter the community of the faithful, the church, and to live out the realities of the future in the present before the eyes of the world in real space-time history. This is why the Great Commission cannot be spoken of as "fulfilled" apart from the larger eschatological context of the consummation of the New Creation.

John Piper has famously noted that "missions exists because worship doesn't," seeking, thereby, to reorient the ultimate motivation for all missionary activity in the glory of God.[5] Piper's perspective is valuable, not

---

5. John Piper, *Let the Nations Be Glad! The Supremacy of God in Missions* (Grand Rapids: Baker, 1993), 11.

only because it reminds us that missions is first and foremost about God and His glory and His plan for the universe (the *missio dei*), but also because it points out that worship brings us into gathered communities with one another and into the presence of the triune God. This helps to reinforce the central theme that missions is about God building His *church*— gathered communities of worshippers. Missions, therefore, is both an act of worship (the church's response to God's revelation) and a participation in the final goal of God's mission, which is the worship of God. I am confident that when Piper speaks about eschatological worship, he intends that to be shorthand for the full revelation of God's purposes for His people for all eternity, in every facet and dimension. While I cannot produce a phrase as memorable or catchy as Piper's, I think that, perhaps, a more precise summary might actually be, "Missions exists because the New Creation has not yet been consummated." We must reconnect our understanding of missions with the larger context of the inbreaking of the New Creation.

The Global Church

Finally, this missiology seeks to move beyond the monocultural paradigms that heretofore have dominated missiological reflection by taking into account the new realities of the global church and reflecting the truth that "it takes the whole church to bring the whole gospel to the whole world." It is a fundamental premise of this work that today all missiologies must be reconceptualized from the perspective of global Christianity. Inevitably, this will challenge at least three notions that have dominated missionary discourse and practice.

First, a missiology seen through the wide lens of the global church challenges the language of "center" and "periphery" in reference to the church and its mission. Traditionally, missions strategy was based on the notion that the mission of the church moves out from some single center of life and vibrancy to the periphery, which is known as the "mission field." The assumption is that we represent the heart of the Christian movement, and "out there" is the mission field. However, today, missions is *from* everywhere *to* everywhere. In the twenty-first century, the church on every continent is simultaneously sending missionaries and receiving missionaries. The rise of global immigration, increased diversity, the impact of globalization, and the increased fragmentation of societies have given rise to a situation where the "center" and the "periphery" have merged in new and surprising ways. The church and the mission field are both "here" and "there." Missions can now be advanced as much by a Western agent relocating to North Africa or to an immigrant community in an urban city of the United States, as by a Brazilian missionary moving to China or an African Christian working in London or Los Angeles. Every region of the world has a Christian center, and every region of the world encompasses people groups without the gospel. Removing the emphasis on unreached people groups from its long-standing captivity to geographic paradigms should serve to heighten, not diminish, our burden for crossing the remaining frontiers that separate thousands of people groups from a viable church witness.

Second, a missiology conceptualized from a global perspective challenges the way we think about the missionary force. For centuries the Protestant church in general (and the Protestant missionary movement in particular) has been dominated by Western missionaries from a European heritage. Essentially, we were the only players on the field. Eventually, with the rise of the Majority World church, various adjustments were made that allowed for a more globalized missionary force, but we retained the role as the central player and the chief financier, as well as the final referee over all that transpired. Strategies were developed, funding was secured, and, finally, Majority World Christians were included in the implementation phase. We gradually recognized the need for greater parity and even adopted the language of "partnership," but it has been a long and difficult transition to not only relinquish control but also recognize that there were many important missions initiatives in which the strategy, funding, and personnel all came from the Majority World church. Today, the work of missions is a cross-cultural team effort with players from all over the world.

If you are a Western person reading this chapter, I want to make it clear that it would be a mistake to envision the future of the Western church as playing only a minor role, sitting by passively, merely "along for the ride." On the contrary, in the twenty-first century we will see major initiatives coming from all quarters of the church's life. We must all become more collaborative. For a time the Western church needed to step back and make it clear that we were simply one part of the global church. However, there are many gifts and perspectives the Western church can offer that will enhance the strength, vitality, and wisdom of the larger global Christian movement.[6] We will continue to play a role in strategic thinking, in funding, and in mobilization, but the difference is that we will be simply one player among many and we will play a much wider array of roles than in the past.

Third, viewing the church from a global perspective enables us to see many new and challenging frontiers, which have not received sufficient attention. Because missionary discourse, even in the post-Lausanne I period, has been dominated by so many geographic, territorially driven paradigms, our ability to recognize many of the most challenging new frontiers that face Christians in the twenty-first century has been hampered. Many of the most important frontiers are intellectual, social, and epistemological and defy the normal geographic parameters. Postmodern epistemology, angry atheism, rampant poverty, and the dissolution of basic social structures such as marriage and the conjugal family unit are examples of challenges many in the church around the world face. Thus the church must mobilize, not only to cross the traditional geographic or ethnic barriers, but also to cross intellectual and epistemological barriers to reach people who are lost and without access to the gospel, even though they may—geographically or ethnically speaking—live right in the midst of a vibrant church.

APPLYING A TRINITARIAN MISSIOLOGY
TO CONTEMPORARY ISSUES

Missions and Missiology

One of the most helpful ways to think about the relationship between missions and missiology is the phrase "missions at sunrise, missiology at sunset." The idea behind this phrase is that missions is inherently optimistic, forward looking, and rooted in action and practice. Field missionaries are busy preaching the gospel and planting churches and often do not have the time or energy for sufficient reflection. When one is experiencing a genuine movement of God, tremendous energy and effort is extended to support and encourage this movement. Over time, however,

---

6. I only gradually realized how much of contemporary missions writings that speak in glowing terms about the rise of the Majority World church have inadvertently caused many Western students to think that they no longer have a meaningful role to play in the world mission of the church because their "day has past." We must be committed to collaborative paradigms that are multidirectional and value the contributions of *all* sectors of the church.

issues and challenges inevitably arise that demand deeper theological reflection. In the New Testament, the classic example of this can be found in the dramatic move of God among Gentiles.

It must have been thrilling to experience firsthand God's transformative work in the hearts and lives of people who were formerly considered unclean pagans. However, difficult and serious questions quickly began to arise: Should Gentile believers be circumcised? Should they be asked to submit to the Jewish Law? The dilemma was real. If they insisted that a Gentile believer submit to the Jewish Law, that could erode the doctrine of justification by faith and the church's proclamation of the sufficiency of the completed work of Christ on behalf of the believer. On the other hand, if they failed to address practical moral guidelines, that could erode the ethical purity of the people of God and give the impression that Christians were antinomian and had abandoned the relationship between faith and faithfulness, between trusting belief and the necessary ethical response. Furthermore, since the earliest believers were Jews, they also risked disrupting shared table fellowship between all the believers, thereby effectively creating two separate churches, two bodies of Christ, one Jew and one Gentile. This would create a fundamental division in the body of Christ in breach of Jesus' high priestly prayer that we might be one (John 17:11).

The Jerusalem Council was called in the wake of a missions movement in order to engage in vital, reflective missiology. They did not gather to discuss theology in some abstract way removed from the life of the church. It was fundamentally a discussion over the terms through which Gentiles would enter the church and enjoy fellowship with believers who were Jews. Missiology happens *after* the missionary advance: missions happens at "sunrise," missiology at "sunset." However, the relationship between "sunrise" and "sunset" should not be forgotten. If missiology is done well, it should in turn stimulate a new "sunrise," which over time raises fresh challenges and new issues that call for further reflection. Missions and missiology each stimulate, support, and lead to the other. Missions is activistic; missiology is more reflective. One could say that missiology is an attempt to answer questions and wrestle with issues that missions has posed from the front lines of engagement. Without a vibrant missionary movement, there are no new questions, and missiology cannot thrive. However, if new questions are raised and they are not given an adequate answer, then the health of the church can be affected, and the missionary movement can become stagnant.

Let me illustrate this with an example from my own experience in India. When the missionary movement began to really take hold among North Indians from a Hindu background, the new believers began to ask whether they should change their names to more biblical ones, since many of them were named after Hindu gods such as Rama or Krishna. It was an important missiological question, which deserved the right response. If the missionaries had insisted that these new believers change their names (as a few did), then it actually would have served to unnecessarily impede the growth of the missionary movement by extracting these Hindu background believers from their own culture. Wisely, more and more believers from Hindu backgrounds are retaining their birth names, which, in turn, helps to stimulate the missions movement because it enables Hindus to see that someone from a Hindu family can *become* a Christian, contrary to the widely held notion that religious adherence is based on one's ethnic and cultural heritage.

I remember how important Romans 16 was to the missiological reflection on this real-life missionary question, even though this chapter is widely neglected in the West because it is merely a long list of names—people whom Paul greets after the "real content" of the letter has been drawn to a close. However, I was powerfully reminded that *all Scripture* is God-breathed and profitable for teaching and training in righteousness (2 Tim. 3:16). An examination of the names of the Christians Paul greets in Rome reveals that several of them were named after pagan deities, such as Narcissus, Hermes, and Olympas.[7]

As the missionary movement crosses new cultural frontiers, it will inevitably give rise to new questions. When I am in India, students frequently ask me, "When my Hindu neighbors offer me *prasad*,[8] should I take it?" When I was in Africa recently, someone asked me, "If a man is married to three wives and then comes to Christ, what should he do to

---

7. The observation that Saul of Tarsus's name was changed after his encounter with the risen Christ on the road to Damascus fails to recognize that Saul continues to use his Jewish name (Saul) after his conversion and only begins to use his Greek name (Paul) as his ministry to Gentiles opens up. The use of the name "Paul" was to further identity with the Greek culture, not to separate from it, as is the case of those who abandon names like "Rama" and "Krishna" and start calling themselves "Abraham" or "Hezekiah."

8. Food sacrificed to idols.

conform to the monogamous practice of the Christian church?" These are just a few examples of questions that have not been seriously discussed in the West, because they are questions that would never naturally arise within Christendom. However, it is inevitable that once a new movement begins to take place, whether it be among postmodern youths in North America or religious Hindus in North India, new questions will arise that call for deeper reflection. If there are no missions, then there will be no missiology. If missionary initiatives advance without missiology, then important issues are ignored and over time the new church movement can become weak and subject to error and experience atrophy.

However, despite the vital relationship between missions and missiology, there will always be a natural tension between the two. If we are honest, we can admit that it is all too easy for missiology to become theoretical and disconnected from the real-world challenges of missionary work. Likewise, missionaries can easily become susceptible to pragmatic and results-oriented strategies that are not theologically sound and have little consideration for the long-term health and vitality of the church. One of the central concerns of this book is not only to reunite missiology and missions to fundamental theological paradigms, but also to set forth a context in which missiology and missions can work together more cooperatively and collaboratively.

Three-Step Process for Engaging New Missiological Questions

I have chosen one example in missions discourse today as a case study in how missiology can serve to enliven, strengthen, and inform our reflection on important new questions. The issue is known as "insider movements." The point of this reflection is to guide the reader through a method for tackling such a difficult matter. I recommend a three-step process when approaching any new issue. First, identify the key theological issues that are raised by the issue at stake. This means looking beyond the "presenting" issue or question and seeking to identity the underlying theological issues at stake. For example, in the case of the Jerusalem Council, the presenting question was, "What are the terms through which a Gentile may gain access to the church?" However, the debate, and often heated discussion, that took place reveals that there were crucial theological considerations that lay beneath the presenting question. There seemed to be broad (even if not total) agreement that the

Gentiles had been saved. The most challenging issue, therefore, was more ecclesiologial than soteriological. This process is crucial, because most readers who approach this issue assume that the primary issue was soteriological (How can a Gentile be saved?) rather than ecclesiological (How can we preserve unity in the church?).

Second, we should reflect on church history, and see if there are any insights from the life and experience of the church through the ages that might shed light on the issue. Only rarely do we face entirely new situations in the life of the church. Most questions have, in one way or another, been faced by earlier Christians. Gaining the insight of Christians who belonged to a different time and place but worshipped Christ and read the same Bible can be very helpful.

Finally, once a potential solution or answer is proposed, it should then be tested by how it looks in light of the four governing themes of good missiology: the *missio dei*, the Trinity, the New Creation, and the global church. The challenge of "insider movements" will now be examined using this process.

Case Study: Insider Movements

In chapter 10 we highlighted the rise of Muslim followers of Jesus who have chosen to remain in the mosque. This phenomenon is known as "insider movements." An insider movement refers to genuine movements toward Christ that have been observed primarily within Hindu and Islamic communities. Herbert Hoefer, in his *Churchless Christianity*, has identified nearly two hundred thousand nonbaptized followers of Jesus who continue to identify themselves as Hindus. They do not identify themselves as Christians but as *Jesu bhakta*, that is, devotees of Jesus, through a provision within popular Hinduism that allows people to worship a particular god, even exclusively, without denying that other gods or goddesses may exist.[9] Likewise, John Travis and Joshua Massey, among others, have written extensively about thousands of Muslims who maintain their cultural and religious identity with the Islamic community but worship Isa (Jesus) as Lord. These are "Messianic Muslims," who have accepted Jesus as their Savior but continue legally, socially, and religiously to identify with the mosque and the wider Islamic community. These movements

---

9. Herbert Hoefer, *Churchless Christianity* (Pasadena, CA: William Carey Library, 2001).

have generated considerable discussion among missionaries, mission organizations, and missiologists in recent years.[10] The scope and purpose of this case study is neither to explore the details of this issue nor to provide a full response. Rather, it is to set forth the broad contours of how this issue should be examined using the three-step process outlined above.

BIBLICAL/THEOLOGICAL TEST

When examining "insider movements," the presenting question is, "Can a Muslim follow Isa (Christ) and stay religiously and culturally within Islam?" Alternatively, the question is sometimes posed as, "Can a Hindu follow Jesus Christ while remaining within his or her sphere of Hindu life and practice (in this case, *bhakti* worship, which focuses exclusively on Jesus)?" While there are many theological issues that might be identified, there seems to be wide agreement that there are two dominant theological issues at stake.

First, our understanding of ecclesiology will play a crucial role in how we respond to the presenting question. How important is it for followers of Jesus to belong to a community that is recognized as a visible fellowship of

---

10. To survey several of the most important articles written on this issue in recent years, see "A Different Kind of Mosque," *Mission Frontiers* 19, nos. 7–10 (July–October 1997): 20–21; Erich Bridges, "Of 'Jesus Mosques' and Muslim Christians," *Mission Frontiers* 19, nos. 7–10 (July–October 1997): 19; Rick Brown, "What Must One Believe About Jesus for Salvation?" *International Journal of Frontier Missions* 17, no. 4 (2000): 13–21; Robby Butler, "Unlocking Islam," *Mission Frontiers* 13, no. 1 (January–March 1991): 24; Frank Decker, "When 'Christian' Does Not Translate," *Mission Frontiers* 27, no. 5 (September–October 2005): 8; Herbert Hoefer, *Churchless Christianity* (Pasadena: William Carey Library: 2002), "Proclaiming a 'Theologyless' Christ," *International Journal of Frontier Missions* 22, no. 3 (2005): 97–100; Joshua Massey, "God's Amazing Diversity in Drawing Muslims to Christ," *International Journal of Frontier Missions* 17, no. 1 (2000): 5–14; "Misunderstanding C-5: His Ways Are Not Our Orthodoxy," *Evangelical Missions Quarterly* 40, no. 3 (2004): 296–304; "Misunderstanding C-5 and the Infinite Translatability of Christ: Why C-5 Has Been So Misunderstood by Its Critics," *Evangelical Missions Quarterly* 40, no. 1 (2004): 1–18. Unabridged online edition at http://bgc.gospelcom.net/emis/pdfs/Misunderstanding_C5.pdf; and "His Ways Are Not Our Ways," *Evangelical Missions Quarterly* 35, no. 2 (1999): 188–97; Timothy Tennent, "Followers of Jesus (Isa) in Islamic Mosques: A Closer Examination of C-5 'high spectrum' Contextualization," *International Journal of Frontier Missions* 23, no. 3 (Fall 2006): 101–15; "The Challenge of Churchless Christianity: An Evangelical Assessment," *International Bulletin of Missionary Research* 29 (October 2005): 171–77; and *Theology in the Context of World Christianity* (Grand Rapids: Zondervan, 2007), chap. 8; John Travis, "Messianic Muslim Followers of Jesus," *International Journal of Frontier Missions* 17, no. 1 (2000): 53–59; "Two Responses: Must All Muslims Leave 'Islam' to Follow Jesus?" *Evangelical Missions Quarterly* 34, no. 4 (1998): 411–15; and "The C1 to C6 Spectrum," *Evangelical Missions Quarterly* 34, no. 4 (1998): 407–8; Mark Williams, "Aspects of High-Spectrum Contextualization in Ministries to Muslims," *Journal of Asian Mission* 5, no. 1 (2003): 75–91; Ralph Winter, "Can We Trust Insider Movements?" *Mission Frontiers* 27, no. 5 (September–October 2005): 4.

the church? Second, our understanding of soteriology also will be critical to how we respond to the issue. In this particular case, the two doctrines often seem to stand in conflict with one another. If salvation is primarily a personal issue, then the role of the church is significantly diminished and salvation is interpreted in a minimalistic way—in essence, what is the least someone has to do to be a follower of Christ? Our understanding of soteriology will dramatically frame whether or not public baptism or identification with other believers from around the world are determinative in how we resolve the issue. Rick Brown, in his analysis of insider movements, has written an article entitled "What Must One Believe About Jesus for Salvation?" His affirmation of insider movements is clearly made possible because of his underlying low view of the church and his minimalistic understanding of salvation. In contrast, Lesslie Newbigin's more negative assessment of insider movements is based on his higher ecclesiology and his unwillingness to equate salvation with justification.[11]

Once the key doctrines are identified, it is then helpful to identify whether quotations of key scriptural passages, either in favor of or in opposition to insider movements, are rooted in reliable exegesis or the writers are merely proof-texting to provide biblical support for what they already have determined is the right missiological solution to the presenting question. Ultimately, all good theology must be substantiated and supported by good exegesis. Hermetically sealed theological systems must always be open to careful scrutiny by the Word of God to be certain that important biblical insights have not been neglected in our own formulation of theology.

CHURCH HISTORY TEST

Once this process is complete, it is helpful to see if any lessons can be learned from church history, when similar situations have been encountered. This often serves to either confirm our earlier theological reflection or, in some cases, to cause us to go back and reexamine the text afresh. In the case of insider movements, it is helpful to examine how the church in the sixteenth century wrestled with ecclesiology once the Reformers broke from the magisterial authority of the Roman Catholic Church. Even if the Reformation is understood as primarily a struggle over biblical

---

11. Compare Brown's, "What Must One Believe About Jesus for Salvation?" to Lesslie Newbigin's *The Finality of Christ* (London: SCM, 1969).

soteriology, it was also a major struggle over the doctrine of ecclesiology, which had been understood in territorial and institutional ways. Luther's concept of the "invisible church" is frequently cited by supporters of insider movements, even though Luther's concern was to acknowledge the presence of unbelievers inside the institutional church, whereas proponents of insider movements are concerned with the presence of believers inside Islam or Hinduism.[12]

MAJOR THEMES OF SALVATION HISTORY TEST

Finally, as with any new presenting issue, one must see how it fits within the larger, overarching themes of biblical revelation. We will now explore how we might better understand Christians from "insider movements" in light of the four overarching themes of the *missio dei*, the Trinity, the New Creation, and the global church.

Missio Dei

The *missio dei* reminds us that God takes initiatives quite distinct from our own expectations and organizations. Therefore, insider movements may be an example of a sovereign initiative that has caught us by surprise. Could this represent a kind of "Reformation in reverse?"[13] In other words, our own Reformation history is the story of people who initially saw themselves as Christians because they belonged to the formal, ecclesial structure of Christianity; that is, they were members of Christendom. Among other things, the Reformation was the gradual recognition over several hundred years by "Christians" that they were, in fact, not Christians at all and needed to become Christians, even though they were baptized Christians in the public, formal sense. In the case of insider movements, could the exact opposite be taking place—a kind of Reformation in reverse? Could there be tens of thousands of people who belong to Islam or Hinduism in a public, formal sense who, over many years, gradually realize that they are no longer Muslims or Hindus but Christians? Could we, for example, someday see thousands of Muslim followers of Jesus, who

---

12. In an earlier article, I have explored in more detail how the doctrine of ecclesiology in church history helps us to better understand the issues presented by insider movements. See Tennent, "The Challenge of Churchless Christianity," 171–77.

13. I am indebted to Jonathan Bonk, director of the Overseas Ministries Study Center in New Haven, CT, for this insight.

currently are wrongly trying to maintain their Islamic identity, gradually come to see that their truest identity is with the people of God?

Trinity
Insider movements also must be tested by the doctrine of the Trinity. For example, any movement that does not clearly and decisively identify and proclaim the fullness of the person and work of Jesus Christ and the Holy Spirit will, in the long run, fail to continue as a viable expression of Christian faithfulness. While more research needs to be done, early indications are that followers of Jesus who remain within the mosque or temple frequently have a deficient, truncated understanding of Jesus Christ and the Holy Spirit. More needs to be done to disciple these new believers and if, over time, they emerge with a biblical view of the Trinity, it will do much to commend this movement.

New Creation
It is also important to observe the life and witness of those who follow Christ as insiders within other religious and cultural structures. Does their life and witness exhibit the inbreaking of God's rule? Are there clear and identifiable examples of the Holy Spirit's work in their midst? Are the gifts and fruits of the Spirit active and growing? This is an assessment that will need to be done by missionaries who are in direct contact with these believers, as it is quite difficult to assess from a remote location.

In the book of Acts the Jewish followers of Jesus were caught off guard by the dramatic extension of the gospel into the lives of Gentiles. The church at Jerusalem wisely sent Barnabus to Antioch to make a firsthand assessment of what was, at the time, an astonishing and seemingly implausible development. Acts records:

> News of this reached the ears of the church at Jerusalem, and they sent Barnabus to Antioch. When he arrived and saw the evidence of the grace of God, he was glad and encouraged them all to remain true to the Lord with all their hearts. (Acts 11:22–23)

It is vital that we not only examine doctrinal and theological issues closely but also look for evidence of the grace of God.

At the Council of Jerusalem, recorded in Acts 15, the leaders of the church in Jerusalem not only discussed the theological issues at stake, but they also listened to those who were in relationship with these new believers.

> The whole assembly became silent as they listened to Barnabus and Paul telling about the miraculous signs and wonders God had done among the Gentiles through them. (Acts 15:12)

After hearing these testimonies, the assembly went back and reexamined the Scriptures afresh. James, one of the leaders of the Jerusalem church, concluded that the dramatic extension of the gospel among the Gentiles was indeed consistent with the Scriptures. In fact, Acts records that James quoted an important text in Amos 9:11–12 to substantiate that a day was prophesied when Gentiles would be included among the people of God. Amos's prophecy that a "remnant of men may seek the Lord, and all the Gentiles who bear my name" (Acts 15:17) is most likely cited in Acts as a single example among many texts that were reflected on to provide the necessary broad scriptural support for this astonishing work of God. The recognition of God's work among the Gentiles, of course, was not the end of the story. This spurred the church on to make certain these new believers were properly discipled and could participate in fellowship with the rest of the church as full and secure members of the body of Christ.

Global Church

Finally, as a testimony to the cultural translatability of the Christian gospel and a candid admission that the church in every culture and throughout time has its own share of blind spots, it is important to reflect on how an issue might be viewed from various perspectives across the global church. Having spent considerable time interacting with Christians from different continents, I have frequently observed that the blind spots of North American evangelicalism are often readily apparent to those of a different culture, even as their blind spots are evident to me. Amazingly, however, we are each unaware of our own.

In reflecting on insider movements, it is helpful to gain the perspective and input of mature believers from the actual cultural settings in which insider movements have arisen. Exploring the issue of Muslims who follow Isa in the mosque with mature believers from the Middle East or Bangladesh enables us to see the whole issue in a fresh light, and frequently new insights are gained. For example, mature Muslim leaders have pointed out to me some of the cultural and ethical difficulties followers of Isa who remain in the mosque face, which may not be readily apparent to those of us who are observing the issue from the outside.

Likewise, I have discovered the great complexity of insider movements when viewed through the eyes of those in the culture. For example, I once asked a woman who was following Christ within Hinduism why she remained in the temple, even though she was now a devoted follower of Jesus Christ. She responded that her extended family was very supportive of her worshipping Christ as long as she did not break from Hinduism. However, in their words, if she "forsook her culture" and "embraced the foreign Christians," then they would disinherit all her children. In this particular case, this woman eventually was able to become fully and publicly identified with the church, but her story does underscore some of the pastoral challenges when considering these issues. Furthermore, this is another reminder that the more missiologists stay connected to the life and work of missionaries on the field and the actual challenges that are faced around the world, the better we will be able to maintain a healthy relationship between missiology and missions. Missiology must not be allowed to drift too far from field-based realities, and those on the front lines of the missionary movement must be regularly reminded of the importance of grounding their work and practice on solid theological and missiological reflection.

We have demonstrated a process through which new issues that arise on the field can be reflected on theologically and missiologically. While we chose to examine the issue of insider movements, a whole host of contemporary issues could have been chosen, including major trends in missions such as business as missions and short-term missions. This process also works well in reflecting on particular questions that demand more missiological reflection, such as whether it is advisable to use the Qur'an in witnessing to Muslims or whether the words God and Allah can be used interchangeably. Without such a process, these issues will almost inevitably be evaluated on pragmatic, rather than theological and biblical, grounds. However, with such a process in place, missions practice will stimulate good missiological reflection and this, in turn, will help to stimulate more effective missions *and* missiology: missions at sunrise, missiology at sunset, each leading to and stimulating the other.

CONCLUSION

This book began with a survey of seven megatrends that are influencing missions in the twenty-first century. We are living in the seam between two major epochs in Christian history, as evidenced by the collapse of Christendom, the rise of the Majority World church, the rapid pace of globalization and technology, the epistemological challenges of postmodernism, and the growth of relativistic influences, among other things. It is clear that we cannot afford to pursue a business-as-usual approach to missions. Contemporary missions strategy, mobilization, deployment of resources, and field practice all over the world need to be more reflective and set more securely within a larger biblical and theological context.

The current practice of building missions practice on social science models served the church in past generations because it assumed that those who studied missions already held a theological framework into which they could insert their missiology. However, with the erosion of biblical/theological foundations in the wider church, this assumption is no longer tenable. Today, robust missions practice coupled with a confident missionary force demands a more thoroughgoing biblical and theological perspective. The Trinitarian framework of this missiology, which roots missions in the *missio dei* and places it within the larger eschatological context of the New Creation and the emergence of the global church, seeks to provide the necessary basis for a healthy missiology for the twenty-first century. Missions must increasingly be seen as flowing forth from God's initiative to Abraham to bless all nations (Gen. 12:3) and moving toward that day in the New Creation when men and women "from every nation, tribe, people and language" will be worshipping our Lord Jesus Christ (Rev. 7:9). Until that day, may God's grace rest upon His church as we seek to embody His glory and majesty in all creation.

Bibliography

"A Different Kind of Mosque." *Mission Frontiers* 19, nos. 7–10 (July–October 1997): 20–21.

"Acts of the Holy Apostle Thomas." In *The Ante-Nicene Fathers*, edited by Alexander Roberts and James Donaldson. Vol. 8. Peabody, MA: Hendrickson, 1999.

Aikman, David. *Jesus in Beijing: How Christianity Is Transforming China and Changing the Global Balance of Power.* Washington, D.C.: Regnery, 2003.

Allier, Raoul. "Missions and the Soul of a People." *International Review of Missions* 18 (1929): 282–84.

Amaladdos, Michael. "Dialogue and Mission: Conflict or Convergence?" *International Review of Missions* 75, no. 299 (1986): 224–41.

Anderson, Allan. *An Introduction to Pentecostalism.* Cambridge: Cambridge University Press, 2004.

———. "To All Points of the Compass: The Azusa Street Revival and Global Pentecostalism." *Enrichment Journal*, online journal of the General Council of the Assemblies of God, http://enrichmentjournal. ag.org/200602/200602_164_AllPoints.cfm (accessed June 30, 2008).

Andrew, Brother, ed. *Destined to Suffer? African Christians Face the Future.* Orange, CA: Open Doors, 1979.

Appasamy, Aiyadurai Jesudasen, and E. H. M. Waller. *Temple Bells: Readings from Hindu Religious Literature.* Mysore, India: Student Christian Movement Press, 1930.

Arndt, William F., and F. Wilbur Gingrich. *A Greek-English Lexion of the New Testament.* 2nd ed., adaptation and translation of Walter Bauer's 4th ed. Chicago: University of Chicago Press, 1979.

Ash, Timothy Garton. "Christian Europe, RIP." *Guardian*, April 29, 2005.
    http://www.guardian.co.uk/world/2005/apr/21/catholicism.religion5.
Augustine. *Confessions*. Translated by Henry Chadwick. Oxford World's
    Classics. New York: Oxford University Press, 1998.
———. "Confessions." In *The Nicene and Post-Nicene Fathers*, edited by Philip
    Schaff and Henry Wace. Vol. 1. Peabody, MA: Hendrickson, 1999.
Aune, David ed. *The Westminster Dictionary of New Testament and Early
    Christian Literature and Rhetoric*. Louisville: Westminister John Knox
    Press, 2003.
Baltzer, Klaus. *Deutero-Isaiah*. Minneapolis: Augsburg Fortress Press, 2001.
Banks, Robert J. *Paul's Idea of Community*. Rev. ed. Peabody, MA: Hendrickson,
    2007.
Barrett, David, ed. *World Christian Encyclopedia: A Comparative Survey of
    Churches and Religions in the Modern World*, A.D. *1900 to 2000*. New York:
    Oxford University Press, 1982.
Barrett, David B., and Todd M. Johnson, eds. "Annual Statistical Table on
    Global Mission: 2001." *International Bulletin of Missionary Research* 25,
    no.1 (2001): 24.
———. *World Christian Trends, AD 30—AD 2200: Interpreting the Annual
    Christian Megacensus*. Pasadena, CA: William Carey Library, 2001.
Barrett, David B., Todd M. Johnson, and Peter F. Crossing. "Missiometrics 2008:
    Reality Checks for Christian World Communions." *International Bulletin
    of Missionary Research* 32, no. 1 (January 2008): 27–30.
Barrett, David B., George T. Kurian, and Todd M. Johnson, eds. *World
    Christian Encyclopedia: A Comparative Survey of Churches and Religions in
    the Modern World*. 2nd ed. New York: Oxford University Press, 2001.
Barth, Karl. *God in Action*. Translated by E. G. Homrighausen and Karl J. Ernst.
    Manhasset, NY: Round Table Press, 1936.
———. *Theology and Church: Shorter Writings 1920–1928*. Translated by Louise
    Pettibone Smith. New York: Harper & Row, 1962.
Bauckham, Richard. *God Crucified: Monotheism and Christology in the New
    Testament*. Grand Rapids: Eerdmans, 1998.
Bavinck, J. H. *The Church Between Temple and Mosque: A Study of the
    Relationship Between the Christian Faith and Other Religions*. Grand Rapids:
    Eerdmans, 1966.
———. *Introduction to the Science of Missions*. Translated by David H. Freeman.
    Philadelphia: Presbyterian and Reformed Publishing, 1960.

Beale, Greg. *The Temple and the Church's Mission.* Downers Grove, IL: InterVarsity Press, 2004.

Beaver, R. Pierce, ed. *To Advance the Gospel: Selections from the Writings of Rufus Anderson.* Grand Rapids: Eerdmans, 1967.

Bediako, Kwame. *Christianity in Africa: The Renewal of a Non-Western Religion.* Maryknoll, NY: Orbis, 1995.

Benz, Ernst. "Pietist and Puritan Sources of Early Protestant World Missions." In *Christianity and Missions, 1450–1800,* edited by J. S. Cummins, 315–42. Brookfield, VT: Ashgate, 1997.

Berger, Peter L. "The Desecularization of the World: A Global Overview." In *The Desecularization of the World: Resurgent Religion and World Politics,* edited by Peter L. Berger, 1–18. Grand Rapids: Eerdmans; Washington, D.C.: Ethics and Public Policy Center, 1999.

Berkhof, Louis. *Systematic Theology.* Grand Rapids: Eerdmans, 1941.

Bettenson, Henry, ed. *Documents of the Christian Church.* New York: Oxford University Press, 1977.

Bodley, John H. *Cultural Anthropology: Tribes, States and the Global System.* Mountain View, CA: Mayfield, 1997.

Boer, Harry. *Pentecost and Missions.* Grand Rapids: Eerdmans, 1961.

Bonk, Jonathan. Foreword to *Missions in the Third Millennium,* by Stan Guthrie, xi–xiii. Waynesboro, GA: Paternoster Press, 2000.

Bonner, Anthony, ed. *Doctor Illuminatus: A Ramon Lull Reader.* Princeton, NJ: Princeton University Press, 1985.

Bosch, David. "The Structure of Mission: An Exposition of Matthew 28:16–20." In *Exploring Church Growth,* edited by Wilbert R. Shenk, 218–48. Grand Rapids: Eerdmans, 1983.

———. *Transforming Mission: Paradigm Shifts in Theology of Mission.* Maryknoll, NY: Orbis, 1991.

Bowie, Fiona. "Reclaiming Women's Presence." In *Women and Missions: Past and Present: Anthropological and Historical Perceptions,* edited by Fiona Bowie, Deborah Kirkwood, and Shirley Ardener, 1–19. Providence: Berg, 1993.

Brandon, S. G. F. *The Fall of Jerusalem and the Christian Church: A Study of the Effects of the Jewish Overthrow of* A.D *70 on Christianity.* London: SPCK, 1951.

Bria, Ion, ed. *Martyria/Mission: The Witness of the Orthodox Church Today.* Geneva: World Council of Churches, 1980.

Bridges, Erich. "Of 'Jesus Mosques' and Muslim Christians." *Mission Frontiers* 19, nos. 7–10 (July–October 1997): 19.

Brown, G. Thompson. *Christianity in the People's Republic of China*. Atlanta: John Knox Press, 1986.

Brown, Rick. "What Must One Believe About Jesus for Salvation?" *International Journal of Frontier Missions* 17, no. 4 (2000): 13–21.

Buhlmann, Walbert. *The Coming of the Third Church: An Analysis of the Present and Future Church*. Maryknoll, NY: Orbis, 1978.

Bush, Richard C., Jr. *Religion in Communist China*. Nashville: Abingdon Press, 1970.

Butler, Robby. "Unlocking Islam." *Mission Frontiers* 13, no. 1 (January–March 1991): 24.

Cahill, Elizabeth Kirkland. "A Bible for the Plowboy: Tyndale at the New York Public Library." *Commonweal* 124, no. 7 (1997): 19–20.

Calvin, John. *The Epistles of Paul the Apostle to the Corinthians*. Translated by John W. Fraser. Grand Rapids: Eerdmans, 1960.

———. *Institutes of the Christian Religion*. Vol. 1. Translated by Henry Beveridge. Grand Rapids: Eerdmans, 1957.

Cardoz-Orlandi, Carlos F. *Mission: An Essential Guide*. Nashville: Abingdon Press, 2002.

Carey, William. *An Enquiry into Obligations of Christians to Use Means for the Conversion of the Heathens*. 1792. A facsimile of the first edition. London: Carey Kingsgate, 1961.

Carson, D. A. "The Purpose of the Fourth Gospel: John 20:31 Reconsidered." *Journal of Biblical Literature* 106, no. 4 (1987): 639–51.

Carter, Craig A. *Rethinking Christ and Culture: A Post-Christendom Perspective*. Grand Rapids: Brazos Press, 2006.

Carus-Wilson, Ashley. "A World Parliament on Missions: The Meaning and Methods of the Edinburgh Conference of 1910." *The Quiver* 45 (1910): 631–35.

"Catechism of the Catholic Church. Article 9: I Believe in the Holy Catholic Church." United States Conference of Catholic Bishops. http://www.usccb.org/catechism/text/pt1sect2chpt3art9.shtml.

Chai, Soo-il. "*Missio Dei*—Its Development and Limitations in Korea." *International Review of Missions* 92, no. 367 (2003): 538–49.

Chan, Simon. *Liturgical Theology*. Downers Grove, IL: InterVarsity Press, 2006.

Charbonnier, Jean-Pierre. *Christians in China*. San Francisco: Ignatius Press, 2007.

The Children's Bible in 365 Stories. Oxford, England: Lion Children's Books, 1995.

Clements, Keith. *Faith on the Frontiers: A Life of J. H. Oldham*. Edinburgh: T & T Clark; Geneva: World Council of Churches, 1999.

Colson, Charles. *The Body: Being Light in Darkness*. Dallas: Word Publishing, 1992.

Cone, James. *Black Theology and Black Power*. Maryknoll, NY: Orbis, 1969, 1999.

Conzelmann, Hans. *The Theology of St. Luke*. Translated by G. Buswell. Philadelphia: Fortress Press, 1982.

Corrie, John, ed. *Dictionary of Mission Theology: Evangelical Foundations*. Downers Grove, IL: InterVarsity Press, 2007.

Cox, Harvey. *Fire from Heaven: The Rise of Pentecostal Spirituality and the Reshaping of Religion in the Twenty-first Century*. Reading, MA: Addison-Wesley, 1995.

———. *The Secular City: Secularization and Urbanization in Theological Perspective*. New York: Macmillan, 1966.

Cunningham, David S. *These Three Are One: The Practice of Trinitarian Theology*. Malden, MA: Blackwell Publishers, 1998.

Cunningham, Scott. *Through Many Tribulations: The Theology of Persecution in Luke-Acts*. Sheffield, England: Sheffield Academic Press, 1997.

Cyprian. "The Epistles of Cyprian." In *The Ante-Nicene Fathers*, edited by Alexander Roberts and James Donaldson. Vol. 5. Peabody, MA: Hendrickson, 1999.

———. "The Treatises of Cyprian." In *The Ante-Nicene Fathers*, edited by Alexander Roberts and James Donaldson. Vol. 5. Peabody, MA: Hendrickson, 1999.

Daneel, Marthinus. *Old and New in Southern Shona Independent Churches*. Vol. 1. The Hague: Mouton, 1971.

Darwin, Charles. *On the Origin of Species by Means of Natural Selection*. London: J. Murray, 1859.

Davis, John Jefferson. "'Teaching Them to Observe All That I Have Commanded You': The History of the Interpretation of the 'Great Commission' and Implications for Marketplace Ministries." *Evangelical Review of Theology* 25, no. 1 (January 2001): 65–80.

Decker, Frank. "When 'Christian' Does Not Translate." *Mission Frontiers* 27, no. 5 (September–October 2005): 8.

Demarest, Bruce. *General Revelation*. Grand Rapids: Zondervan, 1982.

Deutsch E., and J. A. B. van Buitenen, eds. *A Source Book of Advaita Vedanta*. Honolulu: University of Hawaii Press, 1971.

Dhimmi Watch. https://www.jihadwatch.org/dhimmiwatch/.

"Dogmatic Constitution on the Church." Documents of the II Vatican Council. http://www.vatican.va/archive/hist_councils/ii_vatican_council/documents/vat-ii_const_19641121_lumen-gentium_en.html.

Duhm, Bernard. *Das Buch Jesaia*. Tubingen: Tubingen University Press, 1892.

Eagleton, Terry. *The Idea of Culture*. Malden, MA: Blackwell Publishers, 2000.

Edwards, Jonathan. *The Works of Jonathan Edwards*. Edited by John E. Smith et al. Vol. 8. *Ethical Writings*. New Haven: Yale University Press, 1972.

Endo, Shusaku. *Silence*. Translated by William Johnston. New York: Taplinger, 1980.

Escobar, Samuel. "A Missiological Approach to Latin American Protestantism." *International Review of Mission* 87, no. 345 (April 1998): 161–73.

———. "Mission from the Margins to the Margins: Two Case Studies from Latin America." *Missiology: An International Review* 26, no. 1 (January 1998): 87–95.

Farquhar, J. N. *The Crown of Hinduism*. 1913. Reprint. New Delhi: Oriental Books Reprint Corporation, 1971.

"Fastest Growing Church in the Hemisphere." *Time* (November 2, 1962).

Fee, Gordon D. *God's Empowering Presence: The Holy Spirit in the Letters of Paul*. Peabody, MA: Hendrickson, 1994.

Fernando, Ajith. "Grounding Our Reflections in Scripture: Biblical Trinitarianism and Mission." In *Global Missiology for the 21st Century: The Iguassu Dialogue*, edited by William Taylor, 189–256. Grand Rapids: Baker Academic, 2000.

Fiedler, Klaus. *The Story of Faith Missions: From Hudson Taylor to the Present*. Irvine, CA: Regnum Books, International, 1994.

France, R. T. *The Gospel of Matthew*. New International Commentary on the New Testament. Grand Rapids: Eerdmans, 2007.

Fraser, J. N., and K. B. Marathe. *The Poems of Tukaram*. Madras: Christian Literature Society, 1909.

Friesen, Abraham. *Erasmus, the Anabaptists, and the Great Commission*. Grand Rapids: Eerdmans, 1998.

Friesen, Duane K. *Artists, Citizens and Philosophers: Seeking the Peace of the City*. Scottdale, PA: Herald Press, 2000.

Frow, John. *Cultural Studies and Cultural Value.* Oxford: Clarendon Press, 1995.

Gairdner, W. H. T. *Edinburgh 1910: An Account and Interpretation of the World Missionary Conference.* Edinburgh: Oliphant, Anderson and Ferrier, 1910.

Garrison, David. "Church Planting Movements vs. Insider Movements: Missiological Realities vs. Mythiological Speculations." *International Journal of Frontier Missions* 21, no. 4 (Winter 2004): 151–54.

Gayle, Clement. *George Liele: Pioneer Missionary of Jamaica.* Kingston, Jamaica: Jamaica Baptist Union, 1982.

Geertz, Clifford. *The Interpretation of Cultures.* New York: Basic Books, 1973.

George, Timothy. "Letters." *Christianity Today* 46, no. 4 (2002): 12.

Gilliland, Dean. "Context Is Critical in 'Islampur' Case." *Evangelical Missions Quarterly* 34, no. 4 (October 1998): 415–17.

Gillman, Ian, and Hans-Joachim Klimkeit. *Christians in Asia Before 1500.* Surrey, UK: Curzon Press, 1999.

Glaser, Arthur. "Salvation Today and the Kingdom." In *Crucial Issues in Mission Tomorrow,* edited by Donald McGavran, 33–53. Chicago: Moody Press, 1972.

Goen, C. C., ed. *Works of Jonathan Edwards.* Vol. 4, *The Distinguishing Marks.* New Haven: Yale University Press, 1972.

"Go Figure." *Christianity Today* 47, no. 7 (2003): 13.

Goheen, Michael W. *As the Father Has Sent Me, I Am Sending You: J. E. Lesslie Newbigin's Missionary Ecclesiology.* Zoetermeer, Netherlands: Uitgeverij Boekencentrum, 2000.

Goodall, Norman, ed. *Missions Under the Cross: Addresses Delivered at the Enlarged Meeting of the Committee of the International Missionary Council at Willingen, in Germany, 1952.* London: Edinburgh House Press, 1953.

Gordon, A. J. *The Ministry of the Spirit.* Philadelphia: American Baptist Publication Society, 1894.

Gorringe, T. J. *Furthering Humanity: A Theology of Culture.* Burlington, VT: Ashgate Publishing, 2004.

Gorski, John F. "How the Catholic Church in Latin America Became Missionary." *International Bulletin of Missionary Research* 27, no. 2 (April 2003): 59–64.

Green, Joel. "Salvation to the End of the Earth (Acts 13:47): God as Saviour in the Acts of the Apostles." In *Witness to the Gospel: The Theology of Acts,* edited by I. Howard Marshall and David Peterson, 80–106. Grand Rapids: Eerdmans, 1998.

Gustafson, James W. "The Integration of Development and Evangelism."
    Missiology: An International Review 26, no. 2 (April 1998): 131–42.
Guthrie, Stan. *Missions in the Third Millennium: 21 Key Trends for the 21st
    Century.* Waynesboro, GA: Paternoster Press, 2000.
Hackett, Stuart. *The Reconstruction of the Christian Revelation Claim.* Grand
    Rapids: Baker, 1984.
Hall, Douglas John. *God and Human Suffering: An Exercise in the Theology of
    the Cross.* Minneapolis: Augsburg Publishing House, 1986.
Harris, Paul. "Denominationalism and Democracy: Ecclesiastical Issues
    Underlying Rufus Anderson's Three-Self Program." In *North American
    Foreign Missions, 1810–1914,* edited by Wilbert R. Shenk, 61–85. Grand
    Rapids: Eerdmans, 2006.
Hastings, Adrian. *The Church in Africa, 1450–1950.* Oxford: Clarendon Press,
    1994.
———. *A History of African Christianity 1950–1975.* New York: Cambridge
    University Press, 1979.
Hatcher, Mark J. "Contextualizing the Creed Through Structured Bible Study."
    Missiology: An International Review 26, no. 3 (July 1998): 315–28.
Hattaway, Paul. *Back to Jerusalem.* Carlisle, UK: Piquant Press; Waynesboro,
    GA: Authentic Media, 2003.
Heim, S. Mark. *The Depth of Riches: A Trinitarian Theology of Religious Ends.*
    Grand Rapids: Eerdmans, 2001.
Henry, Carl. *The Uneasy Conscience of American Fundamentalism.* Grand
    Rapids: Eerdmans, 1947.
Herder, J. G. *Herder on Social and Political Culture.* Edited and translated by
    F. M. Barnard. Cambridge: Cambridge University Press, 1969.
Hesselgrave, David J. *Communicating Christ Cross-Culturally: An Introduction
    to Missionary Communication.* 2nd ed. Grand Rapids: Zondervan, 1991.
Hesselgrave, David, and Edward Rommen. *Contextualization: Meanings,
    Methods and Models.* Pasadena, CA: William Carey Library, 2000.
Hick, John. *An Interpretation of Religion.* New Haven: Yale University Press,
    1989.
———. *The Metaphor of God Incarnate.* London: SCM Press, 1993.
Hiebert, Paul G. *Anthropological Insights for Missionaries.* Grand Rapids: Baker,
    1985.
———. *Anthropological Reflections on Missiological Issues.* Grand Rapids: Baker,
    1994.

Hillman, E. *The Wider Ecumenism: Anonymous Christianity and the Church.* New York: Herder and Herder; London: Burns and Gates, 1968.

Hoefer, Herbert. *Churchless Christianity.* Pasadena, CA: William Carey Library, 2001.

———. "Proclaiming a 'Theologyless' Christ." *International Journal of Frontier Missions* 22, no. 3 (2005): 97–100.

Hollenweger, Walter. *Pentecostalism: Origins and Developments Worldwide.* Peabody, MA: Hendrickson, 1997.

Holloway, Richard. *Signs of Glory.* London: Darton, Longman and Todd, 1982.

Holmes, E. A. "George Liele: Negro Slavery's Prophet of Deliverance." *Baptist Quarterly* 20 (October 1964): 340–51.

Hoover, Willis C. *History of the Pentecostal Revival in Chile.* Santiago, Chile: Imprenta Ebenezer, 2000.

Horne, Donald. *The Public Culture.* London: Pluto Press, 1994.

Huizenga, Leroy Andrew. "The Incarnation of the Servant: The 'Suffering Servant' and Matthean Christology." *Horizons in Biblical Theology* 27, no. 1 (2005): 25–28.

Hunter, Alan, and Kim-Kwong Chan. *Protestantism in Contemporary China.* Cambridge: Cambridge University Press, 1993.

Hurtado, Larry. *Lord Jesus Christ.* Grand Rapids: Eerdmans, 2003.

Imunde, Lawford, and Dr. T. John Padwick. "Advancing Legal Empowerment of the Poor: The Role and Perspective of the African Independent Churches." Organisation for African Instituted Churches (OAIC). http://www.wcrp.org/files/AICs%20and%20Legal%20empowerment.FINAL_.doc (accessed January 2008).

The Inclusive New Testament. Hyattsville, MD: AltaMira (Priests for Equality), 1996.

Inglis, Fred. *Culture.* Malden, MA: Polity Press, 2004.

Isichei, Elizabeth. *A History of Christianity in Africa.* Grand Rapids: Eerdmans, 1995.

Jenkins, Philip. *God's Continent: Christianity, Islam, and Europe's Religious Crisis.* New York: Oxford University Press, 2007.

———. *The Next Christendom: The Coming of Global Christianity.* Oxford: Oxford University Press, 2002.

Johnson, L. T. *The Acts of the Apostles.* Sacra Pagina. Collegeville, MN: Liturgical Press, 1992.

Johnson, Todd M. "Three Waves of Christian Renewal: A 100-Year Snapshot." *International Bulletin of Missionary Research* 30, no. 2 (April 2006): 75–76.

Johnson, Todd M., K. R. Ross, and S. S. K. Lee, eds. *Atlas of Global Christianity.* Edinburgh: Edinburgh University Press, 2010 (forthcoming).

Johnson, Todd M., and Sun Young Chung. "Tracking Global Christianity's Statistical Centre of Gravity, AD 33–AD 2100." *International Review of Missions* 93, no. 369 (2004): 166–81.

Johnson, Todd M., Sarah Tieszen, and Thomas Higgins. "Counting Christians in India, AD 52–2200." *Dharma Deepika* (forthcoming).

Johnstone, Patrick, Robyn Johnstone, and Jason Mandryk. *Operation World: When We Pray God Works.* Carlisle, England: Paternoster Lifestyle, 2001.

Jordan, Clarence. *Cotton Patch Version of Matthew and John, Cotton Patch Version of Luke and Acts, Cotton Patch Version of Hebrews and General Epistles.* El Monte, CA: New Win Publishing, 1970–1997.

Justin Martyr. "Second Apology." In *The Ante-Nicene Fathers*, edited by Alexander Roberts and James Donaldson. Vol. 1. Peabody, MA: Hendrickson, 1999.

Kaiser, Walter C., Jr. *Mission in the Old Testament: Israel as a Light to the Nations.* Grand Rapids: Baker, 2000.

Kallestad, Walt. *Entertainment Evangelism: Taking the Church Public.* Nashville: Abingdon Press, 1996.

Karkkainen, Veli-Mati. "Are Pentecostals Oblivious to Social Justice? Theological and Ecumenical Perspectives." *Missiology: An International Review* 29, no. 4 (October 2001): 417–31.

———. *Trinity and Religious Pluralism.* Burlington, VT: Ashgate Publishing, 2004.

Kaufman, Gordon. "Religious Diversity, Historical Consciousness, and Christian Theology." In *The Myth of Christian Uniqueness*, edited by John Hick and Paul F. Knitter. Maryknoll, NY: Orbis, 1987.

Keesing, Roger. *Cultural Anthropology: A Contemporary Perspective.* New York: Holt, Rinehart, and Winston, 1981.

Kerr, Hugh T., ed. *A Compend of Luther's Theology.* Philadelphia: Westminster Press, 1966.

Kierkegaard, Soren. *Kierkegaard's Attack Upon "Christendom" 1854–1855.* Translated by Walter Lowrie. Princeton, NJ: Princeton University Press, 1944.

Kirkwood, Deborah. "Protestant Missionary Women." In *Women and Missions: Past and Present: Anthropological and Historical Perceptions*, edited by Fiona Bowie, Deborah Kirkwood, and Shirley Ardener, 23–42. Providence: Berg, 1993.

Kittel, Gerhard, and G. Friedrich, eds. *Theological Dictionary of the New Testament*. Translated by G. W. Bromiley. 10 vols. Grand Rapids: Eerdmans, 1964–1976.

Knitter, Paul F. *Introducing Theologies of Religions*. Maryknoll, NY: Orbis, 2002.

Koschorke, Klaus, Frieder Ludwig, and Mariano Delgado. *A History of Christianity in Asia, Africa and Latin America, 1450–1990*. Grand Rapids: Eerdmans, 2007.

Kraemer, Hendrick. *The Christian Message in a Non-Christian World*. London: Edinburgh House Press, 1938.

Kruger, Danny. "There's Plenty of Life Left in the Churches." *Telegraph*, October 13, 2005. http://www.telegraph.co.uk/opinion/main.jhtml?xml=/ opinion/2005/10/13/do1302.xml.

Kuzmic, Peter. "To Suffer with Our Lord: Christian Responses to Religious Persecution. "*Brandywine Review of Faith and International Affairs* 2, no. 3 (Winter, 2004–2005): 35–42.

LaGrand, James. *The Earliest Christian Mission to 'All Nations' in the Light of Matthew's Gospel*. Atlanta: Scholar's Press, 1995.

LaHaye, Tim, and Jerry Jenkins. *Left Behind*. Wheaton, IL: Tyndale, 1996.

Lambert, Tony. *The Resurrection of the Chinese Church*. Wheaton, IL: Shaw, 1994.

Laqueur, Walter. *The Last Days of Europe: Epitaph for an Old Continent*. New York: Thomas Dunne Books/St. Martin's Press, 2007.

Larkin, William J., Jr. "Mission in Luke." In *Mission in the New Testament: An Evangelical Approach*, edited by William J. Larkin Jr. and Joel F. Williams, 152–69. Maryknoll, NY: Orbis, 1998.

Latourette, Kenneth Scott. *A History of Christianity*. 2 vols. Peabody, MA: Prince, 2000 .

———. *A History of the Expansion of Christianity*. Vol. 6. *The Great Century: North Africa and Asia*. Grand Rapids: Zondervan, 1970.

Lausanne Movement. "The Lausanne Covenant." http://www.lausanne.org/ lausanne-1974/lausanne-covenant.html.

Lewis, Jeff. *Cultural Studies: The Basics*. London: Sage Publications, 2002.

Liddell, Henry George, and Robert Scott. *A Greek-English Lexicon*. Oxford: Clarendon Press, 1996.

Lindbeck, George. *Nature of Doctrine: Religion and Theology in a Postliberal Age*. Philadelphia: Westminster Press, 1984.

Lindsey, Hal. *The Late Great Planet Earth*. 25th ed. Grand Rapids: Zondervan, 1998.

Longenecker, Richard N. "Acts." In *The Expositor's Bible Commentary*, vol. 9, edited by Frank E. Gaebelein, 207–573. Grand Rapids: Zondervan, 1981.

Lull, Raymond. *The Tree of Love*. Translated by Edgar Allison Peers. London: SPCK, 1926.

Luther, Martin. *Luther's Works*. Vol. 14. *Selected Psalms III*. Edited by Jaroslav Pelikan. St. Louis: Concordia, 1958.

Lyotard, Jean-Francois. *The Postmodern Condition: A Report on Knowledge*. Minneapolis: University of Minnesota Press, 1985.

MacGregor, Neil. *The Image of Christ*. London: National Gallery, 2000.

Malchow, Bruce. "Social Justice in the Israelite Law Codes." *Word and World* 4, no. 3 (Summer 1984): 299–306.

Malkovsky, B. "The Personhood of Śankara's Para Brāhman." *Journal of Religion* 77, no. 4 (October 1997): 541–62.

Marostica, Matthew. "The Defeat of Denominational Culture in the Argentine Evangelical Movement." In *Latin American Religion in Motion*, edited by Christian Smith and Joshua Prokopy, 148–72. New York and London: Routledge, 1999.

Marshall, I. Howard. *The Gospel of Luke*. New International Greek Testament Commentary. Grand Rapids: Eerdmans, 1978.

Massey, Joshua. "God's Amazing Diversity in Drawing Muslims to Christ." *International Journal of Frontier Missions* 17, no. 1 (2000): 5–14.

———. "His Ways Are Not Our Ways." *Evangelical Missions Quarterly* 35, no. 2 (1999): 188–97.

———. "Misunderstanding C-5: His Ways Are Not Our Orthodoxy." *Evangelical Missions Quarterly* 40, no. 3 (2004): 296–304.

———. "Misunderstanding C-5 and the Infinite Translatability of Christ: Why C-5 Has Been So Misunderstood by Its Critics." *Evangelical Missions Quarterly* 40, no. 1 (2004): 1–18. Unabridged online ed., http://bgc.gospelcom.net/emis/pdfs/Misunderstanding_C5.pdf.

Matthews, Basil. *John R. Mott, World Citizen*. New York: Harper and Brothers, 1934.

Mbiti, John. "Theological Impotence and the Universality of the Church." In *Mission Trends No. 3: Third World Theologies*, edited by Gerald H. Anderson and Thomas F. Stransky, 6–18. New York: Paulist; Grand Rapids: Eerdmans, 1976.

McCarty, Jennifer, and Timothy Foecke. *What Really Sank the Titanic: New Forensic Discoveries*. New York: Citadel, 2008.

McDaniel, Ferris L. "Mission in the Old Testament." In *Mission in the New Testament: An Evangelical Approach*, edited by William J. Larkin Jr. and Joel F. Williams, 11–20. Maryknoll, NY: Orbis, 1998.

McDermott, Gerald R. *Can Evangelicals Learn from World Religions?* Downers Grove, IL: InterVarsity Press, 2000.

McEvedy, Colin, and Richard Jones. *Atlas of World Population History*. New York: Penguin, 1978.

McGavran, Donald. *Understanding Church Growth*. Rev. ed. Grand Rapids: Eerdmans, 1990.

McLoughlin, William G., and Robert Bellah, eds. *Religion in America*. Boston: Houghton Mifflin, 1968.

McPolin, James, S. J. "Mission in the Fourth Gospel." *Irish Theological Quarterly* 36 (1969): 113–22.

Menzies, William W. "The Holy Spirit in Christian Theology." In *Perspectives on Evangelical Theology*, edited by Kenneth Kantzer and Stanley Gundry, 67–79. Grand Rapids: Baker, 1979.

Merwin, Wallace, and Francis Jones, eds. *Documents of the Three-Self Movement: Source Materials for the Study of the Protestant Church in Communist China*. New York: National Council of Churches, 1963.

Metzger, Paul Louis. *The Word of Christ and the World of Culture*. Grand Rapids: Eerdmans, 2003.

Meyer, Ben. *The Early Christians: Their World Mission and Self-Discovery*. Wilmington, DE: Michael Glazier, 1986.

Migliore, Daniel L. *Faith Seeking Understanding: An Introduction to Christian Theology*. 2nd ed. Grand Rapids: Eerdmans, 2004.

Miley, George. *Loving the Church, Blessing the Nations*. Carlise, UK: Authentic Media, 1969.

Moffett, Samuel. *A History of Christianity in Asia*. Vol. 1. *Beginnings to 1500*. Maryknoll, NY: Orbis, 1998.

———. *A History of Christianity in Asia*. Vol. 2. *1500 to 1900*. Maryknoll, NY: Orbis, 2005.

Moltmann, Jürgen. *The Church in the Power of the Spirit*. London: SCM Press, 1975.

Montgomery, John Warwick. "Luther and Missions." *Evangelical Missions Quarterly* 3, no. 4 (1967): 193–202.

Moon, Steve Sang-Cheol. "The Acts of Koreans: A Research Report on Korean Missionary Movement." Korea Research Institute for Missions. http://krim .org/files/The_Acts_of_Koreans.doc.

———. "The Protestant Missionary Movement in Korea: Current Growth and
    Development." *International Bulletin of Missionary Research* 32, no. 2
    (April 2008): 59–64.
———. "The Recent Korean Missionary Movement: A Record of Growth, and
    More Growth Needed." *International Bulletin of Missionary Research* 27,
    no. 1 (January 2003): 11–17.
Moreau, A. Scott, ed. *Evangelical Dictionary of World Missions*. Grand Rapids:
    Baker, 2000.
Mott, John. *The Evangelization of the World in This Generation*. 3rd ed. London:
    Student Volunteer Missionary Union, 1903.
Müller, Max. *Origin and Growth of Religion*. Varanasi, India: Indological
    Book House, 1964.
Mundadan, Mathias. *History of Christianity in India*. Vol. 1. *Beginnings to 1572*.
    Bangalore: Theological Publications in India, 1984.
Nash, Ronald. *Is Jesus the Only Savior?* Grand Rapids: Zondervan, 1994.
Neander, Augustus. *General History of the Christian Religion and Church*.
    Translated by Joseph Torrey. Boston: Crocker and Brewster, 1854.
Neill, Stephen. *A History of Christianity in India, 1707–1858*. New York and
    London: Cambridge University Press, 1985.
———. *A History of Christian Missions*. Baltimore: Penguin, 1964.
Netland, Harold. *Dissonant Voices*. Grand Rapids: Eerdmans, 1991.
———. *Encountering Religious Pluralism*. Downers Grove, IL: InterVarsity, 2001.
Neuleip, James W. *Intercultural Communication: A Contextual Approach*.
    Thousand Oaks, CA: Sage Publications, 2006.
Newbigin, Lesslie. *The Finality of Christ*. London: SCM Press, 1969.
———. *The Gospel in a Pluralist Society*. Grand Rapids: Eerdmans, 1989.
———. *Honest Religion for Secular Man*. Philadelphia: Westminster Press, 1966.
———. *Household of God: Lectures on the Nature of the Church*. London: SCM Press,
    1953.
———. "The Logic of Missions." In *New Directions in Mission and
    Evangelization*, edited by James Scherer and Stephan Bevans, 16–25.
    Maryknoll, NY: Orbis, 1994.
———. *The Open Secret: An Introduction to the Theology of Mission*. Rev. ed.
    Grand Rapids: Eerdmans, 1995.
———. *The Relevance of Trinitarian Doctrine for Today's Mission*. Commission
    on World Mission and Evangelism Study Pamphlets 2. London: Edinburgh
    House, 1963.

Newport, John P. *Life's Ultimate Questions*. Dallas: Word, 1989.

Niebuhr, H. Richard. *Christ and Culture*. New York: Harper and Brothers, 1951.

Nolland, John. *The Gospel of Matthew*. New International Greek Testament Commentary. Grand Rapids: Eerdmans, 2005.

———. *Luke 9:21–18:34*. Word Biblical Commentary. Vol. 35b. Dallas: Word, 1993.

O'Brien, Peter T. *Colossians, Philemon*. Word Biblical Commentary. Vol. 44. Waco: Word, 1982.

Ockenga, Harold John. "Theological Education." *Bulletin of Fuller Theological Seminary* 4 (October–December 1954): 4–8.

Oden, Thomas. *The Rebirth of Orthodoxy*. New York: HarperSanFrancisco, 2003.

Olson, Roger E., and Christopher A. Hall. *The Trinity*. Grand Rapids: Eerdmans, 2002.

Packer, J. I., and Thomas C. Oden. *One Faith: The Evangelical Consensus*. Downers Grove, IL: InterVarsity Press, 2004.

Padilla, C. Rene. "Evangelism and the World." In *Let the Earth Hear His Voice*, edited by J. D. Douglas, 116–46. Minneapolis: World Wide Publications, 1975.

Panikkar, R. G. "The Brāhman of the Upanishads and the God of the Philosophers." *Religion and Society* 7, no. 2 (September 1960): 12–19.

———. *The Unknown Christ of Hinduism*. London: Darton, Longman and Todd, 1964.

Parekh, Bhikhu. *Rethinking Multiculturalism: Cultural Diversity and Political Theory*. New York: Palgrave, 2000.

Parshall, Phil. "Danger! New Directions in Contextualization." *Evangelical Missions Quarterly* 34, no. 4 (1998): 404–17.

Patterson, Richard. "The Widow, Orphan, and the Poor in the Old Testament and in Extra-Biblical Literature." *Bibliotheca Sacra* 130, no. 519 (July–September 1973): 223–34.

Pelikan, Jaroslav. *Acts*. Grand Rapids: Brazos Press, 2005.

———. *The Christian Tradition: A History of the Development of Doctrine*. Vol. 1. *The Emergence of the Catholic Tradition (100–600)*. Chicago: University of Chicago Press, 1971.

———. *Jesus Through the Centuries: His Place in the History of Culture*. New Haven: Yale University Press, 1985.

Pelikan, Jaroslav, and Helmut T. Lehman, eds. *Luther's Works*. 55 vols. St. Louis: Concordia, 1959–1986.

Pinnock, Clark. "Toward an Evangelical Theology of Religions." *Journal of the Evangelical Theological Society* 33, no. 3 (1990): 359–68.

———. *A Wideness in God's Mercy: The Finality of Jesus Christ in a World of Religions.* Grand Rapids: Zondervan, 1992.

Piper, John. *Let the Nations Be Glad! The Supremacy of God in Missions.* Grand Rapids: Baker, 1993.

Pocock, Michael, Gailyn Van Rheenen, and Douglas McConnell. *The Changing Face of World Missions: Engaging Contemporary Issues and Trends.* Grand Rapids: Baker Academic, 2005.

Pommerville, Paul A. *The Third Force in Missions.* Peabody, MA: Hendrickson, 1985.

Powell, Charles R. "Spiritual Awakening in China Today: Out from, and Returning to, Jerusalem, Vol. 1." D.Min. diss., Gordon-Conwell Theological Seminary, 2003.

Pretorius, Hennie, and Lizo Jafta. "A Branch Springs Out: African Initiated Churches." In *Christianity in South Africa: A Political, Social and Cultural History*, edited by Richard Elphick and T. Davenport, 211–26. Berkeley: University of California Press, 1998.

Priest, Robert. "Christian Theology, Sin, and Anthropology." In *Explorations in Anthropology and Theology*, edited by Frank A. Salamone and Walter Randolph Adams, 23–37. New York: University Press of America, 1997.

Pulliam, Sarah. "In the Aftermath of a Kidnapping: The South Korean Missionary Movement Seeks to Mature Without Losing Its Zeal." *Christianity Today* 51, no. 11 (2007): 64–65.

Rahner, Karl. "Christianity and the Non-Christian Religions." In *Christianity and Other Religions*, edited by John Hick and Brian Hebblethwaite, 52–79. Philadelphia: Fortress Press, 1980.

———. *Theological Investigations.* 20 vols. New York: Seabury, 1966–1983.

———. *Trinity.* New York: Seabury, 1997.

Ro, Bong Rin, ed. *Christian Suffering in Asia.* Taichung, Taiwan: Asia Theological Association, 1989.

Robeck, Cecil M., Jr. "Pentecostals and the Apostolic Faith: Implications for Ecumenism." *Pneuma: The Journal of the Society for Pentecostal Studies* 9, no. 1 (Spring 1987): 61–84.

Roberts, Alexander, and James Donaldson, eds. *The Ante-Nicene Fathers.* 10 vols. Peabody, MA: Hendrickson Publishers, 1999.

Robinson, Charles. *History of Christian Missions.* Edinburgh: T & T Clark, 1915.

Robinson, John. *Honest to God.* Philadephia: Westminster Press, 1963.

Rommen, Edward, and Gary Corwin, eds. *Missiology and the Social Sciences: Contributions, Cautions and the Conclusions.* Evangelical Missiological Society Series 4. Pasadena, CA: William Carey Library, 1996.

Rowell, John. *To Give or Not to Give.* Tyrone, GA: Authentic Publishing, 2007.

Roxburgh, Alan. "Rethinking Trinitarian Missiology." In *Global Missiology for the 21st Century: The Iguassu Dialogue*, edited by William Taylor, 179–88. Grand Rapids: Baker Academic, 2000.

Ruether, Rosemary Radford. *New Woman, New Earth: Sexist Ideologies and Human Liberation.* New York: Seabury, 1975.

Rutledge, Fleming. *The Undoing of Death.* Grand Rapids: Eerdmans, 2002.

Sanders, E. P. *Jesus and Judaism.* Philadelphia: Fortress Press, 1985.

Sanders, John. *No Other Name: An Investigation into the Destiny of the Unevangelized.* Grand Rapids: Eerdmans, 1992.

Sanneh, Lamin. "The Horizontal and Vertical in Mission: An African Perspective." *International Bulletin of Missionary Research* 7, no. 4 (October 1983): 165–71.

———. *Translating the Message: The Missionary Impact on Culture.* Maryknoll, NY: Orbis, 1989.

———. *Whose Religion Is Christianity? The Gospel Beyond the West.* Grand Rapids: Eerdmans, 2003.

Savage, Timothy M. "Europe and Islam." *Washington Quarterly* 27, no. 3 (Summer 2004): 25–50.

Schaff, Philip, and Henry Wace, eds. *Nicene and Post-Nicene Fathers.* Vol. 14. *The Seven Ecumenical Councils.* 2nd series. Peabody, MA: Hendrickson, 1999.

Schwartz, Glenn J. *When Charity Destroys Dignity: Overcoming Unhealthy Dependency in the Christian Movement.* Lancaster, PA: World Mission Associates, 2007.

Scriven, Charles. *The Transformation of Culture.* Scottdale, PA: Herald Press, 1988.

Seitz, Chrisopher R., ed. *Nicene Christianity: The Future for a New Ecumenism.* Grand Rapids: Brazos Press, 2001.

Semple, Rhonda Anne. *Missionary Women: Gender, Professionalism and the Victorian Idea of Christian Mission.* Rochester, NY: Boydell Press, 2003.

Shenk, Calvin E. *Who Do You Say That I Am? Christians Encounter Other Religions.* Scottdale, PA: Herald Press, 1997.

Showalter, Richard. "Bands and Bonds: Authentic Missionary Practice for the Twenty-First Century." D.Min. diss., Gordon-Conwell Theological Seminary, 2004.

Simpson, E. K., and F. F. Bruce. *The Epistles to the Ephesians and Colossians*. The New International Commentary on the New Testament. Grand Rapids: Eerdmans, 1982.

Slater, T. E. *Higher Hinduism in Relation to Christianity*. London: E. Stock, 1903.

Smith, David. *Mission After Christendom*. London: Darton, Longman and Todd, 2003.

Soneson, Jerome Paul. *Pragmatism and Pluralism*. Minneapolis: Fortress Press, 1993.

Speer, Robert. *The Unfinished Task in Foreign Missions*. New York: Fleming H. Revell, 1926.

Spencer, Aida Besancon, and William David Spencer. *Joy Through the Night*. Downers Grove, IL: InterVarsity Press, 1991.

Spencer, William. *Dread Jesus*. London: SPCK, 1999.

Spener, Philip Jacob. *Pia Desideria*. Philadelphia: Fortress Press, 1964.

Stinton, Diane B. *Jesus of Africa: Voices of Contemporary African Christology*. Maryknoll, NY: Orbis, 2004.

Stock, Eugene. *History of the Church Missionary Society: Its Environment, Its Men, and Its Work*. Vol. 1. London: Christian Missionary Society, 1899.

Stoll, David. *Is Latin America Turning Protestant? The Politics of Evangelical Growth*. Los Angeles: University of California Press, 1990.

———. "A Protestant Reformation in Latin America?" *Christian Century* 107, no. 2 (1990): 44–48.

Stone, Bryan. *Evangelism After Christendom: The Theology and Practice of Christian Witness*. Grand Rapids: Brazos Press, 2007.

Studebaker, John A., Jr. *The Lord Is the Spirit: The Authority of the Holy Spirit in Contemporary Theology and Church Practice*. Eugene, OR: Pickwick Publications, 2008.

Sumner, George. *The First and the Last*. Grand Rapids: Eerdmans, 2004.

Sundkler, Bengt. *Bantu Prophets in South Africa*. London: Lutterworth Press, 1948.

Tagawa, Kenzo. "People and Community in the Gospel of Matthew." *New Testament Studies* 16 (1969–1970): 149–62.

Tennent, Timothy C. "Adoniram Judson and the Mission Societies of the Great Century." *American Baptist Evangelicals Journal* 11, no. 3 (2003): 20–24.

———. "The Challenge of Churchless Christianity: An Evangelical Assessment." *International Bulletin of Missionary Research* 29, no. 4 (2005): 171–77.

———. *Christianity at the Religious Roundtable: Evangelicalism in Conversation with Hinduism, Buddhism and Islam.* Grand Rapids: Baker Academic, 2002.

———. "The Church: What Are Its Boundaries?" *American Baptist Evangelicals Journal* 9, nos. 1–2 (March and June 2001): 3–9.

———. "Followers of Jesus (*Isa*) in Islamic Mosques: A Closer Examination of C-5 'High Spectrum' Contextualization." *International Journal of Frontier Missions* 23, no. 3 (Fall 2006): 101–15.

———. "Ministries for Which We Teach: A World Cafe Model." In *Revitalizing Practice: Collaborative Models for Theological Faculties*, edited by Malcolm L. Warford, 99–135. New York: Peter Lang, 2008.

———. *Theology in the Context of World Christianity.* Grand Rapids: Zondervan, 2007.

Tertullian. "Apology." In *The Ante-Nicene Fathers*, edited by Alexander Roberts and James Donaldson. Vol. 3. Peabody, MA: Hendrickson, 1999.

———. "The Prescription Against Heretics." In *The Ante-Nicene Fathers*, edited by Alexander Roberts and James Donaldson. Vol. 3. Peabody, MA: Hendrickson, 1999.

Theological Education Fund. *Ministry in Context: The Third Mandate Programme of the Theological Education Fund, 1970–1977.* Bromley, England: Theological Education Fund, 1972.

Thiessen, Henry C. *Lectures in Systematic Theology.* Rev. ed. Grand Rapids: Eerdmans, 1979.

Thomas, M. M. *Towards an Evangelical Social Gospel: A New Look at the Reformation of Abraham Malpan.* Madras: CLS, 1977.

Thomas, Norman E., ed. *Classic Texts in Mission and World Christianity.* Maryknoll, NY: Orbis, 2003.

Thompson, T. Jack. "African Independent Churches in Britain: An Introductory Survey." In *New Religions and the New Europe*, edited by Robert Towler, 224–31. Aarhus, Denmark: Aarhus University Press, 1995.

Tiessen, Terry. "God's Work of Grace in the Context of the Religions." Διδασκαλια 18, no. 1 (Winter 2007): 165–91.

Tieszen, Charles L. *Re-Examining Religious Persecution: Constructing a Theological Framework for Understanding Persecution.* Kempton Park, Johannesburg: AcadSA, 2008.

Tillich, Paul. *Kairos: Zur Geisteslage und Geisteswendung.* Darmstadt, Germany: Otto Reichl Verlag, 1926.

———. *Systematic Theology.* Vol. 3. Chicago: University of Chicago Press, 1963.

"Top 100 Most Important Events in Church History." *Christian History* 9, no. 4 (1990).

Travis, John. "The C1 to C6 Spectrum." *Evangelical Missions Quarterly* 34, no. 4 (1998): 407–8.

———. "Messianic Muslim Followers of Jesus." *International Journal of Frontier Missions* 17, no. 1 (2000): 53–59.

———. "Two Responses: Must All Muslims Leave 'Islam' to Follow Jesus?" *Evangelical Missions Quarterly* 34, no. 4 (1998): 411–15.

Tucker, Ruth A. *From Jerusalem to Irian Jaya: A Biographical History of Christian Missions.* Grand Rapids: Zondervan, 1983.

Turner, Harold. *Religious Innovation in Africa.* Boston: G. K. Hall, 1979.

Turner, Max. "The 'Spirit of Prophecy' as the Power of Israel's Restoration and Witness." In *Witness to the Gospel: The Theology of Acts,* edited by I. Howard Marshall and David Peterson, 327–48. Grand Rapids: Eerdmans, 1998.

Tylor, Edward B. *Primitive Culture.* Vol. 1. London: Murray Publishers, 1871.

Uddin, Rafique. "Contextualized Worship and Witness." In *Muslims and Christians on the Emmaus Road,* edited by J. Dudley Woodberry, 269–72. Monrovia, CA: MARC, 1989.

"An Uncertain Road: Muslims and the Future of Europe." The Pew Forum on Religion and Public Life. http://pewforum.org/docs/index.php?DocID=60.

Van Dusen, Henry P. "The Third Force in Christendom." *Life* (June 9, 1958).

Van Rooy, J. A. "Christ and the Religions: The Issues at Stake." *Missionalia* 13, no. 1 (1985): 3–13.

Vanhoozer, Kevin J. *The Drama of Doctrine: A Canonical-Linguistic Approach to Christian Theology.* Louisville: Westminster John Knox Press, 2005.

———. "One Rule to Rule Them All? Theological Method in an Era of World Christianity." In *Global Theologizing,* edited by Harold Netland and Craig Ott, 85–126. Grand Rapids: Baker Academic, 2006.

Verkuyl, Johannes. *Contemporary Missiology: An Introduction.* Grand Rapids: Eerdmans, 1978.

Vicedom, Georg. *The Mission of God: An Introduction to the Theology of Mission.* Translated by Gilbert A. Thiele and Dennis Hilgendorf. St. Louis: Concordia, 1965.

Wagner, C. Peter. *Church Growth and the Whole Gospel.* San Francisco: Harper and Row, 1981.

———. "The Greatest Church Growth Is Beyond Our Shores." *Christianity Today* 28, no. 8 (1984): 24–31.

Wallis, Jim. *The Soul of Politics.* New York: Harvest Books, 1995.

Walls, Andrew F. *The Cross-Cultural Process in Christian History.* Maryknoll, NY: Orbis, 2002.

———. "Eusebius Tries Again: Reconceiving the Study of Christian History." *International Bulletin of Missionary Research* 24, no. 3 (July 2000): 105–8, 110–11.

———. *The Missionary Movement in Christian History: Studies in the Transmission of Faith.* Maryknoll, NY: Orbis, 1996.

———. "Old Athens and New Jerusalem: Some Signposts for Christian Scholarship in the Early History of Mission Studies." *International Bulletin of Missionary Research* 21, no. 4 (October 1997): 146–53.

———. "Towards an Understanding of Africa's Place in Christian History." In *Religion in a Pluralistic Society*, edited by J. S. Pobee, 180–89. Leiden: E. J. Brill, 1976.

Wan, Enoch. "Critiquing the Method of the Traditional Western Theology and Calling for Sino-Theology." *Chinese Around the World* (November 1999): 13–16.

Ware, James. *The Mission of the Church in Paul's Letter to the Philippians in the Context of Ancient Judaism.* Leiden, Netherlands; Boston: E. J. Brill, 2005.

Warfield, B. B. *Counterfeit Miracles.* New York: Charles Scribner's Sons, 1918.

Watanabe, Teresa. "Global Convention Testifies to Pentecostalism's Revival." *Los Angeles Times,* May 31, 2001.

Watson, Russell. "Latin America: John Paul Goes to War." *Newsweek* (February 12, 1996).

Webber, Robert. *The Younger Evangelicals: Facing the Challenge of a New World.* Grand Rapids: Baker, 2002.

Weber, Linda J., and Dotsey Welliver, eds. *Mission Handbook: U.S. and Canadian Protestant Ministries Overseas, 2007–2009.* Wheaton, IL: EMIS, 2007.

Weigel, George. *The Cube and the Cathedral: Europe, America, and Politics Without God.* New York: Basic Books, 2006.

"Weird Babble of Tongues." *Los Angeles Times,* April 18, 1906.

Welliver, Dotsey, and Minnette Northcutt, eds. *Mission Handbook: U.S. and Canadian Protestant Ministries Overseas, 2004–2006.* Wheaton, IL: EMIS, 2004.

Wells, David. *God in the Wasteland: The Reality of Truth in a World of Fading Dreams*. Grand Rapids: Eerdmans, 1994.

Wenham, John. *Easter Enigma*. Eugene, OR: Wipf and Stock, 2005.

Westmeier, Karl-Wilhelm. *Protestant Pentecostalism in Latin America*. London: Associated University Presses, 1999.

Williams, Mark. "Aspects of High-Spectrum Contextualization in Ministries to Muslims." *Journal of Asian Mission* 5, no. 1 (2003): 75–91.

Wilson, Everett A. "Latin American Pentecostals—Their Potential for Ecumenical Dialogue." *Pneuma: The Journal of the Society of Pentecostal Studies* 9, no. 1 (Spring 1987): 85–90.

Winter, Ralph D. "Can We Trust Insider Movements?" *Mission Frontiers* 27, no. 5 (September–October 2005): 4.

———. "The Two Structures of God's Redemptive Mission." In *Perspectives on the World Christian Movement*, edited by Ralph D. Winter and Steven C. Hawthorne, 220–30. Pasadena, CA: William Carey Library, 1999.

Winter, Ralph, and Bruce Koch. "Finishing the Task: the Unreached Peoples Challenge." *International Journal of Frontier Missions* 19, no. 4 (2002): 15–24.

———. *International Journal of Mission Frontiers* (June 2000): 22–33.

Wishard, Luther. *A New Programme of Missions*. New York: Fleming H. Revell, 1895.

World Christian Database. http://www.worldchristiandatabase.org.

Wright, Christopher J. H. *The Mission of God*. Grand Rapids: IVP Academic, 2006.

———. "An Upside-Down World." *Christianity Today* 51, no. 1 (2007): 42–46.

Wright, N. T. *Evil and the Justice of God*. London: SPCK, 2006.

Yancey, Philip. *The Jesus I Never Knew*. Grand Rapids: Zondervan, 1995.

Yannoulatos, Anastasios. "Discovering the Orthodox Missionary Ethos." In *Martyria/Mission: The Witness of the Orthodox Churches Today*, edited by Ion Bria, 20–37. Geneva: World Council of Churches, 1980.

Yates, Timothy. *Christian Mission in the Twentieth Century*. New York: Cambridge University Press, 1994.

Yeoman, Barry. "The Stealth Crusade." *Mother Jones* 48 (May–June 2002): 42–49.

Ye'or, Bat. *The Decline of Eastern Christianity Under Islam: From Jihad to Dhimmitude*. London: Associated University Press, 1996.

———. *Eurabia: The Euro-Arab Axis*. Madison: Fairleigh Dickinson University Press, 2005.

Yoder, John. "How H. Richard Niebuhr Reasoned: A Critique of Christ and Culture." In *Authentic Transformation: A New Vision of Christ and Culture*, edited by Glen H. Stassen, 31–89. Nashville: Abingdon Press, 1996.

Yong, Amos. *Beyond the Impasse: Toward a Pneumatological Theology of Religions*. Grand Rapids: Baker Academic, 2003.

Youth Bible, The. Nashville: Word, 2002

Zizioulas, J. *Being and Communion: Studies in the Personhood and Church*. New York: St. Vladimir's Seminary Press, 1985.

Scripture Index

Subject Index